DICTIONARY OF
ACCOUNTING

second edition

D0869499

English Dictionaries

English Dictionary for Students	1-901659-06-2
English Study Dictionary	1-901659-63-1
Children's English Dictionary	1-901659-86-0
Dictionary of Accounting, 2nd ed	1-901659-85-2
Dictionary of Aeronautical English	1-901659-10-0
Dictionary of Agriculture, 2nd ed	0-948549-78-5
Dictionary of American Business, 2nd ed	1-901659-22-4
Dictionary of Astronomy, 2nd ed	1-901659-72-0
Dictionary of Automobile Engineering	0-948549-66-1
Dictionary of Banking & Finance, 2nd ed	1-901659-30-5
Dictionary of Business, 3rd ed	1-901659-50-X
Dictionary of Computing, 4th ed	1-901659-46-1
Dictionary of Ecology & Environment, 4th ed	1-901659-61-5
Dictionary of Government & Politics, 2nd ed	0-948549-89-0
Dictionary of Hotels, Tourism, Catering Management	0-948549-40-8
Dictionary of Human Resources & Personnel, 2nd ed	0-948549-79-3
Dictionary of Information Technology, 3rd ed	1-901659-55-0
Dictionary of Law, 3rd ed	1-901659-43-7
Dictionary of Library & Information Management	0-948549-68-8
Dictionary of Marketing	0-948549-73-4
Dictionary of Medicine, 3rd ed	1-901659-45-3
Dictionary of Military Terms	1-901659-24-0
Dictionary of Multimedia, 3rd ed	1-901659-51-8
Dictionary of PC & the Internet, 3rd ed	1-901659-52-6
Dictionary of Printing & Publishing, 2nd ed	0-948549-99-8

Check Your Vocabulary workbooks for:

Aeronautical English	1-901659-81-X
American Business	1-901659-32-1
Banking & Finance	0-948549-96-3
Business, 2nd ed	1-901659-27-5
Colloquial English	0-948549-97-1
Computing, 2nd ed	1-901659-28-3
English for Academic Purposes	1-901659-53-4
English for FCE	1-901659-11-9
English for IELTS	1-901659-60-7
English for TOEFL	1-901659-68-2
Hotels, Tourism, Catering	0-948549-75-0
Law, 2nd ed	1-901659-21-6
Marketing	1-901659-48-8
Medicine, 2nd ed	1-901659-47-X
Military English	1-901659-58-5

Visit our website for full details of all our books: **www.petercollin.com**

DICTIONARY OF
ACCOUNTING

second edition

P.H. Collin
David York
Adrian Joliffe

PP

PETER COLLIN PUBLISHING

Second edition published 2001

First published in Great Britain 1992

Published by Peter Collin Publishing Ltd
32-34 Great Peter Street, London, SW1P 2DB

British Library Cataloguing-in-Publication Data

A catalogue record for this book is available from the British Library

ISBN 1-901659-85-2

Text computer typeset by PCP
Printed and bound in Finland by WS Bookwell
Cover artwork by Gary Weston

Preface to the first edition

This dictionary provides a basic vocabulary of terms used in the fields of accounting, bookkeeping and general finance. It covers both British and American usage.

The main words and phrases are defined in simple English, and many examples are given to show how the words may be used in context. Explanatory comments are given in some cases to expand the definitions. There are also quotations from newspapers and specialist magazines.

The supplement at the back of the book gives a list of common abbreviations, and sample documents and financial statements.

We would like to thank in particular Adrian Joliffe, who read the text and contributed many helpful comments.

Preface to the second edition

Many changes have taken place in the terminology of accounting since the first edition of this dictionary was published. The text has been entirely updated and expanded, including new explanatory comments and quotations.

Because the pronunciation of some specialized words can pose problems, we have added the IPA phonetic transcription for all the main words.

We thank in particular David York who has contributed much to this second edition.

Phonetics

The following symbols have been used to show the pronunciation of the main words in the dictionary.

Stress has been indicated by a main stress mark ('), but these are only guides as the stress of the word may change according to its position in the sentence.

Vowels			*Consonants*	
æ	back		b	buck
ɑː	harm		d	dead
ɒ	stop		ð	other
aɪ	type		dʒ	jump
aʊ	how		f	fare
aɪə	hire		g	gold
aʊə	hour		h	head
ɔː	course		j	yellow
ɔɪ	loyalty		k	cab
e	head		l	leave
eə	fair		m	mix
eɪ	make		n	nil
ə	abroad		ŋ	bring
əʊ	float		p	post
əʊə	lower		r	rule
ɜː	word		s	save
iː	keep		ʃ	shop
ɪ	fit		t	take
ɪə	near		tʃ	change
u	supreme		χ	loch
uː	pool		θ	theft
ʊ	book		v	value
ʌ	shut		w	work
			z	zone
			ʒ	measure

Aa

Schedule A ['ʃedjuːl 'eɪ] schedule to the Finance Acts under which tax is charged on rental income from land or buildings

Table A ['teɪbl 'eɪ] model articles of association of a limited company set out in the Companies Act, 1985

A, AA, AAA ['sɪŋgleɪ or 'dʌbəleɪ or 'trɪpl'eɪ] letters indicating that a share, bond or bank has a certain rating for reliability; *these bonds have a AAA rating*

QUOTE the rating concern lowered its rating to single-A from double-A, and its senior debt rating to triple-B from single-A
Wall Street Journal

COMMENT: the AAA rating is given by Standard & Poor's or by Moody's, and indicates a very high level of reliability for a corporate or municipal bond in the US

A list ['eɪ 'lɪst] *noun* list of members of a company at the time it is wound up who may be liable for the company's unpaid debts

'A' shares ['eɪ 'ʃeəz] *noun* ordinary shares with limited voting rights or no right to vote at all

COMMENT: a company may be set up with two classes of share: 'A' shares, which are available to the general investor, and 'B' shares which are only bought by certain individuals, such as the founder and his family. Such division of shares is becoming less usual nowadays

AAA = AMERICAN ACCOUNTING ASSOCIATION

AAT = ASSOCIATION OF ACCOUNTING TECHNICIANS

abandonment [ə'bændənmənt] *noun* act of giving something up voluntarily (such as the right to a property); **abandonment of a claim** = giving up a claim in a civil action

abatement [ə'beɪtmənt] *noun* act of reducing; **tax abatement** = reduction of tax

ab initio ['æb ɪn'ɪʃɪəʊ] *Latin phrase* meaning 'from the beginning'

abnormal [əb'nɔːməl] *adjective* not normal, not usual; **abnormal gain** = gain which is more than the normal or expected gain; **abnormal loss** = loss which is higher than the normal or expected loss

above par [ə'bʌv 'pɑː] *phrase* (share) with a market or issue price higher than its par value

above the line [ə'bʌv ðə 'laɪn] *phrase* **(a)** *(companies)* income and expenditure before tax; *exceptional items are noted above the line in company accounts* **(b)** revenue items in a government budget dealing with taxes and government expenditure

abroad [ə'brɔːd] *adverb* not in the United Kingdom (in a country outside England, Scotland, Wales and Northern Ireland); *income from land or proerty abroad must be declared in the Foreign Pages of the Income Tax return*

absolute ['æbsəluːt] *adjective* perfect or complete; **absolute monopoly** = situation where only one producer or supplier produces or supplies something; *the company has an absolute monopoly of imports of French wine*; **absolute value** = size or value of a number regardless of its sign; *the absolute value of -62.34 is 62.34*

absorb [əb'zɔːb] *verb* **(a)** to take in a small item so as to form part of a larger one; **to absorb overheads** = to include a proportion of overhead costs into a production cost (this is done at a certain rate, called 'absorption rate'); **to absorb a surplus** = to take back surplus stock so that it does not affect a business; **overheads have absorbed all our profits** = all our profits have gone in paying overhead expenses; **to absorb a loss by a subsidiary** = to write a subsidiary company's loss into the group accounts; *see also* OVERABSORBED, UNDERABSORBED **(b)** business which has been absorbed by a competitor = a small business which has been acquired by a larger one

absorption [əb'zɔːpʃən] *noun* **(a)** making a smaller business part of a larger one, so that the smaller company in effect no longer exists

(b) absorption costing = costing a product to include both the direct costs of production and the overhead costs which are absorbed as well; **absorption rate** = rate at which overhead costs are absorbed into each unit of production

COMMENT: absorption costing follows three stages: 'allocation' of actual overhead costs directly to the cost centre to which they relate; 'apportionment', by which common overhead costs are divided between various cost centres in proportion to the estimated benefit to each cost centre; 'absorption', by which the total costs are charged to each unit of production

abstract ['æbstrækt] *noun* short form of a report or document; *to make an abstract of the company accounts*

a/c *or* **acc** = ACCOUNT

ACA = ASSOCIATE OF THE INSTITUTE OF CHARTERED ACCOUNTANTS IN ENGLAND AND WALES

ACAUS = ASSOCIATION OF CHARTERED ACCOUNTANTS IN THE UNITED STATES

ACCA = ASSOCIATE OF THE ASSOCIATION OF CHARTERED CERTIFIED ACCOUNTANTS; ASSOCIATION OF CHARTERED CERTIFIED ACCOUNTANTS

accelerate [æk'seləreɪt] *verb* **(a)** to make something go faster; *we will try to accelerate the payment of your invoice* **(b)** to make a maturity date become closer

QUOTE in a separate development, the Geneva-based bank confirmed that it has accelerated the six Swiss bond issues. Acceleration means the bonds become payable immediately and allows bondholders to rank alongside the company's other creditors
Times

accelerated depreciation
[æk'seləreɪtɪd dɪpriːʃɪ'eɪʃən] *noun* system of depreciation which reduces the value of assets at a high rate in the early years to encourage companies, because of tax advantages, to invest in new equipment

COMMENT: this tax treatment was introduced in several economies at a time of high inflation. It applied generally in the UK until 1984; companies could depreciate new equipment at 100% in the first year. Subsequently this method was allowed for restricted classes of fixed assets to stimulate investment in new technology, for example in computer equipment. From 1980 to 1987 in

the USA, accelerated depreciation rules were made more generous by the accelerated cost recovery system introduced by the Economic Recovery Tax Act of 1981

acceleration clause [ækselə'reɪʃn 'klɔːz] *noun* section of a contract which explains how a loan may be required to be repaid early if the borrower defaults on other clauses of the contract; *the bank called the whole loan in early under the acceleration clause because the company failed to pay interest when due*

accept [ək'sept] *verb* **(a)** to take something which is being offered; **to accept a bill of exchange** = to sign a bill of exchange to indicate that you promise to pay it **(b)** to say yes, or to agree to something; *60% of shareholders have accepted the offer*

acceptable [ək'septəbl] *adjective* which can be accepted; *the offer is not acceptable to the shareholders*

acceptance [ək'septəns] *noun* **(a)** (i) act of signing a bill of exchange to show that you agree to pay it; (ii) a bill which has been accepted; **to present a bill for acceptance** = to apply for payment by the person who has accepted it; **acceptance credit** = letter of credit, where the bank accepts bills of exchange drawn on the bank by the beneficiary: the bank then discounts the bills and pays them when they mature; the company or person who opened the letter of credit owes the bank for the bills but these are covered by money deposited with the bank; **acceptance house** *US* **acceptance bank** = ACCEPTING HOUSE **(b)** act of accepting an offer of new shares for which you have applied **(c) acceptance of an offer** = agreeing to an offer; **to give an offer a conditional acceptance** = to accept provided that certain things happen or that certain terms apply; **we have his letter of acceptance** = we have received a letter from him accepting the offer **(d) acceptance sampling** = testing a small part of a batch to see if the whole batch is good enough

accepting house *or* **acceptance house** [ək'septɪŋ 'haʊs *or* ək'septəns 'haʊs] *noun* firm (usually a merchant bank) which accepts bills of exchange (i.e. promises to pay them) at a discount, in return for immediate payment to the issuer, in this case the Bank of England; **Accepting Houses Committee** = the main London merchant banks, which act as accepting houses; they receive slightly better discount rates from the Bank of England

acceptor [ək'septə] *noun* person or company which signs a bill of exchange, and so undertakes to pay it

access ['ækses] **1** *noun* **to have access to something** = to be able to obtain or reach something; *he has access to large amounts of venture capital*; *she has access to the company's deposit account* **2** *verb* to call up (data) which is stored in a computer; *she accessed the address file on the computer*; **access time** = time taken by a computer to find data stored in it

accommodation [əkɒmə'deɪʃən] *noun* **(a)** money lent for a short time **(b) to reach an accommodation with creditors** = to agree terms for settlement **(c) accommodation bill** = bill of exchange where the drawee signing is helping another company (the drawer) to raise a loan; it is given on the basis of trade debts owed to the borrower

account [ə'kaʊnt] **1** *noun* **(a)** record of financial transactions over a period of time, such as money paid, received, borrowed or owed; *please send me your account; a detailed or an itemized account*; **expense account** = money which a businessman is allowed by his company to spend on travelling and entertaining clients in connection with his business; *he charged his hotel bill to his expense account* **(b)** *(in a shop)* arrangement which a customer has to buy goods and pay for them at a later date (usually the end of the month); *to have an account or a charge account or a credit account with Harrods*; *put it on my account or charge it to my account*; *(of a customer)*; **to open an account** = to ask a shop to supply goods which you will pay at a later date; *(of a shop)*; **to open an account** *or* **to close an account** = to start or to stop supplying a customer on credit; **to settle an account** = to pay all the money owed on an account; **to stop an account** = to stop supplying a customer until he has paid what he owes **(c) on account** = as part of a total bill; **to pay money on account** = to pay or to settle part of a bill; **advance on account** = money paid as a part payment **(d)** customer who regularly does a large amount of business with a firm and has an account; *he is one of our largest accounts*; *our salesmen call on their best accounts twice a month*; **account executive** = employee who looks after certain customers or who is the link between certain customers and his company **(e) the accounts of a business** *or* **a company's accounts** = detailed record of a company's financial affairs; **to keep the accounts** = to write each sum of money in the books of account; *the*

accountant's job is to enter all the money received in the accounts; **annual accounts** = accounts prepared at the end of a financial year; **management accounts** = financial information (sales, expenditure, credit, and profitability) prepared for a manager so that he or she can take decisions; **account form** = balance sheet laid out in horizontal form (it is the opposite of 'report' or 'vertical' form); **period of account** = accounting period, the period usually covered by a company's accounts; **profit and loss account (P&L account)** = statement of company expenditure and income over a period of time, almost always one calendar year, showing whether the company has made a profit or loss (the balance sheet shows the state of a company's finances at a certain date; the profit and loss account shows the movements which have taken place since the last balance sheet) (NOTE: the American equivalent is the **profit and loss statement** or **income statement**; **account form** = a balance sheet laid out in horizontal form (it is the opposite of 'report' or 'vertical' form); **accounts department** = department in a company which deals with money paid, received, borrowed or owed; **accounts manager** = manager of an accounts department; **accounts payable** = money owed by a company for purchases of goods and services; **accounts receivable** = money owed to a company by its customers **(f) bank account** *US* **banking account** = arrangement to keep money in a bank; *he put the money into his building society account*; *he has an account with Barclays*; *I have an account with the Lambeth Building Society*; *to put or to deposit money in(to) your account*; *to take money out of your account or to withdraw money from your account*; **budget account** = account where you plan income and expenditure to allow for periods when expenditure is high; **current account** *or* **cheque account** *US* **checking account** = account which pays no interest but from which the customer can withdraw money when he wants by writing cheques; **deposit account** = account which pays interest but on which notice usually has to be given to withdraw money; **external account** = account in a British bank of someone who is living in another country; **frozen account** = account where the money cannot by used or moved because of a court order; **joint account** = account for two people; *most married people have joint accounts so that they can each take money out when they want it*; **overdrawn account** = account where you have taken out more money than you have put in (i.e. where the bank is lending you money); **savings account** = account where you put money in regularly and which pays interest, often at a higher rate than a deposit account; **to open an account** = to start an account by putting money in; *she opened an account with the Halifax*; **to close an account** = to take all money out of a bank account and stop the account; *he closed his account with Lloyds* **(g)** *(Stock Exchange)* period during which shares are traded for credit, and at the end of which the shares bought must be paid for; **account day** *or* **settlement day** = day on which shares which have been bought must be paid for; *share prices rose at the end of the account or the account end*; **trading for the account** *or* **dealing for the account** *or* **account trading** = buying shares and selling the same shares during an account, which means that the dealer has only to pay the difference between the price of the shares bought and the price obtained for them when they are sold; *US* **rolling account** = system where there are no fixed account days, but stock exchange transactions are paid at a fixed period after each transaction has taken place **(h)** notice; **to take account of inflation** *or* **to take inflation into account** = to assume that there will be a certain percentage inflation when making calculations **2** *verb* **to account for** = to explain and record a money transaction; *to account for a loss or a discrepancy*; *the reps have to account for all their expenses to the sales manager*

COMMENT: for stock exchange transactions, the account system was necessary before computerization and on-line trading made earlier settlement possible under a rolling account. On the London Stock Exchange the account period is three business days from the day of trade

accountability [əkaʊntə'bɪləti] *noun* being responsible to someone for something (such as the accountability of directors to the shareholders)

accountable [ə'kaʊntəbl] *adjective* (person) who is responsible for something (such as to record and then explain a money transaction) (NOTE: you are accountable **to** someone **for** something)

accountancy [ə'kaʊntənsi] *noun* work of an accountant (as a course of study); *he is studying accountancy* *or* *he is an accountancy student* (NOTE: American English uses **accounting** in the meaning of the subject studied)

accountant [ə'kaʊntənt] *noun* (i) a person who keeps a company's accounts and

prepares financial statements; (ii) an expert in accounting and financial matters generally; (iii) a person who examines a company's accounts; *the chief accountant of a manufacturing group*; *I send all my income tax queries to my accountant*; **certified accountant** = accountant who has passed the professional examinations and is a member of the Association of Chartered Certified Accountants (ACCA); *US* **certified public accountant** = accountant who has passed professional examinations; **chartered accountant (ACA** *or* **FCA)** = accountant who has passed the professional examinations and is an associate of the Institute of Chartered Accountants in England and Wales, or a member of the Institute of Chartered Accountants in Scotland; **cost accountant** = accountant who gives managers information about their business costs; **Financial Accountant** = qualified accountant, a member of the Institute of Financial Accountants, who advises on accounting matters or who works as the financial director of a company; **management accountant** = accountant who prepares financial information for managers so that they can take decisions; *US* **accountant's opinion** = report of the audit of a company's books, carried out by a certified public accountant (also called 'audit opinion')

COMMENT: there are separate institutes for England and Wales, Ireland and Scotland. Members of the Association of Chartered Certified Accountants (ACCA) may be referred to as 'certified' or, less often, 'chartered certified'. Members of the Chartered Institute of Management Accountants may be refered to as 'chartered management accountants' but this is less usual as a formal title is more relevant to accountants in private practice. A firm may describe itself as 'Chartered Accountants' even though a large number of its partners are not

accounting [ə'kaʊntɪŋ] *noun* **(a)** work of recording money paid, received, borrowed or owed; *accounting methods or accounting procedures*; *accounting system*; **accounting bases** = the possible ways in which accounting concepts may be applied to financial transactions (the methods used to depreciate assets, how intangible assets or work in progress are dealt with, etc.); **accounting concept** = general assumption on which accounts are prepared (the main concepts are: that the business is a going concern, that revenue and costs are noted when they are incurred and not when cash is received or paid, that the present accounts are drawn up following the same principles as the previous accounts, that the revenue or costs are only recorded if it is certain that they will be incurred; see FRS 18); **accounting date** = the date on which an accounting period ends (usually 31st December for annual accounts, but it can in fact be any date); **accounting entity** = any unit which takes part in a financial transaction which is recorded in a set of accounts (it can be a department, a sole trader, a plc, etc.); **accounting fees** = fees paid to an accountant for preparing accounts (such fees are deductible against tax); **accounting period** = period usually covered by a company's accounts (the balance sheet shows the state of the company's affairs at the end of the accounting period, while the profit-and-loss account shows the changes which have taken place since the end of the previous period); **accounting policies** = the accounting bases used by a company when preparing its financial statements (see FRS 18); **Accounting Principles Board (APB)** = the US body which issued Opinions that formed much of US Generally Accepted Accounting Principles up to 1973 when the Financial Accounting Standards Board (FASB) took over that role; **accounting rate of return (ARR)** = method of valuing shares in a company where the company's estimated future profits are divided by the rate of return required by investors; **accounting standards** = rules of accounting practice recommended by the Accounting Standards Board (or FASB in the USA); *see also* FAS, GAAP, SSAP; **Accounting Standards Board (ASB)** = body set up in 1990 by British accounting institutions to set accounting standards; it issues Financial Reporting Standards (FRSs) and has adopted the Statements of Standard Accounting Practice (SSAPs) issued by its predecessor body, the Accounting Standards Committee; **Accounting Standards Committee (ASC)** = UK accounting standards issuing body whose functions were taken over by the ASB in 1990; **accounting technician** = person who assists in the preparation of accounts but who is not a fully qualified accountant; **accounting unit** = ACCOUNTING ENTITY; **cost accounting** = preparing special accounts of manufacturing and sales costs; **current cost accounting** = method of accounting which notes the cost of replacing assets at current prices, rather than valuing assets at their original cost; **financial accounting** = recording financial transactions in monetary terms according to accounting standards and legal requirements; **management accounting** = providing information to managers, which helps them to plan, to control their businesses and to take decisions which will make them run their

businesses more efficiently **(b)** accountancy, the work of an accountant as a course of study

COMMENT: note the various theoretical bases for accountancy, moving from the general to the specific: 'accounting concepts' are general: so various concepts, such as the 'accruals concept' may apply to depreciation; 'accounting bases' are more specific, so in the case of depreciation, the bases could be straight-line depreciation, reducing balance depreciation, etc.; 'accounting policies' are the policies applied by a company, so the company policy could be to apply straight-line depreciation in its financial statements

accrete [ə'kriːt] *verb* to add to, especially to add interest to a fund

accretion [ə'kriːʃn] *noun* **(a)** adding interest to a fund over a period of time **(b)** *US* adjustment of the difference between the par value of a bond and the discounted price paid for it when it was bought

accrual [ə'kruːəl] *noun* **(a)** noting financial transactions when they take place, and not when payment is made; **accruals concept** = concept that accounts are prepared with financial transactions accrued (revenue and costs are both reported during the accounting period to which they refer; see FRS 18) **(b)** **accruals** = accrued liabilities and accrued income **(c)** gradual increase by addition; **accrual of interest** = automatic addition of interest to capital

accrue [ə'kruː] *verb* **(a)** to record a financial transaction in accounts when it takes place, and not when payment is made or received; **accrued liabilities** = liabilities which are recorded, although payment has not yet been made (this refers to liabilities such as rent, rates, etc.) (NOTE: American English is also **accrued expenses**); **accrued income** *or* **accrued revenue** = revenue entered in accounts, although payment has not yet been received **(b)** to increase and be due for payment at a later date; *interest accrues from the beginning of the month*; *accrued interest is added quarterly*; **accrued dividend** = dividend earned since the last dividend was paid; **accrued interest** = interest which has been earned by an interest-bearing investment

acct = ACCOUNT

accumulate [ə'kjuːmjʊleɪt] *verb* to grow larger by adding (as by adding interest to capital); *to allow dividends to accumulate*; **accumulated depreciation** = total amount by which an asset has been depreciated since it was purchased; **accumulated profit** = profit which is not paid as dividend but is taken over into the accounts of the following year; *US* **accumulated earnings tax** *or* **accumulated profits tax** = tax on earnings above a specified limit which are unjustifiably retained in a business to avoid paying higher personal income tax; **accumulated reserves** = reserves which a company has put aside over a period of years

accumulation [əkjuːmjʊˈleɪʃn] *noun* growing larger by adding (as by adding interest or dividends to capital); **accumulation units** = type of units in a unit trust, where dividends accumulate and form more units (as opposed to income units, where the investor receives the dividends as income)

ACH *US* = AUTOMATED CLEARING HOUSE

achieve [əˈtʃiːv] *verb* to succeed in doing something, to do something successfully; *the company has achieved great success in the Far East*; *we achieved all our objectives in 1998*

> QUOTE the company expects to move to profits of FFr 2m for 1999 and achieve equally rapid growth in following years
> Financial Times

acid test ratio [ˈæsɪd ˈtest ˈreɪʃɪəʊ] *noun* ratio of liquid assets (that is, current assets less stocks, but including debtors) to current liabilities, giving an indication of a company's solvency (NOTE: also called **quick ratio** *or* **liquidity ratio**)

ACMA = ASSOCIATE OF THE CHARTERED INSTITUTE OF MANAGEMENT ACCOUNTANTS

acquire [əˈkwaɪə] *verb* to buy; *to acquire a company*

acquirer [əˈkwaɪərə] *noun* person or company which buys something

acquisition [ækwɪˈzɪʃən] *noun* **(a)** thing bought; *the chocolate factory is his latest acquisition* **(b)** act of getting or buying something **(c)** takeover of a company; *the company has a record of making profitable acquisitions of traders in the retail sector* **(d)** business combination that is not a merger (see FRS 6); **acquisition accounting** *US* **purchase acquisition** = full consolidation, where the identifiable assets and liabilities of a subsidiary company acquired are included

in the acquirer's consolidated balance sheet at their fair value at the date of acquisition

> COMMENT: the results and cash flows of the acquired company are brought into the group accounts only from the date of acquisition; the figures for the previous period for the reporting entity should not be adjusted. The difference between the fair value of the net identifiable assets acquired and the fair value of the purchase consideration is goodwill (See FRS 6)

across-the-board [əˈkrɒs ðə ˈbɔːd] *adjective* applying to everything or everyone; *an across-the-board price increase*; **across-the-board tariff increase** = increase in duty which applies to a whole range of items

ACT = ADVANCE CORPORATION TAX

act [ækt] **1** *noun* **(a)** law passed by a parliament which must be obeyed by the people; *GB* **Companies Act** = Act which rules how companies should do their business; **Finance Act** = annual Act of Parliament which gives the government power to raise taxes as proposed in the budget; **Financial Services Act** = Act of the British Parliament which regulates the offering of financial services to the public **(b)** **act of God** = something you do not expect to happen, and which cannot be avoided (such as storms or floods); acts of God may be referred to in commercial contracts as one aspect of 'force majeure' **2** *verb* **(a)** to work; *to act as an agent for an American company*; *to act for someone or to act on someone's behalf*; **to act as insolvency practitioner** = to administer the affairs of an insolvent company **(b)** to do something; *the board will have to act quickly if the company's losses are going to be reduced*; *the lawyers are acting on our instructions*; **to act on a letter** = to do what a letter asks to be done; *(of several people)*; **to act in concert** = to work together to achieve an aim, such as to take over a company, especially in such a way as to defraud other investors; *see also* CONCERT PARTY

active [ˈæktɪv] *adjective* busy; **active account** = bank account which is used (i.e., money is deposited and withdrawn) frequently; **active partner** = partner who works in the company; *an active demand for oil shares*; *oil shares are very active*; *an active day on the Stock Exchange*; *business is active*

activity [ækˈtɪvəti] *noun* being active or busy; *a low level of business activity*; *there was a lot of activity on the Stock Exchange*; **activity chart** = plan showing work which has been done so that it can be compared to the plan of work to be done; **monthly activity report** = report by a department on what has been done during the past month; **ordinary activity** = normal trading of a company, that is, what the company normally does (see FRS 3)

> QUOTE preliminary indications of the level of business investment and activity during the March quarter will provide a good picture of economic activity in 2000
> *Australian Financial Review*

actual ['æktʃʊəl] **1** *adjective* real or correct; *what is the actual cost of one unit?*; *the actual figures for directors' expenses are not shown to the shareholders*; **actual price** = price for a commodity which is for immediate delivery (NOTE: also called **cash price, physical price, spot price**) **2** *noun* **(a)** actuals = real figures based on what has really happened, not what might happen in the future; *these figures are the actuals for 2000* **(b)** physical commodity which is ready for delivery (as opposed to futures) (NOTE: also called **cash, physical** or **spot**)

actuarial [æktjʊ'eərɪəl] *adjective* calculated by an actuary; *the premiums are worked out according to actuarial calculations*; **actuarial tables** = lists showing how long people of certain ages are likely to live, used to calculate life assurance premiums; **actuarial method** = (i) way of calculating the value of an asset which is paid for in instalments being partly capital and partly interest charges on the credit; (ii); *US* method of calculating an employer's contributions to a pension plan

actuary ['æktjʊəri] *noun* person employed by an insurance company or other organization to calculate the risk involved in an insurance, and therefore the premiums payable by persons taking out insurance; **consulting actuary** = independent actuary who advises individuals, or large corporations such as large pension funds, on questions of pensions and insurance

> COMMENT: in the UK, actuaries are qualified after passing the examinations of the Institute of Actuaries

add [æd] *verb* to put figures together to make a total; *to add interest to the capital*; *interest is added monthly*; **added value** = amount added to the value of a product or service, being the difference between its cost and the amount received when it is sold (wages, taxes, etc., are deducted from the

added value to give the retained profit); *see also* VALUE ADDED

> COMMENT: various added-value ratios can be used to calculate the overall efficiency of a company. Some of these are: added value per employee (the total of added value divided by the number of employees); added value/direct labour costs (added value divided by the total direct labour costs); added value/overheads; etc.

addend ['ædend] *noun* number added to the augend in an addition

addition [ə'dɪʃən] *noun* arithmetical operation of putting numbers together to make a sum

additional [ə'dɪʃənl] *adjective* extra which is added; **additional costs**; **additional charges**; **additional clauses to a contract**; *additional duty will have to be paid*; **additional voluntary contributions (AVCs)** = extra money paid by an individual into a company pension scheme to improve the benefits he will receive on retirement; *see also* FREESTANDING ADDITION VOLUNTARY CONTRIBUTIONS

address [ə'dres] **1** *noun* **(a)** details of number, street and town where an office is or a person lives; *my business address and phone number are printed on the card*; **accommodation address** = address used for receiving messages but which is not the real address of the company; **forwarding address** = address to which a person's mail can be sent on; **home address** = address of a house or flat where someone lives; *please send the documents to my home address*; **address list** = list of addresses; *we keep an address list of two thousand addresses in Europe* **(b)** *(computing)* number allowing a central processing unit to reference a location in a storage medium **2** *verb* **(a)** to write the details of an address on an envelope, etc.; *to address a letter or a parcel*; *please address your enquiries to the manager*; *a letter addressed to the managing director*; *an incorrectly addressed package* **(b)** *(in computing)* to refer to a location in a storage medium

addressee [ædre'siː] *noun* person to whom a letter or package is addressed

addressing machine [ə'dresɪŋ mə'ʃiːn] *noun* machine which puts addresses on envelopes automatically

add up ['æd 'ʌp] *verb* to put several figures together to make a total; *to add up a column* *of figures*; **the figures do not add up** = the total given is not correct

add up to ['æd 'ʌp tʊ] *verb* to make a total; *the total expenditure adds up to more than £1,000*

adeem [ə'diːm] *verb* to remove a legacy from a will because the item mentioned no longer exists (as when the person who made the will sells the item before he dies)

ademption [ə'demʃn] *noun* removing a legacy from a will, because the item concerned no longer exists

adequacy ['ædɪkwəsi] *noun* having enough of something; **capital adequacy ratio** = amount of money which a bank has to have in the form of shareholders' capital, shown as a percentage of its assets (this has been agreed internationally at 8%)

adequate ['ædɪkwət] *adjective* large enough; **to operate without adequate cover** = to act without being completely protected by insurance

adjudicate [ə'dʒuːdɪkeɪt] *verb* to give a judgement between two parties in law; to decide a legal problem; *to adjudicate a claim*; *to adjudicate in a dispute*; **he was adjudicated bankrupt** = he was declared legally bankrupt

adjudication [ədʒuːdɪ'keɪʃən] *noun* act of giving a judgement or of deciding a legal problem; **adjudication order** *or* **adjudication of bankruptcy** = order by a court making someone bankrupt; **adjudication tribunal** = group which adjudicates in industrial disputes

adjudicator [ə'dʒuːdɪkeɪtə] *noun* **(a)** person who gives a decision on a problem; *an adjudicator in an industrial dispute* **(b)** **the Adjudicator** = official who examines complaints from individuals and businesses about how the Inland Revenue handles their affairs, but does not deal with questions of tax liability

adjust [ə'dʒʌst] *verb* to change something to fit new conditions; *to adjust prices to take account of inflation*; *prices are adjusted for inflation*; **adjusting entry** = entry in accounts which is made to correct a mistake in the accounts

QUOTE inflation-adjusted GNP moved up at a 1.3% annual rate
Fortune

QUOTE Saudi Arabia will no longer adjust its production to match short-term supply with demand
Economist

adjustable [ə'dʒʌstəbl] *adjective* which can be adjusted; **adjustable peg** = situation where one currency is pegged to another, but with the possibility of adjusting the exchange rate from time to time; *US* **adjustable rate mortgage (ARM)** = mortgage where the interest rate changes according to the current market rates; **adjustable rate preferred stock (ARPS)** = preference shares on which dividends are paid in line with the interest rate on Treasury bills

adjuster [ə'dʒʌstə] *noun* person who calculates losses for an insurance company; **average adjuster** = person who calculates how much of a maritime insurance is to be paid by the insurer against a claim; **loss adjuster** = person who calculates how much insurance should be paid on a claim

adjustment [ə'dʒʌstmənt] *noun* **(a)** act of adjusting; slight change; *tax adjustment*; *wage adjustment*; *to make an adjustment to salaries*; *adjustment of prices to take account of rising costs*; **average adjustment** = calculation of the share of cost of damage or loss of a ship; *US* **adjustment credit** = short-term loan from the Federal Reserve to a commercial bank **(b)** entry in accounts which is made to make the accounts correct **(c)** change in the exchange rates to correct a balance of payment deficit; **adjustment trigger** = factor (such as a certain level of inflation) which triggers an adjustment in exchange rates

adjustor [ə'dʒʌstə] *noun* = ADJUSTER

ad litem ['æd 'liːtem] *Latin phrase meaning* 'referring to the case at law'; **guardian ad litem** = person who acts on behalf of a minor who is a defendant in a court case

administer [əd'mɪnɪstə] *verb* to organize, to manage; *he administers a large pension fund US* **administered price** = price fixed by a manufacturer which cannot be varied by a retailer (NOTE: in the UK, this is called **resale price maintenance**)

administration [ədmɪnɪ'streɪʃən] *noun* **(a)** organization, control or management of a company; **administration costs** *or* **expenses of the administration** *or* **administration expenses** = costs of management, not including production, marketing or distribution costs **(b)** appointment by a court of a person to manage the affairs of a company; **administration order** = (i) order by a court, appointing an administrator for a company; (ii) order by a court, by which the court arranges for a debtor to repay his debts in instalments; **letters of administration** = letter given by a court to allow someone to deal with the estate of a person who has died

QUOTE his repeated failure to get any of the money paid to the UK finally exhausted the patience of bank creditors, which have been pressing for the company to put itself into administration since the end of last week. Administration involves the appointment of an outside administrator by the court to oversee a reorganization of the company's affairs and orderly disposal of its assets for the benefit of all its creditors

Financial Times

administrative [əd'mɪnɪstrətɪv] *adjective* referring to administration; **administrative expenses** = costs of administration; **administrative receiver** = receiver appointed by a debenture holder to liquidate the assets of a company on his behalf; **administrative receivership** = appointment of an administrative receiver by a debenture holder

administrator [əd'mɪnɪstreɪtə] *noun* **(a)** person who directs the work of other employees in a business **(b)** (i) person or bank appointed by a court to manage the affairs of someone who dies without leaving a will; (ii) person appointed by a court to administer the affairs of a company

ADP = AUTOMATIC DATA PROCESSING

ADR = AMERICAN DEPOSITARY RECEIPT

ad valorem ['æd və'lɔːrəm] *Latin phrase* meaning 'according to value', showing that a tax is calculated as a percentage of the value of the goods taxed; *ad valorem duty*; *ad valorem tax*

advance [əd'vɑːns] **1** *noun* **(a)** money paid as a loan or as a part of a payment to be made later; *she asked if she could have a cash advance*; *to receive an advance from the bank*; *we paid her an advance on account*; *to make an advance of £100 to someone*; *to pay someone an advance against a security*; *can I have an advance of £50 against next month's salary?* **(b)** **in advance** = early, before something happens; *to pay in advance*; *freight payable in advance*; *price fixed in advance* **2** *adjective* early; *advance holiday bookings are up on last year*; *you must give seven days' advance notice of withdrawals*

from the account **3** *verb* **(a)** to pay money in advance; to lend; *the bank advanced him £10,000 against the security of his house* **(b)** to make something happen earlier; *the date of the AGM has been advanced to May 10th*; *the meeting with the German distributors has been advanced from 11.00 to 09.30*

Advance Corporation Tax (ACT)

[əd'vɑːns kɔːpə'reɪʃn 'tæks] *noun* tax paid by a company in advance of its main corporation tax payments; it is paid when dividends are paid to shareholders and is deducted from the main tax payment when that falls due; it appears on the tax voucher attached to a dividend warrant

COMMENT: in the UK, over the four years from April 1999, ACT was being phased out in favour of a system of quarterly advance payments of corporation tax

adverse ['ædvɜːs] *adjective* bad, not helpful; **adverse balance of trade** = situation when a country imports more than it exports; *US* **adverse opinion** = an auditor's report that a company's financial statement is not a fair representation of the company's actual financial position; **adverse trading conditions** = bad conditions for trade; **adverse variance** = variance which shows that the actual result is worse than expected

advice [əd'vaɪs] *noun* **(a) advice note** = (i) written notice to a customer giving details of goods ordered and shipped but not yet delivered; (ii) written notice from a bank to a customer, showing that a sum has been debited or credited to his account; **as per advice** = (i) according to what is written on the advice note; (ii) advising that a bill of exchange has been drawn **(b)** opinion as to what action to take; *the accountant's advice was to send the documents to the police*; *we sent the documents to the police on the advice of the accountant* or *we took the accountant's advice and sent the documents to the police*; **to take legal advice** = to ask a lawyer to say what should be done

advise [əd'vaɪz] *verb* **(a)** to tell someone what has happened; *we are advised that the shipment will arrive next week* **(b)** to suggest to someone what should be done; *we are advised to take the shipping company to court*; *the accountant advised us to send the documents to the police*

advise against [əd'vaɪz ə'genst] *verb* to suggest that something should not be done; *the bank manager advised against closing the account*; *my stockbroker has advised against buying those shares*

adviser _or_ **advisor** [əd'vaɪzə] _noun_ person who suggests what should be done; _he is consulting the company's legal adviser_; **financial adviser** = person or company which gives advice on financial problems for a fee

advisory [əd'vaɪzəri] _adjective_ as an adviser; _he is acting in an advisory capacity_; **an advisory board** = a group of advisers; **advisory funds** = funds placed with a financial institution to invest on behalf of a client, the institution investing them at its own discretion

AFA = ASSOCIATE OF THE INSTITUTE OF FINANCIAL ACCOUNTANTS

AFBD = ASSOCIATION OF FUTURES BROKERS AND DEALERS

affect [ə'fekt] _verb_ to change, to have a effect on (something); _the new government regulations do not affect us_; _the company's sales in the Far East were seriously affected by the embargo_

QUOTE the dollar depreciation has yet to affect the underlying inflation rate
Australian Financial Review

affiliate [ə'fɪlɪeɪt] _noun_ company which partly owns another company, or is partly owned by the same holding company as another

affiliated [ə'fɪlɪeɪtɪd] _adjective_ connected with or partly owned by another company; **affiliated enterprise** _or_ **affiliated company** = company which is partly owned by another (though less than 50%), and where the share-owning company exerts some management control or has a close trading relationship with the associate; _one of our affiliated companies_

afterdate ['ɑːftədeɪt] _noun_ bill of exchange payable at a date later than that on the bill

after-hours ['ɑːftə'aʊəz] _adjective_ **after-hours buying** _or_ **selling** _or_ **dealing** _or_ **trading** = buying, selling or dealing in shares after the Stock Exchange has officially closed for the day, such deals being subject to normal Stock Exchange rules (in this way, dealers can take advantage of the fact that because of time differences, the various stock exchanges round the world are open almost all twenty-four hours of the day)

aftermarket ['ɑːftəmɑːkɪt] _noun_ market in new shares, which starts immediately after

trading in the shares begins (i.e., a secondary market)

after tax ['ɑːftə 'tæks] _phrase_ after tax has been paid; **real return after tax** = return calculated after deducting tax and inflation; **after-tax profit** = profit after tax has been deducted

against [ə'genst] _preposition_ relating to, part of; compared with; _to pay an advance against a security_; _can I have an advance against next month's salary?_; _the bank advanced him £10,000 against the security of his house_

QUOTE investment can be written off against the marginal rate of tax
Investors Chronicle

aged debtors analysis _or_ **ageing schedule** ['eɪdʒd 'detəz ə'næləsɪs _or_ 'eɪdʒɪŋ 'ʃedjuːl] _noun_ list which analyses a company's debtors, showing the number of days their payments are outstanding (NOTE: American spelling is **aging**)

COMMENT: an ageing schedule shows all the debtors of a company and lists (usually in descending order of age) all the debts that are outstanding: they are usually listed as 'under 30 days', 'under 60 days', 'under 90 days' and 'over 90 days'

agency ['eɪdʒənsi] _noun_ **(a)** office or job of representing another company in an area; _they signed an agency agreement_ _or_ _an agency contract_; **sole agency** = agreement to be the only person to represent a company or to sell a product in a certain area; _he has the sole agency for Ford cars_ **(b)** office or business which arranges things for other companies; _US_ **agency bank** = bank which does not accept deposits, but acts as an agent for another (usually foreign) bank; **agency bill** = bill of exchange drawn on the local branch of a foreign bank; **agency broker** = dealer who acts for a client, buying and selling shares for a commission; **agency worker** = person who is employed by an agency to work for another company (he or she is taxed as an employee of the agency, not of the company where he or she actually works); **employment agency** = office which attempts to find jobs for its clients

agenda [ə'dʒendə] _noun_ list of items to be discussed at a meeting

agent ['eɪdʒənt] _noun_ **(a)** person who represents a company or another person in an area; _to be the agent for IBM_; **sole agent** = person who has the sole agency for a company in an area; _he is the sole agent for Ford cars_; **agent's commission** = money (often a percentage of sales) paid to an agent **(b)** person in charge of an agency; **commission agent** = agent who is paid by commission, not by fee; **forwarding agent** = person or company which arranges shipping and customs documents; **insurance agent** = person who arranges insurance for clients **(c)** *US* **(business) agent** = chief local official of a trade union **(d)** *US* **agent bank** = bank which uses the credit card system set up by another bank

age-related ['eɪdʒrɪ'leɪtɪd] *adjective* connected with a person's age; **age-related allowance** = extra tax allowance which a person over 65 may be entitled to

aggregate ['ægrɪgət] *adjective* total, with everything added together; **aggregate demand** = total demand for goods and services from all sectors of the economy (from individuals, companies and the government); **aggregate risk** = risk which a bank runs in lending to a customer; **aggregate supply** = total supply of goods and services to meet the aggregate demand

agio ['ædʒɪəʊ] *noun* **(a)** charge made for changing money of one currency into another, or for changing banknotes into cash **(b)** difference between two values, such as between the interest charged on loans made by a bank and the interest paid by the bank on deposits, or the difference between the values of two currencies, or between a gold coin and paper currency of the same face value

AGM ['eɪdʒiː'em] = ANNUAL GENERAL MEETING

agree [ə'griː] *verb* **(a)** to approve, to verify; *the auditors have agreed the accounts*; *the figures were agreed between the two parties*; *we have agreed the budgets for next year*; *terms of the contract are still to be agreed* **(b)** to say yes, or to accept; *it has been agreed that the lease will run for 25 years*; *after some discussion he agreed to our plan*; *we all agreed on the plan* (NOTE: to agree **to** *or* **on** a plan) **(c)** to agree to do something = to say that you will do something; *she agreed to be chairman*; *will the finance director agree to resign?*; *the bank will never agree to lend the company £250,000*

agreed [ə'griːd] *adjective* which has been accepted by everyone; **agreed takeover bid** = takeover bid which is accepted by the target company and recommended by the directors to the shareholders

agreement [ə'griːmənt] *noun* contract between two parties which explains how they will act; **written agreement**; **unwritten** *or* **verbal agreement**; **to draw up** *or* **to draft an agreement**; **to break an agreement**; **to sign an agreement**; **to witness an agreement**; **an agreement has been reached** *or* **concluded** *or* **come to**; **to reach an agreement** *or* **to come to an agreement on prices** *or* **salaries**; **an international agreement on trade**; **exclusive agreement** = agreement where a company is appointed sole agent for a product in a market; **gentleman's agreement** *US* **gentlemen's agreement** = verbal agreement between two parties who trust each other; **agreement to sell** = contract between two parties, where one agrees to sell something to the other at a date in the future

> QUOTE after three days of tough negotiations the company has reached agreement with its 1,200 unionized workers
> *Toronto Star*

agree with [ə'griː wɪð] *verb* **(a)** to say that your opinions are the same as someone else's; *I agree with the chairman that the figures are lower than normal* **(b)** to be the same as; *the auditors' figures do not agree with those of the accounts department*

AICPA = AMERICAN INSTITUTE OF CERTIFIED PUBLIC ACCOUNTANTS

algorithm ['ælgərɪðm] *noun* rules used to define or perform a specific task, or to solve a specific problem

alien corporation ['eɪlɪən kɔːpə'reɪʃn] *noun US* company which is incorporated in another country

alimony ['ælɪmənɪ] *noun* money which a court orders a husband to pay regularly to his separated or divorced wife; *alimony payments may be taxable* (NOTE: in British English this is usually referred to as **maintenance**)

> COMMENT: alimony can occasionally be applied to a wife who is ordered to support her divorced husband

allocate ['æləkeɪt] *verb* **(a)** to divide (a sum of money) in various ways and share it out; *we allocate 10% of revenue to publicity*; *$2,500 was allocated to office furniture* **(b)** to charge overhead costs directly to the cost centre to which they relate; **allocated costs** = overhead costs which have been allocated to a certain cost centre; *see also comment at* APPORTION

allocation [ælə'keɪʃən] *noun* **(a)** dividing a sum of money in various ways; *allocation of capital*; *allocation of funds to a project* **(b)**

way in which overhead expenses are related to various cost centres; *see COMMENT at* ABSORPTION **(c) share allocation** *or* **allocation of shares** = spreading the number of shares available among a large group of people who have applied for them

allonge [ə'lɒnʒ] *noun* piece of paper attached to a bill of exchange, so that endorsements can be written on it

allot [ə'lɒt] *verb* to share out; **to allot shares** = to give a certain number of shares to people who have applied for them (NOTE: **allotting - allotted)**

allotment [ə'lɒtmənt] *noun* **(a)** sharing out funds by giving money to various departments; *allotment of funds to a project* **(b)** giving new shares in a company to people who have applied for them; *share allotment*; *payment in full on allotment*; **letter of allotment** *or* **allotment letter** = letter which tells someone who has applied for new shares in a company how many shares he has been allotted (the letter acts as a temporary share certificate)

allow [ə'lau] *verb* **(a)** to say that someone can do something; *junior members of staff are not allowed to use the chairman's lift; the company allows all members of staff to take six days' holiday at Christmas* **(b)** to give; *to allow someone a discount; to allow 5% discount to members of staff; to allow 10% interest on large sums of money* **(c)** to agree, to accept legally; *to allow a claim or an appeal*

allowable [ə'lauəbl] *adjective* legally accepted; **allowable deductions** = deductions from income which are allowed by the Inland Revenue, and which reduce the tax payable; **allowable expenses** = expenses which can be claimed against tax; **allowable losses** = losses (as on the sale of assets) which are allowed to be set off against gains (NOTE: the opposite is **disallowable)**

allowance [ə'lauəns] *noun* **(a)** money which is given for a special reason; **cost-of-living allowance** = addition to normal salary to cover increases in the cost of living; **entertainment allowance** = money which a manager is allowed to spend each month on meals with visitors **(b)** **allowances against tax** *or* **tax allowances** *or* **personal allowances** = part of someone's income which is not taxed; **capital allowances** = allowances based on the value of fixed assets which may be deducted from a company's profits and so reduce its tax liability; **writing-down allowance** = a form of capital allowance

giving tax relief to companies acquiring fixed assets which are then depreciated; **allowance for bad debts** = provision made in a company's accounts for debts which may never be paid **(c)** money removed from an invoice because the goods supplied are damaged, imperfect, etc. **(d)** *US* = PROVISION

> QUOTE the compensation plan includes base, incentive and car allowance totalling $50,000+
> Globe and Mail (Toronto)

allow for [ə'lau fɔː] *verb* to give a discount for, to make an adjustment for something; *to allow for money paid in advance; to allow 10% for packing; delivery is not allowed for* = delivery charges are not included; **allow 28 days for delivery** = calculate that delivery will take at least 28 days

alpha ['ælfə] *noun* **(a)** anticipated performance of a share, compared to the market in general **(b)** rate of return on a unit trust or mutual fund, compare with typical returns for that category of trust; *see also* BETA

amalgamate [ə'mælgəmeɪt] *verb* to join two or more companies together to form a single new company

amalgamation [əmælgə'meɪʃn] *noun* joining two or more companies together to form a single new company

American Accounting Association (AAA) [ə'merɪkən ə'kauntɪŋ əsəusɪ'eɪʃn] association of American accountants which publishes mainly academic studies on contemporary accounting issues

American Depositary Receipt (ADR) [ə'merɪkən dɪ'pɒzɪtri rɪ'siːt] *noun* document issued by an American bank to US citizens, making them unregistered shareholders of companies in foreign countries; the document allows them to receive dividends from their investments, and ADRs can themselves be bought or sold

> QUOTE we constantly stare at the idea of having an ADR facility, but I am not sure it would be worthwhile. We could get a NASDAQ quote as a service to institutions in the US, but when it comes to dealing they usually just pick up the phone and deal through London. There was a trend for British companies to get the Big Board listing, but I don't go for that. We get some institutional interest in our shares in the US without having an ADR
> Money Observer

COMMENT: buying and selling ADRs is easier for American investors than buying or selling the actual shares themselves, as it avoids stamp duty and can be carried out in dollars without incurring exchange costs

American Institute of Certified Public Accountants (AICPA)

[ə'merıkən 'ınstıtjuːt əv 'sɜːtıfaıd 'pʌblık ə'kaʊntəns] professional association representing Certified Public Accountants (CPAs)

amortizable [æmɔː'taızəbl] *adjective* which can be amortized; *the capital cost is amortizable over a period of ten years*

amortization [əmɔːtaı'zeıʃn] *noun* **(a)** act of amortizing; *amortization of a debt*; *amortization of a lease*; **amortization period** = length of a lease, used when depreciating the value of the asset leased **(b)** *US* = DEPRECIATION

amortize ['æmɔːtaız] *verb* **(a)** to pay off (a debt) by instalments or by putting money aside regularly over a period of time **(b)** to depreciate or to write down the capital value of an asset over a period of time in a company's accounts; *the capital cost is amortized over five years*; *see also* SINKING FUND

amount [ə'maʊnt] **1** *noun* quantity of money; *amount paid*; *amount deducted*; *amount owing*; *amount written off*; *what is the amount outstanding?*; *a small amount invested in gilt-edged stock* **2** *verb* **to amount to** = to make a total of; *their debts amount to over £1m*

analyse *or* **analyze** ['ænəlaız] *verb* to examine in detail; *to analyse a statement of account*

analysis [ə'næləsıs] *noun* detailed examination and report; *analysis of the financial situation of a company*; *to make a detailed analysis of the cashflow situation*; **cost analysis** = examination of the costs of a product or service; **systems analysis** = (i) analysing a process or system to see if it could be more efficiently carried out by a computer; (ii) examining an existing system with the aim of improving or replacing it (NOTE: plural is **analyses)**

analyst ['ænəlıst] *noun* person who makes analyses; **investment analyst** = person working for a stockbroking firm, who analyses the performance of companies in certain sectors of the market, or the performance of a market sector as a whole, or economic trends in general

annual ['ænjʊəl] *adjective* for one year; *annual statement of income*; *he has six weeks' annual leave*; **annual accounts** = balance sheet and profit and loss account for a company at the end of a year's trading; **annual depreciation provision** = allocation of the cost of an asset to a single year of the asset's expected year; **annual exemptions** = amount of income which is exempt from tax (as in the case of capital gains, where the first œ7,000 in any one year is exempt from tax); **annual report and accounts** = report from the directors on the company's financial situation at the end of a year, together with the balance sheet, profit and loss account, statement of source and application of funds, and the auditor's report, all prepared for the shareholders of the company each year; **annual return** = official report which a registered company has to make each year to the Registrar of Companies; **on an annual basis** = each year; *the figures are revised on an annual basis*

QUOTE real wages have risen at an annual rate of only 1% in the last two years
Sunday Times

QUOTE the remuneration package will include an attractive salary, profit sharing and a company car together with four weeks annual holiday
Times

annual general meeting (AGM)

['ænjʊəl 'dʒenrəl 'miːtıŋ] *noun* annual meeting of all the members (that is, the shareholders) of a company, when the company's financial situation is presented by and discussed with the directors, when the accounts for the past year are approved, when dividends are declared and auditors are appointed, etc. (NOTE: the American term is **annual meeting** or **annual stockholders' meeting)**

annualized ['ænjʊəlaızd] *adjective* shown on an annual basis; **annualized percentage rate** = yearly percentage rate, calculated by multiplying the monthly rate by twelve (not as accurate as the APR, which includes fees and other charges)

annually ['ænjʊəli] *adverb* each year; *the figures are updated annually*

Annual Percentage Rate (APR)

['ænjʊəl pə'sentıdʒ 'reıt] *noun* rate of interest (such as on a hire-purchase agreement) shown on an annual compound basis, including fees and charges

QUOTE ever since October, when the banks' base rate climbed to 15 per cent, the main credit card issuers have faced the prospect of having to push interest rates above 30 per cent APR. Though store cards have charged interest at much higher rates than this for some years, 30 per cent APR is something the banks fight shy of
Financial Times Review

COMMENT: because hire purchase agreements quote a flat rate of interest covering the whole amount borrowed or a monthly repayment figure, the Consumer Credit Act, 1974, forces lenders to show the APR on documentation concerning hire purchase agreements, so as to give an accurate figure of the real rate of interest as opposed to the nominal rate. The APR includes various fees charged (such as the valuation of a house for mortgage); it may also vary according to the sum borrowed - a credit card company will quote a lower APR if the borrower's credit limit is low

annuitant [ə'njuːɪtənt] *noun* person who receives an annuity

annuity [ə'njuːəti] *noun* money paid each year to a retired person, usually in return for a lump-sum payment; the value of the annuity depends on how long the person lives, as it cannot be passed on to another person; annuities are fixed payments, and lose their value with inflation, whereas a pension can be index-linked; *to buy or to take out an annuity*; **annuity certain** = annuity which is payable over a fixed period of time; **annuity contract** = contract under which a person is paid a fixed sum regularly for life; **annuity for life** *or* **life annuity** = annual payments made to someone as long as he is alive; **reversionary annuity** = annuity paid to someone on the death of another person

antedate ['æntɪdeɪt] *verb* to put an earlier date on a document; *the invoice was antedated to January 1st*

anti- ['ænti] *prefix* against

anticipate [æn'tɪsɪpeɪt] *verb* to expect something to happen; **anticipated balance** = balance which is forecast from a deposit when it matures

anti-dumping ['ænti'dʌmpɪŋ] *adjective* which protects a country against dumping; *anti-dumping legislation*

anti-inflationary ['æntiɪn'fleɪʃnəri] *adjective* which tries to restrict inflation; *anti-inflationary measures*

anti-trust ['ænti'trʌst] *adjective* which attacks monopolies and encourages competition; **anti-trust laws** *or* **legislation** = laws in the US which prevent the formation of monopolies

APB *GB* = AUDITING PRACTICES BOARD *US (formerly)* = ACCOUNTING PRINCIPLES BOARD

applicant ['æplɪkənt] *noun* person who applies for something; *applicant for a job or job applicant*; *there were thousands of applicants for shares in the new company*

application [æplɪ'keɪʃən] *noun* **(a)** way in which something is used; **application of funds** = details of the way in which funds have been spent during an accounting period; *see also* SOURCE AND APPLICATION OF FUNDS STATEMENT **(b)** asking for something, usually in writing; *application for shares*; *shares payable on application*; *application for a job or job application*; **application form** = form to be filled in when applying for a new issue of shares *or* for a job; *to fill in an application (form) for an issue of shares or a share application (form)*; *attach the cheque to the share application form*

apply [ə'plaɪ] *verb* **(a)** to ask for something, usually in writing; *to apply for a job*; *to apply for shares*; *to apply in writing*; *to apply in person* **(b)** to affect, to relate to; *this clause applies only to deals outside the EC*

appoint [ə'pɔɪnt] *verb* to choose someone to do a job; *to appoint an official receiver*

appointment [ə'pɔɪntmənt] *noun* being appointed to a job; **on his appointment as receiver** = when he was made receiver of the company

apportion [ə'pɔːʃən] *verb* to share out (costs); *costs are apportioned according to projected revenue*

COMMENT: several methods can be used to apportion costs which are incurred in common (such as administrative costs, storage, cleaning, staff canteen and sports club, etc.). Cost can be split according to the number of employees in each cost centre, according to the floor area or the total cubic space occupied by the cost centre; they can also be related to the total wage bill of the cost centre, the number of hours worked, etc.

apportionment [ə'pɔːʃənmənt] *noun* sharing out of common overhead costs among various cost centres; *see COMMENT at* ABSORPTION

appraisal [ə'preɪzəl] *noun* calculation of the value of someone or something; **capital investment appraisal** = analysis of the future profitability of capital purchases as an aid to good management; **staff appraisals** = reports on how well each member of staff is working

appraise [ə'preɪz] *verb* to assess or to calculate the value of something

appreciate [ə'priːʃieɪt] *verb* **(a)** *(of currency, stocks)* to increase in value; *the dollar has appreciated in terms of the yen; these shares have appreciated by 5%* **(b)** to notice how good something is; *the customer always appreciates efficient service; tourists do not appreciate long delays at banks*

COMMENT: although most assets depreciate in value during an accounting period some, such as land, buildings and investments, may actually appreciate. If this happens, the company may want to show these assets in the balance sheet at the higher value

appreciation [əpriː'eɪʃən] *noun* **(a)** *(of currency, stocks)* increase in value; *these shares show an appreciation of 10%; the appreciation of the dollar against the peseta* **(b)** valuing something highly; *he was given a rise in appreciation of his excellent work*

appro ['æprəʊ] *noun* = APPROVAL; **to buy something on appro** = to buy something which you will only pay for if it is satisfactory

appropriate [ə'prəʊprieɪt] *verb* to put a sum of money aside for a special purpose; *to appropriate a sum of money for a capital project*

appropriation [əprəʊpri'eɪʃən] *noun* act of putting money aside for a special purpose; *appropriation of funds to the reserve;* **appropriation account** = part of a profit and loss account which shows how each part of the profit has been dealt with (i.e. how much has been given to the shareholders as dividends, how much is being put into the reserves, what proportion of the profits comes from subsidiary companies, etc.)

approval [ə'pruːvəl] *noun* **(a)** agreement; *to submit a budget for approval;* **certificate of approval** = document showing that an item has been approved officially **(b) on approval** = sale where the buyer only pays for goods if they are satisfactory; *to buy a photocopier on approval*

approve [ə'pruːv] *verb* **(a) to approve of** = to think something is good; *the chairman approves of the new company letter heading; the sales staff do not approve of interference from the accounts division* **(b)** to agree to something officially; *to approve the terms of a contract; the proposal was approved by the board;* **approved scheme** = pension scheme

or share purchase scheme which has been approved by the Inland Revenue; *US* **approved securities** = state bonds which can be held by banks to form part of their reserves (the list of these bonds is the 'approved list')

approximate [ə'prɒksɪmət] *adjective* not exact, but almost correct; *the sales division has made an approximate forecast of expenditure*

approximately [ə'prɒksɪmətli] *adverb* almost correctly; *expenditure is approximately 10% down on the previous quarter*

approximation [əprɒksɪ'meɪʃən] *noun* rough calculation; *approximation of expenditure; the final figure is only an approximation*

APR = ANNUAL PERCENTAGE RATE

arbitrage ['ɑːbɪtreɪdʒ] *noun* **(a)** making a profit from the difference in value of various assets, such as: selling foreign currencies or commodities on one market and buying on another at almost the same time to profit from different exchange rates; buying currencies forward and selling them forward at a later date, to benefit from a difference in prices; buying a security and selling another security to the same buyer with the intention of forcing up the value of both securities **(b) risk arbitrage** = buying shares in companies which are likely to be taken over and so rise in price; **arbitrage syndicate** = group of people formed to raise the capital to invest in arbitrage deals

arbitrager *or* **arbitrageur** ['ɑːbɪtreɪdʒə *or* ɑːbɪtrɑː'ʒɜː] *noun* **(risk) arbitrageur** = person whose business is risk arbitrage

COMMENT: arbitrageurs buy shares in companies which are potential takeover targets, either to force up the price of the shares before the takeover bid, or simply as a position while waiting for the takeover bid to take place. They also sell shares in the company which is expected to make the takeover bid, since one of the consequences of a takeover bid is usually that the price of the target company rises while that of the bidding company falls. Arbitrageurs may then sell the shares in the target company at a profit, either to one of the parties making the takeover bid, or back to the company itself. See also GREENMAIL

arbitration [ɑːbɪ'treɪʃən] *noun* settlement of a dispute by the two parties concerned, using an arbitrator, an outside person, chosen by both sides; *to submit a dispute to arbitration; to refer a question to arbitration; to take a dispute to arbitration;*

to go to arbitration; **arbitration board** *or* **arbitration tribunal** = group which arbitrates; **industrial arbitration tribunal** = court which decides in industrial disputes

arbitrator ['ɑːbɪtreɪtə] *noun* person not concerned with a dispute who is chosen by both sides to try to settle it; *they refused to accept or they rejected the arbitrator's ruling*

ARM = ADJUSTABLE RATE MORTGAGE

around [ə'raʊnd] *preposition* **(a)** approximately; *the office costs around £2,000 a year to heat*; *his salary is around $85,000* **(b)** *(in foreign exchange dealings)* with a premium or discount; **5 points around** = with a 5-point premium and a 5-point discount, both calculated on the spot price

ARPS = ADJUSTABLE RATE PREFERRED STOCK

ARR = ACCOUNTING RATE OF RETURN

arrangement fee [ə'reɪndʒmənt 'fiː] *noun* charge made by a bank to a client for arranging credit facilities; **scheme of arrangement** = scheme drawn up by an individual or company to offer ways of paying debts, so as to avoid bankruptcy proceedings

> QUOTE on the upside scenario the outlook is reasonably optimistic, bankers say, the worst scenario being that a scheme of arrangement cannot be achieved, resulting in liquidation
>
> *Irish Times*

arrears *or* **arrear** [ə'rɪəz] *noun* money which is owed, but which has not been paid at the right time; *arrears of interest*; *to allow the payments to fall into arrears*; *salary with arrears effective from January 1st*; **in arrears** = owing money which should have been paid earlier; *the payments are six months in arrears*; *he is six weeks in arrears with his rent*; **calls in arrear(s)** = money called up for shares, but not paid at the correct time (the shares may be forfeited) and a special calls in arrear account is set up to debit the sums owing

article ['ɑːtɪkl] *noun* **(a)** product or thing for sale; *to launch a new article on the market*; *a black market in luxury articles* **(b)** section of a legal agreement; *see article 10 of the contract*; **article 8 currency** = strong convertible currency (according to the IMF) **(c) articles of association** = document which lays down the rules for a company regarding the issue of shares, the conduct of meetings, the appointment of directors, etc. (NOTE: in

the USA, called **bylaws**) *director appointed under the articles of the company*; *this procedure is not allowed under the articles of association of the company US* **articles of incorporation** = document which sets up a company and lays down the relationship between the shareholders and the company (NOTE: in the UK called **Memorandum of Association)**; **Memorandum (and Articles) of Association** = legal documents setting up a limited company and giving details of its name, aims, authorized share capital, conduct of meetings, appointment of directors, and registered office

asap ['eɪ'es'eɪ'piː *or* 'æsæp] = AS SOON AS POSSIBLE

ASB = ACCOUNTING STANDARDS BOARD

ASC = ACCOUNTING STANDARDS COMMITTEE (replaced by the Accounting Standards Board)

ascending tops [ə'sendɪŋ 'tɒps] *noun* term used by chartists to refer to an upward trend in the market, where each peak is higher than the preceding one

asked price ['ɑːskt 'praɪs] *noun* price at which a commodity or stock is offered for sale by a seller (also called 'offer price' in the UK)

asking price ['ɑːskɪŋ 'praɪs] *noun* price which the seller asks for the goods being sold; *the asking price is £24,000*

assay mark [ə'seɪ 'mɑːk] *noun* mark put on gold or silver items to show that the metal is of the correct quality

assess [ə'ses] *verb* to calculate the value of something; *to assess damages at £1,000*; *to assess a property for the purposes of insurance*; *tax for the year was assessed at £20,000*

assessment [ə'sesmənt] *noun* calculation of value; *assessment of damages*; *assessment of property*; **tax assessment** = calculation by a tax inspector of the amount of tax a person owes (NOTE: in the UK this has now been replaced by self-assessment); **staff assessments** = reports on how well members of staff are working

asset ['æsɪt] *noun* **(a)** thing which belongs to company or person, and which has a value (an asset can be tangible or intangible, current, fixed, etc.); *he has an excess of assets over liabilities*; *her assets are only £640 as against liabilities of £24,000* **(b)** **assets** = liabilities plus owners' equity;

capital assets *or* **fixed assets** = property or machinery which a company owns and uses in its business, but which the company does not buy or sell as part of its regular trade (fixed assets are divided into tangible fixed assets, intangible fixed assets, and investments); **current assets** = assets used by a company in its ordinary work (such as materials, finished goods, cash, monies due) and which are held for a short time only; **frozen assets** = assets of a company which cannot be sold because someone has a claim against them; **intangible (fixed) assets** = assets which are not visible, such as patents, licences, copyrights, development costs (see FRS10), but which have a value; **liquid assets** = cash, or investments or other assets which can be quickly converted into cash; **personal assets** = moveable assets which belong to a person; **tangible assets** = assets which are visible (such as furniture, jewels or cash); **tangible assets** *or* **property** = assets which are visible (such as machinery, buildings, furniture, jewellery, etc.); **tangible (fixed) assets** = assets such as land, buildings, plant and equipment, etc., that have physical substance and are held for use in the production or supply of goods or services, for rental to others, or for administrative purposes on a continuing basis in a reporting entity's activities (see FRS 15); **asset backing** = support for a share price provided by the value of the company's assets; **valuation of a company on an assets basis** = calculating the value of a company on the basis of the value of its assets (as opposed to a valuation on an earnings or dividend yield basis); **asset cover** = ratio of assets to borrowings; **asset-rich company** = company with valuable tangible assets, such as property, which provide firm backing for its shares; **asset stripper** = person who buys a company to sell its assets; **asset stripping** = buying a company at a lower price than its asset value, and then selling its assets; **asset value** = value of a company calculated by adding together all its assets

QUOTE many companies are discovering that a well-recognised brand name can be a priceless asset that lessens the risk of introducing a new product
Duns Business Month

QUOTE assets are probable future economic benefits obtained or controlled by a particular entity as a result of past transactions or events
FASB Concepts Statement No. 3

COMMENT: a company's balance sheet will show assets in various forms: current assets, fixed assets, intangible assets, etc. A company's assets are made up of any of the following resources: land, buildings, plant, equipment, stocks of raw materials, finished or semi-finished products; intangibles such as patents, goodwill and copyrights; money, and money owed; investments in other companies

asset-backed ['æsɪt'bækt] *adjective* (shares) which are backed by the security of assets

assign [ə'saɪn] *verb* **(a)** to give legally; *to assign a right to someone*; *to assign shares to someone* **(b)** to give someone a job of work; *he was assigned the job of checking the sales figures*

assignation [æsɪg'neɪʃən] *noun* legal transfer; *assignation of shares to someone*; *assignation of a patent*

assignee [æsaɪ'ni:] *noun* person who receives something which has been assigned to him

assignment [ə'saɪnmənt] *noun* **(a)** legal transfer of a property or of a right to a payment; *assignment of a patent or of a copyright*; *to sign a deed of assignment* **(b)** particular job of work; *he was appointed managing director with the assignment to improve the company's profits*; *the oil team is on an assignment in the North Sea*

assignor [æsaɪ'nɔ:] *noun* person who assigns a right to someone

associate [ə'səʊsɪət] **1** *adjective* linked; **associate company** = ASSOCIATED COMPANY; **associate director** = director who attends board meetings, but has not been elected by the shareholders **2** *noun* **(a)** person who works in the same business as someone; *she is a business associate of mine* **(b)** = ASSOCIATED COMPANY **(c)** person or company linked to another in a takeover bid **(d)** title given to a junior member of a professional organization (senior members are usually called 'fellows')

associated company [ə'səʊsɪeɪtɪd 'kʌmpəni] *noun* company which is partly owned by another (though less than 50%), and where the share-owning company exerts some management control or has a close trading relationship with the associate (see FRS 9); *Smith Ltd and its associated company, Jones Brothers*

association [əsəʊsɪ'eɪʃən] *noun* **(a)** group of people or of companies with the same interest; *trade association*; *employers'* *association*; *manufacturers' association*; **Association of Accounting Technicians (AAT)** = organization which groups accounting technicians and grants membership to people who have passed its examinations; **Association of Authorized Public Accountants** = organization which groups accountants who have been authorized by the government to work as auditors; **Association of Chartered Accountants in the United States (ACAUS)** = organization representing Chartered Accountants from Australia, Canada, England and Wales, Ireland, New Zealand, Scotland and South Africa who are based in the United States; **Association of Chartered Certified Accountants (ACCA)** = professional association of certified accountants in the UK; it holds examinations and successful students car called Chartered Certified Accountants; **Association of Corporate Treasurers** = organization which groups company treasurers and awards membership to those who have passed its examinations; **Association of Futures Brokers and Dealers (AFBD)** = self-regulating organization which regulates the activities of dealers in futures and options **(b)** **Memorandum of Association** = document drawn up at the same time as the articles of association of a company, in which the company's objects are defined, the details of the share capital, directors, registered office, etc. are set out (NOTE: in the USA, called **articles of incorporation)**

assumable mortgage [ə'sju:məbl 'mɔ:gɪdʒ] *noun US* mortgage which can be passed to another person, such as a person buying the property from the mortgagor

assume [ə'sju:m] *verb* to take; *to assume all risks; he has assumed responsibility for marketing*

assumption [ə'sʌmpʃən] *noun* the act of taking; *assumption of risks*

assurance [ə'ʃʊərəns] *noun* insurance, agreement that in return for regular payments, a company will pay compensation for loss of life; *assurance company*; *assurance policy*; **life assurance** = insurance which pays a sum of money when someone dies

assure [ə'ʃʊə] *verb* to insure, to have a contract with a company where if regular payments are made, the company will pay compensation if you die; *to assure someone's life; he has paid the premiums to have his wife's life assured*; **the life assured** = the person whose life has been covered by the life assurance

assurer *or* **assuror** [ə'ʃʊərə] *noun* insurer, company which insures (NOTE: **assure, assurer,** and **assurance** are used in Britain for insurance policies relating to something which will certainly happen (such as death); for other types of policy (i.e., those against something which may or may not happen, such as an accident) use the terms **insure, insurer,** and **insurance)**

AST = AUTOMATED SCREEN TRADING

at arm's length [ət 'ɑːmz 'leŋθ] *phrase* **to deal with someone at arm's length** = to deal as if there were no connection between the two parties (as when a company buys a service from one of its own subsidiaries); *the directors were required to deal with the receiver at arm's length*

> QUOTE it is desirable that all dealing should be done at arm's length, but there are a number of grey areas; for example the so-called 'soft' commissions, whereby fund managers can pay commission out of the fund to stockbrokers, and themselves receive back services as a form of rebate on these commissions
> Financial Times Review

at best ['æt 'best] *phrase* **sell at best** *or* **sell at the market** = instruction to a stockbroker to sell shares at the best price possible

at call ['æt 'kɔːl] *phrase* immediately available; **money at call** = loans which the lender can ask to be repaid at any time

ATM ['eɪtiː'em] = AUTOMATED TELLER MACHINE

> QUOTE Swiss banks are issuing new Eurocheque cards which will guarantee Eurocheque cash operations but will also allow cash withdrawals from ATMs in Belgium, Denmark, Spain, France, the Netherlands, Portugal and Germany
> Banking Technology

at par ['æt 'pɑː] *phrase* equal to the face value; **share at par** = share whose value on the stock market is the same as its face value

at sight ['æt 'saɪt] *phrase* (financial instrument) which is payable when it is presented

attach [ə'tætʃ] *verb* **(a)** to fasten or to link; *I am attaching a copy of my previous letter; please find attached a copy of my letter of June 24th; the machine is attached to the floor so it cannot be moved; the bank attaches great importance to the deal* **(b)** to add a computer file to an email

attachment [ə'tætʃmənt] *noun* **(a)**
computer file sent with an email **(b)** holding a
debtor's property to prevent it from being sold
until debts are paid; **attachment of earnings**
= legal power to take money from a person's
salary to pay money, which is owed, to the
court; **attachment of earnings order** = court
order to make an employer pay part of an
employee's salary to the court to pay off
debts; **attachment order** = order from a court
to hold a debtor's property to prevent it being
sold until debts are paid

attest [ə'test] **1** *noun* formal statement,
such as a statement by an auditor that a
company's financial position is correctly
stated in the company's accounts **2** *verb* to
sign (a document such as a will) in the
presence of a witness who also signs as
evidence that the signature is real

attestation [ætes'teɪʃn] *noun* signing a
document (such as a will) in the presence of a
witness to show that the signature is genuine;
attestation clause = clause showing that the
signature of the person signing a legal
document has been witnessed

COMMENT: the attestation clause is usually
written: 'signed sealed and delivered by ... in
the presence of ...'

attract [ə'trækt] *verb* to bring something or
someone to something; *the deposits attract
interest at 15%*

QUOTE airlines offer special
stopover rates and hotel packages to
attract customers and to encourage
customer loyalty
                    Business Traveller

attractive [ə'træktɪv] *adjective* which
attracts; **attractive prices** = prices which are
cheap enough to make buyers want to buy;
attractive salary = good salary to make
high-quality applicants apply for the job

attributable profit [ə'trɪbjʊtəbl 'prɒfɪt]
noun part of the total profit expected from a
long-term contract which relates to the work
already done (see SSAP9)

auction ['ɔːkʃən] **1** *noun* **(a)** selling of
goods where people offer bids, and the item is
sold to the person who makes the highest
offer; *to sell goods by auction US at auction*;
to put something up for auction = to offer an
item for sale at an auction; **Dutch auction** =
auction where the auctioneer offers an item
for sale at a high price and gradually reduces
the price until someone makes a bid **(b)**
method of selling government stock, where
all stock on issue will be sold, and the highest
price offered will be accepted (as opposed to

tendering, where not all the stock may be sold
if the tender prices are too low); *(Stock
Exchange)*; **auction system** = system where
prices are struck as the result of marketmakers
offering stock for sale on the trading floor (as
opposed to a quote system, where prices are
quoted on a computerized screen) **2** *verb* to
sell at an auction; *the factory was closed and
the machinery was auctioned off*

QUOTE the Canadian government
auctioned $1.3 billion in two-year
bonds due March 5, 1993, at an
average yield of 9.292 per cent
                    Toronto Globe & Mail

auctioneer [ɔːkʃə'nɪə] *noun* person who
conducts an auction

audit ['ɔːdɪt] **1** *noun* examination of the
books and financial records of a company; *to
carry out the annual audit*; **external audit** *or*
independent audit = audit carried out by an
independent auditor (who is not employed by
the company); **internal audit** = audit carried
out by a department inside the company;
audit fee = fee charged by an auditor for
auditing a company's accounts; *US* **audit
opinion** = report of the audit of a company's
books, carried out by a certified public
accountant (also called 'accountant's
opinion'); **audit programme** = listing of all
the steps to be taken when auditing a
company's accounts; **audit report** =
AUDITORS' REPORT; **audit risk** = the risk
that auditors may give an inappropriate audit
opinion on financial statements; *see also*
RISK; **audit trail** = (i) series of checks
showing how a final figure in the audited
accounts was arrived at; (ii) checking a series
of computer transactions for errors or
irregularities (one of the ways of detecting
fraud on a Stock Exchange) **2** *verb* to examine
the books and financial records of a company;
to audit the accounts; *the books have not yet
been audited*; **to audit the stock** = to carry
out a stock control, in front of witnesses, so as
to establish the exact quantities and value of
stock

Audit Commission ['ɔːdɪt kə'mɪʃən]
noun British government agency whose duty
is to audit the accounts of ministries and other
government departments (NOTE: the
American equivalent is the **General
Accounting Office**)

auditing ['ɔːdɪtɪŋ] *noun* action of
examining the books and accounts or systems
and controls of a company

Auditing Practices Board (APB)
official body which determines the standards

for external auditors in the UK and Ireland (the principles are published in regular Statements of Auditing Standards (SASs)

auditor ['ɔːdɪtə] *noun* person, firm or partnership which audits; **external auditor** = independent person who audits the company's accounts; **internal auditor** = member of staff who examines a company's internal controls; **auditors' fees** = fees paid to a company's auditors, which are approved by the shareholders at an AGM; **auditors' report** = report written by a company's auditors after they have examined the accounts of the company (if they are satisfied, the report certifies that, in the opinion of the auditors, the accounts give a 'true and fair' view of the company's financial position); *see also* QUALIFICATION

COMMENT: auditors are appointed by the company's directors and voted by the AGM. In the USA, audited accounts are only required by corporations which are registered with the SEC, but in the UK all limited companies must provide audited annual accounts if they exceed the size criteria for audit exemption

augend ['ɔːgənd] *noun (in an addition)* the number to which another number (the addend) is added to produce the sum

authenticate [ɔː'θentɪkeɪt] *verb* to say that something is true, especially when stating that gold is of a correct quality

authorization [ɔːθəraɪ'zeɪʃən] *noun* permission, power to do something; *do you have authorization for this expenditure?*; *he has no authorization to act on our behalf*

authorize ['ɔːθəraɪz] *verb* **(a)** to give permission for something to be done; *to authorize payment of £10,000* **(b)** to give someone the authority to do something; *to authorize someone to act on the company's behalf*

QUOTE in 1934 Congress authorized President Franklin D. Roosevelt to seek lower tariffs with any country willing to reciprocate
Duns Business Month

authorized ['ɔːθəraɪzd] *adjective* permitted; **authorized capital** *or* **authorized (capital) stock** = amount of capital in the form of shares which a company is allowed to issue, as stated in the memorandum of association (not all the shares need to be issued); **authorized unit trusts (AUTs)** = official name for unit trusts which have to be managed according to EU directives

automated ['ɔːtəmeɪtɪd] *adjective* worked automatically by machines; **automated screen trading (AST)** = system where securities are bought, sold and matched automatically by computer; *US* **Automated Clearing House (ACH)** = organization set up by the federal authorities to settle securities transactions by computer; **Automated Teller Machine (ATM)** = machine which gives out cash when a special card is inserted and special instructions given; *see also* PIN

automatic [ɔːtə'mætɪk] *adjective* which works or takes place without any person making it happen; *there is an automatic increase in salaries on January 1st*; **automatic data processing (ADP)** = data processing done by a computer; **automatic telling machine (ATM)** = machine which gives out money when a special card is inserted and special instructions given; *see also* PIN

automatically [ɔːtə'mætɪkəli] *adverb* working without a person giving any instructions; *the invoices are sent out automatically*; *a demand note is sent automatically when the account is overdue*

automation [ɔːtə'meɪʃən] *noun* use of machines to do work with very little supervision by people

availability [əveɪlə'bɪləti] *noun* being obtainable; **offer subject to availability** = the offer is valid only if the goods are available

available [ə'veɪləbl] *adjective* which can be obtained or bought; *funds which are made available for investment in small businesses*; **available capital** = capital which is ready to be used

aval [æ'væl] *noun* term used in Europe to refer to a bill or promissory note which is guaranteed by a third party

AVC = ADDITIONAL VOLUNTARY CONTRIBUTION

average ['ævərɪdʒ] **1** *noun* **(a)** number calculated by adding together several figures and dividing by the number of figures added; *the average for the last three months or the last three months' average*; *sales average or average of sales*; **moving average** = average of share prices on a stock market, where the calculation is made over a period which moves forward regularly: the commonest are 100-day or 200-day averages, or 10- or 40-week moving averages; the average is calculated as the average figure for the whole period, and moves forward one day or week at a time (these averages are often used by chartists); **weighted average** = average which is calculated taking several factors into account, giving some more value than others; **average cost** *or* **price** = method of calculating the cost of stocks issued to production or in hand at the end of a period, based on average prices (as opposed to FIFO or LIFO methods); **simple average cost** *or* **price** = average cost of stock received during a period calculated at the end of the period as the average unit price of each delivery of stock rather than an average price of each unit delivered (as in weighted average price); **weighted average cost** *or* **price** = average price per unit of stock delivered in a period, calculated either at the end of the period or each time a new delivery is received **(b) on average** = in general; *on average, £15 worth of goods are stolen every day* **(c)** sharing of the cost of damage or loss of a ship between the insurers and the owners; **average adjuster** = person who calculates how much of a maritime insurance is to be paid by the insurer against a claim **2** *adjective* middle (figure); *average cost per unit; average price; average sales per representative; the average figures for the last three months; the average increase in prices* **3** *verb* to produce as an average figure; *price increases have averaged 10% per annum; days lost through sickness have averaged twenty-two over the last four years*

QUOTE a share with an average rating might yield 5 per cent and have a PER of about 10
Investors Chronicle

QUOTE the average price per kilogram for this season to the end of April has been 300 cents
Australian Financial Review

average due date ['ævərɪdʒ 'djuː 'deɪt] *noun* the average date when several different payments fall due

average out ['ævərɪdʒ 'aʊt] *verb* to come to a figure as an average; *it averages out at 10% per annum; sales increases have averaged out at 15%*

averager ['ævərɪdʒə] *noun* person who buys the same share at various times and at various prices to give an average price

average-sized ['ævərɪdʒ'saɪzd] *adjective* not large or small; *it is an average-sized company; he has an average-sized office*

averaging ['ævərɪdʒɪŋ] *noun* **(a)** buying or selling shares at different times and at different prices to establish an average price **(b) pound-cost averaging** = buying securities at different times, but always spending the same amount of money (NOTE: in the USA, this is called **dollar cost averaging)**

avoid [ə'vɔɪd] *verb* to try not to do something; *the company is trying to avoid bankruptcy; my aim is to avoid paying too much tax; we want to avoid direct competition with Smith Ltd* (NOTE: you avoid something or avoid **doing** something)

avoidance [ə'vɔɪdəns] *noun* trying not to do something; *avoidance of an agreement or of a contract;* **tax avoidance** = trying (legally) to pay as little tax as possible

award [ə'wɔːd] **1** *noun* decision which settles a dispute or claim; *the latest pay award has just been announced; an award by an industrial tribunal; the arbitrator's award was set aside on appeal* **2** *verb* to decide the amount of money to be given to someone; *to award someone a salary increase; to award damages; the judge awarded costs to the defendant;* **to award a contract to someone** = to decide that someone will have the contract to do work

Bb

Schedule B ['ʃedjuːl 'biː] *noun* formerly, a schedule to the Finance Acts under which tax was charged on income from woodlands (abolished in 1988)

Table B ['teɪbl 'biː] *noun* model memorandum of association of a limited company set out in the Companies Act, 1985

'B' shares ['biː 'ʃeəz] *plural noun* ordinary shares with special voting rights (often owned by the founder of a company and his family); *see* COMMENT *at* 'A' SHARES

baby bonds ['beɪbi 'bɒndz] *plural noun* US bonds in small denominations (i.e. $100) which the small investor can afford to buy

back [bæk] **1** *noun* opposite side to the front; *the conditions of sale are printed on the back of the invoice*; *please endorse the cheque on the back* **2** *adjective* referring to the past; **back duty** = duty or tax which is due but has not yet been paid; **back interest** = interest not yet paid; **back payment** = paying money which is owed; *the salesmen are claiming for back payment of unpaid commission*; **back rent** = rent owed; *the company owes £100,000 in back rent*; **back tax** = tax which is due but which has not as yet been paid **3** *adverb* as things were before; *he will pay back the money in monthly instalments*; *the store sent back the cheque because the date was wrong* **4** *verb* **(a)** to **back someone** = to help someone financially; *the bank is backing him to the tune of £100,000*; *he is looking for someone to back his project* **(b)** to **back a bill** = to sign a bill promising to pay it if the person it is addressed to is not able to do so

> QUOTE the businesses we back range from start-up ventures to established companies in need of further capital for expansion
>
> *Times*

backdate ['bækdeɪt] *verb* to put an earlier date on a cheque or an invoice than the date of writing; *backdate your invoice to April 1st*

back-end loaded ['bækend 'ləʊdɪd] *adjective* (insurance or investment scheme) where commission is charged when the investor withdraws his money from the scheme; *compare* FRONT-END

backer ['bækə] *noun* **(a)** person who gives someone financial support; *he has an Australian backer*; *one of the company's backers has withdrawn* **(b) backer of a bill** = person who backs a bill

backing ['bækɪŋ] *noun* **(a)** financial support; *he has the backing of an Australian bank*; *the company will succeed only if it has sufficient backing*; *who is providing the backing for the project* or *where does the backing for the project come from?* **(b) asset backing** = support for a share price provided by the value of the company's assets

> QUOTE the company has received the backing of a number of oil companies who are willing to pay for the results of the survey
>
> Lloyd's List

backlog ['bæklɒg] *noun* work (such as orders or letters) which has piled up waiting to be done; *the office is trying to cope with a backlog of share deals*; *my secretary can't cope with the backlog of paperwork*; **backlog depreciation** = depreciation which has not been provided in previous accounts because of an increase in the value of the asset during the current year due to inflation

back office ['bæk 'ɒfɪs] *noun* (i) the part of a broking firm where the paperwork involved in buying and selling shares is processed; (ii) US part of a bank where cheques are processed, statements of account drawn up, etc.

back out ['bæk 'aʊt] *verb* to stop being part of a deal or an agreement; *the bank backed out of the contract*; *we had to cancel the project when our German partners backed out*

back-to-back ['bæktə'bæk] *adjective* **back-to-back credit** = (i) credit facilities for the purchase of goods (the credit is asked for by the purchaser, but is granted to a middleman, who buys the goods, then sells them on to the final purchaser, and uses the credit as a basis for obtaining further credit facilities); (ii) credit in a currency allowed to a foreign trader on the basis of credit which has been granted by a bank in the trader's own country; **back-to-back loan** = loan from one company to another in one currency arranged against a loan from the second company to the first in another currency (used by international companies to get round exchange controls)

back up ['bæk 'ʌp] *verb* **(a)** to support, to help; *he brought along a file of documents to back up his claim*; *the finance director said the managing director had refused to back him up in his argument with the VAT office* **(b)** *US (of a market)* to go into reverse; **to back up a portfolio** = to sell long-term bonds and replace them by short-term bonds

backup ['bækʌp] **1** *noun* support or help **2** *adjective* supporting or helping; *we offer a free backup service to customers*; *after a series of sales tours by representatives, the sales director sends backup letters to all the contacts*; **backup copy** = copy of a computer disk to be kept in case the original disk is damaged; **backup credit** = credit provided by banks for a eurocurrency note; *US* **backup line** = credit provided by banks against the security of commercial bills of exchange

backwardation [bækwə'deɪʃən] *noun* **(a)** penalty paid by the seller when postponing delivery of shares to the buyer **(b)** (i) situation where the spot price of a commodity or currency is higher than the futures price; (ii) difference between the spot and futures prices (NOTE: the opposite is **forwardation** or **contango)**

BACS [bæks] system owned by the major clearing banks and building societies, which facilitates making payments from one bank account to another, usually taking only three days to complete the transaction

bad [bæd] *adjective* not good; **bad bargain** = item which is not worth the price asked; **bad buy** = thing bought which was not worth the money paid for it; **bad cheque** = cheque which is returned to the drawer for any reason

bad debt ['bæd 'det] *noun* debt which will not be paid (usually because the debtor has gone out of business) and which has to be written off in the accounts; *the company has written off £30,000 in bad debts*; **bad debts account** = special account set up to deal with bad debts (it is an account to which debts are transferred as they become bad); **bad debt provision** *or* **provision for bad debts** = an accounting estimate of the amount of debts thought likely to have to be written off

COMMENT: the bad dept provision is deducted from trade debtors for balance sheet presentation; the change in the provision from one year to the next together with any bad debts written off is the charge for bad debts in the profit and loss account

badges of trade ['bædʒɪz əv 'treɪd] *noun* collection of principles established by case law to determine whether or not a person is trading (if so, he is taxed under different rules from non-traders)

bailee [beɪ'liː] *noun* person who receives property by way of bailment

bailment ['beɪlmənt] *noun* **(a)** transfer of goods by someone (the bailor) to someone (the bailee) who then holds them until they have to be returned to the bailor (as when leaving a coat in a cloakroom or at the cleaner's) **(b)** placing personal property for safekeeping with someone (such as putting jewels in a bank's safe deposit box)

bailor [beɪ'lɔː] *noun* person who transfers property by way of bailment

bail out ['beɪl 'aʊt] *verb* **(a)** to rescue a company which is in financial difficulties **(b)** to sell one's holdings in a company **(c) to bail someone out** = to pay money to a court as a guarantee that someone will return to face charges; *she paid $3,000 to bail him out*

balance ['bæləns] **1** *noun* **(a)** amount to be put in one of the columns of an account to make the total debits and credits equal; **balance in hand** = cash held to pay small debts; **closing balance** = balance at the end of an accounting period; **balance brought down** *or* **forward** = the closing balance of the previous period used as the opening balance of the current period; **balance carried down** *or* **forward** = the closing balance of the current period **(b)** rest of an amount owed; *you can pay £100 deposit and the balance within 60 days*; **balance due to us** = amount owed to us which is due to be paid; **balance certificate** = share certificate given to an investor who has sold part of his shareholding (the certificate refers to the balance of the shares he has retained) **(c) balance of trade** *or* **trade balance** = record of the international trading position of a country in merchandise, excluding invisible trade; **adverse** *or* **unfavourable balance of trade** = situation where a country imports more than it exports; **favourable trade balance** = situation where a country exports more than it imports; *the country has had an adverse balance of trade for the second month running* **(d) bank balance** = state of an account at a bank at a particular time; **credit balance** = balance on an account showing that more money is owed or has been paid by the company than is due or has been received by the company; **debit balance** = balance in an account showing that more money is owed to or has been received by the company than is owed or has been paid by the company **2** *verb* **(a)** *(of two sides in a balance sheet)* to be equal (i.e., the assets owned must always equal the total liabilities plus capital) **(b)** to calculate the amount needed to make the two sides of an account equal; *I have finished balancing the accounts for March*; **the February accounts do not balance** = the two sides are not equal; **to balance off the accounts** = to make the two sides of an account balance at the end of an accounting period, by entering a debit balance in the credit side or a credit balance in the debit side, and carrying the balance forward into the next period; **balancing item** *or* **balancing figure** = item introduced into a balance sheet to make the two sides balance **(c)** to plan a budget so that expenditure and income are equal; **balanced budget** = budget where expenditure and income are equal

COMMENT: note that in accounting, the words 'debit' and 'credit' mean the exact opposite of bank debits and credits. Therefore if a company's bank account is £1000 'in credit' it will appear in the ledger accounts as a *debit* balance of £1000

balance of payments (BOP) ['bæləns əv 'peɪmənts] *noun* comparison between total receipts and payments arising from international trade in goods, services and financial transactions; **balance of payments capital account** = items in a country's balance of payments which refer to capital investments made in or by other countries; **balance of payments current account** = record of imports and exports of goods and services and the flows of money between countries arising from investments; **long-term balance of payments** = record of movements of capital relating to overseas investments and the purchase of companies overseas; **overall balance of payments** = the total of current and long-term balance of payments; **balance of payments deficit** = situation where a country buys more from other countries than it sells as exports; **balance of payments surplus** = situation where a country sells more to other countries than it buys from them

balance sheet ['bæləns 'ʃiːt] *noun* statement of the financial position of a company, trader or partnership at a particular time, such as the end of the financial year or the end of a quarter, showing the company's assets and liabilities; *the company balance sheet for the year shows a substantial loss*; *the accountant has prepared the balance sheet for the first half-year*; **balance sheet asset value** = value of a company calculated by adding together all its assets; **balance sheet date** = the date (usually the end of a financial or accounting year) when a balance sheet is drawn up

COMMENT: the balance sheet shows the state of a company's finances at a certain date; the profit and loss account shows the movements which have taken place since the end of the previous accounting period. A balance sheet must balance, with the basic equation that assets (i.e., what the company owns, including money owed to the company) must equal liabilities (i.e., what the company owes to its creditors) plus capital (i.e., what it owes to its shareholders). A balance sheet can be drawn up either in the horizontal form, with liabilities and capital on the left- hand side of the page (in the USA, it is the reverse) or in the vertical form, with assets at the top of the page, followed by liabilities, and capital at the bottom. Most are usually drawn up in the vertical format, as opposed to the more old-fashioned horizontal style

balloon [bə'luːn] *noun* (i) loan where the last repayment is larger than the others; (ii) large final payment on a loan, after a number of periodic smaller loans; *US* **balloon mortgage** = mortgage where the final payment (called a 'balloon payment') is larger than the others

band [bænd] *noun* range of figures between low and high, within which a figure can move (used for the range of movement which a currency is allowed to make against other currencies)

bank [bæŋk] **1** *noun* **(a)** business which holds money for its clients, which lends money at interest, and trades generally in money; *Lloyds Bank*; *The First National Bank*; *The Royal Bank of Scotland*; *he put all his earnings into his bank*; *I have had a letter from my bank telling me my account is overdrawn*; **bank loans** *or* **bank advances** = loans from a bank; *he asked for a bank loan to start his business*; **bank borrowing** = money borrowed from a bank; *the new factory was financed by bank borrowing*; **bank borrowings have increased** = loans given by banks have increased; **bank deposits** = all money placed in banks by private or corporate customers; **bank identification number (BIN)** = internationally organized six-digit number which identifies a bank for charge card

purposes; **bank mandate** = written order to a bank, asking them to open an account and allowing someone to sign cheques on behalf of the account holder, giving specimen signatures, etc.; **bank reconciliation** = making sure that the bank statements agree with the company's ledgers; **bank return** = statement of the financial position of a central bank **(b) central bank** = main government-controlled bank in a country, which controls the financial affairs of the country by fixing main interest rates, issuing currency and controlling the foreign exchange rate; **the Federal Reserve Banks** = central banks in the USA which are owned by the state, and directed by the Federal Reserve Board; *US* **national bank** = bank which is chartered by the federal government and is part of the Federal Reserve system (as opposed to a 'state bank'); **state bank** = commercial bank licensed by the authorities of a state, and not necessarily a member of the Federal Reserve system (as opposed to a 'national bank'); **the World Bank** = central bank, controlled by the United Nations, whose funds come from the member states of the UN and which lends money to member states **(c) commercial bank** = bank which offers banking services to the public, as opposed to a merchant bank; **merchant bank** = bank which lends money to companies and deals in international finance; **savings bank** = bank where you can deposit money and receive interest on it; **the High Street banks** = main British banks which accept deposits from and allow withdrawals by individuals **2** *verb* to deposit money into a bank or to have an account with a bank; *he banked the cheque as soon as he received it*; *where do you bank?* = where do you have a bank account?; *I bank at or with Barclays*

bankable ['bæŋkəbl] *adjective* which a bank will accept as security for a loan; *a bankable paper*

bank account ['bæŋk ə'kaʊnt] *noun* account which a customer has with a bank, where the customer can deposit and withdraw money; *to open a bank account*; *to close a bank account*; *how much money do you have in your bank account?*; *she has £100 in her savings bank account*; *if you let the balance in your bank account fall below £100, you have to pay bank charges*

bank balance ['bæŋk 'bæləns] *noun* the amount of money in a bank account at any particular time; *our bank balance went into the red last month*

bank bill ['bæŋk 'bɪl] *noun* **(a)** *GB* bill of exchange by one bank telling another bank (usually in another country) to pay money to someone (bank bills are more secure than trade bills, which are issued by companies) **(b)** *US* piece of printed paper money

bank book ['bæŋk 'bʊk] *noun* book, given by a bank, which shows the amount of money which you deposit or withdraw from your savings account

bank card ['bæŋk 'kɑːd] *noun* card issued by a bank to a customer, used to withdraw money from a cash dispenser or as a cheque guarantee card

bank charges ['bæŋk 'tʃɑːdʒɪz] *plural noun* charges which a bank makes for carrying out work for a customer (NOTE: in American English this is **a service charge)**

bank clerk ['bæŋk 'klɑːk] *noun* person who works in a bank, but not a manager

bank draft ['bæŋk 'drɑːft] *noun* (i) order by one bank telling another bank (usually in another country) to pay money to someone; (ii) certified cheque drawn by a bank on its account with another bank

banker ['bæŋkə] *noun* **(a)** person who is in an important position in a bank; **merchant banker** = person who has a high position in a merchant bank **(b)** generally, a bank; *the company's banker is Barclays US* **banker's acceptance** = bill of exchange guaranteed by a bank; **banker's bill** = order by one bank telling another bank (usually in another country) to pay money to someone; **banker's credit card** = credit card issued by (or backed by) a bank, as opposed to cards issued by stores (typical cards are Visa, Access, MasterCard, etc.); **banker's draft** = (i) order by one bank telling another bank (usually in another country) to pay money to someone; (ii) certified cheque drawn by a bank on its account with another bank; **banker's order** = order written by a customer asking a bank to make a regular payment; *he pays his subscription by banker's order*

Bank for International Settlements (BIS) bank (based in Basle) which acts as a clearing bank for the central banks of various countries, through which they settle their currency transactions

bank giro ['bæŋk 'dʒaɪrəʊ] *noun GB* method used by clearing banks to transfer money rapidly from one account to another (used by individuals when paying bills)

bank holiday ['bæŋk 'hɒlədi] *noun* a weekday which is a public holiday when the banks are closed; *New Year's Day is a bank holiday*

banking ['bæŋkɪŋ] *noun* the business of banks; *he is studying banking*; *she has gone into banking* US **banking account** = account which a customer has with a bank; **a banking crisis** = crisis affecting the banks; **banking hours** = hours when a bank is open for its customers; *you cannot get money out of the bank after banking hours*; **internet banking** = operation of a bank account over the internet (to make transfers etc.); **telephone banking** = operation of a bank account over the telephone (to make transfers tec.); **Banking Ombudsman** = official whose duty is to investigate complaints by members of the public against banks; **banking products** = goods and services produced by banks for customers, such as statements, direct debits, etc.

bank manager ['bæŋk 'mænɪdʒə] *noun* person in charge of a branch of a bank; *he asked his bank manager for a loan*

bank note *or* **banknote** ['bæŋknəʊt] *noun* **(a)** piece of printed paper money (in England, issued by the Bank of England; in Scotland, commercial banks can issue notes); *he pulled out a pile of used bank notes* (NOTE: American English is **bill**) **(b)** *US* interest-bearing certificate issued by a bank

Bank of England ['bæŋk əv 'ɪŋlənd] central British bank, owned by the state, which, together with the Treasury, regulates the nation's finances

COMMENT: the Bank of England issues banknotes which carry the signatures of its officials. It is the lender of last resort to commercial banks and supervises banking institutions in the UK. Its Monetary Policy Committee is independent of the government, and sets interest rates. The Governor of the Bank of England is appointed by the government

bankrupt ['bæŋkrʌpt] **1** *adjective & noun* (person or company) which declares itself or has been declared by a court not to be capable of paying its debts and whose affairs are put into the hands of a receiver; *he was adjudicated or declared bankrupt*; *a bankrupt property developer*; *he went bankrupt after two years in business*; **certificated bankrupt** = bankrupt who has been discharged from bankruptcy with a certificate to show he was not at fault;

discharged bankrupt = person who has been released from being bankrupt because he has paid his debts; **undischarged bankrupt** = person who has been declared bankrupt and has not been released from that state **2** *verb* to make someone become bankrupt; *the recession bankrupted my father*

bankruptcy ['bæŋkrəpsi] *noun* state of being bankrupt; *the recession has caused thousands of bankruptcies*; **adjudication of bankruptcy** *or* **declaration of bankruptcy** *or* **bankruptcy order** = legal order making someone bankrupt; **discharge in bankruptcy** = being released from bankruptcy after paying debts; **bankruptcy petition** = petition to the Court asking for an order making someone bankrupt; **to file a petition in bankruptcy** = to apply officially to be made bankrupt, to ask officially for someone else to be made bankrupt; **bankruptcy proceedings** = court case to make someone bankrupt; *see also* CHAPTER 11

COMMENT: in the UK, 'bankruptcy' is applied only to individual persons, but in the USA the term is also applied to corporations. In the UK, a bankrupt cannot hold public office (for example, he cannot be elected an MP) and cannot be the director of a company. He also cannot borrow money. In the USA, there are two types of bankruptcy: 'involuntary', where the creditors ask for a person or corporation to be made bankrupt; and 'voluntary', where a person or corporation applies to be made bankrupt (in the UK, this is called 'voluntary liquidation')

bank statement ['bæŋk 'steɪtmənt] *noun* written statement from a bank showing the balance of an account

bar [bɑː] **1** *noun* thing which stops you doing something; *government legislation is a bar to foreign trade* **2** *verb* to prohibit or to exclude; *he barred from membership of the association*

bar chart ['bɑː 'tʃɑːt] *noun* chart where values or quantities are represented by columns of different heights

bargain ['bɑːgɪn] **1** *noun* **(a)** agreement on the price of something; *to make a bargain*; **to drive a hard bargain** = to be a difficult negotiator, to agree a deal which is favourable to you; **it is a bad bargain** = it is not worth the price **(b)** thing which is cheaper than usual; *that car is a (real) bargain at £500*; **bargain hunter** = person who looks for cheap deals; **bargain hunting** = looking for cheap deals, which no one has noticed **(c)** sale and purchase of one lot of shares on the Stock Exchange; **bargains done** = number of deals made on the Stock Exchange during a day **2**

verb to discuss a price for something; *you will have to bargain with the dealer if you want a discount; they spent two hours bargaining about* or *over the price*

bargaining ['bɑːgɪnɪŋ] *noun* act of discussing a price, usually wage increases for workers; **(free) collective bargaining** = (unrestricted right to conduct) negotiations between employers and workers' representatives over wage increases and conditions; **bargaining power** = strength of one person or group when discussing prices or wage settlements; **bargaining position** = statement of position by one group during negotiations

barren ['bærən] *adjective* (money) which is not earning any interest

barrier ['bærɪə] *noun* thing which stops someone doing something, especially sending goods from one place to another; **customs barriers** or **tariff barriers** = customs duty intended to make trade more difficult; **to impose trade barriers on certain goods** = to restrict the import of certain goods by charging high duty; **to lift trade barriers from imports** = to remove restrictions on imports

```
QUOTE a senior European Community
official has denounced Japanese
trade barriers, saying they cost
European producers $3 billion a year
                              Times
```

```
QUOTE to create a single market out
of the EC member states, physical,
technical and tax barriers to free
movement of trade between member
states must be removed. Imposing VAT
on importation of goods from other
member states is seen as one such tax
barrier
                        Accountancy
```

barter ['bɑːtə] **1** *noun* system where goods are exchanged for other goods and not sold for money; **barter agreement** or **barter arrangement** or **barter deal** = agreement to exchange goods by barter; *the company has agreed a barter deal with Bulgaria* **2** *verb* to exchange goods for other goods, but not buy them for money; *they agreed a deal to barter tractors for barrels of wine*

```
QUOTE under the barter agreements,
Nigeria will export 175,000 barrels
a day of crude oil in exchange for
trucks, food, planes and chemicals
                   Wall Street Journal
```

bartering ['bɑːtərɪŋ] *noun* act of exchanging goods for other goods and not for money

base [beɪs] **1** *noun* **(a)** lowest or first position; *turnover increased by 200%, but starting from a low base*; **base currency** = currency against which exchange rates of other currencies are quoted; **(bank) base rate** = basic rate of interest on which the actual rate a bank charges on loans to its customers is calculated; *see also* DATABASE; **base-weighted index** = index which is weighted according to the base year; **base year** = first year of an index, against which later years' changes are measured; **capital base** = the capital structure of a company (shareholders' capital plus certain loans and retained profits) used as a way of assessing the company's worth **(b)** place where a company has its main office or factory, place where a businessman has his office; *the company has its base in London and branches in all European countries*; *he has an office in Madrid which he uses as a base while he is travelling in Southern Europe* **2** *verb* **(a)** to start to calculate or to negotiate from a position; *we based our calculations on the forecast turnover*; **based on** = calculating from; *based on last year's figures*; *based on population forecasts* **(b)** to set up a company or to establish a person in a place; *the European manager is based in our London office*; *our overseas branch is based in the Bahamas*; *a London-based bank*

```
QUOTE the base lending rate, or prime
rate, is the rate at which banks lend
to their top corporate borrowers
                     Wall Street Journal
```

```
QUOTE other investments include a
large stake in the Chicago-based
insurance company
                          Lloyd's List
```

basic ['beɪsɪk] **1** *adjective* **(a)** normal; **basic balance** = balance of current account and long-term capital accounts in a country's balance of payments; **basic discount** = normal discount without extra percentages; *our basic discount is 20%, but we offer 5% extra for rapid settlement*; **basic pay** or **basic salary** or **basic wage** = normal salary without extra payments; **basic rate** = minimum rate for a job; **basic rate tax** = main or first rate of income tax, currently 22%, levied on taxable income after the lowest, or starting, rate, and running until the higher rate threshold is reached **(b)** most important; **basic commodities** = ordinary farm produce, produced in large quantities (such as corn, rice, sugar, etc.) **(c)** simple, from which everything starts; *he has a basic knowledge of the market; to work at the cash desk, you need a basic qualification in maths*

basis ['beɪsɪs] *noun* **(a)** point or number from which calculations are made; *we forecast the turnover on the basis of a 6% price increase*; **basis period** = the period during which transactions occur (used for the purpose of deciding in which they should be assessed for taxation); **basis point** = one hundredth of a percentage point (0.01%), the basic unit used in measuring market movements or interest rates; **basis price** = (i) price agreed between buyer and seller on the over-the- counter market; (ii) price of a bond shown as its annual percentage yield to maturity; **basis swap** = exchange of two financial instruments, each with a variable interest calculated on a different rate **(b) accounting bases** = the possible ways in which accounting concepts may be applied to financial transactions (the methods used to depreciate assets, how intangible assets or work in progress are dealt with, etc.); **basis of apportionment** = way in which common overhead costs are shared among various cost centres; *see note at* APPORTIONMENT; **basis of assessment** = method of deciding in which year financial transactions should be assessed for taxation **(c)** *US* the difference between the cash price and futures price for a commodity **(d)** general terms of an agreement; **on a short-term** *or* **long-term basis** = for a short, long period; *he has been appointed on a short-term basis*; *we have three people working on a freelance basis* (NOTE: the plural is **bases**)

batch [bætʃ] **1** *noun* **(a)** group of items which are made at one time; *this batch of shoes has the serial number 25-02*; **batch costing** = method of calculating the price of one item as part of a batch of items made at the same time **(b)** group of documents which are processed at the same time; *a batch of invoices*; *today's batch of orders*; *the accountant signed a batch of cheques*; *we deal with the orders in batches of fifty*; **batch processing** = system of data processing where information is collected into batches before being loaded into the computer **2** *verb* *to batch invoices or cheques*

batch number ['bætʃ 'nʌmbə] *noun* number attached to a batch; *when making a complaint always quote the batch number on the packet*

b/d
= BROUGHT DOWN

bear [beə] **1** *noun (Stock Exchange)* person who sells shares (or commodities or currency) because he thinks the price will fall and he

will be able to buy again more cheaply later; **covered bear** = bear who holds the stock which he is selling; **uncovered bear** = person who sells stock which he does not hold, hoping to be able to buy stock later at a lower price when he needs to settle; **bear covering** = point in a market where dealers who sold stock short, now buy back (at lower prices) to cover their positions; **bear market** = period when share prices fall because shareholders are selling since they believe the market will fall further; **bear position** = short position, that is, selling shares which you do not own (you will buy them later at a lower price so as to be able to settle); **taking a bear position** = acting on the assumption that the market is likely to fall; **bear raid** = selling large amounts of stock (which the seller does not hold), in order to depress the market so as to be able to pick up stock again later at lower prices; **bear squeeze** = (i) action by banks to raise exchange rates, forcing currency bear sellers to buy back currency at a loss (i.e., at a higher price); (ii) operation by marketmakers to increase the price of shares, so as to force bears to buy at higher prices than they intended (NOTE: the opposite of bear is **bull**) **2** *verb* **(a)** to give interest; *government bonds which bear 5% interest* **(b)** to have (a name); to have something written on it; *the cheque bears the signature of the company secretary*; *envelope which bears a London postmark*; *a letter bearing yesterday's date*; *the share certificate bears his name* **(c)** to pay costs; *the costs of the exhibition will be borne by the company*; *the company bore the legal costs of both parties* (NOTE: **bearing - bore - has borne**)

bearer ['beərə] *noun* person who holds a cheque, certificate or financial document; **the cheque is payable to bearer** = the cheque will be paid to the person who holds it, not to any particular name written on it

bearer bond *or* **bearer security** ['beərə 'bɒnd *or* sɪ'kjuːrəti] *noun* bond which is payable to the bearer and does not have a name written on it (useful if the owner wishes to avoid being identified by the income tax authorities)

bearing ['beərɪŋ] *adjective* which bears or which produces; *a deposit bearing interest at 5%*; *interest-bearing deposits*

bed-and-breakfast deal ['bedənd'brekfəst 'diːl] *noun* formerly, an arrangement where shares were sold one day and bought back the following day, in order to establish a profit or loss for tax declaration

(doing such deals was called 'bed-and-breakfasting')

COMMENT: this is no longer possible, since a period of thirty days has to elapse between the sale and repurchase of the same shares to allow a new price to be established

bellwether ['belwðə] *noun* leading share which is thought of as an indicator of market trends as a whole (such as LloydsTSB in the UK)

QUOTE the Treasury's bellwether 30-year bond declined 3/32 to 98 20/32, yielding 7.99 per cent
Toronto Globe & Mail

QUOTE Monday seemed to whet investors' appetite for the technology bellwether
Barron's

QUOTE more than 24 hours before semiconductor giant and market bellwether Intel will report its quarterly earnings
Wall Street Journal

below par [bɪ'ləʊ 'pɑː] *phrase* (share) with a market price lower than its par value; *compare* ABOVE PAR

below-the-line [bɪ'ləʊðə'laɪn] **1** *adjective* **below-the-line expenditure** = payments which do not arise from a company's normal activities (such as redundancy payments) **2** *noun* (i) part of a budget referring to receipts from redeemed debts and expenditure covered by borrowings; (ii) extraordinary items which are shown in the profit and loss account below net profit after taxation (as opposed to exceptional items which are included in the figure for profit before taxation)

benchmark ['bentʃmɑːk] *noun* figure or indicator which is important, and can be used to compare with other figures

QUOTE the US bank announced a cut in its prime, the benchmark corporate lending rate, from 10+% to 10%
Financial Times

QUOTE the dollar dropped below three German marks - a benchmark with more psychological than economic significance - for the first time since October
Fortune

QUOTE the benchmark 11³/₄% Treasury due 2003/2007 was quoted at 107 11/32, down 13/32 from Monday
Wall Street Journal

beneficial [benɪ'fɪʃəl] *adjective* **beneficial occupier** = person who occupies a property but does not own it fully; **beneficial interest** = interest which allows someone to occupy or receive rent from a property, but not to own it

beneficiary [benɪ'fɪʃəri] *noun* person who gains money from something; *the beneficiaries of a will*

QUOTE the pound sterling was the main beneficiary of the dollar's weakness
Business Times (Lagos)

benefit ['benɪfɪt] **1** *noun* **(a) state benefits** = payments which are made to someone under a national or private scheme; *she receives £60 a week as unemployment benefit; the sickness benefit is paid monthly; the insurance office sends out benefit cheques each week*; **death benefit** = money paid to the family of someone who dies **(b) benefits from employment** *or* **fringe benefits** = extra items given by a company to workers in addition to their salaries (such as company cars, private health insurance) **2** *verb* **(a)** to make better, to improve; *a fall in inflation benefits the exchange rate* **(b) to benefit from** *or* **by something** = to be improved by something, to gain more money because of something; *exports have benefited from the fall in the exchange rate; the employees have benefited from the profit-sharing scheme*

QUOTE the retail sector will also benefit from the expected influx of tourists
Australian Financial Review

QUOTE what benefits does the executive derive from his directorship? Compensation has increased sharply in recent years and fringe benefits for directors have proliferated
Duns Business Month

QUOTE salary is negotiable to £80,000, plus car and a benefits package appropriate to this senior post
Financial Times

QUOTE California is the latest state to enact a program forcing welfare recipients to work for their benefits
Fortune

Benford's Law ['benfədz 'lɔː] *noun* law discovered by Dr Benford in 1938, which shows that in sets of random numbers, it is more likely that the set will begin with the number 1 than with any other number

bequeath [bɪ'kwiːð] *verb* to leave (property, but not freehold land) to someone in a will; *he bequeathed his shares to his daughter*

bequest [bɪˈkwest] *noun* giving of property, money, etc. (but not freehold land) to someone in a will; *he made several bequests to his staff*

| COMMENT: freehold land given in a will is a **devise**

at best [ˈæt ˈbest] *phrase* **sell at best** *or* **sell at the market** = instruction to stockbroker to sell shares at the best price possible

best-selling [ˈbestˈselɪŋ] *adjective* which sells very well; *these computer disks are our best-selling line*

beta [ˈbiːtə] *noun* measurement of the return on investment in a certain stock compared against a one percentage point return on the stock market in general: it shows the volatility in the price of the share compared to the FTSE All-Share Index

b/f
= BROUGHT FORWARD

bi- [baɪ] *prefix* twice; **bi-monthly** = twice a month; **bi-annually** = twice a year

bid [bɪd] **1** *noun* **(a)** offer to buy something (such as a share, currency, commodity, or a unit in a unit trust) at a certain price; **to make a bid for something** = to offer to buy something; *he made a bid for the house*; *the company made a bid for its rival*; **to make a cash bid** = to offer to pay cash for something; **to put in a bid for something** *or* **to enter a bid for something** = to offer (usually in writing) to buy something; **bid basis** = pricing of unit trusts at a lower bid price to encourage buyers; **bid market** = market where there are more bids to buy than offers to sell (the opposite is an 'offered' market); **bid price** = (i) highest price at which a purchaser will buy shares on the Stock Exchange; (ii) price at which units in a unit trust are sold back to the trust by an investor (the opposite, i.e. the price offered by the purchaser, is called the 'offer' price; the difference between the two is the 'spread'); **bid rate** = rate of interest offered on deposits **(b)** *(at an auction)*; **opening bid** = first bid; **closing bid** = last bid at an auction, the bid which is successful **(c)** offer to do some work at a certain price; *he made the lowest bid for the job* **(d)** *US* offer to sell something at a certain price; *they asked for bids for the supply of spare parts* **(e)** **takeover bid** = offer to buy all or a majority of shares in a company so as to control it; *to make a takeover bid for a company*; *to withdraw a takeover bid*; *the*

company rejected the takeover bid = the directors recommended that the shareholders should not accept it **2** *verb (at an auction)*; **to bid for something** = to offer to buy something; *he bid £1,000 for the jewels* = he offered to pay £1,000 for the jewels (NOTE: **bidding - bid - has bid**)

bidder [ˈbɪdə] *noun* person who makes a bid (usually at an auction); *several bidders made offers for the house*; *the property was sold to the highest bidder* = the property was sold to the person who had made the highest bid or who offered the most money; *the tender will go to the lowest bidder* = to the person who offers the best terms or the lowest price for services

bidding [ˈbɪdɪŋ] *noun* action of making offers to buy (usually at an auction); *the bidding started at £1,000* = the first and lowest bid was £1,000; *the bidding stopped at £250,000* = the last bid (and the successful bid) was for £250,000; *the auctioneer started the bidding at £100* = he suggested that the first bid should be £100

Big Four [ˈbɪg ˈfɔː] *noun* **(a)** the four large British commercial banks: Barclays, LloydsTSB, HKSB and RBS/Natwest **(b)** the four largest Japanese securities houses: Daiwa, Nikko, Nomura, Yamaichi

bilateral [baɪˈlætərəl] *adjective* between two parties or countries; *the minister signed a bilateral trade agreement*; **bilateral clearing** = the system of annual settlements of accounts between certain countries, where accounts are settled by the central banks; **bilateral credit** = credit allowed by banks to other banks in a clearing system (to cover the period while cheques are being cleared)

bill [bɪl] **1** *noun* **(a)** written list of charges to be paid; *the salesman wrote out the bill*; *does the bill include VAT?*; *the bill is made out to Smith Ltd*; *the builder sent in his bill*; *he left the country without paying his bills*; **to foot the bill** = to pay the costs **(b)** list of charges in a restaurant; *can I have the bill please?*; *the bill comes to £20 including service*; *does the bill include service?*; *the waiter has added 10% to the bill for service* (NOTE: American English is **check**) **(c)** written paper promising to pay money; **bills payable (B/P)** = bills (especially bills of exchange) which a company will have to pay (to its creditors); **bills receivable (B/R)** = bills (especially bills of exchange) which are due to be paid to a company's debtors; **due bills** = bills which are owed but not yet paid; **Treasury Bill** *US* **T-Bill** = short-term financial instrument which does not give any interest and is sold by the government at a discount through the central bank **(d) bill of lading** = list of goods being shipped,which the transporter gives to the person sending the goods to show that the goods have been loaded **(e)** *US* piece of paper money; *a $5 bill* **(f) bill of sale** = document which the seller gives to the buyer to show that the sale has taken place **(g)** draft of a new law which will be discussed in Parliament **2** *verb* to present a bill to someone so that it can be paid; *the builders billed him for the repairs to his neighbour's house*

bill of exchange ['bɪl əv ɪks'tʃeɪnʒ] *noun* document signed by the person authorizing it, which tells another to pay money unconditionally to a named person on a certain date (usually used in payments in foreign currency); **accommodation bill** = bill of exchange where the person signing is helping someone else to raise a loan; **bank bill** = bill of exchange endorsed by a bank; **bill broker** = discount house, a firm which buys and sells bills of exchange for a fee; **demand bill** = bill of exchange which must be paid when payment is asked for; **trade bill** = bill of exchange between two companies who are trading partners (it is issued by one company and accepted by the other); **to accept a bill** = to sign a bill of exchange to show that you promise to pay it; **to discount a bill** = to sell a bill of exchange at a lower price than that written on it in order to cash it before its maturity date

> COMMENT: a bill of exchange is a document raised by a seller and signed by a purchaser, stating that the purchaser accepts that he owes the seller money, and promises to pay it at a later date. The person raising the bill is the 'drawer', the person who accepts it is the 'drawee'. The seller can then sell the bill at a discount to raise cash. This is called a 'trade bill'. A bill can also be accepted (i.e. guaranteed) by a bank, and in this case it is called a 'bank bill'

billing ['bɪlɪŋ] *noun US* writing of invoices or bills; *the payment will be processed before the next billing*

billion ['bɪljən] *number* one thousand million (NOTE: in American English it has always meant one thousand million, but in British English it formerly meant one million million, and it is still sometimes used with this meaning. With figures it is usually written **bn**: **$5bn** say 'five billion dollars')

bin [bɪn] *noun* part of a warehouse in which stock is kept; **bin card** = stock record card, showing how much stock there is in a bin

BIN = BANK IDENTIFICATION NUMBER

bind [baɪnd] *verb* to tie or to attach; *the company is bound by its articles of association*; *he does not consider himself bound by the agreement which was signed by his predecessor* (NOTE: **binding - bound**)

binder ['baɪndə] *noun* **(a)** stiff cardboard cover for papers; **ring binder** = cover with rings in it which fit into small holes made in sheets of paper **(b)** *US* temporary agreement for insurance sent before the insurance policy is issued (NOTE: the British English for this is **cover note**)

binding ['baɪndɪŋ] *adjective* which legally forces someone to do something; *a binding contract*; *this document is not legally binding*; *the agreement is binding on all parties* = all parties signing it must do what is agreed

BIS = BANK FOR INTERNATIONAL SETTLEMENTS

black [blæk] **1** *adjective* **(a) black economy** = goods and services which are paid for in cash, and therefore not declared for tax **(b) in the black** = in credit; *the company has moved into the black*; *my bank account is still in the black* **2** *verb* to forbid trading in certain goods or with certain suppliers; *three firms were blacked by the government*; *the union has blacked a trucking firm*

black market ['blæk 'mɑːkɪt] *noun* buying and selling goods or currency in a way which is not allowed by law (as in a time of rationing); *there is a flourishing black market in spare parts for cars*; *you can buy gold coins on the black market*; **to pay black market prices** = to pay high prices to get items which are not easily available

blank [blæŋk] **1** *adjective* with nothing written; **a blank cheque** = a cheque with no amount of money or name written on it, but signed by the drawer **2** *noun* space on a form which has to be completed; *fill in the blanks and return the form to your local office*

blanket lien ['blæŋkɪt 'liːn] *noun US* lien or claim on a person's property (including personal effects)

blind trust ['blaɪnd 'trʌst] *noun* trust set up to run a person's affairs without the details of any transaction being known to the person concerned (set up by politicians to avoid potential conflicts of interest)

block [blɒk] **1** *noun* series of items grouped together; *he bought a block of 6,000 shares*; **block booking** = booking of several seats or rooms at the same time; *the company has a block booking for twenty seats on the plane or for ten rooms at the hotel*; **block trading** = trading in very large numbers of shares **2** *verb* to stop something taking place; *he used his casting vote to block the motion*; *the planning committee blocked the redevelopment plan*; **blocked account** = bank account which cannot be used, usually because a government has forbidden its use; **blocked currency** = currency which cannot be taken out of a country because of government exchange controls; *the company has a large account in blocked roubles*

blowout ['bləʊaʊt] *noun US* rapid sale of the whole of a new stock issue

blue [bluː] *adjective* **blue-chip share** *or* **blue chip** = share of a good company, with a good record of dividends; **blue-chip investments** = shares of very large established companies which are generally low-risk investments; *US* **blue sky laws** = state laws to protect investors against fraudulent traders in securities

Blue Book ['bluː 'bʊk] *noun GB* annual publication of national statistics of personal incomes and spending patterns

Blue list ['bluː 'lɪst] *noun US* daily list of municipal bonds and their ratings, issued by Standard & Poor's

bn ['bɪljən] = BILLION

board [bɔːd] **1** *noun* **(a)** *see* BOARD OF DIRECTORS **(b)** *US (informal)* the board of governors of the Federal Reserve **(c)** group of people who run an organization, trust or society; **advisory board** = group of advisors; **editorial board** = group of editors; **Board of Customs and Excise** = ruling body of the Customs and Excise; **Board of Inland Revenue** = ruling body of the Inland Revenue, appointed by the Treasury **(d) on board** = on a ship, plane, train or truck; **free on board (f.o.b.)** = price includes all the seller's costs until the goods are on the vehicle for transportation **2** *verb* to go on to a ship, plane or train; *customs officials boarded the ship in the harbour*

board of directors ['bɔːd əv daɪ'rektəz] *noun* **(a)** *GB* group of directors elected by the

shareholders to run a company; *the bank has two representatives on the board*; *he sits on the board as a representative of the bank*; *two directors were removed from the board at the AGM*; **she was asked to join the board** = she was asked to become a director; **board meeting** = meeting of the directors of a company **(b)** *US* group of people elected by the shareholders to draw up company policy and to appoint the president and other executive officers who are responsible for managing the company

QUOTE a proxy is the written authorization an investor sends to a stockholder meeting conveying his vote on a corporate resolution or the election of a company's board of directors

Barrons

QUOTE CEOs, with their wealth of practical experience, are in great demand and can pick and choose the boards they want to serve on

Duns Business Month

COMMENT: directors are elected by shareholders at the AGM, though they are usually chosen by the chairman or chief executive. A board will consist of a chairman (who may be non-executive), a chief executive or managing director, and a series of specialist directors in charge of various activities of the company (such as a finance director, production director or sales director). The company secretary will attend board meetings, but need not be a director. Apart from the executive directors, who are in fact employees of the company, there may be several non-executive directors, appointed either for their expertise and contacts, or as representatives of important shareholders such as banks. The board of an American company may be made up of a large number of non-executive directors and only one or two executive officers; a British board has more executive directors

bona fide ['bəʊnə 'faɪdi] *adjective* trustworthy, which can be trusted; **a bona fide offer** = an offer which is made honestly

bona vacantia ['bəʊnə və'kæntiə] *noun* property with no owner, or which does not have an obvious owner, and which usually passes to the Crown, as in the case of the estate of a person dying intestate and with no living relatives

bond [bɒnd] *noun* **(a)** contract document promising to repay money borrowed by a company or by the government at a certain date, and paying interest at regular intervals; **government bonds** *or* **treasury bonds** = bonds issued by the central government; **municipal bond** *or* **local authority bond** =

bond issued by a town or district; **bond discount** = the difference between the face value of a bond and the lower price at which it is issued; **bond market** = market in which government or municipal bonds are traded; **bond premium** = the difference between the face value of a bond and a higher price at which it is issued; **bearer bond** = bond which is payable to the bearer and does not have a name written on it; **debenture bond** = certificate showing that a debenture has been issued; **mortgage bond** = certificate showing that a mortgage exists and that property is security for it; *GB* **premium bond** = government bond, part of the National Savings scheme, which pays no interest, but gives the owner the chance to win a weekly or monthly prize; **bond rating** = rating of the reliability of a company or government or local authority which has issued a bond (the highest rating is AAA); **bond yield** = income produced by a bond, shown as a percentage of its purchase price **(b)** form of insurance fund which is linked to a unit trust (there is no yield because the income is automatically added to the fund) **(c) goods (held) in bond** = goods held by the customs until duty has been paid; **entry of goods under bond** = bringing goods into a country in bond; **to take goods out of bond** = to pay duty on goods so that they can be released by the customs

> COMMENT: bonds are in effect another form of long-term borrowing by a company or government. They can carry a fixed interest or a floating interest, but the yield varies according to the price at which they are bought; bond prices go up and down in the same way as share prices. Note that in the USA, only the word 'bonds' is used of government borrowings, while in the UK, these are also referred to as 'stocks': see the note at STOCK

bonded ['bɒndɪd] *adjective* held in bond; **bonded warehouse** = warehouse where goods are stored in bond until duty is paid

bondholder ['bɒndhəʊldə] *noun* person who holds bonds

bondized ['bɒndaɪzd] *adjective* (insurance fund) linked to a unit trust

bond-washing ['bɒndwɒʃɪŋ] *noun* selling American Treasury bonds with the interest coupon, and buying them back ex coupon, so as to reduce tax

bonus ['bəʊnəs] *noun* **(a)** extra payment (in addition to a normal salary); **capital bonus** = extra payment by an insurance company which is produced by a capital gain; **cost-of-living bonus** = money paid to meet the increase in the cost of living; **Christmas bonus** = extra payment made to staff at Christmas; **incentive bonus** = extra pay offered to a worker to encourage him to work harder; **productivity bonus** = extra payment made because of increased productivity **(b) bonus issue** = scrip issue or capitalization issue, where a company transfers money from reserves to share capital and issues free extra shares to the shareholders (the value of the company remains the same, and the total market value of shareholders' shares remains the same, the market price being adjusted to account for the new shares (NOTE: the American equivalent is **stock split** or **stock dividend**); **bonus share** = extra share given to an existing shareholder **(c) no-claims bonus** = reduction of premiums on an insurance because no claims have been made

book [bʊk] *noun* **(a)** set of sheets of paper attached together; **a company's books** = the financial records of a company; **book debt** = debt which is written (or should have been written) into the accounts of a company; **order book** = record of orders; **the company has a full order book** = it has sufficient orders to keep the workforce occupied; **book sales** = sales as recorded in the accounts; **book value** = value of an asset as recorded in the company's balance sheet; **statutory books** = company records required by law, such as a register of members **(b) bank book** = book which shows money which you have deposited or withdrawn from a bank account; **cheque book** = book of new cheques **(c)** *(of a marketmaker)*; **to make a book** = to have a list of shares which you are prepared to buy or sell on behalf of clients **(d)** *(in foreign exchange dealing)* statement of a dealer's exposure to the market (i.e. the amount which he is due to pay or has borrowed); **book-squaring** = reducing the dealer's exposure to the market to nil

bookkeeper ['bʊkkiːpə] *noun* person who keeps the financial records of a company

bookkeeping ['bʊkkiːpɪŋ] *noun* keeping of the financial records of a company or an organization; **single-entry bookkeeping** = recording a transaction with only one entry, as in a cash book; **double-entry bookkeeping** = method of bookkeeping, where both debit and credit entries are recorded in the accounts at the same time (e.g. as a sale is credited to the sales account the purchaser's debt is debited to the debtors account); **bookkeeping transaction** = transaction (such as the issue of bonus shares) which involves changes to a company's books of account, but does not alter the value of the company in any way

book of account ['bʊk əv ə'kaʊnt] *noun* account book, book which records financial transactions

COMMENT: the books of account record a company's financial transactions. These are: sales (sales day book and sales returns book); purchases (purchases day book and purchases returns book); cash payments and receipts (cash book) and adjustments (journal). These books are commonly known as the 'books of prime entry', but in addition, a company's accounting records usually include the ledger accounts (nominal ledger, sales ledger and purchases ledger) which may also be referred to as 'books of account'

boom [buːm] **1** *noun* time when sales, production or business activity are increasing; *a period of economic boom*; *the boom of the 1970s*; **boom industry** = industry which is expanding rapidly; **a boom share** = share in a company which is expanding; **the boom years** = years when there is an economic boom **2** *verb* to expand, to become prosperous; *business is booming*; *sales are booming*

booming ['buːmɪŋ] *adjective* which is expanding or becoming prosperous; *a booming industry or company*; *technology is a booming sector of the economy*

boost [buːst] **1** *noun* encouragement; *this publicity will give sales a boost*; *the government hopes to give a boost to industrial development* **2** *verb* to make something increase; *we expect our publicity campaign to boost sales by 25%*; *the company hopes to boost its market share*; *incentive schemes are boosting production*

QUOTE the company expects to increase turnover this year to FFr 16bn from FFr 13.6bn last year
Financial Times

BOP = BALANCE OF PAYMENTS

border ['bɔːdə] *noun* frontier between two countries; **border tax adjustment** = deduction of indirect tax paid on goods being exported or imposition of local indirect tax on goods being imported

borrow ['bɒrəʊ] *verb* **(a)** to take money from someone for a time, possibly paying interest for it, and repaying it at the end of the period; *he borrowed £1,000 from the bank*; *the company had to borrow heavily to repay its debts*; *they borrowed £25,000 against the security of the factory*; **to borrow short** *or* **long** = to borrow for a short or long period **(b)**

(on a commodity market) to buy at spot prices and sell forward at the same time

borrower ['bɒrəʊə] *noun* person who borrows; *borrowers pay 12% interest on loans from the bank*

borrowing ['bɒrəʊɪŋ] *noun* **(a)** action of borrowing money; *the new factory was financed by bank borrowing*; **borrowing costs** *or* **cost of borrowing** = the interest and other charges paid on money borrowed; **borrowing power** = amount of money which a company or person can borrow; **Public Sector Borrowing Requirement (PSBR)** = amount of money which a government has to borrow to pay for its own spending **(b) borrowings** = money borrowed; *the company's borrowings have doubled*; **bank borrowings** = money borrowed from banks; **gross borrowings** = total of all monies borrowed by a company (such as overdrafts, long-term loans, etc.) but without deducting cash in bank accounts and on deposit; **net borrowings** = total of all borrowings less the cash in bank accounts and on deposit

COMMENT: borrowings are sometimes shown as a percentage of shareholders' funds (i.e. capital and money in reserves); this gives a percentage which is the 'gearing' of the company

bottom ['bɒtəm] **1** *noun* lowest part or point; **sales have reached rock bottom** = the very lowest point of all; **the bottom has fallen out of the market** = sales have fallen below what previously seemed to be the lowest point possible; **rock-bottom price** = lowest price of all **2** *verb* **to bottom (out)** = to reach the lowest point; **the market has bottomed out** = has reached the lowest point and does not seem likely to fall further

bottom line ['bɒtəm 'laɪn] *noun* final result, the last line of a profit and loss account indicating total profit or loss; **the boss is interested only in the bottom line** = he is only interested in the final profit

bought [bɔːt] *see* BUY; **bought day book** *or* **purchases day book** = book used to record purchases made on credit (i.e., for which cash is not paid immediately); **bought ledger** = set of accounts recording separately the money owed to each supplier (i.e., the creditors of a company); **bought ledger clerk** = office worker who deals with the bought ledger

bounce [baʊns] *verb* (*of a cheque*) to be returned to the person who has tried to cash it, because there is not enough money in the payer's account to pay it; *he paid for the car with a cheque that bounced*

bounty ['baʊnti] *noun* government subsidy made to help an industry

B/P
= BILL PAYABLE

B/R
= BILL RECEIVABLE

bracket ['brækɪt] **1** *noun* (i) group of items or people taken together; (ii) one of the various groups of underwriters underwriting a loan; **people in the middle-income bracket** = people with average incomes, not high or low; **he is in the top tax bracket** = he pays the highest level of tax **2** *verb* **to bracket together** = to treat several items together in the same way; *in the sales reports, all the European countries are bracketed together*

branch [brɑːntʃ] *noun* a local office of a bank or large business; local shop of a large chain of shops; *the bank has branches in most towns in the south of the country*; *the insurance company has closed its branches in South America*; *he is the manager of our local branch of Lloyds bank*; *we have decided to open a branch office in Chicago*; *the manager of our branch in Lagos or of our Lagos branch*; **branch accounts** = accounts showing transactions belonging to the branches of a large organization (i.e., between a branch and other branches or its head office, or other companies outside the organization); **branch manager** = manager of a branch

QUOTE a leading manufacturer of business, industrial and commercial products requires a branch manager to head up its mid-western Canada operations based in Winnipeg
Globe and Mail (Toronto)

brand [brænd] *noun* the make of a product, which can be recognized by its name or its design, and which gives the company making it an advantage over its competitors; **brand accounting** = valuation of brands as intangible fixed assets in the balance sheet of a company

COMMENT: ED52, published by the ASC in 1990, proposed a separate SSAP on brand accounting which would allow brands to be shown as part of goodwill on acquisition but not as separate intangible assets in the balance sheet, as some companies have done since 1988

breach [briːtʃ] *noun* failure to carry out the terms of an agreement; **breach of contract** = failing to do something which is in a contract; **the company is in breach of contract** = it has failed to carry out the duties of the contract; **breach of trust** = failure on the part

of a trustee to act properly regarding a trust; **breach of warranty** = supplying goods which do not meet the standards of the warranty applied to them

break [breɪk] **1** *noun* sharp fall in prices **2** *verb* **(a)** to fail to carry out the duties of a contract; **to break an engagement to do something** = not to do what has been agreed **(b)** to cancel (a contract); *the company is hoping to be able to break the contract* (NOTE: **breaking - broke - has broken**)

breakages ['breɪkɪdʒɪz] *plural noun* items of stock which have been broken (such items do not count as assets when taking stock)

break down ['breɪk 'daʊn] *verb* **(a)** to stop working because of mechanical failure; *the fax machine has broken down*; *what do you do when your photocopier breaks down?* **(b)** to stop; *negotiations broke down after six hours* **(c)** to show all the items in a total list of costs or expenditure; *we broke the expenditure down into fixed and variable costs*; *can you break down this invoice into spare parts and labour?*

breakdown ['breɪkdaʊn] *noun* **(a)** stopping work because of mechanical failure; *we cannot communicate with our Nigerian office because of the breakdown of the telex lines* **(b)** stopping talking; *a breakdown in wage negotiations* **(c)** showing details item by item; *give me a breakdown of investment costs*

break even ['breɪk 'iːvən] *verb* to balance costs and receipts, so as to make neither a profit nor a loss; *last year the company only just broke even*; *we broke even in our first two months of trading*

breakeven [breɪk'iːvn] *noun* situation where there is neither a profit nor a loss; **breakeven analysis** = calculation which shows at what point a product will break even; **breakeven chart** = chart which shows the breakeven analysis in the form of a diagram; **breakeven point** = (i) point at which sales income exactly covers total costs, so that neither a profit nor a loss is made; (ii) *(Stock Exchange)* transaction which does not show a profit or loss

break-out ['breɪk'aʊt] *noun* movement of a share price above or below its previous trading level

break up ['breɪk 'ʌp] *verb* to split something large into small sections; *the company was broken up and separate divisions sold off*; **break-up value** = value of a company if its assets are sold separately (rather than its value as an existing business)

bribe [braɪb] **1** *noun* money given to someone in authority to get him to help; *the minister was dismissed for taking bribes* **2** *verb* to pay someone money to get him to do something for you; *we had to bribe the minister's secretary before she would let us see her boss*

bricks and mortar [ˈbrɪks ənd ˈmɔːtə] *noun (informal)* fixed assets of a company, especially its buildings

bridge finance [ˈbrɪdʒ faɪˈnæns] *noun* loans to cover short-term needs

bridging loan *US* **bridge loan** [ˈbrɪdʒɪŋ ˈləʊn *or* ˈbrɪdʒ ˈləʊn] *noun* short-term loan to help someone buy a new house when he has not yet sold his old one

bring down [ˈbrɪŋ ˈdaʊn] *verb* **(a)** to reduce; *oil companies have brought down the price of petrol* **(b)** = BRING FORWARD (b)

bring forward [ˈbrɪŋ ˈfɔːwəd] *verb* **(a)** to move to an earlier date or time; *to bring forward the date of repayment*; *the date of the next meeting has been brought forward to March* **(b)** to take an account balance from the end of the previous period as the starting point for the current period; *balance brought forward: £365.15*

bring in [ˈbrɪŋ ˈɪn] *verb* to earn (dividend or interest); *the shares bring in a small amount*

broker [ˈbrəʊkə] *noun* **(a)** person who acts as a middleman between a seller and a buyer; **foreign exchange broker** = person who buys and sells foreign currency on behalf of other people; **insurance broker** = person who sells insurance to clients **(b) (stock)broker** = person or firm that buys and sells shares or bonds on behalf of clients; **agency broker** = dealer who acts as the agent for an investor, buying and selling for a commission; **discount broker** = broker who charges a lower commission than other brokers; **broker-dealer** = dealer who makes a market in shares (i.e. buys shares and holds them for resale) and also deals on behalf of investor clients; **broker's commission** = payment to a broker for a deal carried out (formerly, the commission charged by brokers on the London Stock Exchange was fixed, but since 1986 commissions are variable)

brokerage [ˈbrəʊkərɪdʒ] *noun* **(a)** broker's commission, the payment to a broker for a deal carried out **(b)** = BROKING; **brokerage**

firm *or* **brokerage house** = firm which buys and sells shares for clients

broking [ˈbrəʊkɪŋ] *noun* dealing in stocks and shares

brought down (b/d) *or* **brought forward (b/f)** [ˈbrɔːt ˈdaʊn *or* ˈbrɔːt ˈfɔːwəd] *phrase* balance on an account from the previous period taken as the starting point for the current period; *balance brought down or balance brought forward: £365.15*

buck [bʌk] **1** *noun US informal* dollar; **to make a quick buck** = to make a profit very quickly **2** *verb* **to buck the trend** = to go against the trend

bucket shop [ˈbʌkɪt ˈʃɒp] *noun* **(a)** *GB* travel agency which specializes in selling cut-price air tickets **(b)** *US* brokerage firm which tries to encourage the sale of certain securities

budget [ˈbʌdʒɪt] **1** *noun* **(a)** plan of expected expenditure and income (usually for one year); *to draw up a budget*; *we have agreed the budgets for next year*; **budget centre** = part of an organization for which a separate budget is prepared; **budget period** = period of time covered by a budget; **advertising budget** = money planned for spending on advertising; **capital (expenditure) budget** = budget for planned purchases of fixed assets during the budget period; **cash budget** = plan of cash income and expenditure; **fixed budget** = budget which refers to a certain level of business (i.e., a certain sales turnover which produces a certain level of profit); **flexed** *or* **flexible budget** = budget which changes in response to changes in sales turnover and output; **master budget** = budget prepared by amalgamating budgets from various profit and cost centres (sales, production, marketing, administration, etc.) to provide a main budget for the whole accounting entity; **overhead budget** = plan of probable overhead costs; **publicity budget** = money allowed for expected expenditure on publicity; **sales budget** = plan of probable sales **(b) the Budget** = the annual plan of taxes and government spending proposed by a finance minister; *the minister put forward a budget aimed at boosting the economy*; **to balance the budget** = to plan income and expenditure so that they balance; *the president is planning for a balanced budget*; *(in the UK)*; **Budget Day** = day (usually in March, but with an advance budget statement in November) when the Chancellor of the Exchequer presents his budget to Parliament; **budget deficit** = deficit in a country's planned budget, where income from taxation will not be sufficient to pay for the government's expenditure **(c)** *US* **Office of Manpower and Budget (OMB)** = government department which prepares the US federal budget; **Director of the Budget** = member of the government in charge of the preparation of the US budget (the equivalents in the UK are the **Chief Secretary to the Treasury** and the **Financial Secretary) (d) budget account** = (i) *(in a shop)* arrangement where a customer has credit facilities in return for regular small payments into the account; (ii) *(in a bank)* bank account where you plan income and expenditure to allow for periods when expenditure is high, by paying a set amount each month **(e)** *(in shops)* cheap; **budget department** = department selling cheap goods; **budget prices** = low prices **2** *verb* to plan probable income and expenditure; *we are budgeting for £10,000 of sales next year*

QUOTE he budgeted for further growth of 150,000 jobs (or 2.5 per cent) in the current financial year
Sydney Morning Herald

QUOTE the minister is persuading the oil, gas, electricity and coal industries to target their advertising budgets towards energy efficiency
Times

QUOTE the Federal government's budget targets for employment and growth are within reach according to the latest figures
Australian Financial Review

budgetary ['bʌdʒɪtəri] *adjective* referring to a budget; **budgetary policy** = policy of planning income and expenditure; **budgetary control** = using budgets to control the performance of a company; **budgetary requirements** = expenditure or income required to meet the budget forecasts

budgeting ['bʌdʒɪtɪŋ] *noun* preparing of budgets to help plan expenditure and income

buffer stocks ['bʌfə 'stɒks] *noun* (i) stocks of raw materials or work in progress required by a production department to meet sales demand when these are planned, or otherwise unplanned changes in the rate of production; (ii) stocks of a commodity bought by an international body when prices are low and held for resale at a time when prices have risen, with the intention of removing sharp fluctuations in world prices of the commodity

buildings ['bɪldɪŋz] *noun* constructions (offices, houses, factories, etc.) which are fixed tangible assets

COMMENT: the valuation of buildings is difficult. Some appreciate over a period of time, while others can deteriorate and so have to be depreciated in the accounts. The asset value can also vary independently of the building itself as general property values rise or fall

building and loan association ['bɪldɪŋ ənd 'ləʊn əsəʊsɪ'eɪʃən] *noun US* = SAVINGS AND LOAN ASSOCIATION

building society ['bɪldɪŋ sə'saɪəti] *noun GB* financial institution which accepts and pays interest on deposits and lends money to people who are buying property against the security of the property; *he put his savings into a building society or into a building society account; I have an account with the Lambeth Building Society; I saw the building society manager to ask for a mortgage*

COMMENT: building societies are mutual institutions and belong to their members; they mainly invest the money deposited with them as mortgages on properties, but a percentage is invested in government securities. Societies can now offer a range of banking services, such as cheque books, standing orders, overdrafts, etc., and now operate in much the same way as banks. Several have demutualized and have become plcs. The comparable US institutions are the Savings & Loan Associations, or 'thrifts'

build into ['bɪld 'ɪntʊ] *verb* to add something to something; *you must build all the forecasts into the budget; we have built 10% for contingencies into our cost forecast* = we have added 10% to our basic forecast to allow for items which may appear suddenly

build up ['bɪld 'ʌp] *verb* **(a)** to create something by adding pieces together; *he bought several shoe shops and gradually built up a chain* **(b)** to expand something gradually; *to build up a profitable business; to build up a team of salesmen*

buildup ['bɪldʌp] *noun* gradual increase; *a buildup in sales or a sales buildup; there will be a big publicity buildup before the launch of the new model*

bull [bʊl] *noun (Stock Exchange)* person who believes the market will rise, and therefore buys shares (or commodities or currency) to sell at a higher price later; **bull market** = period when share prices rise because people are optimistic and buy shares; **bull position** = buying shares in the hope that they will rise (NOTE: the opposite of bull is **bear**)

> QUOTE lower interest rates are always a bull factor for the stock market
> *Financial Times*

> QUOTE another factor behind the currency market's bullish mood may be the growing realisation that Japan stands to benefit from the current combination of high domestic interest rates and a steadily rising exchange rate
> *Far Eastern Economic Review*

bullet ['bulɪt] *noun US* repayment of the capital of a loan, when it matures; **bullet bond** = eurobond which is only redeemed when it is mature (it is used in payments between central banks and also acts as currency backing); **bullet loan** = loan which is repaid in a single payment

bullion ['buljən] *noun* gold or silver bars; *the price of bullion is fixed daily*; *to fix the bullion price for silver*

bumping ['bʌmpɪŋ] *noun US* situation where a senior person takes precedence over a junior (in a restaurant, an aircraft or in a job)

business ['bɪznəs] *noun* (a) occupation or trade; *business is expanding*; *business is slow*; *he does a thriving business in repairing cars*; *what's your line of business?*; **business call** = visit to talk to someone about business; **business centre** = part of a town where the main banks, shops and offices are located; **business correspondent** = journalist who writes articles on business news for newspapers; **business cycle** = regular rise and fall in trade; **business day** = day (a normal weekday, excluding public holidays) when banks and stock exchanges are open for business; **business hours** = time (usually 9 a.m. to 5 p.m.) when a business is open; **business plan** = document drawn up to show how a business is planned to work, with cash flow forecasts, sales forecasts, etc. (often used when trying to raise a loan, or when setting up a new business); **business travel** = travel costs incurred in the course of work (as opposed to private travel or daily travel to your normal place of work); **to be in business** = to run a commercial firm; **to go into business** = to start a commercial firm; *he went into business as a car dealer*; **to go out of business** = to stop trading; *the firm went out of business during the recession*; **on business** = on commercial work; *he had to go abroad on business*; *the chairman is in*

Holland on business (b) commercial company; *he owns a small car repair business*; *she runs a business from her home*; *he set up in business as an insurance broker*; **business address** = details of number, street and town where a company is located; **business card** = card showing the name of a businessman or businesswoman and the name and address of the company he or she works for; **business combination** = action when one or more businesses become subsidiaries of another business; **business correspondence** = letters concerned with a business; **business expenses** = money spent on running a business, not on stock or assets; **business name** = name used by a company for trading purposes; **business review** = report on business carried out over the past year (it forms part of the directors' report); **business segment** = section of a company which can be distinguished from the rest of the company by its own revenue and expenditure (c) **big business** = very large commercial firms; **small business** = commercial firm with a few employees and a low turnover; *see also* SMALL (d) affairs discussed; *the main business of the meeting was finished by 3 p.m.*; **any other business (AOB)** = item at the end of an agenda, where any matter can be raised

business agent ['bɪznəs 'eɪdʒənt] *noun US* chief local official of a trade union

businessman *or* **businesswoman** ['bɪznɪsmæn *or* 'bɪznɪswumən] *noun* man or woman engaged in business; *she's a good businesswoman* = she is good at commercial deals; *a small businessman* = man who owns a small business

bust [bʌst] *adjective (informal)*; **to go bust** = to become bankrupt

buy [baɪ] **1** *verb* to get something by paying money; *he bought 10,000 shares*; *the company has been bought by its leading supplier*; *to buy wholesale and sell retail*; *to buy for cash*; **to buy at best** = to buy securities at the best price available, even if it is high; **to buy forward** = to buy foreign currency before you need it, in order to be sure of the exchange rate (NOTE: **buying - bought**) **2** *noun* **good buy** *or* **bad buy** = thing bought which is or is not worth the money paid for it; *that watch was a good buy*; *this car was a bad buy*

buy back ['baɪ 'bæk] **1** *verb* to buy something which you have sold; *he sold the shop last year and is now trying to buy it back* **2** *noun* (a) type of loan agreement to repurchase bonds or securities at a later date for the same price as they are being sold **(b)** international trading agreement where a company builds a factory in a foreign country and agrees to buy all its production

buyer ['baɪə] *noun* **(a)** person who buys; **there were no buyers** = no one wanted to buy; **a buyers' market** = market where shares, commodities or products are sold cheaply because there are few buyers (NOTE: the opposite is a **seller's market**); **impulse buyer** = person who buys something when he sees it, not because he was planning to buy it **(b)** person who buys stock on behalf of a trading organization for resale or for use in production; **head buyer** = most important buyer in an organization; *she is the shoe buyer for a London department store*; *he is the paper buyer for a large magazine chain*

buy in ['baɪ 'ɪn] *verb* **(a)** *(of a seller at an auction)* to buy the thing which you are trying to sell because no one will pay the price you want **(b)** *(Stock Exchange)* to buy stock to cover a position **(c)** *(of a company)* to buy its own shares

buyin ['baɪɪn] *noun* **management buyin (MBI)** = purchase of a company by a group of outside executives

buying ['baɪɪŋ] *noun* getting something for money; **bulk buying** = getting large quantities of goods at low prices; **forward buying** *or* **buying forward** = buying shares or commodities or currency for delivery at a later date; **impulse buying** = buying items which you have just seen, not because you had planned to buy them; **panic buying** = rush to buy something at any price because stocks may run out; **buying department** = department in a company which buys raw materials or goods for use in the company; **buying power** = ability to buy; *the buying power of the pound has fallen over the last few years*

buyout ['baɪaʊt] *noun* purchase of a controlling interest in a company; **employee buyout** = purchase of a company by its employees; **management buyout (MBO)** = takeover of a company by a group of employees (usually senior managers and directors); **leveraged buyout (LBO)** = buying all the shares in a company by borrowing money against the security of the shares to be bought

QUOTE we also invest in companies whose growth and profitability could be improved by a management buyout
Times

QUOTE in a normal leveraged buyout, the acquirer raises money by borrowing against the assets or cash flow of the target company
Fortune

BV *Dutch* = BESLOTEN VENOOTSCHAP Limited Company

bylaws ['baɪlɔːz] *noun US* rules governing the internal running of a corporation (the number of meetings, the appointment of officers, etc.) (NOTE: in the UK, called **Articles of Association**)

by-product ['baɪprɒdʌkt] *noun* product made as a result of manufacturing a main product and which can be sold for profit

COMMENT: from the point of view of preparation of accounts, it is necessary to decide how much of the development costs of the main product should be apportioned to the by-product

Cc

Schedule C [ˈʃedjuːl ˈsiː] *noun* schedule to the Finance Acts under which tax was charged on income from public sources such as government stock

Table C [ˈteɪbl ˈsiː] *noun* model memorandum and articles of association set out in the Companies Act 1985 for a company limited by guarantee having no share capital

CA = CHARTERED ACCOUNTANT (a member of the Institute of Chartered Accountants of Scotland)

cage [keɪdʒ] *noun US* **(a)** the part of a broking firm where the paperwork involved in buying and selling shares is processed (NOTE: the British equivalent is the **back office) (b)** section of a bank where a teller works (surrounded by glass windows)

calculate [ˈkælkjʊleɪt] *verb* **(a)** to find the answer to a problem using numbers; *the bank clerk calculated the rate of exchange for the dollar* **(b)** to estimate; *I calculate that we have six months' stock left*

calculation [kælkjʊˈleɪʃən] *noun* answer to a problem in mathematics; **rough calculation** = approximate answer; *I made some rough calculations on the back of an envelope*; *according to my calculations, we have six months' stock left*; **we are £20,000 out in our calculations** = we have £20,000 too much or too little

calculator [ˈkælkjʊleɪtə] *noun* electronic machine which works out the answers to problems in mathematics; *my pocket calculator needs a new battery*; *he worked out the discount on his calculator*

calendar [ˈkæləndə] *noun* book or set of sheets of paper showing the days and months in a year, often attached to pictures; **financial calendar** = list of significant events and dates in a company's financial reporting year; **calendar month** = a whole month as on a calendar, from the 1st to the 30th or 31st; **calendar year** = year from the 1st January to 31st December; **calendar variance** = variance which occurs if a company uses calendar months for the financial accounts but uses the number of actual working days to calculate overhead expenses in the cost accounts

call [kɔːl] **1** *noun* **(a)** demand for repayment of a loan by a lender; **call account** = type of current account where money can be withdrawn without notice; **call loan** = bank loan repayable at call; **money at call** *or* **money on call** *or* **call money** = money loaned for which repayment can be demanded without notice (used by commercial banks, placing money on very short-term deposit with discount houses); **call rate** = rate of interest on money at call **(b)** *(Stock Exchange)* (i) demand to pay for new shares, which then become paid up; (ii) price established during a trading session; **at call** = immediately available; **call option** = option to buy shares at a future date and at a certain price (NOTE: the opposite is **put**); **call price** = price to be paid on redemption of a US bond; **call purchase** *or* **call sale** = transaction where the seller or purchaser can fix the price for future delivery; **call rule** = price fixed on a Stock Exchange at the end of a day's trading and which remains valid until trading starts again the next day; **calls in arrear** = money called up for shares, but not paid at the correct time (the shares may be forfeited) and a special calls in arrear account is set up to debit the sums owing **2** *verb* to ask for a loan to be repaid immediately

callable [ˈkɔːləbl] *adjective* **callable bond** = bond which can be redeemed before it matures; **callable capital** = the part of a company's capital which has not been called up

call-back pay [ˈkɔːlbæk ˈpeɪ] *noun* pay given to a worker who has been called back to work after his normal working hours

called up capital [ˈkɔːld ʌp ˈkæpɪtl] *noun* share capital in a company which has been called up but not yet paid for

call in [ˈkɔːl ˈɪn] *verb* to ask for a debt to be paid; **call-in pay** = CALL-BACK PAY

call-over price [ˈkɔːlˈəʊvə ˈpraɪs] *noun (on commodity markets)* price which is applied when selling is conducted by a chairman, and not by open outcry

call up ['kɔːl 'ʌp] *verb* to ask for share capital to be paid

cancel ['kænsəl] *verb* **(a)** to stop something which has been agreed or planned; *to cancel an appointment or a meeting*; *to cancel a contract*; *the government has cancelled the order for a fleet of buses* **(b)** *to cancel a cheque* = to stop payment of a cheque which has been signed (NOTE: British English spelling is **cancelling - cancelled** but American English spelling is **canceling - canceled**)

cancellation [kænsə'leɪʃən] *noun* stopping something which has been agreed or planned; *cancellation of an appointment*; *cancellation of an agreement*; **cancellation clause** = clause in a contract which states the terms on which the contract may be cancelled

cancel out ['kænsəl 'aʊt] *verb* to balance and so make invalid, or to make even; *the two clauses cancel each other out*; *costs have cancelled out the sales revenue*

cap [kæp] **1** *noun* upper limit placed on something, such as an interest rate (the opposite, i.e. a lower limit, is a 'floor'); *see also* EARNINGS CAP **2** *verb* to place an upper limit on something; **capped floating rate note** = floating rate note which has an agreed maximum rate

capacity [kə'pæsəti] *noun* **(a)** amount which can be produced or amount of work which can be done; *industrial or manufacturing or production capacity*; **to work at full capacity** = to do as much work as possible; **to use up spare *or* excess capacity** = to make use of time or space which is not fully used; **capacity utilization** = output shown as a percentage of capacity; **capacity variance** = variance caused by the difference between planned and actual hours worked; **overhead capacity variance** = difference between the overhead absorbed based on budgeted hours and actual hours worked **(b)** amount of space; **storage capacity** = space available for storage; **warehouse capacity** = space available in a warehouse **(c)** (i) ability; (ii) *(of a borrower)* ability to pay back a loan; **earning capacity** = amount of money someone is able to earn

> QUOTE analysts are increasingly convinced that the industry simply has too much capacity
>
> *Fortune*

capita ['kæpɪtə] *see* PER CAPITA

capital ['kæpɪtl] *noun* **(a)** money, property and assets used in a business; *company with £10,000 capital or with a capital of £10,000*; **authorized capital *or* registered capital *or* nominal capital** = maximum capital which is permitted by a company's memorandum of association; **capital account** = account containing the capital invested in a partnership or company; **capital adequacy ratio *or* capital-to-asset ratio** = amount of money which a bank has to have in the form of shareholders' capital, shown as a percentage of its assets (internationally agreed at 8%); **capital assets *or* fixed assets** = property or machinery which a company owns and uses, but which the company does not buy or sell as part of its regular trade (fixed assets are divided into tangible fixed assets, intangible fixed assets, and investments); **capital asset pricing model (CAPM)** = model of the stock market which can be used to estimate different returns from high and low risk investments as well as the value of a company's shares; **capital base** = the capital structure of a company (shareholders' capital plus long-term loans and retained profits) used as a way of assessing the company's worth; **capital bonus** = bonus payment by an insurance company which is produced by capital gain; **capital (expenditure) budget** = budget for planned purchases of fixed assets during the next budget period; **capital commitments** = expenditure on assets which has been authorized by directors, but not yet spent at the end of a financial period; **capital employed** = shareholders' funds plus long-term borrowings of a business; *see also* RETURN ON CAPITAL EMPLOYED; **capital equipment** = equipment which a factory or office uses in production; **capital expenditure *or* investment *or* outlay** = money spent on fixed assets (property, machines, furniture, etc.); **capital goods** = goods used to manufacture other goods (i.e. machinery); **capital levy** = tax on the value of a person's property and possessions; **capital loss** = loss made when selling fixed assets; **capital profit** = profit made by selling an asset (same as capital gain); **capital ratio** = CAPITAL ADEQUACY RATIO; **capital reconstruction** = putting a company into voluntary liquidation and then selling its assets to another company with the same name and same shareholders, but with a larger capital base; **capital reorganization** = changing the capital structure of a company by amalgamating or dividing existing shares to form shares of a higher or lower nominal value; **capital reserves** = reserves of a company which cannot be distributed to the shareholders, except if the company is wound up (also known as 'undistributable reserves'; **capital shares** = shares in a unit trust which rise in value as the capital value of the units rises, but do not receive any income (the other form of shares in a split-level investment trust are income shares, which receive income from the investments, but do not rise in value); **capital structure of a company** = way in which a company's capital is made up of various sources of capital; **capital transfer tax** = formerly, tax on gifts or bequests of money or property; **circulating capital** = capital in the form of cash or debtors, raw materials, finished products and work in progress required for a company to carry on its business; **cost of capital** = minimum return required from an investment; **equity capital** = a company's capital which is owned by its ordinary shareholders (note that preference shares are not equity capital; if the company were wound up, none of the equity capital would be distributed to preference shareholders; **fixed capital** = capital in the form of fixed assets; **issued capital** or **subscribed capital** = amount of capital issued as shares to the shareholders; **junior capital** = capital in the form of shareholders' equity, which is repaid only after secured loans (senior capital) if the firm goes into liquidation; **paid-up capital** = amount of money paid for the issued share capital (it does not include called-up capital which has not yet been paid for); **risk capital** or **venture capital** = capital for investment usually in high-risk projects at an early stage of development; **senior capital** = capital in the form of secured loans to a company (it is repaid before junior capital, such as shareholders' equity, in the event of liquidation); **(nominal) share capital** = the total face value of all the shares which a company is authorized to issue according to its memorandum of association (also known as 'authorized share capital'); **working capital** = capital in the form of cash, stocks and debtors (less creditors) used by a company in its day-to-day operations **(b)** money for investment; **movements of capital** = changes of investments from one country to another; **capital exports** = movement of capital out of a country (in the form of overseas investments, or of loans to overseas countries); **flight of capital** = rapid movement of capital out of one country because of lack of confidence in that country's economic future; **capital markets** = (i) places where companies can look for long-term investment capital; (ii)

international markets where money can be raised for investment in businesses

capital account ['kæpɪtl ə'kaʊnt] *noun* **(a)** account of dealings (money invested in a business, or profits left in a business) by the partners or proprietors **(b)** items in a country's balance of payments which refer to capital investments made in or by other countries **(c)** *US* account showing the total owners' equity in a business

capital allowances ['kæpɪtl ə'laʊənsɪz] *noun* allowances based on the value of fixed assets which may be deducted from a company's profits and so reduce its tax liability

COMMENT: under current UK law, depreciation is not allowable for tax on profits, whereas capital allowances, based on the value of fixed assets owned by the company, are tax-allowable

capital gain ['kæpɪtl 'geɪn] *noun* money made by selling fixed assets or certain other types of property (such as works of art, leases, etc.; if the asset is sold for less than its purchase price, the result is a capital loss); **capital gains expenses** = expenses incurred in buying or selling assets, which can be deducted when calculating a capital gain or loss; **capital gains tax (CGT)** = tax paid on capital gains

COMMENT: in the UK, capital gains tax is payable on capital gains from the sale of assets, in particular shares and properties, above a certain minimum level

capitalism ['kæpɪtəlɪzəm] *noun* economic system where each person has the right to invest money in a business and to profit from trading

capitalist ['kæpɪtəlɪst] **1** *noun* person who invests money in a business **2** *adjective* working according to the principles of capitalism; *a capitalist economy*; *the capitalist system*; *the capitalist countries*

capitalization [kæpɪtəlaɪ'zeɪʃən] *noun* **market capitalization** = (i) value of a company calculated by multiplying the price of its shares on the Stock Exchange by the number of shares issued; (ii) value of all the shares listed on a stock market; *company with a £1m capitalization*; **capitalization issue** *or* **bonus issue** *or* **free issue** *or* **scrip issue** = issue of shares, where a company transfers money from reserves to share capital and issues free extra shares to the shareholders (the value of the company remains the same, and the total market value of shareholders' shares remains the same, the market price being adjusted to account for the new shares); **capitalization of costs** = including costs normally charged to the profit and loss account in the balance sheet (the effect is that profits are higher than if such costs are matched with revenues in the same accounting period); **capitalization of reserves** = issuing free bonus shares to shareholders

capitalize ['kæpɪtəlaɪz] *verb* **(a)** to authorize a company to issue shares up to a certain limit; **company capitalized at £10,000** = company with an authorized share capital of £10,000 **(b)** to convert reserves into share capital **(c)** to calculate the value of a business (two methods are used: the present value of future income or the share price multiplied by the number of the shares in issue)

QUOTE at its last traded price the bank was capitalized at around $1.05 billion with 60 per cent in the hands of the family
South China Morning Post

capitalize on ['kæpɪtəlaɪz ɒn] *verb* to make a profit from; *to capitalize on one's market position*

CAPM = CAPITAL ASSET PRICING MODEL

captive market ['kæptɪv 'mɑːkɪt] *noun* market where one supplier has a monopoly and the buyer has no choice over the product which he must purchase

car [kɑː] *noun* **company car** = car which belongs to a company and is lent to an employee to use for business or other purposes

COMMENT: if a car or van is provided for you by your company for private use as well for us on company business, you will have to declare it as a benefit to the Inland Revenue, and pay tax on it

card [kɑːd] *noun* small piece of stiff paper or plastic; **business card** = card showing a businessman's name and the address of the company he works for; **cash card** = plastic card used to obtain money from a cash dispenser; **charge card** = credit card for which a fee is payable, but which does not allow the user to take out a loan (he has to pay off the total sum charged at the end of each month); **cheque (guarantee) card** = plastic card from a bank which guarantees payment of a cheque up to a certain amount, even if the user has no money in his account; **credit card** = plastic card which allows you to borrow money or to buy goods without paying for them immediately; **debit card** = plastic card, similar to a credit card, but which debits the holder's account immediately through an EPOS system; **punched card** = card with holes punched in it which a computer can read; **smart card** = credit card with a microchip, used for withdrawing money from ATMs, or for purchases at EFTPOS terminals; **store card** = credit card issued by a department store

QUOTE ever since October, when the banks' base rate climbed to 15 per cent, the main credit card issuers have faced the prospect of having to push interest rates above 30 per cent APR. Though store cards have charged interest at much higher rates than this for some years, 30 per cent APR is something the banks fight shy of
Financial Times Review

cardholder ['kɑːdhəʊldə] *noun* person who holds a credit card or bank cash card

carriage ['kærɪdʒ] *noun* transporting goods from one place to another; cost of transport of goods; *to pay for carriage*; *to allow 10% for carriage*; *carriage is 15% of the total cost*; **carriage free** = deal where the customer does not pay for the shipping; **carriage paid** = deal where the seller has paid for the shipping; **carriage forward** = deal where the customer will pay for the shipping when the goods arrive

carry ['kæri] **1** *noun* cost of borrowing to finance a deal; **positive carry** = deal where the cost of the finance is less than the return; **negative carry** = deal where the cost of finance is more than the return on the capital used **2** *verb* **(a)** to take from one place to another; *to carry goods*; *a tanker carrying oil from the Gulf*; *the train was carrying a consignment of cars for export* **(b)** to vote to approve; **the motion was carried** = the motion was accepted after a vote **(c)** to produce; *the bonds carry interest at 10%*

carry back ['kæri 'bæk] *verb* to take back to an earlier accounting period

| COMMENT: losses or expenses (such as contributions to pension funds) can be carried back to earlier periods to set against tax

carry forward ['kæri 'fɔːwəd] *verb* **(a)** to take an account balance at the end of the current period as the starting point for the next period; **balance carried forward** *or* **balance c/f** = amount entered in an account at the end of a period or page of an account book to balance the debit and credit entries; it is then taken forward to start the next period or page **(b)** to take forward to a later accounting period

| COMMENT: substantial losses made in one year can be carried forward to succeeding years and set against tax

carry down ['kæri 'daʊn] *verb* to take an account balance at the end of the current period as the starting point for the next period; **balance carried down** *or* **balance c/d** = amount entered in an account at the end of a period or page of an account book to balance the debit and credit entries; it is then taken forward to start the next period or page

carry over ['kæri 'əʊvə] *verb* **(a)** **to carry over a balance** = to take a balance from the end of one page or period to the beginning of the next **(b)** **to carry over stock** = to hold stock from the end of one stocktaking period to the beginning of the next

carryover ['kærɪəʊvə] *noun* **(a)** stock of a commodity held at the beginning of a new financial year **(b)** not paying an account on settlement day, but later

cartel [kɑː'tel] *noun* group of companies which try to fix the price, or to regulate the supply of a product, because they can then profit from this situation

cash [kæʃ] **1** *noun* **(a)** money in coins or notes; **cash in hand** *US* **cash on hand** = money and notes, kept to pay small amounts but not deposited in the bank; **hard cash** = money in notes and coins, as opposed to cheques or credit cards; **petty cash** = small amounts of money; **ready cash** = money which is immediately available; **cash account** = account which records the money

(cash and cheques) which is received and spent; **cash advance** = loan in cash against a future payment; **cash balance** = balance in cash, as opposed to amounts owed; **cash book (CB)** = book in which cash transactions are entered; **cash box** = metal box for keeping cash; **cash budget** = plan of cash income and expenditure; **cash card** = card used to obtain money from a cash dispenser; **cash desk** = place in a store where you pay for the goods bought; **cash dispenser** *or* **cash machine** = machine which gives out money when a special card is inserted and instructions given; **cash dividend** = dividend paid in cash, as opposed to a dividend in the form of bonus shares; **cash economy** = black economy, where goods and services are paid for in cash, and therefore not declared for tax; **cash float** = cash put into the cash box at the beginning of the day or week to allow change to be given to customers; **cash inflow** = receipts of cash or cheques; **cash limit** = fixed amount of money which can be spent during a certain period; **cash market** = the gilt-edged securities market (where purchases are paid for almost immediately, as opposed to the futures market); **cash offer** = offer to pay in cash, especially offer to pay cash when buying shares in a takeover bid; **cash outflow** = expenditure in cash or cheques; **cash payment** = payment in cash; **cash position** = state of the cash which a company currently has available; *(on commodity markets)*; **cash price** = price of a commodity which is for immediate delivery (also called actual price or spot price); **cash purchases** = purchases made in cash; **cash ratio** = (i) ratio of cash or other liquid assets to the current liabilities in a business; (ii) ratio of cash to deposits in a bank (usually a percentage laid down by the central bank); **cash register** *or* **cash till** = machine which shows and adds the prices of items bought, with a drawer for keeping the cash received; **cash reserves** = a company's reserves in cash, deposits or bills, kept in case of urgent need **(b)** using money in coins or notes; **cash discount** *or* **discount for cash** = discount given to a customer who is paying cash; **to pay cash down** = to pay in cash immediately; **cash equivalent** = the equivalent in cash terms of an asset which is enjoyed; **cash price** *or* **cash terms** = lower price or terms which apply if the customer pays cash; **cash price** *or* **spot price** = price for buying a commodity for immediate delivery (as opposed to the price for future delivery); **settlement in cash** *or* **cash settlement** = (i) paying a bill in cash; (ii) paying for government securities immediately on purchase; **cash sale** *or* **cash transaction** = transaction paid for in cash; **cash on delivery**

(COD) = payment in cash when goods are delivered; **terms: cash with order (CWO)** = terms of sale showing that the payment has to be made in cash when the order is placed **2** *verb* **to cash a cheque** = to exchange a cheque for cash

cashable ['kæʃəbl] *adjective* which can be cashed; *a crossed cheque is not cashable at any bank*

cash and carry ['kæʃ ənd 'kæri] *noun* **(a)** large store, selling goods at low prices, where the customer pays cash and has to take the goods away himself; *cash and carry warehouse* **(b)** buying a commodity for cash and selling the same commodity on the futures market

cashback ['kæʃbæk] *noun* payment of cash to a purchaser as an incentive to encourage him or her to make the purchase

> COMMENT: cashbacks are offered by car dealers or house builders, and must be declared on a tax return

cash basis ['kæʃ 'beɪsɪs] *noun* method of preparing the accounts of a business, where revenues and costs are shown at the time when they are received or paid (as opposed to showing them when they are earned or incurred; also called 'receipts and payments basis')

cash cow ['kæʃ 'kaʊ] *noun* product or subsidiary company that consistently generates good profits but does not provide growth

cash crops ['kæʃ 'krɒps] *noun* agricultural crops grown for sale to other buyers or to other countries, rather than for domestic consumption

cash flow ['kæʃ 'fləʊ] *noun* cash which comes into a company from sales (cash inflow) or the money which goes out in purchases or overhead expenditure (cash outflow); **cash flow accounting (CFA)** = measuring the financial activities of a company in terms of cash receipts and payments, without recording accruals, prepayments, debtors, creditors and stocks; **cash flow budget** = cash budget, a plan of cash income and expenditure; **cash flow forecast** = forecast of when cash will be received or paid out; **cash flow statement** = report which shows inflows and outflows during a given period; **net cash flow** = difference between the money coming in (cash inflow) and the money going out (cash outflow); **negative cash flow** = situation where more money is going out of a company

than is coming in; **positive cash flow** = situation where more money is coming into a company than is going out; **the company is suffering from cash flow problems** = cash income is not coming in fast enough to pay the expenditure going out

cashier [kæˈʃɪə] *noun* **(a)** person who takes money from customers in a shop **(b)** person who deals with customers' money in a bank; *US* **cashier's check** = a bank's own cheque, drawn on itself and signed by the cashier or other bank official

cash in ['kæʃ 'ɪn] *verb* to sell (shares) for cash

cash in on ['kæʃ 'ɪn ɒn] *verb* to profit from; *the company is cashing in on the interest in computer games*

cashless society ['kæʃləs səˈsaɪəti] *noun* society where no one uses cash, all purchases being made by credit cards, charge cards or cheques

cash up ['kæʃ 'ʌp] *verb* to add up the cash in a shop at the end of the day

casual ['kæʒjʊəl] *adjective* not permanent, not regular; **casual labour** = workers who are hired for a short period; **casual work** = work where the workers are hired for a short period; **casual labourer** *or* **casual worker** = worker who can be hired for a short period

CAT = CERTIFIED ACCOUNTING TECHNICIAN

CB = CASH BOOK

CCA = CURRENT COST ACCOUNTING

CCAB = CONSULTATIVE COMMITTEE OF ACCOUNTANCY BODIES

CD [siːˈdiː] = CERTIFICATE OF DEPOSIT

c/d = CARRIED DOWN

CE = CHIEF EXECUTIVE

ceiling ['siːlɪŋ] *noun* highest point, such as the highest interest rate, the highest amount of money which a depositor may deposit, etc.; *there is a ceiling of $100,000 on deposits*; *to fix a ceiling to a budget*; **ceiling price** *or* **price ceiling** = highest price that can be reached

central ['sentrəl] *adjective* organized at one main point; **central government** = the main government of a country (as opposed to municipal, local, provincial or state governments); **central office** = main office which controls all smaller offices; **central processing unit (CPU)** = component that provides all the functions that control your computer and run software programs; **central purchasing** = purchasing organized by a central office for all branches of a company

central bank [ˈsentrəl ˈbæŋk] *noun* main government-controlled bank in a country, which controls the financial affairs of the country by fixing main interest rates, issuing currency, supervising the commercial banks and controlling the foreign exchange rate; **central bank discount rate** = rate at which a central bank discounts bills, such as treasury bills; **central bank intervention** = action by a central bank to change base interest rates, to impose exchange controls, to buy or sell the country's own currency, in an attempt to influence international money markets

QUOTE central bankers in Europe and Japan are reassessing their intervention policy

Duns Business Month

centralization [sentrəlaɪˈzeɪʃən] *noun* organization of everything from a central point

centralize [ˈsentrəlaɪz] *verb* to organize from a central point; *all purchasing has been centralized in our main office*; *the group benefits from a highly centralized organizational structure*

centre *US* **center** [ˈsentə] *noun* **(a)** **business centre** = part of a town where the main banks, shops and offices are **(b)** important town or region; *industrial centre*; *manufacturing centre*; *the centre for the shoe industry* **(c)** group of items in an account; **cost centre** = person or group whose costs can be itemized and to which costs can be allocated for control purposes; **profit centre** = person or department considered separately for the purposes of calculating a profit

CEO [ˈsiːiːˈəʊ] = CHIEF EXECUTIVE OFFICER

certain [ˈsɜːtn] *adjective* **(a)** sure; *the chairman is certain we will pass last year's total sales* **(b)** a certain number *or* a certain quantity = some; **certain annuity** = annuity which will be paid for a certain number of years only

certificate [səˈtɪfɪkət] *noun* official document which shows that something is owned by someone or that something is true; **clearance certificate** = document showing that goods have been passed by customs;

savings certificate = document showing you have invested money in a government savings scheme; **share certificate** = document proving that you own shares; **certificate of approval** = document showing that an item has been officially approved; **certificate to commence business** = document issued by the Registrar of Companies which allows a registered company to trade; **certificate of incorporation** = document showing that a company has been officially registered; **certificate of origin** = document showing where imported goods come from or were made; **certificate of quality** = certificate showing the grade of a soft commodity; **certificate of registration** = document showing that an item has been registered

certificated [səˈtɪfɪkeɪtɪd] *adjective* **certificated bankrupt** = bankrupt who has been discharged from bankruptcy with a certificate to show that he was not at fault

certificate of deposit (CD) [səˈtɪfɪkət əv dɪˈpɒzɪt] *noun* document from a bank showing that money has been deposited at a certain guaranteed interest rate for a certain period of time

COMMENT: a CD is a bearer instrument, which can be sold by the bearer. It can be sold at a discount to the value, so that the yield on CDs varies

QUOTE interest rates on certificates of deposit may have little room to decline in August as demand for funds from major city banks is likely to remain strong. After delaying for months, banks are now expected to issue a large volume of CDs. If banks issue more CDs on the assumption that the official discount rate reduction will be delayed, it is very likely that CD rates will be pegged for a longer period than expected

Nikkei Weekly

certify [ˈsɜːtɪfaɪ] *verb* to make an official declaration in writing; *I certify that this is a true copy*; *the document is certified as a true copy*; **certified accountant** = accountant who has passed the professional examinations and is a member of the Association of Chartered Certified Accountants; **Certified Accounting Technician (CAT)** = person who has passed the first stage course of the Association of Chartered Certified Accountants (ACCA); **certified cheque** *US* **certified check** = cheque which a bank says is good and will be paid out of money put aside from the payer's bank account; *US* **Certified Public Accountant (CPA)** = accountant who has passed the examinations of the AICPA and been given a certificate by a state, allowing him or her to practise in that state

cessation [se'seɪʃn] *noun* stopping (of an activity or work); *see also* POST-CESSATION

cession ['seʃən] *noun* giving up property to someone (especially a creditor)

c/f
= CARRIED FORWARD

CFA = CASH FLOW ACCOUNTING

CFO ['siːefˈəʊ] = CHIEF FINANCIAL OFFICER

CGT = CAPITAL GAINS TAX

chairman ['tʃeəmən] *noun* person who presides over the board meetings of a company; *the chairman of the board or the company chairman*; **the chairman's report** *or* **chairman's statement** = annual report from the chairman of a company to the shareholders

COMMENT: Note that in a UK company, the chairman is less important than the managing director, although one person can combine both posts. In the US, a company president is less important than the chairman of the board

QUOTE the corporation's entrepreneurial chairman seeks a dedicated but part-time president. The new president will work a three-day week

Globe and Mail (Toronto)

Chamber of Commerce ['tʃeɪmbər əv 'kɒməs] *noun* group of local businessmen who meet to discuss problems which they have in common and to promote commerce in their town

Chancellor of the Exchequer ['tʃɑːnsələr əv ði: ɪks'tʃekə] *noun GB* chief finance minister in the British government (NOTE: the American equivalent is the **Secretary of the Treasury**)

change [tʃeɪndʒ] **1** *noun* **(a)** money in coins or small notes; **small change** = coins; **to give someone change for £10** = to give someone coins or notes in exchange for a ten pound note; **change machine** = machine which gives small change for a larger coin or a note **(b)** money given back by the seller, when the buyer can pay only with a larger note or coin than the amount asked; *he gave me the wrong change*; *you paid the £5.75 bill with a £10 note, so you should have £4.25 change*; **keep the change** = keep it as a tip (said to waiters, etc.) **(c)** different way of working; **change in**

accounting principles = using a method to state a company's accounts which is different from the method used in the previous acocunts, (this will have to be agreed with the auditors, and possibly with the Inland Revenue) **2** *verb* **(a) to change a £10 note** = to give change in smaller notes or coins for a £10 note **(b)** to give one type of currency for another; *to change £1,000 into dollars*; *we want to change some traveller's cheques* **(c) to change hands** = to be sold to a new owner; *the shop changed hands for £100,000*

channel ['tʃænl] **1** *noun* physical connection between two points that allows data to be transmitted, such as a link between a CPU and a peripheral **2** *verb* to send in a certain direction; *they are channelling their research funds into developing European communication systems*

CHAPS [tʃæps] = CLEARING HOUSE AUTOMATED PAYMENTS SYSTEM computerized system for clearing cheques organized by the banks; *compare* BACS

chapter ['tʃæptə] *noun US* section of an Act of Congress; **Chapter 7** = section of the Bankruptcy Reform Act 1978, which sets out the rules for the liquidation of an incorporated company; **Chapter 11** = section of the Bankruptcy Reform Act 1978, which allows a corporation to be protected from demands made by its creditors for a period of time, while it is reorganized with a view to paying its debts; the officers of the corporation will negotiate with its creditors as to the best way of reorganizing the business; **Chapter 13** = section of the Bankruptcy Reform Act 1978, which allows a business to continue trading and to pay off its creditors by regular monthly payments over a period of time

QUOTE the company filed under Chapter 11 of the federal bankruptcy code, the largest failure ever in the steel industry

Fortune

QUOTE the firm, whose trademark dates back to 1871, has been desperately trying to cut costs to compete with manufacturers in cheaper countries, but has also been hit by management problems. It said the filing for Chapter 11 protection should have little impact on customers and employees and would allow it to restructure

Times

character ['kærəktə] *noun* graphical symbol which appears as a printed or displayed mark, such as one of the letters of the alphabet, a number or a punctuation mark;

character set = list of all the characters which can be printed or displayed

charge [tʃɑːdʒ] **1** *noun* **(a)** money which must be paid; price of a service; *to make no charge for delivery*; *to make a small charge for rental*; *there is no charge for service or no charge is made for service*; **admission charge** *or* **entry charge** = price to be paid before going into an exhibition, etc.; **bank charges** *US* **service charge** = charges made by a bank for carrying out work for a customer; **handling charge** = money to be paid for packing, invoicing or dealing with goods which are being shipped; **inclusive charge** = charge which includes all items; **interest charges** = money paid as interest on a loan; **scale of charges** = list showing various prices; **service charge** = charge added to a bill in a restaurant to pay for service; *a 10% service charge is added*; *does the bill include a service charge?*; **charge account** = arrangement which a customer has with a store to buy goods and to pay for them at a later date, usually when the invoice is sent at the end of the month; the customer will make regular monthly payments into the account and is allowed credit of a multiple of those payments; **charge card** = credit card for which a fee is payable, but which does not allow the user to take out a loan (he has to pay off the total sum charged at the end of each month); **charges forward** = charges which will be paid by the customer; **a token charge is made for heating** = a small charge is made which does not cover the real costs at all; **free of charge** = free, with no payment to be made **(b)** guarantee of security for a loan, for which assets are pledged; **fixed charge** = charge linked to certain specified assets, such as property; **floating charge** = charge linked to any of the company's assets of a certain type, but not to any specific item; **charge by way of legal mortgage** = way of borrowing money on the security of a property, where the mortgagor signs a deed which gives the mortgagee an interest in the property **(c)** sum deducted from revenue in the profit and loss account **2** *verb* **(a)** to ask someone to pay for services; to ask for money to be paid; *to charge £5 for delivery*; *how much does he charge?*; **to charge the packing to the customer** *or* **to charge the customer with the packing** = the customer has to pay for packing; **he charges £6 an hour** = he asks to be paid £6 for an hour's work **(b)** to record an expense or other deduction from revenue in the profit and loss account **(c)** to take something as guarantee for a loan; **charging order** = court order to make someone liable to

pay a sum owed by placing a charge on his assets

chargeable ['tʃɑːdʒəbl] *adjective* which can be charged; *repairs chargeable to the occupier*; **chargeable asset** = asset which will produce a capital gain when sold (assets which are not chargeable include your family home, cars, and some types of investments such as government stocks); **chargeable business asset** = asset which is owned by a business and is liable to capital gains if sold; **chargeable gain** = capital gain on which capital gains tax is assessed; **sums chargeable to the reserve** = sums which can be debited to a company's reserves

chargee [tʃɑːˈdʒiː] *noun* (i) person who holds a charge over a property; (ii) person who has the right to force a debtor to pay

charitable ['tʃærɪtəbl] *adjective* which benefits the general public as a charity; **charitable deductions** = deductions from taxable income for contributions to charity; **charitable purposes** = the aims of a charity; **charitable trust** *US* **charitable corporation** = trust which benefits the public as a whole, which promotes education or religion, which helps the poor or or which does other useful work

charity ['tʃærəti] *noun* body which aims not to make a profit, but to benefit the general public by helping the poor, by promoting education or religion or by doing other useful work; **the Charity Commissioners** = UK body which governs charities and sees that they follow the law and use their funds for the purposes intended

COMMENT: a charity must benefit the general public or a specific group within the general public. A charity cannot benefit its own members at the expense of the public

chart [tʃɑːt] *noun* diagram showing information as a series of lines or blocks, etc.; **bar chart** = diagram where quantities and values are represented by thick columns of different heights or lengths; **flow chart** = diagram showing the arrangement of various work processes in a series; **organization chart** = diagram showing how a company or an office is organized; **pie chart** = diagram where information is shown as a circle cut up into sections of different sizes; **sales chart** = diagram showing how sales vary over time

charter ['tʃɑːtə] **1** *noun* **(a)** bank charter = official government document allowing the establishment of a bank **(b)** hiring transport for a special purpose; **charter flight** = flight in an aircraft which has been hired for that purpose; **charter plane** = plane which has been chartered **2** *verb* to hire for a special purpose; *to charter a plane or a boat or a bus*

chartered ['tʃɑːtəd] *adjective* **(a)** (body) which has been set up by royal charter, and not registered under the Companies Act; **chartered bank** = bank which has been set up by government charter (formerly used in England, but now only done in the USA and Canada); **chartered company** = (company) which has been set up by royal charter, and not registered under the Companies Act **(b)** **chartered ship** *or* **bus** *or* **plane** = ship, bus or plane which has been hired for a special purpose

chartered accountant ['tʃɑːtəd ə'kauntənt] *noun* accountant who has passed the professional examinations and is an associate of the Institute of Chartered Accountants in England and Wales, or a member of the Institute of Chartered Accountants in Scotland; *see also* CERTIFIED

Chartered Institute of Management Accountants (CIMA) professional association of management accountants, which holds examinations for membership; its members are associates (ACMA) or fellows (FCMA)

Chartered Institute of Public Finance and Accounting (CIPFA) professional association for accountants working in the public services

Chartered Institute of Taxation professional body which promotes the study of taxation, and offers examinations which qualify its members to advise on taxation matters

Chartered Tax Adviser person who has passed the qualifying examinations of the Chartered Institute of Taxation

charting ['tʃɑːtɪŋ] *noun* using charts to analyze stock market trends and forecast future rises or falls

chartist ['tʃɑːtɪst] *noun* person who studies stock market trends and forecasts future rises or falls

chattel mortgage ['tʃætl 'mɔːɡɪdʒ] *noun* US mortgage using personal property as security

chattels ['tʃætlz] *noun* goods and chattels = moveable property (but not freehold real estate); **chattels real** = leaseholds; **chattels personal** = any property that is not real property; **incorporeal chattels** = intangible properties (such as patents or copyrights)

cheat [tʃiːt] *verb* to trick someone so that he loses money; *he cheated the Inland Revenue out of thousands of pounds*; *she was accused of cheating clients who came to ask her for advice*

check [tʃek] **1** *noun* **(a)** sudden stop; **to put a check on imports** = to stop some imports **(b)** **check digit** = last digit of a string of computerized reference numbers, used to validate the transaction; **check sample** = sample to be used to see if a consignment is acceptable **(c)** investigation or examination; *the auditors carried out checks on the petty cash book* **(d)** US *(in restaurant)* bill **(e)** *US* = CHEQUE; **check routing symbol** = number shown on an American cheque which identifies the Federal Reserve district through which the cheque will be cleared (similar to the British 'bank sort code') **(f)** *US* mark on paper to show that something is correct; *make a check in the box marked 'R'* (NOTE: British English is **tick**) **2** *verb* **(a)** to stop or to delay; *to check the entry of contraband into the country* **(b)** to examine or to investigate; *to check that an invoice is correct; to check and sign for goods; he checked the computer printout against the invoices* = he examined the printout and the invoices to see if the figures were the same **(c)** *US* to mark with a sign to show that something is correct; *check the box marked 'R'*

checkable ['tʃekəbl] *adjective* US (deposit account) on which checks can be drawn

checking account ['tʃekɪŋ ə'kaunt] *noun* US bank account on which you can write cheques

checkoff ['tʃekɒf] *noun* system where union dues are automatically deducted by the employer from a worker's pay cheque

cheque [tʃek] *noun* note to a bank asking them to pay money from your account to the account of the person whose name is written on the note; *a cheque for £10 or a £10 cheque*; **cheque account** = bank account which allows the customer to write cheques; **cheque to bearer** = cheque with no name written on it, so that the person who holds it can cash it; **crossed cheque** = cheque with two lines across it showing that it can only be deposited at a bank and not exchanged for cash; **open** *or*

uncrossed cheque = cheque which can be cashed anywhere; **blank cheque** = cheque with the amount of money and the payee left blank, but signed by the drawer; **pay cheque** *or* **salary cheque** *US* **pay check** = monthly cheque by which an employee is paid; **traveller's cheques** *US* **traveler's checks** = cheques taken by a traveller, which can be cashed in a foreign country; **dud cheque** *or* **bouncing cheque** *or* **cheque which bounces** *US* **rubber check** = cheque which cannot be cashed because the person writing it has not enough money in his account to pay it **(b) to cash a cheque** = to exchange a cheque for cash; **to endorse a cheque** = to sign a cheque on the back to show that you accept it; **to make out a cheque to someone** = to write someone's name on a cheque; *who shall I make the cheque out to?*; **to pay by cheque** = to pay by writing a cheque, and not using cash or a credit card; **to pay a cheque into your account** = to deposit a cheque into a bank account; **the bank referred the cheque to drawer** = returned the cheque to the person who wrote it because there was not enough money in the account to pay it; **to sign a cheque** = to sign on the front of a cheque to show that you authorize the bank to pay the money from your account; **to stop a cheque** = to ask a bank not to pay a cheque which has been signed and sent

cheque book *US* **checkbook** ['tʃekbʊk] *noun* booklet with new cheques

cheque (guarantee) card ['tʃek gæærən'tiː 'kɑːd] *noun* plastic card from a bank which guarantees payment of a cheque up to a certain amount, even if there is no money in the account

Chicago school [ʃɪ'kɑːgəʊ 'skuːl] *noun* school of monetarists, based at the University of Chicago, led by Professor Milton Friedman

chief [tʃiːf] *adjective* most important; *he is the chief accountant of an industrial group*; **chief cashier** = main cashier in a bank (NOTE: the American equivalent is **head teller**); **chief executive (CE)** *US* **chief executive officer (CEO)** = executive in charge of the management of all of a company (often the same person as the managing director); **chief financial officer (CFO)** = executive in charge of a company's financial operations, reporting to the CEO

Chinese wall ['tʃaɪniːz 'wɔːl] *noun* imaginary barrier between departments in the same organization, set up to avoid insider dealing or conflict of interest (as when a merchant bank is advising on a planned takeover bid, its investment department

should not know that the bid is taking place, or they would advise their clients to invest in the company being taken over)

chip [tʃɪp] *noun* **(a)** a computer chip = device used in computers, consisting of a small piece of crystal of a semiconductor, onto which are etched a number of components such as transistors, resistors or capacitors, which together perform a function **(b)** blue chip = very safe investment, risk-free share in a good company

CHIPS = CLEARING HOUSE INTERBANK PAYMENTS SYSTEM the computerized clearing bank system used in New York

chop [tʃɒp] *noun* (*in the Far East*) stamp, a mark made on a document to show that it has been agreed, acknowledged, paid, or that payment has been received

chose [ʃəʊz] *French word meaning* 'item' or 'thing'; **chose in action** = personal right which can be enforced or claimed as if it were property (such as a patent, copyright, debt or cheque); **chose in possession** = physical thing which can be owned (such as a piece of furniture)

churning ['tʃɜːnɪŋ] *noun* **(a)** keeping a bank account very active by making many payments and receipts before fraudulently diverting funds from it **(b)** practice employed by stockbrokers, where they buy and sell on a client's discretionary account in order to earn their commission (the deals are frequently of no advantage to the client) **(c)** practice employed by insurance salesmen where the salesman suggests that a client should change his insurance policy solely in order to earn the salesman a commission

> QUOTE more small investors lose money through churning than almost any other abuse, yet most people have never heard of it. Churning involves brokers generating income simply by buying and selling investments on behalf of their clients. Constant and needless churning earns them hefty commissions which bites into the investment portfolio
>
> *Guardian*

c.i.f. *or* **CIF** = COST, INSURANCE AND FREIGHT

CIMA = CHARTERED INSTITUTE OF MANAGEMENT ACCOUNTANTS

CIPFA = CHARTERED INSTITUTE OF PUBLIC FINANCE AND ACCOUNTANCY

circular ['sɜːkjʊlə] **1** *adjective* sent to many people; **circular letter of credit** = letter of credit sent to all branches of the bank which issues it **2** *noun* **(a)** leaflet or letter sent to many people; *they sent out a circular offering a 10% discount* **(b)** leaflet sent by a broker to clients, with information about companies and shares

circularize ['sɜːkjʊləraɪz] *verb* to send a circular to; *the committee has agreed to circularize the members*; *they circularized all their customers with a new list of prices*

circulate ['sɜːkjʊleɪt] *verb* **(a)** *(of money)*; **to circulate freely** = to move about without restriction by the government **(b)** to send or to give out without restrictions; **to circulate money** = to issue money, to make money available to the public and industry; **circulating asset** = floating asset, an asset which it is assumed will be consumed during the company's normal trading cycle and will be replaced by the same type of asset **(c)** to send information to; *they circulated a new list of prices to all their customers*

circulating capital ['sɜːkjʊleɪtɪŋ 'kæpɪtəl] *noun* capital in the form of cash or debtors, raw materials, finished products and work in progress required for a company to carry on its business

circulation [sɜːkjʊ'leɪʃən] *noun* **(a)** movement; *the company is trying to improve the circulation of information between departments*; **circulation of capital** = movement of capital from one investment to another **(b)** **to put money into circulation** = to issue new notes to business and the public; *the amount of money in circulation increased more than was expected*

> QUOTE the level of currency in circulation increased to N4.9 billion in the month of August
> Business Times (Lagos)

city ['sɪti] *noun* **(a)** large town; *the largest cities in Europe are linked by hourly flights*; **capital city** = main town in a country, where the government is located; **inter-city** = between cities; *inter-city train services are often quicker than going by air* **(b)** **the City (of London)** = old centre of London, where banks and large companies have their main offices; the British financial centre; *he works in the City* or *he is in the City*; **City Code on Takeovers and Mergers** see TAKEOVER CODE; **City desk** = section of a newspaper office which deals with business news; **City editor** = business or finance editor of a British paper; **they say in the City that the company has been sold** = the business world is saying that the company has been sold

civil ['sɪvl] *adjective* **civil action** = court case brought by a person or a company against someone who has done them wrong; **civil law** = laws relating to people's rights and agreements between individuals

claim [kleɪm] **1** *noun* **(a)** asking for money; **wage claim** = asking for an increase in wages; **the union put in a 6% wage claim** = the union asked for a 6% increase in wages for its members **(b)** **legal claim** = statement that you think you own something legally; *he has no legal claim to the property* **(c)** **insurance claim** = asking an insurance company to pay for damages or for loss; **claims department** = department of an insurance company which deals with claims; **claim form** = form to be filled in when making an insurance claim; **claims manager** = manager of a claims department; **no claims bonus** = lower premium paid because no claims have been made against the insurance policy; **to put in a claim** = to ask the insurance company officially to pay damages; *to put in a claim for repairs to the car*; *she put in a claim for £250,000 damages against the driver of the other car*; **to settle a claim** = to agree to pay what is asked for; *the insurance company refused to settle his claim for storm damage* **(d)** **small claim** = claim for less than £5000 in the County Court; **small claims court** = court which deals with disputes over small amounts of money **2** *verb* **(a)** to ask for money; *he claimed £100,000 damages against the cleaning firm*; *she claimed for the rest of the car repairs from her insurance company* **(b)** to say that something is your property; *he is claiming possession of the house*; *no one claimed the umbrella found in my office* **(c)** to state that something is a fact; *he claims he never received the goods*; *she claims that the shares are her property*

claimant ['kleɪmənt] *noun* person who claims; **rightful claimant** = person who has a legal claim to something (NOTE: this term has now replaced **plaintiff**. The other side in a case is the **defendant**)

claimer ['kleɪmə] *noun* = CLAIMANT

class [klɑːs] *noun* **(a)** category or group into which things are classified according to quality or price; **first-class** = top quality, most expensive; *he is a first-class accountant* **(b)** *US* classification of common stock (Class A stock is similar to the British 'A' Shares)

46393

classify ['klæsɪfaɪ] *verb* to put (expenses, such as electricity, rent, salaries, postage, etc.) into classes or categories

clause [klɔːz] **1** *noun* section of a contract; *there are ten clauses in the contract; according to clause six, payments will not be due until next year*; **exclusion clause** = clause in an insurance policy or warranty which says which items are not covered by the policy; **penalty clause** = clause which lists the penalties which will be imposed if the contract is not fulfilled; **termination clause** = clause which explains how and when a contract can be terminated **2** *verb* to list details of the relevant parties to a bill of exchange

claw back ['klɔː 'bæk] *verb* to take back money which has been allocated; *income tax claws back 24% of pensions paid out by the government; of the £1m allocated to the project, the government clawed back £100,000 in taxes*

clawback ['klɔːbæk] *noun* **(a)** money taken back **(b)** allocation of new shares to existing shareholders, so as to maintain the value of their holdings

clean bill of lading ['kliːn 'bɪl əv 'leɪdɪŋ] *noun* bill of lading with no note to say the shipment is faulty or damaged

clean float ['kliːn 'fləʊt] *noun* floating a currency freely on the international markets, without any interference from the government; *compare* DIRTY FLOAT

clear [klɪə] **1** *adjective* **(a) clear profit** = profit after all expenses have been paid; *we made $6,000 clear profit on the sale* **(b)** free or total period of time; **three clear days** = three whole working days; *allow three clear days for the cheque to be paid into the bank* **2** *verb* **(a)** to sell cheaply in order to get rid of stock; *'demonstration models to clear'* **(b) to clear goods through customs** = to have all documentation passed by customs so that goods can leave the country **(c) to clear 10%** *or* **$5,000 on the deal** = to make 10% or $5,000 clear profit; **we cleared only our expenses** = the sales revenue only paid for the costs and expenses without making any profit **(d) to clear a cheque** = to pass a cheque through the banking system, so that the money is transferred from the payer's account to another; *the cheque took ten days to clear* *or* *the bank took ten days to clear the cheque*

clearance ['klɪərəns] *noun* **(a) customs clearance** = passing goods through customs so that they can enter or leave the country; **to**

effect customs clearance = to clear goods through customs; **clearance certificate** = certificate showing that goods have been passed by customs **(b) clearance sale** = sale of items at low prices to get rid of stock **(c) clearance of a cheque** = passing of a cheque through the banking system, transferring money from one account to another; *you should allow six days for cheque clearance*

clearing ['klɪərɪŋ] *noun* **(a) clearing of goods through customs** = passing of goods through customs **(b) clearing of a debt** = paying all of a debt **(c)** settling of a banking or stock exchange transaction through a centralized system; **clearing member** = member firm of a stock exchange which is also a member of the stock exchange clearing house

clearing agency ['klɪərɪŋ 'eɪdʒənsi] *noun* *US* central office where where stock exchange or commodity exchange transactions are settled (NOTE: British English is **clearing house**)

clearing bank ['klɪərɪŋ 'bæŋk] *noun* bank which clears cheques, one of the major British High Street banks, specializing in normal banking business for ordinary customers (loans, cheques, overdrafts, interest-bearing deposits, etc.)

clearing house ['klɪərɪŋ 'haʊs] *noun* central office where clearing banks exchange cheques, or where stock exchange or commodity exchange transactions are settled; **Clearing House Automated Payments System (CHAPS)** = computerized system for clearing cheques (NOTE: in the USA, the equivalent is the **Clearing House Interbank Payments System (CHIPS)**

clear off ['klɪər 'ɒf] *verb* **to clear off a debt** = to pay all of a debt

client ['klaɪənt] *noun* person with whom business is done; person who pays for a service; **client account** = bank account opened by a solicitor or estate agent to hold money on behalf of a client

clientele [kliːənˈtel] *noun* all the clients of a business; all the customers of a shop

close 1 [kləʊz] *noun* end of a day's trading session on a stock or commodity exchange; *at the close of the day's trading the shares had fallen 20%* **2** [kləʊs] *adjective* **close to** = very near, almost; *the company was close to bankruptcy; we are close to meeting our sales targets* **3** [kləʊz] *verb* to end **(a)** to stop doing business for the day; *the office closes at*

5.30; *we close early on Saturdays* **(b) to close (off) the accounts** = to come to the end of an accounting period and take the closing balances on the ledger accounts to the profit and loss account; **to close a position** = to arrange one's affairs so that one no longer has any liability to pay (as by selling all one's securities or when a purchaser of a futures contract takes on a sales contract for the same amount to offset the risk) **(c) to close an account** = (i) to stop supplying a customer on credit; (ii) to take all the money out of a bank account and stop the account; **he closed his building society account** = he took all the money out and stopped using the account **(d) the shares closed at $15** = at the end of the day's trading the price of the shares was $15

QUOTE Toronto stocks closed at an all-time high, posting their fifth straight day of advances in heavy trading
           Financial Times

QUOTE declines in unlisted outpaced the losses of listed stocks, and the NASDAQ composite dropped 13.01 per cent to close August at 381.21
           Financial Times Review

close company *US* **closed corporation** ['kləʊs 'kʌmpənɪ *or* kɔːpə'reɪʃən] *noun* company controlled by a few shareholders (in the UK, five or less) or its directors, where the public owns only a small proportion of the shares

closed [kləʊzd] *adjective* **(a)** shut, not open or not doing business; *the office is closed on Mondays*; *all the banks are closed on the National Day* **(b)** restricted; **closed shop** = system where a company agrees to employ only union members in certain jobs; *a closed shop agreement*; *the union is asking the management to agree to a closed shop*; **closed economy** = type of economy where trade and financial dealings are tightly controlled by the government; **closed fund** = fund, such as an investment trust, where the investor buys shares in the trust and receives dividends (as opposed to an open-ended trust, such as a unit trust, where the investor buys units, and his investment is used to purchase further securities for the trust); **closed market** = market where a supplier deals only with one agent or distributor and does not supply any others direct; *they signed a closed market agreement with an Egyptian company*

close-ended *US* **closed-end** ['kləʊz'endɪd] *adjective* which is fixed, and cannot be increased; **closed-end fund** = investment company with a fixed capital which investments can only be made by buying shares in the company

closely held ['kləʊslɪ 'held] *adjective* (shares in a company) which are controlled by only a few shareholders

close off ['kləʊz 'ɒf] *verb* to come to the end of an accounting period and take the closing balances in the ledger accounts to the profit and loss account

closing ['kləʊzɪŋ] **1** *adjective* **(a)** final, coming at the end; **closing bid** = last bid at an auction, the bid which is successful; **closing date** = last date; *the closing date for tenders to be received is May 1st*; **closing price** = price of a share at the end of a day's trading **(b)** at the end of an accounting period; **closing balance** = balance at the end of an accounting period; **closing entry** = entry which closes an account; **closing stock** = value of stock held at the end of an accounting period **2** *noun* **(a)** shutting of a shop; being shut; **closing time** = time when a shop or office stops work; **early closing day** = weekday (usually Wednesday or Thursday) when shops close in the afternoon **(b) closing of an account** = act of stopping supply to a customer on credit

closing down sale ['kləʊzɪŋ 'daʊn 'seɪl] *noun* sale of goods when a shop is closing for ever

closing out ['kləʊzɪŋ 'aʊt] *noun* ending of a futures contract by selling the relevant commodity

closure ['kləʊʒə] *noun* act of closing

C/N = CREDIT NOTE

Co. [kəʊ] = COMPANY *J. Smith & Co. Ltd*

co- [kəʊ] *prefix* working or acting together; **co-financing** = arranging finance for a project from several different sources

co-creditor ['kəʊ'kredɪtə] *noun* person who is a creditor of the same company as another person

COD *or* **c.o.d.** ['siːəʊ'diː] = CASH ON DELIVERY

code [kəʊd] *noun* **(a)** system of signs, numbers or letters which mean something; **bar code** = system of lines printed on a product which can be read by a computer to give a reference number or price; **machine-readable codes** = sets of signs or letters (such as bar codes or post codes) which can be read by computers; **post code** *US* **ZIP code** =

letters and numbers used to indicate a town or street in an address on an envelope; **stock code** = numbers and letters which refer to an item of stock; **tax code** = number given to indicate the amount of tax allowances a person has **(b)** set of rules; **code of practice** US **code of ethics** = rules drawn up by an association which the members must follow when doing business (as in the code of professional ethics drawn up by the AICPA); *see also* TAKEOVER CODE

codicil ['kəʊdəsɪl] *noun* document executed in the same way as a will, making additions or changes to an existing will

coding ['kəʊdɪŋ] *noun* attaching codes to something (such as codes on income tax assessments or on stock control cards); **notice of coding** = notice which informs someone of the code number given to indicate the amount of tax allowances a person has

co-director [kəʊdɪ'rektə] *noun* person who is a director of the same company as another person

co-insurance [kəʊɪn'ʃʊərəns] *noun* insurance policy where the risk is shared among several insurers

COLA *US* = COST OF LIVING ADJUSTMENT

cold [kəʊld] *adjective* without being prepared; **cold call** = sales call (either a visit or a telephone call) where the salesman has no appointment and the client is not an established customer; **cold start** = starting a new business or opening a new shop where there was none before

collar ['kɒlə] *noun* purchasing fixed minimum and maximum rates ('floors' and 'caps') of interest, dividends or repayments at the same time

COMMENT: if a company has money in variable rate investments and wants to protect its income, it will buy a floor; instead of paying the premium for this purchase it will simultaneously sell a cap, so effectively creating a 'collar' round its investments

collateral [kɒ'lætərəl] *adjective & noun* (security, such as negotiable instruments, shares, goods) used to provide a guarantee for a loan

collateralization [kɒlætərəlaɪ'zeɪʃn] *noun* securing a debt by selling long-term receivables to another company which secures them on the debts

QUOTE examiners have come to inspect the collateral that thrifts may use in borrowing from the Fed
Wall Street Journal

collateralize [kɒ'lætərəlaɪz] *verb* to secure a debt on a collateral

collect [kə'lekt] **1** *verb* **(a)** to make someone pay money which is owed; **to collect a debt** = to go and make someone pay a debt **(b)** to take things away from a place; *we have to collect the stock from the warehouse; can you collect my letters from the typing pool?* **2** *adverb & adjective US* (phone call) where the person receiving the call agrees to pay for it; *to make a collect call; he called his office collect*

collectables *or* **collectibles** [kə'lektəblz] *noun* things which can be collected as a hobby but can also be considered as an investment (such as stamps, old coins, etc.)

collectibility [kəlektə'bɪləti] *noun* ability of cash owed to be collected

collecting agency [kə'lektɪŋ 'eɪdʒənsi] *noun* agency which collects money owed to other companies for a commission; **collecting bank** = bank into which a person has deposited a cheque, and which has the duty to collect the money from the account of the writer of the cheque; **debt collecting** = collecting money which is owed

collection [kə'lekʃən] *noun* **(a)** getting money together; making someone pay money which is owed; **tax collection** *or* **collection of tax**; **debt collection** = collecting money which is owed; **debt collection agency** = company which collects debts for other companies for a commission; **bills for collection** = bills where payment is due **(b)** fetching of goods; *the stock is in the warehouse awaiting collection*; **collection charges** *or* **collection rates** = charge for collecting something; **to hand something in for collection** = to leave something for someone to come and collect **(c) collections** = money which has been collected

collector [kə'lektə] *noun* person who makes people pay money which is owed; **collector of taxes** *or* **tax collector** = person who collects taxes for the Inland Revenue; **debt collector** = person who collects debts owing to others

column ['kɒləm] *noun* series of numbers, one under the other; *to add up a column of figures; put the total at the bottom of the column*; **credit column** = right-hand side of an account showing decreases in assets or increases in liabilities; **debit column** = left-hand side of an account showing increases in assets or decreases in liabilities

comfort ['kʌmfət] *noun* **letter of comfort** *or* **comfort letter** = (i) letter supporting a subsidiary company which is trying to get a loan; (ii) letter from a company to someone who intends to lend money to one of its subsidiaries, in which the company supports its subsidiary

QUOTE comfort letters in the context of a group of companies can take the form of (a) an undertaking by a holding company to provide finance to a subsidiary; (b) an undertaking to meet the debts and liabilities of a subsidiary as they fall due. Comfort letters are encountered in numerous other situations: where a bank is to grant finance to a subsidiary company, it may seek a comfort letter from the parent to the effect that the parent will not dispose of its interest in the subsidiary

Accountancy

commerce ['kɒmɜːs] *noun* business, buying and selling of goods and services; **Chamber of Commerce** = group of local businessmen who meet to discuss problems which they have in common and to promote business in their town

commercial [kə'mɜːʃəl] *adjective* **(a)** referring to business; **commercial aircraft** = aircraft used to carry cargo or passengers for payment; **commercial attaché** = diplomat who represents and tries to promote his country's business interests; **commercial bank** = bank which offers banking services to the public, as opposed to a merchant bank; **commercial bill** = bill of exchange issued by a company (a trade bill) or accepted by a bank (a bank bill) (as opposed to treasury bills which are issued by the government); **commercial directory** = book which lists all the businesses and business people in a town; **commercial district** = part of a town where offices and shops are; **commercial law** = laws regarding business; **commercial lawyer** = lawyer who specializes in business and company law; **commercial paper (CP)** = IOU issued by a company to raise a short-term loan; **commercial port** = port which has only goods traffic; **commercial property** = building used for offices or shops; **sample only - of no commercial value** = not worth anything if sold **(b)** profitable; **not a commercial proposition** = not likely to make a profit

commercially [kə'mɜːʃəli] *adverb* in a business way; **not commercially viable** = not likely to make a profit

commission [kə'mɪʃən] *noun* **(a)** money paid to a salesman, agent or stockbroker, usually a percentage of the sales made or the business done; **she gets 10% commission on everything she sells**; **he charges 10% commission** = he asks for 10% of sales as his payment; **commission agent** = agent who is paid a percentage of sales; **broker's commission** = commission paid to a broker who buys or sells for a client; *US* **commission broker** = stockbroker who works for a commission; **commission house** = firm which buys or sells (usually commodities) for clients, and charges a commission for this service; **commission rep** = representative who is not paid a salary, but receives a commission on sales; **commission sale** *or* **sale on commission** = sale where the salesman is paid a commission; *see also* HALF-COMMISSION MAN **(b)** group of people officially appointed to examine some problem; **the government has appointed a commission of inquiry to look into the problems of small exporters**; **he is the chairman of the government commission on export subsidies**

commissioner [kə'mɪʃənə] *noun* person appointed to examine a certain problem or to direct a certain organization; **Commissioner of Inland Revenue (IRC)** = person appointed officially to supervise the collection of taxes, including income tax, capital gains tax and corporation tax, but not Value Added Tax

commit [kə'mɪt] *verb* **to commit oneself to** = to guarantee (a loan issue)

commitment [kə'mɪtmənt] *noun* agreement by an underwriting syndicate to underwrite a note issuance facility; **commitment fee** = fee paid to a bank which has arranged a line of credit which has not been fully used

commodity [kə'mɒdəti] *noun* thing sold in very large quantities, especially raw materials and food such as metals or corn; **primary** *or* **basic commodities** = farm produce grown in large quantities, such as corn, rice, cotton; **staple commodity** = basic food or raw material which is most important in a country's economy; **commodity market** *or* **commodity exchange** = place where people buy and sell commodities; **commodity futures** = trading in commodities for delivery at a later date; **coffee rose 5% on the commodity futures market yesterday**;

commodity trader = person whose business is buying and selling commodities

COMMENT: commodities are either traded for immediate delivery (as 'actuals or 'physicals'), or for delivery in the future (as 'futures'). Commodity markets deal either in metals (aluminium, copper, lead, nickel, silver, zinc) or in 'soft' items, such as cocoa, coffee, sugar and oil. In London the exchanges are the London Metal Exchange and the London Commodity Exchange. Gold is traded on the London Gold Market, petroleum on the International Petroleum Exchange (IPE). In the USA, the New York Commodity Exchange (COMEX) deals in metals, the Chicago Board of Trade (CBT) in metals, soft commodities and financial futures, and the Chicago Mercantile Exchange (CME) in livestock and livestock futures

common ['kɒmən] *adjective* belonging to several different people or to everyone; **common carrier** = firm which carries goods or passengers, and which anyone can use; **common cost** *or* **common overhead** = cost which is apportioned to two or more cost centres; *US* **common dividend** = dividend payable on common stock; **common ownership** = ownership of a company or a property by a group of people; **common pricing** = illegal fixing of prices by several businesses so that they all charge the same price; *US* **common stock** = ordinary shares in a company, giving shareholders a right to vote at meetings and to receive dividends

common law ['kɒmən 'lɔ:] *noun* **(a)** law as laid down in decisions of courts, rather than by statute **(b)** general system of laws which formerly were the only laws existing in England, and which in some cases have been superseded by statute (NOTE: you say **at common law** when referring to something happening according to the principles of common law)

Common Market ['kɒmən 'mɑ:kɪt] *noun* former name for the European Community

commute [kə'mju:t] *verb* to change a right into cash; *he decided to commute part of his pension rights into a lump sum payment*

commuting [kə'mju:tɪŋ] *noun* ordinary **commuting** = travel between your home and your place of work (the cost is not tax-deductible)

company ['kʌmpəni] *noun* **(a)** business, a group of people organized to trade in goods and services for profit; **to put a company into liquidation** = to close a company by selling its assets for cash; **to set up a company** = to start a company legally **(b)** *(forms of company)*; **associate company** = company

which is partly owned by another company; **family company** = company where most of the shares are owned by members of a family; **holding company** = company which exists only to own shares in subsidiary companies; **joint-stock company** = company whose shares are held by many people; **limited (liability) company** = company where a shareholder is responsible for repaying the company's debts only to the face value of the shares he owns; **listed company** = company whose shares can be bought or sold on the Stock Exchange; **parent company** = company which owns more than half of another company's shares; **private (limited) company** = company with a small number of shareholders, whose shares are not traded on the Stock Exchange; **public limited company (plc)** = company in which the public can invest and whose shares and loan stock can usually be bought on the Stock Exchange; **subsidiary company** = company which is owned by a parent company **(c)** **finance company** = company which buys goods or equipment which it then hires or leases to companies or individuals; **insurance company** = company whose business is insurance; **shipping company** = company whose business is in transporting goods or passengers in ships; **a tractor** *or* **aircraft** *or* **chocolate company** = company which makes tractors, aircraft or chocolate **(d)** **company auditor** = person or firm appointed to audit a company's accounts; **company car** = car which belongs to a company and is lent to an employee to use for business or other purposes; **company doctor** = (i) doctor who works for a company and looks after sick workers; (ii) specialist businessman who advises companies which are in difficulties on methods of becoming profitable again; **company director** = person appointed by the shareholders to help run a company; **company law** = laws which refer to the way companies may work; **company secretary** = person responsible for the company's legal and financial affairs; *GB* **the Companies Acts** = Acts of Parliament which regulate the workings of companies, stating the legal limits within which companies may do their business; **Companies Registration Office (CRO)** *or* **Companies House** = official organization where the records of companies must be deposited, so that they can be inspected by the public

COMMENT: a company can be incorporated (with memorandum and articles of association) as a private limited company, and adds the initials 'Ltd' after its name, or as a public limited company, when its name must end in 'plc'. Unincorporated companies are partnerships such as firms of solicitors, architects, accountants, etc., and they add the initials Co. after their name

comparable ['kɒmpərəbl] *adjective* which can be compared; *the two sets of figures are not comparable*; **which is the nearest company comparable to this one in size?** = which company is of a similar size and can be compared with this one?

compare with [kəm'peə 'wɪð] *verb* to put two things together to see how they differ; *how do the sales this year compare with last year's?*; *compared with 1998, last year was a boom year*

compensate ['kɒmpenseɪt] *verb* to pay for damage done; *to compensate a salesman for loss of commission*; **compensating balance** = money which someone has to deposit a bank in order to qualify for a loan from the bank; **compensating errors** = two or more errors which are set against each other so that the accounts still balance (NOTE: you compensate someone **for** something)

QUOTE it was rumoured that the government was prepared to compensate small depositors
South China Morning Post

compensation [kɒmpen'seɪʃən] *noun* **(a)** **compensation for damage** = payment for damage done; **compensation for loss of office** = payment to a director who is asked to leave a company before his contract ends; **compensation for loss of earnings** = payment to someone who has stopped earning money or who is not able to earn money; **compensation fund** = fund operated by the Stock Exchange to compensate investors for losses suffered when members of the Stock Exchange default **(b) compensation deal** = deal where an exporter is paid (at least in part) in goods from the country to which he is exporting **(c)** *US* salary; **compensation package** = salary, pension and other benefits offered with a job

QUOTE golden parachutes are liberal compensation packages given to executives leaving a company
Publishers Weekly

compete [kəm'piːt] *verb* to compete with someone *or* with a company = to try to do better than another person or another company; *we have to compete with cheap imports from the Far East*; *they were competing unsuccessfully with local companies on their home territory*; **the two companies are competing for market share**

or **for a contract** = each company is trying to win a larger part of the market or to win the contract

competing [kəm'piːtɪŋ] *adjective* which competes; **competing firms** = firms which compete with each other; **competing products** = products from different companies which have the same use and are sold in the same markets at similar prices

competition [kɒmpə'tɪʃən] *noun* **(a)** trying to do better than another supplier; **free competition** = being free to compete without government interference; **keen competition** = strong competition; *we are facing keen competition from European manufacturers* **(b) the competition** = companies which are trying to compete with your product; *we have lowered our prices to beat the competition*; *the competition have brought out a new range of products*

QUOTE profit margins in the industries most exposed to foreign competition are worse than usual
Sunday Times

QUOTE competition is steadily increasing and could affect profit margins as the company tries to retain its market share
Citizen (Ottawa)

competitive [kəm'petɪtɪv] *adjective* which competes effectively; **competitive devaluation** = devaluation of a currency to make a country's goods more competitive on the international markets; **competitive price** = low price aimed to compete with a rival product; **competitive pricing** = putting low prices on goods so as to compete with other products; **competitive products** = products which compete well with existing products

QUOTE the company blamed fiercely competitive market conditions in Europe for a £14m operating loss last year
Financial Times

competitiveness [kəm'petɪtɪvnəs] *noun* being competitive

QUOTE farmers are increasingly worried by the growing lack of competitiveness for their products on world markets
Australian Financial Review

competitor [kəm'petɪtə] *noun* person or company which competes; *two German firms are our main competitors*

complete [kəm'pli:t] *verb* to sign a contract for the sale of a property and to exchange it with the other party, so making it legal

completion [kəm'pli:ʃən] *noun* act of finishing something; **completion date** = date when something will be finished; **completion of a contract** = signing of a contract for the sale of a property when the buyer pays and the seller passes ownership to the buyer

compliance [kəm'plaɪəns] *noun* (i) agreement to do what is ordered; (ii) doing what has been ordered; **compliance department** = department in a stockbroking firm which makes sure that the Stock Exchange rules are followed and that confidentiality is maintained in cases where the same firm represents rival clients; **compliance officer** = person working in the compliance department of a stockbroking firm

comply [kəm'plaɪ] *verb* **to comply with a court order** = to obey an order given by a court

composition [kɒmpə'zɪʃən] *noun* agreement between a debtor and creditor, where the creditor will accept part repayment of the existing debt

compound 1 ['kɒmpaʊnd] *adjective* **compound interest** = interest which is added to the capital and then earns interest itself **2** [kəm'paʊnd] *verb* **(a)** to agree with creditors to settle a debt by paying only part of what is owed **(b)** to add interest to capital; *$1,000 at 10% compounded twice a year will produce $1102.50 at the end of the year, while if it is compounded once a year it will produce only $1100.00*

comprehensive insurance [kɒmprɪ'hensɪv ɪn'ʃʊərəns] *noun* insurance policy which covers you against all risks which are likely to happen

COMMENT: the term is commonly used in motor insurance to differentiate from third-party insurance, which only covers damage to any person who is not one of the people named in the insurance contract

compromise ['kɒmprəmaɪz] **1** *noun* agreement between two sides, where each side gives way a little to settle a dispute; *management offered £5 an hour, the union asked for £9, and a compromise of £7.50 was*

reached **2** *verb* to reach an agreement by giving way a little; *he asked £15 for it, I offered £7 and we compromised on £10*

comptable [kɒn'ta:bl] *French* accountant

comptroller [kən'trəʊlə] *noun* financial controller; **Comptroller and Auditor General** = official whose duty is to examine the accounts of ministries and government departments; *US* **Comptroller General** = official whose duty is to examine the accounts of government departments (he or she is the head of the General Accounting Office); **Comptroller of the Currency** = official of the US government responsible for the regulation of US national banks (that is, banks which are members of the Federal Reserve)

compulsory liquidation *or* **compulsory winding up** [kəm'pʌlsəri lɪkwɪ'deɪʃn *or* 'waɪndɪŋ ʌp] *noun* liquidation which is ordered by a court

computable [kəm'pju:təbl] *adjective* which can be calculated

computation [kɒmpjʊ'teɪʃən] *noun* calculation

computational [kɒmpjʊ'teɪʃənl] *adjective* **computational error** = mistake made in calculating

compute [kəm'pju:t] *verb* to calculate, to do calculations

computer [kəm'pju:tə] *noun* electronic machine which calculates, stores information and processes it automatically; **computer bureau** = office which offers to do work on its computers for companies which do not have their own computers; **computer department** = department in a company which manages the company's computers; **computer error** = mistake made by a computer; **computer file** = section of information on a computer (such as the payroll, list of addresses, customer accounts); **computer language** = system of signs, letters and words used to instruct a computer; **computer listing** = printout of a list of items taken from data stored in a computer; **computer manager** = person in charge of a computer department; **computer network** = number of computers, terminals and peripherals connected together to allow communication between each; **computer program** = instructions to a computer, telling it to do a particular piece of work; **computer programmer** = person who writes computer programs; **computer services** = work using a computer, done by a computer bureau; **computer time** = time when a computer is being used (paid for at an hourly rate); *running all those sales reports costs a lot in computer time*; **business computer** = powerful small computer which is programmed for special business uses; **personal computer** *or* **home computer** = small computer which can be used in the home

computerize [kəm'pju:təraɪz] *verb* to change from a manual system to one using computers; *our stock control has been completely computerized*

computerized [kəm'pju:təraɪzd] *adjective* worked by computers; *a computerized invoicing system*

computer-readable
[kəm'pju:tə'ri:dəbl] *adjective* which can be read and understood by a computer; *computer-readable codes*

computing [kəm'pju:tɪŋ] *noun* referring to computers; **computing speed** = speed at which a computer calculates

concealment of assets [kən'si:lmənt əv 'æsɪts] *noun* hiding assets so that creditors do not know they exist

concept ['kɒnsept] *noun* **accounting concept** = general assumption on which accounts are prepared (the main concepts are: that the business is a going concern; that revenue and costs are noted when they are incurred and not when cash is received or paid; that the present accounts are drawn up following the same principles as the previous accounts ('consistency'); that revenue or costs are only recorded if it is certain that they will be incurred; that transactions are only recorded if they have monetary value; see FRS 18); **historical cost concept** *or* **historical cost convention** = basis for treatment of assets in financial statements where they are recorded at their historical cost, without adjustment for inflation or other price variations; **matching concept** *or* **matching convention** = the basis for preparing accounts which says that profits can only be recognised if sales are fully matched with costs accrued during the same period; **concept of capital maintenance** = idea that profit is only recorded if the capital of the company, measured in terms of its net assets, increases during an accounting period (assets can be measured at historical cost or in units of constant purchasing power); **concept of maintenance of operating capacity** = concept of capital maintenance measured in terms of the changes in the current values of fixed assets, stock and working capital (profit

can only be taken if the total value of these assets, called the 'net operating assets', including adjustments for changes in prices affecting these assets, increases during an accounting period)

concern [kən'sɜ:n] *noun* business or company; *his business is a going concern* = the company is working (and making a profit); **sold as a going concern** = sold as an actively trading company

concert ['kɒnsət] *noun (of several people)*; **to act in concert** = to work together to achieve an aim (this is illegal if the aim is to influence a share price by all selling or buying together)

concert party ['kɒnsət 'pɑ:ti] *noun* arrangement where several people or companies work together in secret (usually to acquire another company through a takeover bid)

concession [kən'seʃn] *noun* **(a)** right to use someone else's property for business purposes; **mining concession** = right to dig a mine on a piece of land **(b)** right to be the only seller of a product in a place; *she runs a jewellery concession in a department store* **(c)** allowance; **tax concession** = allowing less tax to be paid

concessionaire [kənseʃə'neə] *noun* person who has the right to be the only seller of a product in a place

concessionary [kən'seʃnəri] *adjective* **concessionary fare** = reduced fare for certain types of passenger (such as employees of the transport company, or old age pensioners)

conciliation [kənsɪlɪ'eɪʃən] *noun* bringing together the parties in a dispute so that the dispute can be settled

condition [kən'dɪʃən] *noun* **(a)** term of a contract; duties which have to be carried out as part of a contract; something which has to be agreed before a contract becomes valid; **conditions of employment** *or* **conditions of service** = terms of a contract of employment; **conditions of sale** = agreed ways in which a sale takes place (such as discounts or credit terms); **on condition that** = provided that; *they were granted the lease on condition that they paid the legal costs* **(b)** general state; *the union has complained of the bad working conditions in the factory*; *item sold in good condition*; *what was the condition of the car* *when it was sold?*; *adverse trading conditions*

conditional [kən'dɪʃənl] *adjective* **(a)** provided that certain things take place; **to give a conditional acceptance** = to accept, provided that certain things happen or certain terms apply; **he made a conditional offer** = he offered to buy, provided that certain terms applied; **conditional sale** = sale which is subject to certain conditions, such as a hire-purchase agreement **(b) conditional on** = subject to (certain conditions); **the offer is conditional on the board's acceptance** = the offer is only valid provided the board accepts

conditionality [kəndɪʃə'næləti] *noun* state of having conditions attached, such as a loan from the IMF

confirm [kən'fɜːm] *verb* to say that orders from foreign purchasers are agreed, and that the sellers will be paid for these orders

confirmation [kɒnfə'meɪʃən] *noun* agreement that orders from foreign purchasers will be paid

conflict of interest ['kɒnflɪkt əv 'ɪntrest] *noun* (i) situation where a person may profit personally from decisions which he takes in his official capacity; (ii) situation where a firm may be recommending a course of action to clients which is not in their best interest, but may well profit the firm, or where different departments of the same firm are acting for rival clients

conglomerate [kən'glɒmərət] *noun* group of subsidiary companies linked together and forming a group making very different types of products

consensus ad idem [kɒn'sensəs 'æd 'ɪdem] *Latin phrase meaning* 'agreement to this same thing': real agreement to a contract by both parties

conservative [kən'sɜːvətɪv] *adjective* careful, not overestimating; *a conservative estimate of sales*; *his forecast of expenditure is very conservative*; **at a conservative estimate** = calculation which probably underestimates the final figure; *their turnover has risen by at least 20% in the last year, and that is probably a conservative estimate*

conservatively [kən'sɜːvətli] *adverb* not overestimating; *the total sales are conservatively estimated at £2.3m*

conservator ['kɒnsərveɪtə] *noun US* official appointed by a court to manage a person's affairs

consider [kən'sɪdə] *verb* to think seriously about something; **to consider the terms of a contract** = to examine and discuss if the terms are acceptable

consideration [kənsɪdə'reɪʃən] *noun* **(a)** serious thought; *we are giving consideration to moving the head office to Scotland* **(b)** something valuable exchanged as part of a contract (not always money, it could be an issue of shares as part of the purchase price when taking over a company); **for a small consideration** = for a small fee or payment; **deferred consideration** = instalment payments for the acquisition of new subsidiaries usually made in the form of cash and shares, where the balance due after the initial deposit depends on the performance of the business acquired (also called 'earn-outs')

consign [kən'saɪn] *verb* **to consign goods to someone** = to send goods to someone for him to use or to sell for you

consignation [kɒnsaɪ'neɪʃən] *noun* act of consigning

consignee [kɒnsaɪ'niː] *noun* person who receives goods from someone for his own use or to sell on behalf of the sender

consignment [kən'saɪnmənt] *noun* **(a)** sending of goods to someone who will sell them for you; **goods on consignment** = goods kept for another company to be sold on their behalf for a commission; **consignment accounts** = accounts kept by both consignee and consignor, showing quantities, dates of shipment, and payments for stocks held **(b)** group of goods sent for sale; *a consignment of goods has arrived*; *we are expecting a consignment of cars from Japan*; **consignment note** = note saying that goods have been sent

consignor [kən'saɪnə] *noun* person who consigns goods to someone

| COMMENT: the goods remain the property of the consignor until the consignee sells or pays for them

consistency [kən'sɪstənsi] *noun* one of the basic accounting concepts, that items in the accounts should be treated in the same way from year to year

consolidate [kən'sɒlɪdeɪt] *verb* **(a)** to include the accounts of several subsidiary companies as well as the holding company in a single set of accounts; **consolidated accounts** = accounts where the financial position of several different accounting entities (i.e., a holding company and its subsidiaries) are recorded together; **consolidated balance sheet** = balance sheets of the holding company and its subsidiary companies grouped together into a single balance sheet; **consolidated profit and loss account** = profit and loss accounts of the holding company and its subsidiary companies grouped together into a single profit and loss account **(b)** to group goods together for shipping; **consolidated shipment** = goods from different companies grouped together into a single shipment **(c)** *GB* **Consolidated Fund** = money in the Exchequer which comes from tax revenues and is used to pay for government expenditure

consolidated stock [kən'sɒlɪdeɪtɪd 'stɒk] = CONSOLS

Consolidating Act [kən'sɒlɪdeɪtɪŋ 'ækt] *noun* Act of Parliament which brings together several previous Acts which relate to the same subject

consolidation [kənsɒlɪ'deɪʃən] *noun* **(a)** action of preparing consolidated accounts; **Consolidation Act** = CONSOLIDATING ACT **(b)** grouping together of goods for shipping **(c)** taking profits from speculative investments and investing them safely in blue-chip companies

consols ['kɒnsɒlz] *plural noun GB* irredeemable government bonds (they pay an interest but do not have a maturity date)

consortium [kən'sɔːtjəm] *noun* group of companies which are brought together for a special purpose; *a consortium of Canadian companies or a Canadian consortium; a consortium of French and British companies is planning to construct the new aircraft*

constant ['kɒnstənt] *adjective* which does not change; *US* **constant dollar accounting** = method of accounting for transactions which attempts to relate each monetary amount to the same base period and so remove the distortions caused by inflation; **constant purchasing power** = CURRENT PURCHASING POWER

consult [kən'sʌlt] *verb* to ask an expert for advice; *he consulted his accountant about his tax problems*

consultancy [kən'sʌltənsi] *noun* act of giving specialist advice; *a consultancy firm; he offers a consultancy service*

consultant [kən'sʌltənt] *noun* specialist who gives advice; *management consultant; tax consultant*

Consultative Committee of Accountancy Bodies (CCAB) committee formed of representatives of various accountancy bodies, such as the AAT, ICAEW, ACCA, etc., which draws up recommendations regarding competence in accounting

consulting [kən'sʌltɪŋ] *adjective* person who gives specialist advice; **consulting actuary** = independent actuary who advises large pension funds

consumable goods *or* **consumables** [kən'sjuːməbl 'gʊdz *or* kən'sjuːməblz] *noun* goods which are bought by companies and used up in administrative work rather than in production (such as stationery)

consumer [kən'sjuːmə] *noun* person or company which buys and uses goods and services; *gas consumers are protesting at the increase in prices; the factory is a heavy consumer of water;* **consumer council** = group representing the interests of consumers; **consumer credit** = credit given by shops, banks and other financial institutions to consumers so that they can buy goods; lenders have to be licensed under the Consumer Credit Act, 1974 (the American equivalent is also called **installment credit)**; **Consumer Credit Act, 1974** = Act of Parliament which licenses lenders, and requires them to state clearly the full terms of loans which they make (including the APR); **consumer goods** = goods bought by consumers, by members of the public; **consumer hire agreement** = agreement by which a customer hires something for his own use for a period of time; **consumer panel** = group of consumers who report on products they have used so that the manufacturers can improve them or use what the panel says about them in advertising; **consumer price index (CPI)** = American index showing how prices of consumer goods have risen over a period of time (the British equivalent is the Retail Prices Index or RPI); **consumer protection** = protecting consumers against unfair or illegal traders; **consumer research** = research into why consumers buy goods and what goods they really want to buy; **consumer resistance** = lack of interest by consumers in buying a product; **consumer society** = type of society where consumers are encouraged to buy goods; **consumer spending** = spending by private households on goods and services

contable [kɒn'tæbleɪ] *Spanish* accountant

contango [kən'tæŋɡəʊ] *noun* **(a)** payment of interest to a stockbroker for permission to carry payment for shares from one account day to the next; **contango day** = day when the rate of contango payments is fixed **(b)** *(on commodity markets)* cash price which is lower than the forward price (NOTE: also called **forwardation;** the opposite is **backwardation)**

contemnor [kən'temnə] *noun* person who commits a contempt of court

contempt of court [kən'temt əv 'kɔːt] *noun* being rude to a court, as by bad behaviour in court or by refusing to carry out a court order

contested takeover [kən'testɪd 'teɪkəʊvə] *noun* takeover where the board of the target company does not recommend it to the shareholders and tries to fight it

contingency [kən'tɪndʒənsi] *noun* something which may possibly take place, but which is not certain to happen (see FRS 12); **contingency fund** *or* **contingency reserve** = money set aside in case it is needed urgently; **contingency plans** = plans which will be put into action if something happens which no one expects; **to add on 10% to provide for contingencies** = to provide for further expenditure which may be incurred; *we have built 10% for contingencies into our cost forecast*

contingent [kən'tɪndʒənt] *adjective* **(a)** **contingent expenses** = expenses which will be incurred only if something happens; **contingent gain** *or* **contingent loss** = gain or loss which is incurred only if something happens; **contingent liability** = liability which may or may not occur, but for which provision is made in a company's accounts (as opposed to 'provisions', where money is set aside for an anticipated expenditure) **(b)** **contingent policy** = insurance policy which pays out only if something happens (e.g. if the person named in the policy dies before the person due to benefit)

continuous [kən'tɪnjʊəs] *adjective* which goes on without stopping; **continuous stocktaking** *US* **continuous inventory** = method of stock control used in large companies where each day a different group of stock items is counted and compared with what the records indicate should be in stock

contra ['kɒntrə] **1** *noun* **contra account** = account which offsets another account (where a company's supplier is not only a creditor in that company's books but also a debtor because it has purchased goods on credit); **contra entry** = entry made in the opposite side of an account to offset an earlier entry; **per contra** *or* **as per contra** = words showing that a contra entry has been made **2** *verb* **to contra an entry** = to enter a similar amount in the opposite side of an account

contract 1 ['kɒntrækt] *noun* **(a)** legal agreement between two parties; *to draw up a contract*; *to draft a contract*; *to sign a contract*; **the contract is binding on both parties** = both parties signing the contract must do what is agreed; **under contract** = bound by the terms of a contract; *the firm is under contract to deliver the goods by November*; **to void a contract** = to make a contract invalid; **contract of employment** = contract between management and employee showing all conditions of work; **contract of service** *or* **service contract** = contract between a company and a person showing all conditions of work which the person will carry out for the company as an employee; **exchange of contracts** = point in the sale of a property when the buyer and seller both sign the contract of sale which then becomes binding **(b)** **contract law** *or* **law of contract** = laws relating to written agreements; **by private contract** = by private legal agreement **(c)** *(Stock Exchange)* deal to buy or sell shares; agreement to purchase options or futures; **contract note** = note showing that shares have been bought or sold but not yet paid for, also including the commission; **futures contract** = contract for the purchase of commodities for delivery at a date in the future; **financial futures contract** = contract for the purchase of gilt-edged securities for delivery at a date in the future (NOTE: a futures contract is a contract to purchase; if an investor is bullish, he will buy a contract, but if he feels the market will go down, he will sell one) **(d)** agreement for supply of a service or goods; *contract for the supply of spare parts*; *to enter into a contract to supply spare parts*; *to sign a contract for £10,000 worth of spare parts*; **to put work out to contract** = to decide that work should be done by another company on a contract, rather than employing members of staff to do it; **to award a contract to a company** *or* **to place a contract with a**

company = to decide that a company shall have the contract to do work for you; **to tender for a contract** = to put forward an estimate of cost for work under contract; **breach of contract** = breaking the terms of a contract; **the company is in breach of contract** = the company has failed to do what was agreed in the contract; **contract costing** = method of costing large projects, where the contracted work will run over several accounting periods; **contract work** = work done according to a written agreement **2** ['kɒntrækt or kən'trækt] *verb* to agree to do some work by contract; **to contract to supply spare parts** or **to contract for the supply of spare parts**; **the supply of spare parts was contracted out to Smith Ltd** = Smith Ltd was given the contract for supplying spare parts; **to contract out of an agreement** = to withdraw from an agreement with the written permission of the other party

COMMENT: a contract is an agreement between two or more parties to create legal obligations between them. Some contracts are made 'under seal', i.e. they are signed and sealed by the parties; most contracts are made orally or in writing. The essential elements of a contract are: (a) that an offer made by one party should be accepted by the other; (b) consideration; (c) the intention to create legal relations. The terms of a contract may be express or implied. A breach of contract by one party entitles the other party to sue for damages or in some cases to seek specific performance

contracting party [kən'træktɪŋ 'pɑːti] *noun* person or company which signs a contract

contractor [kən'træktə] *noun* person or company which does work according to a written agreement; **haulage contractor** = company which transports goods under contract; **government contractor** = company which supplies the government with goods under contract

contractual [kən'træktjʊəl] *adjective* according to a contract; **contractual liability** = legal responsibility for something as stated in a contract; **to fulfil your contractual obligations** = to do what you have agreed to do in a contract; **he is under no contractual obligation to buy** = he has signed no agreement to buy; **contractual savings** = savings in the form of regular payments into long-term investments such as pension schemes

contractually [kən'træktjʊəli] *adverb* according to a contract; *the company is contractually bound to pay his expenses*

contribute [kən'trɪbjuːt] *verb* to give money, to add money to; *to contribute 10% of the profits*; *he contributed to the pension fund for 10 years*

contribution [kɒntrɪ'bjuːʃən] *noun* **(a)** money paid to add to a sum; **contribution of capital** = money paid to a company as additional capital; **employer's contribution** = money paid by an employer towards a worker's pension; **National Insurance contributions (NIC)** = money paid each month by a worker and the company to the National Insurance; **pension contributions** = money paid by a company or worker into a pension fund **(b)** difference between sales value and the variable costs of a unit sold (it goes to cover fixed costs and provide the profit)

contributor [kən'trɪbjʊtə] *noun* **contributor of capital** = person who contributes capital

contributory [kən'trɪbjʊtəri] **1** *adjective* **(a) contributory pension plan** or **scheme** = pension plan where the employee as well as the employer has to contribute a percentage of salary **(b)** which helps to cause; *rising exchange rates have been a contributory factor in the company's loss of profits* **2** *noun* person who is liable to contribute funds to a company if the company is wound up, such as a shareholder who has not paid for his shares in full

control [kən'trəʊl] **1** *noun* **(a)** power; being able to direct something; *the company is under the control of three shareholders*; *the family lost control of its business*; **to gain control of a company** = to buy more than 50% of the shares so that you can direct the business; **to lose control of a company** = to find that you have less than 50% of the shares in a company, and so are no longer able to direct it **(b)** restricting or checking something; making sure that something is kept in check; **under control** = kept in check; *expenses are kept under tight control*; *the company is trying to bring its overheads back under control*; **out of control** = not kept in check; *costs have got out of control*; **budgetary control** = using budgets to control the performance of a company; **credit control** = checking that customers pay on time and do not exceed their credit limits; **quality control** = making sure that the quality of a product is good; **stock control** = making sure that the correct level of stock is maintained (to always meet demand while keeping the costs of holding stock to a minimum) **(c) control account** = account used to record the total amounts entered in a number of different ledger accounts; it also acts as a means of checking the accuracy of the ledger accounts **(d) exchange controls** = government restrictions on changing the local currency into foreign currency in order to make payments to people or companies abroad; *the government has imposed exchange controls*; *they say the government is going to lift exchange controls*; **price controls** = legal measures to prevent prices rising too fast **2** *verb* **(a) to control a company** = to be able to direct the business of a company, because you own more than 50% of the shares; *the business is controlled by a company based in Luxembourg*; *the company is controlled by the majority shareholder* **(b)** to make sure that something is kept in check or is not allowed to develop; *the government is fighting to control inflation or to control the rise in the cost of living*

controlled [kən'trəuld] *adjective* ruled, kept in check; **government-controlled** = ruled by a government; **controlled company** = company where more than 50% (or in the USA, 25%) of the shares belong to one owner; **controlled economy** = economy where the most business activity is directed by orders from the government

controller [kən'trəulə] *noun* **(a)** person who controls (especially the finances of a company); **credit controller** = member of staff whose job is to try to get payment of overdue invoices; **finance controller** = accountant whose main task is to manage the company's monetary resources; **stock controller** = person who tries to maintain stock at the correct level; **Controller of Audit** = head of the Audit Commission **(b)** *US* chief accountant in an organization, reponsible for internal auditing, tax affairs and the reporting of the orgnaization's accounts

controlling [kən'trəulɪŋ] *adjective* **to have a controlling interest in a company** = to own more than 50% of the shares so that you can direct how the company is run

convention [kən'venʃn] *noun* **historical cost convention** *or* **historical cost concept** = basis for treatment of assets in financial statements where they are recorded at their historical cost, without adjustment for inflation or other price variations; **matching convention** *or* **matching concept** = the basis for preparing accounts which says that profits can only be recognised if sales are fully matched with costs accrued during the same period

conversion [kən'vɜːʃən] *noun* change **(a) conversion costs** = cost of changing raw materials into finished or semi-finished products, including wages, other direct production costs and the production overhead **(b) conversion price** *or* **conversion rate** = rate at which a currency is changed into a foreign currency; price at which preference shares are converted into ordinary shares **(c)** changing convertible loan stock into ordinary shares; **conversion discount** *or* **conversion premium** = difference between the price of convertible stock and the ordinary shares into which they are to be converted (if the convertible stock is cheaper, the difference is a 'conversion premium'; if the stock is dearer, the difference is a 'conversion discount'; **conversion issue** = issue of new bonds timed to coincide with the date of maturity of older bonds, with the intention of persuading investors to reinvest; **conversion period** = time during which convertible loan stock may be changed into ordinary shares; **conversion value** = value of convertible stock, including the extra value of the ordinary shares into which they may be converted **(d) conversion of funds** = using money which does not belong to you for a purpose for which it is not supposed to be used

convert [kən'vɜːt] *verb* **(a)** to change money of one country for money of another; *we converted our pounds into Swiss francs* **(b) to convert funds to one's own use** = to use someone else's money for yourself

convertibility [kənvɜːtə'bɪləti] *noun* (i) ability to exchange one currency for another easily; (ii) ability to exchange a currency for gold or SDRs

convertible [kən'vɜːtəbl] **1** *adjective* **convertible currency** = currency which can be exchanged for another easily; **convertible debentures** *or* **convertible loan stock** = debentures or loan stock which can be exchanged for ordinary shares at a later date **2** *noun* **convertibles** = CONVERTIBLE LOAN STOCK

conveyance [kən'veɪəns] *noun* legal document which transfers a property from the seller to the buyer

conveyancer [kən'veɪənsə] *noun* person who draws up a conveyance

conveyancing [kən'veɪənsɪŋ] *noun* legally transferring a property from a seller to a buyer; **do-it-yourself conveyancing** = drawing up a legal conveyance without the help of a lawyer

cooling off period ['ku:lɪŋ ɒf 'pi:rɪəd] *noun* (i) during an industrial dispute, a period when negotiations have to be carried on and no action can be taken by either side; (ii) period when a person is allowed to think about something which he has agreed to buy on hire-purchase and possibly change his mind; (iii) period of ten days during which a person who has signed a life assurance policy may cancel it

cooperative ['kəʊ'ɒpərətɪv] **1** *noun* business *or* organization run by a group of workers who are the owners and who share the profits **2** *adjective* willing to work together; **cooperative society** = society where the customers and workers are partners and share the profits; **cooperative store** = store owned by those who shop there as well as by its workers

coproprietor [kəʊprə'praɪətə] *noun* person who owns a property with another person or several other people

coproperty [kəʊ'prɒpəti] *noun* ownership of property by two or more people together

copyright ['kɒpiraɪt] **1** *noun* an author's legal right to publish his or her own work and not to have it copied (lasting fifty years after the author's death under the Berne Convention); similar right of an artist, film maker or musician; **Copyright Act** = an Act of Parliament (such as the Copyright Acts 1911, 1956, 1988, etc.) making copyright legal, and controlling the copying of copyright material; **copyright deposit** = depositing a copy of a published work in a copyright library (usually the main national library), which is part of the formal copyrighting of copyright material; **copyright holder** *or* **copyright owner** = person who owns the copyright in a work; **copyright law** = laws concerning the protection of copyright; **copyright line** = COPYRIGHT NOTICE; **work which is out of copyright** = work by a writer, etc., who has been dead for fifty years, and which anyone can publish; **work still in copyright** = work by a living writer, or by a writer who has not been dead for fifty years; **infringement of copyright** *or* **copyright infringement** = act of illegally copying a work which is in copyright; **copyright notice** = note in a book showing who owns the copyright and the date of ownership **2** *verb* to confirm the copyright of a written work by printing a copyright notice and publishing the work **3** *adjective* covered by the laws of copyright; *it is illegal to take copies of a copyright work*

COMMENT: Copyright exists in original written works, in works of art and works of music; it covers films, broadcasts, recordings, etc.; it also covers the layout of books, newspapers and magazines. Copyright only exists if the work is created by a person who is qualified to hold a copyright, and is published in a country which is qualified to hold a copyright. There is no copyright in ideas, items of news, historical events, items of information, or in titles of artistic works. When a copyright is established, the owner of the copyright can copy his work himself, sell copies of it to the public, perform his work or exhibit it in public, broadcast his work, or adapt it in some way. No other person has the right to do any of these things. Copyright lasts for 50 years after the author's death according to the Berne Convention, and for 25 years according to the Universal Copyright Convention. In the USA, copyright is for 50 years after the death of an author for books published after January 1st, 1978. For books published before that date, the original copyright was for 28 years after the death of the author, and this can be extended for a further 28 year period up to a maximum of 75 years. In 1995, the European Union adopted a copyright term of 70 years after the death of the author. The copyright holder has the right to refuse or to grant permission to copy copyright material, though under the Paris agreement of 1971, the original publishers (representing the author or copyright holder) must, under certain circumstances, grant licences to reprint copyright material. The copyright notice has to include the symbol ©, the name of the copyright holder and the date of the copyright (which is usually the date of first publication). The notice must be printed in the book and usually appears on the reverse of the title page. A copyright notice is also printed on other forms of printed material such as posters

corp *US* = CORPORATION

corporate ['kɔ:pərət] *adjective* referring to a whole corporation; **corporate bonds** = bonds issued by corporations to raise capital; **corporate finance** = financing of a corporation; **corporate image** = idea which a corporation would like the public to have of it; **corporate loan** = loan issued by a corporation; **corporate plan** = plan for the future work of a whole corporation; **corporate planning** = planning the future work of a whole corporation; **corporate profits** = profits of a corporation; **corporate raider** = person or company which buys a stake in another company before making a hostile takeover bid

QUOTE the prime rate is the rate at which banks lend to their top corporate borrowers
Wall Street Journal

> QUOTE corporate profits for the first quarter showed a 4 per cent drop from last year
> Financial Times

> QUOTE if corporate forecasts are met, sales will exceed $50 million
> Citizen (Ottawa)

corporate governance [ˈkɔːpərət ˈgʌvənəns] *noun* the way a company or other organisation is run including the powers of the board of directors, audit committees, ethics, environmental impact, treatment of workers, directors' salaries and internal control

> QUOTE the chairman has committed the cardinal sin in corporate governance - he acted against the wishes and interests of the shareholders
> Investors Chronicle

COMMENT: corporate governance reporting in the UK developed from the 1992 Cadbury Committee on the Financial Aspects of Corporate Governance. That was followed by the Greenbury report on directors' remuneration. Both were later updated by the Hampel Committee. In 1999 the Turnbull Report dealing with internal control introduced the concept that companies should adopt a system to analyse all the risks to the business, not just narrow financial ones. In the USA, corporate governance is mostly prescribed by state law, though the Securities and Exchange Commission has imposed a degree of conformity federally

corporation [kɔːpəˈreɪʃən] *noun* **(a)** a body (such as a company) which the law regards as a separate entity from its members; **finance corporation** = company which provides money for hire purchase; **corporation tax (CT)** = tax on profits and capital gains made by companies, calculated before dividends are paid; *see also* ADVANCE CORPORATION TAX, MAINSTREAM CORPORATION TAX **(b)** *US* company which is incorporated in the United States; **corporation income tax** = tax on profits made by incorporated companies **(c)** *GB* municipal authority; **corporation loan** = loan issued by a local authority

COMMENT: a corporation is formed by registration with the Registrar of Companies under the Companies Act (in the case of public and private companies) or other Acts of Parliament (in the case of building societies and charities). A corporation can also be created by Royal Charter (such as ACCA and CIMA)

correct [kəˈrekt] *verb* **correcting entry** = entry made in accounts to make something right which was previously wrong

correction [kəˈrekʃən] *noun* making something correct; change which makes something correct; **technical correction** = situation where a share price or a currency moves up or down because it was previously too low or too high, because of technical factors

> QUOTE now the market is having a correction, or a bear market, which is correspondingly worse than others round the world. The bear market is signalled when the index cuts below its 200-day moving average
> Money Observer

COSA = COST OF SALES ADJUSTMENT

cost [kɒst] **1** *noun* **(a)** amount of money which has to be paid for something; **to cover costs** = to produce enough money in sales to pay for the costs of production; *the sales revenue barely covers the costs of advertising or the manufacturing costs*; **to sell at cost** = to sell at a price which is the same as the cost of manufacture or the wholesale cost **(b)** **allocated costs** = overhead costs which have been allocated to a certain cost centre; **direct costs** = all costs (e.g. materials, labour and expenses)which can be directly related to the making of a product; **fixed costs** = business costs which do not change with the quantity of the product made; **historic(al) cost** = actual cost of purchasing something which was purchased some time ago; **incremental cost** = cost of changing the level of activity (such as the cost of making one thousand extra units above the number already planned; this may then include further fixed costs); **indirect costs** = costs which are not directly related to the making of a product (such as cleaning, rent, administration); **labour costs** = cost of hourly-paid workers employed to make a product; **indirect labour costs** = cost of paying workers which cannot be allocated to a cost centre (such as workers who are not directly involved in making a product, like secretaries in a typing pool, cleaners, etc.); **manufacturing costs** *or* **production costs** = costs of making a product; **marginal cost** = cost of making a single extra unit above the number already planned; **operating costs** *or* **running costs** = cost of the day-to-day organization of a company; **overhead costs** = total cost of materials, salaries and other expenses (including selling, administration and finance costs) which are not directly related to the making of a product; **variable costs** = production costs which increase with the quantity of the product made (such as wages, raw materials) **(c)** **cost accountant** =

accountant who gives managers information about their business costs; **cost accounting** = branch of management accounting concerned with the recording of manufacturing and sales costs, budgets and the calculation of profitability; **cost allocation** = way in which overhead expenses are related to various cost centres; **cost analysis** = examination of the costs of a product or service; **cost apportionment** = sharing out of common overhead costs among various cost centres; **cost centre** = person or group whose costs can be itemized and to which costs can be allocated for control purposes; **cost of control** = goodwill which is incurred when the cost of acquiring a company is higher than the asset value of the company; **cost, insurance and freight (CIF)** = estimate of a price, which includes the cost of the goods, the insurance and the transport charges; **cost of goods sold** = COST OF SALES; **cost price** = selling price which is the same as the price which the seller paid for the item (i.e. either the manufacturing cost or the wholesale price); **cost of sales** = all the costs of a product sold, including manufacturing costs and the staff costs of the production department, before general overheads are calculated; **cost of sales adjustment (COSA)** = adjustment made in current cost accounting to a company's historical cost profit figure to take into account the effect of inflation on the value of materials used in production during the accounting period (if prices are rising, the COSA will reduce historical cost profit); **cost-volume-profit (CVP) analysis** = analysis of the relationship between gross profit and costs of production at different selling prices and output volumes **(b) cost of borrowing** or **cost of money** = interest rate paid on borrowed money **(c) costs** = expenses involved in a court case; **to pay costs** = to pay the expenses of a court case; *the judge awarded costs to the defendant*; *costs of the case will be borne by the prosecution* **2** *verb* **(a)** to have a price; *how much does the machine cost?*; *this cloth costs £10 a metre* **(b) to cost a product** = to calculate how much money will be needed to make a product, and so work out its selling price

cost-benefit analysis ['kɒst'benɪfɪt ə'næləsɪs] *noun* comparing the costs and benefits of different possible ways of using available resources

cost-cutting ['kɒst'kʌtɪŋ] *noun* reducing costs; *we have taken out the telex as a cost-cutting exercise*

cost-effective ['kɒstɪ'fektɪv] *adjective* which gives a good result in relation to its cost; *we find advertising in the Sunday newspapers very cost-effective*

cost-effectiveness ['kɒstɪ'fektɪvnəs] *noun* being cost-effective; *can we calculate the cost-effectiveness of air freight against shipping by sea?*

costing ['kɒstɪŋ] *noun* calculation of the manufacturing costs, and so the selling price of a product; *the costings give us a retail price of $2.95*; *we cannot do the costing until we have details of all the production expenditure*; **absorption costing** = costing a product to include both the direct costs of production and the overhead costs which are absorbed as well; **incremental costing** or **differential costing** = costing method which shows the difference in costs which results from different levels of activity (such as the cost of making one thousand or ten thousand extra units); **marginal costing** = costing a product on the basis of its variable costs only, excluding fixed costs

costly ['kɒstli] *adjective* expensive, which costs a lot of money

cost of living ['kɒst əv 'lɪvɪŋ] *noun* money which has to be paid for food, heating, rent etc.; *to allow for the cost of living in the salaries*; **cost-of-living allowance** *US* **cost of living adjustment** = addition to normal salary to cover increases in the cost of living (in the USA, called COLA); **cost-of-living bonus** = extra money paid to meet the increase in the cost of living; **cost-of-living increase** = increase in salary to allow it to keep up with the increased cost of living; **cost-of-living index** = way of measuring the cost of living which is shown as a percentage increase on the figure for the previous year; similar to the consumer price index, but including other items such as the interest on mortgages

cost plus ['kɒst 'plʌs] *noun* system of charging, where the buyer pays the costs plus a percentage commission to the seller; *we are charging for the work on a cost plus basis*

council ['kaʊnsl] *noun* governing body of an organization, such as the Stock Exchange council

counselling *US* **counseling** ['kaʊnsəlɪŋ] *noun* giving advice; **debt counselling** = advising people in debt as to the best way of arranging their finances to pay off their debts

count [kaʊnt] *verb* **(a)** to add figures together to make a total; *he counted up the* *sales for the six months to December* (b) to include; *did you count my trip to New York as part of my sales expenses?*

counter- ['kaʊntə] *prefix* against

counterbid ['kaʊntəbɪd] *noun* higher bid in reply to a previous bid; *when I bid £20 he put in a counterbid of £25*

counter-claim ['kaʊntəkleɪm] **1** *noun* claim for damages made in reply to a previous claim; *Jones claimed £25,000 in damages against Smith, and Smith entered a counter-claim of £50,000 for loss of office* **2** *verb* to put in a counter-claim; *Jones claimed £25,000 in damages and Smith counter-claimed £50,000 for loss of office*

counterfeit ['kaʊntəfɪt] **1** *adjective* false or imitation (money) **2** *verb* to make imitation money

counterfoil ['kaʊntəfɔɪl] *noun* slip of paper kept after writing a cheque, an invoice or a receipt, as a record of the deal which has taken place

countermand ['kaʊntəmɑːnd] *verb* **to countermand an order** = to say that an order must not be carried out

counter-offer ['kaʊntər'ɒfə] *noun* higher offer made in reply to another offer; *Smith Ltd made an offer of £1m for the property, and Black & Son replied with a counter-offer of £1.4m*

> QUOTE the company set about paring costs and improving the design of its product. It came up with a price cut of 14%, but its counter-offer – for an order that was to have provided 8% of its workload next year – was too late and too expensive
> *Wall Street Journal*

counterparty ['kaʊntəpɑːti] *noun* the other party in a deal

counterpurchase ['kaʊntəpɜːtʃəs] *noun* international trading deal, where a company agrees to use money received on a sale to purchase goods in the country where the sale was made

countersign ['kaʊntəsaɪn] *verb* to sign a document which has already been signed by someone else; *all cheques have to be countersigned by the finance director; the purchasing manager countersigns all my orders*

countertrade ['kaʊntətreɪd] *noun* trade which does not involve payment of money, but rather barter, buy-back deals, etc.

countervailing duty ['kaʊntəveɪlɪŋ 'djuːti] *noun* duty imposed by a country on imported goods, where the price of the goods includes a subsidy from the government in the country of origin

counting house ['kaʊntɪŋ 'haʊs] *noun* department dealing with cash

coupon ['kuːpɒn] *noun* **(a)** piece of paper used in place of money; **gift coupon** = coupon from a store which is given as a gift and which must be exchanged in that store **(b)** (i) slip of paper attached to a government bond certificate which can be cashed to provide the annual interest; (ii) the interest on a government bond; **cum coupon** = with a coupon attached or before interest due on a security is paid; **ex coupon** = without the interest coupons or after interest has been paid; **zero-coupon bond** = bond which carries no interest, but which is issued at a discount and can be redeemed at its face value, so providing a capital gain; **coupon rate** = percentage fixed interest rate on a government bond or a debenture; *US* **coupon security** = government security which carries a coupon and pays interest, as opposed to one which pays no interest but is sold at a discount to its face value

covenant ['kʌvənənt] **1** *noun* legal contract; **deed of covenant** = official signed agreement by which someone agrees to certain conditions, such as the payment of a certain sum of money each year **2** *verb* to agree to pay a sum of money each year by contract; *to covenant to pay £10 per annum*

> COMMENT: when payments are made under covenant to a charity, the charity can reclaim the tax paid by the person making the covenant

cover ['kʌvə] **1** *noun* **(a) insurance cover** = protection guaranteed by an insurance policy; *do you have cover against theft?*; **to operate without adequate cover** = without being protected by insurance; **to ask for additional cover** = to ask the insurance company to increase the amount for which you are insured; **full cover** = insurance against all risks; **cover note** = letter from an insurance company giving details of an insurance policy and confirming that the policy exists (NOTE: the American English for this is **binder) (b)** security to guarantee a loan or future purchases; forward contract which is entered into to protect against exchange rate falls; *do you have sufficient cover for this loan?* **(c) dividend cover** = ratio of profits to dividend **(d) cover price** = retail price of a newspaper, magazine or book, shown on the cover **2** *verb*

(a) to earn enough money to pay for costs, expenses, etc.; *we do not make enough sales to cover the expense of running the shop*; *breakeven point is reached when sales cover all costs*; **the dividend is covered four times** = profits are four times the dividend paid out **(b)** to have enough money to pay; **to cover a position** = to have enough money to be able to pay for a forward purchase; **covered bear** = bear who holds the stock which he sells; *see also* UNCOVERED **(c)** to take steps to give yourself security against a possible loss; **the damage was covered by the insurance** = the insurance company paid for the damage; **to cover a risk** = to be protected by insurance against a risk; **to be fully covered** = to have insurance against all risks; *the insurance covers fire, theft and loss of work*

QUOTE three export credit agencies have agreed to provide cover for large projects in Nigeria
Business Times (Lagos)

coverage ['kʌvərɪdʒ] *noun US* protection guaranteed by insurance; *do you have coverage against fire damage?*

covering letter *or* **covering note** ['kʌvərɪŋ 'letə *or* 'kʌvərɪŋ 'nəʊt] *noun* letter or note sent with documents to say why you are sending them

CP = COMMERCIAL PAPER

CPA *US* = CERTIFIED PUBLIC ACCOUNTANT

CPI = CONSUMER PRICE INDEX

CPM = CRITICAL PATH METHOD

CPP = CURRENT PURCHASING POWER

CPU = CENTRAL PROCESSING UNIT group of circuits which perform the basic functions of a computer

Cr *or* **CR** = CREDIT

creative accountancy *or* **creative accounting** [krɪ'eɪtɪv ə'kaʊntənsi *or* ə'kaʊntɪŋ] *noun* adaptation of a company's figures to present a better picture than is correct (to appear to make a company more attractive to a potential buyer, or for some other reason which may not be strictly legal); **creative financing** = finding methods of financing a commercial project that are different from the normal methods of raising money

COMMENT: 'creative accounting' is the term used to cover accounting practices which, although legal, may be used to mislead banks, investors and shareholders about the profitability or liquidity of a business. These practices include: changes in depreciation policies between accounting periods, the use of extraordinary items to reduce the effect on earnings-per-share, pre-acquisition write-downs, contingent liabilities (potential liabilities are not shown on the balance sheet), off-balance sheet finance, capitalization of costs, and brand accounting. In the UK, the Accounting Standards Board has issued many financial reporting standards designed to curb creative accounting. For example, FRS 3 'Reporting financial performance', changed the definition of extraordinary items so as to prevent companies disclosing such items. Several books have been published dealing with creative accounting. The most significant was 'Accounting for Growth' by Terry Smith which introduced a 'blob guide' to score companies on how many creative accounting techniques they used

QUOTE Terry identified exactly the same problems that we did with the accountancy world. I think that of the 12 issues he highlighted, we have now dealt with nine of them.
Chairman of the ASB (1993)

credere ['kreɪdəri] *see* DEL CREDERE

credit ['kredɪt] **1** *noun* **(a)** amount entered in accounts to show a decrease in assets or expenses or an increase in liabilities, revenue or capital (in accounts, credits are entered in the right-hand column); *compare* DEBIT *to enter £100 to someone's credit*; *to pay in £100 to the credit of Mr Smith*; **debits and credits** = figures which are entered in the accounts to record increases or decreases in assets, expenses, liabilities, revenue or capital; **credit balance** = difference between debits and credits in an account where the value of credits is greater; *the account has a credit balance of £1,000* (NOTE: in bank statements, a credit balance is shown by an asterisk or the letters CR after the figure); **credit column** = right-hand side of an account showing decreases in assets or increases in liabilities; **credit entry** = entry on the credit side of an account; **credit note** **(C/N)** = note showing that money is owed to a customer; *the company sent the wrong order and so had to issue a credit note*; **credit side** = right-hand side of an account showing the value of income receivable, cash paid or money owed to others; **account in credit** = account where the credits are higher than the debits; *US* **adjustment credit** = short-term loan from the Federal Reserve to a commercial bank; **bank credit** = loans or overdrafts from a bank to a customer; **tax credit** = part of a dividend on which the company has already paid advance corporation tax which is deducted from the shareholder's income tax charge **(b)** period of time a customer is allowed before he has to pay a debt incurred for goods or services; *to give someone six months' credit*; *to sell on good credit terms*; **extended credit** = credit on very long repayment terms; **interest-free credit** = arrangement to borrow money (to purchase a good or service) without paying interest on the loan; **long credit** = terms allowing the borrower a long time to pay; **open credit** = bank credit given to good customers without security; **short credit** = terms allowing the customer only a short time to pay; **trade credit** = credit offered by one company when trading with another; **credit account** = account which a customer has with a shop which allows him to buy goods and pay for them later; **credit agency** *US* **credit bureau** = company which reports on the creditworthiness of customers to show whether they should be allowed credit; **credit bank** = bank which lends money; **credit control** = (i) check that customers pay on time and do not owe more than their credit limit; (ii) limits on bank lending imposed by a government; **credit controller** = member of staff whose job is to try to get payment of overdue invoices; **credit facilities** = arrangement with a bank or supplier to have credit so as to buy goods; **credit freeze** *or* **credit squeeze** = period when lending by banks is restricted by the government; **letter of credit** = document issued by a bank on behalf of a customer, authorizing payment to a supplier when the conditions specified in the document are met in full; **irrevocable letter of credit** = letter of credit which cannot be cancelled; **credit limit** = fixed amount which is the most a customer can owe on credit; **he has exceeded his credit limit** = he has borrowed more money than he is allowed; **to open a line of credit** *or* **a credit line** = to make credit available to someone; *US* **credit line** = overdraft, the amount by which a person can draw money from an account with no funds, with the agreement of the bank; **credit rating** = amount which a credit agency feels a customer should be allowed to borrow; **credit reference** = a credit rating or other indication of the creditworthiness of a company or individual; **credit risk** = risk that a borrower may not be able to repay a loan **(c)** **on credit** = without paying immediately; *to live on credit*; *we buy everything on sixty days' credit*; *the company exists on credit from its suppliers* **2** *verb* to put money into someone's account; to record money received in an account; *to credit an account with £100 or to credit £100 to an account*

credit card ['kredɪt 'kɑːd] *noun* plastic card which allows the cardholder to borrow money and to buy goods up to a certain limit without paying for them immediately; *see also* DEBIT CARD

creditor ['kredɪtə] *noun* person or company that is owed money (a company's creditors are its liabilities); **creditors** = list of all liabilities in a set of accounts, including overdrafts, amounts owing to other companies in the group, trade creditors, payments received on account for goods not yet supplied, etc.; **trade creditors** = companies which are owed money by a company (the amount owed to trade creditors is shown in the annual accounts); **creditors' meeting** = meeting of all persons to whom an insolvent company owes money, to decide how to obtain the money owed

credit union ['kredɪt 'juːnjən] *noun US* group of people who pay in regular deposits or subscriptions which earn interest and are used to make loans to other members of the group

creditworthiness ['kredɪtwɜːðɪnəs] *noun* ability of a customer to pay for goods bought on credit

creditworthy ['kredɪtwɜːði] *adjective* (person or company) trusted to be able to pay for goods supplied on credit

crisis ['kraɪsɪs] *noun* serious economic situation where decisions have to be taken rapidly; *international crisis*; *banking crisis*; *financial crisis*; **crisis management** = management of a business or a country's economy during a period of crisis; **to take crisis measures** = to take severe measures rapidly to stop a crisis developing (NOTE: plural is **crises)**

critical path analysis ['krɪtɪkəl 'pɑːθ ə'næləsɪs] *noun* defining tasks or jobs and the time each requires, arranged in order to achieve certain goals (NOTE: also called **PERT (Program Evaluation and Review Techniques)**

critical path method (CPM) ['krɪtɪkəl 'pɑːθ 'meθəd] *noun* use of analysis and projection of each critical step in a large project to help a management team

CRO = COMPANIES REGISTRATION OFFICE

crore [krɔː] *noun (in India)* ten million (NOTE: one crore equals 100 lakh)

cross [krɒs] *verb* **to cross a cheque** = to write two lines across a cheque to show that it has to be paid into a bank; **crossed cheque** = cheque which has to be paid into a bank

COMMENT: crossed cheques have the words 'A/C payee' printed in the space between the two vertical lines: all British cheques are now printed in this way. This means that the cheque can only be paid into a bank, and only into the account of the person whose name is written on it - it cannot be endorsed to a third party

cross-border ['krɒs 'bɔːdə] *adjective* across borders of countries, from one country to another; **cross-boder services** = accountancy services provided by an accountancy firm in one country for a client in another country

cross holding ['krɒs 'həʊldɪŋ] *noun* situation where two companies hold shares in each other (to prevent each from being taken over)

cross out ['krɒs 'aʊt] *verb* to put a line through something which has been written; *she crossed out £250 and put in £500*

cross-selling ['krɒs'selɪŋ] *noun* selling insurance or other financial services at the same time as a mortgage

crown [kraʊn] *noun* word used in English to refer to the currencies of several countries, such as the Czech Republic, Norway, Sweden, etc.

crown jewels ['kraʊn 'dʒuːlz] *noun* most valuable assets of a company (the reason why other companies may want to make takeover bids)

crystallization [krɪstəlaɪ'zeɪʃn] *noun* process by which a floating charge becomes fixed (usually by the appointment of a receiver)

crystallize ['krɪstəlaɪz] *verb* to become chargeable on an asset; *a deferred gain is crystallized when you realize the gain by selling the asset*

CT = CORPORATION TAX

cum [kʌm] *preposition* with; **cum all** = price of a share including all entitlements; **cum dividend** = price of a share including the next dividend still to be paid; **cum coupon** = with an interest coupon attached; the price of a bond including the right to receive the next interest payment; **cum rights** = shares sold with the right to purchase new shares in a rights issue; *see also* EX

cumulative ['kjuːmjʊlətɪv] *adjective* which is added to the total previously calculated; **cumulative interest** = interest which is added to the capital each year; **cumulative preference share** *US* **cumulative preferred stock** = preference share which will have the dividend paid at a later date even if the company is not able to pay a dividend in the current year; **cumulative weighted average cost** *or* **price** = average price per unit of stock delivered in a period calculated each time a new delivery is received (as opposed 'periodic weighted average')

currency ['kʌrənsi] *noun* **(a)** money in coins and notes which is used in a particular country; **convertible currency** = currency which can easily be exchanged for another; **foreign currency** = currency of another country (see SSAP 20); **foreign currency account** = bank account in the currency of another country (e.g. a dollar account in the UK); **foreign currency reserves** = a country's reserves in currencies of other countries; **hard currency** = currency of a country which has a strong economy and which can be changed into other currencies easily; *to pay for imports in hard currency*; *to sell raw materials to earn hard currency*; **legal currency** = money which is legally used in a country; **soft currency** = currency of a country with a weak economy, which is cheap to buy and difficult to exchange for other currencies; **currency backing** = gold or securities which maintain the international strength of a currency; **dual currency bond** = bond which is paid for in one currency but which is repayable in another; **currency note** = bank note **(b)** foreign currency; **currency band** = exchange rate levels between which a currency is allowed to move without full revaluation or devaluation; **currency basket** *or* **basket of currencies** = group of currencies, each weighted and calculated together as a single unit against which another currency can be measured; **currency clause** = clause in a contract which avoids problems of payment caused by changes in exchange rates, by fixing the exchange rate for the various transactions covered by the contract; **currency futures** = purchases of foreign currency for delivery at a future date; **currency mismatching** *see* MISMATCHING; **currency movements** =

changes in exchange rates between countries; **currency swap** = (i) agreement to use a certain currency for payments under a contract in exchange for another currency (the two companies involved each can buy one of the currencies at a more favourable rate than the other); (ii) buying (or selling) a fixed amount of foreign currency on the spot market and selling (or buying) the same amount of the same currency on the forward market

QUOTE the strong dollar's inflationary impact on European economies, as national governments struggle to support their sinking currencies and push up interest rates
Duns Business Month

QUOTE today's wide daily variations in exchange rates show the instability of a system based on a single currency, namely the dollar
Economist

QUOTE the level of currency in circulation increased to N4.9 billion in the month of August
Business Times (Lagos)

current ['kʌrənt] *adjective* referring to the present time; **current assets** = assets used by a company in its ordinary work (such as materials, finished products, monies owed by customers, cash); **current cost** = the amount it would cost to replace an asset at current prices; **current cost accounting (CCA)** *or* **current value accounting** = method of accounting which records a company's costs and revenues after taking into account changes in prices affecting those items and the value of assets at current replacement cost (NOTE: the same as replacement cost accounting, as opposed to historical cost accounting); **current liabilities** = debts which a company has to pay within the next accounting period (in a company's annual accounts, these would be debts which must be paid within the year and are usually payments for goods or services received); **current price** = (i) today's price; (ii) price which has been adjusted for inflation; **current purchasing power (CPP)** = method of accounting which takes inflation into account by using constant monetary units (actual amounts multiplied by a general price index); **current rate of exchange** = today's rate of exchange; **current ratio** = ratio of a company's current assets to its current liabilities; **current standard** = standard which is used for the current accounting period (i.e., a standard which is only applicable in the short term); **current year** = the year in which an accounting period falls; **under self-assessment, income is taxed on a current year basis - i.e. it is taxed in the year in which it is received**; **current yield** = dividend calculated as a percentage of the current price of a share on the stock market

current account ['kʌrənt ə'kaʊnt] *noun* **(a)** account in an bank from which the customer can withdraw money when he wants (current accounts do not always pay interest) (NOTE: the American equivalent is a **checking account**) **(b)** account of a partner in a partnership, showing the partner's share of debts together with his drawings **(c)** account of a sole trader for the current accounting period; account of intergroup transactions held by each company within the group (these are then amalgamated into the group accounts) **(d)** account of the balance of payments recording a country's imports and exports of goods and services and the money paid on or received from investments

QUOTE crude oil output plunged during the past month and is likely to remain at its current level for the near future
Wall Street Journal

QUOTE customers' current deposit and current accounts also rose to $655.31 million at the end of December
Hongkong Standard

curve [kɜːv] *noun* line which bends round; *the graph shows an upward curve*; **learning curve** = line on a graph which shows the relationship between experience in doing something and competence at carrying it out; **sales curve** = graph showing how sales increase or decrease

cushion ['kʊʃən] *noun* money which allows a company to pay interest on its borrowings or to survive a loss; *we have sums on deposit which are a useful cushion when cash flow is tight*

custom ['kʌstəm] *noun* **(a)** use of a shop by regular shoppers; **to lose someone's custom** = to do something which makes a regular customer go to another shop; **custom-built** *or* **custom-made** = made specially for one customer; *he drives a custom-built Rolls Royce* **(b)** **the customs of the trade** = general way of working in a trade

customer ['kʌstəmə] *noun* person or company which buys goods; *the shop was full of customers*; *can you serve this customer first, please?*; *he is a regular customer of ours*; **customer appeal** = what attracts customers to a product; **customer service department** = department which deals with customers and their complaints, orders and enquiries

customize ['kʌstəmaɪz] *verb* to change something to fit the special needs of a customer; *we used customized computer terminals*

customs ['kʌstəmz] *plural noun* **H.M. Customs and Excise** = (i) British government department which organizes the collection of taxes on imports, excise duty on alcohol, etc., and VAT; (ii) office of this department at a port or airport; **to go through customs** = to pass through the area of a port or airport where customs officials examine goods; *he was stopped at the customs checkpoint; her car was searched by customs*; **customs barrier** = customs duty intended to prevent imports; **customs broker** = person or company which takes goods through customs for a shipping company; **customs clearance** = document given by customs to a shipper to show that customs duty has been paid and the goods can be shipped; *to wait for customs clearance*; **customs declaration** = statement showing goods being imported on which duty will have to be paid; *to fill in a customs (declaration) form*; **customs duty** = tax paid on goods brought into or taken out of a country; **the crates had to go through a customs examination** = the crates had to be examined by customs officials; **customs formalities** = declaration of goods by the shipper and examination of them by customs; **customs officers** *or* **customs officials** = people working for customs; **customs tariff** = list of duties to be paid on imported goods; **customs union** = agreement between several countries that goods can travel between them, without paying duty, while goods from other countries have to pay special duties

cut [kʌt] **1** *noun* **(a)** sudden lowering of a price, salary or numbers of jobs; *price cuts or cuts in prices; salary cuts or cuts in salaries*; **job cuts** = reductions in the number of jobs; **he took a cut in salary** = he accepted a lower salary **(b)** share in a payment; *he introduces*

new customers and gets a cut of the salesman's commission **2** *verb* **(a)** to lower suddenly; *we are cutting prices on all our models*; **to cut (back) production** = to reduce the quantity of products made; *the company has cut back its sales force*; *we have taken out the photocopier in order to try to cut costs* **(b)** to reduce the number of something; **to cut jobs** = to reduce the number of jobs by making people redundant; **he cut his losses** = he stopped doing something which was creating a loss (NOTE: **cutting - cut - has cut**)

QUOTE state-owned banks cut their prime rates a percentage point to 11%
Wall Street Journal

QUOTE the US bank announced a cut in its prime from 10+ per cent to 10 per cent
Financial Times

cutback ['kʌtbæk] *noun* reduction; *cutbacks in government spending*

cut down (on) ['kʌt 'daʊn ɒn] *verb* to reduce suddenly the amount of something used; *the government is cutting down on welfare expenditure*; *the office is trying to cut down on electricity consumption*; *we have installed a word-processor to cut down on paperwork*

cutting ['kʌtɪŋ] *noun* **cost-cutting** = reducing costs; *we have made three secretaries redundant as part of our cost-cutting programme*; **price-cutting** = sudden lowering of prices; **price-cutting war** = competition between companies to get a larger market share by cutting prices

CVP = COST-VOLUME-PROFIT

CWO = CASH WITH ORDER

cycle ['saɪkl] *noun* period of time when something leaves its original position and then returns to it; **economic cycle** *or* **trade cycle** *or* **business cycle** = period during which trade expands, then slows down and then expands again

cyclical ['sɪklɪkəl] *adjective* which happens in cycles; **cyclical factors** = way in which a trade cycle affects businesses

Dd

Schedule D ['ʃedjuːl 'diː] *noun* schedule to the Finance Acts under which tax is charged on profits of trades and professions. It is sub-divided into six categories, called Cases: Case I: income from a trade (such as a builder) carried on in the UK; Case II: income from a profession (such as an accountant) carried out in the UK; Case III: annual investment income from National Savings and annuities; Case IV: investment income from outside the UK; Case V: income from professions carried out abroad; Case VI: income from various sources not covered by the other schedules

Table D ['teɪbl 'diː] *noun* model memorandum and articles of association of a company with share capital limited by guarantee, set out in the Companies Act, 1985

Daimyo bond ['daɪmjəʊ 'bɒnd] *noun* Japanese bearer bond which can be cleared through European clearing houses

damages ['dæmɪdʒɪz] *noun* (i) money claimed by a claimant from a defendant as compensation for harm done; (ii) money awarded by a court as compensation to a claimant; *to claim £1,000 in damages*; *to be liable for or in damages*; *to pay £25,000 in damages*; **to bring an action for damages against someone** = to take someone to court and claim damages; **aggravated damages** = damages awarded by court against a defendant who has behaved maliciously or wilfully; **compensatory damages** = damages which compensate for the loss or harm suffered; **exemplary** *or* **punitive damages** = heavy damages which punish the defendant for the loss or harm caused to the claimant, awarded to show that the court feels the defendant has behaved badly towards the claimant; **general damages** = damages awarded by court to compensate for a loss which cannot be calculated (such as an injury); **measure of damages** = calculation of how much money a court should order one party to pay another to compensate for a tort or breach; **mitigation of damages** = reduction in the extent of damages awarded; **nominal damages** = very small amount of damages, awarded to show that the loss or harm suffered was technical rather than actual; **special damages** = damages awarded by court to compensate for a loss which can be calculated (such as the expense of repairing something)

data ['deɪtə] *noun* information (letters or figures) available on computer; **data acquisition** *or* **data capture** = getting information; keyboarding information onto a database; **bank of data** = DATABANK; **data processing (DP)** = selecting and examining data in a computer to produce useful information or to organize data files (NOTE: **data** is usually singular: **the data is easily available**)

databank ['deɪtəbæŋk] *noun* store of information in a computer

database ['deɪtəbeɪs] *noun* store of information in a computer from which other types of information can be produced; *we can extract the lists of potential customers from our database*

Datastream ['deɪtəstriːm] *noun* data system available online, giving information about securities, prices, stock exchange transactions, etc.

date [deɪt] **1** *noun* **(a)** number of day, month and year; *I have received your letter of yesterday's date*; **date stamp** = rubber stamp for marking the date on letters received; **date of bill** = date when a bill will mature; **maturity date** = date when a financial instrument will mature; **date of receipt** = date when something is received; **date of record** *or* **record date** = date when a shareholder must be registered to qualify for a dividend; **return date** = date by which a company has to file its annual return with the Companies Registration Office; **tax date** = date on which a transaction occurs for tax purposes, particularly relevant to invoices on which VAT is charged **(b) to date** = up to now; **interest to date** = interest up to the present time **2** *verb* to put a date on a document; *the cheque was dated March 24th*; *you forgot to date the cheque*; **to date a cheque forward** = to put a later date than the present one on a cheque

dated ['deɪtɪd] *adjective* with a date written on it; **dated securities** *or* **dated stocks** = securities with a date for redemption (as opposed to undated securities); **long-dated bill** = bill which is payable in more than three months' time from now; **long-dated stocks** = government stocks which mature in over fifteen years' time (NOTE: also called **'longs'**); **short-dated bill** = bill which is payable within a few days; **short-dated gilts** = government stocks which mature in less than five years time (NOTE: also called **'shorts'**)

dawn raid ['dɔːn 'reɪd] *noun* sudden planned purchase of a large number of a company's shares at the beginning of a day's trading (up to 15% of a company's shares may be bought in this way, and the purchaser must wait for seven days before purchasing any more shares; sometimes a dawn raid is the first step towards a takeover of the target company)

day [deɪ] *noun* **(a)** period of 24 hours; *there are thirty days in June*; *the first day of the month is a public holiday*; **settlement day** = (i) day when accounts have to be settled; (ii) account day, the day on which shares which have been bought must be paid for (usually a Monday ten days after the end of an account); **three clear days** = three whole working days; *to give ten clear days' notice*; *allow four clear days for the cheque to be paid into the bank*; **day order** = order to a stockbroker to buy or sell on a certain day; **day trader** = trader who buys and sells the same futures on the same day **(b)** period of work from morning to night; *she took two days off* = she did not come to work for two days; *he works three days on, two days off* = he works for three days, then has two days' holiday; **to work an eight-hour day** = to spend eight hours at work each day; **day shift** = shift which works during the daylight hours such as from 8 a.m. to 5.30 p.m.; *there are 150 men on the day shift*; *he works the day shift*; **day release** = arrangement where a company allows a worker to go to college to study for one or two days each week; *the junior sales manager is attending a day release course*

day book ['deɪ 'bʊk] *noun* book with an account of sales or purchases made each day

DCF = DISCOUNTED CASH FLOW

dead [ded] *adjective* not working; **dead account** = account which is no longer used; **dead loss** = total loss; *the car was written off as a dead loss*; **dead money** = money which is not invested to make a profit; **dead season** = time of year when there are few tourists about

deal [diːl] **1** *noun* business agreement, affair or contract; *to arrange a deal or to set up a deal or to do a deal*; *to sign a deal*; *the sales director set up a deal with a Russian bank*; *the deal will be signed tomorrow*; *they did a deal with an American airline*; **to call off a deal** = to stop an agreement; *when the chairman heard about the deal he called it off*; **cash deal** = sale done for cash; **package deal** = agreement where several different items are agreed at the same time; *they agreed a package deal, which involves the construction of the factory, training of staff and purchase of the product* **2** *verb* **(a)** to deal with = to organize; *leave it to the filing clerk - he'll deal with it*; **to deal with an order** = to supply an order **(b)** to trade, to buy and sell; **to deal with someone** = to do business with someone; **to deal in leather** *or* **to deal in options** = to buy and sell leather or options; **he deals on the Stock Exchange** = his work involves buying and selling shares on the Stock Exchange for clients

dealer ['diːlə] *noun* **(a)** person who buys and sells; **foreign exchange dealer** = person who buys and sells foreign currencies; **retail dealer** = person who sells to the general public; **wholesale dealer** = person who sells in bulk to retailers **(b)** *(Stock Exchange)* person or firm which buys or sells on their own account, not on behalf of clients; **broker-dealer** = dealer who makes a market in shares (i.e. buys shares and holds them for resale) and also deals on behalf of investor clients

dealing ['diːlɪŋ] *noun* **(a)** buying and selling on a Stock Exchange or commodities exchange; **dealing for the account** *or* **within the account** = buying shares and selling the same shares during an account, which means that the dealer has only to pay the difference between the price of the shares bought and the price obtained for them when they are sold; **fair dealing** = legal trade, legal buying and selling of shares; **foreign exchange dealing** = buying and selling foreign currencies; **forward dealings** = buying or selling commodities forward; **insider dealing** = illegal buying or selling of shares by staff of a company who have secret information about the company's plans; **option dealing** = buying and selling share options; **dealing floor** = (i) area of a broking house where dealing in securities is carried out by phone, using monitors to display current prices and stock exchange transactions; (ii) part of a stock exchange where dealers trade in securities (NOTE: also called the **trading floor;** the American English for this is the **pit) (b)**

buying and selling goods; **to have dealings with someone** = to do business with someone

dear [dɪə] *adjective* expensive, costing a lot of money; *property is very dear in this area*; **dear money** = money which has to be borrowed at a high interest rate, and so restricts expenditure by companies

death [deθ] *noun* act of dying; **death benefit** = insurance benefit paid to the family of someone who dies; **death in service** = insurance benefit or pension paid when someone dies while employed by a company; *US* **death duty** *or* **death tax** = tax paid on the property left by a dead person (NOTE: the British equivalent is **inheritance tax)**

debenture [dɪ'bentʃə] *noun* acknowledgement of a debt issued by a limited company (debentures pay a fixed interest and are very long-dated; they use the company's assets as security); *the bank holds a debenture on the company*; **convertible debenture** = debenture which can be converted into ordinary shares at a certain date; **floating debenture** = debenture secured on all the company's assets which runs until the company is wound up, when the debenture becomes fixed; **mortgage debenture** = debenture where the loan is secured against the company's fixed assets; **debenture issue** *or* **issue of debentures** = borrowing money against the security of the company's assets; **debenture bond** = (i) certificate showing that a debenture has been issued; (ii) *US* long-term unsecured loan; **debenture capital** = capital borrowed by a company, using its assets as security; **debenture holder** = person who holds a debenture for money lent; **debenture register** *or* **register of debentures** = list of debenture holders of a company; **debenture stock** = stock in a company which is secured on the company's assets

COMMENT: in the UK, debentures are always secured on the company's assets; in the USA, debenture bonds are not secured

debit ['debɪt] **1** *noun* entry in accounts which shows an increase in assets or expenses or a decrease in liabilities, revenue or capital (entered in the left-hand side of an account); *compare* CREDIT; **debits and credits** = figures which are entered in the accounts to record increases or decreases in assets, expenses, liabilities, revenue or capital; **debit balance** = difference between debits and credits in an account where the value of debits is greater; **debit card** = plastic card, similar to a credit card, but which debits the holder's account immediately through an EPOS

system; **debit column** = left-hand side of an account showing increases in assets or decreases in liabilities; **debit entry** = entry on the debit side of an account; **debit side** = left-hand side of an account showing the value of assets purchased, expenses incurred, cash received or money owed by others; **debit note** = note showing that a customer owes money; *we undercharged Mr Smith and had to send him a debit note for the extra amount*; **direct debit** = system where a customer allows a company to charge costs to his bank account automatically and where the amount charged can be increased or decreased with the agreement of the customer; *I pay my electricity bill by direct debit* **2** *verb* **to debit an account** = to charge an account with a cost; *his account was debited with the sum of £25*

debitable ['debɪtəbl] *adjective* which can be debited

debt [det] *noun* **(a)** (i) any money owed; (ii) money borrowed by a company to finance its activities; *the company stopped trading with debts of over £1 million*; **to be in debt** = to owe money; *he is in debt to the tune of £250* = he owes £250; **to get into debt** = to start to borrow more money than you can pay back; **the company is out of debt** = the company does not owe money any more; **to pay back a debt** = to pay all the money owed; **to pay off a debt** = to finish paying money owed; **to reschedule a debt** = to arrange for the repayment of a debt to be put off to a later date; **to service a debt** = to pay interest on a debt; *the company is having problems in servicing its debts*; **bad debt** = debt which will not be paid (usually because the debtor has gone out of business) and which has to be written off in the accounts; *the company has written off £30,000 in bad debts*; **bad debts account** = special account set up to deal with bad debts (it is an account to which debts are transferred as they become bad); **bad debt provision** *or* **provision for bad debts** = money put aside in accounts to cover potential bad debts; **secured debts** *or* **unsecured debts** = debts which are guaranteed or not guaranteed by assets; **debt collecting** *or* **debt collection** = collecting money which is owed; **debt collection agency** = company which collects debts for a commission; **debt collector** = person who collects debts; **debt counselling** = advising people in debt as to the best way of arranging their finances to pay off their debts; **debts due** = money owed which is due for repayment; **debt factoring** = business of buying debts at a discount (a factor collects a company's debts when due, and pays the creditor in advance part of the sum to be collected, so 'buying' the debt); **debt ratio** = the debts of a company shown as a percentage of its equity plus loan capital; **debt swap** = method of reducing exposure to a long-term Third World debt by selling it at a discount to another bank **(b) funded debt** = (i) short-term debt which has been converted into long-term by selling long-term securities such as debentures to raise the money; (ii) part of the British National Debt which pays interest, but where there is no date for repayment of the principal; **the National Debt** = money borrowed by a government

debt-convertible   bond

['detkən'vɜːtəbl 'bɒnd] *noun* floating-rate bond which can be converted to a fixed rate of interest; *see also* DROPLOCK

debtor ['detə] *noun* **(a)** person who owes money to an accounting entity **(b) debtors** = all money owed to an accounting entity; **debtors control** = ensuring that customers do not take too long to pay what they owe; *see also* CREDIT CONTROL; **debtors control account** = account used to summarize the balances on the individual sales ledger accounts; **debtors cycle** = normal credit time allowed to debtors, together with the time taken for them to place repeat orders; **debtors ledger** = sales ledger; **debtor side** = debit side of an account; **trade debtors** = debtors who owe money to a company in the normal course of that company's trading

> QUOTE the United States is now a debtor nation for the first time since 1914, owing more to foreigners than it is owed itself
>
> *Economist*

decile ['desaɪl] *noun* **(a)** one of a series of nine figures below which one tenth or several tenths of the total fall **(b)** each of the ten groups separated by these figures

decimal ['desɪməl] *noun* **decimal system** = system based on the number 10; **correct to three places of decimals** = correct to three figures after the decimal point (e.g. 3.485); **decimal point** = dot which indicates the division between the whole unit and its smaller parts (such as 4.75)

> COMMENT: the decimal point is used in the UK and USA. In most European countries a comma is used to indicate a decimal, so 4,75% in Germany means 4.75% in the UK

decimalization [desɪmǝlaɪ'zeɪʃn] *noun* changing to a decimal system

decimalize ['desɪmǝlaɪz] *verb* to change to a decimal system

decision [dɪ'sɪʒən] *noun* making up your mind to do something; **decision making** = act of coming to a decision; **decision maker** = person who has to decide; **decision support system** = computer-based system which presents auditor judgements in a structured way and can be used to create audit programmes or document the assessment of business risk; **decision table** = chart showing the relationship between certain variables and actions available when certain conditions are met; **decision tree** = graph showing a decision table, with possible paths and actions if different conditions are met

declaration [deklǝ'reɪʃən] *noun* (i) any official statement; (ii) statement that someone is taking up an option; **declaration of bankruptcy** = official statement that someone is bankrupt; **declaration of income** = statement declaring income to the tax authorities; *US* **declaration date** = date on which a board of directors declares the dividend to be paid; **customs declaration** = statement declaring goods brought into a country on which customs duty should be paid; **VAT declaration** = statement declaring VAT income to the VAT office

declare [dɪ'kleə] *verb* to make an official statement, to announce to the public; *to declare someone bankrupt*; *to declare a dividend of 10%*; **to declare goods to customs** = to state that you are importing goods which are liable to duty; *the customs officials asked him if he had anything to declare*; **to declare an interest** = to state in public that you own shares in a company being discussed or that you are related to someone who can benefit from your contacts, etc.

declared [dɪ'kleəd] *adjective* which has been made public or officially stated; **declared value** = value of goods entered on a customs declaration

decline [dɪ'klaɪn] *verb* to fall slowly; *US* **declining balance method** = REDUCING BALANCE METHOD

decrease 1 ['diːkriːs] *noun* fall or reduction; *decrease in price*; *decrease in value*; *decrease in imports*; *exports have registered a decrease*; *sales show a 10% decrease on last year* **2** [dɪ'kriːs] *verb* to fall or to become less; *imports are decreasing*; *the value of the pound has decreased by 5%*

deduct [dɪ'dʌkt] *verb* to remove money from a total; *to deduct £3 from the price*; *to deduct a sum for expenses*; *after deducting costs the gross margin is only 23%*; *expenses* *are still to be deducted*; **tax deducted at source** = tax which is removed from a salary, interest payment or dividend payment before the money is paid

deductible [dɪ'dʌktəbl] *adjective* which can be deducted; **tax-deductible** = which can be deducted from an income before tax is paid; *these expenses are not tax-deductible* = tax has to be paid on these expenses

deduction [dɪ'dʌkʃən] *noun* **(a)** removing of money from a total; *net salary is salary after deduction of tax and social security* **(b)** money removed from a total; **deductions from salary** *or* **salary deductions** *or* **deductions at source** = money which a company removes from salaries to give to the government as tax, national insurance contributions, etc.; **tax deductions** = (i) money removed from a salary to pay tax; (ii) business expenses which can be claimed against tax

deed [di:d] *noun* legal document or written agreement; **deed of arrangement** = document which sets out the agreement between an insolvent person and his creditors; **deed of assignment** = document which legally transfers a property from a debtor to a creditor; **deed of covenant** = signed legal agreement to pay someone a sum of money every year; **deed of partnership** = agreement which sets up a partnership; **deed of transfer** = document which transfers the ownership of shares; **title deeds** = document showing who owns a property; *we have deposited the deeds of the house in the bank*

deep discount ['di:p 'dɪskaʊnt] *noun* very large discount; **deep-discount** *or* **deep-discounted bond** = bond which is issued at a very large discount but which produces little or no interest; *compare* ZERO-COUPON; **deep-discounted rights issue** = rights issue where the new shares are priced at a very low price compared to their current market value

QUOTE as the group's shares are already widely held, the listing will be via an introduction. It will also be accompanied by a deeply discounted œ25m rights issue, leaving the company cash positive
Sunday Times

deep pocket ['di:p 'pɒkɪt] *noun* company which provides finance for another

defalcation [di:fæl'keɪʃən] *noun* illegal use of money by someone who is not the owner but who has been trusted to look after it

default [dɪ'fɔ:lt] **1** *noun* failure to carry out the terms of a contract, especially failure to pay back a debt; **in default of payment** = with no payment made; **the company is in default** = the company has failed to carry out the terms of the contract; **by default** = because no one else will act; **he was elected by default** = he was elected because all the other candidates withdrew **2** *verb* to fail to carry out the terms of a contract, especially to fail to pay back a debt; **to default on payments** = not to make payments which are due under the terms of a contract

defaulter [dɪ'fɔ:ltə] *noun* person who defaults

defence US **defense** [dɪ'fens] *noun* **(a)** protecting someone or something against attack, as defending a company against a takeover bid; *the merchant bank is organizing the company's defence against the takeover bid*; **defence document** = document published by a company which is the subject of a takeover bid, saying why the bid should be rejected **(b)** fighting a lawsuit on behalf of a defendant; **defence counsel** = lawyer who represents the defendant in a lawsuit

defend [dɪ'fend] *verb* to fight to protect someone or something which is being attacked, such a company which is the subject of a takeover bid; *the company is defending itself against the takeover bid*; *he hired the best lawyers to defend him against the tax authorities*; **to defend a lawsuit** = to appear in court to state your case when accused of something; **defended takeover** = contested takeover, takeover where the board of the target company does not recommend it to the shareholders and tries to fight it

defendant [dɪ'fendənt] *noun* person who is sued or who is accused of doing something to harm someone (NOTE: the other side in a case is the **claimant**)

defer [dɪ'fɜ:] *verb* to put back to a later date, to postpone; *to defer payment*; *the decision has been deferred until the next meeting* (NOTE: **deferring - deferred**)

deferment [dɪ'fɜ:mənt] *noun* postponement, putting back to a later date; *deferment of payment*; *deferment of a decision*

deferral method [dɪ'fɜ:rəl 'meθəd] *noun* way of computing deferred tax using current tax rates rather than estimated future rates of tax (see FRS 19)

deferred [dɪ'fɜːd] *adjective* put back to a later date; *US* **deferred charges** = charges incurred now but which are carried over to the future (such as insurance and rent); **deferred coupon note** *or* **deferred interest bond** = bond where the interest is not paid immediately, but only after a certain date; **deferred consideration** *see* CONSIDERATION; **deferred creditor** = person who is owed money by a bankrupt but who is paid only after all other creditors; **deferred equity** = share ownership at a later date (i.e. as part of convertible loan stock); **deferred expenditure** = expenditure incurred now but reflected in the accounts of future years; **deferred payment** = payment for goods by instalments over a long period; **deferred revenue** = revenue carried forward to future accounting periods; **deferred ordinary shares** *or* **deferred stock** = shares which receive a dividend after all other dividends have been paid; **deferred tax** *or* **deferred taxation** = tax which can be explained by the different treatment of certain transactions in the accounts and the tax computation (see FRS 15 and FRS 19)

deficiency [dɪ'fɪʃənsi] *noun* amount of money which is lacking; *there is a £10 deficiency in the petty cash*; **to make up a deficiency** = to put money into an account to balance it

deficit ['defɪsɪt] *noun* amount by which spending is higher than income; **the accounts show a deficit** = the accounts show a loss; **to make good a deficit** = to put money into an account to balance it; **balance of payments deficit** *or* **trade deficit** = situation when a country imports more than it exports and so pays out more in foreign currency than it earns; **deficit financing** = planning by a government to cover the shortfall between tax income and expenditure by borrowing money

deflate [dɪ'fleɪt] *verb* **to deflate the economy** = to reduce activity in the economy by cutting the supply of money or reducing the level of government expenditure

deflation [dɪ'fleɪʃən] *noun* reduction in economic activity (falls in output, wages, prices, etc.)

deflationary [dɪ'fleɪʃnəri] *adjective* which can cause deflation; *the government has introduced some deflationary measures in the budget*

QUOTE the strong dollar's deflationary impact on European economies as national governments push up interest rates
Duns Business Month

deflator [dɪ'fleɪtə] *noun* amount by which a country's GNP is reduced to take inflation into account

degearing [diːˈɡɪərɪŋ] *noun* reduction in gearing, reducing a company's loan capital in relation to the value of its ordinary shares plus reserves

del credere [del 'kreɪdəri] *noun* amount added to a charge to cover the possibility of not being paid; **del credere agent** = agent who receives a high commission because he guarantees payment by customers

delinquency [dɪ'lɪŋkwənsi] *noun US* being overdue in payment of an account

delinquent [dɪ'lɪŋkwənt] *adjective US* (account or payment of tax) which is overdue

deliver [dɪ'lɪvə] *verb* to transport goods to a customer; **goods delivered free** *or* **free delivered goods** = goods transported to the customer's address at a price which includes transport costs; **goods delivered free on board** = goods transported free to the ship or plane but not to the customer's warehouse; **delivered price** = price which includes packing and transport

delivery [dɪ'lɪvəri] *noun* **(a) delivery of goods** = transport of goods to a customer's address; *parcels awaiting delivery*; *free delivery* *or* *delivery free*; *delivery date*; *delivery within 28 days*; *allow 28 days for delivery*; *delivery is not allowed for* *or* *is not included*; **delivery note** = list of goods being delivered, given to the customer with the goods; **delivery order** = instructions given by the customer to the person holding his goods, to tell him where and when to deliver them; **delivery time** = number of days before something will be delivered; **delivery van** = goods van for delivering goods to retail customers; **express delivery** = very fast delivery; **recorded delivery** = mail service where the letters are signed for by the person receiving them; *we sent the documents (by) recorded delivery*; **cash on delivery (COD)** = payment in cash when the goods are delivered; **to take delivery of goods** = to accept goods when they are delivered; *we took delivery of the stock into our warehouse on the 25th* **(b)** goods being delivered; *we take in three deliveries a day*; *there were four items missing in the last delivery* **(c)** transport of a commodity to a purchaser; **delivery**

month = month in a futures contract when actual delivery will take place **(d)** transfer of a bill of exchange

demand [dɪˈmɑːnd] **1** *noun* **(a)** asking for payment; **payable on demand** = which must be paid when payment is asked for; **demand bill** = bill of exchange which must be paid when payment is asked for; **demand deposit** = (i) money in an account which can be taken out when you want it in cash or by writing a cheque; (ii) *US* = CURRENT ACCOUNT; **demand draft** = DEMAND BILL; **demand note** = promissory note which must be paid when it is presented; **final demand** = last reminder from a supplier, after which he will sue for payment **(b)** need for goods at a certain price; *there was an active demand for oil shares on the stock market*; **to meet a demand** *or* **to fill a demand** = to supply what is needed; *the factory had to increase production to meet the extra demand*; *the factory had to cut production when demand slackened*; *the office cleaning company cannot keep up with the demand for its services*; **there is not much demand for this item** = not many people want to buy it; **this book is in great demand** *or* **there is a great demand for this book** = many people want to buy it; **effective demand** = actual demand for a product which can be paid for; **demand price** = price at which a certain quantity of goods will be bought; **supply and demand** = amount of a product which is available and the amount which is wanted by customers; **law of supply and demand** = general rule that the amount of a product which is available is related to the needs of potential customers **2** *verb* to ask for something and expect to get it; *she demanded a refund*; *the suppliers are demanding immediate payment of their outstanding invoices*

```
QUOTE spot prices are now relatively
stable in the run-up to the winter's
peak demand
                              Economist
```

```
QUOTE the demand for the company's
products remained strong throughout
the first six months of the year with
production    and    sales    showing
significant increases
                   Business Times (Lagos)
```

```
QUOTE growth in demand is still
coming from the private rather than
the public sector
                          Lloyd's List
```

demerge [diːˈmɜːdʒ] *verb* to separate a company into various separate parts

demerger [diːˈmɜːdʒə] *noun* separation of a company into several separate parts (especially used of a companies which have grown by acquisition)

demise [dɪˈmaɪz] **1** *noun* **(a)** death; *on his demise the estate passed to his daughter* **(b)** granting of a property on a lease **2** *verb* to grant property on a lease

demonetization [diːmʌnɪtaɪˈzeɪʃn] *noun* stopping a coin or note being used as money

demonetize [diːˈmʌnətaɪz] *verb* to stop a coin or note being used as money

demurrage [dɪˈmʌrɪdʒ] *noun* money paid to a customer when a shipment is delayed at a port or by customs

demutualization [diːmjʊtjʊəlaɪˈzeɪʃn] *noun* changing the status of a building society from being mutual to normal share ownership

demutualize [diːˈmjʊtjʊəlaɪz] *verb* to cease to be mutual, as when the members of a building society vote to end the society's mutual status and become a plc

denomination [dɪnɒmɪˈneɪʃən] *noun* unit of money (written on a coin, banknote or stamp); *coins of all denominations*; *small denomination notes*

department [dɪˈpɑːtmənt] *noun* **(a)** specialized section of a large company; *complaints department*; *design department*; *dispatch department*; *export department*; *legal department*; **accounts department** = section in a company which deals with all aspects of accounting; **new issues department** = section of a bank which deals with issues of new shares; **personnel department** = section of a company dealing with the staff; **head of department** *or* **department head** *or* **department manager** = person in charge of a department **(b)** section of a large store selling one type of product; *you will find beds in the furniture department*; **budget department** = department in a large store which sells cheaper goods **(c)** section of the British government containing several ministries; **the Department of Trade and Industry (DTI)** = British government department which supervises and regulates commercial dealings and promotes British trade overseas

departmental [diːpɑːtˈmentl] *adjective* referring to a department; **departmental accounts** = accounts which analyze the sales of different departments or products of a company; **departmental manager** = manager of a department

depletion [dɪ'pliːʃn] *noun* depreciation of an asset, such as a gold mine, which is gradually being used up

deposit [dɪ'pɒzɪt] **1** *noun* **(a)** money placed in a bank for safe keeping or to earn interest; **certificate of deposit (CD)** = document from a bank showing that money has been deposited at a certain guaranteed interest rate for a certain period of time; **bank deposits** = all the money placed in banks; *bank deposits are at an all-time high*; **demand deposit** = (i) money in an account which can be taken out when you want it in cash or by writing a cheque; (ii) *US* = CURRENT ACCOUNT; **fixed deposit** = deposit which pays a fixed interest over a fixed period; **deposit account** = bank account which pays interest but on which notice has to be given to withdraw money (NOTE: in the USA, called a **time deposit**); **deposit at 7 days' notice** = money deposited which you can withdraw by giving seven days' notice; **deposit slip** = piece of paper stamped by the cashier to prove that you have paid money into your account; **deposit-taking business** *or* **institution** *or* **licensed deposit-taker (LDT)** = institution such as a building society, bank or friendly society, which is licensed to receive money on deposit from private individuals and to pay interest on it **(b) safe deposit** = bank safe where you can leave jewellery or documents; **safe deposit box** = small box which you can rent, in which you can keep jewellery or documents in a bank's safe **(c)** money given in advance so that the thing which you want to buy will not be sold to someone else; *to pay a deposit on a watch*; *to leave £10 as deposit* **2** *verb* **(a)** to put documents somewhere for safe keeping; *to deposit shares with a bank*; *we have deposited the deeds of the house with the bank*; *he deposited his will with his solicitor* **(b)** to put money into a bank or building society account

depositary [dɪ'pɒzɪtəri] *noun US* person or corporation which can place money or documents for safekeeping with a depository; *see also* AMERICAN DEPOSITARY RECEIPT (NOTE: do not confuse with **depository)**

depositor [dɪ'pɒzɪtə] *noun* person who deposits money in a bank, building society, etc.

depository [dɪ'pɒzɪtəri] *noun* **(a) furniture depository** = warehouse where you can store household furniture **(b)** bank or company with whom money or documents can be deposited (NOTE: do not confuse with **depositary)**

depreciable [dɪ'priːʃəbl] *adjective* which can be depreciated; **depreciable asset** = asset which will be used over more than one accounting period, but which has a limited life and so can be depreciated; **depreciable cost** = an expense which may be set against the profits of more than one accounting period

depreciate [dɪ'priːʃieɪt] *verb* **(a)** to reduce the value of assets in the accounts; *we depreciate our company cars over three years* **(b)** to lose value; *a share which has depreciated by 10% over the year*; *the pound has depreciated by 5% against the dollar*

> QUOTE this involved reinvesting funds on items which could be depreciated against income for three years
> *Australian Financial Review*

> QUOTE buildings are depreciated at two per cent per annum on the estimated cost of construction
> *Hongkong Standard*

depreciation [dɪpriːʃi'eɪʃən] *noun* **(a)** reduction in value, writing down the capital value of an asset over a period of time in a company's accounts (see FRS 15); **depreciation rate** = rate at which an asset is depreciated each year in the accounts; **accelerated depreciation** = system of depreciation which reduces the value of assets at a high rate in the early years to encourage companies, as a result of tax advantages, to invest in new equipment; **annual depreciation** = reduction in the book value of an asset at a certain rate per year; **backlog depreciation** = depreciation which has not been provided in previous accounts because of an increase in the value of the asset during the current year due to inflation; **historic cost depreciation** = depreciation based on the original cost of the asset; **replacement cost depreciation** = depreciation based on the actual cost of replacing the asset in the current year; **straight line depreciation** = depreciation calculated by dividing the cost of an asset, less its expected residual value, by the number of years it is likely to be used **(b)** loss of value; *a share which has shown a depreciation of 10% over the year*; *the depreciation of the pound against the dollar*

> COMMENT: various methods of depreciating assets are used, such as the 'straight line method', where the asset is depreciated at a constant percentage of its cost each year and the 'reducing balance method', where the asset is depreciated at a higher rate in the early years and at a lower rate later (the depreciation rate is a constant percentage but it is applied to the cost of the asset after each of

the previous year's depreciation has been deducted)

depress [dɪ'pres] *verb* to reduce; *reducing the money supply has the effect of depressing demand for consumer goods*

depressed [dɪ'prest] *adjective* **depressed area** = part of a country suffering from depression; **depressed market** = market where there are more goods than customers

dept [dɪ'pɑːtmənt] = DEPARTMENT

deregulate [diː'regjʊleɪt] *verb* to remove government controls from an industry; *the US government deregulated the banking sector in the 1980s*

deregulation [diːregjʊ'leɪʃn] *noun* reducing government control over an industry; *the deregulation of the airlines*

derivative instrument [dɪ'rɪvətɪv 'ɪnstrəmənt] *noun* form of security, such as option contracts, which is derived from ordinary bonds and shares

descending tops [dɪ'sendɪŋ 'tɒps] *noun* term used by chartists to refer to a falling market, where each peak is lower than the one before

desk [desk] *noun* **(a)** writing table in an office, usually with drawers for stationery; *desk diary; desk drawer; desk light;* **a three-drawer desk** = desk with three drawers; **desk pad** = pad of paper kept on a desk for writing notes **(b)** **cash desk** *or* **pay desk** = place in a store where you pay for goods bought; *please pay at the desk* **(c)** *US* section of a bank dealing with a particular type of business, such as the foreign exchange desk (NOTE: the British equivalent is **department**) **(d)** section of a newspaper; **the City desk** = the department which deals with business news

despatch [dɪ'spætʃ] = DISPATCH

detailed account ['diːteɪld ə'kaʊnt] *noun* separate account which lists items separately, the totals then being entered into the main accounts

determine [dɪ'tɜːmɪn] *verb* to fix, to arrange or to decide; *to determine prices or quantities; conditions still to be determined*

devaluation [diːvæljʊ'eɪʃn] *noun* reduction in value of a currency against other currencies; *the devaluation of the franc*

devalue [diː'væljuː] *verb* to reduce the value of a currency against other currencies; *the pound has been devalued by 7%; the government has devalued the pound by 7%*

develop [dɪ'veləp] *verb* **(a)** to plan and produce; *to develop a new product* **(b)** to plan and build an area; *to develop an industrial estate*

developer [dɪ'veləpə] *noun* **a property developer** = person who plans and builds a group of new houses or new factories, or who renovates old buildings

developing country *or* **developing nation** [dɪ'veləpɪŋ 'kʌntri *or* dɪ'veləpɪŋ 'neɪʃən] *noun* country which is not fully industrialized

development [dɪ'veləpmənt] *noun* **(a)** planning the production of a new product; **research and development (R & D)** = scientific investigation which leads to making new products or improving existing products (see SSAP13); *the company spends millions on research and development*; **research and development costs** = the costs involved in R & D; **research and development expenditure** = money spent on R & D; **development costs** = costs of developing new or improved products **(b)** **industrial development** = planning and building of new industries in special areas; **property development** = renovating old buildings or building new ones on their sites, seen as a business activity; **development area** *or* **development zone** = area which has been given special help from a government to encourage businesses and factories to be set up there

devise [dɪ'vaɪz] **1** *noun* giving freehold land to someone in a will **2** *verb* to give freehold property to someone in a will

devisee *noun* person who receives freehold property in a will

COMMENT: giving of other types of property is a **bequest**

differential [dɪfə'renʃəl] **1** *adjective* which shows a difference; **differential costing** = incremental costing, method of costing which shows the difference in costs which results from different levels of activity (such as the cost of making one thousand or ten thousand extra units); **differential tariffs** = different tariffs for different classes of goods (as, for example, when imports from certain countries are taxed more heavily than similar imports from other countries) **2** *noun* **price differential** = difference in price between products; **wage differentials** = differences in salary between workers in similar types of jobs; **to erode wage differentials** = to reduce differences in salary gradually

digit ['dɪdʒɪt] *noun* single number; *a seven-digit phone number*; **sum of digits method** = method of depreciating a fixed asset where the cost of the asset (less its residual value) is multiplied by a fraction based on the number of years of its expected useful life (the fraction changes each year and charges the highest costs to the earliest years)

COMMENT: an example of the sum of digits method of depreciation: if an asset has an expected life of four years, the sum of the digits is ten (1 + 2 + 3 + 4). In the first year, 4/10 of the cost of the asset is charged to depreciation, in the second year 3/10 of the original cost, in the third year 2/10 and in the final year 1/10

digital ['dɪdʒɪtl] *adjective* **digital clock** = clock which shows the time as a series of figures (such as 12:05:23); **digital computer** = computer which calculates on the basis of numbers

digital analysis ['dɪdʒɪtl ə'næləsɪs] *noun* auditing techniques that investigate the digits in accounting numbers to reveal fraud and error

COMMENT: digital analysis makes use of computers to test whether accounting amounts, such as cheque payments, exhibit characteristics that may indicate fraud or systematic error. For example if many cheques are issued for £9,999 when the signatory's authority limit is £10,000 it may indicate a problem. Benford's law predicts the frequency of occurrence of leading digits (the most likely being the number 1) and is an important element in digital analysis

dilute [daɪ'luːt] *verb* to make less valuable; *conversion of the loan stock will dilute the assets per share by 5%*; **fully diluted earnings per share** = earnings per share calculated over the whole number of shares including convertible shares (i.e., shares which may in future be converted to ordinary shares)

dilution [daɪ'luːʃən] *noun* **dilution of equity** *or* **of shareholding** = situation where the ordinary share capital of a company has been increased but without an increase in the assets, so that each share is worth less than before

dime [daɪm] *noun US (informal)* ten cent coin

diminish [dɪ'mɪnɪʃ] *verb* to become smaller; *our share of the market has diminished over the last few years*; **law of**

diminishing returns = general rule that as more factors of production (land, labour and capital) are added to the existing factors, so the amount they produce is proportionately smaller

direct [daɪ'rekt] **1** *verb* to manage or to organize; *he directs our South-East Asian operations*; *she was directing the development unit until last year* **2** *adjective* straight, with no interference; **direct business** = insurance business transacted between an insurance company and the person taking out the insurance (without going through a broker); **direct cost** = cost which can be directly related to the making of a product; **direct cost variance** = difference between the planned direct costs for a product and the actual direct costs; *US* **direct costing** = costing a product on the basis of its variable costs only, excluding fixed costs (NOTE: British English for this is **marginal costing**); **direct debit** = system where a customer allows a company to charge costs to his bank account automatically and where the amount charged can be increased or decreased with the agreement of the customer; **direct expense** = cost which is not the cost of materials or labour, but which is incurred in the production of the product; **direct labour cost** = cost of the workers employed in making a product; **direct mail** = selling a product by sending publicity material to possible buyers through the post; *these calculators are only sold by direct mail*; *the company runs a successful direct-mail operation*; **direct-mail advertising** = advertising by sending leaflets to people through the post; **direct material cost** = cost of the materials which are used in making a product; **direct selling** = selling a product direct to the customer without going through a shop; **direct share ownership** = ownership of shares by private individuals, buying or selling through brokers, and not via holdings in unit trusts; **direct taxation** = tax, such as income tax, which is deducted from income directly; *the government raises more money by direct taxation than by indirect* **3** *adverb* straight, with no third party involved; *we pay income tax direct to the government*; **to dial direct** = to contact a phone number yourself without asking the operator to do it for you; *you can dial New York direct from London if you want*

directional testing [dɪ'rekʃnl 'testɪŋ] *noun* auditing technique by which work is reduced by testing debits only for overstatement and credits only for understatement

COMMENT: once hugely popular, directional testing has been declining because of the rise of more modern audit approaches that solve the main problem with this technique, i.e. that it results in very large sample sizes on profit-and-loss items such as sales and cost of sales

directive [daɪˈrektɪv] *noun (in the EU)* legislation which is binding, but which member states can implement as they wish; *the Commission issued a directive on food prices*

COMMENT: a directive is binding as to the result to be achieved, but leaves to the national authorities the choice of form and method (Article 189 EC)

director [daɪˈrektə] *noun* **(a)** person appointed by the shareholders to help run a company; **managing director** = director who is in charge of the whole company; **chairman and managing director** = managing director who is also chairman of the board of directors; **board of directors** = (i) *GB* group of directors elected by the shareholders to run a company; (ii) *US* group of people elected by the shareholders to draw up company policy, to declare dividends and to appoint the president and other executive officers who are responsible for managing the company; **directors' fees** = fees paid to directors (these are not part of a director's salary); **directors' report** = annual report from the board of directors to the shareholders; **directors' salaries** = salaries of directors (which have to be listed in the company's profit and loss account); **associate director** = director who attends board meetings but has not been elected by the shareholders; **executive director** = director who actually works full-time in the company; **non-executive director** = director who attends board meetings only to give advice; **outside director** = director who is not employed by the company **(b)** person who is in charge of a project, an official institute, etc.; *the director of the government research institute; she was appointed director of the organization*

directorate [daɪˈrektərət] *noun* group of directors

directorship [daɪˈrektəʃɪp] *noun* post of director; *he was offered a directorship with Smith Ltd*

COMMENT: directors are elected by shareholders at the AGM, though they are usually chosen by the chairman or chief executive. A board will consist of a chairman (who may be non- executive), a chief executive or managing director, and a series of specialist directors in change of various

activities of the company (such as a finance director, production director or sales director). The company secretary will attend board meetings, but need not be a director. Apart from the executive directors, who are in fact employees of the company, there may be several non-executive directors, appointed either for their expertise and contacts, or as representatives of important shareholders such as banks. The board of an American company may be made up of a large number of non-executive directors and only one or two executive officers; a British board has more executive directors

QUOTE the research director will manage and direct a team of business analysts reporting on the latest developments in retail distribution throughout the UK

Times

QUOTE what benefits does the executive derive from his directorship? In the first place compensation has increased sharply in recent years

Duns Business Month

dirty float [ˈdɜːti ˈfləʊt] *noun* floating a currency, where the government intervenes to regulate the exchange rate (NOTE: also called a **managed float**) *compare* CLEAN FLOAT

disallow [dɪsəˈlaʊ] *verb* not to accept a claim for insurance or for tax relief; *he claimed £2,000 for fire damage, but the claim was disallowed; the Inspector of Taxes disallowed the company's claim for relief on entertainment expenditure*

disallowable [dɪsəˈlaʊəbl] *adjective* which cannot be allowed for tax relief; *the use of a car for private travel is a disallowable expense*

disburse [dɪsˈbɜːs] *verb* to pay money

disbursement [dɪsˈbɜːsmənt] *noun* payment of money

discharge [dɪsˈtʃɑːdʒ] **1** *noun* **(a) discharge in bankruptcy** = being released from bankruptcy **(b)** payment of debt; **in full discharge of a debt** = paying a debt completely; **final discharge** = final payment of what is left of a debt **(c) in discharge of his duties as director** = carrying out his duties as director **2** *verb* **(a) to discharge a bankrupt** = to release someone from bankruptcy because he has paid his debts **(b) to discharge a debt** *or* **to discharge one's liabilities** = to pay a debt or one's liabilities in full **(c)** to dismiss or to sack; *to discharge an employee*

disclaimer [dɪsˈkleɪmə] *noun* **(a)** legal refusal to accept responsibility or to accept a right **(b)** clause in a contract where a party disclaims responsibility for something **(c)** refusing to accept property bequeathed to you under someone's will **(d)** auditors' report stating that they cannot form an opinion on the accounts as a whole

disclose [dɪs'kləʊz] *verb* to tell details; *the bank has no right to disclose details of my account to the tax office*

disclosure [dɪs'kləʊʒə] *noun* act of telling details; *the disclosure of the takeover bid raised the price of the shares*; **disclosure of shareholding** = making public the fact that someone owns shares in a company (if someone owns or buys 5% of the shares in a listed company, this holding must be declared to the Stock Exchange)

discount ['dɪskaʊnt] **1** *noun* **(a)** percentage by which a full price is reduced to a buyer by the seller; *to give a discount on bulk purchases*; **to sell goods at a discount** *or* **at a discount price** = to sell goods below the normal price; **basic discount** = normal discount without extra percentages; *we give 25% as a basic discount, but can add 5% for cash payment*; **quantity discount** = discount given to people who buy large quantities; **10% discount for quantity purchases** = you pay 10% less if you buy a large quantity; **cash discount** = discount given to a customer who is paying cash; **10% discount for cash** *or* **10% cash discount** = you pay 10% less if you pay in cash; **trade discount** = discount given to a trader in the same trade (as opposed to a retail customer); **discount allowed** = amount by which the seller agrees to reduce his price to the customer; **discount received** = amount by which the purchaser receives a reduction in price from the seller **(b) discount broker** = broker who deals for a smaller commission than other brokers; **discount house** = (i) financial company which specializes in buying and selling bills at a discount, using money which has been borrowed short-term from commercial banks to finance the operation; (ii) shop which specializes in selling cheap goods bought at a high discount; **discount market** = market for borrowing and lending money, through Treasury bills, certificates of deposit, etc.; **discount rate** = (i) interest rate used to calculate the discount on the sale of commercial bills to the central bank, e.g. to the Bank of England; (ii) rate at which the face value of a bill of exchange is reduced when payment is made before its maturity date; (iii) percentage used in a discounting calculation, e.g. to find the present value of future income; **discount store** = shop which specializes in cheap

goods bought at a high discount; *US* **discount window** = way in which the Federal Reserve grants loans to a bank by giving advances on the security of Treasury bills which the bank is holding **(c)** amount by which something is sold for less than its value; **currency at a discount** = currency whose future value is less than its spot value; **shares which stand at a discount** = shares which are lower in price than their asset value or their par value (NOTE: the opposite are shares which are **at a premium**) **2** *verb* **(a)** to reduce prices to increase sales **(b)** to discount *or* to re-discount bank bills = to sell bills, issued by banks, at less than their face value (the Central Bank buys the bills and in this way is able to provide the banks with cash); **to discount bills of exchange** = to sell bills of exchange for less than the value written on them in order to cash them before their maturity date **(c)** to calculate the value of future income or expenditure in present value terms; **discounted value** = difference between the face value of a share and its lower market price **(d)** to react to something which may happen in the future (such as a possible takeover bid or currency devaluation); **shares are discounting a rise in the dollar** = shares have risen in advance of a rise in the dollar price

> QUOTE pressure on the Federal Reserve Board to ease monetary policy and possibly cut its discount rate mounted yesterday
> *Financial Times*

> QUOTE banks refrained from quoting forward US/Hong Kong dollar exchange rates as premiums of 100 points replaced the previous day's discounts of up to 50 points
> *South China Morning Post*

> QUOTE a 100,000 square-foot warehouse generates ten times the volume of a discount retailer; it can turn its inventory over 18 times a year, more than triple a big discounter's turnover
> *Duns Business Month*

discountable [dɪs'kaʊntəbl] *adjective* which can be discounted; *these bills are not discountable*

discounted cash flow (DCF) [dɪs'kaʊntɪd 'kæʃfləʊ] *noun* calculating the forecast return on capital investment by discounting future cash flows from the investment, usually at a rate equivalent to the company's minimum required rate of return

COMMENT: the present value of the net return on an investment is found by discounting the expected cash flows from that investment. Discounting is the exact opposite of compounding, and is necessary because it is generally accepted that money held today is worth more than money to be received in the future. The effect of discounting is to reduce future income or expenses to their 'present value'. Once discounted, future cash flows can be compared directly with the initial cost of a capital investment which is already stated in present value terms. If the present value of income is greater than the present value of costs the investment can be said to be worthwhile

discounter [dɪs'kaʊntə] *noun* person or company which discounts bills or sells goods at a discount

discrepancy [dɪs'krepənsi] *noun* error or inconsistency such as where totals do not add up correctly in accounts; **there is a discrepancy in the accounts** = there is an error; **statistical discrepancy** = amount by which sets of figures differ

discretion [dɪs'kreʃən] *noun* being able to decide what should be done; **I leave it to your discretion** = I leave it for you to decide what to do; **at the discretion of someone** = if someone decides; *membership is at the discretion of the committee*

discretionary [dɪs'kreʃənəri] *adjective* which can be done if someone wants; **discretionary account** = a client's account with a stockbroker, where the broker invests and sells at his own discretion; **on a discretionary basis** = way of managing a client's funds, where the fund manager uses his discretion to do as he wants, without the client giving him any specific instructions; **discretionary client** = client whose funds are managed on a discretionary basis; **discretionary funds** = funds managed on a discretionary basis; **discretionary trust** = trust where the trustees decide how to invest the income and when and how much income should be paid to the beneficiaries

QUOTE churning is most common with portfolios managed on a discretionary basis where clients leave all the investment decisions to their adviser

Guardian

diseconomies of scale [dɪsi:'kɒnəmi:z əv 'skeɪl] *noun* situation where increased production actually increases unit cost

COMMENT: after having increased production using the existing workforce and machinery, giving economies of scale, the company finds that in order to increase production further it has to employ more workers and buy more machinery, leading to an increase in unit cost

disenfranchise [dɪsɪn'fræntʃaɪz] *verb* to take away someone's right to vote; *the company has tried to disenfranchise the ordinary shareholders*

disequilibrium [dɪsi:kwɪ'lɪbriəm] *noun* being in a state of imbalance; *the sudden increase in demand has caused temporary disequilibrium between supply and demand*

dishonour US **dishonor** [dɪs'ɒnə] *verb* **to dishonour a bill** = not to pay a bill; **dishonoured cheque** = cheque which the bank will not pay because there is not enough money in the account to pay it

disinvest [dɪsɪn'vest] *verb* to reduce investment by not replacing capital assets when they wear out

disinvestment [dɪsɪn'vestmənt] *noun* reduction in capital assets by not replacing them when they wear out

disk [dɪsk] *noun* round flat plate, used to store information in computers; **floppy disk** = small flexible disk for storing computer information; **hard disk** = solid disk in a sealed case which will store a large amount of computer information; **zip disk** = high capacity removable disk capable of storing one or two hundred megabytes of data; **disk drive** = part of a computer which makes a disk spin round in order to read it or store information on it

diskette [dɪs'ket] *noun* small floppy disk used in most PCs

dispatch *or* **despatch** [dɪs'pætʃ] *verb* to send; **dispatch note** = advice note, a written notice to a customer giving details of goods ordered and shipped but not yet delivered

dispensation [dɪspən'seɪʃn] *noun* arrangement between an employer and the Inland Revenue by which business expenses paid to an employee are not declared for tax

disposable [dɪs'pəʊzəbl] *adjective* **disposable personal income** = income left after tax and national insurance have been deducted (also called 'take-home' pay)

disposal [dɪs'pəʊzəl] *noun* **(a)** sale; *disposal of securities or of property*; **lease** *or*

business for disposal = lease *or* business for sale **(b) disposals** = assets which have been sold or scrapped

dispose [dɪs'pəʊz] *verb* **to dispose of** = to get rid of or to sell cheaply; *to dispose of excess stock*; *to dispose of one's business*

disqualification [dɪskwɒlɪfɪ'keɪʃn] *noun* **(a)** making someone disqualified to do something **(b)** court order which forbids a person from being a director of a company

QUOTE Even 'administrative offences' can result in disqualification. A person may be disqualified for up to five years following persistent breach of company legislation in terms of failing to file returns, accounts and other documents with the Registrar
Accountancy

disqualify [dɪs'kwɒlɪfaɪ] *verb* to make a person unqualified to do something, such as to be a director of a company

dissolution [dɪsə'luːʃən] *noun* ending (of a partnership)

dissolve [dɪ'zɒlv] *verb* to bring to an end; **to dissolve a partnership** = to end a partnership because one of the partners has died or has retired, or because a new partner is coming into the business

distrain [dɪ'streɪn] *verb* to seize (goods) to pay for debts

distress [dɪ'stres] *noun* taking someone's goods to pay for debts; *US* **distress merchandise** = goods sold cheaply to pay a company's debts; **distress sale** = sale of goods at low prices to pay a company's debts

distributable [dɪ'strɪbjuːtəbl] *adjective* which can be distributed; **distributable profits** = profits which are available to be paid to shareholders as dividends

distribute [dɪ'strɪbjuːt] *verb* **(a)** to share out dividends; **distributed profits** = profits passed to shareholders in the form of dividends **(b)** to send out goods from a manufacturer's warehouse to retail shops; *Smith Ltd distributes for several smaller companies*

distribution [dɪstrɪ'bjuːʃən] *noun* **(a)** act of sending goods from the manufacturer to the wholesaler and then to retailers; **distribution cost** *or* **distribution expense** = expenditure involved in warehousing, packing and sending stocks for sale; **channels of distribution** *or* **distribution channels** = ways

of sending goods from the manufacturer to the retailer; **distribution network** = series of points or small warehouses from which goods are sent all over a country; **distribution overhead** = DISTRIBUTION COST **(b)** **distribution slip** = paper attached to a document or a magazine showing all the people in an office who should read it **(c)** **distribution of income** *or* **distributions** = payment of dividends to shareholders

distributor [dɪ'strɪbjuːtə] *noun* company which sells goods for another company which makes them; **sole distributor** = retailer who is the only one in an area who is allowed by the manufacturer to sell a certain product; **a network of distributors** = a series of distributors spread all over a country

distributorship [dɪ'strɪbjuːtəʃɪp] *noun* position of being a distributor for a company

diversification [daɪvɜːsɪfɪ'keɪʃən] *noun* (i) adding another quite different type of business to a firm's existing trade; (ii) placing money in a wide spread of investments; **product diversification** *or* **diversification into new products** = adding new types of products to the range already made

diversify [daɪ'vɜːsɪfaɪ] *verb* **(a)** to add new types of business to existing ones; *to diversify into new products* **(b)** to invest in different types of shares or savings so as to spread the risk of loss

divest [daɪ'vest] *verb* **to divest oneself of something** = to get rid of something; *the company had divested itself of its US interests*

divestiture [daɪ'vestɪtʃə] *noun* sale of an asset

dividend ['dɪvɪdend] *noun* **(a)** part of a company's profits paid to shareholders; **to raise** *or* **to increase the dividend** = to pay out a higher dividend than in the previous year; **to maintain the dividend** = to keep the same dividend as in the previous year; **to pass the dividend** *US* **to omit the dividend** = to pay no dividend; **final dividend** = dividend paid at the end of a year's trading, which has to be approved by the shareholders at an AGM; **gross dividend per share** = dividend per share paid before tax is deducted; **interim dividend** = dividend paid during a financial year; **dividend cover** = the ratio of profits to dividends paid to shareholders; **the dividend is covered four times** = the profits are four times the dividend; **dividend forecast** = forecast of the amount of an expected dividend; **forecast dividend** *or* **prospective**

dividend = dividend which a company expects to pay at the end of the current year; **dividend per share** = amount of money paid as dividend for each share held; **dividend mandate** = authorization by a shareholder to the company, to pay his dividends directly into his bank account; **dividend warrant** = cheque which makes payment of a dividend (NOTE: the American equivalent is **dividend check**); **dividend yield** = dividend expressed as a percentage of the current market price of a share; **cum dividend** = share sold with the dividend still to be paid; **ex dividend** = share sold after the dividend has been paid; **the shares are quoted ex dividend** = the share price does not include the right to the dividend **(b)** sum paid to unsecured creditors in an insolvency

divisor [dɪ'vaɪzə] *noun* operand used to divide a dividend in a division operation

document ['dɒkjʊmənt] *noun* paper with writing on it; **formal documents** = documents giving full details of a takeover bid (the official timetable for the bid starts with the sending out of the formal documents)

documentary [dɒkjʊ'mentəri] *adjective* in the form of documents; **documentary credit** = LETTER OF CREDIT

documentation [dɒkjʊmen'teɪʃən] *noun* all documents referring to something; *please send me the complete documentation concerning the sale*

dollar ['dɒlə] *noun* **(a)** unit of currency used in the USA and other countries, such as Australia, Bahamas, Barbados, Bermuda, Brunei, Canada, Fiji, Hong Kong, Jamaica, New Zealand, Singapore, Zimbabwe; *the US dollar rose 2%*; *it costs six Australian dollars*; **five dollar bill** = banknote for five dollars **(b)** *(in particular)* the currency used in the USA; **dollar area** = area of the world where the US dollar is the main trading currency; **dollar balances** = a country's trade balances expressed in US dollars; **dollar cost averaging** *see* AVERAGING; **dollar crisis** = fall in the exchange rate for the US dollar; **dollar gap** *or* **dollar shortage** = situation where the supply of US dollars is not enough to satisfy the demand for them from overseas buyers; **dollar stocks** = shares in US companies (NOTE: usually written $: **$250**. The currencies used in different countries can be shown by the initial letter of the country: **C$** (Canadian dollar) **A$** (Australian dollar), etc.)

domicile ['dɒmɪsaɪl] **1** *noun* country where someone is deemed to live permanently or where a company's office is registered (especially for tax purposes); **domicile of origin** = domicile which a person has from birth (usually the domicile of the father); **domicile of choice** = country where someone has chosen to live, which is not the domicile of origin **2** *verb* **he is domiciled in Denmark** = he lives in Denmark officially; **bills domiciled in France** = bills of exchange which have to be paid in France

donatio mortis causa [də'nɑːtiəʊ 'mɔːtɪs 'kaʊzə] *Latin phrase meaning* 'gift because of death': transfer of property made when death is imminent

donation [də'neɪʃn] *noun* gift (especially to a charity)

donee [dəʊ'niː] *noun* person who receives a gift from a donor

donor ['dəʊnə] *noun* person who gives property to another

dormant ['dɔːmənt] *adjective* not active; **dormant account** = bank account which is no longer used; **dormant company** = company which has not made any transactions during an accounting period

double ['dʌbl] **1** *adjective* **(a)** twice as large, two times the size; *their turnover is double ours*; **to be on double time** = to earn twice the usual wages for working on Sundays or other holidays; **double-entry bookkeeping** = method of bookkeeping, where both debit and credit entries are recorded in the accounts at the same time (e.g. as a sale is credited to the sales account the purchaser's debt is debited to the debtors account); **double option** = option to buy or sell at a certain price in the future (a combination of call and put options); **double taxation** = taxing the same income twice; **double taxation agreement** = agreement between two countries that a person living in one country shall not be taxed in both countries on the income earned in the other country; **double taxation relief** = reduction of tax payable in one country by the amount of tax on income, profits or capital gains already paid in another country **(b) in double figures** = with two figures, 10 to 99; *inflation is in double figures*; *we have had double-figure inflation for some years* **2** *verb* to become twice as big; to make something twice as big; *we have doubled our profits this year or our profits have doubled this year*; *the company's borrowings have doubled*

doubtful ['daʊtfəl] *adjective* which is not certain; **doubtful debt** = debt which may never be paid; **doubtful loan** = loan which may never be repaid

down [daʊn] *adverb & preposition* in a lower position or to a lower position; *the inflation rate is gradually coming down*; *shares are slightly down on the day*; *the price of petrol has gone down*; **to pay money down** = to make a deposit; *he paid £50 down and the rest in monthly instalments*

downgrade [daʊn'greɪd] *verb* (i) to reduce the forecast for a share; (ii) to reduce the credit rating for a bond

down payment ['daʊn 'peɪmənt] *noun* part of a total payment made in advance; *he made a down payment of $100*

downside ['daʊnsaɪd] *noun* **downside factor** *or* **downside potential** = possibility of making a loss (in an investment); **downside risk** = risk that an investment will fall in value (NOTE: the opposite is **upside**)

downtick ['daʊntɪk] *noun US* price of stock sold which is lower than the price of the previous sale

down time ['daʊn 'taɪm] *noun* time when a machine is not working because it is broken or being mended, or when a worker cannot work because machines have broken down or because components are not available, etc.

downturn ['daʊntɜːn] *noun* movement towards lower prices, sales or profits; *a downturn in the market price*; *the last quarter saw a downturn in the economy*

DP = DATA PROCESSING selecting and examining data in a computer to produce useful information or to organize data files

Dr *or* **DR** = DEBTOR

draft [drɑːft] **1** *noun* **(a)** order for money to be paid by a bank; **banker's draft** = draft payable by a bank in cash on presentation; **to make a draft on a bank** = to ask a bank to pay money for you; **sight draft** = bill of exchange which is payable when it is

presented **(b)** first rough plan or document which has not been finished; *draft of a contract or draft contract*; *he drew up the draft agreement on the back of an envelope*; *the first draft of the contract was corrected by the managing director*; *the finance department has passed the final draft of the accounts*; **rough draft** = plan of a document which may have changes made to it before it is complete **2** *verb* to make a first rough plan of a document; *to draft a letter*; *to draft a contract*; *the contract is still being drafted or is still in the drafting stage*

drafter ['drɑːftə] *noun* person who makes a draft; *the drafter of the agreement*

drafting ['drɑːftɪŋ] *noun* act of preparing the draft of a document; *the drafting of the contract took six weeks*

drain [dreɪn] **1** *noun* gradual loss of money flowing away; *the costs of the London office are a continual drain on our resources* **2** *verb* to remove something gradually; *the expansion plan has drained all our profits*; *the company's capital resources have drained away*

draw [drɔː] *verb* **(a)** to take money away; *to draw money out of an account*; **to draw a salary** = to have a salary paid by the company; *the chairman does not draw a salary* **(b)** to write a cheque; *he paid the invoice with a cheque drawn on an Egyptian bank* (NOTE: **drawing - drew - has drawn**)

drawback ['drɔːbæk] *noun* **(a)** thing which is not convenient, likely to cause problems; *one of the main drawbacks of the scheme is that it will take six years to complete* **(b)** refund of customs duty when imported goods are then re-exported

drawdown ['drɔːdaʊn] *noun* **(a)** taking yearly income from a pension scheme rather than using the money accumulated in the scheme to purchase an annuity **(b)** drawing money which is available under a credit agreement

drawee [drɔː'iː] *noun* person or bank asked to make a payment by a drawer

drawer ['drɔːə] *noun* person who writes a cheque or a bill asking a drawee to pay money to a payee; *the bank returned the cheque to*

drawer = the bank would not pay the cheque because the person who wrote it did not have enough money in the account to pay it

drawing ['drɔːɪŋ] *noun* **(a) drawing account** = bank current account, from which the customer may take money when he wants; **drawing rights** = right of a member country of the IMF to borrow money from the fund in a foreign currency; *see also* SPECIAL DRAWING RIGHTS **(b) drawings** = money or trading stock taken by a partner from a partnership, or by a sole trader from his business; **drawings account** = account showing amounts drawn by partners in a partnership

draw up ['drɔː 'ʌp] *verb* to write a legal document; *to draw up a contract or an agreement*; *to draw up a company's articles of association*

drop [drɒp] **1** *noun* fall; *drop in sales*; *sales show a drop of 10%*; *a drop in prices* **2** *verb* to fall; *sales have dropped by 10% or have dropped 10%*; *the pound dropped three points against the dollar* (NOTE: **dropping - dropped**)

> QUOTE while unemployment dropped by 1.6 per cent in the rural areas, it rose by 1.9 per cent in urban areas during the period under review
> Business Times (Lagos)

> QUOTE corporate profits for the first quarter showed a 4 per cent drop from last year's final three months
> Financial Times

> QUOTE since last summer American interest rates have dropped by between three and four percentage points
> Sunday Times

droplock bond ['drɒplɒk 'bɒnd] *noun* floating rate bond which will convert to a fixed rate of interest if interest rates fall to a certain point; *see also* DEBT CONVERTIBLE BOND

DTI = DEPARTMENT OF TRADE AND INDUSTRY

dual ['djuːəl] *adjective* referring to two things at the same time; **dual currency bond** = bond which is paid for in one currency but which is repayable in another; **dual listing** = listing a share on two stock exchanges; **dual pricing** = giving different prices to the same product depending on the market in which it is sold; **dual resident** = person who is legally resident in two countries

dud [dʌd] *adjective & noun (informal)* false; not good (coin or banknote); *the £50 note was a dud*; **dud cheque** = cheque which the bank refuses to pay because the person writing it has not enough money in his account to pay it

due [djuː] *adjective* **(a)** owed; *sum due from a debtor*; *bond due for repayment*; **to fall due** *or* **to become due** = to be ready for payment; **bill due on May 1st** = bill which has to be paid on May 1st; **balance due to us** = amount owed to us which should be paid; **due bills** = amounts which are owed but not yet paid **(b) in due form** = written in the correct legal form; *receipt in due form*; *contract drawn up in due form*; **after due consideration of the problem** = after thinking seriously about the problem

> QUOTE many expect the US economic indicators for April, due out this Thursday, to show faster economic growth
> Australian Financial Review

dues [djuːz] *plural noun* **(a) dock dues** *or* **port dues** *or* **harbour dues** = payment which a ship makes to the harbour authorities for the right to use the harbour **(b)** orders taken but not supplied until new stock arrives

dump [dʌmp] *verb* to **dump goods on a market** = to get rid of large quantities of excess goods cheaply in an overseas market

dumping ['dʌmpɪŋ] *noun* act of getting rid of excess goods cheaply in an overseas market; *the government has passed anti-dumping legislation*; *dumping of goods on the European market*; **panic dumping of sterling** = rush to sell sterling at any price because of possible devaluation

> QUOTE a serious threat lies in the 400,000 tonnes of subsidized beef in EC cold stores. If dumped, this meat will have disastrous effects in Pacific Basin markets
> Australian Financial Review

Dun & Bradstreet (D&B) ['dʌn ən 'brædstriːt] organization which produces reports on the financial rating of companies; it also acts as a debt collection agency

duplicate 1 ['djuːplɪkət] *noun* copy; *he sent me the duplicate of the contract*; **duplicate receipt** *or* **duplicate of a receipt** = copy of a receipt; **in duplicate** = with a copy; **receipt in duplicate** = two copies of a receipt; *to print an invoice in duplicate* **2** ['djuːplɪkeɪt] *verb* **(a)** *(of a bookkeeping entry)*; **to duplicate with another** = to repeat another entry, to be the same as another entry **(b) to duplicate a letter** = to make a copy of a letter

duplication [dju:plɪ'keɪʃən] *noun* copying of documents; **duplication of work** = work which is done twice without being necessary

Dutch [dʌtʃ] *adjective* referring to the Netherlands; **Dutch auction** = auction where the auctioneer offers an item for sale at a high price and then gradually reduces the price until someone makes a bid; **to go Dutch** = to share a bill (as in a restaurant)

> QUOTE Dutch government bonds: prices were about 0.12 point lower as market participants awaited auction results for the new 10-year 9% state loan. The issue is being sold via a Dutch-style auction, which means that all paper is sold at the lowest accepted price
> *Wall Street Journal*

dutiable ['dju:tjəbl] *adjective* **dutiable goods** *or* **dutiable items** = goods on which a customs duty has to be paid

duty ['dju:ti] *noun* tax which has to be paid; *to take the duty off alcohol; to put a duty on cigarettes;* **ad valorem duty** = duty calculated on the sales value of the goods; **customs duty** *or* **import duty** = tax on goods imported into a country; **excise duty** = tax on certain goods (such as alcohol and petrol) which are produced in the country; **goods which are liable to duty** = goods on which customs or excise tax has to be paid; **duty-paid goods** = goods where the duty has been paid; **stamp duty** = tax on legal documents (such as the conveyance of a property to a new owner); **estate duty** *US* **death duty** = tax paid on the property left by a dead person

> QUOTE Canadian and European negotiators agreed to a deal under which Canada could lower its import duties on $150 million worth of European goods
> *Globe and Mail (Toronto)*

> QUOTE the Department of Customs and Excise collected a total of N79m under the new advance duty payment scheme
> *Business Times (Lagos)*

duty-free ['dju:ti'fri:] *adjective & adverb* sold with no duty to be paid; *he bought a duty-free watch at the airport or he bought the watch duty-free;* **duty-free shop** = shop at an airport or on a ship where goods can be bought without paying duty

Ee

e- *prefix* meaning electronic

> COMMENT: many words can be prefixed by 'e-' to indicate that they are 'electronic', though this has taken on a meaning related to using the Internet. For example 'ecommerce' is commerce involving electronic communication, such as buying from a web site. Sometimes a word is formed by dropping a letter or letters, for example 'etailing' is electronic retailing from a web site. Many such words are short lived and informal. Some possible words, such as 'ecrime' are not often used as the alternative and older prefix 'cyber-' is used instead (as in 'cybercrime' meaning computer crime, which may or may not involve use of the Internet)

e.& o.e. = ERRORS AND OMISSIONS EXCEPTED

Schedule E ['ʃedjuːl 'iː] schedule to the Finance Acts under which tax is charged on wages, salaries, and other income from employment (including directors' fees) and pensions: it is sub-divided into three sections: Case I: UK residents; Case II people who are resident outside the UK; Case III: people who are resident in the UK but who work abroad

Table E ['teɪbl 'iː] model memorandum and articles of association of an unlimited company with share capital, set out in the Companies Act

early withdrawal ['ɜːli wɪθ'drɔːəl] *noun* withdrawing money from a deposit account before due date; *early withdrawal usually incurs a penalty*

earmark ['ɪəmɑːk] *verb* to reserve for a special purpose; *to earmark funds for a project*; *the grant is earmarked for computer systems development*

earn [ɜːn] *verb* **(a)** to be paid money for working; *to earn £50 a week*; *our agent in Paris certainly does not earn his commission*; *earned income* = income from wages, salaries, pensions, etc. (as opposed to 'unearned' income from investments) **(b)** to produce interest or dividends; *what level of dividend do these shares earn?*; *account which earns interest at 10%*

earnest ['ɜːnɪst] *noun* money paid as a down payment

earning ['ɜːnɪŋ] *noun* **earning capacity** *or* **earning power** = amount of money someone should be able to earn; *he is such a fine dress designer that his earning power is very large*; **earning potential** = (i) amount of money a person should be able to earn; (ii) amount of dividend a share should produce; **earning power** = ability of a company to be more profitable and so pay higher dividends

earnings ['ɜːnɪŋz] *noun* **(a)** salary or wages, profits and dividends or interest received; **pensionable earnings** = earnings of a member of a pension scheme on which the member's final pension is calculated; **compensation for loss of earnings** = payment to someone who has stopped earning money or who is not able to earn money; **earnings-related contributions** = social security contributions which are linked to salary or wages; **earnings cap** = top limit of earnings which can be used in calculating a retirement pension paid from an occupational pension scheme; *US* **earnings credit** = allowance which reduces service charges on checking accounts; *see also* NET RELEVANT EARNINGS **(b)** profit of a business; **earnings basis** = method of valuing a business by calculating its future profits, as opposed to calculating its assets; **earnings per share (EPS** *or* **eps)** = money earned in profit per share (the total profits after tax and dividend on preference shares, but before extraordinary items, divided by the number of ordinary shares) (see FRS 14); **earnings yield** = ratio between earnings per share and the current market price of one share; **gross earnings** = earnings before tax and other deductions; **retained earnings** = profits which are not paid out to shareholders as dividend; *see also* PRICE/EARNINGS RATIO

> QUOTE if corporate forecasts are met, sales will exceed $50 million in 1985 and net earnings could exceed $7 million
>
> Citizen (Ottawa)

earn-outs ['ɜːnaʊts] *see* DEFERRED CONSIDERATION

ease [iːz] **1** *noun* slight fall in prices **2** *verb* (*of prices, interest rates, etc.*) to fall a little; *the share index eased slightly today*

easy ['iːzi] *adjective* **(a)** not difficult; **easy terms** = terms which are not difficult to accept, price which is easy to pay; *the shop is let on very easy terms*; **the loan is repayable in easy payments** = with very small sums paid back regularly; **easy money** = (i) money which can be earned with no difficulty; (ii) money available on easy repayment terms; **easy money policy** = government policy of expanding the economy by making money more easily available (lower interest rates, easy access to credit, etc.) **(b)** **easy market** = market where few people are buying, so prices are lower than they were before; *the Stock Exchange was easy yesterday*; **share prices are easier** = prices have fallen slightly

e-business ['iːbɪznəs] *noun* the business of dealing with other businesses over the Internet; *e-business is a rising part of the economy*

EC ['iː'siː] = EUROPEAN COMMUNITY (NOTE: now called the **European Union (EU)**

ECB ['iː'siː'biː] = EUROPEAN CENTRAL BANK

ECGD ['iːsiːdʒiː'diː] = EXPORT CREDIT GUARANTEE DEPARTMENT

e-commerce ['iːkɒmɜːs] *noun* system of buying and selling goods and services over the Internet

econometrics [iːkɒnə'metrɪks] *noun* study of the statistics of economics, using computers to analyze statistics and make forecasts using mathematical models

economic [iːkə'nɒmɪk] *adjective* **(a)** which provides enough money; *the flat is let at an economic rent*; *it is hardly economic for the company to run its own warehouse*; **economic order quantity (EOQ)** = optimum quantity of stocks which a company should hold based on the costs of ordering and warehousing, availability of bulk discount (lower unit costs because of higher quantities purchased will be offset by higher warehousing costs), the rate at which stocks are used and the time it takes for suppliers to deliver new orders **(b)** referring to the financial state of a country; *economic planner*; *economic planning*; *the government's economic policy*; *the economic situation*; *the country's economic system*; *economic trends*; **economic crisis** *or* **economic depression** = state where a country is in financial collapse; *the government has introduced import controls to solve the current economic crisis*; **economic cycle** = period during which trade expands, then slows down, then expands again; **economic development** = expansion of the commercial and financial situation; *the economic development of the region has totally changed since oil was discovered there*; **economic growth** = increase in the national income; *the country enjoyed a period of economic growth in the 1960s*; **economic indicators** = statistics which show how the economy is going to perform in the short or long term (unemployment rate, overseas trade, etc.); **economic sanctions** = restrictions on trade with a country in order to make its government change policy; *the western nations imposed economic sanctions on the country*

economical [iːkə'nɒmɪkəl] *adjective* which saves money or materials, or which is cheap; **economical car** = car which does not use much petrol; **economical use of resources** = using resources as carefully as possible

economics [iːkə'nɒmɪks] *noun* **(a)** study of production, distribution, selling and use of goods and services **(b)** study of financial structures to show how a product or service is costed and what returns it produces; *the economics of town planning*; *I do not understand the economics of the coal industry*

> QUOTE believers in free-market economics often find it hard to sort out their views on the issue
> Economist

economist [ɪ'kɒnəmɪst] *noun* person who specializes in the study of economics; *agricultural economist*

economy [ɪ'kɒnəmi] *noun* **(a)** being careful not to waste money or materials; **an economy measure** = an action to save money or materials; **to introduce economies** *or* **economy measures into the system** = to start using methods to save money or materials; **economies of scale** = making a product more profitable by manufacturing it in larger quantities and so reducing unit costs; *compare* DISECONOMIES; **economy car** = car which does not use much petrol; **economy class** = cheapest class on a plane; *to travel economy class*; **economy drive** = campaign to save money or materials; **economy size** = large size or large packet, which is a bargain **(b)** financial state of a country, the way in which a country makes and uses its money; *the country's economy is in ruins*; **black economy** = work which is paid for in cash or goods, but not declared to the tax authorities; **capitalist economy** = system where each person has the right to invest money in a business and to make profits from trading, with no restrictions from the state; **controlled economy** = system where business activity is controlled by orders from the government; **free market economy** = system where the government does not interfere in business activity in any way; **mixed economy** = system which contains both government-controlled industries and private enterprise; **planned economy** = system where the government plans all business activity

> QUOTE the European economies are being held back by rigid labor markets and wage structures, huge expenditures on social welfare programs and restrictions on the free movement of goods within the Common Market
> Duns Business Month

ECP = EUROCOMMERCIAL PAPER

ED = EXPOSURE DRAFT

EDI ['iːdiː'aɪ] = ELECTRONIC DATA INTERCHANGE

EDP ['iːdiː'piː] = ELECTRONIC DATA PROCESSING

EEA ['iːiː'eɪ] = EUROPEAN ECONOMIC AREA

EEIG ['iːiː'aɪ'dʒiː] = EUROPEAN ECONOMIC INTEREST GROUPING

effect [ɪ'fekt] **1** *noun* **(a)** result; *the effect of the pay increase was to raise productivity levels*; **terms of a contract which take effect** *or* **come into effect from January 1st** = terms which start to operate on January 1st; **prices are increased 10% with effect from January 1st** = new prices will apply from January 1st; **to remain in effect** = to continue to be applied **(b)** meaning; **clause to the effect that** = clause which means that; **we have made provision to this effect** = we have put into the contract terms which will make this work **2** *verb* to carry out; **to effect a payment** = to make a payment; **to effect customs clearance** = to clear goods through customs; **to effect a settlement between two parties** = to bring two parties together and make them agree to a settlement

effective [ɪ'fektɪv] *adjective* **(a)** real; **effective control of a company** = situation where someone owns a large number of shares in a company, but less than 50%, and so in effect controls the company because no other single shareholder can outvote him; **effective demand** = actual demand for a product which can be paid for; **effective exchange rate** = rate of exchange for a currency calculated against a basket of currencies; **effective price** = share price which has been adjusted to allow for a rights issue; **effective rate** = real interest rate on a loan or deposit (i.e., the APR); **effective units of stock** = equivalent units of stock which are used to calculate stock valuation; **effective yield** = actual yield shown as a percentage after adjustments have been made **(b)** **effective date** = date on which a rule or a contract starts to be applied, or on which a transaction takes place; **clause effective as from January 1st** = clause which starts to be applied on January 1st **(c)** which is able to produce the desired effect; *an effective solution to a problem*; *a highly effective management team*; *see also* COST-EFFECTIVE

effectiveness [ɪˈfektɪvnəs] *noun* working, producing results; *I doubt the effectiveness of television advertising*; *see* COST-EFFECTIVENESS

efficiency [ɪˈfɪʃənsi] *noun* ability to work well, to produce the right result or the right work quickly; **with a high degree of efficiency**; *a business efficiency exhibition*; *an efficiency expert*; **efficiency variance** = difference between the standard cost of making a product and actual costs of production (a separate variance can be calculated for materials, labour and overheads)

> QUOTE increased control means improved efficiency in purchasing, shipping, sales and delivery
> Duns Business Month

COMMENT: in a 'weak efficiency' market share prices do no depend on information about companies, while, at the other extreme, in a 'strong efficiency' market share prices are very sensitive to all types of information, including information which has not been made public

efficient [ɪˈfɪʃənt] *adjective* able to work well, or to produce the right result quickly; *the efficient working of a system*; *he needs an efficient secretary to look after him*; *efficient machine*; **efficient market hypothesis (EMH)** = theory that stock markets respond with varying degrees of efficiency to information about the companies listed

efficiently [ɪˈfɪʃəntli] *adverb* in an efficient way; *she organized the sales conference very efficiently*

efflux [ˈeflʌks] *noun* flowing out; *efflux of capital to North America* (NOTE: the opposite is **influx**)

EFT = ELECTRONIC FUNDS TRANSFER

EFTA [ˈeftə] = EUROPEAN FREE TRADE ASSOCIATION

EFTPOS [ˈeftpɒs] = ELECTRONIC FUNDS TRANSFER AT POINT OF SALE

EGM [ˈiːdʒiːˈem] = EXTRAORDINARY GENERAL MEETING

EIB [ˈiːaɪˈbiː] = EUROPEAN INVESTMENT BANK

eighty-twenty law *or* **eighty/twenty rule** [ˈeɪtɪˈtwentɪ ˈlɔː *or* ˈruːl] rule that a small percentage of customers may account for a large percentage of sales; *see* PARETO'S LAW

EIS = ENTERPRISE INVESTMENT SCHEME

elastic [ɪˈlæstɪk] *adjective* which can expand or contract easily (as in consumer demand for certain products which changes a lot as a result of only small changes in price: such products are said to be 'price-elastic')

elasticity [ɪlæsˈtɪsəti] *noun* (i) ability to change easily; (ii) the rate of change in response to change in a related factor; **elasticity of supply and demand** = changes in supply and demand of an item in response to changes in its market price

eldercare [ˈeldəkeə] *noun* assurance services sold to elderly people and their families

elect [ɪˈlekt] *verb* **(a)** choose someone by a vote *to elect the officers of an association*; *she was elected president* **(b)** to choose to take a certain course of action

-elect [ɪˈlekt] *suffix* person who has been elected but has not yet started the term of office; *she is the president-elect* (NOTE: the plural is **presidents-elect**)

election [ɪˈlekʃən] *noun* **(a)** act of choosing by vote; *the election of officers of an association*; *the election of directors by the shareholders* **(b)** choosing to take a certain course of action, such as deciding that part of your income should be taxed in a certain way; *he made an election to regard his London flat as his main residence*

electronic [elekˈtrɒnɪk] *adjective* **electronic banking** = using computers to carry out banking transactions, such as withdrawals through cash dispensers, transfer of funds at point of sale, etc.; **electronic data interchange (EDI)** = system of exchange of information between banks using computers; **electronic data processing (EDP)** = selecting and examining data stored in a computer to produce information; **electronic funds transfer (EFT)** = system for transferring money from one account to another electronically (as when using a smart card); **electronic funds transfer at point of sale (EFTPOS)** = system for transferring money directly from the purchaser's account to the seller's, when a sale is made using a plastic card; **Electronic Lodgement Service (ELS)** British system for filing your tax return electronically; **electronic mail** *or* **email** = system of sending messages from one computer terminal to another, via telephone lines; **electronic point of sale (EPOS)** = system where sales are charged automatically to a customer's credit card and stock is controlled by the shop's computer; **Electronic Version of the Tax Return (EVR)** = method of making an individual's tax return using email

element ['elɪmənt] *noun* basic part; *the elements of a settlement*

eligibility [elɪdʒə'bɪləti] *noun* being eligible; *the chairman questioned her eligibility to stand for re-election*

eligible ['elɪdʒəbl] *adjective* which can be chosen; **eligible bill** *or* **eligible paper** = bill which will be accepted by the Bank of England or the US Federal Reserve, and which can be used as security against a loan; **eligible liabilities** = liabilities which go into the calculation of a bank's reserves

eliminate [ɪ'lɪmɪneɪt] *verb* to remove; *to eliminate defects in the system*; *using a computer should eliminate all possibility of error*

ELS = ELECTRONIC LODGEMENT SERVICE

email ['iː'meɪl] = ELECTRONIC MAIL **1** *noun* **(a)** system of sending messages from one computer to another, via a network or a modem and the Internet; *you can contact me by phone or email if you want*; **email address** = series of characters which make up an address for email; *I'll give you my email address*; *my email address is: peter_pcp.co.uk* **(b)** message sent by this means; *I had six emails from him today*; **email attachment** = computer file sent with an email **2** *verb* to send a message from one computer to another, using a modem and telephone lines; *she emailed her order to the warehouse*; *I emailed him about the meeting*

emailing ['iː'meɪlɪŋ] *noun* sending something by email

embargo [em'bɑːgəʊ] **1** *noun* **(a)** government order which stops a type of trade, such as exports to, or other commercial activity with, another country; **arms embargo** = embargo on the export of arms to a country at war or a country suspected of human rights abuses; **to lay** *or* **put an embargo on trade with a country** = to say that trade with a country must not take place; *the government has put an embargo on the export of computer equipment*; **to lift an embargo** = to allow trade to start again; *the government has lifted the embargo on the export of computers*; **to be under an embargo** = to be forbidden **(b)** period of time

during which certain information in a press release must not be published (NOTE: plural is **embargoes) 2** *verb* **(a)** to stop trade, not to allow trade; *the government has embargoed trade with the Eastern countries* **(b)** not to allow publication of information for a period of time; *the news of the merger has been embargoed until next Wednesday*

> QUOTE the Commerce Department is planning to loosen export controls for products that have been embargoed but are readily available elsewhere in the West
>
> *Duns Business Month*

embezzle [ɪm'bezl] *verb* to use money which is not yours, or which you are looking after for someone; *he was sent to prison for six months for embezzling his clients' money*

embezzlement [ɪm'bezlmənt] *noun* act of embezzling; *he was sent to prison for six months for embezzlement*

embezzler [ɪm'bezlə] *noun* person who embezzles

emergency [ɪ'mɜːdʒənsi] *noun* critical situation which needs rapid action to control; *US* **emergency credit** = credit given by the Federal Reserve to an organization which has no other means of borrowing

EMH = EFFICIENT MARKET HYPOTHESIS

emoluments [ɪ'mɒljʊmənts] *noun* wages, salaries, fees, or any monetary benefit from an employment

employ [ɪm'plɔɪ] *verb* to give someone regular paid work; **to employ twenty staff** = to have twenty people working for you; **to employ twenty new staff** = to give work to twenty new people

> QUOTE 70 per cent of Australia's labour force was employed in service activity
>
> *Australian Financial Review*

employed [ɪm'plɔɪd] **1** *adjective* **(a)** in regular paid work; **he is not gainfully employed** = he has no regular paid work; **self-employed** = working for yourself; *he worked in a bank for ten years but now is self-employed* **(b)** (money) used profitably; **capital employed** = shareholders' funds plus long-term borrowings of a business; **return on capital employed (ROCE)** = profit shown as a percentage of capital employed **2** *plural noun* people who are working; *the employers and the employed*; **the self-employed** = people who work for themselves

employee [emplɔɪ'iː] *noun* worker, person employed by a company or firm; *employees of the firm are eligible to join a profit-sharing scheme*; *relations between management and employees have improved*; *the company has decided to take on new employees*; **employee buyout** = purchase of a company by its employees; **employee contribution** = contribution paid by an employee towards his or her pension; **employee share ownership plan** *US* **employee stock ownership plan (ESOP)** = scheme which allows employees to obtain shares in the company for which they work (though tax may be payable if the shares are sold to employees at a price which is lower than the current market price)

QUOTE companies introducing robotics think it important to involve individual employees in planning their introduction
Economist

employer [ɪm'plɔɪə] *noun* person or company which has regular workers and pays them; **employers' organization** *or* **association** = group of employers with similar interests; **employer's contribution** = money paid by an employer towards a worker's pension

employment [ɪm'plɔɪmənt] *noun* regular paid work; **full employment** = situation where everyone in a country who can work has a job; **full-time employment** = work for all of a working day; **part-time employment** = work for part of a working day; **temporary employment** = work which does not last for more than a few months; **to be without employment** = to have no work; **to find someone alternative employment** = to find another job for someone; **conditions of employment** = terms of a contract where someone is employed; **contract of employment** *or* **employment contract** = contract between employer and an employee stating all the conditions of work; **security of employment** = feeling by a worker that he has the right to keep his job until he retires; **employment income** = money received from an employer (salary, fees, commission, bonus, fringe benefits, etc.)

QUOTE the blue-collar unions are the people who stand to lose most in terms of employment growth
Sydney Morning Herald

EMU = EUROPEAN MONETARY UNION

encash [ɪn'kæʃ] *verb* to cash a cheque, to exchange a cheque for cash

encashable [ɪn'kæʃəbl] *adjective* which can be cashed

encashment [ɪn'kæʃmənt] *noun* act of exchanging for cash

encumbrance [ɪn'kʌmbrəns] *noun* liability (such as a mortgage or charge) which is attached usually to a property or land

end [end] **1** *noun* final point or last part; *at the end of the contract period*; **at the end of six months** = after six months have passed; **account end** = the end of an accounting period; **month end** *or* **year end** = the end of the month or year, when accounts have to be drawn up; **end product** = manufactured product, made at the end of a production process; **end user** = person who actually uses a product **2** *verb* to finish; *the chairman's speech ended on a weak note*

endorse [ɪn'dɔːs] *verb* to endorse a bill *or* a cheque = to sign a bill or a cheque on the back to show that you pass ownership of it to someone else

COMMENT: by endorsing a cheque (i.e., signing it on the back), a person whose name is on the front of the cheque is passing ownership of it to another party, such as the bank, which can then accept it and pay him cash for it. If a cheque is deposited in an account, it does not need to be endorsed. Cheques can also be endorsed to another person: a cheque made payable to Mr A. Smith can be endorsed by Mr Smith on the back, with the words: 'Pay to Brown Ltd', and then his signature. This has the effect of making the cheque payable to Brown Ltd, and to no one else. In Britain, cheques are now printed as crossed cheques with the words 'A/C Payee' printed in the space between the two vertical lines. These cheques can only be paid to the person whose name is written on the cheque and cannot be endorsed

endorsee [endɔː'siː] *noun* person whose name is written on a bill or a cheque as having the right to cash it

endorsement [ɪn'dɔːsmənt] *noun* **(a)** act of endorsing; signature on a document (such as a cheque) which endorses it **(b)** note on an insurance policy which adds conditions to the policy

endorser [ɪn'dɔːsə] *noun* person who endorses a bill or cheque which then is passed to another person

endowment [ɪn'daʊmənt] *noun* giving money to provide a regular income; **endowment assurance** *or* **endowment insurance** *or* **endowment policy** = insurance policy where a sum of money is paid to the insured person on a certain date, or to his heirs if he dies earlier

endowment mortgage [ɪnˈdaʊmənt ˈmɔːgɪdʒ] *noun* mortgage backed by an endowment policy

COMMENT: the borrower pays interest on the mortgage in the usual way, but does not repay the capital; the endowment assurance (a life insurance) is taken out to cover the total capital sum borrowed, and when the assurance matures the capital is paid off, and a further lump sum is usually available for payment to the borrower. This is the theory, though in some cases the assurance is not sufficient to pay off the capital and the borrower has to pay a further lump sum to end the mortgage. A mortgage where the borrower repays both interest and capital is called a 'repayment mortgage'

energy [ˈenədʒi] *noun* power from electricity or petrol, etc.; *we try to save energy by switching off the lights when the rooms are empty*; *if you reduce the room temperature to eighteen degrees, you will save energy*; **energy costs** = costs of gas, electricity, etc., as shown in accounts; **energy shares** = shares in companies (gas, electricity, etc.) which provide energy

enforce [ɪnˈfɔːs] *verb* to make sure something is done or that a rule is obeyed; *to enforce the terms of a contract*

enforcement [ɪnˈfɔːsmənt] *noun* making sure that something is obeyed; *enforcement of the terms of a contract*

engage [ɪnˈgeɪdʒ] *verb* **(a)** to engage someone to do something = to make someone do something legally; *the contract engages us to a minimum annual purchase* **(b)** to employ; *we have engaged the best commercial lawyer to represent us*; *the company has engaged twenty new salesmen* **(c)** to be engaged in = to be busy with; *he is engaged in work on computers*; *the company is engaged in trade with Africa*

engagement [ɪnˈgeɪdʒmənt] *noun* agreement to do something; **to break an engagement to do something** = not to do what you have legally agreed; *the company broke their engagement not to sell our rivals' products*; **engagement letter** = letter, usually required by professional standards, sent by an accountant to a client setting out the work the accountant is to do and further administrative matters, such as any limit on the accountant's liability

enquire [ɪnˈkwaɪə] = INQUIRE

enquiry [ɪnˈkwaɪəri] = INQUIRY

entail [ɪnˈteɪl] **1** *noun* legal condition which passes ownership of a property only to certain persons **2** *verb* to involve; *itemizing the sales figures will entail about ten days' work*

enter [ˈentə] *verb* **(a)** to write; *to enter a name on a list*; *the clerk entered the interest in my bank book*; *to enter an item in a ledger*; **to enter a bid for something** = to offer (usually in writing) to buy something; **to enter a caveat** = to warn legally that you have an interest in a case, and that no steps can be taken without your permission **(b) to enter into** = to begin; *to enter into a partnership with a legal friend*; *to enter into an agreement or a contract*

entering [ˈentərɪŋ] *noun* act of writing items in a record

enterprise [ˈentəpraɪz] *noun* **(a)** system of carrying on a business; **free enterprise** = system of business free from government interference; **enterprise investment scheme (EIS)** = UK scheme to promote investment in unquoted companies by which qualifying gains are exempt from capital gains tax; **private enterprise** = businesses which are owned privately, not by the state; *the project is completely funded by private enterprise*; **enterprise zone** = area of the country where businesses are encouraged to develop by offering special conditions such as easy planning permission for buildings, reduction in the business rate, etc. **(b)** business; **a small-scale enterprise** = a small business; **a state enterprise** = a state-controlled company; *bosses of state enterprises are appointed by the government*

entertain [entəˈteɪn] *verb* to offer meals or hotel accommodation, theatre tickets, etc. to (business) visitors

entertainment [entəˈteɪnmənt] *noun* offering meals, etc. to business visitors; **entertainment allowance** = money which a manager is allowed by his company to spend on meals, etc. with visitors; **entertainment expenses** = money spent on giving meals, etc. to business visitors

entitle [ɪnˈtaɪtl] *verb* to give the right to something; *he is entitled to a discount* = he has the right to be given a discount

entitlement [ɪnˈtaɪtlmənt] *noun* right; **holiday entitlement** = number of days' paid holiday which a worker has the right to take; *she has not used up all her holiday entitlement*; **pension entitlement** = amount of pension which someone has the right to receive when he retires; *(Australia)* **entitlement issue** = rights issue

entity ['entɪti] *noun* single separate body or organization; **accounting entity** = any unit which takes part in financial transactions which are recorded in accounts (a sole trader, a department of a large business, a limited company, etc.); **reporting entity** = any organization, such as a limited company, which reports its accounts to its shareholders

entrepreneur [ɒntrəprə'nɜː] *noun* person who directs a company and takes commercial risks

entrepreneurial [ɒntrəprə'nɜːrɪəl] *adjective* taking commercial risks; *an entrepreneurial decision*

entry ['entri] *noun* **(a)** written information put in an accounts ledger; **credit entry** *or* **debit entry** = entry on the credit or debit side of an account; **single-entry bookkeeping** = recording only one entry per transaction (usually in the cash book); **double-entry bookkeeping** = system of bookkeeping where both debit and credit entries are recorded in the accounts at the same time (e.g., as a sale is credited to the sales account the purchaser's debt is debited to the debtors account); **to make an entry in a ledger** = to write in details of a transaction; **closing entry** = entry which closes an account; **contra entry** = entry made in the opposite side of an account to offset an earlier entry; **to contra an entry** = to enter a similar amount on the opposite side of the account; **entry price** = price at which an accounting entity buys (i.e., the current replacement cost) **(b)** act of going in; place where you can go in; *to pass a customs entry point*; *entry of goods under bond*; **entry visa** = visa allowing someone to go into a country; **multiple entry visa** = entry visa which allows someone to enter a country as often as he likes

EOQ ['iː'əʊ'kjʊ] = ECONOMIC ORDER QUANTITY

epos *or* **EPOS** ['iːpɒs] = ELECTRONIC POINT OF SALE

eps *or* **EPS** = EARNINGS PER SHARE

equal ['iːkwəl] **1** *adjective* exactly the same; *male and female workers should have equal pay*; **equal opportunities programme** = programme to avoid discrimination in employment (NOTE: the American equivalent is **affirmative action**) **2** *verb* to be the same as; *production this month has equalled our best*

month ever (NOTE: **equalling - equalled** but American spelling is **equaling - equaled**)

equalize ['iːkwəlaɪz] *verb* to make equal; *to equalize dividends*

equally ['iːkwəli] *adverb* in the same way, to the same degree; *costs will be shared equally between the two parties*; *they were both equally responsible for the disastrous launch*

equate [ɪ'kweɪt] *verb* to treat something as being equal with another

equation [ɪ'kweɪʒn] *noun* set of mathematical rules applied to solve a problem; *the basic accounting equation is that assets equal liabilities plus capital*

equilibrium [iːkwɪ'lɪbriəm] *noun* being in a state of balance, as where a country's balance of payments is neither in deficit nor in surplus; *compare* DISEQUILIBRIUM

equities ['ekwətiz] *noun* ordinary shares

equity ['ekwəti] *noun* **(a)** the value of a company which is the property of its ordinary shareholders (the company's assets less its liabilities, not including the ordinary share capital) (also called 'shareholders' equity' or 'capital'); **equity accounting** = including part of the profits of an associated company in the investor company's profit and loss account and showing the balance sheet value of the investment as cost plus a share of the associate's retained profit **(b)** the ordinary shares in a company; **equity capital** = a company's capital which is invested by holders of ordinary shares giving them the right to unlimited returns (as opposed to preference shareholders who are only entitled to a fixed maximum return); **equity earnings** = profits after tax, which are available for distribution to shareholders in the form of dividends, or which can be retained in the company for future development; **equity finance** = finance for a company in the form of ordinary shares paid for by shareholders; **equity gearing** = ratio of a company's borrowings to its ordinary share capital; **equity sweetener** = incentive to encourage people to lend a company money, in the form of a warrant giving the right to buy shares at a later date and at a certain price (NOTE: in American English also called **equity kicker**) **(c)** fair system of laws, the system of British law which developed in parallel with the common law to make the common law fairer, summarized in the maxim 'equity does not suffer a wrong to be without a remedy'; **equity of redemption** = right of a mortgagor to redeem the estate by paying off the principal and interest

COMMENT: 'equity' (also called 'capital' or 'shareholders' equity' or 'shareholders' capital' or 'shareholders' funds') is the current net value of the company including, but not restricted to, the nominal value of the shares in issue. After several years a company would expect to increase its net worth above the value of the starting capital. 'Equity capital' on the other hand is only the nominal value of the shares in issue

QUOTE in the past three years commercial property has seriously underperformed equities and dropped out of favour as a result
Investors Chronicle

QUOTE investment trusts can raise more capital but this has to be done as a company does it, by a rights issue of equity
Investors Chronicle

equivalence [ɪ'kwɪvələns] *noun* being equivalent

equivalent [ɪ'kwɪvələnt] **1** *adjective* **to be equivalent to** = to have the same value as, or to be the same as; *the total dividend paid is equivalent to one quarter of the pretax profits*; **equivalent unit** = unit of unfinished production calculated for valuation purposes when work started during the period is not finished at the end of the period, or when work started during the previous period is finished during the current period **2** *noun* thing which has the same value as another; *shares at £3.00 are the equivalent of £6.00 before the share split*; *the invoice is for £100, payable in sterling or the dollar equivalent*; **cash equivalent** = the equivalent in cash terms of an asset which is enjoyed

ERDF = EUROPEAN REGIONAL DEVELOPMENT FUND

error ['erə] *noun* mistake; *he made an error in calculating the total*; *the secretary must have made a typing error*; **clerical error** = mistake made in an office; **computer error** = mistake made by a computer; **margin of error** = degree of inaccuracy or number of mistakes which can be accepted in a document or in a calculation; **errors and omissions excepted (e. & o.e.)** = words written on an invoice to show that the company has no responsibility for mistakes in the invoice; **error rate** = number of mistakes per thousand entries or per page

escalate ['eskəleɪt] *verb* to increase steadily

escalation [eskə'leɪʃən] *noun* **escalation of prices** = steady increase in prices; **escalation clause** = ESCALATOR CLAUSE

escalator clause ['eskəleɪtə 'klɔːz] *noun* clause in a contract allowing for regular price increases because of increased costs

escape [ɪs'keɪp] *noun* getting away from a difficult situation; **escape clause** = clause in a contract which allows one of the parties to avoid carrying out the terms of the contract under certain conditions

escrow ['eskrəʊ] *noun* agreement between two parties that something should be held by a third party until certain conditions are fulfilled; **in escrow** = held in safe keeping by a third party; **document held in escrow** = document given to a third party to keep and to pass on to someone when money has been paid; **escrow account** = account where money is held in escrow until a contract is signed or until goods are delivered, etc.

ESOP = EMPLOYEE SHARE OWNERSHIP PLAN

establish [ɪs'tæblɪʃ] *verb* to set up or to open; *the company has established a branch in Australia*; *the business was established in Scotland in 1823*; *it is a young company - it has been established for only four years*; **to establish oneself in business** = to become successful in a new business

establishment [ɪs'tæblɪʃmənt] *noun* **(a)** commercial business; *he runs an important printing establishment* **(b)** number of people working in a company; **to be on the establishment** = to be a full-time employee; **office with an establishment of fifteen** = office with a budgeted staff of fifteen; **establishment charges** = cost of people and property in a company's accounts

estate [ɪs'teɪt] *noun* **(a) real estate** = property (land or buildings); **estate agency** = office which arranges for the sale of property; **estate agent** = person in charge of an estate agency **(b)** property left by a dead person; **estate duty** = formerly, tax on property left by a dead person (now called 'inheritance tax')

estimate 1 ['estɪmət] *noun* **(a)** calculation of probable cost, size or time of something; **rough estimate** = very approximate calculation; **at a conservative estimate** = calculation which probably underestimates the final figure; *their turnover has risen by at least 20% in the last year, and that is a conservative estimate*; *these figures are only an estimate* = these are not the final, accurate figures; *can you give me an estimate of how much time was spent on the job?* **(b)** calculation of how much something is likely to cost in the future, given to a client so as to get him to make an order; *estimate of costs or of expenditure*; *before we can give the grant we must have an estimate of the total costs involved*; *to ask a builder for an estimate for building the warehouse*; **to put in an estimate** = to give someone a written calculation of the probable costs of carrying out a job; *three firms put in estimates for the job* **2** ['estɪmeɪt] *verb* **(a)** to calculate the probable cost, size or time of something; *to estimate that it will cost £1m or to estimate costs at £1m*; *we estimate current sales at only 60% of last year's* **(b) to estimate for a job** = to state in writing the future costs of carrying out a piece of work so that a client can make an order; *three firms estimated for the fitting of the offices*

estimated ['estɪmeɪtɪd] *adjective* calculated approximately; *estimated sales*; *estimated figure*

estimation [estɪ'meɪʃən] *noun* approximate calculation

estimator ['estɪmeɪtə] *noun* person whose job is to calculate estimates for carrying out work

estoppel [ɪ'stɒpəl] *noun* rule of evidence whereby someone is prevented from denying or asserting a fact in legal proceedings; **estoppel of or by record** = rule that a person cannot reopen a matter which has already been decided by a court; **estoppel by deed** = rule that a person cannot deny having done something which is recorded in a deed; **estoppel by conduct or in pais** = rule that no one can deny things which he has done or failed to do which have had an effect on other persons' actions if that person has acted in a way which relied on the others' behaviour; *see also* PROMISSORY

euro ['jʊərəʊ] *noun* currency adopted as legal tender in several European countries from January 1st, 1999; *many articles are priced in euros*; *what's the exchange rate for the euro?*; **euro account** = bank account in euros (NOTE: written € before numbers: €250: strictly speaking, you should say: 'two hundred and fifty euro' - as the plural should be 'euro' not 'euros')

QUOTE cross-border mergers in the European Union have shot up since the introduction of the euro
Investors Chronicle

COMMENT: the countries which are joined together in the European Monetary Union and adopted the euro as their common currency in 1999 are: Austria, Belgium, Finland, France, Germany, Ireland, Italy, Luxembourg, the Netherlands, Portugal, and Spain. The conversion of these currencies to the euro was fixed on 1st January 1999. Greece joined on 1st January 2001

Euro- ['jʊərəʊ] *prefix* referring to Europe or the European Community

eurobond ['jʊərəʊbɒnd] *noun* long-term bearer bond issued by an international corporation or government outside its country of origin and sold to purchasers who pay in a eurocurrency (sold on the Eurobond market)

Eurocheque ['jʊərəʊtʃek] *noun* cheque which can be cashed in any European bank (the Eurocheque system is based in Brussels)

Eurocommercial paper (ECP) [jʊərəʊkə'mɜːʃəl 'peɪpə] *noun* form of short-term borrowing in eurocurrencies

eurocredit [jʊərəʊ'kredɪt] *noun* large bank loan in a eurocurrency (usually provided by a group of banks to a large commercial undertaking)

eurocurrency ['jʊərəʊkʌrənsi] *noun* any currency used for trade within Europe but outside its country of origin (the eurodollar, euroyen, etc., are eurocurrencies); *a eurocurrency loan*; *the eurocurrency market*

eurodeposit [jʊərəʊdɪ'pɒzɪt] *noun* deposit of eurodollars in a bank outside the USA

eurodollar ['jʊərəʊdɒlə] *noun* US dollar deposited in a bank outside the USA, used for trade within Europe; *a Eurodollar loan*; *the Eurodollar markets*

euroequity [jʊərəʊ'ekwɪti] *noun* share in an international company traded on European stock markets outside its country of origin

euronote [jʊərəʊ'nəʊt] *noun* short-term eurocurrency bearer note

euro-option [jʊərəʊ'ɒpʃn] *noun* option to buy European bonds at a later date

Europe ['jʊərəp] *noun* **(a)** group of countries to the West of Asia and the North of Africa; *most of the countries of Western Europe are members of the Common Market*; *Canadian exports to Europe have risen by 25%* **(b)** *used to refer to* the European Community

European [jʊərə'piːən] *adjective* referring to Europe; **the European Parliament** = parliament of members (MEPs) elected in each member country of the EC

European Central Bank (ECB)

[jʊrə'piən 'sentrəl 'bæŋk] *noun* central bank for most of the countries in the European Union, those which have accepted European Monetary Union and have the euro as their common currency

QUOTE the ECB begins with some $300 billion of foreign exchange reserves, far more than any other central bank

Investors Chronicle

QUOTE any change in the European bank's statutes must be agreed and ratified by all EU member nations

The Times

European Commission

[jʊərə'piːən kə'mɪʃn] *noun* the administration of the European Union, made up of members nominated by each member state (NOTE: also called the **Commission of the European Community)**

European Economic Area (EEA)

[jʊərə'piːən iːkə'nɒmɪk 'eərɪə] agreement on trade between the EU and the members of EFTA

European Economic Interest Grouping (EEIG)

[jʊərə'piːən iːkə'nɒmɪk 'ɪntrəst 'gruːpɪŋ] association linking companies in different EU countries which is aimed at facilitating its members' economic activities

COMMENT: an EEIG is a legal entity, and is a form of non-profit-making organization in which each member company is legally liable

European Free Trade Association (EFTA)

[jʊərə'piːən 'friː 'treɪd əsəʊsi'eɪʃn] group of countries (Iceland, Liechtenstein, Norway and Switzerland) formed to encourage freedom of trade between its members, and linked with the EU in the European Economic Area

European Investment Bank (EIB)

[jʊərə'piːən ɪn'vestmənt 'bæŋk] international European bank set up to provide loans to European countries

European Monetary Union (EMU)

['jʊərəpiːən 'mʌnɪtəri 'juːnɪən] the process by which some of the member states of the EU joined together to adopt the euro as their common currency on 1st January 1999

European Regional Development Fund (ERDF)

[jʊərə'piːən 'riːdʒənəl dɪ'veləpmənt 'fʌnd] fund set up to provide grants to underdeveloped parts of Europe

European Union (EU)

[jʊərə'piːən 'juːnɪən] (formerly called the European Economic Community (EEC) or the Common Market) a group of European countries linked together by the Treaty of Rome, basing their cooperation on the four fundamental freedoms of movement: of goods, capital, people and services

COMMENT: the European Community was set up in 1957 and changed its name to the European Union when it adopted the Single Market. It has now grown to include fifteen member states. These are: Austria, Belgium, Denmark, Finland, France, Germany, Greece, Ireland, Italy, Luxembourg, the Netherlands, Portugal, Spain, Sweden and the United Kingdom; other countries are negotiating to join. The member states of the EU are linked together by the Treaty of Rome in such a way that trade is more free, that money can be moved from one country to another freely, that people can move from one country to another more freely, and that people can work more freely in other countries of the group. See also comment at EURO

euroyen ['jʊərəʊjen] *noun* Japanese yen deposited in a European bank and used for trade within Europe

Eurozone ['jʊərəʊzəʊn] *noun* the European countries which use the euro as a common currency, seen as a group

QUOTE the European Central Bank left the door open yesterday for a cut in Eurozone interest rates

Financial Times

QUOTE a sustained recovery in the euro will require either a sharp slowdown in US growth or a rise in inflation and interest rates in the eurozone beyond that already discounted

Investors Chronicle

evade [ɪ'veɪd] *verb* to try to avoid something; **to evade tax** = to try illegally to avoid paying tax

evaluate [ɪ'væljʊeɪt] *verb* to calculate a value; *to evaluate costs*

evaluation [ɪvæljʊ'eɪʃən] *noun* calculation of value; **job evaluation** = examining different jobs within a company to see what skills and qualifications are needed to carry them out; **stock evaluation** = measuring the value of stock held at a certain point in time; *see also* STOCKTAKING

evasion [ɪ'veɪʒən] *noun* avoiding; **tax evasion** = illegally trying not to pay tax

EVR = ELECTRONIC VERSION OF THE TAX RETURN

ex *or* **ex-** [eks] *preposition & prefix* **(a)** out of or from; **price ex warehouse** = price for a product which is to be collected from the manufacturer's or agent's warehouse and so does not include delivery; **price ex works** *or* **ex factory** = price not including transport from the maker's factory **(b)** without; **ex-all (xa)** share price where the share is sold without the dividend, rights issue, or any other current issue; **ex-capitalization** *or* **ex cap (xc)** = share price where the share is sold without a recent scrip issue; **ex-coupon** = bond sold without the current interest coupon; **share quoted ex dividend** *or* **ex div (xd)** = share price not including the right to receive the next dividend; *the shares went ex dividend yesterday*; **ex-rights (xr)** = share price where the share is sold without a recent rights issue (NOTE: the opposite of **ex** is **cum**)

exact [ɪg'zækt] *adjective* very correct; *the exact time is 10.27*; *the salesgirl asked me if I had the exact sum, since the shop had no change* US **exact interest** = annual interest calculated on the basis of 365 days (as opposed to ordinary interest, calculated on 360 days)

exactly [ɪg'zæktli] *adverb* very correctly; *the total cost was exactly £6,500*

examination [ɪgzæmɪ'neɪʃən] *noun* **(a)** looking at something very carefully to see if it is acceptable; **customs examination** = looking at goods or baggage by customs officials **(b)** test to see if someone has passed a course; *he passed his accountancy examinations*; *she came first in the final examination for the course*; *he failed his proficiency examination and so had to leave his job*

examine [ɪg'zæmɪn] *verb* to look at someone or something very carefully to see if it can be accepted; *the customs officials asked to examine the inside of the car*; *the police are examining the papers from the managing director's safe*

examiner [ɪg'zæmɪnə] *noun* person who examines something to see if it is correct; *(in Ireland)* court-appointed administrator for a company

QUOTE bankers to the group said that the interim report of the examiner held few surprises for them and that they were ready to begin the hard task of negotiation with the examiner and company representatives
Irish Times

exceed [ɪk'siːd] *verb* to be more than; *discount not exceeding 15%*; *last year costs exceeded 20% of income for the first time*; **he has exceeded his credit limit** = he has borrowed more money than he is allowed

except [ɪk'sept] *preposition & conjunction* not including; *VAT is levied on all goods and services except books, newspapers and children's clothes*; *sales are rising in all markets except the Far East*

excepted [ɪk'septɪd] *adverb* not including; **errors and omissions excepted** = note on an invoice to show that the company has no responsibility for mistakes in the invoice

exceptional [ɪk'sepʃənl] *adjective* not usual, different; **exceptional items** = items which arise from normal trading but which are unusual because of their size or nature

COMMENT: such items are shown separately in a note to the company's accounts but not on the face of the P & L account unless they are profits or losses on the sale or termination of an operation, or costs of a fundamental reorganization or restructuring that have a material effect on the nature and focus of the reporting entity's operations, or profits or losses on the disposal of fixed assets (see FRS3)

excess 1 [ɪk'ses] *noun* amount which is more than what is allowed or needed; *an excess of expenditure over revenue* **2** ['ekses] *adjective* **excess capacity** = spare capacity which is not being used; **excess liquidity** = cash held by a bank above the normal requirement for that bank; **excess profits** = profit which is more than what is thought to be normal; **excess profits tax** = tax on excess profits; **excess stock** = stocks held which are higher than the optimum stock level

QUOTE control of materials provides manufacturers with an opportunity to reduce the amount of money tied up in excess materials
Duns Business Month

excessive [ɪk'sesɪv] *adjective* too large; *excessive management charges*

exchange [ɪks'tʃeɪndʒ] **1** *noun* **(a)** giving of one thing for another; **part exchange** = giving an old product as part of the payment for a new one; *to take a car in part exchange*;

exchange of contracts = point in the sale of property when the buyer and the seller both sign the contract of sale which then becomes binding **(b) foreign exchange** = (i) exchanging the money of one country for that of another; (ii) money of another country; *the company has more than £1m in foreign exchange*; **foreign exchange broker** = person who buys and sells foreign currency on behalf of other people; **foreign exchange market** = dealings in foreign currencies; *he trades on the foreign exchange market*; *foreign exchange markets were very active after the dollar devalued*; **rate of exchange** *or* **exchange rate** = price at which one currency is exchanged for another; *the current rate of exchange is 9.95 francs to the pound*; **exchange rate mechanism (ERM)** = former method of stabilizing exchange rates within the European Monetary System, where currencies could only move up or down within a narrow band (usually 2.25% either way, but for certain currencies this is widened to 6%) without involving a realignment of all the currencies in the system; **exchange control** = control by a government of the way in which its currency may be exchanged for foreign currencies; *the government had to impose exchange controls to stop the rush to buy dollars*; **exchange cross rates** = rates of exchange for various currencies, shown in terms of each other; **exchange dealer** = person who buys and sells foreign currency; **exchange dealings** = buying and selling foreign currency; *GB* **Exchange Equalization Account** = account with the Bank of England used by the government when buying or selling foreign currency to influence the sterling exchange rate; **exchange gain** *or* **exchange loss** = gain or loss made from changes in the exchange rate which take place during the period of the transaction; **exchange premium** = extra cost above the normal rate for buying a foreign currency **(c) bill of exchange** = document which tells a bank to pay a person (usually used in foreign currency payments) **(d)** market for shares, commodities, futures, etc.; **Stock Exchange** = place where stocks and shares are bought and sold; *the company's shares are traded on the New York Stock Exchange*; *he works on the Stock Exchange*; **commodity exchange** = place where commodities are bought and sold **2** *verb* **(a)** to exchange one article for another = to give one thing in place of something else; *he exchanged his motorcycle for a car*; *if the trousers are too small you can take them back and exchange them for a larger pair*; *goods can be exchanged only on production of the sales slip* **(b)** to exchange contracts =

to sign a contract when buying a property (done by both buyer and seller at the same time) **(c)** to change money of one country for money of another; *to exchange francs for pounds*

QUOTE under the barter agreements, Nigeria will export crude oil in exchange for trucks, food, planes and chemicals
Wall Street Journal

QUOTE can free trade be reconciled with a strong dollar resulting from floating exchange rates
Duns Business Month

QUOTE a draft report on changes in the international monetary system casts doubt on any return to fixed exchange-rate parities
Wall Street Journal

exchangeable [ɪksˈtʃeɪndʒəbl] *adjective* which can be exchanged

exchanger [ɪksˈtʃeɪndʒə] *noun* person who buys and sells foreign currency

Exchequer [ɪksˈtʃekə] *noun* GB **the Exchequer** = (i) fund of all money received by the government of the UK from taxes and other revenues; (ii) the British government's account with the Bank of England; (iii) British government department dealing with public revenue; **the Chancellor of the Exchequer** = the chief British finance minister; **Exchequer stocks** = Treasury stocks, British government stocks used to finance government expenditure

excise [ˈeksaɪz] *noun* **(a) excise duty** = tax on certain goods produced in a country (such as alcohol or cigarettes) (NOTE: duty on goods imported into a country is **customs duty**); **excise licence** = licence issued (against payment) to allow someone to trade in products which are subject to excise duty, such as making wine; *US* **excise tax** = tax levied for a particular purpose **(b) Customs and Excise** *or* **Excise Department** = government department which deals with taxes on imports and on products such as alcohol produced in the country; it also deals with VAT

exciseman [ˈeksaɪzmæn] *noun* person who works in the Excise Department

exclude [ɪksˈkluːd] *verb* to keep out, not to include; *the interest charges have been excluded from the document*; *damage by fire is excluded from the policy*

exclusion [ɪksˈkluːʒən] *noun* act of not including; **exclusion clause** = clause in an insurance policy or warranty which says which items are not covered

exclusive [ɪksˈkluːsɪv] *adjective* **(a)** **exclusive agreement** = agreement where a person is made sole agent for a product in a market; **exclusive right to market a product** = right to be the only person to market the product **(b)** **exclusive of** = not including; *all payments are exclusive of tax*; *the invoice is exclusive of VAT*

exclusivity [ekskluːˈsɪvəti] *noun* exclusive right to market a product

execute [ˈeksɪkjuːt] *verb* to carry out (an order)

execution [eksɪˈkjuːʃən] *noun* carrying out of an order or a contract; **stay of execution** = temporary stopping of a legal order; *the court granted the company a two-week stay of execution*

executive [ɪgˈzekjʊtɪv] **1** *adjective* which puts decisions into action; **executive committee** = committee which runs a society or a club; **executive director** = director who actually works full-time in the company; **executive powers** = right to put decisions into action; *he was made managing director with full executive powers over the European operation*; **executive program** = master program in a computer system, that controls the execution of other programs **2** *noun* person in a business who takes decisions, a manager or director; *sales executive*; *senior or junior executive*; **account executive** = employee who is the link between his company and certain customers; **chief executive** = executive director in charge of a company; **executive share option scheme** = scheme where executives of a company receive options to buy shares in the company at a certain price in the future

executor [ɪgˈzekjʊtə] *noun* person or firm that sees that the terms of a will are carried out; *he was named executor of his brother's will*

executory [ɪgˈzekjʊtəri] *adjective* which is still being carried out; **executory consideration** = consideration where one party makes a promise in exchange for a counter-promise from the other party

executrix [ɪgˈzekjʊtrɪks] *noun* female executor

exempt [ɪgˈzempt] **1** *adjective* not covered by a law; not forced to obey a law; **exempt from tax** *or* **tax-exempt** = not required to pay tax, not taxable; *as a non-profit-making*

organization we are exempt from tax; *winnings on the national Lottery are tax-exempt*; **exempt assets** = assets (such as cars) which are not subject to capital gains tax when sold; **exempt supplies** = sales of goods or services which are exempt from VAT **2** *verb* to free something from having tax paid on it or from having to pay tax; *non-profit-making organizations are exempted from tax*; *food is exempted from sales tax*; *the government exempted trusts from tax*

exemption [ɪgˈzempʃən] *noun* act of exempting something from a contract or from a tax; **exemption clause** = clause in a contract exempting a party from certain liabilities; **exemption from tax** *or* **tax exemption** = being free from having to pay tax; *as a non-profit-making organization you can claim tax exemption*

exercise [ˈeksəsaɪz] **1** *noun* **(a)** use of something; **exercise of an option** = using an option, putting an option into action; **exercise date** = date when an option can be put into effect; **exercise price** = price at which an option will be put into effect **(b)** financial year; *during the current exercise* **2** *verb* to use; **to exercise an option** = to put an option into action; *only 25% of the shareholders exercised their option to purchase shares at £1.57p*; *he exercised his option to acquire sole marketing rights for the product*; *the chairwoman exercised her veto to block the motion*

ex gratia [eks ˈgreɪʃə] *adjective* **an ex gratia payment** = payment made as a gift, with no other obligations

exit price [ˈegsɪt ˈpraɪs] *noun* planned price at which an investor sells an investment

QUOTE Under an option agreement the exit price in five years is 117p per share to give an equivalent tax-free compound annual return of 13.38%.
Accountancy

ex officio [eks əˈfɪʃɪəʊ] *adjective & adverb* because of an office held; *the treasurer is ex officio a member or an ex officio member of the finance committee*

exor = EXECUTOR

expand [ɪkˈspænd] *verb* to increase, to get bigger or to make something bigger; *an expanding economy*; *the company is expanding fast*; *we have had to expand our sales force*

expansion [ɪkˈspænʃən] *noun* increase in size (either by using funds to increase production and sales, or by acquiring another company); *the expansion of the domestic market*; *the company had difficulty in financing its current expansion programme*

> QUOTE inflation-adjusted GNP moved up at a 1.3% annual rate, its worst performance since the economic expansion began
> *Fortune*

> QUOTE the businesses we back range from start-up ventures to established businesses in need of further capital for expansion
> *Times*

> QUOTE the group is undergoing a period of rapid expansion and this has created an exciting opportunity for a qualified accountant
> *Financial Times*

ex parte ['eks 'pɑːteɪ] *Latin phrase meaning* 'on behalf of'; **an ex parte application** = application made to a court where only one side is represented and no notice is given to the other side (often where the application is for an injunction); *the wife applied ex parte for an ouster order against her husband*

expect [ɪk'spekt] *verb* to hope that something is going to happen; *they are expecting a cheque from their agent next week*; *the company was sold for more than the expected price*

> QUOTE he observed that he expected exports to grow faster than imports
> *Sydney Morning Herald*

> QUOTE American business as a whole has seen profits well above the levels normally expected at this stage of the cycle
> *Sunday Times*

expectancy [ɪk'spektənsi] *noun* **life expectancy** = number of years a person is likely to live

expected value [ɪk'spektɪd 'væljuː] *noun* future value of a certain course of action, weighted according to the probability that the course of action will actually occur

> COMMENT: if the possible course of action produces income of £10,000 and has a 10% chance of occurring, its expected value is 10% of £10,000 or £1,000

expenditure [ɪk'spendɪtʃə] *noun* amounts of money spent; **below-the-line expenditure** = payments which do not arise a company's normal activities (such as redundancy payments); **capital expenditure** = money spent on fixed assets (such as property or machinery); **the company's current expenditure programme** = the company's spending according to the current plan; **heavy expenditure on equipment** = spending large sums of money on equipment (NOTE: usually singular, but American English uses the plural **expenditures**)

expense [ɪk'spens] *noun* **(a)** money spent; *it is not worth the expense*; *the expense is too much for my bank balance*; **at great expense** = having spent a lot of money; *he furnished the office regardless of expense* = without thinking how much it cost **(b)** **expense account** = money which a businessman is allowed by his company to spend on travelling and entertaining clients in connection with his business; *I'll put this lunch on my expense account*; *expense account lunches form a large part of our current expenditure*

expenses [ɪk'spensɪz] *noun* money paid for doing something in the course of business, but not for manufacturing a product or for purchasing stock or for paying labour; *the salary offered is £10,000 plus expenses*; **all expenses paid** = with all costs paid by the company; *the company sent him to San Francisco all expenses paid*; **to cut down on expenses** = to try to reduce spending; **allowable expenses** = business expenses which are allowed against tax; **business expenses** = money spent on running a business, not on stock or assets; **direct expenses** = expenses (excluding materials, labour or purchase of stock for resale) which are incurred in making a product; **entertainment expenses** = money spent on giving meals to business visitors; **fixed expenses** = expenses which do not vary with different levels of production (such as rent, secretaries' salaries, insurance); **incidental expenses** = small amounts of money spent at various times, in addition to larger amounts; **indirect expenses** = expenses (excluding materials, labour or purchase of stock for resale) which are incurred by a business, but which cannot be allocated to any particular product; **legal expenses** = money spent on fees paid to lawyers; **overhead expenses** *or* **general expenses** *or* **running expenses** = money spent on the day-to-day running of a business; **travelling expenses** = money spent on travelling and hotels for business purposes

expert system ['eksp3ːt 'sɪstəm] *noun* system that applies the knowledge, advice and rules defined by experts in a particular field to a user's data to help solve a problem

COMMENT: once thought to be potentially highly significant, expert systems have proved very difficult to design and implement in the real world. Auditors commonly use 'decision support systems' instead. These present auditor judgements in a structured way and may be used to create audit programmes or document the assessment of business risk

expiration [ekspɪˈreɪʃən] *noun* coming to an end; *expiration of an insurance policy*; *to repay before the expiration of the stated period*; **on expiration of the lease** = when the lease comes to an end; **expiration date** = EXPIRY DATE

expire [ɪkˈspaɪə] *verb* to come to an end; *the option expired last Tuesday*; *our lease expires in 1997*; **his passport has expired** = his passport is no longer valid

expiry [ɪkˈspaɪəri] *noun* coming to an end; *expiry of an option or of an insurance policy*; **expiry date** = (i) date when something will end, such as the last date for exercising an option; (ii) the last date on which a credit card can be used

exponent [eksˈpəʊnənt] *noun* number indicating the power to which a base number is to be raised

export 1 [ˈekspɔːt] *noun* **(a) exports** = goods sent to a foreign country to be sold; *exports to Africa have increased by 25%* **(b)** action of sending goods to a foreign country to be sold; *the export trade or the export market*; **export department** = section of a company which deals in sales to foreign countries; **export duty** = tax paid on goods sent out of a country for sale; **export house** = company which specializes in the export of goods made by other manufacturers; **export licence** = government permit allowing something to be exported; *the government has refused an export licence for computer parts*; **export manager** = person in charge of an export department in a company; **Export Credits Guarantee Department (ECGD)** = British government department which insures sellers of exports sold on credit against the possibility of non-payment by the purchasers **2** [ɪkˈspɔːt] *verb* to send goods to foreign countries for sale; *50% of our production is exported*; *the company imports raw materials and exports the finished products*

exportation [ekspɔːˈteɪʃən] *noun* act of sending goods to foreign countries for sale

exporter [eksˈpɔːtə] *noun* person, company or country which sells goods in foreign countries; *a major furniture exporter; Canada is an important exporter of oil or an important oil exporter*

exporting [eksˈpɔːtɪŋ] *adjective* which exports; **oil exporting countries** = countries which produce oil and sell it to other countries

exposure [ɪkˈspəʊʒə] *noun* **(a)** showing something **(b)** amount of risk which a lender or investor has; *he is trying to cover his exposure in the property market; see also* OVEREXPOSURE

COMMENT: exposure can be the amount of money lent to a customer (a bank's exposure to a foreign country) or the amount of money which an investor may lose if his investments collapse (such as his exposure in the Australian market)

exposure draft (ED) [ɪkˈspəʊʒə ˈdrɑːft] *noun* document produced by a body before a new authorative pronouncement is published; it invites accountants and other interested parties to comment on matters raised by the draft

COMMENT: The UK Accounting Standards Committee issued drafts of SSAPs in a numbered series eg. ED24, ED25 etc. Exposure drafts issued by the UK Accounting Standards Board are known as FREDs (Financial Reporting Exposure Drafts)

express [ɪkˈspres] **1** *adjective* **(a)** rapid, very fast; *express letter; express delivery* **(b)** clearly shown in words; *the contract has an express condition forbidding sale in Africa* **2** *verb* **(a)** to put into words or diagrams; *this chart shows home sales expressed as a percentage of total turnover* **(b)** to send by fast mail or courier; *we expressed the order to the customer's warehouse*

expressly [ɪkˈspresli] *adverb* clearly in words; *the contract expressly forbids sales to the United States*

extend [ɪkˈstend] *verb* **(a)** to make available, or to give; *to extend credit to a customer* **(b)** to make longer; *to extend a contract for two years*

extended credit [ɪkˈstendɪd ˈkredɪt] *noun* **(a)** credit allowing the borrower a very long time to pay; *we sell to Australia on extended credit* **(b)** *US* extra long credit used by commercial banks borrowing from the Federal Reserve

extension [ɪkˈstenʃən] *noun* **(a)** allowing longer time; **to get an extension of credit** = to get more time to pay back; **extension of a contract** = continuing the contract for a further period **(b)** *(in an office)* individual telephone linked to the main switchboard;

can you get me extension 21?; extension 21 is engaged; the sales manager is on extension 53

extensive [ɪk'stensɪv] *adjective* very large, covering a wide area; *an extensive network of sales outlets*

QUOTE the White House refusal to ask for an extension of the auto import quotas

Duns Business Month

external [ɪk'stɜːnl] *adjective* **(a)** outside a country; **external account** = (i) account with a British bank of someone who is living in another country; (ii) a country's balance of payments account with other countries; **external debt** = money owed by foreign countries; **external debts** *or* **external funds** = money which a company has borrowed from outside sources (such as a bank) as opposed to money raised from debentureholders or shareholders; **external trade** = trade with foreign countries **(b)** outside a company; **external audit** = audit carried out by an independent auditor; **external auditing** = action of auditing a set of accounts by an external auditor; **external auditor** = auditor who carries out audits of a company's accounts but is not employed by that company; **external growth** = growth by buying other companies, rather than by expanding existing sales or products; **external liabilities** = money owed to lenders and other creditors outside a company

extract ['ekstrækt] *noun* printed document which is part of a larger document; *he sent me an extract of the accounts*

extraordinary [ɪk'strɔːdənəri] *adjective* different from normal; **Extraordinary General Meeting (EGM)** = special meeting of shareholders to discuss an important matter which cannot wait until the next AGM (such as a change in the company's articles of association)

extraordinary items [ɪk'strɔːdənəri 'aɪtəmz] *noun* formerly, large items of income or expenditure which did not arise from normal trading and which did not occur every year (they were shown separately on the face of the P&L account, after taxation; see FRS 3); *compare* EXCEPTIONAL ITEMS *see* COMMENT *at* ORDINARY ACTIVITIES

extraordinary resolution [ɪk'strɔːdənəri rezə'luːʃn] *noun* resolution which needs 75% of the votes before it can be carried

COMMENT: notice that an extraordinary resolution will be put to a meeting must be given, but no minimum period is specified by law, as opposed to a 'special resolution' for which 21 days' notice must be given. An extraordinary resolution could be a proposal to wind up a company voluntarily, but changes to the articles of association, such as a change of name, or of the objects of the company, need a special resolution

Ff

Schedule F ['ʃedjuːl 'ef] schedule to the Finance Acts under which tax is charged on income from dividends paid by UK companies and unit trusts

FA = FINANCE ACT

face value ['feɪs 'væljuː] *noun* value written on a coin, banknote, share certificate or bill of exchange

QUOTE travellers cheques cost 1% of their face value - some banks charge more for small amounts
Sunday Times

facility [fə'sɪləti] *noun* (a) being able to do something easily; *we offer facilities for payment* (b) loan; **credit facilities** = arrangement with a bank or supplier to have credit so as to buy goods; **overdraft facility** = arrangement with a bank to have an overdraft; **facility fee** = arrangement fee, a charge made by a bank to a client for arranging credit facilities

factor ['fæktə] 1 *noun* (a) thing which is important or which influences; *the drop in sales is an important factor in the company's lower profits*; **cost factor** = problem of cost; **cyclical factors** = way in which a trade cycle affects businesses; **deciding factor** = most important factor which influences a decision; **limiting factor** = factor which limits a company's ability to achieve its goals (e.g. sales demand being too low for the company to make enough profit); **factors of production** = things needed to produce a product (land, labour, machinery and capital) (b) number used in multiplication to produce another number; **by a factor of ten** = ten times (c) (i) person who acts for another and is paid a commission; (ii) person or company which is responsible for collecting debts for companies, by buying debts at a discount to their face value 2 *verb* to buy debts from a company at a discount

COMMENT: a factor collects a company's debts when due, and pays the creditor in advance part of the sum to be collected, so 'buying' the debt; the debtors are informed of this arrangement (i.e., that the debt has been assigned), as opposed to invoice discounting, where the debtor is not told

factorial [fæk'tɔːriəl] *noun* the product of all the numbers below a number; *example: 4 factorial = 1x2x3x4 = 24* (NOTE: **4 factorial** is written **4!**)

factoring ['fæktərɪŋ] *noun* business of buying debts at a discount; **factoring charges** = cost of selling debts to a factor for a commission

factory overhead ['fæktri 'əʊvəhed] *noun* production overhead, indirect costs of production which are absorbed into the cost of goods produced

FAE = FINAL ADMITTING EXAM

fail [feɪl] *verb* (a) not to do something which you were trying to do; *the company failed to notify the tax office of its change of address* (b) to be unsuccessful commercially; **the company failed** = the company went bankrupt; *he lost all his money when the bank failed*

failure ['feɪljə] *noun* (a) breaking down or stopping; *the failure of the negotiations* (b) **failure to pay a bill** = not having paid the bill (c) **commercial failure** = financial collapse or bankruptcy; *he lost all his money in the bank failure*

fair [feə] 1 *noun* **trade fair** = large exhibition and meeting for advertising and selling a certain type of product 2 *adjective* (a) honest or correct; **fair deal** = arrangement where both parties are treated equally; **fair dealing** = legal buying and selling of shares; **fair price** = good price for both buyer and seller; **fair trade** = (i) international business system where countries agree not to charge import duties on certain items imported from their trading partners; (ii) *US* = RESALE PRICE MAINTENANCE *US* **fair trade price** = retail price which is fixed by the manufacturer and which cannnot be changed by the retailer; **fair trading** *or* **fair dealing** = way of doing business which is reasonable and does not harm the consumer; *GB* **Office of Fair Trading** = government department which protects consumers against unfair or illegal business; **fair wear and tear** = acceptable damage caused by normal use; *the insurance policy covers most damage, but not fair wear and tear to the machine* **(b) fair copy** = document which is written or typed with no mistakes

fair value *US* **fair market value** ['feə 'væljuː] *noun* **(a)** price paid by a buyer who knows the value of what he is buying to a seller who also knows the value of what he is selling (i.e., neither is cheating the other) **(b)** method of valuing the assets and liabilities of a business based on the amount for which they could be sold to independent parties at the time of valuation

COMMENT: fair values are particularly relevant to acquisitions of whole companies, and relate to the valuation of the net assets purchased as well as the consideration (i.e. the purchase price) which may be made up of cash and securities. FRS6 defines fair value as 'the amount at which an asset or liability could be exchanged in an arm's length transaction between informed and willing parties, other than in a forced or liquidation sale'

fall [fɔːl] **1** *noun* sudden drop, suddenly becoming smaller; loss of value; *a fall in the exchange rate; fall in the price of gold; a fall on the Stock Exchange; profits showed a 10% fall* **2** *verb* **(a)** to drop suddenly to a lower price; *shares fell on the market today; gold shares fell 10% or fell 45 cents on the Stock Exchange; the price of gold fell for the second day running; the pound fell against the dollar* **(b)** to happen, to take place; *the public holiday falls on a Tuesday;* **payments which fall due** = payments which are now due to be made (NOTE: **falling - fell - has fallen)**

QUOTE market analysts described the falls in the second half of last week as a technical correction to the market
Australian Financial Review

QUOTE for the first time since mortgage rates began falling in March a financial institution has raised charges on homeowner loans
Globe and Mail (Toronto)

fall away [fɔːl ə'weɪ] *verb* to become less; *hotel bookings have fallen away since the tourist season ended*

fall back [fɔːl 'bæk] *verb* to become lower or cheaper after rising in price; *shares fell back in light trading*

fall behind [fɔːl bɪ'haɪnd] *verb* to be late in doing something; *he fell behind with his mortgage repayments*

falling ['fɔːlɪŋ] *adjective* which is growing smaller or dropping in price; **a falling market** = market where prices are coming down; **the falling pound** = the pound which is losing its value against other currencies

QUOTE falling profitability means falling share prices
Investors Chronicle

fall off [fɔːl 'ɒf] *verb* to become lower, cheaper or less; *sales have fallen off since the tourist season ended*

false [fɔːls] *adjective* not true, not correct; *to make a false entry in the accounts;* **false accounting** = criminal offence of changing, destroying or hiding accounting records for a dishonest purpose, such as to gain money; **false market** = market in shares caused by persons or companies conspiring to buy or sell and so influence the share price to their advantage; **false pretences** = doing or saying something to cheat someone; *he was sent to prison for obtaining money by false pretences*

falsification [fɔːlsɪfɪ'keɪʃən] *noun* action of making false entries in accounts

falsify ['fɔːlsɪfaɪ] *verb* to change something to make it wrong; *to falsify the accounts*

FAS = FINANCIAL ACCOUNTING STANDARDS (accounting standards applied in the USA)

FASB = FINANCIAL ACCOUNTING STANDARDS BOARD (the body which regulates accounting standards in the USA)

favourable *US* **favorable** ['feɪvərəbl] *adjective* which gives an advantage; **favourable balance of trade** = situation where a country's exports are more than it imports; **on favourable terms** = on good terms which give an advantage; *the shop is let on very favourable terms;* **favourable variance** = variance which shows that the actual result is better than expected

fax [fæks] **1** *noun* (i) system for sending facsimile copies of documents via the telephone lines; (ii) document sent by this method; *we received a fax of the order this morning; can you confirm the booking by fax?* **2** *verb* to send a message by fax; *the* *details of the offer were faxed to the brokers this morning*

> COMMENT: banks will not accept fax messages as binding instructions (as for example, a faxed order for money to be transferred from one account to another)

FCA = FELLOW OF THE INSTITUTE OF CHARTERED ACCOUNTANTS IN ENGLAND AND WALES

FCCA = FELLOW OF THE ASSOCIATION OF CHARTERED CERTIFIED ACCOUNTANTS

FCMA = FELLOW OF THE CHARTERED INSTITUTE OF MANAGEMENT ACCOUNTANTS

the Fed [ðə 'fed] *US informal* = FEDERAL RESERVE BOARD; **Fed Funds** = FEDERAL FUNDS

> QUOTE indications of weakness in the US economy were contained in figures from the Fed on industrial production for April
> *Financial Times*

> QUOTE the half-point discount rate move gives the Fed room to reduce the federal funds rate further if economic weakness persists. The Fed sets the discount rate directly, but controls the federal funds rate by buying and selling Treasury securities
> *Wall Street Journal*

federal ['fedərəl] *adjective* **(a)** referring to a system of government where a group of states are linked together in a federation **(b)** referring to the central government of the United States; *most federal offices are in Washington*; **federal credit agencies** = agencies which provide credit to individual borrowers and are backed by the federal government; **federal funds** *or* **fed funds** = deposits by commercial banks with the Federal Reserve Banks, which can be used for short-term loans to other banks; **fed funds rate** = the rate charged by banks for lending money deposited with the Federal Reserve to other banks

> QUOTE federal examiners will determine which of the privately-insured savings and loans qualify for federal insurance
> *Wall Street Journal*

> QUOTE since 1978 America has freed many of its industries from federal rules that set prices and controlled the entry of new companies
> *Economist*

Federal Home Loans Banks ['fedərəl 'həʊm 'ləʊnz 'bæŋks] *US* small group of banks which lend to Savings and Loans Associations, and to other institutions which lend money to homeowners against mortgages

Federal Reserve ['fedərəl rɪ'zɜːv] system of federal government control of the US banks, where the Federal Reserve Board regulates money supply, prints money, fixes the discount rate and issues government bonds

> COMMENT: the Federal Reserve system is the central bank of the USA. The system is run by the Federal Reserve Board, under a chairman and seven committee members (or 'governors') who are all appointed by the President. The twelve Federal Reserve Banks act as lenders of last resort to local commercial banks. Although the board is appointed by the president, the whole system is relatively independent of the US government

Federal Reserve Bank ['fedərəl rɪ'zɜːv 'bæŋk] *US* one of the central banks in the USA which are owned by the state and directed by the Federal Reserve Board

Federal Reserve Board ['fedərəl rɪ'zɜːv 'bɔːd] *US* committee which runs the central banks in the USA

> QUOTE pressure on the Federal Reserve Board to ease monetary policy mounted yesterday with the release of a set of pessimistic economic statistics
> *Financial Times*

Federal Trade Commission ['fedərəl 'treɪd kə'mɪʃən] federal agency established to keep business competition free and fair

federation [fedə'reɪʃən] *noun* group of societies, companies or organizations which have a central organization which represents them and looks after their common interests; *federation of trades unions*; *employers' federation*

Fédération des Experts Comptables Européens (FEE) [feɪdeɪ'ræsɪɒn deɪz 'ekspeə 'kɒntæbl 'ɜːrəʊpeɪæn] European organization which includes all national accounting organizations

fee [fiː] *noun* **(a)** money paid for work carried out by a professional person (such as an accountant, a doctor or a lawyer); *we charge a small fee for our services*; *director's fees*; *consultant's fee* **(b)** money paid for something; *entrance fee or admission fee*; *registration fee* **(c)** *(legal)* **fee simple** =

freehold ownership of land with no restrictions to it; *to hold an estate in fee simple*; **fee tail** = interest in land which is passed on to the owner's direct descendants, and which cannot be passed to anyone else

fellow ['feləʊ] *noun* title given to senior members of a professional association (junior members are usually called 'associates')

fiat money ['fiːæt 'mʌni] *noun* coins or notes which are not worth much as paper or metal, but are said by the government to have a value

fictitious assets [fɪk'tɪʃəs 'æsɪts] *noun* assets (such as prepayments) which do not have a resale value, but are entered as assets in the balance sheet

fiddle ['fɪdl] **1** *noun (informal)* cheating; *it's all a fiddle*; **he's on the fiddle** = he is trying to cheat **2** *verb informal* to cheat; *he tried to fiddle his tax returns*; *the salesman was caught fiddling his expense account*

fide ['faɪdi] *see* BONA FIDE

fiduciary [fɪ'djuːʃjəri] *adjective & noun* (person) in a position of trust; *directors have fiduciary duty to act in the best interests of the company*; **fiduciary deposits** = bank deposits which are managed for the depositor by the bank

FIFO ['faɪfəʊ] = FIRST IN FIRST OUT

fifty-fifty ['fɪfti'fɪfti] *adjective & adverb* half; **to go fifty-fifty** = to share the costs equally; **he has a fifty-fifty chance of making a profit** = he has an equal chance of making a profit or a loss

figure ['fɪgə] *noun* **(a)** number; income or expense written in numbers; *the figure in the accounts for heating is very high*; **he put a very low figure on the value of the lease** = he calculated the value of the lease as very low **(b) figures** = written numbers; **sales figures** = total sales; **to work out the figures** = to calculate; **his income runs into five figures** *or* **he has a five-figure income** = his income is more than £10,000; **in round figures** = not totally accurate, but correct to the nearest 10 or 100; *they have a workforce of 2,500 in round figures* **(c) figures** = results for a company; *the figures for last year or last year's figures*

file [faɪl] **1** *noun* **(a)** cardboard holder for documents, which can fit in the drawer of a filing cabinet; *put these letters in the customer file*; *look in the file marked 'Scottish sales'*; **box file** = cardboard box for

holding documents **(b)** documents kept for reference; **to place something on file** = to keep a record of something; **to keep someone's name on file** = to keep someone's name on a list for reference; **file copy** = copy of a document which is kept for reference in an office **(c)** section of data on a computer (such as payroll, address list, customer accounts); *how can we protect our computer files?*; **file maintenance** = process of updating a file by adding, deleting or changing entries; **file processing** = applying a set of rules or search limits to a file, in order to update it or to find information **2** *verb* **(a)** to **file documents** = to put documents in order so that they can be found easily; *the correspondence is filed under 'complaints'* **(b)** to make an official request; **to file a petition in bankruptcy** = (i) to ask officially to be made bankrupt; (ii) to ask officially for someone else to be made bankrupt **(c)** to **file an application for a patent**; *to file a return to the tax office*; **filing date** = date by which income tax returned must be filed with the Inland Revenue

FIMBRA = FINANCIAL INTERMEDIARIES, MANAGERS AND BROKERS REGULATORY ASSOCIATION

final ['faɪnl] *adjective* last, coming at the end of a period; *to pay the final instalment*; *to make the final payment*; *to put the final details on a document*; **final accounts** = accounts produced at the end of an accounting period, including the balance sheet and profit and loss account; **Final Admitting Exam (FAE)** = final examination set by the ICAEW to admit student accountants as members (i.e. as Chartered Accountants); **final date for payment** = last date by which payment should be made; **final closing date** = last date for acceptance of a takeover bid, when the bidder has to announce how many shareholders have accepted his offer; **final demand** = last reminder from a supplier, after which he will sue for payment; **final discharge** = last payment of what is left of a debt; **final dividend** = dividend paid at the end of a year's trading, which has to be approved by the shareholders; **final product** = manufactured product, made at the end of a production process; **final settlement** = last payment which settles a debt

finalize ['faɪnəlaɪz] *verb* to agree final details; *we hope to finalize the agreement tomorrow*; *after six weeks of negotiations the loan was finalized yesterday*

finance 1 ['faɪnæns] *noun* **(a)** money used by a company, provided by the shareholders or by loans; **finance charge** = (i) the cost of borrowing money; (ii) additional charge made to a customer who asks for extended credit; **finance company** *or* **finance corporation** *or* **finance house** = company, usually part of a commercial bank, which buys goods or equipment which it then hires or leases to companies or individuals; **finance house deposits** = amount of money deposited by banks with finance houses and used by them to provide credit to clients for the purchase of goods or equipment; **finance lease** = lease which requires the lessee company to show the asset acquired under the lease in its balance sheet and to depreciate it in the normal way (see SSAP21); *see also* OPERATING LEASE; **finance market** = place where large sums of money can be lent or borrowed; **high finance** = lending, investing and borrowing of very large sums of money, organized by financiers **(b)** money (of a club, local authority, etc.); *she is the secretary of the local authority finance committee* **(c)** finances = money or cash which is available; *the bad state of the company's finances* **2** [fɪ'næns] *verb* to provide money to pay for something; *to finance an operation*

Finance Act (FA) ['faɪnæns 'ækt] *noun* *GB* annual act of parliament which gives the government the power to obtain money from taxes as proposed in the Budget (NOTE: when referring to a particular Finance Act, use the abbreviation **FA: 'see Sch 10 to FA 1985'**)

Finance Bill ['faɪnæns 'bɪl] *noun* **(a)** *GB* bill which lists the proposals in a Chancellor of the Exchequer's budget and which is debated before being voted into law as the Finance Act **(b)** *US* short-term bill of exchange which provides credit for a corporation so that it can continue trading

Finance Secretary ['faɪnæns 'sekrətri] *noun* member of the British government responsible for the Inland Revenue and tax

financial [fɪ'nænʃəl] *adjective* concerning money; **Financial Accountant** = qualified accountant, a member of the Institute of Financial Accountants, who advises on accounting matters or who works as the financial director of a company; **financial accounting** = recording financial transactions in monetary terms according to accounting standards and legal requirements; **financial adviser** = person or company which gives advice on financial matters for a fee; *see also* INDEPENDENT, TIED; **financial assistance** = help in the form of money; **financial correspondent** = journalist who writes articles on money matters for a newspaper; **financial futures** = investment in gilt-edged stocks, eurodollars, etc., for delivery at a date in the future; **financial institution** = organization such as a building society, pension fund or insurance company, which invests large amounts of money in securities; **financial instrument** = any form of investment in the stock market or in other financial markets, such as shares, government stocks, certificates of deposit, bills of exchange, etc.; **financial intermediary** = institution which takes deposits or loans from individuals and lends money to clients (banks, building societies, hire purchase companies, are all types of financial intermediaries); **financial management** = management of the acquisition and use of long- and short-term capital by a business; **financial position** = financial state of a company (i.e., its assets and liabilities); **financial resources** = money which is available for investment; *a company with strong financial resources*; **financial risk** = possibility of losing money; *there is no financial risk in selling to East European countries on credit*; **financial statements** = documents which show the financial situation of a company at the end of an accounting period as well as the effect of transactions during that period; *see also* STATEMENT; **the Financial Statement** = document which sets out the details of the budget presented by the Chancellor of the Exchequer (it is published on Budget Day); **financial supermarket** = company which offers a range of financial services (a bank may offer loans, mortgages, pensions, insurance as well as the normal personal banking services); **financial year** = (i) the twelve month period for which a company produces accounts (not necessarily the same as a calendar year); (ii) for corporation tax purposes, the period 1st April to 31st March of the following year

Financial Accounting Standards (FAS) [fɪ'nænʃəl ə'kauntɪŋ 'stændədz] accounting standards applied in the USA

Financial Accounting Standards Board (FASB) [fɪ'nænʃəl ə'kauntɪŋ 'stændədz 'bɔːd] the body which regulates accounting standards in the USA

Financial Intermediaries, Managers and Brokers Regulatory Association (FIMBRA) one of the self-regulatory bodies replaced by the FSA, originally set up to regulate the activities of financial advisers, insurance brokers, etc., giving financial advice or arranging financial services for small clients

financially [fɪˈnænʃəli] *adverb* regarding money; **company which is financially sound** = company which is profitable and has strong assets

Financial Reporting Exposure Draft (FRED) [fɪˈnænʃəl rɪˈpɔːtɪŋ ɪkˈspəʊʒə ˈdrɑːft] document produced by the UK Accounting Standards Board before a new authorative pronouncement is published; it invites accountants and other interested parties to comment on matters raised by the draft

Financial Reporting Standard (FRS) [fɪˈnænʃəl rɪˈpɔːtɪŋ ˈstændədz] standard issued by the Accounting Standards Board; the first FRS was FRS1, issued in 1991 to replace SSAP10

Financial Reporting Standard for Smaller Entities (FRSSE) [fɪˈnænʃəl rɪˈpɔːtɪŋ ˈstændəd fə ˈsmɔːlə ˈentɪtiːz *or* ˈfrʌzi] reporting standards specially devised for small businesses

Financial Reporting Review Panel (FRRP) [fɪˈnænʃəl rɪˈpɔːtɪŋ rɪˈvjuː ˈpænəl] *noun* UK body that receives and investigates complaints about the annual accounts of companies in respect of apparent departures from the accounting requirements of the Companies Act, including the requirement to give a true and fair view

financials [fɪˈnænʃəlz] *noun* = FINANCIAL FUTURES

Financial Services Act [fɪˈnænʃəl ˈsɜːvɪsɪz ˈækt] Act of the British Parliament which regulates the offering of financial services to the general public and to private investors

Financial Services Authority (FSA) [fɪˈnænʃəl ˈsɜːvɪsɪz ɔːˈθɒrəti] government agency set up to regulate all financial services, such as banks, stockbrokers, unit trusts, pension companies, professional bodies, stock exchanges, etc., including the ombudsmen for these services

Financial Times (FT) [faɪˈnænʃəl ˈtaɪmz] important British financial daily newspaper (printed on pink paper); **FT Actuaries Share Indices** = several indices based on prices on the London Stock Exchange, which are calculated by and published in the Financial Times; **FT All-Share Index** = index based on the market price of about 700 companies listed on the London Stock Exchange (it includes the companies on the FT 500 Index, plus shares in financial institutions) (NOTE: also simply called the **All-Share Index**); **FT Industrial Group Share Index** = index based on the market prices of more than 470 leading industrial companies; **FT-Stock Exchange 100 Share Index (FT-SE 100** *or* **Footsie)** = index based on the prices of one hundred leading companies (this is the main London index); **FT 500 Share Index** = index based on the market prices of 500 leading companies in the manufacturing, retailing and service sectors

financier [faɪˈnænsɪə] *noun* person who organizes deals involving large amounts of money

financing [fɪˈnænsɪŋ] *noun* providing money; *the financing of the project was done by two international banks*; **deficit financing** = planning by a government to borrow money to cover the shortfall between expenditure and income from taxation

finder's fee [ˈfaɪndəz ˈfiː] *noun* fee paid to a person who finds a client for another (as for example, someone who introduces a client to a stockbroking firm)

fine [faɪn] **1** *noun* money paid because of something wrong which has been done; *he was asked to pay a $25,000 fine*; *we had to pay a $10 parking fine* **2** *verb* to punish someone by making him pay money; *to fine someone £2,500 for obtaining money by false pretences* **3** *adjective* very small; **fine rate of discount** = lowest rate of discount on offer **4** *adverb* very thin, very small; **we are cutting our margins very fine** = we are reducing our margins to the smallest possible; **fine-tuning** = making small adjustments to interest rates, the tax bands, the money supply, etc., to improve a nation's economy

finish [ˈfɪnɪʃ] **1** *noun* end of a day's trading on the Stock Exchange; *oil shares rallied at the finish* **2** *verb* to come to an end; *the market finished the day on a stronger note*; **finished goods** = goods which have been through the production processes and are now ready for sale

fire sale [ˈfaɪə ˈseɪl] *noun* (i) sale of fire-damaged goods; (ii) sale of anything at a very low price

firm [fɜːm] **1** *noun* business or partnership; *he is a partner in a law firm*; *a manufacturing firm*; *an important publishing firm* **2** *adjective* **(a)** which cannot be changed; *to make a firm offer for something*; *to place a firm offer for two aircraft*; *they are quoting a firm price of £1.22 per unit*; **firm order** = (i) confirmed order, which the purchaser cannot withdraw; (ii) order to a broker to sell or buy on a certain date; **firm sale** = sale which does not allow the purchaser to return the goods **(b)** not dropping in price, and possibly going to rise; *sterling was firmer on the foreign exchange markets*; *shares remained firm* **3** *verb* (*Stock Exchange*) to remain at a price and gradually go up; *the shares firmed at £1.50*

QUOTE some profit-taking was noted, but underlying sentiment remained firm
Financial Times

COMMENT: strictly speaking, a 'firm' is a partnership or other trading organization which is not a limited company. In practice, it is better to use the term for unincorporated businesses such as 'a firm of accountants' or 'a firm of stockbrokers', rather than for 'a major aircraft construction firm' which is likely to be a plc

firmness [ˈfɜːmnəs] *noun* being steady at a price, being likely to rise; *the firmness of the pound*

QUOTE Toronto failed to mirror New York's firmness as a drop in gold shares on a falling bullion price left the market closing on a mixed note
Financial Times

firm up [ˈfɜːm ˈʌp] *verb* to finalize, to agree final details; *we expect to firm up the deal at the next trade fair*

first [fɜːst] *noun* person or thing which is there at the beginning, or which is earlier than others; *our company was one of the first to sell to the European market*; **first half** *or* **first half-year** = six-month period from January to the end of June; **first mortgage** = mortgage taken out on a property, usually when buying the property (the lender has a lien on the property; if the first mortgage is not sufficient, a second mortgage can be taken out, but the second lender will have less security than the first, and will charge more); **first year allowance (FYA)** = allowance which can be claimed on capital expenditure by a business or self-employed person during the year in which the purchase was made (after the first year, the written down allowance (WDA) applies)

first-class [ˈfɜːstˈklɑːs] *adjective & noun* **(a)** top quality; most expensive; *he is a first-class accountant* **(b)** most expensive and comfortable type of travel or hotel; *to travel first-class*; *first-class travel provides the best service*; *a first-class ticket to stay in first-class hotels*; **first-class mail** = (i) *GB* most expensive mail service, designed to be faster; (ii) *US* mail service for letters and postcards; *a first-class letter should get to Scotland in a day*

first in first out (FIFO) [ˈfɜːst ˈɪn ˈfɜːst ˈaʊt] *phrase* (i) accounting policy where it is assumed that stocks in hand were purchased last, and that stocks sold during the period were purchased first; (ii) redundancy policy, where the people who have been working longest are the first to be made redundant; *compare* LIFO

first quarter [ˈfɜːst ˈkwɔːtə] *noun* three-month period from January to the end of March

fiscal [ˈfɪskəl] *adjective* referring to tax, to government revenues; *the government's fiscal policies*; **fiscal agent** = bank which acts as an agent for a eurobond issue; **fiscal drag** = negative effect on an individual's work of higher personal taxation; **fiscal measures** = tax changes made by a government to improve the working of the economy; **fiscal year** = (i) twelve-month period on which taxes are calculated (in the UK, April 6th to April 5th); (ii) any twelve-month period used by a company as the period for calculating its taxes

QUOTE the standard measure of fiscal policy - the public sector borrowing requirement - is kept misleadingly low
Economist

fittings [ˈfɪtɪŋz] *plural noun* items in a property which are sold with it but are not permanently fixed (such as carpets or shelves); *see also* FIXTURES

fix [fɪks] *verb* **(a)** to arrange, to agree; *to fix a budget*; *to fix a meeting for 3 p.m.*; *the date has still to be fixed*; *the price of gold was fixed at $300*; *the mortgage rate has been fixed at 8%* **(b)** to mend; *the technicians are coming to fix the telephone switchboard*; *can you fix the photocopier?*

QUOTE coupons are fixed by reference to interest rates at the time a gilt is first issued
Investors Chronicle

fixation [fɪks'eɪʃn] *noun* (i) stating of a price on an options market; (ii) fixing of a price, such as the price of gold

fixed [fɪkst] *adjective* permanent, which cannot be removed; **fixed assets** = property, machinery which a company owns and uses, but which the company does not buy or sell as part of its regular trade, including the company's investments in shares of other companies; **tangible fixed assets** = assets which are visible, such as land, buildings, machinery, equipment; **intangible fixed assets** = assets which are not visible, such as patents, licences, copyrights, development costs (see FRS10); **fixed budget** = budget which refers to a certain level of business (i.e., a certain sales turnover, which produces a certain level of profit); **fixed capital** = capital in the form of fixed assets; **fixed charge** = charge linked to certain specified assets, such as a mortgage on a property; **fixed costs** = costs incurred in making a product which do not change with the amount of product made (such as rent or insurance); **fixed deduction** = deduction agreed by the Inland Revenue and a group of employees, such as a trade union, which covers general expenditure on clothes or tools used in the course of employment; **fixed deposit** = deposit which pays a stated interest over a set period; **fixed exchange rate** = rate of exchange of one currency against another which cannot fluctuate, and can only be changed by devaluation or revaluation; **fixed expenses** *or* **fixed overhead costs** = FIXED COSTS; **fixed income** = income which does not change (as from an annuity); **fixed rate** = rate (such as an exchange rate) which does not change; **fixed rate loan** = loan on which the rate of interest stays the same for the duration of the loan; **fixed scale of charges** = rate of charging which cannot be altered

QUOTE you must offer shippers and importers fixed rates over a reasonable period of time
Lloyd's List

fixed-interest [fɪkst'ɪntrest] *adjective* (investment) which produces an interest which does not vary; **fixed-interest investments** = investments producing an interest which does not change; **fixed-interest securities** = securities (such as government bonds) which produce an interest which does not change

fixed-price [fɪkst'praɪs] *noun* which has a fixed price which cannot be changed; **fixed-price agreement** = agreement where a company provides a service or a product at a price which stays the same for the whole period of the agreement; **fixed-price offer for sale** = offer to purchase shares in a new company for a price which has been fixed at flotation (as opposed to tendering)

fixer ['fɪksə] *noun (informal)* person who has a reputation for arranging business deals (often illegally)

fixing ['fɪksɪŋ] *noun* **(a)** arranging; *fixing of charges*; *fixing of a mortgage rate* **(b)** price fixing = illegal agreement between companies to charge the same price for competing products **(c)** regular meeting to set a price; **gold fixing** = system where the world price for gold is set twice a day in US dollars on the London Gold Exchange and in Paris and Zurich

fixture ['fɪkstʃə] *noun* item in a property which is permanently attached to it (such as a sink or lavatory) and which passes to a new owner with the property itself; **fixtures and fittings (f. & f.)** = objects in a property which are sold with the property, both those which cannot be removed and those which can (a category of fixed assets)

flat [flæt] **1** *adjective* **(a)** (market prices) which do not fall or rise because of low demand; *the market was flat today* **(b)** fixed, not changing; **flat rate** = charge which always stays the same; *we pay a flat rate for electricity each quarter*; *he is paid a flat rate of £2 per thousand*; **flat yield** = interest rate as a percentage of the price paid for fixed-interest stock **2** *noun* set of rooms for one family in a building with other sets of similar rooms; **company flat** = flat owned by a company and used by members of staff from time to time (NOTE: American English is **apartment**)

QUOTE the government revised its earlier reports for July and August. Originally reported as flat in July and declining by 0.2% in August, industrial production is now seen to have risen by 0.2% and 0.1% respectively in those months
Sunday Times

flexed budget ['flekst 'bʌdʒɪt] *see* FLEXIBLE BUDGET

flexibility [fleksə'bɪləti] *noun* being easily changed; *there is no flexibility in the company's pricing policy*

flexible ['fleksəbl] *adjective* which can be altered or changed; *flexible prices*; *flexible pricing policy*; **flexible budget** *or* **flexed budget** = budget which changes in response to changes in sales turnover or output; **flexible disk** = FLOPPY DISK; **flexible working hours** = system where workers can start or stop work at different hours of the morning or evening provided that they work a certain number of hours per day or week; *we work flexible hours*

flight of capital ['flaɪt əv 'kæpɪtəl] *noun* rapid movement of capital out of one country because of lack of confidence in that country's economic future; **flight to quality** = tendency of investors to buy safe blue-chip securities when the economic outlook is uncertain

float [fləʊt] **1** *noun* **(a)** cash taken from a central supply and used for running expenses; *the sales reps have a float of £100 each*; **cash float** *or* **till float** = cash put into the cash box at the beginning of the day to allow change to be given to customers; *we start the day with a £20 float in the cash desk* **(b)** selling shares or securities of a public company on the Stock Exchange; *the float of the new company was a complete failure* **(c)** allowing a currency to settle at its own exchange rates, without any government intervention; **dirty float** *or* **managed float** = floating a currency, where the government intervenes to regulate the exchange rate; **clean float** = floating a currency freely on the international markets, without any interference from the government **2** *verb* **(a) to float a company** = to arrange the sale of shares or securities of a company on the Stock Exchange; **to float a loan** = to raise a loan on the financial market by asking banks and companies to subscribe to it **(b)** to let a currency find its own exchange rate on the international markets and not be fixed; *the government has let sterling float*; *the government has decided to float the pound*

floater ['fləʊtə] *noun US* loan with a variable interest rate

floating ['fləʊtɪŋ] **1** *noun* **(a) floating of a company** = selling shares or securities of a company on the Stock Exchange, thus raising new finance and, usually, increasing the number of owners of the business **(b) the floating of the pound** = letting the pound find its own exchange rate on the international market **2** *adjective* which is not fixed; *floating exchange rates*; *the floating pound*; **floating asset** = circulating asset, an asset which it is assumed will be consumed during the company's normal trading cycle and will be replaced by the same type of asset; **floating charge** = charge linked to any or all of the company's assets of a certain type, but not to

any specific item; **floating debenture** = debenture secured on all the company's assets which runs until the company is wound up, when the debenture becomes fixed; **floating rate** = (i) rate of interest on a loan which is not fixed, but can change with the current bank interest rates; (ii) exchange rate for a currency which can vary according to market demand, and is not fixed by the government; **floating-rate notes (FRNs)** = eurocurrency loans arranged by a bank which are not at a fixed rate of interest (they mature in 5-7 years); **floating point notation** = notation in which a fractional number is represented with a point after the first digit and a power, so that any number can be stored in a standard from; *the fixed number 56.47 in floating-point arithmetic would be 0.5647 and a power of 2*

floor [flɔ:] *noun* **(a)** part of the room on which you walk; **floor space** = area of floor in an office, shop or warehouse; *we have 3,500 square metres of floor space to let*; **the factory floor** = main works of a factory; **on the shop floor** = in the works, in the factory, or among the ordinary workers; *the feeling on the shop floor is that the manager does not know his job* **(b)** all rooms on one level in a building; *the shoe department is on the first floor*; *her office is on the 26th floor* **(c) dealing floor** *or* **trading floor** = (i) area of a broking house where dealing in securities is carried out by phone, using monitors to display current prices and stock exchange transactions; (ii) part of a stock exchange where dealers trade in securities (NOTE: American English for this is also **pit**) *US* **floor broker** = stockbroker who is a member of a brokerage house; *US* **floor trader** = independent trader on a stock exchange, who buys and sells on his own account **(d)** bottom level of something (such as the lowest exchange rate which a government will accept for its currency or the lower limit imposed on an interest rate; the opposite is the 'ceiling' or 'cap'); **to establish a floor at an auction** = to fix the bottom price below which the seller will not sell; **floor price** = lowest price, price which cannot go any lower

flop [flɒp] **1** *noun* failure, not being a success; *the new model was a flop* **2** *verb* to fail, not to be a success; *the flotation of the new company flopped badly* (NOTE: **flopping - flopped**)

floppy disk *or* **floppy** ['flɒpi 'dɪsk *or* 'flɒpi] *noun* secondary storage device in the form of a flat circular flexible disk onto which data can be stored in a magnetic form (a floppy disk cannot store as much data as a hard disk, but is easily removed, and is protected by a flexible paper or plastic sleeve)

florin ['flɒrɪn] *noun* another name for the Dutch guilder (NOTE: the abbreviation for the guilder is **fl**)

flotation [fləʊ'teɪʃən] *noun* **the flotation of a new company** = starting a new public company by selling shares in it

flow [fləʊ] **1** *noun* **(a)** movement; *the flow of capital into a country*; *the flow of investments out of Japan* **(b) cash flow** = cash which comes into a company from sales and goes out in purchases or overhead expenditure; **discounted cash flow (DCF)** = calculation of the forecast return on capital investment by discounting future cash flows from the investment, usually at a rate equivalent to the company's minimum required rate of return; **the company is suffering from cash flow problems** = cash income is not coming in fast enough to pay for the expenditure going out; *see also* FUNDS FLOW **(c) flow chart** *or* **flow diagram** = chart which shows the arrangement of work processes in a series **2** *verb* to move smoothly; *production is now flowing normally after the strike*

fluctuate ['flʌktjʊeɪt] *verb* to move up and down; *prices fluctuate between £1.10 and £1.25*; *the pound fluctuated all day on the foreign exchange markets*

fluctuating ['flʌktjʊeɪtɪŋ] *adjective* moving up and down; *fluctuating dollar prices*

fluctuation [flʌktjʊ'eɪʃən] *noun* up and down movement; *the fluctuations of the franc*; *the fluctuations of the exchange rate*

FOB *or* **f.o.b.** ['efəʊ'biː] = FREE ON BOARD

folio ['fəʊlɪəʊ] **1** *noun* **(a)** page with a number, especially two facing pages in an account book which have the same number **(b)** reference letter or number written in the column next to the entries in a ledger showing the other page to which an entry refers **2** *verb* to put a number on a page

foot [fʊt] *verb* **(a) to foot the bill** = to pay the bill; *the director footed the bill for the department's Christmas party* **(b)** *US* **to foot up an account** = to add up a column of figures

FOR ['efəʊ'ɑː] = FREE ON RAIL

force [fɔːs] **1** *noun* **(a)** strength; **to be in force** = to be operating or working; *the rules have been in force since 1946*; **to come into force** = to start to operate or to work; *the new regulations will come into force on January 1st* **(b)** group of people; **labour force** *or* **workforce** = all the workers in a company or in an area; *the management has made an increased offer to the labour force*; *we are opening a new factory in the Far East because of the cheap local labour force*; **sales force** = group of salesmen **(c) force majeure** = something which happens which is out of the control of the parties who have signed a contract (such as strike, war, storm) **2** *verb* to make someone do something; *competition has forced the company to lower its prices*

forced [fɔːst] *adjective* **forced sale** = sale which takes place because a court orders it or because it is the only way to avoid a financial crisis

forecast ['fɔːkɑːst] **1** *noun* description or calculation of what will probably happen in the future; *the chairman did not believe the sales director's forecast of higher turnover*; *we based our calculations on the forecast turnover*; **cash flow forecast** = forecast of when cash will be received or paid out; **dividend forecast** = forecast of the amount of an expected dividend; **forecast dividend** = dividend which a company expects to pay at the end of the current year (NOTE: also called **prospective dividend**); **sales forecast** = calculation of future sales **2** *verb* to calculate, to say what will probably happen in the future; *he is forecasting sales of £2m*; *economists have forecast a fall in the exchange rate* (NOTE: **forecasting - forecast**)

forecaster ['fɔːkɑːstə] *noun* person who says what he thinks will happen in the future; **economic forecaster** = person who says how he thinks a country's economy will perform in the future

forecasting ['fɔːkɑːstɪŋ] *noun* calculating what will probably happen in the future; **manpower forecasting** = calculating how many workers will be needed in the future, and how many will actually be available

foreclose [fɔː'kləʊz] *verb* to force the sale of a property because the owner cannot repay money which he has borrowed using the property as security; *the bank foreclosed on the farm*

foreclosure [fɔːˈkləʊʒə] *noun* act of foreclosing

foreign [ˈfɒrən] *adjective* not belonging to one's own country; *foreign cars have flooded our market*; *we are increasing our trade with foreign countries*; **foreign banks** = banks from other countries which have branches in a country; **foreign branch** = branch of a company in another country (the accounts of foreign branches may cause problems because of varying exchange rates); **foreign company** = company which is not resident in the UK; **foreign currency** = money of another country; **foreign earnings** = earning received from employment outside the UK; **foreign emoluments** = salary paid to a person who is not domiciled in the UK by a company which itself is not resident in the UK; **foreign entity** = person or incorporated company outside the UK; **foreign income** = income which comes from outside the UK; **foreign investments** = money invested in other countries; **foreign money order** = money order in a foreign currency which is payable to someone living in a foreign country; **foreign taxation** = taxation in another country (often subject to double taxation agreements); **foreign trade** = trade with other countries

QUOTE a sharp setback in foreign trade accounted for most of the winter slowdown
Fortune

QUOTE the treasury says it needs the cash to rebuild its foreign reserves which have fallen from $19 billion when the government took office to $7 billion in August
Economist

foreign exchange (forex) [ˈfɒrən ɪksˈtʃeɪndʒ] *noun* **(a)** exchanging the money of one country for that of another; **foreign exchange broker** *or* **dealer** = person who deals on the foreign exchange market; **foreign exchange dealing** = buying and selling foreign currencies; **the foreign exchange markets** = market where people buy and sell foreign currencies **(b)** foreign currencies; **foreign exchange reserves** = foreign money held by a government to support its own currency and pay its debts; **foreign exchange transfer** = sending of money from one country to another

QUOTE the dollar recovered a little lost ground on the foreign exchanges yesterday
Financial Times

forensic [fəˈrenzɪk] *adjective* referring to the courts or to the law in general; **forensic partner** = partner in an accountancy firm who deals with litigation

foreseeable loss [fɔːˈsiːəbl ˈlɒs] *noun* loss which is expected to occur during a long-term contract (see SSAP9)

forex *or* **Forex** [ˈfɔːreks] = FOREIGN EXCHANGE

QUOTE the amount of reserves sold by the authorities were not sufficient to move the $200 billion Forex market permanently
Duns Business Month

forfaiting [ˈfɔːfɪtɪŋ] *noun* providing finance for exporters, where an agent (the forfaiter) accepts a bill of exchange from an overseas customer; he buys the bill at a discount, and collects the payments from the customer in due course

forfeit [ˈfɔːfɪt] **1** *noun* taking something away as a punishment; **forfeit clause** = clause in a contract which says that goods or a deposit will be taken away if the contract is not obeyed; **the goods were declared forfeit** = the court said that the goods had to be taken away from their owner **2** *verb* to have something taken away as a punishment; **to forfeit a deposit** = to lose a deposit which was left for an item because you have decided not to buy that item; **to forfeit a patent** = to lose a patent because payments have not been made; **to forfeit shares** = to be forced to give back shares if money called up is not paid on time

forfeiture [ˈfɔːfɪtʃə] *noun* act of forfeiting a property

forint [ˈfɒrɪnt] currency used in Hungary

form [fɔːm] **1** *noun* **(a) form of words** = words correctly laid out for a legal document; **receipt in due form** = correctly written receipt; **form letter** = letter which is sent without any change to several correspondents (such as a letter chasing payment) **(b) account form** = balance sheet laid out in horizontal form (it is the opposite of 'report' or 'vertical' form) **(c)** official printed paper with blank spaces which have to be filled in with information; *you have to fill in form A20*; *customs declaration form*; *a pad of order forms*; **application form** = form which has to be filled in to apply for something; **claim form** = form which has to be filled in when making an insurance claim **2** *verb* to start, or to organize; *the brothers have formed a new company*

forma ['fɔːmə] *see* PRO FORMA

formal ['fɔːməl] *adjective* clearly and legally written; *to make a formal application*; *to send a formal order*; **formal documents** = documents giving full details of a takeover bid (the official timetable for the bid starts with the sending out of the formal documents)

formality [fɔːˈmæləti] *noun* something which has to be done to obey the law; **customs formalities** = declaration of goods by the shipper and examination of them by the customs

formation *or* **forming** [fɔːˈmeɪʃən *or* 'fɔːmɪŋ] *noun* act of organizing; *the formation of a new company*

formula investing ['fɔːmjələ ɪnˈvestɪŋ] *noun* method of investing according to a set plan (such as purchasing a certain value of shares each month, or only investing in shares of companies with a capitalization of less than £25m)

fortune ['fɔːtʃuːn] *noun* large amount of money; *he made a fortune from investing in oil shares*; *she left her fortune to her three children*

forward ['fɔːwəd] **1** *adjective* in advance, to be paid at a later date; **forward buying** *or* **buying forward** = buying shares, currency or commodities at a price fixed today for delivery at a later date; **forward contract** = one-off agreement to buy foreign currency, shares or commodities for delivery at a later date at a certain price; **forward cover** = arrangement to cover the risks on a forward contract by buying foreign currency forward; **forward delivery** = delivery at some date in the future which has been agreed between the buyer and seller; **forward margin** = difference between the current (or spot) price and the forward price; **forward market** = market for purchasing foreign currency, oil or commodities for delivery at a later date (these are one-off deals, as opposed to futures contracts which are continuous); **forward (exchange) rate** = rate for purchase of foreign currency at a fixed price for delivery at a later date; *what are the forward rates for the pound?*; **forward sales** = sales for delivery at a later date **2** *adverb* **(a) to date a cheque forward** = to put a later date than the present one on a cheque; **carriage forward** *or* **freight forward** = deal where the customer pays for transporting the goods; **charges forward** = charges which will be paid by the customer **(b) to buy forward** = to buy foreign currency before you need it, in order to be certain of the exchange rate; **to sell forward** =

to sell foreign currency for delivery at a later date **(c) balance brought forward** = balance on an account from the previous period taken to be the starting point of the period; **balance carried forward** = amount entered in an account to balance the debit and credit entries which is taken forward to start the next period

forwardation [fɔːwəˈdeɪʃn] *noun (on commodity markets)* cash price which is lower than the forward price (NOTE: also called **contango**; the opposite is **backwardation**)

foul [faʊl] *adjective* **foul bill of lading** = bill of lading which says that the goods were in bad condition when received by the shipper

founder ['faʊndə] *noun* person who starts a company; **founder's shares** = special shares issued to the person who starts a company

401(K) Plan *noun US* plan by which an employee can take part of his or her salary and invest it in securities, through a fund provided by the employer (no tax is paid on the investment until it is withdrawn by the employee)

fourth quarter ['fɔːθ 'kwɔːtə] *noun* period of three months from October to the end of the year

fraction ['frækʃən] *noun* very small amount; *only a fraction of the new share issue was subscribed*; **cash fraction** = small amount of cash paid to a shareholder to make up the full amount of part of a share which has been allocated in a share split

fractional ['frækʃənl] *adjective* very small; **fractional certificate** = certificate for part of a share

franc [fræŋk] *noun* **(a)** currency used with the euro in France and Belgium, also in Switzerland and many other countries; *French francs or Belgian francs or Swiss francs*; *it costs twenty-five Swiss francs* **(b)** specifically, the currency used with the euro in France; **franc account** = bank account in francs; **franc zone** = currency area consisting of the former French colonies in Africa or in the Pacific (it uses the CFA franc or the CFP franc as unit of currency) (NOTE: in English usually written **Fr** before the figure: **Fr2,500** (say: 'two thousand, five hundred francs'). Currencies of different countries can be shown by the initial letters of the countries: **FFr** (French francs); **SwFr** (Swiss francs); **BFr** (Belgian francs))

franchise ['fræntʃaɪz] **1** *noun* licence to trade using a brand name and paying a royalty for it; *he has bought a printing franchise or a hot dog franchise* **2** *verb* to sell licences for people to trade using a brand name and paying a royalty; *his sandwich bar was so successful that he decided to franchise it*

franchisee [fræntʃaɪˈziː] *noun* person who is licensed to run a franchise

franchiser [ˈfræntʃaɪzə] *noun* person who licenses a franchise

franchising [ˈfræntʃaɪzɪŋ] *noun* act of selling a licence to trade as a franchise; *he runs his sandwich chain as a franchising operation*

franchisor [ˈfræntʃaɪzə] *noun* = FRANCHISER

franco [ˈfræŋkəʊ] *adverb* free

franked [fræŋkt] *adjective* on which tax has already been paid; **franked investment income** = dividends plus tax credits received by a company from another company in which it owns shares (the tax credits can be set off against advance corporation tax if it makes its own dividend payments); **franked payment** = dividends plus tax credits paid by a company to shareholders

fraud [frɔːd] *noun* making money by making people believe something which is not true; *he got possession of the property by fraud*; *he was accused of frauds relating to foreign currency*; **to obtain money by fraud** = to obtain money by saying or doing something to cheat someone; **Serious Fraud Office (SFO)** = government department in charge of investigating major fraud in companies

fraudulent [ˈfrɔːdjʊlənt] *adjective* not honest, aiming to cheat people; *a fraudulent transaction*; **fraudulent trading** = carrying on the business of a company, knowing that the company is insolvent

fraudulently [ˈfrɔːdjʊləntli] *adverb* not honestly; *goods obtained fraudulently*

FRED = FINANCIAL REPORTING EXPOSURE DRAFT

free [friː] **1** *adjective & adverb* **(a)** not costing any money; *to be given a free ticket to the exhibition*; *the price includes free delivery*; *goods are delivered free*; *catalogue sent free on request*; **carriage free** = the customer does not pay for the shipping; **free gift** = present given by a shop to a customer

who buys a certain amount of goods; **free issue** *or* **scrip issue** *or* **capitalization issue** = issue of shares, where a company transfers money from reserves to share capital and issues free extra shares to the shareholders (the value of the company remains the same, and the total market value of shareholders' shares remains the same, the market price being adjusted to account for the new shares); **free sample** = sample given free to advertise a product; **free trial** = testing of a machine with no payment involved; *to send a piece of equipment for two weeks' free trial*; **free of charge** = with no payment to be made; **free on board (FOB)** = (i) price including all the seller's costs until the goods are on the ship for transportation; (ii) price including all the seller's costs until the goods are delivered to a certain place; **free on rail (FOR)** = price including all the seller's costs until the goods are delivered to the train for shipment **(b)** with no restrictions; **free capital** = amount of a company's capital in shares which are available for trading on a Stock Exchange; **free collective bargaining** = negotiations over wage increases and working conditions between the management and the trade unions; **free competition** = being free to compete without government interference; **free currency** = currency which is allowed by the government to be bought and sold without restriction; **free enterprise** = system of business with no interference from the government; **free market** = market which has no restrictions placed on it (either by a government or by a company); **free market economy** = system where the government does not interfere in business activity in any way; **free port** *or* **free trade zone** = port or area where there are no customs duties; **free reserves** = part of a bank's reserves which are above the statutory level and so can be used for various purposes as the bank wishes; **free trade** = system where goods can go from one country to another without any restrictions; **free trade area** = group of countries practising free trade; **free trader** = person who is in favour of free trade; **free of tax** *or* **tax-free** = with no tax having to be paid; **interest-free credit** *or* **loan** = credit or loan where no interest is paid by the borrower; **free of duty** *or* **duty-free** = with no duty to be paid; *to import wine free of duty* *or* *duty-free* **2** *verb* to make something available or easy; *the government's decision has freed millions of pounds for investment*

QUOTE American business as a whole is increasingly free from heavy dependence on manufacturing
Sunday Times

QUOTE can free trade be reconciled
with a strong dollar resulting from
floating exchange rates?
Duns Business Month

QUOTE free traders hold that the
strong dollar is the primary cause of
the nation's trade problems
Duns Business Month

freehold property ['fri:həʊld 'prɒpəti]
noun property which the owner holds for ever
and on which he pays no rent (NOTE: also
called **fee simple)**

freeholder ['fri:həʊldə] *noun* person who
owns a freehold property

**freestanding addition voluntary
contributions (FSAVCs)** *noun* extra
contributions to a pension scheme which is
not part of an employer's scheme

freeze [fri:z] **1** *noun* **credit freeze** = period
when lending by banks is restricted by the
government; **wages and prices freeze** *or* **a
freeze on wages and prices** = period when
wages and prices are not allowed to be
increased **2** *verb* to keep money, costs, etc., at
their present level and not allow them to rise;
*we have frozen expenditure at last year's
level*; *to freeze wages and prices*; *to freeze
credits*; *to freeze company dividends* (NOTE:
freezing - froze - has frozen)

freight [freɪt] *noun* **(a)** cost of transporting
goods by air, sea or land; *at an auction, the
buyer pays the freight*; **freight charges** *or*
freight rates = money charged for
transporting goods; *freight charges have
gone up sharply this year*; **freight costs** =
money paid to transport goods; **freight
forward** = deal where the customer pays for
transporting the goods **(b) air freight** =
shipping of goods in an aircraft; *to send a
shipment by air freight*; **air freight charges**
or **rates** = money charged for sending goods
by air

freightage ['freɪtɪdʒ] *noun* cost of
transporting goods

friendly society ['frendli sə'saɪəti] *noun*
group of people who pay regular
subscriptions which are used to help members
of the group when they are ill or in financial
difficulties

COMMENT: friendly societies were formerly
regulated by the UK Friendly Societies
Commission which had the power to
authorize friendly societies, both
incorporated and registered, to carry on

insurance business and non-insurance
business. These powers are now with the FSA

fringe benefits ['frɪndʒ 'benɪfɪts] *plural
noun* extra items given by a company to
workers in addition to a salary (such as
company cars, private health insurance)

FRN = FLOATING RATE NOTE

front [frʌnt] *noun* **(a)** business or person
used to hide an illegal trade; *his restaurant is
a front for a drugs organization* **(b) money
up front** *US* **front money** = payment in
advance; *they are asking for £10,000 up
front before they will consider the deal*; *he
had to put money up front before he could
clinch the deal*

front-end ['frʌntend] *adjective* referring to
the start of an investment or insurance;
front-end fee = initial loading of the
management charges into the first premium
paid for an insurance; **front-end loaded** =
where most of the management charges are
incurred in the first year of the investment or
insurance, and are not spread out over the
whole period

frozen ['frəʊzn] *adjective* not allowed to be
changed or used; **frozen account** = bank
account where the money cannot be changed
or used because of a court order; **frozen
assets** = a company's assets which by law
cannot be sold because someone has a claim
against them; **frozen credits** = credit in an
account which cannot be moved; **his assets
have been frozen by the court** = the court
does not allow him to sell his assets; *see also*
FREEZE

FRRP = FINANCIAL REPORTING
REVIEW PANEL

FRS = FINANCIAL REPORTING
STANDARD

FRSSE ['frʌzi] FINANCIAL REPORTING
STANDARD FOR SMALLER ENTITIES

frustrate [frʌs'treɪt] *verb* to prevent
something (especially the terms of a contract)
being fulfilled

frustration [frʌs'treɪʃn] *noun* situation
where the terms of a contract cannot possibly
be fulfilled (as where the contract requires the
use of something which then is destroyed)

FSAVCs = FREESTANDING
ADDITIONAL VOLUNTARY
CONTRIBUTIONS

FT ['ef'ti:] = FINANCIAL TIMES

full [fʊl] *adjective* **(a)** complete, including everything; **we are working at full capacity** = we are doing as much work as possible; **full production costs** = all the costs of manufacturing a product, including both fixed and variable costs; **full cover** = insurance cover against all risks; **in full discharge of a debt** = paying a debt completely; **full price** = price with no discount; **full-price ticket** = ticket which is sold at full price, with no reductions; **full-service banking** = banking offering a whole range of services (including mortgages, loans, pensions, etc.) **(b) in full** = completely; *he accepted all our conditions in full*; *full refund* or *refund paid in full*; **full payment** or **payment in full** = paying all money owed

QUOTE a tax-free lump sum can be taken partly in lieu of a full pension
Investors Chronicle

full-scale ['fʊl'skeɪl] *adjective* complete, very thorough; *the MD ordered a full-scale review of credit terms*

QUOTE the administration launched a full-scale investigation into maintenance procedures
Fortune

fully ['fʊli] *adverb* completely; **the offer was fully subscribed** = all the shares on offer were applied for, so the underwriters to the issue were not forced to buy any; **the shares are fully valued** = the market price of the shares is high enough, possibly too high; **fully-diluted earnings per share** = earnings per share calculated over the whole number of shares including convertible shares (i.e. shares which may in future be converted to ordinary shares); **fully paid-up capital** or **fully-paid shares** = shares where the full face value has been paid

QUOTE issued and fully paid capital is $100 million
Hongkong Standard

function ['fʌŋkʃən] **1** *noun* **(a)** mathematical formula, where a result is dependent upon several other numbers **(b)** sequence of computer program instructions in a main program that perform a certain task **(c)** special feature available in a computer word-processing program; *the word-processor had a spelling-checker function but no built-in text-editing function* **(d)** group of people or department in a company which can be identified by the work that it does (such as

finance, marketing, production, etc.) **2** *verb* to operate or perform correctly; *the new system has not functioned properly since it was installed*

functional ['fʌŋkʃənəl] *adjective* **(a)** which refers to the way something works; **functional diagram** = drawing of the internal workings and processes of a machine or piece of software; **functional specification** = specification which defines the results which a program is expected to produce; **functional unit** = hardware or software that works as it should **(b)** which relates to the various functions within a company; **functional budget** = budget relating to a particular function (such as marketing cost budget, personnel budget, etc.)

function key or **programmable function key** *noun* key or switch that has been assigned a particular task or sequence of instructions; *tags can be allocated to function keys*

COMMENT: function keys often form a separate group of keys on the keyboard, and have specific functions attached to them. They may be labelled F1, F2, etc.

fund [fʌnd] **1** *noun* **(a)** money set aside for a special purpose; **contingency fund** = money set aside in case it is needed urgently; **pension fund** = money which provides pensions for retired members of staff; **sinking fund** = fund built up out of amounts of money put aside regularly to meet a future need, such as the repayment of a loan; **the International Monetary Fund (IMF)** = (part of the United Nations) a bank which helps member states in financial difficulties, gives financial advice to members and encourages world trade **(b)** money invested in an investment trust as part of a unit trust or given to a financial adviser to invest on behalf of a client; **managed fund** or **fund of funds** = unit trust fund which is invested in specialist funds within the group and can be switched from one specialized investment area to another; **fund management** = dealing with the investment of sums of money on behalf of clients **2** *verb* to provide money for a purpose; **to fund a company** = to provide money for a company to operate; *the company does not have enough resources to fund its expansion programme*

QUOTE the S&L funded all borrowers' development costs, including accrued interest
Barrons

fundamental [fʌndə'mentəl] **1** *adjective* basic, most important; **fundamental**

assumptions = the basic assumptions on which the preparation of accounts depends: that the company is a going concern, that the principles on which the accounts are prepared do not change from year to year, that revenues and costs are accrued (i.e., they are written into the accounts when they occur, not when they are received or paid); **fundamental issues** = matters relating to a company's profits or assets; **fundamental research** *or* **analysis** = examination of the basic factors which affect a market; **fundamental uncertainty** = a type of inherent uncertainty that gives rise to a particular form of modified auditors' report; an inherent uncertainty is fundamental when the magnitude of its potential impact is so great that, without clear disclosure of the nature and implications of the uncertainty, the view given by the financial statements would be seriously misleading **2** *noun* **fundamentals** = the basic realities of a stock market or of a company (such as its assets, profitability, dividends, etc.)

> QUOTE with long-term fundamentals reasonably sound, the question for brokers is when does cheap become cheap enough?
> Far Eastern Economic Review

funded ['fʌndɪd] *adjective* backed by long-term loans; *long-term funded capital*; *GB* **funded debt** = (i) short-term debt which has been converted into long-term by selling long-term securities such as debentures to raise the money; (ii) part of the British National Debt which pays interest, but where there is no date for repayment of the principal; **funded scheme** = pension scheme where money is invested in securities to create a fund from which the pension is later paid

funding ['fʌndɪŋ] *noun* **(a)** providing money for spending; *the bank is providing the funding for the new product launch* **(b)** changing a short-term debt into a long-term loan; *the capital expenditure programme requires long-term funding*

funds [fʌndz] *plural noun* **(a)** money which is available for spending; *the company has no funds to pay for the research programme*; **the company called for extra funds** = the company asked for more money; **to run out of funds** = to come to the end of the money available; **public funds** = government money available for expenditure; *the cost was paid for out of public funds*; **shareholders' funds** = the capital and reserves of a company; **conversion of funds** = using money which does not belong to you for a purpose for which it is not supposed to be used; **to convert funds**

to another purpose = to use money for a wrong purpose; **to convert funds to one's own use** = to use someone else's money for yourself; **funds flow method of budgeting** = preparing a budget of funds flow, as opposed to a budget of expenditure; **funds flow statement** = statement which shows the amount of funds (cash and working capital) which have come into a business during the last financial period, the sources of these funds, and the use made of the funds (see FRS1, formerly SSAP10); **budgeted funds flow statement** = plan of anticipated incoming funds and the use to which they will be put; **source and application of funds** *or* **source and use of funds statement** = formerly, an audited statement in SSAP10 of where a company's funds come from and how they have been used during the accounting period (now replaced by cash flow statement, see FRS1) **(b)** *GB* **the Funds** = government stocks and securities; *see also* FED FUNDS

> QUOTE small innovative companies have been hampered for lack of funds
> Sunday Times

> QUOTE the company was set up with funds totalling NorKr 145m
> Lloyd's List

fungibility [fʌndʒɪ'bɪləti] *noun* being exchangeable for something similar

fungible ['fʌndʒəbl] *adjective* (security) which can be exchanged for another of the same type

furnished holiday lettings ['fɜːnɪʃt 'hɒlɪdeɪ 'letɪŋz] *noun* furnished house or flat let furnished during the holiday period (it must be available for at least 240 days in the year)

future ['fjuːtʃə] **1** *adjective* referring to time to come *or* to something which has not yet happened; **future delivery** = delivery at a later date; **future value (FV)** = the value to which a sum of money will increase if invested for a certain period of time at a certain rate of interest **2** *noun* time which has not yet happened; *try to be more careful in future*; *in future all reports must be sent to Australia by air*

futures ['fjuːtʃəz] *plural noun* trading in shares, currency or commodities for delivery at a later date (they refer to fixed amounts, and are always available for sale at various dates); *coffee rose 5% on the commodity futures market yesterday*; **futures contract** = contract for the purchase of commodities for delivery at a date in the future; **financial futures contract** = contract for the purchase of gilt-edged securities for delivery at a date in the future; **futures exchange** = commodity market which only deals in futures; **financial futures market** = market in gilt-edged securities for delivery at a date in the future

COMMENT: a futures contract is a contract to purchase; if an investor is bullish, he will buy a contract, but if he feels the market will go down, he will sell one

FV = FUTURE VALUE

FYA = FIRST YEAR ALLOWANCE

Gg

GAAP = GENERALLY ACCEPTED ACCOUNTING PRINCIPLES

gain [geɪn] **1** *noun* **(a)** increase, becoming larger; **gain in profitability** = becoming more profitable **(b)** increase in profit, price or value; *oil shares showed gains on the Stock Exchange*; *property shares put on gains of 10%-15%*; **capital gain** = money made by selling fixed assets, shares, or certain other types of property, such as works of art, leases, etc.; **capital gains tax** = tax paid on capital gains; **short-term gains** = increase in price made over a short period **(c)** money made by a company which is not from the company's normal trading; **abnormal gain** = gain which is more than the normal or expected gain **2** *verb* **(a)** to get or to obtain; **to gain control of a business** = to buy more than 50% of the shares so that you can direct the business **(b)** to rise in value; *the dollar gained six points on the foreign exchange markets*

galloping inflation [ˈgæləpɪŋ ɪnˈfleɪʃən] *noun* very rapid inflation which is almost impossible to reduce

GAO *US* = GENERAL ACCOUNTING OFFICE

gap [gæp] *noun* empty space; **gap in the market** = opportunity to make a product which is needed but which no one has sold before; *to look for or to find a gap in the market*; *this computer has filled a real gap in the market*; **dollar gap** = situation where the supply of dollars is not enough to satisfy the demand for them from overseas buyers; **trade gap** = difference in value between a country's imports and exports; **gap analysis** = attempting to find ways of improving the company's existing performance to reduce the gap between current results and the long-term objectives of the company; **gap financing** = arranging extra loans (such as a bridging loan) to cover a purchase not covered by an existing loan

garnishee [gɑːnɪˈʃiː] *noun* person who owes money to a creditor and is ordered by a court to pay that money to a creditor of the creditor, and not to the creditor himself

garnishee order *US* **garnishment** [gɑːnɪˈʃiː ˈɔːdə *or* ˈgɑːnɪʃmənt] *noun* court order, making a garnishee pay money not to the debtor, but to a third party

gazump [gəˈzʌmp] *verb* **he was gazumped** = his agreement to buy the house was cancelled because someone offered more money

gazumping [gəˈzʌmpɪŋ] *noun* offering more money for a house than another buyer has done, so as to be sure of buying it

GDP [ˈdʒiːdiːˈpiː] = GROSS DOMESTIC PRODUCT

gear [gɪə] *verb* **(a)** to link to, to connect with; *bank interest rates are geared to American interest rates*; **salary geared to the cost of living** = salary which rises as the cost of living increases **(b) a company which is highly geared** *or* **a highly-geared company** = company which has a high proportion of its funds from borrowings as opposed to its equity capital

gearing *noun* **(a)** ratio of capital borrowed by a company at a fixed rate of interest to the company's total capital; **equity gearing** = ratio between a company's borrowings and its equity (ordinary share capital and reserves); **income gearing** = ratio of the interest a company pays on its borrowing shown as a percentage of its pretax profits (before the interest is paid) **(b)** borrowing money at fixed interest which is then used to produce more money than the interest paid

general ['dʒenərəl] *adjective* **(a)** ordinary, not special; **general expenses** = all kinds of minor expenses, the money spent on the day-to-day costs of running a business; **general fund** = unit trust with investments in a variety of stocks; **general insurance** = insurance covering theft, loss, damage, etc. (not life insurance); **general ledger** = book which records a company's financial transactions in general (but not those recorded in the cash book, the sales ledger or the purchase ledger); **general lien** = lien against the personal possessions of a borrower (but not against his house or land); **general manager** = manager in charge of the administration of a company; **general office** = main administrative office of a company; **general partner** = partner in a partnership whose responsibility for its debts is not limited **(b)** dealing with everything or with everybody; **general audit** = examining all the books and accounts of a company; **general average** = sharing of the cost of lost goods by all parties to an insurance (where some goods have been lost in an attempt to save the rest of the cargo); **general meeting** = meeting of all the shareholders of a company; **Annual General Meeting (AGM)** = meeting of all the shareholders, when the company's financial situation is discussed with the directors; **Extraordinary General Meeting (EGM)** = special meeting of shareholders to discuss an important matter; **general undertaking** = undertaking signed by the directors of a company applying for a Stock Exchange listing, promising to work within the regulations of the Stock Exchange

General Accounting Office (GAO) ['dʒenərəl ə'kauntɪŋ 'ɒfɪs] *US* government department (headed by the Comptroller General) whose duty is to examine the accounts of all government departments (NOTE: the British equivalent is the **Audit Commission**)

General Commissioner ['dʒenərəl kə'mɪʃənə] official appointed to decide on appeals from taxpayers against their tax assessments

Generally Accepted Accounting Principles (GAAP) ['dʒenərəli ək'septɪd ə'kauntɪŋ 'prɪnsɪplz] rules applied to accounting practice in the UK, USA and elsewhere

COMMENT: in the US, people always refer to GAAP. In the UK people may refer instead to Accounting Standards, meaning the UK SSAPs and FRSs, but will also refer to GAAP or more often UK GAAP. When referring to another jurisdiction the appropriate prefix is used,

such as US GAAP, International GAAP, Hong Kong GAAP

gensaki ['gensæki] *noun* Japanese bond market, dealing in bonds issued with agreements to repurchase at less than twelve months' notice

Gesellschaft [gə'zelʃɑːft] *German for* company; **Gesellschaft mit beschränkter Haftung (GmbH)** = private limited company

get back ['get 'bæk] *verb* to receive something which you had before; *he got his initial investment back in two months*

get out ['get 'aut] *verb* **(a)** to produce something (on time); *the accounts department got out the draft accounts in time for the meeting* **(b)** to sell an investment; *he didn't like the annual report, so he got out before the company collapsed*

get out of ['get 'aut əv] *verb* to stop trading in (a product or a market); *the company is getting out of computers; we got out of the South American market*

get round ['get 'raund] *verb* to avoid; *we tried to get round the embargo by shipping from Canada*

gift [gɪft] *noun* thing given to someone; **gift coupon** *or* **gift token** *or* **gift voucher** = card, bought in a store, which is given as a present and which must be exchanged in that store for goods; *we gave her a gift token for her birthday*; **gift aid** = payment above a certain limit made to a registered charity (the charity reclaims the basic rate tax which you have paid on the gift); **gift inter vivos** = present given to another living person; *US* **gift tax** = tax on gifts (the tax is levied on people who have given gifts, only gifts between husband and wife are exempt); **free gift** = present given by a shop to a customer who buys a certain amount of goods

gilt-edged ['gɪlt'edʒd] *adjective* investment which is very safe; **gilt-edged stock** *or* **gilt-edged securities** = (i) *GB* government bonds; (ii) *US* any safe corporate bond with a AAA rating

gilts [gɪlts] *plural noun* UK government bonds, bearing a fixed interest and a guaranteed capital repayment, which are traded on the Stock Exchange

GmbH *German* = GESELLSCHAFT MIT BESCHRANKTER HAFTUNG

GNP ['dʒiːen'piː] = GROSS NATIONAL PRODUCT

go back on ['gəʊ 'bæk ɒn] *verb* not to do what has been promised; *two months later they went back on the agreement*

go-go fund ['gəʊgəʊ 'fʌnd] *noun* fund which aims to give very high returns because it is invested in speculative stocks

going ['gəʊɪŋ] *adjective* **(a)** active or busy; **to sell a business as a going concern** = to sell a business as an actively trading company; **it is a going concern** = the company is working (and making a profit); **accounts prepared on a going-concern basis** = accounts prepared on the assumption that the company will continue to trade (the going concern concept is one of the fundamental accounting concepts in FRS 18); *US* **going concern value** = the value of a corporation as it continues trading (in effect, the goodwill) as opposed to its breakup value **(b)** **the going price** = the usual or current price, the price which is being charged now; *what is the going price for 1975 Volkswagen Beetles?*; **the going rate** = the usual or current rate of payment; *we pay the going rate for typists*; *the going rate for offices is £10 per square metre*

go into ['gəʊ 'ɪntʊ] *verb* **(a)** to go into business = to start in business; *he went into business as a car dealer*; *she went into business in partnership with her son* **(b)** to examine carefully; *the bank wants to go into the details of the inter-company loans*

gold [gəʊld] *noun* **(a)** very valuable yellow metal; *to buy gold*; *to deal in gold*; *gold coins*; **gold bullion** = bars of gold; **gold fixing** = system where the world price for gold is set twice a day in US dollars on the London Gold Exchange and in Paris and Zurich **(b)** a **country's gold reserves** = a country's store of gold kept by a central bank; **the gold standard** = linking of the value of a currency to the value of a quantity of gold; **the pound came off the gold standard** = the pound stopped being linked to the value of gold; **gold point** = amount by which a currency which is linked to gold can vary in price **(c)** **gold shares** *or* **golds** = shares in gold mines

COMMENT: gold is the traditional hedge against investment uncertainties. People buy gold in the form of coins or bars, because they think it will maintain its value when other investments such as government bonds, foreign currency, property, etc. may not be so safe. Gold is relatively portable, and small quantities can be taken from country to country if an emergency occurs. This view, which is prevalent when the political situation is uncertain, has not been borne out in recent years, and gold has not maintained its value for some time

gold card ['gəʊld 'kɑːd] *noun* credit card issued to important customers (i.e., those with a certain level of income), which gives certain privileges, such as a higher spending limit than ordinary credit cards

golden ['gəʊldən] *adjective* made of gold; like gold; **golden hallo** = cash inducement paid to someone to encourage him to change jobs and move to another company; **golden handcuffs** = contractual arrangement to make sure that a valued member of staff stays in his job, by which he is offered special financial advantages if he stays and heavy penalties if he leaves; **golden handshake** = large, usually tax-free, sum of money given to a director who resigns from a company before the end of his service contract; *when the company was taken over, the sales director received a golden handshake of £250,000*; **golden parachute** = special contract for a director of a company, which gives him advantageous financial terms if he has to resign when the company is taken over; **golden share** = share in a privatized company which is retained by the government and carries special privileges (such as the right to veto foreign takeover bids)

goldmine ['gəʊldmaɪn] *noun* mine which produces gold; **that shop is a little goldmine** = that shop is a very profitable business

good [gʊd] *adjective* not bad; **a good buy** = excellent item which has been bought cheaply; **to buy something in good faith** = to buy something thinking it is of good quality, that it has not been stolen or that it is not an imitation

goods [gʊdz] *plural noun* **(a)** **goods and chattels** = moveable personal possessions **(b)** items which can be moved and are for sale; **goods in bond** = imported goods held by the customs until duty is paid; **goods in transit** = goods which have left the sender but which have not arrived at the purchaser's warehouse at the end of his accounting period; **goods received** = goods which have been sent by a seller and received by a purchaser during an accounting period; **goods received note** = internal note within a company which shows the date when goods were received, by whom and in what quantities; **capital goods** = machinery, buildings and raw materials which are used to make other goods; **consumer goods** *or* **consumable goods** = goods bought by the general public and not by businesses; **dry goods** = cloth and clothes; **finished goods** = manufactured goods which are ready to be sold; **household goods** = items which are used in the home; **luxury goods** = expensive items which are not basic necessities; **manufactured goods** = items which are made by machine **(c)** *(in Canada)* **Goods and Services Tax (GST)** = tax on the sale of goods or the provision of services (similar to VAT)

> QUOTE profit margins in the industries most exposed to foreign competition - machinery, transportation equipment and electrical goods
> *Sunday Times*

> QUOTE the minister wants people buying goods ranging from washing machines to houses to demand facts on energy costs
> *Times*

goodwill ['gʊdwɪl] *noun* good reputation of a business, which can be included in a company's intangible asset value (see FRS10 in which purchased goodwill is defined as the difference between the cost of an acquired entity and the aggregate of the fair values of that entity's identifiable assets and liabilities); **negative goodwill** = negative goodwill arises when the aggregate fair values of the identifiable assets and liabilities of the entity exceed the acquisition cost; **positive goodwill** = positive goodwill arises when the acquisition cost exceeds the aggregate fair values of the identifiable assets and liabilities

| COMMENT: positive purchased goodwill should be capitalized and classified as an asset on the balance sheet but internally generated goodwill should not be capitalized

go out ['gəʊ 'aʊt] *verb* **to go out of business** = to stop trading; *the firm went out of business last week*

go private ['gəʊ 'praɪvət] *verb (of a public company)* to become a private company again, by concentrating all its shares in the hands of one or a few shareholders and removing its stock exchange listing

go public ['gəʊ 'pʌblɪk] *verb (of a private company)* to offer its shares to the general public for the first time

govern ['gʌvən] *verb* to rule a country; *the country is governed by a group of military leaders*

governance ['gʌvənəns] *noun* the philosophy of how something should be ruled, whether a country or a company; *see also* CORPORATE GOVERNANCE

government ['gʌvnmənt] *noun* **(a)** organization which administers a country; **central government** = main organization dealing with the affairs of the whole country; **local government** = organizations dealing with the affairs of a small area of the country; **provincial government** *or* **state government** = organization dealing with the affairs of a province or of a state **(b)** coming from the government; referring to the government; *local government finance*; *central government borrowing*; *government intervention or intervention by the government*; *a government ban on investment in the country*; *government regulations state that import duty has to be paid on luxury items*; **government bonds** *or* **government securities** *or* **gilt-edged securities** = bonds or other paper issued by the government on a regular basis as a method of borrowing money for government expenditure; **government grant** = grant of money or assets given by a central government, a local government or a government agency (see SSAP4); **government support** = financial help given by the government; *the computer industry relies on government support*

governmental [gʌvən'mentl] *adjective* referring to a government

government-backed ['gʌvnmənt'bækt] *adjective* backed by the government

government-controlled ['gʌvnməntkən'trəʊld] *adjective* under the direct control of the government; *advertisements cannot be placed in the government-controlled newspapers*

government-regulated ['gʌvnmənt'regjʊleɪtɪd] *adjective* regulated by the government

government-sponsored ['gʌvnmənt'spɒnsəd] *adjective* encouraged by the government and backed by government money; *he is working in a government-sponsored scheme to help small businesses*

governor ['gʌvnə] *noun* **(a)** person in charge of an important institution; **the Governor of the Bank of England** = person (nominated by the British government) who is in charge of the Bank of England (NOTE: the American equivalent is the Chairman of the Federal Reserve Board) **(b)** *US* one of the members of the Federal Reserve Board

grace [greɪs] *noun* favour shown by granting a delay; **grace period** *or* **period of grace** = time given to a debtor to repay a loan; *we decided to give this creditor a period of two weeks' grace*

gradual ['grædʒʊəl] *adjective* slow, step by step; *2000 saw a gradual return to profits*; *his CV describes his gradual rise to the position of company chairman*

gradually ['grædʒʊəli] *adverb* slowly, step by step; *the company has gradually become more profitable*; *she gradually learnt the details of the import-export business*

graduate ['grædʒʊət] *noun* person who has a degree from a university or equivalent educational institution; **graduate entry** = entry of graduates into employment with a company; **graduate training scheme** = training scheme for graduates; **graduate trainee** = person in a graduate training scheme

graduated ['grædʒʊeɪtɪd] *adjective* rising in steps according to quantity; **graduated income tax** = tax which rises in steps (each level of income is taxed at a higher percentage); **graduated pension scheme** = pension scheme which is calculated on the salary of each person in the scheme; **graduated taxation** = tax system where the percentage of tax paid rises as the income rises

grand [grænd] **1** *adjective* important; **grand plan** = major plan; *he explained his grand plan for redeveloping the factory site*; **grand total** = final total made by adding several subtotals **2** *noun informal* one thousand pounds or dollars; *they offered him fifty grand for the information*

grant [grɑːnt] **1** *noun* **government grant** = grant of money or assets given by a central government, a local government or a government agency (see SSAP4); *the laboratory has a government grant to cover the cost of the development programme*; *the government has allocated grants towards the costs of the scheme*; **grant-aided scheme** = scheme which is funded by a government grant; **grant-in-aid** = money given by the central government to local government to help fund a project **2** *verb* to agree to give someone something; *to grant someone a loan* *or* *a subsidy*; *the local authority granted the company an interest-free loan to start up the new factory*

grantor [grɑːnˈtɔː] *noun* person who grants a property to another

graph [grɑːf] *noun* diagram which represents statistical information in the form of a diagram; *to set out the results in a graph*; *to draw a graph showing the rising profitability*; *the sales graph shows a steady rise*; **graph paper** = special paper with many little squares, used for drawing graphs

gratia ['greɪʃə] *see* EX GRATIA

gratis ['grætɪs] *adverb* free, not costing anything; *we got into the exhibition gratis*

gratuity [grəˈtjuːəti] *noun* a tip, money given to someone who has helped you (the person receiving a gratuity must declare it on his or her tax return); *the staff are instructed not to accept gratuities*

greenback ['griːnbæk] *noun US informal* dollar bill

green card ['griːn 'kɑːd] *noun* **(a)** special British insurance certificate to prove that a car is insured for travel abroad **(b)** registration card for a non-US citizen going to live permanently in the USA

green currency ['griːn 'kʌrənsiː] *noun* currency used in the EC for calculating agricultural payments; each country had an exchange rate fixed by the Commission, so there are 'green pounds', 'green francs', 'green Deutschmarks', etc., but these have now been effectively replaced by the euro

green form ['griːn 'fɔːm] *noun* form for giving free or subsidized legal advice to clients who are eligible for Legal Aid; **the green form scheme** = scheme where a solicitor will give advice free of charge or at a subsidized rate, to qualifying people on low incomes if the client has filled in the green form; the scheme provides an initial consultation and the cost is charged to a government agency; the system is open to fraudulent abuse

greenmail ['griːnmeɪl] *noun* making a profit by buying a large number of shares in a company, threatening to take the company over, and then selling the shares back to the company at a higher price

> QUOTE proposes that there should be a limit on greenmail, perhaps permitting payment of a 20% premium on a maximum of 8% of the stock
> Duns Business Month

Green Paper ['griːn 'peɪpə] *noun* report from the British government on proposals for a new law to be discussed in Parliament

green pound ['griːn 'paʊnd] *noun* value of the British pound as used in calculating agricultural prices and subsidies in the EC

green report ['griːn rɪ'pɔːt] *noun* part of a company's annual report dealing with ecological matters

Gresham's Law ['greʃəmz 'lɔː] law that 'bad money will drive out good': where two forms of money with the same denomination exist in the same market, the form with the higher metal value will be driven out of circulation when people hoard it and use the lower-rated form to spend (as when paper money and coins of the same denomination exist in the same market)

grey market ['greɪ 'maːkɪt] *noun* unofficial market run by dealers, where new issues of shares are bought and sold before they officially become available for trading on the Stock Exchange (even before the share allocations are known)

gross [grəʊs] **1** *noun* twelve dozen (144); *he ordered four gross of pens* **2** *adjective* **(a)** total, with no deductions; **gross borrowings** = total of all monies borrowed by a company (such as overdrafts, long-term loans, etc.) but without deducting cash in bank accounts and on deposit; **gross dividend per share** = dividend per share paid before tax is deducted; **gross earnings** = total earnings before tax and other deductions; **gross income** *or* **gross salary** = salary before tax is deducted; **gross income yield** = the yield of an investment before tax is deducted; **gross margin** = (i) percentage difference between the unit manufacturing cost and the received price; (ii) difference between the total interest paid by a borrower and the cost of the loan to the lender; **gross profit** = profit calculated as sales income less the cost of sales; **gross receipts** = total amount of money received before expenses are deducted; **gross sales** = total sales before discounts; **gross turnover** = total turnover including discounts, VAT charged, etc.; **gross yield** = profit from investments before the deduction of tax **(b)**

gross domestic product (GDP) = annual value of goods and services sold inside a country; **gross national product (GNP)** = annual value of goods and services in a country including income from other countries **3** *adverb* with no deductions; *building society accounts can pay interest gross*; *interest on these offshore funds is paid gross* **4** *verb* **(a)** to make a gross profit; *the group grossed £25m last year* **(b) to gross up** = (i) to calculate the percentage rate of a net investment as it would be before tax is deducted; (ii) to calculate gross income by adding income tax paid to net income

> QUOTE news that gross national product increased only 1.3% in the first quarter of the year sent the dollar down on foreign exchange markets
> Fortune

> QUOTE gross wool receipts for the selling season to end June appear likely to top $2 billion
> Australian Financial Review

group [gruːp] **1** *noun* **(a)** several things or people together; *a group of the staff has sent a memo to the chairman complaining about noise in the office* **(b)** several companies linked together in the same organization; *the group chairman* or *the chairman of the group*; *group turnover* or *turnover for the group*; **group accounts** = accounts for a holding company and its subsidiaries, including a consolidated profit-and-loss account and a consolidated balance sheet (see FRS2); **group balance sheet** = consolidated balance sheet (the balance sheets of the holding company and its subsidiary companies grouped together into a single balance sheet as though it were a single company); **group results** = results of a group of companies taken together **2** *verb* **to group together** = to put several items together; *sales from six different agencies are grouped together under the heading 'European sales'*

grow [grəʊ] *verb* to become larger; *the company has grown from a small repair shop to a multinational electronics business*; *turnover is growing at a rate of 15% per annum*; *the computer industry grew fast in the 1980s* (NOTE: **growing - grew - has grown**)

> QUOTE the thrift had grown from $4.7 million in assets in 1980 to $1.5 billion
> Barrons

growth [grəʊθ] *noun* increase in size; **the company is aiming for growth** = is aiming to expand rapidly; **economic growth** = rate at which a country's national income grows; **external growth** = growth by buying other companies, rather than by expanding existing sales or products; **internal growth** = expansion of a company which is based on profits from its existing trading; **a growth area** *or* **a growth market** = an area where sales are increasing rapidly; **a growth industry** = industry which is expanding rapidly; **growth prospects** = potential for growth in a share; **growth rate** = speed at which something grows; **growth share** *or* **growth stock** = share which people think is likely to rise in value

QUOTE a general price freeze succeeded in slowing the growth in consumer prices

Financial Times

QUOTE growth in demand is still coming from the private rather than the public sector

Lloyd's List

QUOTE population growth in the south-west is again reflected by the level of rental values

Lloyd's List

GST = GOODS AND SERVICES TAX (the Canadian equivalent of VAT)

QUOTE because the GST is applied only to fees for brokerage and appraisal services, the new tax does not appreciably increase the price of a resale home

Toronto Globe & Mail

guarantee [gærən'tiː] **1** *noun* **(a)** legal document which promises that goods purchased will work properly or that an item is of good quality; *certificate of guarantee* or *guarantee certificate; the guarantee lasts for two years; it is sold with a twelve-month guarantee;* **the car is still under guarantee** = is still covered by the maker's guarantee **(b)** written promise that someone will pay another person's debts if the latter is unable to pay them; **company limited by guarantee** = company where each member stated in the memorandum of association how much money he will contribute to the company if it becomes insolvent (as opposed to a company limited by shares); **to go guarantee for someone** = to act as security for someone's debts **(c)** thing given as a security; *to leave share certificates as a guarantee* **2** *verb* to give a promise that something will happen; **to guarantee a debt** = to promise that you will pay a debt made by someone else; **to guarantee an associate company** = to promise that an associate company will pay its debts; **to guarantee a bill of exchange** = to promise that the bill will be paid; **the product is guaranteed for twelve months** = the manufacturer says that the product will work well for twelve months, and will mend it free of charge if it breaks down; **guaranteed wage** = wage which a company promises will not fall below a certain figure

guarantor [gærən'tɔː] *noun* person who promises to pay someone's debts; *he stood guarantor for his brother*

guaranty ['gærənti:] *US* = GUARANTEE

Hh

hacker ['hækə] *noun* person who breaks into a computer system for criminal purposes

half [hɑːf] **1** *noun* one of two parts into which something is divided; *the first half of the agreement is acceptable*; **the first half** *or* **the second half of the year** = the periods from January 1st to June 30th or from July 1st to December 31st; **we share the profits half and half** = we share the profits equally (NOTE: plural is **halves**) **2** *adjective* divided into two parts; **half a per cent** *or* **a half per cent** = 0.5%; **his commission on the deal is twelve and a half per cent** = 12.5%; **half a dozen** *or* **a half-dozen** = six; **to sell goods off at half price** = at 50% of the price for which they were sold before; **a half-price sale** = sale of all goods at half the price; **half-commission man** = dealer who introduces new clients to a stockbroker, and takes half the broker's commission as his fee

half-dollar ['hɑːf'dɒlə] *noun US* fifty cents

half-life ['hɑːf'laɪf] *noun* number of years needed to repay half the capital borrowed on mortgage

half-year ['hɑːf'jɜː] *noun* six months of an accounting period; **first half-year** *or* **second half-year** = first six months or second six months of a company's accounting year; **to announce the results for the half-year to June 30th** *or* **the first half-year's results** = results for the period January 1st to June 30th; *we look forward to improvements in the second half-year*

> QUOTE economists believe the economy is picking up this quarter and will do better in the second half of the year
>
> Sunday Times

half-yearly ['hɑːf'jɜːli] **1** *adjective* happening every six months; referring to a period of six months; *half-yearly accounts*; *half-yearly payment*; *half-yearly statement*; *a half-yearly meeting* **2** *adverb* every six months; *we pay the account half-yearly*

hallo [hə'ləʊ] *interjection* **golden hallo** = cash inducement paid to someone to encourage him to change jobs and move to another company

hammer ['hæmə] **1** *noun* **auctioneer's hammer** = wooden hammer used by an auctioneer to hit his desk, showing that an item has been sold; **to go under the hammer** = to be sold by auction; **all the stock went under the hammer** = all the stock was sold by auction **2** *verb* to hit hard; **to hammer the competition** = to attack and defeat the competition; **to hammer prices** = to reduce prices sharply

hammered ['hæməd] *adjective (on the London Stock Exchange)*; **they were hammered** = the firm was removed from the Stock Exchange because it had failed

hammering ['hæmərɪŋ] *noun* **(a)** beating; **the company took a hammering in Europe** = the company had large losses in Europe, or lost parts of its European markets; **we gave them a hammering** = we beat them commercially **(b)** *(on the London Stock Exchange)* announcement of the removal of a member firm because it failed **(c)** *US* massive selling of stock on a stock market

> QUOTE one of Britain's largest independent stockbrokers was hammered by the Stock Exchange yesterday, putting it out of business for good. The hammering leaves all clients of the firm in the dark about the value of their investments and the future of uncompleted financing deals
>
> Guardian

hand [hænd] *noun* **(a) to shake hands** = to hold someone's hand when meeting to show you are pleased to meet him or to show that an agreement has been reached; *the two negotiating teams shook hands and sat down at the conference table*; **to shake hands on a deal** = to shake hands to show that a deal has been agreed **(b) by hand** = using the hands, not a machine; **to send a letter by hand** = to ask someone to carry and deliver a letter personally, not sending it through the post **(c) in hand** = kept in reserve; **balance in hand** *or* **cash in hand** = cash held to pay small debts and running costs; *we have £10,000 in hand*

(NOTE: American English is **on hand**); **work in hand** = work which is in progress but not finished **(d) goods left on hand** = unsold goods left with the retailer or manufacturer; *they were left with half the stock on their hands* **(e) to hand** = here, present; **I have the invoice to hand** = I have the invoice in front of me **(f) show of hands** = vote where people show how they vote by raising their hands; *the motion was carried on a show of hands* **(g) to change hands** = to be sold to a new owner; *the shop changed hands for £100,000* **(h) note of hand** = document where someone promises to pay money at a stated time without conditions; **in witness whereof, I set my hand** = I sign as a witness

handcuffs ['hændkʌfs] *noun* metal rings attached to a person's wrists to prevent him from escaping; **golden handcuffs** = contractual arrangement to make sure that a valued member of staff stays in his job, by which he is offered special financial advantages if he stays and heavy penalties if he leaves

handshake ['hænʃeɪk] *noun* **golden handshake** = large, usually tax-free, sum of money given to a director who resigns from a company before the end of his service contract; *when the company was taken over, the sales director received a golden handshake of £250,000*

hard [hɑːd] *adjective* **(a)** strong, not weak; **to take a hard line in negotiations** = to refuse to accept any proposal from the other side; **hard market** = market which is strong and not likely to fall **(b)** solid; **hard cash** = money in notes and coins which is ready at hand; *he paid out £100 in hard cash for the chair*; **hard copy** = printout of a text which is on a computer, printed copy of a document which is on microfilm; *he made the presentation with diagrams and ten pages of hard copy*; **hard disk** = computer disk which has a sealed case and can store large quantities of information **(c) hard currency** = currency of a country which has a strong economy and which can be changed into other currencies easily; *exports which could earn hard currency are important for the country's economy*; *these goods must be paid for in hard currency*; *a hard currency deal* **(d) hard bargain** = bargain with difficult terms; **to drive a hard bargain** = to be a difficult negotiator; **to strike a hard bargain** = to agree a deal where the terms are favourable to you; **after weeks of hard bargaining** = after weeks of difficult discussions

QUOTE hard disks help computers function more speedily and allow them to store more information
Australian Financial Review

QUOTE few of the paper millionaires sold out and transformed themselves into hard cash millionaires
Investors Chronicle

harden ['hɑːdn] *verb* **prices are hardening** = are settling at a higher price

hardening ['hɑːdnɪŋ] *noun (of a market)* slowly moving upwards; *(of prices)* becoming settled at a higher level

hardness ['hɑːdnəs] *noun* **hardness of the market** = situation where a market is strong, and is not likely to fall

hardware ['hɑːdweə] *noun* physical units, components, integrated circuits, disks and mechanisms that make up a computer and its peripherals

harmless ['hɑːmləs] *see* HOLD HARMLESS LETTER

haven ['heɪvn] *noun* safe place; **tax haven** = country where taxes are low which encourages companies to set up their main offices there

head [hed] **1** *noun* **(a)** most important person; **head of department** *or* **department head** = person in charge of a department **(b)** most important, main; **head clerk**; **head porter**; **head salesman**; **head waiter**; **head buyer** = most important buyer in a company or department store; **head office** = main office, where the board of directors works and meets; *US* **head teller** = main teller in a bank (the UK equivalent is 'chief cashier') **(c) per head** = for each person; *representatives cost on average £25,000 per head per annum*; **head and shoulders** = term used by chartists to refer to a market rise where a gradual rise in prices is followed by a gradual fall **(d) heads of agreement** = draft agreement with not all the details complete **2** *verb* to be first; *the two largest oil companies head the list of stock market results*

heading ['hedɪŋ] *noun* words at the top of a piece of text; *items are listed under several headings*; *look at the figure under the heading 'Costs 85-86'*

headlease ['hedliːs] *noun* lease from a freehold owner to a lessee

headline inflation ['hedlaɪn ɪn'fleɪʃn] *noun* British inflation figure which includes all items (such as mortgage interest and local taxes, which are not included in the inflation figures for other countries)

QUOTE the UK economy is at the uncomfortable stage in the cycle where two years of tight money are having the desired effect on demand: output is falling and unemployment is rising, but headline inflation and earnings are showing no sign of decelerating
Sunday Times

headquarters **(HQ)** [hed'kwɔːtəz] *plural noun* main office, where the board of directors meets and works; *the company's headquarters is in New York*; *divisional headquarters* = main office of a division of a company; **to reduce headquarters staff** = to have fewer people working in the main office

health [helθ] *noun* **(a)** physical and mental condition; *GB* **Health and Safety at Work Act** = Act of Parliament which rules how the health of workers should be protected by the companies they work for; **health insurance** = insurance which pays the cost of treatment for illness, especially when travelling abroad; **a private health scheme** = insurance which will pay for the cost of treatment in a private hospital, not a state one **(b) to give a company a clean bill of health** = to report that a company is trading profitably; **health warning** = notice printed on advertisements for investments, stating that the value of investments can fall as well as rise (this is a legal requirement in the UK)

QUOTE the main US banks have been forced to pull back from international lending as nervousness continues about their financial health
Financial Times

healthy ['helθi] *adjective* being fit and well, not ill; **a healthy balance sheet** = balance sheet which shows high asset values compared to liabilities; **the company made some very healthy profits** *or* **a very healthy profit** = made a large profit

heavily ['hevəli] *adverb* **he is heavily in debt** = he has many debts; **they are heavily into property** = they have large investments in property; **the company has had to borrow heavily to repay its debts** = the company has had to borrow large sums of money; **the issue was heavily stagged** = large numbers of stags applied for the issue of new shares

QUOTE the steel company had spent heavily on new equipment
Fortune

heavy ['hevi] *adjective* **(a)** large, in large quantities; *a programme of heavy investment overseas*; *he had heavy losses on the Stock Exchange*; *the company is a heavy user of steel or a heavy consumer of electricity*; *the government imposed a heavy tax on luxury goods*; **heavy costs** *or* **heavy expenditure** = spending large sums of money; **heavy market** = stock market where prices are falling; **heavy share price** = price (on the London Stock Exchange) which is over £10.00 per share, and so discourages the small investor (if the company wants to encourage more people to buy its shares, it may take steps to reduce the share price by splitting or issuing bonus shares) **(b) heavy industry** = industry which makes large products (such as steel bars, ships or railway lines); **heavy machinery** = large machines

QUOTE heavy selling sent many blue chips tumbling in Tokyo yesterday
Financial Times

hedge [hedʒ] **1** *noun* protection against a possible loss (by taking an action which is the opposite of an action taken earlier); **a hedge against inflation** = investment which should increase in value at a faster rate than the rate of inflation; *he bought gold as a hedge against exchange losses* **2** *verb* to protect oneself (against the risk of a loss); **to hedge one's bets** = to make investments in several areas so as to be protected against loss in one of them; **to hedge against exchange rate losses** = to buy foreign currency forward so as to avoid losses caused by adverse movements in exchange rates; **to hedge against inflation** = to buy investments which should increase in value at a faster rate than the rate of inflation

hedge fund ['hedʒ 'fʌnd] *noun* partnership open to a small number of rich investors, which invests in equities, currency futures and derivatives and may produce high returns but carries a very high risk

COMMENT: originally, hedge funds were funds planned to protect equity investments against possible falls on the stock market. Nowadays the term is applied to funds which take speculative positions in financial futures or equities, and are usually highly-geared: in other words, they do nothing to 'hedge' their holdings. They follow various investment strategies: some invest in 'distressed stocks' (companies which are almost bankrupt) in the hope that they might recover; some only invest in certain sectors or regions, such as oil exploration or emerging markets

QUOTE many hedge funds are actually funds of funds, using a wide portfolio of hedge fund managers to produce a balanced exposure for relatively small investors. They are usually referred to as multi-manager funds

Money Observer

QUOTE hedge funds generally have in common an ability to sell short (that is, sell stocks you do not own), and to increase growth prospects - and risk - by borrowing to enhance the fund's assets

Money Observer

hedging ['hedʒɪŋ] *noun* protecting oneself against possible loss by buying investments or foreign currency at a fixed price for delivery later

QUOTE during the 1970s commercial property was regarded by investors as an alternative to equities, with many of the same inflation-hedge qualities

Investors Chronicle

hereafter [hɪər'ɑːftə] *adverb* from this time on

hereby [hɪə'baɪ] *adverb* in this way, by this letter; *we hereby revoke the agreement of January 1st 1999*

hereditament [herɪ'dɪtəmənt] *noun* property, including land and buildings

herewith [hɪə'wɪð] *adverb* together with this letter; *please find the cheque enclosed herewith*

hidden ['hɪdn] *adjective* which cannot be seen; **hidden asset** = asset which is valued much less in the company's accounts than its true market value; **hidden reserves** = reserves which are not easy to identify in the company's balance sheet (reserves which are illegally kept hidden are called 'secret reserves')

high [haɪ] **1** *adjective* **(a)** large, not low; *high overhead costs increase the unit price; high prices put customers off; they are budgeting for a high level of expenditure; investments which bring in a high rate of return; high interest rates are killing small businesses*; **high finance** = lending, investing and borrowing of very large sums of money organized by financiers; **high flier** = (i) person who is very successful or who is likely to get a very important job; (ii) share whose market price is rising rapidly; **high gearing** = situation where a company has a high level of borrowing compared to its share capital and reserves; **high P/E ratio** = a high figure for the ratio between the market price of a share and the earnings per share (this suggests that investors expect earnings to grow); **high sales** = large amount of revenue produced by sales; **high taxation** = taxation which imposes large taxes on incomes and profits; **higher rate of tax** = top rate of income tax (currently in the UK, 40% on taxable income above œ28,000); **highest tax bracket** = the group which pays the most tax; **high volume (of sales)** = large number of items sold; **high yield** = dividend yield which is higher than is normal for the type of company **(b) highest bidder** = person who offers the most money at an auction; *the property was sold to the highest bidder*; **a decision taken at the highest level** = decision taken by the most important person or group **2** *adverb* **prices are running high** = prices are above their usual level **3** *noun* point where prices or sales are very large; *share prices have dropped by 10% since the high of January 2nd*; **highs and lows on the Stock Exchange** = list of shares which have reached a new high or low price in the previous day's trading; **sales volume has reached an all-time high** = has reached the highest point it has ever been at

high-grade bond ['haɪgreɪd 'bɒnd] *noun* bond which has the highest rating (i.e., AAA)

high-income ['haɪ'ɪnkʌm] *adjective* which gives a high-percentage income; **high-income shares**; *a high-income portfolio*

highly ['haɪli] *adverb* very; **highly-geared company** = company which has a high proportion of its funds from borrowings; **highly-paid** = earning a large salary; **highly-placed** = occupying an important post; *the delegation met a highly-placed official in the Trade Ministry*; **highly-priced** = with a large price; **she is highly thought of by the managing director** = the managing director thinks she is very competent

High Street ['haɪ 'striːt] *noun* main shopping street in a British town; *the High Street shops*; *a High Street bookshop*; **the High Street banks** = main British banks which accept deposits from individual customers

QUOTE American interest rates remain exceptionally high in relation to likely inflation rates

Sunday Times

QUOTE faster economic growth would tend to push US interest rates, and therefore the dollar, higher

Australian Financial Review

QUOTE in a leveraged buyout the acquirer raises money by selling high-yielding debentures to private investors

Fortune

hike [haɪk] **1** *noun US* increase; **pay hike** = increase in salary **2** *verb US* to increase; *the union hiked its demand to $3 an hour*

hire ['haɪə] **1** *noun* **(a)** paying money to rent a car, boat or piece of equipment for a time; *car hire*; *truck hire*; **car hire firm** *or* **equipment hire firm** = company which owns cars or equipment and lends them to customers for a payment; **hire car** = car which has been rented; **hire charge** = money paid for goods which are hired **(b)** *US* **for hire contract** = freelance contract; **to work for hire** = to work freelance **2** *verb* **(a)** to hire **staff** = to engage new staff to work for you; **to hire and fire** = to employ new staff and dismiss existing staff frequently; *we have hired the best lawyers to represent us*; *they hired a small company to paint the offices* **(b) to hire a car** *or* **a crane** = to pay money to use a car or a crane for a time; *he hired a truck to move his furniture* **(c) to hire out cars** *or* **equipment** = to lend cars or equipment to customers who pay for their use

COMMENT: an agreement to hire a piece of equipment, etc., involves two parties: the hirer and the owner. The equipment remains the property of the owner while the hirer is using it. Under a hire-purchase agreement, the equipment remains the property of the owner until the hirer has complied with the terms of the agreement (i.e., until he has paid all monies due). According to standard accounting practice, equipment which is used by a company under an operating lease, and which is financed by a third party, such as a finance house, is not an asset in the balance sheet and forms an 'off balance sheet' item (see SSAP21). Otherwise (for items acquired under hire-purchase agreements or finance leases) such equipment is treated as an asset, and is depreciated in the normal way

hire purchase (HP) ['haɪə 'pɜːtʃəs] *noun* system of buying something on credit by paying a sum regularly each month, which includes part debt repayment and part interest (see SSAP21); *to buy a refrigerator on hire purchase*; **to sign a hire-purchase agreement** = to sign a contract to pay for something by instalments; **hire-purchase company** = company which provides money for hire purchase (NOTE: the American equivalent is **installment credit;** 'to buy something on hire purchase' is **to buy something on an installment plan**)

hirer ['haɪərə] *noun* person who hires something

hiring ['haɪərɪŋ] *noun* employing; *hiring of new personnel has been stopped*

historic *or* **historical** [hɪs'tɒrɪk *or* hɪs'tɒrɪkəl] *adjective* which goes back over a period of time; **historic(al) cost** = actual cost of purchasing something which was bought some time ago; **historical cost accounts** *or* **accounts using the historical cost convention** = accounts which are prepared on the basis of historic(al) cost, with assets valued at their original cost of purchase (as opposed to their current or replacement cost); **historical cost concept** *or* **historical cost convention** = basis for treatment of assets in financial statements where they are recorded at their historical cost, without adjustment for inflation or other price variations (NOTE: use 'historical cost convention' not 'historic cost convention'); **historic cost depreciation** = depreciation based on the original cost of the asset; **historical figures** = figures which were current in the past; **historical trading range** = range of prices at which a share has been sold on the stock exchange over a period of time

QUOTE the Federal Reserve Board has eased interest rates in the past year, but they are still at historically high levels

Sunday Times

COMMENT: by tradition, a company's accounts are usually prepared on the historical cost convention - that assets are costed at their purchase price; with inflation, such assets are undervalued, and current cost accounting or replacement cost accounting may be preferred

hive off ['haɪv 'ɒf] *verb* to split off part of a large company to form a smaller subsidiary, giving shares in this to its existing shareholders

hoard [hɔːd] *verb* to buy and store food in case of need; to keep cash instead of investing it

hoarder ['hɔːdə] *noun* person who buys and stores food in case of need; person who holds gold or cash without investing it

hoarding ['hɔːdɪŋ] *noun* **hoarding of supplies** = stocking large quantities of money or food to keep in case of need

QUOTE as a result of hoarding, rice has become scarce with prices shooting up

Business Times (Lagos)

hold [həʊld] **1** *noun* action of keeping something; **these shares are a hold** = these shares should be kept and not sold **2** *verb* **(a)**

to own or to keep; *he holds 10% of the company's shares* **(b)** not to sell; **you should hold these shares - they look likely to rise** = you should keep these shares and not sell them; *the redemption yield is the yield produced by bonds if they are held until redemption date* **(c)** to make something happen; *to hold a meeting* or *a discussion*; *board meetings are held in the boardroom*; *the AGM will be held on March 24th*; *the receiver will hold an auction of the company's assets*; *the accountants held a review of the company's accounting practices* (NOTE: **holding - held**)

QUOTE as of last night, the bank's shareholders no longer hold any rights to the bank's shares
South China Morning Post

hold back ['həʊld 'bæk] *verb* to wait, not to go forward; **investors are holding back until after the Budget** = investors are waiting until they hear the details of the Budget before they decide whether to buy or sell; **he held back from signing the lease until he had checked the details** = he delayed signing the lease until he had checked the details; **payment will be held back until the contract has been signed** = payment will not be made until the contract has been signed

hold down ['həʊld 'daʊn] *verb* **(a)** to keep at a low level; *we are cutting margins to hold our prices down* **(b) to hold down a job** = to manage to do a difficult job

QUOTE real wages have been held down; they have risen at an annual rate of only 1% in the last two years
Sunday Times

holder ['həʊldə] *noun* **(a)** person who owns or keeps something; *holders of government bonds* or *bondholders*; *holder of stock* or *of shares in a company*; *holder of an insurance policy* or *policy holder*; **credit card holder** = person who has a credit card; **debenture holder** = person who holds a debenture for money lent; **holder of record** = person who is registered as the owner of shares in a company; **holder in due course** = person who holds a negotiable instrument, such as a bill of exchange, and holds it in good faith, without knowing of any other claim against it **(b)** thing which keeps something or which protects something; **card holder** or **message holder** = frame which protects a card or a message; **credit card holder** = plastic wallet for keeping credit cards

hold harmless letter ['həʊld 'hɑːmləs 'letə] *noun* letter issued by parties to a business deal to reporting accountants stating

that the accountants will not be held responsible for any losses suffered on the deal

holding ['həʊldɪŋ] *noun* **(a)** group of shares owned; *he has sold all his holdings in the Far East*; *the company has holdings in German manufacturing companies* **(b) cross holdings** = situation where two companies own shares in each other in order to stop either from being taken over; *the two companies have protected themselves from takeover by a system of cross holdings* **(c)** keeping of stocks; **holding cost** or **stockholding cost** = cost of keeping items of stock (including warehousing and handling costs, insurance, losses through deterioration, wastage, theft, etc. and the cost of capital used to acquire the stock measured in terms of the interest lost on the money which was spent on purchasing the stock in the first place or the interest paid on the loans which were needed to finance the purchase of the stock)

holding company ['həʊldɪŋ 'kʌmpnɪ] *noun* (i) company which owns more than 50% of the shares in another company; (ii) company which exists only or mainly to own shares in subsidiary companies (see FRS2); *see also* SUBSIDIARY

hold on ['həʊld 'ɒn] *verb* to wait, not to change; **the company's shareholders should hold on and wait for a better offer** = they should keep their shares and not sell them

hold out for ['həʊld 'aʊt 'fɔː] *verb* to wait and ask for; **you should hold out for a 10% pay rise** = do not agree to a pay rise of less than 10%

QUOTE he will expect a buyer to pay a premium to the current price of 180p, and is likely to hold out for around 200p a share
Sunday Times

hold to ['həʊld 'tuː] *verb* not to allow something to change; **we will try to hold him to the contract** = we will try to stop him going against the contract; **the government hopes to hold wage increases to 5%** = the government hopes that wage increases will not be more than 5%

hold up ['həʊld 'ʌp] *verb* **(a)** to stay at a high level; *share prices have held up well*; *sales held up during the tourist season* **(b)** to delay; *the shipment has been held up at the customs*; *payment will be held up until the contract has been signed*; *the strike will hold up dispatch for some weeks*

hologram ['hɒləgræm] *noun* three-dimensional picture which is used on credit cards as a means of preventing forgery

holograph ['hɒləgrɑːf] *noun* document written by hand; *he left a holograph will*

home ['həʊm] *noun* place where you live; *payments received for travel between your home and place of work are taxable*; **home banking** = system of banking using a computer terminal in one's own home to carry out various financial transactions (such as paying invoices)

honorarium [ɒnə'reərɪəm] *noun* money paid to a professional person, such as an accountant or a lawyer, when he does not ask for a fee (NOTE: plural is **honoraria**)

honorary ['ɒnərəri] *adjective* person who is not paid a salary; *honorary secretary*; *honorary president*

honour ['ɒnə] *verb* to pay something because it is owed and is correct; *to honour a bill*; *the bank refused to honour his cheque*; **to honour a signature** = to pay something because the signature is correct

horizontal form [hɒrɪ'zɒntl 'fɔːm] *noun* one of the two styles of presenting a balance sheet allowed by the Companies Act (NOTE: also called 'account form') *see comment at* BALANCE SHEET

hotchpot ['hɒtʃpɒt] *noun* bringing together into one fund money to be distributed under a will

hour ['aʊə] *noun* **(a)** period of time lasting sixty minutes; **to work a thirty-five hour week** = to work seven hours a day each weekday; **we work an eight-hour day** = we work for eight hours a day, e.g. from 8.30 to 5.30 with one hour for lunch **(b)** sixty minutes of work; *he earns £4 an hour*; *we pay £6 an hour*; **to pay by the hour** = to pay people a fixed amount of money for each hour worked **(c)** **banking hours** = time when a bank is open for its customers; *you cannot get money out of a bank outside banking hours*; **office hours** = time when an office is open; *do not telephone during office hours*; **outside hours** *or* **out of hours** = when the office is not open; *he worked on the accounts out of hours*; **the shares rose in after-hours trading** = in trading after the Stock Exchange had closed

house [haʊs] *noun* **(a)** building in which someone lives; **house property** = private houses, not shops, offices or factories; **house agent** = estate agent who deals in buying or selling houses **(b)** company or firm; *a French business house*; *the largest London finance house*; *he works for a broking house* **or** *a publishing house*; **clearing house** = central office where clearing banks exchange cheques; **discount house** = financial company which specializes in discounting bills; **export house** = company which specializes in the export of goods manufactured by other companies; **house journal** *or* **house magazine** *US* **house organ** = magazine produced for the workers or shareholders in a company to give them news about the company; **house telephone** = internal telephone for calling from one office to another

HP ['eɪtʃ'piː] = HIRE PURCHASE

HQ ['eɪtʃ'kjuː] = HEADQUARTERS

hyper- ['haɪpə] *prefix meaning* very large

hyperinflation ['haɪpərɪn'fleɪʃn] *noun* inflation which is at such a high percentage rate that it is almost impossible to reduce

hypothecation [haɪpɒθɪ'keɪʃn] *noun* **(a)** using property such as securities as collateral for a loan, but not transferring legal ownership to the lender (as opposed to a mortgage, where the lender holds the title to the property) **(b)** allocating specific sources of revenue to specific expenditure (as in the case of earmarking tax on vehicles to road improvement programmes)

Ii

IAPC = INTERNATIONAL AUDITING PRACTICES COMMITTEE

IAS = INTERNATIONAL ACCOUNTING STANDARD

IASC = INTERNATIONAL ACCOUNTING STANDARDS COMMITTEE

ICAEW = INSTITUTE OF CHARTERED ACCOUNTANTS IN ENGLAND AND WALES

ICAI = INSTITUTE OF CHARTERED ACCOUNTANTS IN IRELAND

ICAS = INSTITUTE OF CHARTERED ACCOUNTANTS OF SCOTLAND

ideal [aɪ'dɪəl] *adjective* the best possible; **ideal standard** = standard which a company wishes to reach (but rarely does so)

idle ['aɪdl] *adjective* **(a)** not working; *2,000 employees were made idle by the recession* **(b) idle machinery** *or* **machines lying idle** = machinery not being used; **idle time** = period of time when a machine is available for production but not doing anything **(c) idle capital** = capital not being used productively; **money lying idle** *or* **idle money** = money which is not being used to produce interest, which is not invested in business

IFA = INDEPENDENT FINANCIAL ADVISER, INSTITUTE OF FINANCIAL ACCOUNTANTS

illegal [ɪ'liːgəl] *adjective* not legal, against the law

illegality [ɪlɪ'gælətɪ] *noun* being illegal

illegally [ɪ'liːgəlɪ] *adverb* against the law; *he was accused of illegally importing arms into the country*

illicit [ɪ'lɪsɪt] *adjective* not legal, not permitted; *illicit sale of alcohol*; *trade in illicit alcohol*

illiquid [ɪ'lɪkwɪd] *adjective* (i) (asset) which is not easy to change into cash; (ii) (company) which has no cash

IMF ['aɪem'ef] = INTERNATIONAL MONETARY FUND

immovable [ɪ'muːvəbl] *adjective & noun* which cannot be moved; **immovable property** *or* **immovables** = land, and houses and other buildings on land

impact ['ɪmpækt] *noun* shock, strong effect

QUOTE the strong dollar's deflationary impact on European economies as governments push up interest rates to support their sinking currencies
Duns Business Month

impair [ɪm'peə] *verb* to harm

QUOTE an asset is deemed to have been impaired if its carrying value falls below the higher of its net realizable value or its value in use
Accountancy

impairment [ɪm'peəmənt] *noun* action of harming something, such as an asset

QUOTE indicators of impairment can be that there is direct evidence of impairment, such as direct damage, or a change in the environment in which the asset exists
Accountancy

implement ['ɪmplɪmənt] *verb* to put into action; *to implement an agreement*

implementation [ɪmplɪmen'teɪʃən] *noun* putting into action; *the implementation of new rules*

implied [ɪm'plaɪd] *adjective* which is presumed to exist; **implied trust** = trust which is implied by the intentions and actions of the parties

import 1 ['ɪmpɔːt] *noun* **(a) imports** = goods brought into a country from abroad for sale; *imports from Poland have risen to $1m a year*; **invisible imports** = services (such as banking, tourism, shipping and insurance) which are paid for in foreign currency; **visible**

imports = real goods which are imported **(b) import ban** = forbidding imports; *the government has imposed an import ban on arms*; **import duty** = tax on goods imported into a country; **import levy** = tax on imports, especially in the EC a tax on imports of farm produce from outside the EC; **import licence** *or* **import permit** = government licence or permit which allows goods to be imported; **import quota** = fixed quantity of a particular type of goods which the government allows to be imported; *the government has imposed an import quota on cars*; **import restrictions** = action taken by a government to reduce the level of imports (by imposing quotas, duties, etc.); **import surcharge** = extra duty charged on imported goods, to try to prevent them from being imported and to encourage local manufacture **2** [ɪmˈpɔːt] *verb* to bring goods from abroad into a country for sale; *the company imports television sets from Japan; this car was imported from France; the union organized a boycott of imported cars*

> QUOTE European manufacturers rely heavily on imported raw materials which are mostly priced in dollars
> Duns Business Month

importation [ɪmpɔːˈteɪʃən] *noun* act of importing; *the importation of arms is forbidden*

importer [ɪmˈpɔːtə] *noun* person or company which imports goods; *a cigar importer; the company is a big importer of foreign cars*

import-export [ˈɪmpɔːt ˈekspɔːt] *adjective* dealing with both bringing foreign goods into a country and sending locally made goods abroad; *import-export trade; he is in import-export*

importing [ɪmˈpɔːtɪŋ] **1** *adjective* which imports; *oil-importing countries; an importing company* **2** *noun* act of bringing foreign goods into a country for sale; *the importing of arms into the country is illegal*

impose [ɪmˈpəʊz] *verb* (i) to put a tax or a duty on goods; (ii) to force someone to comply with an instruction; *to impose a tax on bicycles; they tried to impose a ban on smoking; the government imposed a special duty on oil; the customs have imposed a 10% tax increase on luxury items; the unions have asked the government to impose trade barriers on foreign cars*

imposition [ɪmpəˈzɪʃən] *noun* (i) putting a tax on goods or services; (ii) forcing someone to comply

impound [ɪmˈpaʊnd] *verb* to take something away and keep it until a tax or fine is paid; *the customs impounded the whole cargo*

impounding [ɪmˈpaʊndɪŋ] *noun* act of taking something and keeping it until a tax or fine is paid

imprest system [ˈɪmprest ˈsɪstəm] *noun* system of controlling petty cash, where cash is paid out against a written receipt and the receipt is used to get more cash to bring the float to the original level

improve [ɪmˈpruːv] *verb* to make something better; to become better; *they hope to improve the company's cash flow position; we hope the cash flow position will improve or we will have difficulty in paying our bills; export trade has improved sharply during the first quarter* = export trade has increased; **improved offer** = offer which is larger or has better terms than the previous offer

> QUOTE we also invest in companies whose growth and profitability could be improved by a management buyout
> Times

improvement [ɪmˈpruːvmənt] *noun* **(a)** getting better; *there is no improvement in the cash flow situation; sales are showing a sharp improvement over last year* **(b)** thing which is better; **improvement on an offer** = making a better offer

> QUOTE the management says the rate of loss-making has come down and it expects further improvement in the next few years
> Financial Times

improve on [ɪmˈpruːv ˈɒn] *verb* to do better than; *he refused to improve on his previous offer* = he refused to make a better offer

imputation system [ɪmpjuːˈteɪʃn ˈsɪstəm] *noun* system of taxation of dividends, where the company pays advance corporation tax on the dividends it pays to its shareholders, and the shareholders pay no tax on the dividends received, assuming that they pay tax at the standard rate (the ACT is shown as a tax credit which is imputed to the shareholder; the imputation system has been used in the UK, Ireland, Australia, and other countries); *see also* FRANKED

impute [ɪmˈpjuːt] *verb* to pass the responsibility for something to someone else; **imputed value** = value which is given to figures, for which an accurate value cannot be calculated

IMRO ['imrəʊ] = INVESTMENT MANAGEMENT REGULATORY ORGANIZATION

inactive [in'æktiv] *adjective* not active, not busy; **inactive account** = bank account which is not used (i.e., no deposits or withdrawals are made) over a period of time; **inactive market** = stock market with few buyers or sellers

in arrears [in ə'riəz] *see* ARREARS

Inc [iŋk *or* in'kɔːpəreitid] *US* = INCORPORATED

incentive [in'sentiv] *noun* thing which encourages staff to work better; **staff incentives** = pay and better conditions offered to workers to make them work better; **incentive bonus** *or* **incentive payment** = extra pay offered to a worker to make him work better; **incentive scheme** = plan to encourage better work by paying higher commission or bonuses; *incentive schemes are boosting production*

QUOTE some further profit-taking was seen yesterday as investors continued to lack fresh incentives to renew buying activity
Financial Times

inchoate [in'kəʊət] *adjective* (instrument) which is incomplete (i.e., some of the details need to be filled in)

incidental [insi'dentl] **1** *adjective* which is not important, but connected with something else; **incidental expenses** = small amounts of money spent at various times in addition to larger amounts **2** *noun* **incidentals** = incidental expenses

include [in'kluːd] *verb* to count something along with other things; *the charge includes VAT; the total comes to £1,000 including freight; the total is £140 not including insurance and freight; the account covers services up to and including the month of June*

inclusive [in'kluːsiv] *adjective* which counts something in with other things; *inclusive of tax; not inclusive of VAT; inclusive sum* *or* **inclusive charge** = charge which includes all costs

income ['iŋkʌm] *noun* **(a)** money which a person receives as salary or interest or dividends; **annual income** = money received during a calendar year; **disposable income** = income left after tax and national insurance have been deducted; **earned income** = money received as a salary, wages, fees or rental

income; **fixed income** = income which does not change from year to year; **gross income** = income before tax has been deducted; **gross income yield** = the yield of an investment before tax is deducted; **net income** = income left after tax has been deducted; **private income** = income from dividends, interest or rent which is not part of a salary; **personal income** = income received by an individual person; **retained income** = profits which are not paid out to shareholders as dividends; **unearned income** = money received from interest or dividends **(b) lower** *or* **upper income bracket** = groups of people who earn low or high salaries considered for tax purposes; **he comes into the higher income bracket** = he is in a group of people earning high incomes and therefore paying a higher rate of tax; **income shares** = shares in an investment trust which receive income from the investments, but do not benefit from the rise in capital value of the investments (the other form of shares in a split-level investment trust are capital shares, which increase in value as the value of the investments rises, but do not receive any income); **income units** = units in a unit trust, where the investor receives dividends in the form of income (as opposed to accumulation units where the dividend is left to accumulate as new units); **income yield** = actual percentage yield of government stocks, the fixed interest being shown as a percentage of the market price **(c)** (i) money received by an accounting entity from its normal trading (i.e., not including the sale of fixed assets, which produces capital revenue); (ii) profit (i.e. revenue less expenses) earned by an accounting entity from its normal trading (excluding capital gains); **income gearing** = ratio of the interest a company pays on its borrowings shown as a percentage of its pretax profits (before the interest is paid) **(d)** money which an organization receives as gifts or from investments; *the hospital has a large income from gifts* **(e)** *US* **income statement** = a statement of company expenditure and sales which shows whether the company has made a profit or loss (NOTE: the British equivalent is the **profit and loss account**)

QUOTE there is no risk-free way of taking regular income from your money much higher than the rate of inflation
Guardian

income tax ['iŋkʌm 'tæks] *noun* (i) tax on a person's income (both earned and unearned); (ii) *also US* tax on the profits of a corporation; **income tax form** = form to be completed which declares all income to the tax office; **declaration of income** *or* **income tax return** = statement declaring income to the tax office; *see also* PAYE

> QUOTE the company will be paying income tax at the higher rate in 1990
> Citizen (Ottawa)

inconvertible [ɪnkən'vɜːtəbl] *adjective* (currency) which cannot be easily converted into other currencies

incorporate [ɪn'kɔːpəreɪt] *verb* **(a)** to bring something in to form part of a main group; *income from the 2000 acquisition is incorporated into the accounts* **(b)** to form a registered company or other corporate body; *a company incorporated in 1997*; *an incorporated company*; *J. Doe Incorporated* (NOTE: in the USA, **incorporated** is used as part of the name of the corporation, usually shortened to **Inc.**)

incorporation [ɪnkɔːpə'reɪʃən] *noun* act of incorporating a company or other corporate body

> COMMENT: a corporation (a body which is legally separate from its members) is formed in one of three ways: 1) registration under the Companies Act (the normal method for commercial companies); 2) granting of a royal charter; 3) by a special Act of Parliament. A company is incorporated by drawing up a memorandum and articles of association, which are lodged with Companies House. In the UK, a company is either a private limited company (they print Ltd after their name) or a public limited company (they print Plc after their name). A company must be a Plc to obtain a Stock Exchange listing. In the USA, there is no distinction between private and public companies, and all are called 'corporations'; they put Inc. after their name

increase 1 ['ɪŋkriːs] *noun* **(a)** growth, becoming larger; *increase in tax or tax increase*; *increase in price or price increase*; *profits showed a 10% increase or an increase of 10% on last year*; *increase in the cost of living* = rise in the annual cost of living **(b)** higher salary; *increase in pay or pay increase*; *increase in salary or salary increase*; *the government hopes to hold salary increases to 3%*; *he had two increases last year* = his salary went up twice; *cost-of-living increase* = increase in salary to allow it to keep up with higher cost of living; *merit increase* = increase in pay given to a worker whose work is good* **2** [ɪn'kriːs] *verb* **(a)** to grow bigger or higher; *profits have increased faster than the increase in the rate of inflation*; *exports to Africa have increased by more than 25%*; *the price of oil has increased twice in the past*

week; **to increase in price** = to cost more; **to increase in size** *or* **in value** = to become larger or more valuable **(b) the company increased his salary to £40,000** = the company gave him a rise in salary to £40,000

> QUOTE competition is steadily increasing and could affect profit margins as the company tries to retain its market share
> Citizen (Ottawa)

> QUOTE turnover has potential to be increased to over 1 million dollars with energetic management and very little capital
> Australian Financial Review

increment ['ɪŋkrɪmənt] *noun* (i) amount by which something increases; (ii) regular increase in salary; **salary which rises in annual increments of £500** = each year the salary is increased by £500

incremental [ɪŋkrɪ'mentl] *adjective* which rises in stages; **incremental cost** = cost of changing the level of activity (as the cost of making one thousand extra units above the number already planned: this may then include further fixed costs); **incremental costing** = differential costing, a costing method which shows the difference in costs which results from different levels of activity (such as the cost of making one thousand or ten thousand extra units); **incremental increase** = increase in salary according to an agreed annual increment; **incremental scale** = salary scale with regular annual salary increases

incur [ɪn'kɜː] *verb* to make yourself liable to; **to incur the risk of a penalty** = to make it possible that you risk paying a penalty; **to incur debts** *or* **costs** = to do something which means that you owe money or that you will have to pay costs; *the company has incurred heavy costs to implement the expansion programme* = the company has had to pay large sums of money (NOTE: **incurring - incurred**)

> QUOTE the company blames fiercely competitive market conditions in Europe for a £14m operating loss last year, incurred despite a record turnover
> Financial Times

indebted [ɪn'detɪd] *adjective* owing money to someone; *to be indebted to a property company*

indebtedness [ɪn'detɪdnəs] *noun* **state of indebtedness** = being in debt, owing money

indemnification [ɪndemnɪfɪ'keɪʃən] *noun* payment for damage

indemnify [ɪn'demnɪfaɪ] *verb* **(a)** to pay for damage; *to indemnify someone for a loss* **(b)** to protect from legal responsibility or financial loss

indemnity [ɪn'demnəti] *noun* **(a)** compensation paid after a loss; *he had to pay an indemnity of £100*; **letter of indemnity** = letter promising payment as compensation for a loss **(b)** protection from legal responsibility or loss; **form of indemnity** = from signed by an airline passenger who has lost his ticket, which states that if the original ticket is found it will not be used if a replacement ticket is issued

indent 1 ['ɪndent] *noun* order placed for goods required, as by an importer for goods from overseas or by a company employee requesting the purchase of certain items; *he put in an indent for a new stock of soap* **2** [ɪn'dent] *verb* **to indent for something** = to put in an order for something; *the department has indented for a new computer*

indenture [ɪn'dentʃə] *noun US* formal agreement showing the terms of a bond issue

independent [ɪndɪ'pendənt] *adjective* free, not controlled by anyone; **independent company** = company which is not controlled by another company; **independent financial adviser (IFA)** = qualified person, authorized to act by the Personal Investment Authority, who advises private clients on a wide range of financial products (as opposed to a tied financial adviser, who only advises on products from a single company); **independent trader** *or* **independent shop** = shop which is owned by an individual proprietor, not by a chain; **the independents** = shops or companies which do not belong to a large group or chain

index ['ɪndeks] **1** *noun* **(a)** list of items classified into groups or put in alphabetical order; **index card** = small card used for filing; **index letter** *or* **number** = letter or number of an item in an index **(b)** regular statistical report which gives rises and falls in prices, etc., shown as a percentage of the previous figure; **growth index** = index showing how something has grown; **index number** = number which shows the percentage rise of something over a period of time; **cost-of-living index** = way of measuring the cost of living, shown as a percentage increase on the figure for the same period in the previous year; **retail price index** *US* **consumer price index** = index showing how prices of

consumer goods have risen over a period of time, used as a way of measuring inflation and the cost of living; **wholesale price index** = index showing rises and falls of prices of manufactured goods as they leave the factory **(c)** figure based on the current market price of certain shares on a stock exchange, such as the Financial Times-Stock Exchange 100 Index; **index fund** = investment fund consisting of shares in all the companies which are used to calculate a stock exchange index; **index tracker** = fund which tracks (i.e. follows closely) one of the stock market indices, such as the Footsie (NOTE: also called a **tracker fund**); **index tracking** = investment technique whereby a portfolio is maintained in such a way as to match the growth in a stock market index (NOTE: plural is **indexes** or **indices**) **2** *verb* to link a payment to an index; **indexed portfolio** = portfolio of shares in all the companies which form the basis of a stock exchange index

QUOTE the index of industrial production sank 0.2 per cent for the latest month after rising 0.3 per cent in March

Financial Times

QUOTE an analysis of the consumer price index for the first half of 1985 shows that the rate of inflation went down by 12.9 per cent

Business Times (Lagos)

indexation [ɪndek'seɪʃn] *noun* linking of a payment or value to an index; **indexation of pensions** *or* **of wage increases** = linking of pensions or wage increases to the percentage rise in the cost of living

index-linked ['ɪndeks'lɪŋkt] *adjective* which rises automatically by the percentage increase in the cost of living; **index-linked pensions**; *his pension is index-linked*; **index-linked government bonds**

indicate ['ɪndɪkeɪt] *verb* to show; *the latest figures indicate a fall in the inflation rate*; *our sales for 2000 indicate a move from the home market to exports*

indicator ['ɪndɪkeɪtə] *noun* thing which indicates; **government economic indicators** = statistics which show how the country's economy has performed or is going to perform in the short or long term; **lagging indicator** = indicator (such as the gross national product) which shows a change in economic trends later than other indicators; **leading indicator** = indicator (such as manufacturing order books) which shows a change in economic trends earlier than other indicators

QUOTE it reduces this month's growth in the key M3 indicator from about 19% to 12%

Sunday Times

QUOTE we may expect the US leading economic indicators for April to show faster economic growth

Australian Financial Review

QUOTE other indicators, such as high real interest rates, suggest that monetary conditions are extremely tight

Economist

indirect [ɪndaɪ'rekt] *adjective* **(a)** not direct; (cost) which is not directly related to the making of a product; **indirect expenses** *or* **costs** = expenses which are not directly related to the making of a product (such as cleaning, rent, administration); **indirect labour cost** = cost of paying workers which cannot be allocated to a cost centre (such as workers who are not directly involved in making a product, like secretaries in a typing pool, cleaners, etc.); **indirect material** *or* **materials (cost)** = cost of materials which cannot be allocated to the production of a particular product **(b) indirect taxation** = taxes (such as sales tax) which are not deducted from income directly; *the government raises more money by indirect taxation than by direct*

individual [ɪndɪ'vɪdjʊəl] **1** *noun* one single person; *savings plan made to suit the requirements of the private individual* **2** *adjective* single, belonging to one person; *a pension plan designed to meet each person's individual requirements US* **Individual Retirement Account (IRA)** = private pension scheme, into which persons on lower incomes can make contributions (for people not covered by a company pension scheme); **Individual Voluntary Arrangement (IVA)** = legally binding arrangement between a debtor and his creditors by which the debtor offers the creditors the best deal he can afford by realising his assets, and so the expense of bankruptcy proceedings is avoided

COMMENT: set up under the Insolvency Act 1986, an IVA scheme has to be approved by the creditors representing more than 75% of the total debts; it can result in a significantly better deal for creditors than if they opt for making the debtor bankrupt

inducement [ɪn'djuːsmənt] *noun* thing which helps to persuade someone to do something; *they offered him a company car as an inducement to stay*

ineligible [ɪn'elɪdʒɪbl] *adjective* not eligible; **ineligible bills** = bills of exchange which cannot be discounted by a central bank

inflate [ɪn'fleɪt] *verb* **(a)** to inflate prices = to increase prices without any reason; *tourists don't want to pay inflated London prices* **(b) to inflate the economy** = to make the economy more active by increasing the money supply

inflated [ɪn'fleɪtɪd] *adjective* **(a) inflated costs** = costing system used to take account of losses in stock (as when stock is lost when dividing bulk stock into smaller retail quantities, the cost of the smaller quantity includes an element for the amount lost); **inflated prices** = prices which are increased without any reason **(b) inflated currency** = currency which is too high in relation to other currencies

inflation [ɪn'fleɪʃən] *noun* **(a)** situation where prices rise to keep up with increased production costs, with the result that the purchasing power of money falls; **we have 15% inflation** *or* **inflation is running at 15%** = prices are 15% higher than at the same time last year; *to take measures to reduce inflation*; *high interest rates tend to decrease inflation*; **rate of inflation** *or* **inflation rate** = percentage increase in prices over a twelve-month period; **inflation-proof** = (pension, etc.) which is index-linked, so that its value is preserved in times of inflation; **galloping inflation** *or* **runaway inflation** = very rapid inflation which is almost impossible to reduce; **spiralling inflation** = inflation where price rises make workers ask for higher wages which then increase prices again; **a hedge against inflation** = investment which should increase in value more than the increase in the rate of inflation **(b) inflation accounting** = accounting system, where inflation is taken into account when calculating the value of assets and the preparation of accounts; *see also* CURRENT COST ACCOUNTING, CURRENT PURCHASING POWER, REPLACEMENT ACCOUNTING

QUOTE the decision by the government to tighten monetary policy will push the annual inflation rate above the year's previous high

Financial Times

QUOTE when you invest to get a return, you want a 'real' return - above the inflation rate

Investors Chronicle

COMMENT: the inflation rate in the UK is calculated on a series of figures, including prices of consumer items; petrol, gas and electricity; interest rates, etc. This gives the 'underlying' inflation rate which can be compared to that of other countries. The calculation can also include mortgage interest and local taxes which give the 'headline' inflation figure; this is higher than in other countries because of these extra items. Inflation affects businesses, in that as their costs rise, so their profits may fall and it is necessary to take this into account when pricing products

inflationary [ɪnˈfleɪʃnəri] *adjective* which tends to increase inflation; *inflationary trends in the economy*; **the economy is in an inflationary spiral** = in a situation where price rises encourage higher wage demands which in turn make prices rise; **anti-inflationary measures** = measures to reduce inflation

inflow [ˈɪnfləʊ] *noun* flowing in; **inflow of capital into the country** = capital which is coming into a country in order to be invested

QUOTE the dollar is strong because of capital inflows rather than weak because of the trade deficit
Duns Business Month

influx [ˈɪnflʌks] *noun* rushing in; *an influx of foreign currency into the country*; *an influx of cheap labour into the cities* (NOTE: plural is **influxes**; the opposite is **efflux**)

QUOTE the retail sector will also benefit from the expected influx of tourists
Australian Financial Review

information [ɪnfəˈmeɪʃən] *noun* **(a)** knowledge presented to a person in a form which can be understood **(b)** data that has been processed or arranged to provide facts which have a meaning; **information provider (IP)** = company that provides an information source for use in a videotext system or Internet service (such as the company providing weather information or stock market reports); **information retrieval (IR)** = locating quantities of data stored in a database and producing useful information from the data; **information technology (IT)** = technology involved in acquiring, storing, processing and distributing information by electronic means (including radio, television, telephone, computers); **information theory** = formulae and mathematics concerned with data transmission equipment and signals

inherit [ɪnˈherɪt] *verb* to get something from a person who has died; *when her father died she inherited the shop*; *he inherited £10,000 from his grandfather*

inheritance [ɪnˈherɪtəns] *noun* property which is received from a dead person; **inheritance tax** = tax on wealth or property inherited after the death of someone

inheritance per stirpes [ɪnˈherɪtəns pɜːˈstɜːpiːz] *Latin phrase meaning* 'inheritance by branches': the phrase is used in wills where the entitlement is divided among branches of a family rather than among individuals

in-house [ˈɪnˈhaʊs] *adjective* belonging to or carried out inside an organization; *the accounts were prepared in-house* or *by the in-house accountant*; **in-house (credit) card** = store card, a credit card issued by a large department store, which can only be used for purchases in that store

initial [ɪˈnɪʃəl] **1** *adjective* first, starting; **initial capital** = capital which is used to start a business; *he started the business with an initial expenditure* or *initial investment of £500* US **initial public offering (IPO)** = first sale of shares in a corporation to the public; **initial sales** = first sales of a new product; **initial yield** = expected yield on a new unit trust **2** *noun* **initials** = first letters of the words in a name; *what do the initials IMF stand for? the chairman wrote his initials by each alteration in the contract he was signing* **3** *verb* to write your initials on a document to show you have read and approved it; *to initial an amendment to a contract*; *please initial the agreement at the place marked with an X*

QUOTE the founding group has subscribed NKr 14.5m of the initial NKr 30m share capital
Financial Times

QUOTE career prospects are excellent for someone with potential, and initial salary is negotiable around $45,000 per annum
Australian Financial Review

initiate [ɪˈnɪʃɪeɪt] *verb* to start; *to initiate discussions*

initiative [ɪˈnɪʃɪətɪv] *noun* decision to start something; **to take the initiative** = to decide to do something; **to follow up an initiative** = to take action once someone else has decided to do something

inject [ɪnˈdʒekt] *verb* **to inject capital into a business** = to put money into a business

injection [ɪnˈdʒekʃən] *noun* **a capital injection of £100,000** or **an injection of £100,000 capital** = putting £100,000 into an existing business

injunction [ɪn'dʒʌŋkʃən] *noun* court order telling someone not to do something; *he got an injunction preventing the company from selling his car*; *the company applied for an injunction to stop their rivals from marketing a similar product*

inland ['ɪnlənd] *adjective* **(a)** inside a country; **inland postage** = postage for a letter to another part of the country; **inland freight charges** = charges for carrying goods from one part of the country to another **(b)** *GB* **the Inland Revenue** = British government department dealing with taxes (income tax, corporation tax, capital gains tax, inheritance tax, etc.) but not duties, such as Value Added Tax, which is collected by the Customs and Excise (NOTE: the American equivalent is the **Internal Revenue Service (IRS)); Inland Revenue Commissioner** *or* **Commissioner of Inland Revenue (IRC)** = person appointed officially to supervise the collection of taxes, including income tax, capital gains tax and corporation tax, but not Value Added Tax

input ['ɪnpʊt] **1** *noun* **input of information** *or* **computer input** = data fed into a computer; **input device** = device such as a keyboard or bar code reader, which converts actions or information into a form which a computer can understand and transfers the data to the processor **2** *verb* **to input information** = to put data into a computer

inputs ['ɪnpʊts] *noun* purchases by a company on which VAT has been paid; **input tax** = VAT paid on goods or services which a company buys

input/output (I/O) ['ɪnpʊt 'aʊtpʊt] *noun* receiving or transmitting data between a computer and its peripherals, and other points outside the system; **input/output channel** = link between a processor and peripheral allowing data transfer

inside [ɪn'saɪd] **1** *adjective & adverb* in, especially in a company's office or building; *we do all our design work inside*; **inside information** = information which is passed from people working in a company to people outside (and which can be valuable to investors in the company); **inside worker** = worker who works in the office or factory (not in the open air, not a salesman); *US* **inside director** = director who works full-time in a corporation and is an employee **2** *preposition* in; *there was nothing inside the container*; *we have a contact inside our rival's production department who gives us very useful information*

insider [ɪn'saɪdə] *noun* person who works in an organization and therefore knows its secrets; **insider dealing** *or* **insider trading** = illegal buying or selling of shares by staff of a company or other persons who have secret information about the company's plans; **insider information** *see* INSIDE INFORMATION

insolvency [ɪn'sɒlvənsi] *noun* not being able to pay debts when they are due; *he was in a state of insolvency* = he could not pay his debts; **insolvency practitioner** = person or company involved in work concerning insolvency (such as a liquidator or receiver)

insolvent [ɪn'sɒlvənt] *adjective* not able to pay debts when they are due; *he was declared insolvent* = he was officially stated to be insolvent

COMMENT: a company is insolvent when its liabilities are higher than its assets; if this happens it must cease trading

inspect [ɪn'spekt] *verb* to examine in detail; *to inspect a machine* *or* *an installation*; *to inspect the accounts*

inspection [ɪn'spekʃən] *noun* close examination of something; **to issue an inspection order** = to order an official inspection; **VAT inspection** = visit by officials of the Customs and Excise Department to see if a company is correctly reporting its VAT; **inspection stamp** = stamp placed on something to show it has been inspected

inspector [ɪn'spektə] *noun* official who inspects; **inspector of taxes** *or* **tax inspector** = official of the Inland Revenue who examines tax returns and decides how much tax people should pay

inspectorate [ɪn'spektərət] *noun* all inspectors; **the factory inspectorate** = all inspectors of factories

instability [ɪnstə'bɪləti] *noun* being unstable, moving up and down; **period of instability in the money markets** = period when currencies fluctuate rapidly

instalment *US* **installment** [ɪn'stɔːlmənt] *noun* part of a payment which is paid regularly until the total amount is paid; *the first instalment is payable on signature of the agreement*; *the final instalment is now due* = the last of a series of payments should be paid now; **to pay £25 down and monthly instalments of £20** = to pay a first payment of £25 and the rest in payments of £20 each month; **to miss an instalment** = not to pay an instalment at the right time; **instalment sales** *US* **installment sales** *or* **installment buying** = system of buying something by paying a sum regularly each month until the total sum is paid off; *see also* HIRE PURCHASE

institute ['instɪtjuːt] *noun* professional body which represents its members, and which confers the right of membership on those who have passed its examinations, etc.; such as the Institute of Chartered Accountants in England and Wales (ICAEW), the Institute of Chartered Accountants in Ireland (ICAI), or the Institute of Chartered Accountants of Scotland (ICAS) or the Institute of Financial Accountants (IFA)

institution [ɪnstɪ'tjuːʃən] *noun* organization or society set up for a particular purpose; **financial institution** = bank or investment trust or insurance company whose work involves lending or investing large sums of money

institutional [ɪnstɪ'tjuːʃənl] *adjective* referring to a financial institution; **institutional buying** *or* **selling** = buying or selling shares by financial institutions; **institutional investors** = financial institutions which invest money in securities

QUOTE during the 1970s commercial property was regarded by big institutional investors as an alternative to equities
Investors Chronicle

instruction [ɪn'strʌkʃən] *noun* order which tells what should be done; *he gave instructions to his stockbroker to sell the shares immediately*; **to await instructions** = to wait for someone to tell you what to do; **to issue instructions** = to tell everyone what to do; **failing instructions to the contrary** = unless someone tells you to do the opposite

instrument ['ɪnstrəmənt] *noun* **(a)** tool or piece of equipment; *the technician brought instruments to measure the output of electricity* **(b)** legal document; especially, a document referring to a financial transaction; **financial instrument** = document showing that money has been lent or borrowed or passed from one account to another (such as a bill of exchange, certificate of deposit, IOU, etc.); **negotiable instrument** = document (such as a bill of exchange or a cheque) which can be exchanged for cash

insufficient funds [ɪnsə'fɪʃənt 'fʌndz] *noun US* not enough money in a checking

account to pay a check that has been presented

insurable [ɪn'ʃʊərəbl] *adjective* which can be insured; **insurable interest** = the value of the thing insured which is attributed to the person who is taking out the insurance

insurance [ɪn'ʃʊərəns] *noun* **(a)** agreement that in return for regular small payments, a company will pay compensation for loss, damage, injury or death; **to take out an insurance against fire** = to pay a premium, so that if a fire happens, compensation will be paid; **to take out an insurance on the house** = to pay a premium, so that if the house is damaged compensation will be paid; **the damage is covered by the insurance** = the insurance company will pay for the damage; **to pay the insurance on a car** = to pay premiums to insure a car **(b)** **accident insurance** = insurance which will pay if an accident takes place; **car insurance** *or* **motor insurance** = insuring a car, the driver and passengers in case of accident; **comprehensive insurance** = insurance which covers against all risks which are likely to happen; **endowment insurance** = insurance where a sum of money is paid to the insured person on a certain date or to his heir if he dies before that date; **fire insurance** = insurance against damage by fire; **general insurance** = insurance covering theft, loss, damage, etc. (but not life assurance); **house insurance** = insuring a house and its contents against damage; **key man insurance** = insurance to compensate a company for losses following the death of or a major accident to an important executive; **life insurance** = insurance which pays a sum of money when someone dies; **medical insurance** = insurance which pays the cost of medical treatment, especially when travelling abroad; **term insurance** = life insurance which covers a person's life for a fixed period of time; **third-party insurance** = insurance which pays compensation if someone who is not the insured person incurs loss or injury; **whole-life insurance** = insurance where the insured person pays premiums for all his life and the insurance company pays a sum when he dies **(c)** **insurance agent** *or* **insurance broker** = person who arranges insurance for clients; **insurance claim** = asking an insurance company to pay compensation for damage; **insurance company** = company whose business is to receive payments and pay compensation for loss or damage; **insurance contract** = agreement by an insurance company to insure; **insurance cover** = protection guaranteed by an insurance policy; **insurance policy** =

document which shows the conditions of an insurance; **insurance premium** = payment made by the insured person to the insurer **(d)** *GB* **National Insurance** = state insurance, organized by the government, which pays for medical care, hospitals, unemployment benefits, etc.; **National Insurance contributions (NIC)** = money paid by a worker and the company each month to the National Insurance

insure [ɪnˈʃʊə] *verb* to have a contract with a company where, if regular small payments are made, the company will pay compensation for loss, damage, injury or death; *to insure a house against fire*; *to insure someone's life*; *he was insured for £100,000*; *to insure baggage against loss*; *to insure against bad weather*; *to insure against loss of earnings*; **the insured** = the party who will benefit from an insurance; **the life insured** = the person whose life is covered by a life assurance; **the sum insured** = the largest amount of money that an insurer will pay under an insurance

insurer [ɪnˈʃʊərə] *noun* company which insures (NOTE: that for life insurance, British English prefers to use the terms **assurance, assure, assurer)**

intangible [ɪnˈtændʒəbl] *adjective & noun* which cannot be touched; **intangible fixed assets** *or* **intangibles** = assets which are not visible, such as patents, licences, copyrights, development costs (see FRS10)

integer [ˈɪntɪdʒə] *noun* mathematical term to describe a whole number (it may be positive, negative or zero)

integrate [ˈɪntɪɡreɪt] *verb* to link things together to form one whole group

integration [ɪntɪˈɡreɪʃən] *noun* bringing several businesses together under a central control; **horizontal integration** = joining similar companies, or taking over a company in the same line of business as yourself; **vertical integration** = joining business together which deal with different stages in the production or sale of a product

intensive [ɪnˈtensɪv] *adjective* **capital-intensive industry** = industry which needs a large amount of capital investment in plant to make it work; **labour-intensive industry** = industry which needs large numbers of workers, where labour costs are high in relation to turnover

intent [ɪnˈtent] *noun* what is planned; **letter of intent** = letter which states what a company intends to do if something happens

inter- [ˈɪntə] *prefix* between

inter-bank [ˈɪntəbæŋk] *adjective* between banks; **inter-bank deposits** = money which banks deposit with other banks; **inter-bank loan** = loan from one bank to another; **inter-bank market** = market where banks lend to or borrow from each other; **inter-bank rates** = rates of interest charged on inter-bank loans

inter-company [ˈɪntəˈkʌmpəni] *adjective* between companies; **inter-company dealings** *or* **inter-company transactions** = dealings or transactions between two companies in the same group; **inter-company debenture** = debenture held by a company over another company in the same group; **inter-company comparisons** = comparing the results of one company with those of another, normally in the same product area

interest [ˈɪntrəst] *noun* **(a)** payment made by a borrower for the use of money, calculated as a percentage of the capital borrowed; **simple interest** = interest calculated on the capital only, and not added to it; **compound interest** = interest which is added to the capital and then earns interest itself; **accrual of interest** = automatic addition of interest to capital; **accrued interest** = interest which is accumulating and is due for payment at a later date; **back interest** = interest which has not yet been paid; *US* **exact interest** = annual interest calculated on the basis of 365 days (as opposed to ordinary interest, calculated on 360 days); **fixed interest** = interest which is paid at a set rate; **high** *or* **low interest** = interest at a high or low percentage; *US* **ordinary interest** = annual interest calculated on the basis of 360 days (as opposed to exact interest, calculated on 365 days); **interest charges** = cost of paying interest; **interest cover** = ratio of a company's earnings during a period to the interest payable on borrowings during that period; **interest rate** *or* **rate of interest** = percentage charge for borrowing money; **interest rate margin** = difference between the interest a bank pays on deposits and the interest it charges on loans; **interest rate swap** *see* SWAP; **interest-free credit** *or* **loan** = credit or loan where no interest is paid by the borrower; *the company gives its staff interest-free loans* **(b)** money paid as income on investments or loans; *the bank pays 10% interest on deposits*; *to receive interest at 5%*; *the loan pays 5% interest*; *deposit which yields* *or* *gives* *or* *produces* *or* *bears 5% interest*; *account which earns interest at*

10% or which earns 10% interest; **interest-bearing deposits** = deposits which produce interest; **fixed-interest investments** = investments producing an interest which does not change; **fixed-interest securities** = securities (such as government bonds) which produce an interest which does not change **(c)** part of the ownership of something, such as money invested in a company giving a financial share in it; **beneficial interest** = situation where someone is allowed to occupy or receive rent from a house without owning it; **he has a controlling interest in the company** = he owns more than 50% of the shares and so can direct how the company is run; **life interest** = situation where someone benefits from a property as long as he is alive; **majority interest** *or* **minority interest** = situation where someone owns a majority or a minority of shares in a company; *he has a majority interest in a supermarket chain*; **to acquire a substantial interest in the company** = to buy a large number of shares in a company; **to declare an interest** = to state in public that you have a financial interest in something (such as owning shares in a company) which may influence your views or decisions relating to it; *see also* CONFLICT OF INTEREST

QUOTE since last summer American interest rates have dropped by between three and four percentage points
Sunday Times

QUOTE a lot of money is said to be tied up in sterling because of the interest-rate differential between US and British rates
Australian Financial Review

interested party ['ɪntrestɪd 'pɑːti] *noun* person or company with a financial interest in a company

interim ['ɪntərɪm] **1** *adjective* **interim dividend** = dividend paid during an accounting period, usually at the end of a half-year; **interim payment** = payment of part of a dividend; **interim receiver** = receiver appointed to deal with a person's affairs until a bankruptcy order is made; **interim report** = report given at the end of a half-year; **in the interim** = meanwhile, for the time being **2** *noun* statement of interim profits or dividends

QUOTE the company plans to keep its annual dividend unchanged at Y7.5 per share, which includes a Y3.75 interim payout
Financial Times

intermediary [ɪntə'miːdjəri] *noun* person who is the link between two parties; **financial intermediary** = (i) institution which takes deposits or loans from individuals and lends money to clients; (ii) person or company which arranges insurance for a client, but is not itself an insurance company (banks, building societies, hire purchase companies are all types of financial intermediaries)

intermediate [ɪntə'miːdɪət] *adjective* half way between two extremes; **intermediate debt** *or* **term debt** = debts which have to be repaid between four and ten years' time

intermediation [ɪntəmiːdi'eɪʃn] *noun* arrangement of finance or insurance by an intermediary

internal [ɪn'tɜːnl] *adjective* **(a)** inside a company; **we decided to make an internal appointment** = we decided to appoint an existing member of staff to the post, and not bring someone in from outside the company; **internal audit** = audit carried out by a department within the company; **internal audit department** *or* **internal auditor** = department or member of staff who examines the internal controls of the company he works for; **internal auditing** = examining of internal controls by a company's internal audit department; **internal control** = system set up by the management of a company to monitor and control the company's activities; **internal growth** = expansion of a company which is based on profits from its existing trading (as opposed to external growth, which comes from the acquisition of other companies); **internal liabilities** = liabilities of a company to its shareholders or of a partnership to its partners; **internal rate of return (IRR)** = the discount rate at which the cost of an investment and its future cash inflows are exactly equal; **internal telephone** = telephone which is linked to other phones in an office **(b)** inside a country or a region; **an internal flight** = flight to a town inside the same country; **the internal market** *or* **single European market** = the EC considered as one single market, with no tariff barriers between its member states; *US* **Internal Revenue Service (IRS)** = government department which deals with almost all forms of tax; **internal trade** = trade between various parts of a country

international [ɪntə'næʃnl] *adjective* working between countries; **international law** = laws governing relations between countries; **international money markets** = market, such as the Euromarket, the international market for lending or borrowing in eurocurrencies; **international trade** = trade between different countries

International Accounting Standards (IAS)
accounting standards which are applied internationally

International Accounting Standards Committee (IASC)
committee of accountants from many countries, set up to try to standardize accounting practice internationally

International Bank for Reconstruction and Development
the official name of the World Bank

International Monetary Fund (IMF)
[ɪntə'næʃənl 'mʌnɪtri 'fʌnd] (part of the United Nations) a bank which helps member states in financial difficulties, gives financial advice to members and encourages world trade

intervene [ɪntə'viːn] *verb* to try to make a change in a system; **to intervene in a dispute** = to try to settle a dispute

intervention [ɪntə'venʃən] *noun* acting to make a change in a system; *the government's intervention in the foreign exchange markets*; *the central bank's intervention in the banking crisis*; *the government's intervention in the labour dispute*; **official intervention** = attempt by a government to maintain the exchange rate, by buying or selling foreign currency; **intervention mechanism** = methods used by central banks to maintain exchange rate parities (such as buying or selling of foreign currency); **intervention price** = price at which the EC will buy farm produce which farmers cannot sell, in order to keep prices high; *see note at* TARGET PRICE

inter vivos ['ɪntə 'vaɪvəs] *Latin phrase meaning* 'between living people'; **gift inter vivos** = gift given to another living person; *US* **inter vivos trust** = trust set up by one person for another living person

intestacy [ɪn'testəsi] *noun* dying without having made a will

intestate [ɪn'testət] *adjective* **to die intestate** = to die without having made a will; **intestate succession** = rules which apply when someone dies without having made a will

COMMENT: when someone dies intestate, the property automatically goes to the parents or siblings of an unmarried person or, if married, to the surviving partner, unless there are children

intra vires ['ɪntrə 'vaɪriːz] *Latin phrase meaning* 'within the permitted powers'; *the minister's action was ruled to be intra vires*; *see* ULTRA VIRES

intrinsic value [ɪn'trɪnzɪk 'væljuː] *noun* value which exists as part of something, such as the value of an option (for a call option, it is the difference between the current price and the higher striking price)

introduction [ɪntrə'dʌkʃən] *noun* bringing an established company to the Stock Exchange (i.e., getting permission for the shares to be traded on the Stock Exchange), used when a company moves from the Alternative Investment Market to the main stock market; *compare* OFFER FOR SALE, PLACING

QUOTE as the group's shares are already widely held, the listing will be via an introduction
Sunday Times

invalid [ɪn'vælɪd] *adjective* not valid, not legal; *permit that is invalid*; *claim which has been declared invalid*

invalidate [ɪn'vælɪdeɪt] *verb* to make something invalid; *because the company has been taken over, the contract has been invalidated*

invalidation [ɪnvælɪ'deɪʃən] *noun* making invalid

invalidity [ɪnvə'lɪdəti] *noun* being invalid; *the invalidity of the contract*

inventory ['ɪnvəntri] **1** *noun* **(a)** *especially US* stock or goods in a warehouse or shop; *to carry a high inventory*; *to aim to reduce inventory*; **inventory control** = system of checking that there is not too much stock in a warehouse, but just enough to meet requirements; **inventory financing** = using money from working capital to purchase stock for resale; **inventory turnover** = total value of goods sold during a year (or other period), divided by the average value of the stocks held during the year **(b)** list of the contents of a house for sale, of an office for rent, etc.; *to draw up an inventory of fixtures*; **to agree the inventory** = to agree that the inventory is correct **2** *verb* to make a list of stock or contents (NOTE: the word 'inventory' is used in the USA where British English uses the word 'stock'. So, the American 'inventory control' is 'stock control' in British English)

invest [ɪn'vest] *verb* **(a)** to put money into shares, bonds, a building society, hoping that it will produce interest or dividends and also increase in capital value; *he invested all his money in an engineering business*; *she was advised to invest in real estate or in government bonds*; *to invest abroad* = to put money into shares or bonds in overseas countries **(b)** to spend money on something which you believe will be useful; *to invest money in new machinery*; *to invest capital in a new factory*

investment [ɪn'vestmənt] *noun* **(a)** placing of money so that it will increase in value and produce an income (either in an asset, such as a building, or by purchasing shares, placing money on deposit, etc.); *they called for more government investment in new industries*; *investment in real estate*; *to make investments in oil companies*; *return on investment (ROI)* = (profit) interest or dividends shown as a percentage of the money invested (or capital employed in the case of a business); *see also* ROCE **(b)** shares, bonds, deposits bought with invested money; **long-term investment** *or* **short-term investment** = shares, etc., which are likely to increase in value over a long or short period; **blue-chip investments** = shares of very large established companies which are generally low-risk investments; **safe investment** = shares, etc. which are not likely to fall in value; **he is trying to protect his investments** = he is trying to make sure that the money he has invested is not lost; **quoted investments** = investments which are listed on a Stock Exchange; **unquoted investments** = investments which have no Stock Exchange quotation **(c)** **investment adviser** = (i) person who advises individuals on what investments to make; (ii) in particular, a company contracted to give advice on investments for a fee; **investment analyst** = person working for a stockbroking firm, who analyses the performance of companies in certain sectors of the market, or the performance of a market sector as a whole, or economic trends in general; **investment appraisal** = analysis of the future profitability of capital purchases as an aid to good management; *US* **investment bank** *or* **investment banker** = bank or individual who deals with the underwriting of

new issues, and advises corporations on their financial affairs (the British equivalent of the bank is an 'issuing house'); **investment grant** = government grant to a company to help it to invest in new machinery; **investment income** = income (such as interest and dividends) from investments, not from salary, wages or profits of one's business (also called 'unearned income'); **investment property** = property which is held for letting (see SSAP19); **Investment Management Regulatory Organization (IMRO)** = organization which regulates managers of investment funds, such as pension funds; **investment trust** *or* **investment company** = company whose shares can be bought on the Stock Exchange, and whose business is to make money by buying and selling stocks and shares

investor [ɪn'vestə] *noun* person who invests money; **the small investor** *or* **the private investor** = person with a small sum of money to invest; **the institutional investor** = organization (like a pension fund or insurance company) with large sums of money to invest; **investor protection** = legislation to protect small investors from unscrupulous investment brokers and advisers; **Investors in Industry (3i)** = finance group owned by the big British High Street banks, providing finance, especially to smaller companies

invisible [ɪn'vɪzəbl] **1** *adjective* **invisible assets** = assets which have a value but which cannot be seen (such as goodwill or patents); **invisible earnings** = foreign currency earned by a country by providing services, receiving interests or dividends, but not selling goods; **invisible imports** *or* **exports** *or* **invisible trade** = services which are paid for in foreign currency or earn foreign currency without actually selling a product (such as banking, tourism, shipping or insurance) **2** *plural noun* **invisibles** = invisible imports and exports

invitation [ɪnvɪ'teɪʃən] *noun* asking someone to do something; *to issue an invitation to someone to join the board*; *invitation to tender for a contract*; *invitation to subscribe to a new issue*

invite [in'vait] *verb* to ask someone to do something, to ask for something; *to invite someone to an interview*; *to invite someone to join the board*; *to invite shareholders to subscribe a new issue*; *to invite tenders for a contract*

invoice ['invɔis] **1** *noun* **(a)** note asking for payment for goods or services supplied; *your invoice dated November 10th*; *they sent in their invoice six weeks late*; *to make out an invoice for £250*; *to settle or to pay an invoice*; *the total is payable within thirty days of invoice* = the total sum has to be paid within thirty days of the date on the invoice; **purchase invoice** = invoice received by a purchaser from a seller; **sales invoice** = invoice sent by a seller to a purchaser; **VAT invoice** = invoice which includes VAT **(b) invoice clerk** = office worker who deals with invoices; **invoice discounting** = method of obtaining early payment of invoices by selling them at a discount to a company which will receive payment of the invoices when they are paid (the debtor is not informed of this arrangement, as opposed to factoring, where the debtor is informed); **invoice price** = price as given on an invoice (including discount and VAT); **total invoice value** = total amount on an invoice, including transport, VAT, etc. **2** *verb* to send an invoice to someone; *to invoice a customer*; *we invoiced you on November 10th* = we sent you the invoice on November 10th

invoicing ['invɔisiŋ] *noun* sending of an invoice; *our invoicing is done by the computer*; **invoicing department** = department in a company which deals with preparing and sending invoices; **invoicing in triplicate** = preparing three copies of invoices; **VAT invoicing** = sending of an invoice including VAT

involuntary [in'vɒləntəri] *adjective* not willingly; *US* **involuntary bankruptcy** = application by creditors to have a person or corporation made bankrupt (NOTE: the British equivalent for companies is **compulsory liquidation**)

inward ['inwəd] *adjective* towards the home country; **inward bill** = bill of lading for goods arriving in a country; **inward mission** = visit to your home country by a group of foreign businessmen

IOU ['aiəʊ'juː] *noun* (= I OWE YOU) signed document promising that you will pay back money borrowed; *to pay a pile of IOUs*

IP = INFORMATION PROVIDER

IPO ['ai'piː'əʊ] = INITIAL PUBLIC OFFERING

IRA ['aiɑːr'ei] *US* = INDIVIDUAL RETIREMENT ACCOUNT

IRC = INLAND REVENUE COMMISSIONER

IRR = INTERNAL RATE OF RETURN

irrecoverable [iri'kʌvərəbl] *adjective* which cannot be recovered; **irrecoverable debt** = debt which will never be repaid

irredeemable [iri'diːməbl] *adjective* which cannot be redeemed; **irredeemable bond** = government bond which has no date of maturity and which therefore provides interest but can never be redeemed at full value (in the UK, the War Loan is irredeemable)

irrevocable [i'revəkəbl] *adjective* which cannot be changed; **irrevocable acceptance** = acceptance which cannot be withdrawn; **irrevocable letter of credit** = letter of credit which cannot be cancelled or changed, except if agreed between the two parties involved

IRS ['aiɑːr'es] *US* = INTERNAL REVENUE SERVICE

issuance ['iʃuːəns] *noun* action of issuing new shares or new bonds

issue ['iʃuː] **1** *noun* selling or giving of new shares: **bonus issue** *or* **scrip issue** = new shares given free to shareholders; **issue of debentures** *or* **debenture issue** = borrowing money by giving lenders debentures; **issue of new shares** *or* **share issue** = selling new shares in a company to the public or to institutional investors; **rights issue** = giving existing shareholders the right to buy more shares at a lower price; **new issues department** = section of a bank which deals with issues of new shares in companies; **issue price** = price of shares when they are offered for sale for the first time **2** *verb* to put out or to give out (for the first time); *to issue a letter of credit*; *to issue shares in a new company*; *to issue a writ against someone*; *the government issued a report on London's traffic*

QUOTE the rights issue should overcome the cash flow problems
Investors Chronicle

QUOTE the company said that its recent issue of 10.5 per cent convertible preference shares at A$8.50 a share has been oversubscribed
Financial Times

QUOTE issued and fully paid capital
is $100 million
                        Hongkong Standard

QUOTE new issuance in most currency
sectors has already closed for the
year. Dealers are expecting at least
two more Euroyen issues this week by
Japanese companies. There could
also be some new dollar issuance, but
the deals are likely to be targeted
                        Wall Street Journal

issued ['ıʃuːd] *adjective* **issued capital** =
amount of capital which is formed of money
paid for shares issued to shareholders; **issued
price** = price of shares in a new company
when they are offered for sale for the first time

issuer ['ıʃʊə] *noun* company which issues
shares for sale

issuing ['ıʃʊɪŋ] *noun* which organizes an
issue of shares; **issuing bank** *or* **issuing house**
= (i) bank which organizes the selling of
shares in new companies (the US equivalent
is an investment bank); (ii) bank at which a
letter of credit is opened

item ['aɪtəm] *noun* **(a)** thing for sale; **cash
items** = goods sold for cash; **we are holding
orders for out of stock items** = for goods
which are not in stock; *please find enclosed
an order for the following items from your
catalogue* **(b)** piece of information; *items on
a balance sheet*; **exceptional items** = items in
the accounts which need to be separately
identified; *see also* EXCEPTIONAL; **item of
expenditure** = goods or services which have
been paid for and appear in the accounts **(c)**
point on a list; **we will now take item four on
the agenda** = we will now discuss the fourth
point on the agenda

itemize ['aɪtəmaɪz] *verb* to make a detailed
list of things; *itemizing the sales figures will
take about two days*; **itemized account** =
detailed record of money paid or owed;
itemized statement = bank statement where
each transaction is recorded in detail;
itemized invoice = invoice which lists each
item separately

IVA = INDIVIDUAL VOLUNTARY
ARRANGEMENT

Jj

J curve ['dʒeɪ 'kɜːv] *noun* line on a graph shaped like a letter 'J', with an initial short fall, followed by a longer rise (used to describe the effect of a falling exchange rate on a country's balance of trade)

JIT = JUST-IN-TIME

job [dʒɒb] *noun* **(a)** order being worked on; **job card** = record card relating to a job and giving details of the time taken to do a piece of work and the materials used (used to allocate direct labour and materials costs); **job costs** = all the direct costs relating to a single job of work; **job costing** = calculating the cost of a single job of work (also called 'specific order costing'); **job lot** = small parcel of shares traded on a Stock Exchange **(b)** regular paid work; **office job** *or* **white-collar job** = job in an office; **to give up one's job** = to resign from one's work; **to look for a job** = to try to find work; **to retire from one's job** = to leave work and take a pension; **to be out of a job** = to have no work **(c)** **job analysis** = detailed examination and report on the duties of a job; **job application** *or* **application for a job** = asking for a job in writing; **job centre** = government office which lists jobs which are vacant; **job classification** = describing jobs listed under various classes; **job creation scheme** = government-backed plan to make work for the unemployed; **job description** = official document from the management which says what a job involves; **job evaluation** = examining different jobs within an organization to see what skills and qualifications are needed to carry them out; **job satisfaction** = a worker's feeling that he is happy in his place of work and pleased with the work he does; **job security** = a worker's feeling that he has a right to keep his job, or that he will never be made redundant; **job specification** = very detailed description of what is involved in a job; **job title** = name given to a person in a certain job; **on-the-job training** = training given to workers at their place of work; **off-the-job training** = training given to workers away from their place of work (i.e. at a college)

joint [dʒɔɪnt] *adjective* **(a)** combined, with two or more organizations linked together; **joint commission of inquiry** *or* **joint committee** = commission or committee with representatives of various organizations on it; **joint management** = management done by two or more people; **joint venture** = very large business project where two or more companies join together, often forming a new joint venture company to manage the project (see FRS9) **(b)** one of two or more people who work together or who are linked; *joint beneficiary*; *joint managing director*; *joint owner*; *joint signatory*; **joint account** = bank account for two people; **joint and several liability** = situation where someone who has a claim against a group of people can sue them separately or together as a group; **joint ownership** = owning of a property by several owners; **joint product** = one of several products made at the same time from the same raw materials, each product being equally important; *compare* BY-PRODUCT; **joint-stock bank** = bank which is a public company quoted on the Stock Exchange; **joint-stock company** = a company which issues shares to those who have contributed capital to it (also called a 'company limited by shares', as opposed to a 'company limited by guarantee'); **joint tenancy** = situation where two or more persons acquire interests in a property together where, if one of the joint tenants dies, his share goes to the others who survive him

jointly ['dʒɔɪntli] *adverb* together with one or more other people; *to own a property jointly*; *to manage a company jointly*; *they are jointly liable for damages*

journal ['dʒɜːnl] *noun* book recording all transactions with a note against each showing in which ledger each transaction is (or will be) recorded

COMMENT: in practice, the journal is often a list of adjustments to correct previous errors or omissions in the account

judge [dʒʌdʒ] *noun* person who decides in a legal case; *the judge sent him to prison for embezzlement*

judgement *or* **judgment** ['dʒʌdʒmənt] *noun* legal decision, official decision; **to pronounce judgement** *or* **to give one's judgement on something** = to give an official or legal decision about something; **judgment creditor** = person who has been given a court order making a debtor pay him a debt; **judgment debtor** = debtor who has been ordered by a court to pay a debt (NOTE: the spelling **judgment** is used by lawyers)

junior ['dʒuːnjə] *adjective* less important than something else; **junior capital** = capital in the form of shareholders' equity, which is repaid only after secured loans (called 'senior capital') have been paid if the firm goes into liquidation; **junior mortgage** = second mortgage; **junior security** = security which is repaid after other securities

junk [dʒʌŋk] *noun* rubbish; useless items; **junk bonds** = high-interest bonds raised as debentures on the security of a company which is the subject of a takeover bid (the security has a very low credit rating); **junk mail** = advertising material sent through the post

QUOTE the big US textile company is running deep in the red, its junk bonds are trading as low as 33 cents on the dollar
Wall Street Journal

jurisdiction [dʒʊərɪs'dɪkʃn] *noun* **within the jurisdiction of the court** = in the legal power of a court

just-in-time (JIT) ['dʒʌstɪn'taɪm] *noun* **just-in-time (JIT) purchasing** = purchasing system where goods are purchased immediately before they are needed, so as to avoid carrying high levels of stock

Kk

K *or* **k** [keɪ] *abbreviation* one thousand; 'salary: £15K+ ' = salary of more than £15,000 per annum

keep [ki:p] *verb* **(a)** to do what is necessary; **to keep an appointment** = to be there when you said you would be; **to keep the books of a company** *or* **to keep a company's books** = to record the transactions of a company **(b)** to hold items for sale or for information; **to keep someone's name on file** = to have someone's name on a list for reference **(c)** to hold things at a certain level; *we must keep our mailing list up to date; to keep spending to a minimum; the price of oil has kept the pound at a high level; the government is encouraging firms to keep prices low* (NOTE: keeping - kept)

keep back ['ki:p 'bæk] *verb* to hold on to something which you could give to someone; *to keep back information* *or* *to keep something back from someone; to keep £10 back from someone's salary*

keeping ['ki:pɪŋ] *noun* **safe keeping** = being looked after carefully; *we put the documents into the bank for safe keeping*

Keogh plan ['ki:əʊ 'plæn] *noun US* private pension system allowing self-employed businessmen and professionals to set up pension and retirement plans for themselves

kerb market *or* **kerb trading** ['kɜːb 'mɑːkɪt *or* 'treɪdɪŋ] *noun* unofficial after-hours market in shares, bonds or commodities

key [ki:] *noun* **(a)** piece of metal used to open a lock; **key money** = premium paid when taking over the keys of a flat or office which you are renting **(b)** part of a computer or typewriter which you press with your fingers; *there are sixty-four keys on the keyboard*; **control key** = key on a computer which works part of a program; **shift key** = key which makes a typewriter or computer move to capital letters **(c)** important; *key factor*; *key industry*; *key personnel*; *key post*; *key staff*;

key man insurance = insurance to compensate a company for losses following the death of or a major accident to an important executive; **key rate** = an interest rate which gives the basic rate on which other rates are calculated (the former bank base rate in the UK, or the Federal Reserve's discount rate in the USA)

kickback ['kɪkbæk] *noun* illegal commission paid to someone (especially a government official) who helps in a business deal

kicker ['kɪkə] *noun* special inducement to buy a bond (such as making it convertible to shares at a preferential rate); *US* **equity kicker** = incentive given to people to lend a company money, in the form of a warrant to share in future earnings (the UK equivalent is an 'equity sweetener')

kind [kaɪnd] *noun* **benefit in kind** = any benefit arising from an employment, such as a company car, living expenses, or assets made available for private use; **payment in kind** = payment made by giving goods or food, but not money

kite [kaɪt] **1** *noun* **(a)** **to fly a kite** = to put forward a proposal to try to interest people; **kite flier** = person who tries to impress by putting forward a proposal; **kite-flying** = trying to impress by putting forward grand plans **(b)** *GB* **kite mark** = mark on goods to show they meet official standards **(c)** *(informal)* = ACCOMMODATION BILL **2** *verb* **(a)** *US* (i) to write cheques on one account and deposit them in another, withdrawing money from the second account before the cheques are cleared; (ii) to write a cheque for an amount which is higher than the total amount of money in the account, then deposit enough to cover the cheque **(b)** *GB* to use stolen credit cards or cheque books

kitty ['kɪti] *noun* money which has been collected by a group of people to be used later (such as for an office party)

know-how [ˈnəʊhaʊ] *noun* knowledge about how something works or how something is made; *you need some legal know-how to do this job*; *he needs to acquire computer know-how*; **know-how fund** = fund created by the UK government to provide technical training and advice to countries of Eastern Europe

LI

labour *US* **labor** ['leɪbə] *noun* **(a)** heavy work; **to charge for materials and labour** = to charge for both the materials used in a job and also the hours of work involved; **labour costs** = costs of production personnel employed in a company (full-time, part-time or casual) at any level; **direct labour (costs)** = cost of the workers employed which can be allocated to a product (not including materials or overheads); **indirect labour (costs)** = cost of the workers who are not directly involved in making the product (such as supervisors) and which cannot be allocated directly to a product; **labour is charged at £5 an hour** = each hour of work costs £5; **labour turnover** = the rate at which workers leave a company during a period (the costs involved include advertising for new staff, training, etc.) **(b)** workers, the workforce; **casual labour** = workers who are hired for a short period; **cheap labour** = workers who do not earn much money; **local labour** = workers recruited near a factory, not brought in from somewhere else; **organized labour** = workers who are members of trade unions; **skilled labour** = workers who have special knowledge or qualifications; **labour force** = all workers (either in a country or a company); *the management has made an increased offer to the labour force; we are setting up a factory in the Far East because of the cheap labour available*; **labour hours** = number of hours worked, which can be expressed either in actual terms or as standard hours required for a given output; **labour market** = number of workers who are available for work; **25,000 young people have left school and have come on to the labour market** = 25,000 people have left school and become available for work; **labour shortage** *or* **shortage of labour** = situation where there are not enough workers to fill jobs; **labour-intensive industry** = industry which needs large numbers of workers or where labour costs are high in relation to turnover **(c)** **labour disputes** = arguments between management and workers; **labour laws** *or* **labour legislation** = laws relating to the employment of workers; **labour relations** = relations between management and workers; *US* **labor union** = organization which represents workers who are its members in discussions about wages and conditions of work with management

> QUOTE the possibility that British goods will price themselves back into world markets is doubtful as long as sterling labour costs continue to rise faster than in competitor countries
> *Sunday Times*

> QUOTE 70 per cent of Australia's labour force is employed in service activity
> *Australian Financial Review*

lading ['leɪdɪŋ] *noun* loading, putting goods on a ship; **bill of lading** = list of goods being shipped, which the transporter gives to the person sending the goods to show that they have been loaded

Laffer curve ['læfə 'kɜːv] *noun* chart showing that cuts in tax rates increase output in the economy

lag [læg] *verb* to be behind; to be slower than something; **lagging indicator** = indicator (such as the gross national product) which shows a change in economic trends later than other indicators (NOTE: the opposite is a **leading indicator**)

lakh [læk] *noun (in India)* one hundred thousand (NOTE: ten lakh equal one crore)

land [lænd] **1** *noun* area of earth, which can have plants or buildings on its surface and minerals under the surface (land is a tangible fixed asset); **land agent** = person who runs a farm or a large area of land for someone; *GB* **land register** = register of land, showing who owns it and what buildings are on it; **land registration** = system of registering land and its owners; **land registry** = government office where land is registered; **land taxes** = taxes on the area of land owned **2** *verb* to put goods or passengers on to land after a voyage by sea or by air; **landed costs** = costs of goods which have been delivered to a port, unloaded and passed through customs

landing ['lændɪŋ] *noun* **(a)** arrival of a plane on land; arrival of a passenger on land; **landing charges** = payment for putting goods on land and the customs duties; **landing order** = permit which allows goods to be unloaded into a bonded warehouse without paying customs duty **(b) hard landing** = change in economic strategy to counteract inflation which has serious results for the population (high unemployment, rising interest rates, etc.); **soft landing** = change in economic strategy to counteract inflation, which has only minor effects on the bulk of the population

landlord ['lænlɔːd] *noun* person or company which owns a property which is let; **ground landlord** = person or company which owns the freehold of a property which is then let and sublet

lapse [læps] **1** *noun* **a lapse of time** = a period of time which has passed **2** *verb* to stop being valid, to stop being active; *the guarantee has lapsed; the takeover bid was allowed to lapse when only 13% of the shareholders accepted the offer*; **to let an offer lapse** = to allow time to pass so that an offer is no longer valid; **lapsed option** = option which has not been taken up, and now has expired

last [lɑːst] *adjective & adverb* coming at the end of a series; **last quarter** = period of three months to the end of the financial year

last in first out (LIFO) ['lɑːst 'ɪn 'fɜːst 'aʊt] *noun* **(a)** accounting method where stock is valued at the price of the earliest purchases (it is assumed that the most recently purchased stock is sold first) **(b)** redundancy policy, where the people who have been most recently appointed are the first to be made redundant; *compare* FIFO

launder ['lɔːndə] *verb* to pass illegal profits, money from selling drugs, money which has not been taxed, etc., into the normal banking system; *to launder money through an offshore bank*

laundering ['lɔːndə] *noun* **money laundering** = passing money from illegal activities, such as drug trafficking, through apparently legitimate businesses to allow it to be used further without being detected

LAUTRO = LIFE ASSURANCE AND UNIT TRUST REGULATORY ORGANIZATION

law [lɔː] *noun* **(a) laws** = rules by which a country is governed and the activities of people and organizations controlled; **labour laws** = laws concerning the employment of workers **(b) law** = all the laws of a country taken together; **civil law** = laws relating to arguments between individuals and the rights and duties of individuals; **commercial law** = laws regarding business; **company law** = laws which refer to the way companies work; **contract law** *or* **the law of contract** = laws relating to private agreements; **international law** = laws referring to the way countries deal with each other; **maritime law** *or* **the law of the sea** = laws referring to ships, ports, etc.; **law of succession** = laws relating to how property shall pass to others when the owner dies; **inside the law** *or* **within the law** = obeying the laws of a country; **against** *or* **outside the law** = not according to the laws of a country; **to break the law** = to do something which is not allowed by law **(c)** general rule; **law of supply and demand** = general rule that the amount of a product which is available and the needs of possible customers are brought into equality by market forces; **law of diminishing returns** = general rule that as more factors of production (land, labour and capital) are added to the existing factors, so the amount they produce is proportionately smaller

lawful ['lɔːfʊl] *adjective* acting within the law; **lawful practice** = action which is permitted by the law; **lawful trade** = trade which is allowed by law

lawyer ['lɔːjə] *noun* person who has studied law and can act for people on legal business; **commercial lawyer** *or* **company lawyer** = person who specializes in company law or who advises companies on legal problems; **international lawyer** = person who specializes in international law; **maritime lawyer** = person who specializes in laws concerning ships

lay off ['leɪ 'ɒf] *verb* **(a)** to stop employing staff, because there is no work **(b) to lay off risks** = to protect oneself against risk in one investment by making other investments

lay out ['leɪ 'aʊt] *verb* to spend money; *we had to lay out half our cash budget on equipping the new factory*

layout ['leɪaʊt] *noun* way of putting written information on a page (for example, financial statements can have either a vertical or horizontal layout)

LBO = LEVERAGED BUYOUT

L/C
= LETTER OF CREDIT

LDT = LICENSED DEPOSIT-TAKER

lead [liːd] *noun* most important, in the front; **lead bank** = the main bank in a loan syndicate; **lead manager** = person who organizes a syndicate of underwriters for a new issue of securities; **lead underwriter** = underwriting firm which organizes the underwriting of a share issue (NOTE: the American equivalent is a **managing underwriter**)

> QUOTE market leaders may benefit from scale economies or other cost advantages; they may enjoy a reputation for quality simply by being at the top, or they may actually produce a superior product that gives them both a large market share and high profits
>
>   *Accountancy*

leader ['liːdə] *noun* **(a)** product which sells best; **a market leader** = (i) product which sells most in a market; (ii) company which has the largest share of a market; **loss-leader** = article which is sold at a loss to attract customers who may then buy more expensive items as well **(b)** important share, share which is often bought or sold on the Stock Exchange

leading ['liːdɪŋ] *adjective* most important; which comes first; **leading indicator** = indicator (such as manufacturing order books) which shows a change in economic trends earlier than other indicators (NOTE: the opposite is a **lagging indicator**)

lead time ['liːd 'taɪm] *noun* time between deciding to place an order and receiving the product which has been ordered; *the lead time on this item is more than six weeks*

lease [liːs] **1** *noun* **(a)** written contract for letting or renting a building, a piece of land or a piece of equipment for a period against payment of a fee; **long lease** = lease which runs for fifty years or more ; **short lease** = lease which runs for up to two or three years; **finance lease** = lease which requires the lessee company to show the asset acquired

under the lease in its balance sheet and to depreciate it in the normal way (see SSAP21); **full repairing lease** = lease where the tenant has to pay for all repairs to the property; **headlease** = lease from the freeholder to a tenant; **operating lease** = lease which does not require the lessee company to show the asset acquired under the lease in its balance sheet but the annual rental charge for such assets must be disclosed in a note to the accounts; **sublease** *or* **underlease** = lease from a tenant to another tenant; **the lease expires** *or* **runs out in 2025** = the lease comes to an end in 2025; **on expiration of the lease** = when the lease comes to an end **(b) to hold an oil lease in the North Sea** = to have a lease on a section of the North Sea to explore for oil **2** *verb* **(a)** to let or rent offices, land or machinery for a period; *to lease offices to small firms*; *to lease equipment* **(b)** to use an office, land or machinery for a time and pay a fee; *to lease an office from an insurance company*; *all our company cars are leased*

> QUOTE under a finance lease, the lessee will never acquire legal title to the asset and therefore should not be entitled to claim capital allowances. The lessee is able to claim a trading deduction for the lease rentals incurred in the relevant accounting period
>
>   *Accountancy*

lease back ['liːs 'bæk] *verb* to sell a property or machinery to a company and then take it back on a lease; *they sold the office building to raise cash, and then leased it back for twenty-five years*

lease-back ['liːsbæk] *noun* **sale and lease-back** = arrangement where property is sold and then taken back on a lease; *they sold the office building and then took it back under a lease-back arrangement*

leasehold ['liːshəʊld] *noun & adjective* holding property on a lease from a freeholder (the ground landlord); *leasehold property*; *the company has some valuable leaseholds; to buy a property leasehold*

leaseholder ['liːshəʊldə] *noun* person who holds a property on a lease

leasing ['liːsɪŋ] *noun* which leases; working under a lease; *an equipment-leasing company*; *to run a copier under a leasing arrangement*; **leasing agreement** = contract between an owner and a lessee, by which the lessee has the exclusive use of a piece of equipment for a period of time, against payment of a fee (see SSAP21); *see also* LESSEE; **finance leasing** = leasing a property under a finance lease

ledger ['ledʒə] *noun* book in which accounts are written; **bought ledger** *or* **purchase ledger** = book in which purchases are recorded; **bought ledger clerk** *or* **sales ledger clerk** = office worker who deals with the bought ledger or the sales ledger; **nominal ledger** *or* **general ledger** = book which records a company's transactions in the various accounts (normally, all accounts except those relating to debtors, creditors and cash, which are kept in separate ledgers); **payroll ledger** = list of staff and their salaries; **sales ledger** = book in which sales are recorded; **stock ledger** = book which records quantities and values of stock

left [left] *adjective* not right; *the numbers run down the left side of the page*; *put the debits in the column on the left*

left-hand ['lefthænd] *adjective* belonging to the left side; *the debits are in the left-hand column in the accounts*; *he keeps the personnel files in the left-hand drawer of his desk*

legacy ['legəsi] *noun* property given by someone to someone else at his death

legal ['li:gəl] *adjective* **(a)** according to the law, allowed by the law; *the company's action was completely legal*; **legal currency** = money which is legally used in a country; *US* **legal list** = list of blue-chip securities in which banks and financial institutions are allowed to invest by the state in which they are based; **charge by way of legal mortgage** = way of borrowing money on the security of a property, where the mortgagor signs a deed which gives the mortgagee an interest in the property; **legal tender** = coins or notes which can be legally used to pay a debt (small denominations cannot be used to pay large debts) **(b)** referring to the law; **to take legal action** = to sue someone *or* to take someone to court; **to take legal advice** = to ask a lawyer to advise about a legal problem; **legal adviser** = person who advises clients about the law; *GB* **legal aid** = government scheme where someone who has little money can have his legal expenses paid for him; **legal charge** = charge on a property to secure a debt; **legal claim** = statement that someone owns something legally; **legal costs** *or* **legal charges** *or* **legal expenses** = money spent on fees to lawyers (which may be allowable against tax); **legal department** *or* **legal section** = section of a company dealing with legal matters; **legal expert** = person who

knows a lot about the law; **legal holiday** = day when banks and other businesses are closed; **legal personality** = existence as a body and so ability to be affected by the law

legatee [legə'ti:] *noun* person who receives property from someone who has died

legislation [ledʒɪs'leɪʃən] *noun* laws; **labour legislation** = laws concerning the employment of workers

lend [lend] *verb* to allow someone to use something for a period; *to lend something to someone or to lend someone something*; *he lent the company money or he lent money to the company*; *to lend money against security*; *the bank lent him £50,000 to start his business* (NOTE: **lending - lent**)

lender ['lendə] *noun* person who lends money; **lender of the last resort** = central bank which lends money to commercial banks when they are short of funds

lending ['lendɪŋ] *noun* act of letting someone use money for a time; **lending limit** = limit on the amount of money a bank can lend; **lending margin** = agreed spread (based on the LIBOR) for lending

```
QUOTE Japanese banks, responsible
for half of all new international
lending in the second half of the
1980s, have greatly reduced new
lending
                    Financial Times
```

less [les] **1** *adjective* smaller than, of a smaller size or of a smaller value; *we do not grant credit for sums of less than £100*; *he sold it for less than he had paid for it* **2** *preposition* minus, with a sum removed; *purchase price less 15% discount*; *interest less service charges* **3** *adverb* not as much

lessee [le'si:] *noun* person who has a lease, or who pays money for a property he leases

lessor [le'sɔ:] *noun* owner of a property who grants a lease on it

let [let] **1** *verb* to lend a house, an office or a farm to someone for a payment; **to let an office** = to allow someone to use an office for a time in return for payment of rent; **offices to let** = offices which are available to be leased by companies (NOTE: **letting - let**) **2** *noun* period of the lease of a property; *they took the office on a short let*

letter ['letə] *noun* **(a)** written document sent from one person or company to another to request or give information; **circular letter** = letter sent to many people; **covering letter** =

letter sent with documents to say why they are being sent; **standard letter** = letter which is sent without change to various correspondents **(b) letter of acknowledgement** = letter which says that something has been received; **letters of administration** = letter given by a court to allow someone to deal with the estate of a person who has died; **letter of allotment** or **allotment letter** = letter which tells someone how many shares in a new company he has been allotted; **letter of application** = letter in which someone applies for a job; **letter of appointment** = letter in which someone is appointed to a job; **letter of comfort** = (i) letter supporting someone who is trying to get a loan; (ii) letter from a company to a bank stating that a subsidiary company (which has applied to the bank for a loan) will continue to trade for the forseeable future; see also COMFORT; **letter of indemnity** = letter promising payment of compensation for a loss; **letter of intent** = letter which states what a company intends to do if something happens; **letters patent** = official document which gives someone the exclusive right to make and sell something which he has invented

letter of credit (L/C) ['letə əv 'kredɪt] noun document issued by a bank on behalf of a customer authorizing payment to a supplier when the conditions specified in the document are met (this is a common method of guaranteeing payment by overseas customers); **irrevocable letter of credit** = letter of credit which cannot be cancelled or changed

letting ['letɪŋ] noun **letting agency** = agency which deals in property to let; **furnished lettings** = furnished property to let; **furnished holiday lettings** = furnished property let to people on holiday

level ['levl] **1** noun position; *low levels of productivity* or *low productivity levels*; *to raise the level of employee benefits*; *to lower the level of borrowings*; **high level of investment** = large amount of money invested; **manning levels** or **staffing levels** = number of people required in each department of a company to do the work efficiently **2** verb **to level off** or **to level out** = to stop rising or falling; *profits have levelled off over the last few years*; *prices are levelling out* (NOTE: **levelling - levelled** but American spelling **leveling - leveled**)

QUOTE figures from the Fed on industrial production for April show a decline to levels last seen in June 1984
Sunday Times

QUOTE applications for mortgages are running at a high level
Times

QUOTE employers having got their staff back up to a reasonable level are waiting until the scope for overtime working is exhausted before hiring
Sydney Morning Herald

leverage ['li:vərɪdʒ] noun **(a)** ratio of capital borrowed by a company at a fixed rate of interest to the company's total capital (also called 'gearing') **(b)** borrowing money at fixed interest which is then used to produce more money than the interest paid

COMMENT: high leverage (or high gearing) has the effect of increasing a company's profitability when trading is expanding; if the company's trading slows down, the effect of high fixed-interest charges is to increase the rate of slowdown

leveraged ['li:vərɪdʒd] adjective using borrowings for finance; **leveraged buyout (LBO)** or **leveraged takeover** = buying all the shares in a company by borrowing money against the security of the assets of the company to be bought; **leveraged stock** = stock bought with borrowed money

QUOTE the offer came after management had offered to take the company private through a leveraged buyout for $825 million
Fortune

levy ['levi] **1** noun money which is demanded and collected by the government; **capital levy** = tax on the value of a person's property and possessions; **import levy** = tax on imports, especially in the EC; a tax on imports of farm produce from outside the EC; **training levy** = tax to be paid by companies to fund the government's training schemes **2** verb to demand payment of a tax, or an an extra payment and to collect it; *the government has decided to levy a tax on imported cars*; *to levy a duty on the import of luxury items*

QUOTE royalties have been levied at a rate of 12.5% of full production
Lloyd's List

lex [leks] Latin word meaning 'law'; **lex fori** = law of the place where the case is being heard

liability [laɪə'bɪləti] *noun* **(a)** being legally responsible for damage, loss, etc.; **to accept liability for something** = to agree that you are responsible for something; **to refuse liability for something** = to refuse to agree that you are responsible for something; **contractual liability** = legal responsibility for something as stated in a contract; **employers' liability insurance** = insurance to cover accidents which may happen at work, and for which the company may be responsible; **limited liability** = situation where someone's liability for debt is limited by law; **limited liability company** = company where a shareholder is responsible for repaying the company's debts only to the amount unpaid (if any) on the shares he owns **(b)** responsibility for a payment (such as the repayment of a loan); **liabilities** = debts of a business, including dividends owed to shareholders; *the balance sheet shows the company's assets and liabilities*; **accrued liabilities** = liabilities which are recorded, although payment has not yet been made (especially expenses such as rent, rates, etc.); **current liabilities** = debts which a company has to pay within the next accounting period (in a company's annual accounts, these would be debts which must be paid within the year and include amounts owed for goods or services received, taxation due and bank loans to be repaid; also called 'amounts falling due within one year'); **long-term liabilities** = debts which are due to be paid after one year (also called 'amounts falling due after one year'); **he was not able to meet his liabilities** = he could not pay his debts; **to discharge one's liabilities in full** = to pay everything which you owe

QUOTE liabilities are probable future sacrifices of economic benefits arising from present obligations of a particular entity to transfer assets or provide services to other entities in the future as a result of past transactions or events
FASB Concepts Statement No. 3

liable ['laɪəbl] *adjective* **(a) liable for** = legally responsible for; *the customer is liable for breakages*; *the chairman was personally liable for the company's debts* **(b) liable to** = which is officially due to be paid; *goods which are liable to stamp duty*

LIBID = LONDON INTERBANK BID RATE

LIBOR = LONDON INTERBANK OFFERED RATE

licence *US* **license** ['laɪsəns] *noun* official document which allows someone to do something; **import licence** *or* **export licence** = documents which allow goods to be exported or imported; **goods manufactured under licence** = goods made with the permission of the owner of the copyright or patent

license ['laɪsəns] **1** *noun US* = LICENCE **2** *verb* to give someone official permission to do something; *to license a company to manufacture spare parts*; *she is licensed to run an employment agency*; **licensed dealer** = person who has been licensed by the DTI to buy and sell securities for individual clients; **licensed deposit-taker (LDT)** *or* **licensed institution** = deposit-taking institution, such as a building society, bank or friendly society, which is licensed to receive money on deposit from private individuals and to pay interest on it

licensee [laɪsən'siː] *noun* person who has a licence, especially to manufacture something

licensing ['laɪsənsɪŋ] *noun* which refers to licences; *a licensing agreement*

lien [liːn] *noun* legal right to hold someone's goods and keep them until a debt has been paid; **banker's lien** = lien held against documents which the borrower has lodged in the bank; **general lien** = lien against the personal possessions of a borrower (but not against his house or land)

lieu [ljuː] *noun* **in lieu of** = instead of; *she was given two months' salary in lieu of notice* = she was given two months' salary and asked to leave immediately

life [laɪf] *noun* **(a)** time when a person is alive; **life annuity** *or* **annuity for life** = annual payments made to someone as long as he is alive; **life expectancy** = number of years a person is likely to live; **life interest** = interest in a property which stops when a person dies; **life tenant** *or* **tenant for life** = person who can occupy a property for life and has a life interest in the property; **whole-life insurance** = insurance where the insured person pays a fixed premium each year and the insurance company pays a sum when he dies **(b)** period of time something exists; *the life of a loan*; *during the life of the agreement*; **half-life** = number of years needed to repay half the capital borrowed on mortgage; **life of a contract** = remaining period of a futures contract before it expires

life assurance *or* **life insurance** ['laɪf ə'ʃɔːrəns *or* ɪn'ʃɔːrəns] *noun* insurance which pays a sum of money when someone dies, or at a certain date if he is still alive; **the life assured** *or* **the life insured** = the person whose life has been covered by the life assurance; **life assurance company** = company providing life assurance, but usually also providing other services such as investment advice; **Life Assurance and Unit Trust Regulatory Organization (LAUTRO)** = organization set up to regulate the operations of life assurance companies and unit trusts, now replaced by the FSA

LIFO = LAST IN FIRST OUT

limit ['lɪmɪt] **1** *noun* point at which something ends, point where you can go no further; **to set limits to imports** *or* **to impose import limits** = to allow only a certain amount of imports; **credit limit** = largest amount of money which a customer can borrow; **he has exceeded his credit limit** = he has borrowed more money than he is allowed; **lending limit** = restriction on the amount of money a bank can lend; **time limit** = maximum time which can be taken to do something; **to set a time limit for acceptance of the offer** *US* **limit order** = order to a broker to buy or sell if a security falls to a certain price (NOTE: the British equivalent for a sale is **stop-loss order**); **limit 'up'** *or* **limit 'down'** = upper or lower limits to share price movements which are regulated by some stock exchanges **2** *verb* to stop something from going beyond a certain point; **the banks have limited their credit** = the banks have allowed their customers only a certain amount of credit

limitation [lɪmɪ'teɪʃən] *noun* **(a)** act of allowing only a certain quantity of something; **limitation of liability** = making someone liable for only a part of the damage or loss; **time limitation** = amount of time available; **the contract imposes limitations on the number of cars which can be imported (b) statute of limitations** = law which allows only a certain amount of time (a few years) for someone to claim damages or property

limited ['lɪmɪtɪd] *adjective* restricted, not open; **limited company** *or* **limited liability company** = company where a shareholder is responsible for the company's debts only to the amount unpaid (if any) on his shares; **private limited company** = company with a small number of shareholders, whose shares are not traded on the Stock Exchange (NOTE: shortened to **Ltd**); **Public Limited Company** = company whose shares can be bought on the Stock Exchange (NOTE: written as **plc** *or* **PLC**); **limited partner** = partner in a limited

partnership (he is only liable for the amount of capital he has put into the firm, and takes no part in the management of the firm); **limited partnership** = registered business where the liability of the partners is limited to the amount of capital they have each provided to the business and where the partners may not take part in the running of the business

limiting ['lɪmɪtɪŋ] *adjective* which limits; *a limiting clause in a contract;* **limiting factor** = factor which limits a company's ability to achieve its goals (e.g. sales demand being too low for the company to make enough profit); *the short holiday season is a limiting factor on the hotel trade*

line [laɪn] *noun* **(a)** long mark; *he drew a thick line across the bottom of the column to show which figure was the total* **(b)** row of letters or figures on a page; **bottom line** = last line in accounts, showing the net profit; *the boss is interested only in the bottom line;* **line of credit** = (i) amount of money made available to a customer by a bank as an overdraft or credit facility; (ii) *US* borrowing limit on a credit card; **to open a line of credit** *or* **a credit line** = to make credit available to someone

QUOTE the best thing would be to have a few more plants close down and bring supply more in line with current demand

Fortune

linear ['lɪnɪə] *adjective* **linear program** = computer program that contains no loops or branches; **linear programming** = (i) method of mathematically breaking down a problem so that it can be solved by a computer; (ii) mathematical technique for deciding how to make the best possible use of given resources

link [lɪŋk] *verb* to join, to attach to something else; *to link pensions to inflation; his salary is linked to the cost of living; to link bonus payments to productivity; see also* INDEX-LINKED

liquid ['lɪkwɪd] *adjective* easily converted to cash; containing a large amount of cash; **liquid assets** = cash, or bills which can easily be changed into cash; **to go liquid** = to convert as many assets as possible into cash

liquidate ['lɪkwɪdeɪt] *verb* **to liquidate a company** = to close a company and sell its assets; **to liquidate a debt** = to pay a debt in full; **to liquidate stock** = to sell stock to raise cash

liquidation [lɪkwɪ'deɪʃən] *noun* **(a)** sale of assets for cash; closing of a company and selling of its assets; **the company went into liquidation** = the company was closed and its assets sold; **compulsory liquidation** = liquidation which is ordered by a court at the request of the creditors (the court appoints a liquidator to sell the company's assets for the best possible price and so repay the creditors) (NOTE: the American equivalent is **involuntary bankruptcy**); **voluntary liquidation** = situation where a company itself decides it shall pay its debts and close (the shareholders appoint a liquidator to run the company) **(b) liquidation of a debt** = payment of a debt

liquidator ['lɪkwɪdeɪtə] *noun* person named to supervise the closing of a company which is in liquidation (he sells off the assets and pays the creditors; anything left over will be shared among the shareholders)

liquidity [lɪ'kwɪdəti] *noun* having cash, or assets which can be changed into cash; **liquidity crisis** = not having enough liquid assets; **liquidity ratio** = (i) liquid assets shown as a percentage of current liabilities, or similar ratios relating to a company's ability to meet its immediate liabilities; (ii) proportion of bank deposits which a bank keeps in cash

list [lɪst] **1** *noun* several items written one after the other; catalogue; **list price** = price as given in a catalogue; **price list** = sheet giving prices of goods for sale **2** *verb* **listed company** = company whose shares can be bought or sold on the Stock Exchange; **listed securities** = shares which can be bought or sold on the Stock Exchange or shares which appear on the official Stock Exchange list

listing ['lɪstɪŋ] *noun* **Stock Exchange listing** = being on the official list of shares which can be bought or sold on the Stock Exchange; **the company is planning to obtain a Stock Exchange listing**; **Listing Agreement** = document which a company signs when being listed on the Stock Exchange, in which the company promises to abide by stock exchange regulations; **listing particulars** = (i) details of a company which are published when the company applies for a stock exchange listing (the US equivalent is the 'registration statement'); (ii) details of the institutions which are backing an issue; *US* **listing requirements** = conditions which must be met by a corporation before its stock can be listed on the New York Stock Exchange

QUOTE last month the group announced the £103.3m convertible bond issue to repay some of its debt, but it has been slow to publish listing particulars for the bond issue, and the delay has caused investors to be nervous

Financial Times

QUOTE we could get a NASDAQ quote as a service to institutions in the US, but when it comes to dealing they usually just pick up the phone and deal through London. There was a trend for British companies to get the Big Board listing, but I don't go for that

Money Observer

litigation [lɪtɪ'geɪʃən] *noun* the bringing of a lawsuit against someone

living ['lɪvɪŋ] *noun* **cost of living** = money which a person has to pay for rent, food, heating, etc.; **cost-of-living index** = way of measuring the cost of living which is shown as a percentage increase on the figure for the previous year; **cost-of-living allowance** = addition to normal salary to cover increases in the cost of living

Lloyd's (of London) ['lɔɪdz əv 'lʌndən] *noun* London international insurance market; **Lloyd's broker** = agent who represents a client who wants insurance and who arranges this insurance for him through a Lloyd's underwriting syndicate; **Lloyd's Register** = classified list showing details of all the ships in the world, with a rating of their seaworthiness; **ship which is A1 at Lloyd's** = ship in very good condition

COMMENT: Lloyd's is an old-established insurance market; the underwriters who form Lloyd's are divided into syndicates, each made up of active underwriters who arrange the business and non-working underwriters (called 'names') who stand surety for any insurance claims which may arise. See also NAMES

load [ləʊd] *verb* to put charges into a certain period or into certain payments; **back-end loaded** = (insurance or investment scheme) where commission is only charged when the investor withdraws his money from the scheme; **front-end loaded** = (insurance or investment scheme) where most of the management charges are incurred in the first year of the investment or insurance, and are not spread out over the whole period

loan [ləʊn] **1** *noun* money which has been lent; **loan capital** = part of a company's capital which is a loan from an outside source which has to be repaid at a later date; **loan stock** = stock issued by a company at a fixed rate of interest, as a means of raising a loan; **convertible loan stock** = loan which can be exchanged for shares at a later date; **bank loan** = money lent by a bank; **bridging loan** = short-term loan to help someone buy a new house when he has not yet sold his old one; **government loan** = money lent by the government; **home loan** = loan by a bank or building society to help someone buy a house; **short-term loan** *or* **long-term loan** = loans which have to be repaid within a few weeks or some years; **soft loan** = loan (from a company to an employee or from one government to another) at a very low rate of interest or with no interest payable at all; **unsecured loan** = loan made with no security **2** *verb* to lend

QUOTE over the last few weeks, companies raising new loans from international banks have been forced to pay more, and an unusually high number of attempts to syndicate loans among banks has failed
Financial Times

local ['ləʊkəl] *adjective* referring to a particular area, especially one near where a factory or an office is based; **local area network (LAN)** = network where various terminals and equipment are all at a short distance from one another (such as in the same building, or not more than 500m apart); **local authority** = elected section of government which runs a small area of the country; **local authority bond** = loan raised by a local authority in the form of a fixed-interest bond, repayable at a certain date (they are similar to Treasury bonds; the US equivalent is the municipal bond); **local authority deposits** = money deposited with a local authority to earn interest for the depositor; **local currency** = currency used in the country where a transaction is taking place

QUOTE each cheque can be made out for the local equivalent of £100 rounded up to a convenient figure
Sunday Times

QUOTE EC regulations insist that customers can buy cars in the EC at the local pre-tax price
Financial Times

locking up ['lɒkɪŋ 'ʌp] *noun* the locking up of money in stock = investing money in stock so that it cannot be used for other, possibly more profitable, investments

lock in(to) ['lɒk 'ɪntʊ] *verb* to be fixed to a certain interest rate or exchange rate; *by buying dollars forward the company is in effect locking itself into a favourable euro-dollar exchange rate*

QUOTE the next year or so might well see a significant fall in interest rates. This would be fine for borrowers, but no so good for those relying on income from savings. Fortunately, there are plenty of ways in which investors can lock into the present high level of interest rates for periods of up to five years or more
Money Observer

lock up ['lɒk 'ʌp] *verb* to lock up capital = to have capital invested in such a way that it cannot be used for other investments

lodge [lɒdʒ] *verb* to lodge money with someone = to deposit money with someone; to lodge securities as collateral = to put securities into a bank to be used as collateral for a loan

lodgement ['lɒdʒmənt] *noun* depositing money, cheques, etc., in an account

Lombard Rate ['lɒmbɑd 'reɪt] rate at which the German Bundesbank lends to commercial banks

QUOTE in Frankfurt, call money was steady at 8.15 per cent as dealers regarded any change in official rates as unlikely at today's Bundesbank council meeting. The Lombard rate was increased to 8.50 from 8.00 per cent at the beginning of this month
Financial Times

London Interbank Bid Rate (LIBID) ['lʌndən 'ɪntəbæŋk 'bɪd 'reɪt] rate at which banks are prepared to pay on deposits (in sterling or eurodollars) from other banks

London Interbank Offered Rate (LIBOR) ['lʌndən 'ɪntəbæŋk 'ɒfəd 'reɪt] rate at which banks offer to lend money to other banks (in sterling or eurodollars)

London Stock Exchange (LSE) ['lʌndən 'stɒk ɪk'stʃeɪndʒ] main British stock exchange where securities are bought and sold

long [lɒŋ] **1** *adjective* for a large period of time; **long bond** = bond which will mature in some years' time; **long credit** = credit terms which allow the borrower a long time to pay; **long lease** = lease of more than fifty years; **in the long term** = over a long period of time; **to take the long view** = to plan for a long period before current investment becomes profitable **2** *noun* **longs** = government stocks which mature in over fifteen years' time

long-dated ['lɒŋ'deɪtɪd] *adjective* **long-dated bills** = bills which are payable in more than three months' time; **long-dated stocks =** LONGS

long-range ['lɒŋ'reɪndʒ] *adjective* for a long period of time in the future; **long-range economic forecast =** forecast which covers a period of several years

long-tail business ['lɒŋ'teɪl 'bɪznəs] *noun* insurance business where a claim only arises some years after the insurance contract was taken out

long-term ['lɒŋ'tɜːm] *adjective* **on a long-term basis =** for a long period of time; **long-term borrowings =** borrowings which do not have to be repaid for some years; **long-term debts =** debts which will be repaid more than one year later; **long-term forecast =** forecast for a period of some years; **long-term liabilities =** debts which are due to be paid after one year (also called 'amounts falling due after one year'); **long-term loan =** loan to be repaid many years later; **long-term security =** security which will mature in many years' time

QUOTE land held under long-term leases is not amortized
Hongkong Standard

QUOTE the company began to experience a demand for longer-term mortgages when the flow of money used to finance these loans diminished
Globe and Mail (Toronto)

loophole ['luːphəʊl] *noun* **to find a loophole in the law =** to find a means of legally avoiding the law; **to find a tax loophole =** to find a means of legally not paying tax

QUOTE because capital gains are not taxed but money taken out in profits is taxed, owners of businesses will be using accountants and tax experts to find loopholes in the law
Toronto Star

loose change ['luːs 'tʃeɪndʒ] *noun* money in coins

lose [luːz] *verb* **(a)** not to have something any more; **to lose an order =** not to get an order which you were hoping to get; *during the strike, the company lost six orders to American competitors*; **to lose control of a company =** to find that you have less than 50% of the shares and so are no longer able to direct the company **(b)** to have less money; *he lost £25,000 in his father's computer company*; **the pound has lost value =** the pound is worth less (NOTE: **losing - lost**)

loss [lɒs] *noun* **(a)** compensation for loss of earnings = payment to someone who has stopped earning money or who is not able to earn money; **compensation for loss of office =** payment to a director who is asked to leave a company before his contract ends **(b)** having less money than before, not making a profit; **the company suffered a loss =** the company did not make a profit; **to report a loss =** not to show a profit in the accounts at the end of the year; *the company reported a loss of £1m on the first year's trading*; **capital loss =** loss made by selling assets for less than the purchase price, including expenses; **the car was written off as a dead loss** *or* **a total loss =** the car was so badly damaged that the insurers said it had no value; **paper loss =** loss made when an asset has fallen in value but has not been sold; **trading loss =** situation where the company's receipts from sales are less than its expenditure; **loss relief =** amount of tax not to be paid on one year's profit to offset a loss in a previous year (losses from up to three years ago may be used for tax relief); **at a loss =** making a loss, not making any profit; *the company is trading at a loss*; *he sold the shop at a loss*; **to cut one's losses =** to stop doing something which was losing money

lot [lɒt] *noun* **(a)** group of items sold together at an auction; **to bid for lot 23**; *at the end of the auction half the lots were unsold* **(b)** group of shares which are sold; standard quantity sold on a commodity exchange; **to sell a lot of shares**; **to sell shares in small lots**

lottery ['lɒtəri] *noun* game where numbered tickets are sold and prizes given for some of the numbers

low [ləʊ] **1** *adjective* small, not high; **low coupon stocks =** government bonds which pay a low rate of interest; **low gearing =** not having much borrowing in proportion to one's capital; **low yield =** a share's yield compared to its price which is low for the sector, suggesting that investors anticipate that the company will grow fast, and have pushed up the share price in expectation of growth; **the tender will go to the lowest bidder =** the contract will be awarded to the person who offers the lowest price **2** *noun* point where prices or sales are very small

QUOTE after opening at 79.1 the index touched a peak of 79.2 and then drifted to a low of 78.8
Financial Times

QUOTE the pound which had been as low as $1.02 earlier this year, rose to $1.30
Fortune

QUOTE the trade-weighted dollar chart shows there has been a massive devaluation of the dollar since the mid-'80s and the currency is at its all-time low

Financial Weekly

lowballing ['ləʊbɔːlɪŋ] *noun* undercutting competitors, as by offering a discount for auditing a company's accounts

lower ['ləʊə] **1** *adjective* smaller, less high; *a lower rate of interest*; *sales were lower in December than in November*; **lower of cost or market rate** *or* **lower of cost or net realizable value** = basis of valuation of an asset, especially stock, at its original purchase price, resale value or replacement cost, whichever is lower **2** *verb* to make smaller or less expensive; *to lower prices to secure a larger market share*; *to lower the interest rate*

QUOTE Canadian and European negotiators agreed to a deal under which Canada could keep its quotas but lower its import duties

Globe and Mail (Toronto)

loyalty bonus ['lɔɪəlti 'bəʊnəs] *noun* special privileges given to shareholders who keep their shares for a certain period of time (used especially to attract investors to privatization issues)

LSE = LONDON STOCK EXCHANGE

Ltd ['lɪmɪtɪd] = LIMITED

lump sum ['lʌmp 'sʌm] *noun* money paid in one single amount, not in several small sums; *when he retired he was given a lump-sum bonus*; *she sold her house and invested the money as a lump sum*

Mm

m = METRE, MILE, MILLION

machine [mə'ʃiːn] *noun* **(a)** device which works with power from a motor; **adding machine** = machine which adds numbers; **copying machine** *or* **duplicating machine** = machine which makes copies of documents **(b) machine code** *or* **machine language** = instructions and information shown as a series of figures (0 and 1) which can be read by a computer; **machine hour rate** = method of calculating production overhead absorption rate, where the number of hours the machines are expected to work is divided into the budgeted production overhead to give a rate per hour; **machine-readable codes** = sets of signs or letters (such as bar codes, post codes) which a computer can read

machinery [mə'ʃiːnəri] *noun* machines, taken as a whole (these are a tangible fixed cost)

macro- ['mækrəʊ] *prefix* very large, covering a wide area; **macro-economics** = study of the economics of a whole area, a whole industry, a whole group of the population or a whole country, in order to help in economic planning

magnetic [mæg'netɪk] *adjective* **magnetic card** = plastic card with a strip of magnetic recording material on its surface, allowing data to be stored (used in automatic cash dispensers); **magnetic character reading (MCR)** *or* **magnetic ink character recognition (MICR)** = system that recognises characters by sensing magnetic ink (used on cheques); **magnetic ink** = special ink with magnetic particles in it, used for printing cheques; **magnetic strip** = black strip on credit cards and cashpoint cards, on which personal information about the account is recorded

magnitude ['mægnɪtjuːd] *noun* level or strength of a variable

main [meɪn] *adjective* most important; *main office*; *main building*; *one of our main customers*; **the main market** = the London Stock Exchange (as opposed to the Alternative Investment Market); *US* **Main Street** = most important street in a town, where the shops and banks are

mainframe (computer) ['meɪnfreɪm] *noun* large-scale high-powered computer system that can handle high-capacity memory and backing storage devices as well as a number of operations simultaneously

mainstream corporation tax (MCT) ['meɪnstriːm kɔːpə'reɪʃn 'tæks] *noun* total tax paid by a company on its profits (less any advance corporation tax, which a company has already paid when distributing profits to its shareholders in the form of dividends)

maintain [meɪn'teɪn] *verb* **(a)** to keep something going or working; *to maintain good relations with one's customers*; *to maintain contact with an overseas market* **(b)** to keep something working at the same level; *the company has maintained the same volume of business in spite of the recession*; *to maintain an interest rate at 5%*; *to maintain a dividend* = to pay the same dividend as the previous year

maintenance ['meɪntənəns] *noun* **(a)** keeping something at the same level; **concept of capital maintenance, concept of maintenance of operating capacity** *see* CONCEPT **(b)** payment to a former spouse for living expenses for children; *maintenance payments may be taxable*

majeure [mæ'ʒɜː] *see* FORCE MAJEURE

major ['meɪdʒə] *adjective* important; **major shareholder** = shareholder with a large number of shares

> QUOTE if the share price sinks much further the company is going to look tempting to any major takeover merchant
>
> Australian Financial Review

> QUOTE monetary officials have reasoned that coordinated greenback sales would be able to drive the dollar down against other major currencies
>
> Duns Business Month

> QUOTE a client base which includes many major commercial organizations and nationalized industries
> *Times*

majority [mə'dʒɒrəti] *noun* larger group than all others; **majority of the shareholders** = more than 50% of the shareholders; **the board accepted the proposal by a majority of three to two** = three members of the board voted to accept and two voted against; **majority vote** *or* **majority decision** = decision made after a vote according to the wishes of the largest group; **majority shareholding** *or* **majority interest** = group of more than half of all the shares in a company; **a majority shareholder** = person who owns more than half the shares in a company

make [meɪk] *verb* **(a)** to sign, to agree; *to make a deal or to make an agreement*; *to make a bid for something* = to offer to buy something; *(of a marketmaker)*; **to make a book** = to have a list of shares which he is prepared to buy or sell on behalf of clients; **to make a market in securities** = to offer to buy or sell securities on a selected list at any time; **to make a payment** = to pay; **to make a deposit** **(b)** = to pay money as a deposit to earn; to increase in value; *he makes £50,000 a year or £25 an hour; the shares made $2.92 in today's trading* **(c)** to make a profit *or* to make a loss = to have more money or less money after a deal; **to make a killing** = to make a very large profit (NOTE: **making - made)**

make out ['meɪk 'aʊt] *verb* to write; *to make out an invoice; the bill is made out to Smith & Co.*; **to make out a cheque to someone** = to write someone's name on a cheque

make over ['meɪk 'əʊvə] *verb* to transfer property legally; *to make over the house to one's children*

maker ['meɪkə] *noun* person who makes something; person who signs a promissory note in which he promises to pay money; **decision maker** = person who decides or who takes decisions; **marketmaker** = person who buys or sells shares on the stock market and offers to do so in a certain list of securities (a marketmaker operates a book, listing the securities he is willing to buy or sell, and makes his money by charging a commission on each transaction)

make up ['meɪk 'ʌp] *verb* **(a)** to compensate for something; **to make up a loss** *or* **to make up the difference** = to pay extra so that the loss or difference is covered **(b) to make up accounts** = to complete the accounts

maladministration
['mælədmɪnɪs'treɪʃən] *noun* incompetent administration

manage ['mænɪdʒ] *verb* **(a)** to direct, to be in charge of; *to manage a department*; *to manage a branch office* **(b) to manage property** = to look after rented property for the owner; **managed fund** *or* **managed unit trust** = unit trust fund which is invested in specialist funds within the same group of unit trusts and can be switched from one specialized investment area to another

> QUOTE the research director will manage and direct a team of graduate business analysts reporting on consumer behaviour throughout the UK
> *Times*

management ['mænɪdʒmənt] *noun* **(a)** directing or running a business; *to study management; good management or efficient management; bad management or inefficient management; a management graduate or a graduate in management*; **financial management** = management of the acquisition and use of long- and short-term capital by a business; **fund management** = dealing with the investment of sums of money on behalf of clients; **line management** = organization of a business where each manager is responsible for doing what his superior tells him to do; **portfolio management** = buying and selling shares by a person or by a specialist on behalf of a client; **product management** = directing the making and selling of a product as an independent item; **management accountant** = accountant who prepares specialized information for managers so that they can make decisions; **management accounting** = providing information to managers, which helps them to plan, to control their businesses and to take decisions which will make them run their businesses more efficiently; **management accounts** = financial information prepared for a manager so that he can make decisions (including monthly or quarterly financial statements, often in great detail, with analysis of actual performance against the budget); **management consultant** = person who gives advice on how to manage a business; **management course** = training course for managers; **management information systems (MIS)** = computer systems which provide information to managers; **management by objectives** = way of managing a business by setting work targets for the managers and testing to see if they are achieved correctly and on time; **management team** = a group of managers working together; **management techniques** = ways of managing a business; **management training** = training managers by making them study problems and work out ways of solving them; **management trainee** = young person being trained to be a manager **(b)** group of managers or directors; *the management has decided to give an overall pay increase*; **top management** = the main directors of a company; **middle management** = the department managers of a company who carry out the policy set by the directors and organize the work of a group of workers; **management buyin (MBI)** = purchase of a company by a group of outside directors; **management buyout (MBO)** = takeover of a company by a group of employees (usually senior managers and directors)

QUOTE the management says that the rate of loss-making has come down and it expects further improvement in the next few years

Financial Times

manager ['mænɪdʒə] *noun* **(a)** head of a department in a company; **accounts manager** = head of the accounts department; **area manager** = manager who is responsible for the company's work (usually sales) in an area; **general manager** = manager in charge of the administration in a large company **(b)** person in charge of a branch; *Mr Smith is the manager of our local bank*; *the manager of our Lagos branch is in London for a series of meetings*; **bank manager** = person in charge of a branch of a bank; **branch manager** = person in charge of a branch of a company

QUOTE the No. 1 managerial productivity problem in America is managers who are out of touch with their people and out of touch with their customers

Fortune

managing ['mænɪdʒɪŋ] *adjective* **managing director** = director who is in charge of a whole company; **chairman and managing director** = managing director who is also chairman of the board of directors

mandate ['mændeɪt] *noun* order which allows something to take place; **bank mandate** = written order to a bank, asking them to open an account and allowing someone to sign cheques on behalf of the account holder, giving specimen signatures, etc.; **dividend mandate** = authorization by a

shareholder to the company, to pay his dividends directly into his bank account

mandatory ['mændətəri] *adjective* compulsory; **mandatory bid** = offer to purchase the shares of a company which has to be made when a shareholder acquires 30% of that company's shares; **mandatory injunction** = order from a court which compels someone to do or not to do something; **mandatory meeting** = meeting which all members have to attend

manipulate [mə'nɪpjʊleɪt] *verb* **to manipulate accounts** = to make false accounts so that the company seems profitable; **to manipulate the market** = to work to influence share prices in your favour

manipulation [mənɪpjʊ'leɪʃən] *noun* **stock market manipulation** = trying to influence the price of shares by buying or selling in order to give the impression that the shares are widely traded

manipulator [mə'nɪpjʊleɪtə] *noun* **stock market manipulator** = person who tries to influence the price of shares in his own favour

manufacturing [mænjʊ'fæktʃərɪŋ] *noun* making of products for sale; **manufacturing account** = financial statement which shows production costs only (as opposed to a trading account which shows sales and costs of sales); a manufacturing account will include direct materials and labour costs and the production overhead; **manufacturing profit** = difference between the cost of buying a product from another supplier and the cost to the company of manufacturing it itself

marché ['mɑːʃeɪ] *French* market; **Marché à terme des instruments financiers (MATIF)** = the French financial futures market

margin ['mɑːdʒɪn] *noun* **(a)** difference between the money received when selling a product and the money paid for it; **gross margin** = percentage difference between the received price and the unit manufacturing cost or purchase price of goods for resale; **net margin** = percentage difference between received price and all costs, including overheads; **we are cutting our margins very fine** = we are reducing our margins to the smallest possible to be competitive; **our margins have been squeezed** = profits have been reduced because our margins have to be smaller to stay competitive **(b)** deposit paid when purchasing a futures contract; **margin call** = request for a purchaser of a futures contract or an option to pay more margin, since the fall in the price of the securities or commodity has removed the value of the original margin deposited **(c)** difference between interest charged to borrowers and interest paid to depositors (by a bank, building society, etc.) **(d)** extra space or time allowed; **margin of error** = degree of inaccuracy or number of mistakes which are accepted in a document or in a calculation; **safety margin** = time or space allowed for something to be safe; **margin of safety** = units produced (or sales of these units) which are above the breakeven point

> QUOTE profit margins in the industries most exposed to foreign competition - machinery, transportation equipment and electrical goods - are significantly worse than usual
> *Australian Financial Review*

marginal ['mɑːdʒɪnəl] *adjective* **(a)** **marginal cost** = cost of making a single extra unit above the number already planned; *see also* INCREMENTAL COST; **marginal costing** *US* **direct costing** = costing a product on the basis of its variable costs only, excluding fixed costs; **marginal efficiency of capital** = calculation of the interest rate of capital costs incurred in making a product which equals the cash flow from the product in the future; **marginal pricing** = basing the selling price of a product on its variable costs of production plus a margin, but excluding fixed costs; **marginal rate of tax** *or* **marginal tax rate** = percentage of tax which a taxpayer pays at a higher rate (which he therefore pays on every further pound or dollar he earns); **marginal revenue** = income from selling a single extra unit above the planned number of sales **(b)** not very profitable, hardly worth the money paid; *marginal return on investment*; **marginal land** = land which is almost not worth farming; **marginal purchase** = thing which a buyer feels is only just worth buying

> QUOTE pensioner groups claim that pensioners have the highest marginal rates of tax. Income earned by pensioners above $30 a week is taxed at 62.5 per cent, more than the highest marginal rate
> *Australian Financial Review*

mark down ['mɑːk 'daʊn] *verb* to make lower; **to mark down a price** = to lower the price of something; *this range has been marked down to $24.99*; *we have marked all prices down by 30% for the sale*

mark-down ['mɑːkdaʊn] *noun* **(a)** reduction of the price of something to less than its usual price **(b)** percentage amount by which a price has been lowered; *we have used a 30% mark-down to fix the sale price*

market ['mɑːkɪt] *noun* **(a) the Common Market** = the European Economic Community; *the Common Market agricultural policy*; *the Common Market ministers* **(b)** place where a product might be sold; group of people who might buy a product; **home** *or* **domestic market** = market in the country where the selling company is based; *sales in the home market rose by 22%* **(c)** place where money or commodities are traded; **capital market** = place where companies can look for investment capital; **commodity market** = place where commodities are bought or sold; **the foreign exchange markets** = places where currencies are bought or sold; **forward markets** = places where foreign currency or commodities can be bought or sold for delivery at a later date; **money market** *or* **finance market** = place where large sums of money are lent or borrowed at short-term **(d)** **stock market** = place where shares are bought and sold; *the market in oil shares was very active* *or* *there was a brisk market in oil shares*; **to sell at the market** = instruction to stockbroker to sell shares at the best price possible; **to buy shares in the open market** = to buy shares on the Stock Exchange, not privately; **over-the-counter market** = secondary market in shares which are not listed on the main Stock Exchange; *(of a company)*; **to come to the market** = to apply for a Stock Exchange listing, by offering some of the existing shares for sale, or by floating it as a new company; **to bring a company to the market** = to arrange the flotation of a company's shares on the market; *(of a marketmaker)*; **to make a market in securities** = to offer to buy or sell securities on a selected list at any time **(e) market analysis** = detailed examination and report on a market; **market capitalization** = (i) value of a company calculated by multiplying the price of its shares on the Stock Exchange by the number of shares issued; (ii) value of all the shares listed on a stock market; **market economist** = person who specializes in the study of financial structures and the return on investments in the stock market; **market forces** = influences on the sales which bring about a change in prices; **market forecast** = forecast of prices on the stock market; **market leader** = company with the largest market share; **market opportunities** = possibility of finding new sales in a market; **market penetration** *or* **market share** = percentage of a total market which the sales of a company cover; **market price** = price at which a product can be sold; price at which a share stands a stock market; **market professionals** = people who work in a stock market, as brokers, analysts, etc.; **market rate** = normal price in the market; *we pay the market rate for secretaries* or *we pay secretaries the market rate*; **market research** = examining the possible sales of a product before it is put on the market; **market trends** = gradual changes taking place in a market; **market value** = value of an asset, product or company if sold on the open market today **(f)** possible sales of a certain type of product, demand for a certain type of product; **a growth market** = market where sales are likely to rise rapidly; **the labour market** = number of workers available for work; **25,000 graduates have come on to the labour market** = they have become available for work because they have left college **(g) the black market** = buying and selling goods in a way which is not allowed by law; *there is a flourishing black market in spare parts for cars*; **to pay black market prices** = to pay high prices to get items which are not easily available **(h) a buyer's market** = market where goods are sold cheaply because there is little demand; **a seller's market** = market where the seller can ask high prices because there is a large demand for the product **(i) closed market** = market where a supplier deals with only one agent or distributor and does not supply any others direct; **free market economy** = system where the government does not interfere in business activity in any way; **open market** = market where anyone can buy and sell

marketability [mɑːkɪtəˈbɪləti] *noun* being able to be sold easily; *the marketability of privatization shares*

marketable ['mɑːkɪtəbl] *adjective* which can be sold easily; **marketable loan** = loan which can be bought or sold, such as bearer securities like bonds; **marketable securities** = stocks, shares, CDs, etc., which can be bought or sold on a stock market

marketing ['mɑːkɪtɪŋ] *noun* techniques used in selling a product (such as packaging, advertising, etc.); **marketing agreement** = contract by which one company will market another company's products; **marketing cost** = cost of selling a product, including advertising, packaging, etc.; **marketing department** = department in a company which specializes in using marketing techniques to sell a product; **marketing manager** = person in charge of a marketing department; **marketing policy** or **marketing plans** = ideas of how the company's products are going to be marketed; *to plan the marketing of a new product*

marketmaker ['mɑːkɪtmeɪkə] *noun* person who buys or sells shares on the stock market and offers to do so in a certain list of securities (a marketmaker operates a book, listing the securities he is willing to buy or sell, and makes his money by charging a commission on each transaction)

market overt ['mɑːkɪt 'əʊvɜːt] *noun* market which is open to all, in which a sale gives good title to a buyer, even though the seller's title may be defective

COMMENT: this was only applied to certain open-air antique markets, and has been abolished

mark up ['mɑːk 'ʌp] *verb* to increase; **to mark prices up** = to increase prices; *these prices have been marked up by 10%*

mark-up ['mɑːkʌp] *noun* **(a)** increase in price; *we put into effect a 10% mark-up of all prices in June* **(b)** amount added to the cost price to give the selling price; **we work to a 3.5 times mark-up** or **to a 350% mark-up** = we take the unit cost and multiply by 3.5 to give the selling price

master budget ['mɑːstə 'bʌdʒɪt] *noun* budget prepared by amalgamating budgets from various profit and cost centres (sales, production, marketing, administration, etc.) to provide a main budget for the whole accounting entity

matching ['mætʃɪŋ] *noun* (i) relating costs to sales in order to calculate profits during an accounting period; (ii) relating unallocated cash received to invoices; **matching concept** *or* **matching convention** = the basis for preparing accounts which says that profits can only be recognised if sales are fully matched with costs accrued during the same period

material [mə'tɪərɪəl] **1** *adjective* relevant, important to something (taken to mean that something is an important item in the accounts, which would distort the accounts if it were left out or incorrectly stated) **2** *noun* **materials** = (i) substances (such as steel, glass, plastics) used to make a product; (ii) substances (such as soap, detergent, etc.) used in cleaning, painting, etc.; **raw materials** = basic materials such as wood, iron ore, crude petroleum, which have to be treated or processed in some way before they can be used; **material(s) cost** = cost of the materials used in making a product; **direct material(s) cost** = cost of the materials which are used in making a product and for which costs can be directly related to that product; **indirect material(s) cost** = cost of materials which cannot be allocated to the production of a particular product; **materials requisition** = official note from a production department, asking for materials to be moved from the store to the workshop; **materials returns note** = official note which is made if materials are sent back to the store from the workshop (if too much was requisitioned in the first place); **materials transfer note** = official note made out when materials are moved from one workplace to another

materiality [mətɪərɪ'ælɪti] *noun* being material

MATIF ['matif] *see* MARCHÉ

mature [mə'tjʊə] **1** *adjective* **mature economy** = fully developed economy **2** *verb* **bills which mature in three weeks' time** = bills which will be due for payment in three weeks

maturity [mə'tjʊərɪti] *noun* **date of maturity** *or* **maturity date** = date when a government stock, an assurance policy or a debenture will become due for payment; **amount payable on maturity** = amount received by the insured person when the policy becomes mature; **maturity yield** *US* **yield to maturity** = calculation of the yield on a fixed-interest investment, assuming it is bought at a certain price and held to maturity

maximization [mæksɪmaɪ'zeɪʃən] *noun* making as large as possible; **profit maximization** *or* **maximization of profit**

maximize ['mæksɪmaɪz] *verb* to make as large as possible; **to maximize profits**

maximum ['mæksɪməm] **1** *noun* largest possible number, price or quantity; **up to a maximum of £10** = no more than £10; **to increase exports to the maximum** = as much as possible; *it is the maximum the insurance company will pay* (NOTE: plural is **maxima**) **2** *adjective* largest possible; *maximum income tax rate* *or* *maximum rate of tax*; *maximum load*; *maximum production levels*; *maximum price*; **to increase production to the maximum level** = as much as possible

MBI = MANAGEMENT BUYIN

MBO = MANAGEMENT BUYOUT

MCR = MAGNETIC CHARACTER RECOGNITION

MCT = MAINSTREAM CORPORATION TAX

mean [miːn] **1** *adjective* average; *mean annual increase*; **mean price** = average price of a share in a day's trading **2** *noun* average, figure calculated by adding several figures together and dividing by the number of figures added; *unit sales are over the mean for the first quarter* *or* *above the first quarter mean*

means [miːnz] *plural noun* **(a)** way of doing something; *do we have any means of copying all these documents quickly?* **(b)** money or resources; *the company has the means to launch the new product*; *such a level of investment is beyond the means of a small private company*; **means test** = inquiry into how much money someone earns to see if he is eligible for state benefits; **he has private means** = he has income from dividends, interest or rent which is not part of his salary

measure ['meʒə] **1** *noun* **(a)** way of calculating size or quantity; **as a measure of the company's performance** = as a way of judging if the company's results are good or bad **(b)** type of action; **to take measures to prevent something happening** = to act to stop something happening; **to take crisis** *or* **emergency measures** = to act rapidly to stop a crisis developing; **an economy measure** = an action to save money; **fiscal measures** = tax changes made by the government to improve the working of the economy; **as a precautionary measure** = to prevent something taking place **2** *verb* **to measure a**

company's performance = to judge how well a company is doing

measurement ['meʒəmənt] *noun* way of judging something; *performance measurement* or *measurement of performance*; **measurement of profitability** = way of calculating how profitable something is

median ['miːdjən] *noun* point in the middle of a list of numbers or values

medium ['miːdjəm] **1** *adjective* middle, average; *the company is of medium size* **2** *noun* **(a)** means or method by which something is transmitted; **storage medium** = method of storing computing information **(b) mediums** or **medium-dated stocks** = government stocks which mature in seven to fifteen years' time (NOTE: plural for (a) is **media)**

medium-sized company ['miːdjəm'saɪzd 'kʌmpni] *noun (for UK financial reporting purposes)* a company with at least two of the following characteristics: a turnover of less than œ11.2m; net assets of less than œ5.6m; and not more than 250 staff (companies of this size have certain exemptions available to them relating to filing of accounts with the Registrar of Companies)

COMMENT: small and medium-sized companies together are sometimes referred to as small and medium-sized enterprises. This is usually written as 'SMEs'. The SME sector is often referred to in print

QUOTE With business confidence reviving, large numbers of small and medium-sized enterprises (SMEs) will be looking to expand this year. Growth in the SME area is vital for growth in the economy as a whole.
Accountancy

medium-term ['miːdjəm'tɜːm] *adjective* referring to a point between short term and long term; **medium-term bond** = bond which matures within five to fifteen years; **medium-term forecast** = forecast for two or three years; **medium-term loan** = bank loan for three to five years

meet [miːt] *verb* **(a)** to be satisfactory for; **we will try to meet your price** = we will try to offer a price which is acceptable to you; **they failed to meet the deadline** = they were not able to complete in time **(b)** to pay for; *to meet someone's expenses*; *the company will meet your expenses*; *he was unable to meet his mortgage repayments* (NOTE: **meeting - met)**

QUOTE if corporate forecasts are met, sales will exceed $50 million next year
Citizen (Ottawa)

meeting ['miːtɪŋ] *noun* **(a)** coming together of a group of people; **board meeting** = meeting of the directors of a company; **general meeting** or **meeting of shareholders** or **shareholders' meeting** = meeting of all the shareholders of a company, meeting of all the members of a society; **Annual General Meeting (AGM)** *US* **annual stockholders' meeting** = meeting of all the shareholders when a company's financial situation is discussed with the directors; **Extraordinary General Meeting (EGM)** = special meeting of shareholders to discuss an important matter **(b) to hold a meeting** = to organize a meeting of a group of people; *the meeting will be held in the committee room*; **to open a meeting** = to start a meeting; **to conduct a meeting** = to be in the chair for a meeting; **to close a meeting** = to end a meeting; **to address a meeting** = to speak to a meeting; **to put a resolution to a meeting** = to ask a meeting to vote on a proposal

QUOTE in proportion to your holding you have a stake in every aspect of the company, including a vote in the general meetings
Investors Chronicle

member ['membə] *noun* **(a)** person who belongs to a group or a society, such as a member of a pension plan; **ordinary member** = person who pays a subscription to belong to a group **(b)** shareholder in a company; **members' voluntary winding up** = winding up of a company by the shareholders themselves **(c)** organization which belongs to a society; *the member countries of the EC*; *the members of the United Nations*; *the member companies of a trade association US* **member bank** = bank which is part of the Federal Reserve system; **member firm** = stockbroking firm which is a member of a stock exchange

QUOTE it will be the first opportunity for party members and trade union members to express their views on the tax package
Australian Financial Review

QUOTE in 1984 exports to Canada from the member-states of the European Community jumped 38 per cent
Globe and Mail (Toronto)

membership ['membəʃɪp] *noun* **(a)** belonging to a group; *membership qualifications*; *conditions of membership*; *membership card*; *to pay your membership* or *your membership fees* **(b)** all the members of a group; *the membership was asked to vote for the new president*; **the club has a membership of five hundred** = the club has five hundred members

QUOTE the bargaining committee will recommend that its membership ratify the agreement at a meeting called for June

Toronto Star

memorandum [memə'rændəm] *noun* short message; **memorandum (and articles) of association** = legal documents setting up a limited company and giving details of its name, aims, authorized share capital, conduct of meetings, appointment of directors, and registered office

mercantile ['mɜːkəntaɪl] *adjective* commercial; **mercantile agent** = (i) *GB* agent who trades on behalf of another person or company; (ii) *US* person who supplies credit ratings on corporations; **mercantile country** = country which earns income from trade; **mercantile law** = laws relating to business; **mercantile marine** = all the commercial ships of a country

merchant *noun* **(a)** businessman who buys and sells goods (especially imported goods) in bulk for retail sale **(b)** company, shop, etc., which accepts a certain type of credit card for purchases; **merchant number** = number of the merchant, printed at the top of the report slip when depositing credit card payments

merchant bank ['mɜːtʃənt 'bæŋk] *noun* **(a)** bank which arranges loans to companies and deals in international finance, buys and sells shares, launches new companies on the Stock Exchange but does not provide normal banking services to the general public; **merchant banker** = person who has a high position in a merchant bank **(b)** *US* bank which operates a credit card system (accepting payment on credit cards from retailers)

merge [mɜːdʒ] *verb* to join together; *the two companies have merged*; *the firm merged with its main competitor*

merger ['mɜːdʒə] *noun* joining together of two or more companies (usually as the result of an agreed takeover bid); *as a result of the merger, the company is the largest in the field*; **merger accounting** = method of preparing group accounts where the business combination meets the strict criteria necessary for such accounting (see FRS6); *compare* ACQUISITION ACCOUNTING

COMMENT: merger accounting seeks to treat the combining entities as if they had always been combined. The carrying values of their assets and liabilities are not required to be adjusted to fair value on consolidation. The results and cash flows of all the combining entities are brought into the group accounts from the beginning of the financial year in which the combination occurred. The corresponding figures are restated

method ['meθəd] *noun* way of doing something; *a new method of making something or of doing something*; *what is the best method of payment?*; *his organizing methods are out of date*; *their manufacturing methods or production methods are among the most modern in the country*; **time and method study** = examining the way in which something is done to see if a cheaper or quicker way can be found

mezzanine finance ['metsəniːn faɪ'næns] *noun* provision of finance for a company after the start-up finance has been provided

COMMENT: mezzanine finance is less risky than start-up finance, since the company has usually already started trading; this type of finance is aimed at consolidating the company's trading position before it is floated on a stock exchange

MICR = MAGNETIC INK CHARACTER RECOGNITION

micro ['maɪkrəʊ] *noun* = MICROCOMPUTER

micro- ['maɪkrəʊ] *prefix* very small; **microeconomics** = study of the economics of groups of people or single companies

microcomputer *or* **micro** ['maɪkrəʊkəm'pjuːtə] *noun* complete smallscale, cheap, low-power computer system based around a microprocessor chip and having limited memory capacity

microfiche ['maɪkrəʊfiːʃ] *noun* index sheet, made of several microfilm photographs; *we hold our records on microfiche*

microfilm ['maɪkrəʊfɪlm] **1** *noun* roll of film on which a document is photographed in very small scale; *we hold our records on microfilm* **2** *verb* to make a very small scale photograph; *send the 1995 correspondence to be microfilmed or for microfilming*

mid- [mɪd] *prefix* middle; **from mid-2000** = from the middle of 2000; *the factory is closed until mid-July*

middle ['mɪdl] *adjective* in the centre, between two points; **middle management** = department managers in a company, who carry out the policy set by the directors and organize the work of a group of workers; **middle price** = price between the buying and selling price (usually shown in indices)

middle-income ['mɪdl'ɪŋkʌm] *adjective* **people in the middle-income bracket** = people with average incomes, not very high or very low

mid-month ['mɪd'mʌnθ] *adjective* taking place in the middle of the month; *mid-month accounts*

mid-week ['mɪd'wiːk] *adjective* which happens in the middle of a week; *the mid-week lull in sales*

mill [mɪl] *noun US* one-fifth of a cent

million ['mɪljən] number 1,000,000; *the company lost £10 million in the African market*; *our turnover has risen to $13.4 million* (NOTE: can be written m after figures: **$5m:** say 'five million dollars')

millionaire [mɪljə'neə] *noun* person who has more than one million pounds; **dollar millionaire** = person who has more than one million dollars; **paper millionaire** = person who owns shares which, if sold, would be worth one million pounds or dollars

min = MINUTE, MINIMUM

mini- ['mɪni] *prefix* very small

minimization [mɪnɪmaɪ'zeɪʃn] *noun* making as small as possible; **tax minimization** = working to reduce the tax payable by a client

minimize ['mɪnɪmaɪz] *verb* to make small

minimum ['mɪnɪməm] **1** *noun* smallest possible quantity, price or number; *to keep expenses to a minimum*; *to reduce the risk of a loss to a minimum* (NOTE: plural is **minima** or **minimums**) **2** *adjective* smallest possible; **minimum dividend** = smallest dividend which is legal and accepted by the shareholders; **minimum payment** = smallest payment necessary; **minimum quantity** = smallest quantity which is acceptable; **minimum reserves** = smallest amount of reserves which a commercial bank must hold with a central bank; **minimum stock level** = level of stock in a warehouse (when this level is reached more stock has to be ordered); **minimum wage** *or* **statutory minimum wage** = lowest hourly wage which a company can legally pay its workers

minor ['maɪnə] *adjective* less important; *minor expenditure*; *minor shareholders*

minority [maɪ'nɒrəti] *noun* number or quantity which is less than half of the total; *a minority of board members opposed the chairman*; **minority shareholding** *or* **minority interest** = group of shares which are less than one half of the shares in a company; **minority shareholder** = person who owns a group of shares but less than half of the shares in a company; **in the minority** = being fewer than half

minuend ['mɪnjuend] *noun* number from which another is subtracted

minus ['maɪnəs] **1** *adverb* less or without; *net salary is gross salary minus tax and National Insurance deductions*; *gross profit is sales minus production costs* **2** *adjective* **the accounts show a minus figure** = show that more has been spent than has been received; **minus factor** = unfavourable factor; *to have lost sales in the best quarter of the year is a minus factor for the sales team*

MIRAS = MORTGAGE INTEREST RELIEF AT SOURCE

MIS = MANAGEMENT INFORMATION SYSTEMS

misappropriate [mɪsə'prəuprɪeɪt] *verb* to use illegally money which is not yours, but with which you have been trusted

misappropriation [mɪsəprəuprɪ'eɪʃən] *noun* illegal use of money by someone who is not the owner but who has been trusted to look after it

miscalculate [mɪs'kælkjuleɪt] *verb* to calculate wrongly; *the salesman miscalculated the discount, so we hardly broke even on the deal*

miscalculation [mɪskælkju'leɪʃən] *noun* mistake in calculating

miscount 1 ['mɪskaunt] *noun* mistake in counting **2** [mɪs'kaunt] *verb* to count wrongly; *the shopkeeper miscounted, so we got twenty-five bars of chocolate instead of two dozen*

misfeasance [mɪs'fiːzəns] *noun* doing something improperly

mismanage [mɪs'mænɪdʒ] *verb* to manage badly

mismanagement [mɪs'mænɪdʒmənt] *noun* bad management; *the company failed because of the chairman's mismanagement*

mismatching [mıs'mætʃıŋ] *noun*
currency mismatching = borrowing money
in the currency of a country where interest
rates are low and depositing it in the currency
of a country with higher interest rates (the
potential profit from the interest rate margin
may be offset by changes in the exchange
rates which increase the value of the loan in
the company's balance sheet)

misrepresent [mısreprı'zent] *verb* to
report facts wrongly

misrepresentation
[mısreprızen'teıʃən] *noun* wrongly reporting
facts; **fraudulent misrepresentation** =
giving someone wrong information in order
to cheat him

misuse [mıs'juːs] *noun* wrong use; *misuse
of funds or of assets*

mixed [mıkst] *adjective* (a) of different
sorts or of different types together; **mixed
economy** = system which contains both
nationalized industries and private enterprise
(b) neither good nor bad

> QUOTE prices closed on a mixed note
> after a moderately active trading
> session
> Financial Times

MMC = MONOPOLIES AND MERGERS
COMMISSION

mode [məʊd] *noun* way of doing
something; **mode of payment** = way in which
payment is made (such as cash or cheque)

model ['mɒdl] *noun* **economic model** =
computerized plan of a country's economic
system, used for forecasting economic trends;
pricing model = computerized system for
calculating a price, based on costs, anticipated
margins, etc.

modem ['məʊdem] *noun* device which
links a computer to the telephone line,
allowing data to be sent from one computer to
another

modified accounts ['mɒdıfaıd
ə'kaʊnts] *noun* less detailed annual accounts
which can be deposited with the Registrar of
Companies by small or medium-sized
companies

modulus (MOD) ['mɒdjʊləs] *noun* the
remainder after the division of one number by
another

monetarism ['mʌnıtərızm] *noun* theory
that the amount of money in the economy
affects the level of prices, so that inflation can
be controlled by regulating money supply

monetarist ['mʌnıtərıst] **1** *noun* person
who believes in monetarism and acts
accordingly **2** *adjective* according to
monetarism; *monetarist theories*

monetary ['mʌnıtəri] *adjective* referring to
money or currency; **monetary control** =
control of money supply; **monetary items** =
monetary assets (cash, debtors) and monetary
liabilities (overdraft, creditors) whose values
stay the same in spite of inflation; **the
government's monetary policy** = the
government's policy relating to the money
supply, bank interest rates and borrowing;
monetary standard = fixing of a fixed
exchange rate for a currency; **monetary
targets** = figures such as the money supply,
PSBR, etc., which are given as targets by the
government when setting out its budget for
the forthcoming year; **monetary working
capital adjustment (MCWA)** = an
adjustment in current cost accounting to the
historical cost balance sheet to take account of
the effect of inflation on the value of debtors,
creditors and stocks of finished goods; **the
international monetary system** = methods
of controlling and exchanging currencies
between countries; **the European Monetary
System (EMS)** = system of controlled
exchange rates between member countries of
the European Community important before
the introduction of the euro; **monetary unit** =
standard currency in a country (the dollar, the
yen, etc.) or within a group of countries (e.g.
the euro)

> QUOTE the decision by the government
> to tighten monetary policy will push
> the annual inflation rate above the
> year's previous high
> Financial Times

> QUOTE it is not surprising that the
> Fed started to ease monetary policy
> some months ago
> Sunday Times

> QUOTE a draft report on changes in
> the international monetary system
> Wall Street Journal

money ['mʌni] *noun* (a) coins and notes
used for buying and selling; **to earn money** =
to have a salary; **to earn good money** = to
have a large salary; **to lose money** = to make a
loss, not to make a profit; **the company has
been losing money for months** = the
company has been working at a loss; **to get
your money back** = to make enough profit to
cover your original investment; **to make
money** = to make a profit; **to put money into
the bank** = to deposit money into a bank
account; **to put money into a business** = to
invest money in a business; *he put all his*

redundancy money into a shop; **to put money down** = to pay cash, especially as a deposit; *he put £25 down and paid the rest in instalments*; **money at call** *or* **call money** = money loaned for which repayment can be demanded without notice (used by commercial banks, placing money on very short- term deposit with discount houses); **cheap money** = money which can be borrowed at a low rate of interest; **danger money** = extra salary paid to workers in dangerous jobs; **dear money** = money which has to be borrowed at a high rate of interest; **easy money** = money which can be earned with no difficulty; *selling insurance is easy money*; **hot money** = money which is moved from country to country to get the best returns; **paper money** = money in notes, not coins; **ready money** = cash, money which is immediately available; **money lying idle** = money not being used to produce interest; **they are worth a lot of money** = they are valuable **(b) money broker** = dealer operating in the interbank and foreign exchange markets; **money laundering** = passing money from illegal activities, such as drug trafficking, through apparently legitimate businesses to allow it to be used further without being detected; **money markets** = markets for buying and selling short-term loans or financial instruments such as Treasury bills and CDs, which can be easily converted to cash; *the international money market are nervous*; **money market fund** = investment fund, which only invests in CDs, Treasury bills, etc.; **money market instruments** = short-term investments, such as CDs, which can be easily turned into cash and are traded on the money markets; **money rates** = rates of interest for borrowers or lenders **(c) money order** = document which can be bought for sending money through the post; **foreign money order** *or* **international money order** *or* **overseas money order** = money order in a foreign currency which is payable to someone living in a foreign country

moneylender ['mʌnɪlendə] *noun* person who lends money at interest

money-making ['mʌnɪ'meɪkɪŋ] *adjective* which makes money; *a money-making plan*

money-spinner ['mʌnɪ'spɪnə] *noun* item which sells very well or which is very profitable

monies ['mʌnɪz] *noun* sums of money; *monies owing to the company*; *to collect monies due*

monitor ['mɒnɪtə] **1** *noun* screen (like a television screen) on a computer **2** *verb* to check or to examine how something is working; *he is monitoring the progress of sales*; *how do you monitor the performance of a unit trust?*

monopoly [mə'nɒpəli] *noun* situation where one person or company controls all the market in the supply of a product; **public monopoly** *or* **state monopoly** = situation where the state is the only supplier of a product or service (such as the Post Office); **Monopolies and Mergers Commission (MMC)** = government organization which examines takeover bids at the request of the Office of Fair Trading, to see if a successful bid would result in a monopoly and so harm the consumer by reducing competition

Monte Carlo method ['mɒntɪ 'kɑːləʊ 'meθəd] *noun* statistical analysis technique

month [mʌnθ] *noun* one of twelve periods which make a year; *the company pays him £1000 a month*; *he earns £2,000 a month*; *bills due at the end of the current month*; **calendar month** = whole month as on a calendar; **paid by the month** = paid once each month; **to give a customer two months' credit** = to allow a customer to pay not immediately, but after two months

month end ['mʌnθ 'end] *noun & adjective* the end of a calendar month, when accounts are usually drawn up; *month-end accounts*

monthly ['mʌnθli] **1** *adjective* happening every month, which is received every month; *monthly payments*; *he is paying for his car by monthly instalments*; *my monthly salary cheque is late*; **monthly statement** = statement of the present state of a customer's account, sent out at the end of each month; **monthly ticket** = ticket for travel which is good for one month **2** *adverb* every month; *to pay monthly*; *the account is credited monthly*

moonlight ['muːnlaɪt] *verb informal* to do a second job for cash (often in the evening) as well as a regular job

moonlighter ['muːnlaɪtə] *noun* person who moonlights

moonlighting ['muːnlaɪtɪŋ] *noun* doing a second job; *he makes thousands a year from moonlighting*

moratorium [mɒrə'tɔːrɪəm] *noun* temporary stop to repayments of interest or capital of money owed; *the banks called for a moratorium on payments* (NOTE: plural is **moratoria)**

mortgage ['mɔːgɪdʒ] **1** *noun* **(a)** (i) legal agreement where someone lends money to another person so that he can buy a property, the property being the security; (ii) money lent in this way; *to take out a mortgage on the a house*; *to buy a house with a £20,000 mortgage*; **mortgage payments** = money paid each month as interest on a mortgage, plus repayment of a small part of the capital borrowed; **mortgage relief** = reduction in tax on interest paid on a mortgage; **to foreclose on a mortgaged property** = to sell a property because the owner cannot repay money which he has borrowed, using the property as security; **to pay off a mortgage** = to pay back the principal and all the interest on a loan to buy a property **(b) mortgage bond** = certificate showing that a mortgage exists and that property is security for it; **mortgage debenture** = debenture where the loan is secured against the company's property; **mortgage famine** = situation where there is not enough money available to offer mortgages to house buyers; **mortgage queue** = list of people waiting for mortgages; **first mortgage** = main mortgage on a property; **second mortgage** = further mortgage on a property which is already mortgaged **2** *verb* to accept a loan with a property as security; *the house is mortgaged*; *he mortgaged his house to set up in business*

◇ **endowment mortgage** mortgage backed by an endowment policy (the borrower pays interest on the mortgage in the usual way, but does not repay the capital; the endowment assurance (a life insurance) is taken out to cover the total capital sum borrowed, and when the assurance matures the capital is paid off, and a further lump sum is usually available for payment to the borrower

◇ **repayment mortgage** mortgage where the borrower pays back both interest and capital over the period of the mortgage

> QUOTE mortgage money is becoming tighter. Applications for mortgages are running at a high level and some building societies are introducing quotas
> *Times*

> QUOTE for the first time since mortgage rates began falling a financial institution has raised charges on homeowner loans
> *Globe and Mail (Toronto)*

mortgagee [mɔːgə'dʒiː] *noun* person or company which lends money for someone to buy a property

mortgage interest relief at source (MIRAS) scheme (scrapped in April 2000) by which the borrower repaid interest on a mortgage less the standard rate tax (i.e., he did not pay the full interest and then reclaim the tax)

mortgager *or* **mortgagor** ['mɔːgɪdʒə] *noun* person who borrows money to buy a property

movable *or* **moveable** ['muːvəbl] **1** *adjective* which can be moved; **movable property** = chattels and other objects which can be moved (as opposed to land) **2** *plural noun* **movables** = movable property

move [muːv] *verb* to propose formally that a motion be accepted by a meeting; *he moved that the accounts be agreed*; *I move that the meeting should adjourn for ten minutes*

movement ['muːvmənt] *noun* changing position, going up or down; *movements in the money markets*; *cyclical movements of trade*; **movements of capital** = changes of investments (from one country to another)

mover ['muːvə] *noun* person who proposes a motion

moving average ['muːvɪŋ 'ævrɪdʒ] *noun* average of share prices on a stock market, where the calculation is made over a period which moves forward regularly

> COMMENT: the commonest are 100-day or 200-day averages, or 10- or 40-week moving averages; the average is calculated as the average figure for the whole period, and moves forward one day or week at a time; these averages are often used by chartists

MRD = MUTUAL RECOGNITION DIRECTIVE

multi- ['mʌlti] *prefix* referring to many things

multicurrency [mʌltɪ'kʌrənsi] *adjective* in several currencies; **multicurrency loan** = loan in several currencies

multilateral [mʌltɪ'lætərəl] *adjective* between several parties; *a multilateral agreement*; **multilateral netting** = method of putting together sums from various sources into one currency (used by groups of banks trading in several currencies at the same time); **multilateral trade** = trade between several countries

multimillion [mʌltɪˈmɪljən] *adjective* referring to several million pounds or dollars; *they signed a multimillion pound deal*

QUOTE factory automation is a multi-billion-dollar business

Duns Business Month

multimillionaire [mʌltɪmɪljəˈneə] *noun* person who owns several million pounds or dollars

multiple [ˈmʌltɪpl] **1** *adjective* many; **multiple applications** = several applications for a new issue of shares, made by the same person, but under different names (in some share issues, people making multiple applications may be prosecuted); **multiple store** = one store in a chain of stores; **multiple ownership** = situation where something is owned by several parties jointly **2** *noun* **(a) share on a multiple of 5** = share with a P/E ratio of 5 (i.e. 5 is the result when dividing the current market price by the earnings per share) **(b)** company with stores in several different towns

multiplicand [ˈmʌltɪplɪkənd] *noun* number which is multiplied by another number

multiplication [mʌltɪplɪˈkeɪʃən] *noun* act of multiplying; **multiplication sign** = sign (x) used to show that a number is being multiplied by another

multiplier [ˈmʌltɪplaɪə] *noun* number which multiplies another; factor which tends to multiply something (as the effect of new expenditure on total income and reserves)

multiply [ˈmʌltɪplaɪ] *verb* **(a)** to calculate the sum of various numbers repeated a certain number of times; *to multiply twelve by three; square measurements are calculated by multiplying length by width* **(b)** to grow or to increase; *profits multiplied in the boom years*

multi-user system [ˈmʌltiˈjuːzə ˈsɪstəm] *noun* computer system that can support more than one user at a time

municipal bond [mjuˈnɪsɪpəl ˈbɒnd] *noun* US bond issued by a town or local area (the UK equivalent is a 'local authority bond')

Murphy's law [ˈmɜːfɪz ˈlɔː] *noun* law, based on wide experience, which says that in commercial life if something can go wrong it will go wrong, or that when you are thinking that things are going right, they will inevitably start to go wrong

mutual [ˈmjuːtʃʊəl] **1** *adjective* belonging to two or more people; **mutual (insurance) company** = company which belongs to insurance policy holders (who receive dividends from it); *US* **mutual funds** = organizations which take money from small investors and invest it in stocks and shares for them, the investment being in the form of units in the fund (similar to the British 'unit trusts'); **mutual recognition directive (MRD)** = directive of the EC Commission that each country's accountancy firms and cross-border services should be recognised by other member states of the EC **2** *noun* a commercial enterprise which belongs to its members, such as a building society, insurance company or friendly society; *see also* DEMUTUALIZE

Nn

nail [neɪl] *noun* **to pay on the nail** = to pay promptly, to pay rapidly

naked ['neɪkɪd] *adjective* without any hedge (to protect a position)

name [neɪm] *noun* **(a)** word used to call a thing or a person; **brand name** = name of a particular make of product; **corporate name** = name of a large corporation; **under the name of** = using a particular name; **trading under the name of 'Best Foods'** = using the name 'Best Foods' as a commercial name, but not the name of the company **(b)** person who provides security for insurance arranged by a Lloyds of London syndicate

COMMENT: Lloyd's is an old-established insurance market; the underwriters who form Lloyd's are divided into syndicates, each made up of active underwriters who arrange the business and non-working underwriters (called 'names') who stand surety for any insurance claims which may arise

named ['neɪmd] *adjective* **person named in the policy** = person whose name is given on an insurance policy as the person insured

NAO = NATIONAL AUDIT OFFICE

narration *or* **narrative** [nə'reɪən *or* 'nærətɪv] *noun* series of notes and explanations relating to transactions in the accounts

NASDAQ ['næzdæk] = NATIONAL ASSOCIATION OF SECURITIES DEALERS AUTOMATED QUOTATIONS the NASDAQ system provides quotations via computer for the US over-the-counter market, and also for some large corporations listed on the NYSE

national ['næʃənl] *adjective* referring to a particular country; **National Audit Office (NAO)** = body which investigates the use of public money by central government departments (it acts on behalf of the Parliamentary Public Accounts Committee); *US* **national bank** = bank which is chartered by the federal government and is part of the Federal Reserve system (as opposed to a 'state bank'); **the National Debt** = money borrowed by a government; **national income**

= value of income from the sales of goods and services in a country; *GB* **National Insurance** = state insurance which pays for medical care, hospitals, unemployment benefits, etc.; **National Insurance contributions (NIC)** = money paid into the National Insurance scheme by the employer and the worker; **National Insurance number** = number given to each British citizen, which is the number by which he or she is known to the social security services; **gross national product** = annual value of goods and services in a country including income from other countries; *GB* **National Savings** = savings scheme for small investors run by the Post Office (including a savings bank, savings certificates and premium bonds); **National Savings Stock Register** = organization, run by the Department for National Savings, which gives private individuals the opportunity to buy certain British government stocks by post without going through a stockbroker

nationality [næʃə'næləti] *noun* **he is of British nationality** = he is a British citizen; **nationality declaration** = declaration on some share application forms that the applicant is of a certain nationality (some shares cannot be held by persons who are not British)

natural asset ['nætʃrəl 'æsɪt] *noun* asset which is a natural resource, such as an oil well (its value can be depreciated through depletion)

NAV = NET ASSET VALUE

NBV = NET BOOK VALUE

near-liquid asset *or* **near money** ['nɪə'lɪkwɪd 'æsɪt] *noun* asset which can easily be converted to cash

negative ['negətɪv] *adjective* **the answer was in the negative** = the answer was 'no'; **negative carry** = deal where the cost of finance is more than the return on the capital used; **negative cash flow** = situation where a company is spending more money than it receives; **negative equity** = situation where a house bought with a mortgage becomes less valuable than the money borrowed to buy it (because of falling house prices); **negative yield curve** = situation where the yield on a long-term investment is less than on a short-term investment; *see also* GOODWILL (NOTE: the opposite is **positive**)

negotiable [nɪ'gəʊʃəbl] *adjective* **(a)** which can be negotiated **(b)** (document) which can easily be transferred to another person; **not negotiable** = which cannot be exchanged for cash; **'not negotiable'** = words written on a cheque to show that it can be paid only to a certain person; **negotiable cheque** = cheque made payable to bearer (i.e. to anyone who holds it); **negotiable instrument** = document (such as a bill of exchange, or cheque) which can be exchanged for cash; *US* **negotiable order of withdrawal** = cheque written on a NOW account

QUOTE initial salary is negotiable around $45,000 per annum
Australian Financial Review

negotiate [nɪ'gəʊʃɪeɪt] *verb* **to negotiate with someone** = to discuss a problem formally with someone, so as to reach an agreement; *the management refused to negotiate with the union*; **to negotiate terms and conditions** *or* **to negotiate a contract** = to discuss and agree terms of a contract; *he negotiated a £250,000 loan with the bank* = he came to an agreement with the bank for a loan of £250,000

QUOTE many of the large travel agency chains are able to negotiate even greater discounts
Duns Business Month

negotiation [nɪgəʊʃɪ'eɪʃən] *noun* discussion of terms and conditions to reach an agreement; **contract under negotiation** = contract which is being discussed; **a matter for negotiation** = something which must be discussed before a decision is reached; **to enter into negotiations** *or* **to start negotiations** = to start discussing a problem; **to resume negotiations** = to start discussing a problem again, after talks have stopped for a time; **to break off negotiations** = to refuse to go on discussing a problem; **to conduct negotiations** = to negotiate; **negotiations broke down after six hours** = discussions stopped because no agreement was possible; **pay negotiations** *or* **wage negotiations** = discussions between management and workers about pay

QUOTE after three days of tough negotiations, the company reached agreement with its 1,200 unionized workers
Toronto Star

nest egg ['nest 'eg] *noun* money which someone has saved over a period of time (usually kept in an interest-bearing account, and intended for use after retirement)

net [net] **1** *adjective* **(a)** price, weight, pay, etc. after all deductions have been made; **net asset value (NAV)** *or* **net worth** = total value of an accounting entity after deducting the money owed by it (it is the value of shareholders' capital plus reserves and any money retained from profits); **net asset value per share** = value of a company calculated by dividing the shareholders' funds by the number of shares issued; **net book value (NBV)** = value of an asset in a company's books (i.e., its original purchase price less any depreciation); **net borrowings** = a company's borrowings, less any cash the company is holding in its bank accounts; **net cash flow** = difference between money coming in and money going out of a firm; **net current assets** *or* **working capital** = current assets of a company less any current liabilities; **net current liabilities** = current liabilities of a company less its current assets; **net dividend per share** = dividend per share after deduction of personal income tax; **net earnings** *or* **net income** = total earnings of a business after tax and other deductions; **net income** *or* **net salary** = person's income which is left after taking away tax and other deductions; **net loss** = actual loss, after deducting overheads; **net margin** = net profit shown as a percentage of sales; **net present value (NPV)** = value of future cash inflows less future cash outflows discounted at a certain discount rate, usually the company's cost of capital; **net price** = (i) price of goods or services which cannot be reduced by a discount; (ii) price paid for a share, where no commission is payable to the broker; **net profit** = result where income from sales is more than all expenditure; **net profit before tax** = profit of a company after expenses have been deducted but before tax has been paid; **net realizable value (NRV)** = the price at which goods in stock could be sold, less any costs incurred in making the sale; **net receipts** = receipts after deducting commission, tax, discounts, etc.; **net relevant earnings** = earnings which qualify for calculating pension contributions and against which relief against tax can be claimed (such earnings can be income from employment which is not pensionable, profits of a self-employed sole trader, etc.); **net return** = return on an investment after tax and all expenses have been paid; **net sales** = sales less damaged or returned items, discounts to retailers, etc.; **net working capital** = NET CURRENT ASSETS; **net worth** = NET ASSET VALUE; **net yield** = profit from investments after deduction of tax **(b) terms strictly net** = payment has to be the full price, with no discount allowed **2** *verb* **(a)** to make a true profit; *to net a profit of £10,000* **(b) to net out** = to offset debits and credits to give a net result

QUOTE Out of its earnings a company will pay a dividend. When shareholders receive this it will be net, that is, it will have had tax deducted at 25 per cent
Investors Chronicle

QUOTE in each of the years 1986 to 1989, Japan pumped a net sum of the order of $100bn into foreign securities markets, notably into US government bonds. In 1988, Germany was also a significant supplier of net capital to the tune of $45bn
Financial Times Review

New York Stock Exchange (NYSE)
['nju: 'jɔ:k 'stɒk ɪks'tʃeɪnʒ] the main US stock exchange, situated on Wall Street in New York

next in first out (NIFO) ['nekst 'ɪn 'fɜːst 'aʊt] method of valuing goods held in stock at the end of an accounting period in which the replacement value of the goods is used and not their historical cost

NIC = NATIONAL INSURANCE CONTRIBUTIONS

NIF = NOTE ISSUANCE FACILITY

night [naɪt] *noun* **night safe** *US* **night collection box** = safe in the outside wall of a bank where money and documents can be deposited at night using a special door

nil [nɪl] *noun* zero or nothing; *to make a nil return*; *the advertising budget has been cut to nil*; **nil paid shares** = new shares which have not yet been paid for

No. = NUMBER

no-claims bonus ['nəʊ'kleɪmz 'bəʊnəs] *noun* reduction of premiums on an insurance policy because no claims have been made

nominal ['nɒmɪnl] *adjective* **(a)** very small (payment); *we make a nominal charge for our services*; *they are paying a nominal rent*; **nominal account** = account for recording

transactions relating to a particular type of expense or receipt **(b)** **(nominal) share capital** = the total of the face value of all the shares which a company is authorized to issue according to its memorandum of association; **nominal interest rate** = interest rate expressed as a percentage of the face value of a bond, not on its market value; **nominal ledger** = book which records a company's income and expenditure in general, but not debtors, creditor and cash which are recorded in separate ledgers; **nominal value** *or* **face value** *or* **par value** = value written on a share, a coin or a banknote

nominee [nɒmɪ'ni:] *noun* person who is nominated, especially someone who is appointed to deal with financial matters on behalf of another person; **nominee account** = account held on behalf of someone

COMMENT: shares can be purchased and held in nominee accounts so that the identity of the owner of the shares cannot be discovered

non- [nɒn] *prefix* not

non-acceptance ['nɒnək'septəns] *noun* situation where the person who is to pay a bill of exchange does not accept it

non-cash items ['nɒn'kæʃ 'aɪtəmz] *noun* items in an income statement which are not cash, such as depreciation expenses, gains and losses from investments

non-contributory ['nɒnkən'trɪbjʊtəri] *adjective* **non-contributory pension scheme** = pension scheme where the employee does not make any contributions and the company pays everything; *the company pension scheme is non-contributory*

non-executive **director** ['nɒnɪg'zekjʊtɪv daɪ'rektə] *noun* director who attends board meetings and gives advice, but does not work full-time for the company

non-feasance ['nɒn'fi:zəns] *noun* not doing something which should be done by law

non-historic ['nɒnhɪ'stɒrɪk] *adjective* not calculated on a historical cost basis

nonlinear ['nɒn'lɪniə] *adjective* electronic circuit whose output does not change in direct proportion to its input

non-monetary ['nɒn'mʌnɪtəri] *adjective* (items or assets) which are not money, and can be valued at a higher value than their original purchase price

non-negotiable **instrument** ['nɒnnɪ'gəʊʃəbl 'ɪnstrəmənt] *noun* document (such as a crossed cheque) which cannot be exchanged for cash

non-payment ['nɒn'peɪmənt] *noun* **non-payment of a debt** = not paying a debt due

non-performing loan ['nɒnpə'fɔːmɪŋ 'ləʊn] *noun US* loan where the borrower is not likely to pay (as in the case of loans to Third World countries by western banks)

non-production overhead cost ['nɒnprə'dʌkʃn 'əʊvəhed 'kɒst] *noun* overhead cost, such as administration or marketing, which is not incurred in producing the product

non profit-making organization *US* **non-profit corporation** ['nɒn'prɒfɪt'meɪkɪŋ ɔːɡənaɪ'zeɪʃən *or* 'nɒn'prɒfɪt kɔːpə'reɪʃən] *noun* organization (such as a club) which is not allowed by law to make a profit; *non-profit-making organizations are exempted from tax*

non-recurring ['nɒnrɪ'kɜːrɪŋ 'aɪtəmz] *adjective* **non-recurring items** = special items in a set of accounts which appear only once

non-refundable ['nɒnrɪ'fʌndəbl] *adjective* which will not be refunded; *non-refundable deposit*

non-residence ['nɒn'rezɪdəns] *noun* state of not being resident in a country for tax purposes

non-resident ['nɒn'rezɪdənt] *noun* person who is not considered a resident of a country for tax purposes; *he has a non-resident bank account*

non-statutory ['nɒn'stætjʊtri] *adjective* not covered by legislation

non-taxable ['nɒn'tæksəbl] *adjective* which is not subject to tax; *non-taxable income*

non-taxpayer ['nɒn'tækspeɪə] *noun* person who does not pay tax because he or she has no income, or because his or her income is too low

non-trade creditor ['nɒn'treɪd 'kredɪtə] *noun* creditor who is not owed money in the normal trade of a business (such as a debenture holder or the Inland Revenue)

non-voting shares ['nɒn'vəʊtɪŋ 'ʃeəz] *noun* shares which do not allow the shareholder to vote at meetings (also called 'A' shares)

normal ['nɔːməl] *adjective* usual, which happens regularly; **normal loss** = loss which is usual in the type of business being carried on (such as loss of small quantities of materials during the manufacturing process)

normalize ['nɔːməlaɪz] *verb* **(a)** to convert data into a form which can be read by a particular computer system **(b)** to store and represent numbers in a pre-agreed form, usually to provide maximum precision; **normalized form** = floating point number that has been normalized so that its mantissa is within a certain range

notary public ['nəʊtəri 'pʌblɪk] *noun* lawyer who has the authority to witness documents and spoken statements, making them official (NOTE: plural is **notaries public**)

note [nəʊt] *noun* **(a)** short document, short piece of information; **advice note** = written notice to a customer giving details of goods ordered and shipped but not yet delivered; **contract note** = note showing that shares have been bought or sold but not yet paid for; **cover note** = letter from an insurance company giving details of an insurance policy and confirming that the policy exists; **covering note** = letter sent with documents to explain why you are sending them; **credit note** = note showing that money is owed to a customer; **debit note** = note showing that a customer owes money; *we undercharged Mr Smith and had to send him a debit note for the extra amount*; **delivery note** = list of goods being delivered, given to the customer with the goods; **dispatch note** = note saying that goods have been sent; **note of hand** *or* **promissory note** = document stating that someone promises to pay an amount of money on a certain date **(b)** paper showing that money has been borrowed; **note issuance facility (NIF)** = credit facility where a company obtains a loan underwritten by banks and can issue a series of short-term eurocurrency notes to replace others which have expired; **promissory note** = document stating that someone promises to pay an amount of money on a certain date **(c)** **bank note** *or* **currency note** = piece of printed paper money; *a £20 note*; *he pulled out a pile of used notes* **(d)** short piece of writing; **notes to the accounts** = notes attached to a company's accounts to explain items in the accounts or to explain the accounting policies and principles used

notional ['nəʊʃənl] *adjective* probable but not known exactly, not quantifiable; **notional**

income = invisible benefit which is not money or goods and services; **notional rent** = sum put into accounts as rent where the company owns the building it is occupying and so does not pay an actual rent

nought [nɔːt] number 0; *a million pounds can be written as '£1m' or as one and six noughts* (NOTE: **nought** is commoner in British English; in American English, **zero** is more usual)

novation [nəʊ'veɪʃn] *noun* agreement to change a contract by substituting a third party for one of the two original parties

NOW account ['naʊ ə'kaʊnt] *noun US* (= NEGOTIABLE ORDER OF WITHDRAWAL ACCOUNT) an interest-bearing cheque account in which a minimum of $500 has to be kept at all times (cheques drawn on it are called 'negotiable orders of withdrawal')

NPV = NET PRESENT VALUE

NRV = NET REALIZABLE VALUE

number ['nʌmbə] **1** *noun* **(a)** quantity of things or people; *the number of persons on the payroll has increased over the last year; the number of days lost through strikes has fallen; the number of shares sold* **(b)** written figure; *account number; batch number; cheque number; invoice number; order number; page number; serial number; phone number;* **box number** = reference number used when asking for mail to be sent to a post office or when asking for replies to an advertisement to be sent to the newspaper's offices; *please reply to Box No. 209;* **index number** = (i) number of something in an index; (ii) number showing the percentage rise of something over a period (NOTE: often written **No.** with figures) **2** *verb* to put a figure on a document; *to number an order; I refer to your invoice numbered 1234;* **numbered account** = bank account (usually in Switzerland) which is referred to only by a number, the name of the person holding it being kept secret

numeral ['njuːmərəl] *noun* character or symbol which represents a number; **Arabic numerals** = figures written 1, 2, 3, 4, etc.; **Roman numerals** = figures written I, II, III, IV, etc.

numeric *or* **numerical** [njʊ'merɪk *or* njʊ'merɪkl] *adjective* referring to numbers; **in numerical order** = in the order of figures (such as 1 before 2, 33 before 34); *file these invoices in numerical order;* **numeric data** = data in the form of figures; **numeric keypad** = part of a computer keyboard which is a programmable set of numbered keys

nuncupative will ['nʌnkjupətɪv 'wɪl] *noun* will made orally in the presence of a witness (as by a soldier in time of war)

NYSE = NEW YORK STOCK EXCHANGE

Oo

objective [əb'dʒektɪv] **1** *noun* something which you try to do; *the company has achieved its objectives; we set the sales force certain objectives*; **long-term objective** *or* **short-term objective** = aim which you hope to achieve within a few years or a few months; **management by objectives** = way of managing a business by setting work targets for the managers and testing if they are achieved correctly and on time **2** *adjective* (i) considered from a general point of view not from that of the person involved; (ii) (measure of quantity or value) which carries no opinion and can be checked; *to carry out an objective survey of the market; physical stocktaking is an objective measure* (NOTE: the opposite is **subjective)**

objectivity [ɒbdʒek'tɪvəti] *noun* being objective (i.e. not showing any opinion or bias) (NOTE: the opposite is **subjectivity)**

obligate ['ɒblɪgeɪt] *verb* **to be obligated to do something** = to have a legal duty to do something

obligation [ɒblɪ'geɪʃən] *noun* **(a)** duty to do something; **to be under an obligation to do something** = to feel it is your duty to do something; *there is no obligation to buy; to be under no obligation to do something*; **he is under no contractual obligation to buy** = he has signed no contract which forces him to buy; **to fulfil one's contractual obligations** = to do what is stated in a contract; **two weeks' free trial without obligation** = the customer can try the item at home for two weeks without having to buy it at the end of the test **(b)** duty to pay a debt; **to meet one's obligations** = to pay one's debts

o.b.o. = OR BEST OFFER

obsolescence [ɒbsə'lesəns] *noun* being obsolete; **built-in** *or* **planned obsolescence** = method of ensuring continuing sales of a product by making it in such a way that it will soon become obsolete

obsolete ['ɒbsəliːt] *adjective* out of date, no longer suitable for current use; (product) which has ended its useful life

COMMENT: a product or asset may become obsolete because it is worn out, or because new technology has developed new products to replace it

occupational [ɒkjʊ'peɪʃənl] *adjective* referring to a job; **occupational accident** = accident which takes place at work; **occupational pension scheme** = pension scheme where the worker gets a pension from the company he has worked for

occupier ['ɒkjʊpaɪə] *noun* person who lives in a property; **beneficial occupier** = person who occupies a property but does not own it fully; **owner-occupier** = person who owns the property in which he lives

odd [ɒd] *adjective* **(a) odd numbers** = numbers (like 17 or 33) which cannot be divided by two; *odd-numbered buildings or buildings with odd numbers are on the south side of the street* **(b) a hundred odd** = approximately one hundred; **keep the odd change** = keep the small change which is left over **(c) odd lot** = group of miscellaneous items, such as a small block of shares

Oeics ['əʊɪks] = OPEN-ENDED INVESTMENT COMPANIES

off [ɒf] **1** *adverb* **(a)** taken away from a price; *we give 5% off for quick settlement* **(b)** lower than (a previous price); *the shares closed 2% off* **2** *preposition* **(a)** away from a price; *to take £25 off the price; these carpets are sold at £25 off the marked price; we give 10% off our normal prices* **(b)** not included; **items off balance sheet** *or* **off balance sheet assets** = financial items which do not appear in a company's balance sheet as assets (such as equipment acquired under an operating lease); **off balance sheet financing** = financing by leasing equipment under an operating lease instead of buying it, so that it does not appear in the balance sheet as an asset (see SSAP21)

QUOTE its stock closed Monday at $21.875 a share in NYSE composite trading, off 56% from its high last July

Wall Street Journal

offer ['ɒfə] **1** *noun* **(a)** statement that you are willing to pay a certain amount of money to buy something; *to make an offer for a company*; *he made an offer of £10 a share*; *we made a written offer for the house*; *£1,000 is the best offer I can make*; *to accept an offer of £1,000 for the car*; **the house is under offer** = someone has made an offer to buy the house and the offer has been accepted provisionally; **we are open to offers** = we are ready to discuss the price which we are asking; **cash offer** = being ready to pay in cash; **offer price** = price at which investors buy new shares or units in a unit trust (the opposite, i.e., the selling price, is called the 'bid price'; the difference between the two is the 'spread') **(b)** statement that you are willing to sell something for a certain amount of money; **offer for sale** = situation where a company advertises new shares for sale to the public as a way of launching the company on the Stock Exchange (the other ways of launching a company are a 'tender' or a 'placing') (NOTE: the American equivalent for this is **public offering**) **(c)** statement that a company is prepared to buy another company's shares and take the company over; **offer document** = formal document where a company offers to buy shares at a certain price as part of a takeover bid; **offer period** = time during which a takeover bid for a company is open **(d) he received six offers of jobs** *or* **six job offers** = six companies told him he could have a job with them **(e) bargain offer** = sale of a particular type of goods at a cheap price; *this week's bargain offer - 30% off all carpet prices*; **introductory offer** = special price offered on a new product to attract customers; **special offer** = goods put on sale at a specially low price; *we have a range of men's shirts on special offer* **(f) near offer** *US* **or best offer** *or* **or nearest offer** = or an offer of a price which is slightly less than the price asked; *the car is for sale at £2,000 or near offer* (NOTE: often shortened to **o.n.o., o.b.o.**) **2** *verb* **(a)** to say that you are willing to pay a certain amount of money for something; *to offer someone £100,000 for his house*; *he offered £10 a share*; **offered price** = price at which shares are offered for sale by a marketmaker on the Stock Exchange (the opposite, i.e., the price at which an investor sells shares, is the 'bid price'; the difference

between the two is the 'spread') **(b)** to say that you are willing to sell something; *we offered the house for sale*

offeree [ɒfə'ri:] *noun* person who receives an offer

offering ['ɒfrɪŋ] *noun* action of stating that you are prepared to sell something at a certain price; **offering circular** = document which gives information about a company whose shares are being sold to the public for the first time; **initial public offering (IPO)** = offering new shares in a corporation for sale to the public as a way of launching the corporation on the Stock Exchange (NOTE: also called an **offer for sale**)

offeror ['ɒfərə] *noun* person who makes an offer

office ['ɒfɪs] *noun* **(a)** set of rooms where a company works or where business is done; **branch office** = less important office, usually in a different town or country from the main office; **head office** *or* **main office** = office building where the board of directors works and meets; *GB* **registered office** = office address of a company which is officially registered with the Companies' Registrar **(b)** **office hours** = time when an office is open; *open during normal office hours*; *do not telephone during office hours*; *the manager can be reached at home out of office hours*; **office space** *or* **office accommodation** = space available for offices or occupied by offices; **office staff** = people who work in offices **(c)** room where someone works and does business; **back office** = (i) the part of a broking firm where the paperwork involved in buying and selling shares is processed; (ii) *US* part of a bank where cheques are processed, statements of account drawn up, etc.) **(d)** **employment office** = office which finds jobs for people; **general office** = main administrative office in a company; **information office** = office which gives information to tourists or visitors; **inquiry office** = office where someone can answer questions from members of the public **(e)** *GB* government department; **the Home Office** = ministry dealing with the internal affairs of the country; **Office of Fair Trading (OFT)** = government department which protects consumers against unfair or illegal business; it also decides if a takeover bid is in the interests of the ordinary customers of the two companies concerned, and may refer such a bid to the Monopolies and Mergers Commission for investigation; **Serious Fraud Office (SFO)** = government department in charge of investigating major fraud in companies; *US* **Office of Management and Budget (OMB)** = government department which prepares the budget for the president **(f)** post or position; **compensation for loss of office** = payment to a director who is asked to leave a company before his contract ends

officer ['ɒfɪsə] *noun* person who has an official position; **the company officers** *or* **the officers of a company** = the main executives or directors of a company; **customs officer** = person working for the Customs and Excise Department; **personnel officer** = person who deals with the staff, especially interviewing applicants for jobs; **training officer** = person who deals with the training of staff

official [ə'fɪʃəl] **1** *adjective* from a government department or organization; **speaking in an official capacity** = speaking officially; **to go through official channels** = to deal with officials, especially when making a request; **the official exchange rate** = exchange rate which is imposed by the government; *the official exchange rate is ten to the dollar, but you can get twice that on the black market*; **official intervention** = attempt by a government to influence the exchange rate, by buying or selling foreign currency; **Official List** = daily publication by the London Stock Exchange of the highest and lowest prices recorded for each share during the trading session; **official market** = the market in shares on the London Stock Exchange (as opposed to the grey market); **the Official Receiver** = government official who is appointed to deal with bankruptcies or with companies in liquidation **2** *noun* person working in a government department; **customs official** = person working for the customs

officio [ə'fɪʃɪəʊ] *see* EX OFFICIO

off-line ['ɒf'laɪn] *adverb & adjective* (i) (processor, printer or terminal) that is not connected to a network or central computer (usually temporarily); (ii) (peripheral) connected to a network, but not available for use

offload [ɒf'ləʊd] *verb* to pass something which is not wanted to someone else; **to offload excess stock** = to try to sell excess stock; **to offload costs onto a subsidiary company** = to try to get a subsidiary company to pay some charges so as to reduce tax (NOTE: you offload something **from** a thing or person **onto** another thing or person)

offset [ɒf'set] *verb* to balance one thing against another so that they cancel each other

out; *to offset losses against tax*; *foreign exchange losses more than offset profits in the domestic market* (NOTE: **offsetting - offset**)

offshore ['ɒf'ʃɔː] *adjective & adverb* **(a)** on an island, in the sea near to land; *offshore oil field* **(b)** based outside a country (especially in a tax haven); **offshore banking** = banking in a tax haven; **offshore fund** = fund which is based outside the UK, and usually in a country which has less strict taxation than in the UK, such as the Bahamas, etc.

off-the-job training ['ɒfðə'dʒɒb 'treɪnɪŋ] *noun* training given to workers away from their place of work (such as at a college or school)

off-the-shelf company ['ɒfðə'ʃelf 'kʌmpni] *noun* company which has already been registered by an accountant or lawyer, and which is ready for sale to someone who wants to set up a new company quickly

OFT = OFFICE OF FAIR TRADING

old age pension ['əʊld 'eɪdʒ 'penʃn] *noun* retirement pension, a state pension given to a man who is over 65 or a woman who is over 60 (the pensionable age for women is rising by stages to 65)

OMB = OFFICE OF MANAGEMENT AND BUDGET

ombudsman ['ɒmbʊdzmən] *noun* Parliamentary Commissioner, an official who investigates complaints by the public against government departments or other large organizations

COMMENT: there are several ombudsmen: the main one is the Parliamentary Commissioner, who is a civil servant who investigates complaints against government departments. The Banking Ombudsman and the Building Societies Ombudsman are independent officials who investigate complaints by the public against banks or building societies. The Pensions Ombudsman and Personal Investment Authority Ombudsman investigate complaints about personal pensions and employers' pension schemes, and personal investments such as unit trusts. See also ADJUDICATOR

omission [əʊˈmɪʃən] *noun* thing which has been omitted; **errors and omissions excepted** = words written on an invoice to show that the company has no responsibility for mistakes in the invoice

omit [əʊˈmɪt] *verb* not to do something which should be done; *US* **to omit a dividend** = to pay no dividend in a certain year (NOTE: the British equivalent is **to pass a dividend**)

oncosts [ˈɒnkɒsts] *plural noun* fixed costs, money paid in producing a product which does not rise with the quantity of the product made

one-man [ˈwɒnˈmæn] *adjective* **one-man business** *or* **firm** *or* **company** *or* **operation** = business run by one person alone with no staff or partners

one-off [ˈwɒnˈɒf] *adjective* done or made only once; *one-off item*; *one-off deal*

one-sided [ˈwɒnˈsaɪdɪd] *adjective* which favours one side and not the other in a negotiation; *one-sided agreement*

one-stop banking [ˈwɒnˈstɒp ˈbæŋkɪŋ] *noun* banking organization offering a whole range of services (including mortgages, loans, pensions, etc.) (also called **full-service banking**)

one-year money [ˈwɒnˈjeə ˈmʌni] *noun* money placed for one year

on-line *or* **on line** *or* **online** [ˈɒn ˈlaɪn] *adverb & adjective* (terminal or device) connected to and under the control of a central processor; *the sales office is on line to the warehouse*; *we get our data on line from the stock control department*

o.n.o. = OR NEAR OFFER

open [ˈəʊpən] **1** *adjective* **(a)** at work, not closed; *not all banks are open on Saturdays*; *our offices are open from 9 to 6*; *they are open for business every day of the week* **(b)** ready to accept something; *the job is open to all applicants* = anyone can apply for the job; **open to offers** = ready to accept a reasonable offer; *the company is open to offers for the empty factory* = the company is ready to discuss an offer which is lower than the suggested price **(c)** **open account** = account where the supplier offers the purchaser unsecured credit; **open cheque** = cheque

which is not crossed and can be cashed anywhere; **open credit** = bank credit given to good customers without security up to a certain maximum sum; **open market** = market where anyone can buy or sell; **to buy shares on the open market** = to buy shares on the Stock Exchange, not privately; **open ticket** = ticket which can be used on any date **2** *verb* **(a)** to start a new business working; *she has opened a shop in the High Street*; *we have opened an office in London* **(b)** to start work, to be at work; *the office opens at 9 a.m.*; *we open for business on Sundays* **(c)** to begin; **to open negotiations** = to begin negotiating; *he opened the discussions with a description of the product*; *the chairman opened the meeting at 10.30* **(d)** to start, to allow something to start; *to open a bank account*; *to open a line of credit*; *to open a loan* **(e)** **the shares opened lower** = share prices were lower at the beginning of the day's trading

QUOTE after opening at 79.1 the index touched a peak of 79.2 and then drifted to a low of 78.8
Financial Times

open-ended *US* **open-end** [ˈəʊpənˈendɪd *or* ˈəʊpənˈend] *adjective* with no fixed limit, with some items not specified; **open-ended fund** = fund (such as a unit trust or mutual fund) where investors buy units, the money paid being invested in a range of securities (as opposed to a closed fund, such as an investment trust, where investors buys shares in the trust company, and receive dividends)

Open-ended investment company (Oeic) [ˈəʊpənˈendɪd ɪnˈvestmənt ˈkʌmpni] *noun* form of unit trust, in which the investor purchases shares at a single price, as opposed to the offer/bid pricing system used by ordinary unit trusts

QUOTE Oeics are 'open-ended' accepting any amount of investors' money on an on-going basis, but structured as a company with shares. Most importantly, the shares have a single price for both buying and selling
The Times

opening [ˈəʊpənɪŋ] **1** *noun* **(a)** act of starting a new business; *the opening of a new branch*; *the opening of a new market or of a new distribution network* **(b)** **opening hours** = hours when a shop or business is open **2** *adjective* at the beginning, first; **opening balance** = balance at the beginning of an accounting period; **opening bid** = first bid at an auction; **opening entry** = first entry in an account; **opening price** = price at the start of the day's trading; **opening stock** = stock at the beginning of the accounting period

operand ['ɒpərænd] *noun* data (in a computer instruction) which is to be operated on by the operator

operate ['ɒpəreɪt] *verb* to work, to run; *the new terms of service will operate from January 1st*; *the rules operate on inland postal services*

> QUOTE the company gets valuable restaurant locations which will be converted to the family-style restaurant chain that it operates and franchises throughout most parts of the US
> *Fortune*

operating ['ɒpəreɪtɪŋ] *noun* general running of a business or of a machine; **operating budget** = forecast of trading income and expenditure over a period of time; **operating costs** *or* **operating expenses** = costs of production, selling and administration incurred during normal trading; **operating costing** = costing which is based on the costs of services provided (used when costing service industries); **operating cycle** = the time it takes for purchases of materials for production to generate revenue from sales; **operating lease** = lease which does not require the lessee company to show the asset acquired under the lease in its balance sheet but the annual rental charge for such assets must be disclosed in a note to the accounts; **operating manual** = book which shows how to work a machine; **operating profit** *or* **operating loss** = profit or loss made by a company in its usual business (usually calculated before tax has been paid); **operating system** = the main program which operates a computer; **operating time** = total time required to carry out a task

> QUOTE the company blamed over-capacity and competitive market conditions in Europe for a £14m operating loss last year
> *Financial Times*

operation [ɒpə'reɪʃən] *noun* **(a)** business organization and work; *the company's operations in West Africa*; *he heads up the operations in Northern Europe*; **operation costing** = costing method for batches of goods where materials are related to each batch separately but labour and direct overheads are allocated to the operations through which the batches pass; **operations review** = examining the way in which a company or department works to see how it can be made more efficient and profitable; **a franchising operation** = selling licences to trade as a franchise **(b)** working (of a machine); **operation cycle** = section of the machine cycle during which the instruction is executed; **operation time** = period of time that an operation requires for its operation cycle

> QUOTE a leading manufacturer of business, industrial and commercial products requires a branch manager to head up its mid-western Canada operations based in Winnipeg
> *Globe and Mail (Toronto)*

operational [ɒpə'reɪʃənl] *adjective* referring to how something works; **operational budget** = forecast of revenue and expenditure for planned business activity; **operational costs** = costs of production, selling and administration; **operational gearing** = situation where a company has high fixed costs which are funded by borrowings; **operational planning** = planning how a business is to be run; **operational research** = study of a company's way of working to see if it can be made more efficient and profitable

operator ['ɒpəreɪtə] *noun* **(a)** person who runs a business **(b)** person who makes a machine or process work; **computer operator** = person who operates a computer; **operator's console** = input and output devices used by an operator to control a computer (usually consisting of a keyboard and VDU)

> QUOTE a number of block bookings by American tour operators have been cancelled
> *Economist*

OPM ['əʊpiː'em] = OTHER PEOPLE'S MONEY money which a business 'borrows' from its creditors, such as by not paying invoices on schedule, and so avoids using its own funds

opportunity [ɒpə'tjuːnəti] *noun* situation where you can do something successfully; **investment opportunities** *or* **sales opportunities** = possibilities for making investments or sales which will be profitable; **a market opportunity** = possibility of going into a market for the first time; **opportunity cost** = cost of making a decision about how to use limited resources, expressed in terms of the benefit lost by not making the next best decision

oppose [ə'pəʊz] *verb* to try to stop something happening; to vote against something; *a minority of board members opposed the motion*; *we are all opposed to the takeover*

optimal ['ɒptɪməl] *adjective* best

optimism ['ɒptɪmɪzm] *noun* being sure that everything will work out well; *he has considerable optimism about sales possibilities in the Far East*; **market optimism** = feeling that the stock market will rise

optimum ['ɒptɪməm] *adjective* best; *the market offers optimum conditions for sales*

option ['ɒpʃən] *noun* **(a) option to purchase** *or* **to sell** = giving someone the possibility to buy or sell something within a period of time; **first option** = allowing someone to be the first to have the possibility of deciding something; **to grant someone a six-month option on a product** = to allow someone six months to decide if he wants to be the agent for the product, or if he wants to manufacture it; **to take up an option** *or* **to exercise an option** = to accept the option which has been offered and to put it into action; *he exercised his option or he took up his option to acquire sole marketing rights to the product*; **I want to leave my options open** = I want to be able to decide what to do when the time is right; **to take the soft option** = to decide to do something which involves the least risk, effort or problems **(b)** *(Stock Exchange)* giving someone the right to buy or sell a security, a financial instrument, a commodity, etc., at a certain price on a certain date; **call option** = option to buy shares at a certain price; **double option** = option to buy or sell at a certain price in the future (a combination of call and put options); **put option** = option to sell shares at a certain price; **share option** = right to buy or sell shares at a certain price at a time in the future; **stock option** *or* **share option** = right to buy shares at a cheap price given by a company to its employees; **writer of an option** = person who sells an option; **option contract** = right to buy or sell shares at a fixed price; **option dealing** *or* **option trading** = buying and selling share options; **traded options** = options to buy or sell shares at a certain price at a certain date in the future, which themselves can be bought or sold (in London, this is done through the Traded Options Market or TOM); **option holder** = person who holds an option (i.e., who has bought an option)

optional ['ɒpʃənl] *adjective* which can be added if required; *the insurance cover is optional*

order ['ɔːdə] **1** *noun* **(a)** arrangement of records (filing cards, invoices, etc.); **alphabetical order** = arrangement by the letters of the alphabet (A, B, C, etc.); **chronological order** = arrangement by the order of the dates; **numerical order** = arrangement by numbers **(b)** document which allows money to be paid to someone; *he sent us an order on the Chartered Bank*; **banker's order** *or* **standing order** = order written by a customer asking a bank to make a regular payment; *he pays his subscription by banker's order*; **money order** = document which can be bought for sending money through the post **(c) pay to Mr Smith or order** = pay money to Mr Smith or as he orders; **pay to the order of Mr Smith** = pay money directly into Mr Smith's account; **order cheque** = cheque which is paid to a named person with the words 'or order' after the payee's name, showing that he can endorse it and pass it to someone else if he wishes **(d)** *(Stock Exchange)* instruction to a broker to buy or sell; **order-driven system** = price system on a stock exchange, where prices vary according to the level of orders (as opposed to a 'quote-driven' system) **(e)** official request for goods to be supplied; **to fill** *or* **to fulfil an order** = to supply items which have been ordered; **purchase order** = official document which places an order for something; **order fulfilment** = supplying items which have been ordered; **order processing time** *or* **lead time** = time between deciding to place an order and receiving the product; **economic order quantity (EOQ)** = optimum quantity of stocks which a company should hold based on the costs of ordering and warehousing, availability of bulk discounts (lower unit costs because of higher quantities purchased will be offset by higher warehousing costs), the rate at which stocks are used and the time it takes for suppliers to deliver new orders; **terms: cash with order** = the goods will be supplied only if payment in cash is made at the same time as the order is placed; **items available to order only** = items which will be manufactured only if someone orders them; **on order** = ordered but not delivered; **unfulfilled orders** *or* **back orders** *or* **outstanding orders** = orders received in the past and not yet supplied; **order book** = record of orders; **the company has a full order book** = it has enough orders to work at full capacity; **a pad of order forms** = a pad of blank sheets for orders to be written on **2** *verb* to make a request for goods to be supplied; **ordering costs** = costs of placing an order (i.e., the cost of typing the order form, sending the order, etc.)

```
QUOTE  in  the  view  of  some
professionals,   an   order-driven
market where investors' buy and sell
orders are matched, might prove more
appropriate for private individuals
than   the   present   marketmaking
system which concentrates on high
turnover shares
                        Accountancy
```

ordinarily resident ['ɔːdnrəli 'rezɪdənt] *adjective* normally living in a country; *Mr Schmidt is ordinarily resident in Canada*

ordinary ['ɔːdnri] *adjective* normal, not special; **ordinary commuting** = travel between your home and your place of work (the cost is not tax-deductible); **ordinary resolution** = resolution put before an AGM, usually referring to some general procedural matter, and which requires a simple majority of votes to be accepted; **ordinary shares** = normal shares in a company, which have no special bonuses or restrictions (NOTE: the American term is **common stock**); **ordinary shareholder** = person who owns ordinary shares in a company; **ordinary share capital** = capital of a company in the form of money paid for ordinary shares; **FT Ordinary Share Index** = index based on the market prices of thirty blue-chip companies (this index is the oldest of the FT indices, and is now considered too narrow to have much relevance); *US* **ordinary interest** = annual interest calculated on the basis of 360 days (as opposed to 'exact interest' which is calculated on 365 days)

ordinary activities ['ɔːdnri æk'tɪvɪtiːz] *noun* normal trading of a company, that is, what the company normally does (see FRS3)

COMMENT: FRS3 widened the definition of ordinary activities so as to include any activities which are undertaken by a reporting entity as part of its business and such related activities in which the reporting entity engages in furtherance of, incidental to, or arising from, these activities. This change from an earlier accounting standard meant that 'extraordinary items' disappeared from UK published accounts. Now, ordinary activities include the effects on the reporting entity of any event in the various environments in which it operates, including the political, regulatory, economic and geographical environments, irrespective of the frequency or unusual nature of the events

organic growth [ɔː'gænɪk 'grəʊθ] *noun* internal growth, the expansion of a company which is based on profits from its existing trading (as opposed to external growth, which comes from the acquisition of other companies)

organization [ɔːgənaɪ'zeɪʃən] *noun* **(a)** way of arranging something so that it works efficiently; *the chairman handles the organization of the AGM*; *the organization of the group is too centralized to be efficient*; *the organization of the head office into departments*; **organization and methods (O&M)** = examining how an office works, and suggesting how it can be made more efficient; **organization chart** = list of people working in various departments, showing how a company or office is organized; **line organization** = organization of a business where each manager is responsible for doing what his superior tells him to do **(b)** group or institution which is arranged for efficient work; **a government organization** = official body, run by the government; **a travel organization** = body representing companies in the travel business; **an employers' organization** = group of employers with similar interests

```
QUOTE working with a client base
which   includes   many   major
commercial    organizations    and
nationalized industries
                             Times
```

organizational [ɔːgənaɪ'zeɪʃənl] *adjective* referring to the way in which something is organized; *the paper gives a diagram of the company's organizational structure*

organize ['ɔːgənaɪz] *verb* to arrange something so that it works efficiently; *the company is organized into six profit centres*

```
QUOTE we  organize  a  rate  with
importers who have large orders and
guarantee them space at a fixed rate
so that they can plan their costs
                        Lloyd's List
```

OTC = OVER-THE-COUNTER MARKET

other people's money (OPM) ['ʌðə 'piːplz 'mʌniː] *see* OPM

out [aʊt] *adverb* **to be out** = to be wrong in calculating something; *the balance is £10 out*; **we are £20,000 out in our calculations** = we have £20,000 too much or too little

outflow ['aʊtfləʊ] *noun* **outflow of capital from a country** = capital which is sent out of a country for investment abroad

```
QUOTE Nigeria   recorded   foreign
exchange outflow of N972.9 million
for the month of June 1985
                Business Times (Lagos)
```

outgoings ['aʊtgəʊɪŋz] *plural noun* money which is paid out

outlay ['aʊtleɪ] *noun* money spent, expenditure; **capital outlay** = money spent on fixed assets (such as property, machinery, furniture); **for a modest outlay** = for a small sum

outlook ['aʊtlʊk] *noun* view of what is going to happen in the future; *the economic outlook is not good; the stock market outlook is worrying*

QUOTE American demand has transformed the profit outlook for many European manufacturers
Duns Business Month

out of pocket ['aʊt əv 'pɒkɪt] *adjective & adverb* having paid out money personally; *the deal has left me out of pocket*; **out-of-pocket expenses** = amount of money paid back to an employee for his own money which he has spent on company business

output ['aʊtpʊt] *noun* **(a)** amount which a company or a person or a machine produces; *output has increased by 10%*; *25% of our output is exported*; **output per hour** = amount produced in one hour; **output bonus** = extra payment for increased production; **output tax** = VAT charged by a company on goods or services sold **(b)** information which is produced by a computer

QUOTE crude oil output plunged during the last month and is likely to remain near its present level for the near future
Wall Street Journal

outright ['aʊtraɪt] *adverb & adjective* completely; **to purchase something outright** *or* **to make an outright purchase** = to buy something completely, including all rights to it

outside ['aʊtsaɪd] *adjective & adverb* not in a company's office or building; **to send work to be done outside** = to send work to be done in other offices; **outside office hours** = when the office is not open; **outside accountant** *or* **outside director** = accountant or director who is not employed by the company; **outside shareholders** = minority shareholders; **outside worker** = worker who does not work in a company's offices

outsource ['aʊtsɔːs] *verb* to obtain services from specialist bureaux or other companies, rather than employing full-time members of staff to provide them; *we outsourced our accounting function to reduce costs*; *computer maintenance is often outsourced*

outsourcing ['aʊtsɔːsɪŋ] *noun* obtaining services from specialist bureaux or other companies, rather than employing full-time members of staff to provide them

QUOTE organizations in the public and private sectors are increasingly buying in specialist services - or outsourcing - allowing them to cut costs and concentrate on their core business activities
Financial Times

outstanding [aʊt'stændɪŋ] *adjective* not yet paid or completed; **outstanding cheque** = cheque which has been written and therefore has been entered in the company's ledgers, but which has not been presented for payment and so has not been debited from the company's bank account; **outstanding debts** = debts which are waiting to be paid; **outstanding orders** = orders received but not yet supplied; **what is the amount outstanding?** = how much money is still owed?

COMMENT: note the difference between 'outstanding' and 'overdue'. If a debtor has 30 days credit, then his debts are outstanding until the end of the 30 days, and they only become overdue on the 31st day

outvote [aʊt'vəʊt] *verb* to defeat in a vote; **the chairman was outvoted** = the majority voted against the chairman

overabsorbed overhead ['əʊvəæb'zɔːbd] *noun* absorbed overhead which ends up by being higher than the actual overhead incurred (NOTE: the opposite is **underabsorbed)**

overabsorption [əʊvəæb'zɔːpʃn] *noun* situation where the actual overhead incurred is less than the absorbed overhead (NOTE: the opposite is **underabsorption)**

overall [əʊvər'ɔːl] *adjective* covering or including everything; **although some divisions traded profitably, the company reported an overall fall in profits** = the company reported a general fall in profits; **overall plan** = plan which covers everything

overborrowed [əʊvə'bɒrəʊd] *adjective* (company) which has very high borrowings compared to its assets, and has difficulty in meeting its interest payments

overcapacity [əʊvəkə'pæsəti] *noun* unused capacity for producing something

overcapitalized [əuvə'kæpɪtəlaɪzd] *adjective* with more capital in a company than it needs

overcharge 1 ['əuvətʃɑːdʒ] *noun* charge which is higher than it should be; *to pay back an overcharge* **2** [əuvə'tʃɑːdʒ] *verb* to ask too much money; *they overcharged us for meals*; *we asked for a refund because we had been overcharged*

overdraft ['əuvədrɑːft] *noun* **(a)** *GB* amount of money which a company or person can withdraw from a bank account with the bank's permission, and which is more than there is in the account; *the bank has allowed me an overdraft of £5,000*; **overdraft facility** = arrangement with a bank to have an overdraft; **we have exceeded our overdraft facility** = we have taken out more than the overdraft allowed by the bank **(b)** *US* negative amount of money in an account, i.e. situation where a cheque is more than the money in the account on which it is drawn (American banks do not offer overdraft facilities in the same way as British banks)

overdraw [əuvə'drɔː] *verb* to take out more money from a bank account than there is in it; **your account is overdrawn** *or* **you are overdrawn** = you have paid out more money from your account than you have in it (NOTE: **overdrawing - overdrew - overdrawn)**

overdue [əuvə'djuː] *adjective* (account) which has not been paid on time; **interest payments are three weeks overdue** = interest payments which should have been made three weeks ago; *see comment at* OUTSTANDING

overestimate [əuvər'estɪmeɪt] *verb* to think something is larger or worse than it really is; *he overestimated the amount of time needed to fit out the factory*

overextend [əuvərɪk'stend] *verb* **the company overextended itself** = the company borrowed more money than its assets would allow

overgeared [əuvə'gɪəd] *adjective* (company) which has high borrowings in comparison to its assets

overhang ['əuvəhæŋ] **1** *verb* (of a large number of shares); **to overhang the market** = to be available for sale, and so depress the share price **2** *noun* large quantity of shares available for sale, which has the effect of depressing the share price

overhead ['əuvəhed] **1** *noun* **overheads** *US* **overhead** = costs of the day-to-day running of a business or of part of a business (i.e., any cost, other than the cost of the goods offered for sale); *the sales revenue covers the manufacturing costs but not the overheads*; **to absorb overheads** = to include a proportion of overhead costs into a production cost (this is done at a certain rate, called 'absorption rate') **2** *adjective* **overhead absorption rate** = rate at which production costs are increased to absorb higher overhead costs; *see also* OVERABSORBED, UNDERABSORBED; **overhead costs** *or* **expenses** = costs of materials, salaries and other expenses (including selling, administration and finance costs) which are not directly related to the making of a product; **overhead budget** = plan of probable overhead costs (total); **overhead capacity variance** = difference between the overhead absorbed based on budgeted hours and actual hours worked; **(total) overhead cost variance** = difference between the overhead cost absorbed and the actual overhead costs incurred (both fixed and variable); **overhead efficiency variance** = difference between the overhead absorbed by actual production at the standard rate of absorption and the overhead that should have been incurred given actual hours worked; **overhead expenditure variance** = difference between the budgeted overhead costs and the actual expenditure; **overhead volume variance** = difference in fixed overheads allocated to the production of more or less units than the standard quantity on which the overhead absorption rate has been calculated

overlap profit ['əuvəlæp 'prɒfɪt] *noun* profit which occurs in two accounting periods (ie, when two accounting periods overlap) and on which overlap relief can be claimed

overpaid [əuvə'peɪd] *adjective* paid too much; *our staff are overpaid and underworked*

overpay [əuvə'peɪ] *verb* to pay too much; *we overpaid the invoice by $245*

overpayment [əʊvə'peɪmənt] *noun* paying too much

overrider *or* **overriding commission** ['əʊvəraɪdə *or* 'əʊvəraɪdɪŋ kə'mɪʃən] *noun* special extra commission which is above all other commissions

overseas [əʊvə'siːz] **1** *adjective* across the sea, in or to foreign countries; **overseas bank** = (i) British bank which mainly trades overseas; (ii) foreign bank with branches in the UK; **overseas division** = section of a company dealing with trade with other countries; **overseas markets** = markets in foreign countries; **overseas funds** = investment funds based in other countries; **overseas trade** = trade with foreign countries **2** *noun* foreign countries; *the profits from overseas are far higher than those of the home division*

overspend [əʊvə'spend] *verb* to spend too much; **to overspend one's budget** = to spend more money than is allowed in the budget (NOTE: **overspending - overspent**)

overspending [əʊvə'spendɪŋ] *noun* spending more than is allowed; *the board decided to limit the overspending by the production departments*

overstate [əʊvə'steɪt] *verb* to make something more than it really is; *the company accounts overstate the real profit*

overstatement [əʊvə'steɪtmənt] *noun* making something seem more than it really is

overstock [əʊvə'stɒk] **1** *verb* to have more stock than is needed; **to be overstocked with spare parts** = to have too many spare parts in stock **2** *plural noun US* **overstocks** = more stock than is needed to supply orders; *we will have to sell off the overstocks to make room in the warehouse*

QUOTE Cash paid for your stock: any quantity, any products, overstocked lines, factory seconds
Australian Financial Review

oversubscribe [əʊvəsəb'skraɪb] *verb* **the share offer was oversubscribed six times** = people applied for six times as many new shares as were available

oversubscription [əʊvəsəb'skrɪpʃn] *noun* subscribing for more shares in a new issue than are available

over-the-counter **(OTC)** ['əʊvəðə'kaʊntə] *adjective* **over-the-counter market** = market in shares which are not listed on a Stock Exchange; **over-the-**

counter sales = legal selling of shares which are not listed on an official Stock Exchange (usually carried out by telephone); *this share is available on the over-the-counter market*

overtime ['əʊvətaɪm] **1** *noun* hours worked more than the normal working time; **to work six hours' overtime**; *the overtime rate is one and a half times normal pay*; **overtime ban** = order by a trade union which forbids overtime work by its members; **overtime pay** = pay for extra time worked **2** *adverb* **to work overtime** = to work longer hours than in the contract of employment

overtrading [əʊvə'treɪdɪŋ] *noun (of a company)* increasing sales and production too much and too quickly, so that it runs short of cash

overvalue [əʊvə'væljuː] *verb* to give a higher value than is right; **these shares are overvalued at £1.25** = the shares are worth less than the £1.25 for which they are selling; **the pound is overvalued against the dollar** = the exchange rate gives too many dollars to the pound, given the strength of the two countries' economies (NOTE: the opposite is **undervalued**)

owe [əʊ] *verb* to have to pay money; *he owes the bank £250,000*; **he owes the company for the stock he purchased** = he has not paid for the stock

owing ['əʊɪŋ] *adjective* which is owed; *money owing to the directors*; *how much is still owing to the company by its debtors?*

own [əʊn] *verb* to have or to possess; *he owns 50% of the shares*; **a wholly-owned subsidiary** = a subsidiary which belongs completely to the parent company; **a state-owned industry** = an industry which is nationalized

owner ['əʊnə] *noun* person who owns something; *the owners of a company are its shareholders*; **sole owner** = person who owns something by himself; **owners' equity** = value of the shares in a company held by the owners of the company plus retained profits; **owner-occupier** = person who owns and lives in a house; **goods sent at owner's risk** = situation where the owner has to insure the goods while they are being transported

ownership ['əʊnəʃɪp] *noun* act of owning something; **common** *or* **collective ownership** = situation where a business is owned by the workers who work in it; **joint ownership** = situation where two people own the same property; **public ownership** *or* **state**

ownership = situation where an industry is nationalized; **private ownership** = situation where a company is owned by private shareholders; **the ownership of the company has passed to the banks** = the banks have become owners of the company

Pp

P&L = PROFIT AND LOSS

p.a. = PER ANNUM

package ['pækɪdʒ] *noun* group of different items joined together in one deal; **pay package** *or* **salary package** *US* **compensation package** = salary and other benefits offered with a job; *the job carries an attractive salary package*; **package deal** = agreement where several different items are agreed at the same time

> QUOTE the remuneration package will include an attractive salary, profit sharing and a company car
> *Times*

paid [peɪd] *adjective* money has been given **(a) paid holidays** = holidays where the worker's wages are still paid even though he is not working **(b) paid assistant** = assistant who receives a salary **(c)** (account) which has been settled; *carriage paid*; *tax paid*; **paid bills** = bills which have been settled; *the invoice is marked 'paid'* **(d) paid-in capital** = capital in a business which has been provided by its shareholders (not including the premium paid above the par value of the shares); **paid-up (share) capital** = amount of money paid for the issued capital shares (it does not include called-up capital which has not yet been paid for); **paid-up shares** = shares which have been completely paid for by the shareholders; *see also* PARTLY PAID, PAY UP

panel ['pænl] *noun* **Panel on Takeovers and Mergers** *or* **Takeover Panel** = non-statutory body which examines takeovers and applies the Takeover Code

paper ['peɪpə] *noun* **(a) on paper** = in theory; *on paper the system is ideal, but we have to see it working before we will sign the contract*; **paper loss** = loss made when an asset has fallen in value but has not been sold; **paper profit** = profit made when an asset has increased in value but has not been sold; **paper millionaire** = person who owns shares which, if he sold them, would make him a millionaire **(b)** documents which can represent money (bills of exchange, promissory notes, etc.); **bankable paper** = document which a bank will accept as security for a loan; **negotiable paper** = document which can be transferred from one owner to another for money **(c)** shares in the form of share certificates; **paper offer** = takeover bid, where the purchasing company offers its shares in exchange for shares in the company being taken over (as opposed to a cash offer) **(d) paper money** *or* **paper currency** = banknotes

> QUOTE the profits were tax-free and the interest on the loans they incurred qualified for income tax relief; the paper gains were rarely changed into spending money
> *Investors Chronicle*

paperwork ['peɪpəwɜːk] *noun* office work, especially writing memos and filling in forms; *exporting to Russia involves a large amount of paperwork*

par [pɑː] *adjective & noun* equal, at the same price; **par value** = face value or nominal value, the value printed on a share certificate; **shares at par** = shares whose market or issue price is the same as their face value; **shares above par** *or* **below par** = shares with a market or issue price higher or lower than their par value

parachute ['pærəʃuːt] *noun* **golden parachute** = special contract for a director of a company, which gives him advantageous financial terms if he has to resign when the company is taken over

parameter [pəˈræmɪtə] *noun* fixed limit; *the budget parameters are fixed by the finance director*; *spending by each department has to fall within certain parameters*

parcel ['pɑːsl] *noun* **parcel of shares** = group of shares (such as 50 or 100) which are sold as a group; *the shares are on offer in parcels of 50*

parent company ['peərənt 'kʌmpni] *noun* company which owns more than 50% of the shares of another company; *compare* HOLDING COMPANY

Pareto's Law [pə'riːtəʊz 'lɔː] *noun* the theory that a small percentage of a total is responsible for a large proportion of value or resources (also called the 80/20 law, because 80/20 is the normal ratio between majority and minority figures: so 20% of accounts produce 80% of turnover; 80% of GDP enriches 20% of the population, etc.)

pari passu ['pæri 'pæsuː] *Latin phrase* meaning 'equally'; *the new shares will rank pari passu with the existing ones*

parity ['pærəti] *noun* (i) being equal; (ii) official exchange rate against another currency, such as the dollar; **the pound fell to parity with the dollar** = /D **the pound fell to a point where it was at its official exchange rate with the dollar**

> QUOTE the draft report on changes in the international monetary system casts doubt about any return to fixed exchange-rate parities
> Wall Street Journal

part [pɑːt] *noun* (a) **in part** = not completely; *to contribute in part to the costs or to pay the costs in part* (b) **part-owner** = person who owns something jointly with one or more other persons; *he is part-owner of the restaurant*; **part-ownership** = situation where two or more persons own the same property (c) **part exchange** = giving an old product as part of the payment for a new one; *they refused to take my old car as part exchange for the new one*; **part-paid** = PARTLY PAID; **part payment** = paying of part of a whole payment; *I gave him £250 as part payment for the car*; **part delivery** *or* **part order** *or* **part shipment** = delivering or shipping only some of the items in an order

partial ['pɑːʃəl] *adjective* not complete; **partial loss** = situation where only part of the insured property has been damaged or lost; **he got partial compensation for the damage to his house** = he was compensated for part of the damage

participate [pɑː'tɪsɪpeɪt] *verb* to take part in; **participating preference shares** *US* **participating preferred stock** = preference shares which get an extra bonus dividend if company profits reach a certain level

participator [pɑː'tɪsɪpeɪtə] *noun* person who has an interest in a company (an ordinary or preference shareholder, a creditor, the owner of rights to shares, etc.)

partly ['pɑːtli] *adverb* not completely; **partly-paid capital** = capital which represents partly-paid shares; **partly-paid**

shares = where the shareholders have not paid the full value of the shares issued, usually because the company calls for payment in instalments; **partly-secured creditors** = creditors whose debts are not fully covered by the value of the security

partner ['pɑːtnə] *noun* person who works in a business and shares in its risks and profits with others; *he became a partner in a firm of solicitors*; **active partner** *or* **working partner** = partner who works in a partnership; **junior partner** *or* **senior partner** = person who has a small or large part of the shares in a partnership; **limited partner** = partner in a limited partnership (he is only liable for the amount of capital he has put into the firm, and takes no part in the management of the firm); **sleeping partner** = partner who has a share in a business but does not work in it

partnership ['pɑːtnəʃɪp] *noun* (a) unregistered business where two or more people (but not more than twenty) share the risks and profits according to a partnership agreement; *to go into partnership with someone*; *to join with someone to form a partnership*; **to offer someone a partnership** *or* **to take someone into partnership with you** = to have a working business and bring someone in to share it with you; **to dissolve a partnership** = to bring a partnership to an end (b) **general partnership** = partnership where the liability of each partner is not limited; **limited partnership** = registered business where the liability of the partners is limited to the amount of capital they have each provided to the business and where the partners may not take part in the running of the business; **partnership agreement** = document which sets up a partnership, states what it is called, what the capital is, how much is contributed by each partner, the rights of each partner, profit-sharing ratios, and the way the partnership may be dissolved in due course

party ['pɑːti] *noun* (a) company or person involved in a legal dispute or legal agreement; *one of the parties to the suit has died*; *the company is not a party to the agreement* (b) **third party** = any third person, in addition to the two main people involved in a contract; **third party insurance** *or* **third party policy** = insurance to cover damage to any person who is not one of the people named in the insurance contract (that is, neither the insured person nor the insurance company)

pass [pɑːs] *verb* (a) **to pass a dividend** = to pay no dividend in a certain year (NOTE: American English is also **to omit a dividend**)

(b) to approve; *the finance director has to pass an invoice before it is sent out*; *the loan has been passed by the board*; **to pass a resolution** = to vote to agree to a resolution; *the meeting passed a proposal that salaries should be frozen* **(c)** to be successful; *she has passed all her exams and now is a qualified accountant*

passbook ['pɑːsbʊk] *noun* book given to a customer by a bank or building society, which shows money which the customer deposits or withdraws from the account

> QUOTE instead of customers having transactions recorded in their passbooks, they will present plastic cards and have the transactions printed out on a receipt
> Australian Financial Review

pass off ['pɑːs 'ɒf] *verb* **to pass something off as something else** = to pretend that it is another thing in order to cheat a customer

patent ['peɪtənt *or* 'pætənt] **1** *noun* **(a)** official document showing that a person has the exclusive right to make and sell an invention; *to take out a patent for a new type of light bulb*; *to apply for a patent for a new invention*; **letters patent** = official term for a patent; **patent applied for** *or* **patent pending** = words on a product showing that the inventor has applied for a patent for it; **to forfeit a patent** = to lose a patent because payments have not been made; **to infringe a patent** = to make and sell a product which works in the same way as a patented product and not pay a royalty for it; **infringement of patent** *or* **patent infringement** = act of illegally making or selling a product which is patented **(b) patent agent** = person who advises on patents and applies for patents on behalf of clients; **to file a patent application** = to apply for a patent; **patent office** = government office which grants patents and supervises them; **patent rights** = rights which an inventor holds under a patent **2** *verb* **to patent an invention** = to register an invention with the patent office to prevent other people from copying it

> COMMENT: patents are intangible fixed assets, which are limited by contract (the granting of letters patent)

pawn [pɔːn] **1** *noun* **to put something in pawn** = to leave a valuable object with someone in exchange for a loan which has to be repaid if you want to take back the object; **to take something out of pawn** = to repay the loan and so get back the object which has been pawned; **pawn ticket** = receipt given by the

pawnbroker for the object left in pawn **2** *verb* **to pawn a watch** = to leave a watch with a pawnbroker who gives a loan against it

pawnbroker ['pɔːnbrəʊkə] *noun* person who lends money against the security of valuable objects

pawnshop ['pɔːnʃɒp] *noun* pawnbroker's shop

pay [peɪ] **1** *noun* **(a)** salary, wage, money given to someone for regular work; **back pay** = salary which has not been paid; **basic pay** = normal salary without extra payments; **take-home pay** = pay left after tax and insurance have been deducted; **holidays with pay** = holiday which a worker can take by contract and for which he is paid; **unemployment pay** = money given by the government to someone who is unemployed **(b) pay cheque** = monthly cheque which pays a salary to a worker; **pay day** = day on which wages are paid to workers (usually Friday for workers paid once a week, and during the last week of the month for workers who are paid once a month); **pay negotiations** *or* **pay talks** = discussions between management and workers about pay increases; **pay packet** = envelope containing the pay slip and the cash pay; **pay rise** = increase in pay; **pay slip** = piece of paper showing the full amount of a worker's pay, and the money deducted as tax, pension and National Insurance contributions **(c) pay desk** = place in a store where you pay for goods bought; **pay phone** = telephone which works if you put coins into it **2** *verb* **(a)** to give money to buy an item or a service; *to pay £1,000 for a car*; *how much did you pay to have the office cleaned?*; **to pay in advance** = to give money before you receive the item bought or before the service has been completed; *we had to pay in advance to have the new telephone system installed*; **to pay in instalments** = to give money for an item by giving small amounts regularly; *we are paying for the computer by paying instalments of £50 a month*; **to pay cash** = to pay the complete sum in cash; **'pay cash'** = words written on a crossed cheque to show that it can be paid in cash if necessary; **to pay by cheque** = to pay by giving a cheque, not by using cash or credit card; **to pay by credit card** = to pay, using a credit card and not a cheque or cash **(b)** to give money; **to pay on demand** = to pay money when it is asked for, not after a period of credit; **please pay the sum of £10** = please give £10 in cash or by cheque; **to pay a dividend** = to give shareholders a part of the profits of a company; *these shares pay a dividend of 1.5p*; **to pay interest** = to give money as interest on money borrowed or invested; *building societies pay an interest of 10%* **(c)** to give a worker money for work done; **to be paid by the hour** = to get money for each hour worked; **to be paid at piece-work rates** = to get money for each piece of work finished **(d)** to give money which is owed or which has to be paid; *to pay a bill*; *to pay an invoice*; *to pay duty on imports*; *to pay tax* **(e)** to pay a cheque into an account = to deposit money in the form of a cheque (NOTE: **paying - paid**)

```
QUOTE the yield figure means that if
you buy the shares at their current
price you will be getting 5% before
tax on your money if the company pays
the same dividend as in its last
financial year
                    Investors Chronicle
```

```
QUOTE     recession     encourages
communication not because it makes
redundancies easier, but because it
makes low or zero pay increases
easier to accept
                            Economist
```

payable ['peɪəbl] *adjective* which is due to be paid; **payable in advance** = which has to be paid before the goods are delivered; **payable on delivery** = which has to be paid when the goods are delivered; **payable on demand** = which must be paid when payment is asked for; **payable at sixty days** = which has to be paid by sixty days after the date of invoice; **cheque made payable to bearer** = cheque which will be paid to the person who has it, not to any particular name written on it; **shares payable on application** = shares which must be paid for when you apply to buy them; **accounts payable** = money owed by a company for purchases of goods and services; **bills payable** = bills which a debtor will have to pay; **electricity charges are payable by the tenant** = the tenant (and not the landlord) must pay for the electricity

pay as you earn (PAYE) ['peɪ æz jʊ 'ɜːn] *GB* tax system, where income tax is deducted from the salary before it is paid to the worker

pay-as-you-go ['peɪæzjʊ'gəʊ] **(a)** *US* = PAY AS YOU EARN **(b)** *GB* payment system where the purchaser pays in small instalments as he uses the service

pay back ['peɪ 'bæk] *verb* to give money back to someone; *to pay back a loan*; *I lent him £50 and he promised to pay me back in a month*; *he has never paid me back for the money he borrowed*

payback ['peɪbæk] *noun* paying back money which has been borrowed; **payback clause** = clause in a contract which states the terms for repaying a loan; **payback period** = (i) period of time over which a loan is to be repaid; (ii) time taken for the total interest on an investment to equal the amount of the initial investment

pay-cheque *US* **paycheck** ['peɪtʃek] *noun* salary cheque given to an employee

pay down ['peɪ 'daʊn] *verb* **to pay money down** = to make a deposit; *he paid £50 down and the rest in monthly instalments*

paydown ['peɪdaʊn] *noun US* repayment of part of a sum which has been borrowed

PAYE ['piːeɪwaɪˈiː] = PAY AS YOU EARN

payee [peɪˈiː] *noun* person who receives money from someone; person whose name is on a cheque

payer ['peɪə] *noun* person who gives money to someone; **slow payer** = person or company which does not pay debts on time; *they are well known as slow payers*

paying ['peɪɪŋ] **1** *adjective* **(a)** which makes a profit; *it is a paying business*; **it is not a paying proposition** = it is not a business which is going to make a profit **(b)** which pays; **paying agent** = bank which pays dividend or interest to a bondholder **2** *noun* giving money; *paying of a debt*; **paying-in book** = book of forms for paying money into a bank account or a building society account; **paying-in slip** = form which is filled in when money is being deposited in a bank account or a building society account

payment ['peɪmənt] *noun* **(a)** giving money; *payment in cash or cash payment*; *payment by cheque or cheque payment*; *payment of interest or interest payment*; **payment on account** = paying part of the money owed; **full payment** *or* **payment in full** = paying all money owed; **payment on invoice** = paying money as soon as an invoice is received; **payment in kind** = paying by giving goods or other benefits, but not money; **payment by results** = money given which increases with the amount of work done or goods produced **(b)** money paid; **back payment** = paying money which is owed; **deferred payments** = money paid later than the agreed date; *the company agreed to defer payments for three months*; **down payment** = part of a total payment made in advance; **repayable in easy payments** = repayable with small sums regularly; **incentive payments** = extra pay offered to a worker to make him work better

pay off ['peɪ 'ɒf] *verb* **(a)** to finish paying money which is owed; *to pay off a mortgage*; *to pay off a loan* **(b)** to pay all the money owed to someone and terminate his employment; *when the company was taken over the factory was closed and all the workers were paid off*

payoff ['peɪɒf] *noun* money paid to finish paying something which is owed; **payoff period** = PAYBACK PERIOD

pay out ['peɪ 'aʊt] *verb* to give money; *the company pays out thousands of pounds in legal fees*; *we have paid out half our profits in dividends*

payout ['peɪaʊt] *noun* money paid out; money paid to help a company in difficulties; *the company only exists on payouts from the government*

QUOTE after a period of recession followed by a rapid boost in incomes, many taxpayers embarked upon some tax planning to minimize their payouts
                    Australian Financial Review

payroll ['peɪrəʊl] *noun* list of people employed and paid by a company; money paid by a company in salaries; *the company has 250 on the payroll*; **payroll giving scheme** = scheme by which an employee pays money to a charity directly out of his or her salary (the money is deducted by the employer and paid to the charity; the employee gets tax relief on such donations); **payroll ledger** = list of staff and their salaries; **payroll tax** = tax on the people employed by a company

pay up ['peɪ 'ʌp] *verb* to give money which is owed; *the company only paid up when we sent them a letter from our solicitor*; *he finally paid up six months late*; **amount paid up** = amount paid for a new issue of shares, either the total payment or the first instalment, if the shares are offered with instalment payments; *see also* PAID UP

PCB = PETTY CASH BOOK

P/E ['piː'iː] *abbreviation* = PRICE/EARNINGS; **P/E ratio (price/earnings ratio** *or* **PER)** = ratio between the current market price of a share and the earnings per share (profit after tax divided by the number of shares in issue) calculated by dividing the market price by the earnings per share; *these shares sell at a P/E ratio of 7*

COMMENT: the P/E ratio is an indication of the way investors think a company will perform in the future, as a high market price suggests that investors expect earnings to grow and this gives a high P/E figure; a low P/E figure implies that investors think that earnings are not likely to rise

pecuniary [pɪ'kjuːnjəri] *adjective* referring to money; **he gained no pecuniary advantage** = he made no profit

peg [peg] *verb* to hold something at a certain level or price; **to peg a currency** = to fix an exchange rate for a currency which previously was floating; **to peg prices** = to fix prices to stop them rising; **to peg wage increases to the cost-of-living index** = to limit increases in wages to the increases in the cost-of-living index (NOTE: **pegging - pegged**)

penalize ['piːnəlaɪz] *verb* to punish, to fine; *to penalize a supplier for late deliveries*; *they were penalized for bad service*

penalty ['penlti] *noun* punishment (such as a fine) which is imposed if something is not done or is done incorrectly or illegally; **penalty clause** = clause which lists the penalties which will be imposed if the contract is not obeyed; *the contract contains a penalty clause which fines the company 1% for every week the completion date is late*

pendente lite [pen'denteɪ 'laɪteɪ] *Latin phrase meaning* 'during the lawsuit'

pension ['penʃən] **1** *noun* **(a)** money paid regularly to someone who no longer works, paid either by the state or by a private company (see FRS 17); **retirement pension** *or* **old age pension** = state pension given to a man who is over 65 or a woman who is over 60 (the pensionable age for women is rising by stages to 65); **government pension** *or* **state pension** = pension paid by the state; **occupational pension** = pension which is paid by the company by which a worker has been employed; **portable pension** = pension entitlement which can be moved from one company to another without loss (as a worker changes jobs); **pension contributions** = money paid by a company or worker into a pension fund; **pension entitlement** = amount of pension which someone has the right to receive when he retires; **pension fund** = fund which receives contributions from employers and employees, being the money which provides pensions for retired members of staff; **pension funds** = investments managed by pension companies to produce pensions for investors; **pension income** = income which you receive from a pension scheme **(b)** **pension plan** *or* **pension scheme** = plan worked out by an insurance company which arranges for a worker to pay part of his salary over many years and receive a regular payment when he retires; **company pension scheme** = pension which is organized by a company for its staff; *he decided to join the company's pension scheme*; **contributory pension scheme** = scheme where the worker has to pay a proportion of his salary; **graduated pension scheme** = pension scheme where the benefit is calculated as a percentage of the salary of each person in the scheme; **non-contributory pension scheme** = scheme where the employer pays in all the money on behalf of the worker; **personal pension plan** = pension plan which applies to one worker only (usually a self-employed person or a person not in a company pension scheme) not to a group of people; **portable pension plan** = pension plan which allows a worker to carry his pension entitlements from one company to another as he changes jobs **2** *verb* **to pension someone off** = to ask someone to retire and take a pension

QUOTE permanent workers' pensions are funded on a pay-as-you-go basis, with enterprises contributing a portion of permanent employees' total wages to a pool. Contract workers' pension pools are separately funded: enterprises contribute 15% of contract workers' total wages, plus individual deductions of up to 3%
Far Eastern Economic Review

pensionable ['penʃənəbl] *adjective* able to receive a pension; **pensionable age** = age after which someone can take a pension; **pensionable earnings** = earnings of a member of a pension scheme on which the member's final pension is calculated

pensioner ['penʃənə] *noun* person who receives a pension; **old age pensioner** = person who receives the retirement pension

PEP [pep] = PERSONAL EQUITY PLAN

PER = PRICE/EARNINGS RATIO

per [pɜː] *preposition* **(a) as per** = according to; **as per invoice** = as stated in the invoice; **as per sample** = as shown in the sample; **as per previous order** = according to the details given in our previous order **(b)** at a rate of; **per hour** *or* **per day** *or* **per week** *or* **per year** = for each hour, day, week or year; *the rate is £5 per hour*; *he makes about £250 per month*; *we pay £10 per hour* = we pay £10 for each hour worked; **earnings per share** = earnings (company profits after tax) attributable to by each share; **the average sales per representative** = the average sales achieved by one representative; **per head** = for each person

QUOTE a 100,000 square-foot warehouse generates $600 in sales per square foot of space
Duns Business Month

per annum ['pər 'ænəm] *adverb* in a year; *what is their turnover per annum?*

per capita ['pə 'kæpɪtə] *adjective & adverb* for each person; **average income per capita** *or* **per capita income** = average income of one person; **per capita expenditure** = total money spent divided by the number of people involved

per cent *or* **percent** ['pə 'sent] *adjective & adverb* out of each hundred, for each hundred; **10 per cent** = ten in every hundred; *what is the increase per cent?*; *fifty per cent of nothing is still nothing*

QUOTE this would represent an 18 per cent growth rate - a slight slackening of the 25 per cent turnover rise in the first half
Financial Times

QUOTE buildings are depreciated at two per cent per annum on the estimated cost of construction
Hongkong Standard

percentage [pə'sentɪdʒ] *noun* amount shown as part of one hundred; **percentage discount** = discount calculated at an amount per hundred; **percentage increase** = increase calculated on the basis of a rate per hundred; **percentage point** = one per cent

QUOTE state-owned banks cut their prime rates a percentage point to 11%
Wall Street Journal

QUOTE a good percentage of the excess stock was taken up during the last quarter
Australian Financial Review

QUOTE the Federal Reserve Board, signalling its concern about the weakening American economy, cut the discount rate by one-half percentage point to 6.5%
Wall Street Journal

percentile [pə'sentaɪl] *noun* a percentage point, one of a series of ninety-nine figures below which a certain percentage of the total falls

per diem ['pɜː 'diem] *Latin phrase meaning* 'for each day'; *he economised on* *the cost of evening meals as he was only on a per diem*

COMMENT: expenses may be reimbursed on the basis of a notional amount spent each day (an overnight allowance) that is referred to as a per diem allowance, or simple a per diem

perform [pə'fɔːm] *verb* to do well or badly; **how did the shares perform?** = did the shares go up or down?; **the company** *or* **the shares performed badly** = the company's share price fell; *see also* UNDERPERFORM

performance [pə'fɔːməns] *noun* **(a)** way in which someone does his work; **performance of personnel against objectives** = how personnel have worked, measured against the objectives set; **performance review** = yearly interview between a manager and each worker to discuss how the worker has worked during the year; **job performance** = doing a job well or badly **(b)** way in which a share increases in value; **the poor performance of the shares on the stock market** = the fall in the share price on the stock market; **earnings performance** = way in which shares earn dividends **(c)** the results of a company's trading (measured against its objectives); *last year saw a dip in the company's performance*; **as a measure of the company's performance** = as a way of judging if the company's results are good or bad; **performance fund** = fund invested in shares to provide capital growth, but probably with less dividend income than usual; **performance share** = share which is likely to show capital growth, though perhaps not income; these are usually riskier shares than those which provide income

QUOTE inflation-adjusted GNP edged up at a 1.3% annual rate, its worst performance since the economic expansion began

Fortune

period ['pɪəriəd] *noun* **(a)** length of time; *for a period of time or for a period of months or for a six-year period*; *turnover for a period of three months*; *sales over the holiday period*; *to deposit money for a fixed period*; **period cost** = fixed cost, such as rent or insurance, which is related to a period of time **(b)** **accounting period** *or* **period of account** = period of time at the end of which the company's accounts are made up; **base period** = period of time used as a base for comparison with other similar periods

periodic *or* **periodical** [pɪərɪ'ɒdɪk *or* pɪərɪ'ɒdɪkəl] *adjective* from time to time; *a periodic review of the company's performance*; **periodic stock check** = counting of stock at a certain point in time, usually at the end of an accounting period; **periodic weighted average cost** *or* **price** = average price per unit of stock delivered in a period calculated at the end of the period (as opposed to 'cumulative weighted average')

perks [pɜːks] *noun* extra items given by a company to workers in addition to their salaries (such as company cars, private health insurance, etc.)

permit 1 ['pɜːmɪt] *noun* official document which allows someone to do something; **export permit** *or* **import permit** = official document which allows goods to be exported or imported; **work permit** = official document which allows someone who is not a citizen to work in a country **2** [pə'mɪt] *verb* to allow someone to do something; *this document permits you to export twenty-five computer systems*

permutation [pɜːmjuː'teɪʃn] *noun* number of different ways in which something can be arranged

perpetual inventory system (PIS) [pɜː'petjʊəl 'ɪnventəri 'sɪstəm] *noun* stock recording system where each item of stock purchased is added to the total and each item sold is deducted, so that the figures on the stock records are always correct and up-to-date, so avoiding having to close the warehouse for annual stock checks

per pro ['pɜː 'prəʊ] = PER PROCURATIONEM with the authority of; *the secretary signed per pro the manager*

perquisites ['pɜːkwɪzɪts] *plural noun* = PERKS

person ['pɜːsn] *noun* **(a)** party which is involved in a transaction (a man or woman, partnership, company, etc.); *insurance policy which covers a named person*; **the persons named in the contract** = people whose names are given in the contract; **the document should be witnessed by a third person** = someone who is not named in the document should witness it **(b)** **in person** = someone himself or herself; *this important package is to be delivered to the chairman in person* = the package has to be given to the chairman himself (and not to his secretary, assistant, etc.)

personal ['pɜːsənl] *adjective* referring to one person; **personal allowances** = part of a person's income which is not taxed;

additional personal allowance = tax allowance which can be claimed by a single person who has a child of school age living with them (formerly called the 'single-parent allowance'); **personal assets** = moveable assets which belong to a person; **personal call** = telephone call where you ask the operator to connect you with a particular person; **personal chattels** *or* **chattels personal** = things (furniture, clothes, cars) which belong to a person and which are not land; **personal computer** = small computer which can be used at home; **personal effects** *or* **personal property** = things which belong to someone; **personal estate** *or* **personal property** = things which belong to someone (excluding land) which can be inherited by his heirs; **personal income** = income received by an individual person; **personal loan** = loan to a person for household or other personal use, not for business use; **personal pension plan** = pension plan which applies to one worker only, usually a self-employed person, not to a group; **personal representative** = person who is the executor of a will or the administrator of the estate of a deceased person; **personal sector** = part of the investment market which is owned by private investors (as opposed to the corporate or institutional sector); **apart from the family shares, he has a personal shareholding in the company** = he has shares which he owns himself; **the car is for his personal use** = the car is for him to use himself

Personal Equity Plan (PEP) ['pɜːsənl 'ekwɪtɪ 'plæn] *noun* government-backed scheme to encourage share-ownership and investment in industry, where prior to April 1999, individual taxpayers could each invest a certain amount of money in shares each year, and not pay tax on either the income or the capital gains, provided that the shares were held for a certain period of time (existing schemes have continued since April 1999, but no new investment can be made)

Personal Identification Number (PIN) ['pɜːsənl aɪdentɪfɪ'keɪʃn 'nʌmbə] *noun* unique number allocated to the holder of a cash card or credit card, by which he or she can enter an automatic banking system, as, for example, to withdraw cash from an ATM

personalized ['pɜːsnəlaɪzd] *adjective* with the name or initials of a person printed on it; *personalized cheques*; *personalized briefcase*

personalty ['pɜːsnəltɪ] *noun* personal property or chattels (as opposed to land)

per stirpes ['pɜː 'stɜːpiːz] *Latin phrase meaning* 'by branches': phrase used in wills where the entitlement is divided among branches of a family rather than among individuals (which is 'per capita')

PERT = PROGRAM EVALUATION AND REVIEW TECHNIQUES definition of tasks or jobs and the time each requires, arranged in order to achieve a goal

petition [pə'tɪʃn] *noun* written application to a court; **bankruptcy petition** = application to a court asking for an order making someone bankrupt; **to file a petition in bankruptcy** = to apply to the court to be made bankrupt, or to ask for someone else to be made bankrupt; **winding up petition** = application to a court for an order that a company be put into liquidation

petroleum [pə'trəuljəm] *noun* raw natural oil, found in the ground; **crude petroleum** = raw petroleum which has not been processed; **petroleum exporting countries** = countries which produce petroleum and sell it to others; **petroleum industry** = industry which uses petroleum to make other products (petrol, soap, etc.); **petroleum products** = products (such as petrol, soap, paint) which are made from crude petroleum; **petroleum revenues** = income from selling oil; **petroleum revenue tax** = British tax on revenues from companies extracting oil from the North Sea

petty ['petɪ] *adjective* not important; **petty cash** = small amount of money kept in an office to pay small debts or expenses; **petty cash book (PCB)** = book in which petty cash payments are noted; **petty cash box** = locked metal box in an office where the petty cash is kept; **petty cash voucher** = piece of paper showing the amount and reason for petty cash expenditure; **petty expenses** = small sums of money spent

phase [feɪz] **1** *noun* period, part of something which takes place; *the first phase of the expansion programme* **2** *verb* to divide an accounting period into sections

phase in ['feɪz 'ɪn] *verb* to bring something in gradually; *the new invoicing system will be phased in over the next two months*

> QUOTE the budget grants a tax exemption for $500,000 in capital gains, phased in over the next six years
>
> Toronto Star

phase out ['feɪz 'aut] *verb* to remove something gradually; *Smith Ltd will be phased out as a supplier of spare parts*

phoenix company ['fi:nɪks 'kʌmpni] *noun* company formed by the directors of a company which has gone into receivership, which trades in the same way as the first company, and in most respects (except its name) seems to be exactly the same as the first company

physical ['fɪzɪkl] **1** *adjective* **(a)** physical **inventory** = counting actual items of stock; **physical stock** = the actual items of stock held in a warehouse; **physical stock check** *or* **physical stocktaking** = counting actual items of stock (and then checking this figure against stock records) **(b)** **physical market** = commodity market where purchasers actually buy the commodities (as opposed to the futures market, where they buy and sell the right to purchase commodities at a future date); **physical price** = current cash price for a commodity for immediate delivery **2** *noun* **physicals** = actual commodities which are sold on the current market (as opposed to futures)

piece rate ['pi:s 'reɪt] *noun* rate of pay for a product produced or for a piece of work done and not paid for at an hourly rate; *to earn piece rates*

piecework ['pi:swɜ:k] *noun* work for which workers are paid for the products produced or the piece of work done and not at an hourly rate (usually there is a basic guaranteed minimum payment, but this is increased as the number of units produced increases)

pie chart ['paɪ 'tʃɑ:t] *noun* diagram where information is shown as a circle cut up into sections of different sizes

pilferage *or* **pilfering** ['pɪlfərɪdʒ *or* 'pɪlfərɪŋ] *noun* stealing items of stock (this has to be taken into account when calculating the quantity of stock used)

PIN (number) ['pɪn 'nʌmbə] = PERSONAL IDENTIFICATION NUMBER

P&L = PROFIT AND LOSS (ACCOUNT)

place [pleɪs] *verb* **(a)** to put; *to place $25,000 on deposit*; **to place money in an account** = to deposit money in an account; **to place a contract** = to decide that a certain company shall have the contract to do work; **to place something on file** = to file something **(b)** **to place a block of shares** = to find a buyer for a block of shares; **to place an issue** = to find buyers (usually a small number of investors) for all of a new issue of shares

placement ['pleɪsmənt] *noun* **(a)** finding work for someone **(b)** *US* finding buyers for an issue of new shares; **direct placement** = placing new shares directly with purchasers, without going through a broker (NOTE: the British equivalent is **placing)**

placing ['pleɪsɪŋ] *noun* finding a single buyer or a group of institutional buyers for a large number of shares in a new company or a company that is going public; **the placing of a line of shares** = finding a purchaser for a block of shares which was overhanging the market; **public placing** = offering a new issue of shares to the public; **vendor placing** = arranging for an issue of new shares to be bought by institutions, as a means of financing the purchase of another company

plain vanilla swap ['pleɪn və'nɪlə 'swɒp] *noun* interest rate swap, where a company with fixed interest borrowings may swap them for variable interest borrowings of another company; *see also* SWAP

plan [plæn] **1** *noun* **(a)** organized way of doing something; **contingency plan** = plan which will be put into action if something happens which no one expects to happen; **the government's economic plans** = the government's proposals for running the country's economy; **a Five-Year Plan** = proposals for running a country's economy over a five-year period **(b)** way of saving or investing money; *investment plan*; *pensions plan*; *savings plan* **2** *verb* to organize carefully how something should be done; **to plan for an increase in bank interest charges** = to change a way of doing things because you think there will be an increase in bank interest charges; **to plan investments** = to propose how investments should be made (NOTE: **planning - planned)**

> QUOTE the benefits package is attractive and the compensation plan includes base, incentive and car allowance totalling $50,000+
> Globe and Mail (Toronto)

planning ['plænɪŋ] *noun* organizing how something should be done, especially how a company should be run to make increased profits; *long-term planning* *or* *short-term planning*; **economic planning** = planning the future financial state of the country for the government; **corporate planning** = planning the future financial state of a group of companies; **manpower planning** = planning to get the right number of workers in each job

plant [plɑːnt] *noun* **plant and machinery** = equipment used to help someone trade (trucks, tools, office furniture, computers, ladders, etc., all count as plant and machinery)

plastic money ['plæstɪk 'mʌni] *noun* credit cards and charge cards

PLC *or* **plc** ['piːel'siː] = PUBLIC LIMITED COMPANY

pledge [pledʒ] **1** *noun* object given to a pawnbroker as security for money borrowed (possession of the object is transferred to the pledgee); **to redeem a pledge** = to pay back a loan and interest and so get back the security; **unredeemed pledge** = pledge which the borrower has not taken back because he has not repaid the loan **2** *verb* **to pledge share certificates** = to deposit share certificates with a lender as security for money borrowed (the title to the certificates is not transferred and the certificates are returned when the debt is repaid)

pledgee [pledʒ'iː] *noun* person who receives an item as a pledge against a loan

pledgor [pledʒ'ɔː] *noun* person who pledges his property as security for a loan

plough back *US* **plow back** ['plaʊ 'bæk] *verb* **to plough back profits into the company** = to invest the profits in the business (and not pay them out as dividends to the shareholders) by using them to buy new equipment or create new products

plus [plʌs] **1** *preposition* **(a)** added to; *his salary plus commission comes to more than £25,000*; *production costs plus overheads are higher than revenue* **(b)** more than; *houses valued at £160,000 plus* = houses valued at over £160,000 **2** *adjective* favourable, or good and profitable; *a plus factor for the company is that the market is much larger than they had originally thought*; **on the plus side** = this is a favourable point; *on the plus side, we must take into account the new product line* **3** *noun* a good or favourable point; *to have achieved £1m in new sales in less than six months is certainly a plus for the sales team*

pm = PREMIUM

pocket ['pɒkɪt] *noun* **to be £25 in pocket** = to have made a profit of £25; **to be £25 out of pocket** = to have lost £25; **out-of-pocket**

expenses = amount of money paid back to an employee for his own money which he has spent on company business

point [pɔɪnt] *noun* **(a)** place or position; **breakeven point** = position at which sales cover costs but do not show a profit; **customs entry point** = place at a border between two countries where goods are declared to customs **(b) decimal point** = dot which indicates the division between a whole unit and its smaller parts (such as 4.25) **(c)** a unit for calculations; **basis point** = one hundredth of a percentage point (0.01%), the basic unit used in measuring market movements; **percentage point** = 1 per cent; **half a percentage point** = 0.5 per cent; **the dollar gained two points** = the dollar increased in value against another currency by two hundredths of a cent; **government stocks rose by one point** = they rose by £1; **the exchange fell ten points** = the stock market index fell by ten units

QUOTE sterling M3, the most closely watched measure, rose by 13% in the year to August - seven percentage points faster than the rate of inflation

Economist

QUOTE banks refrained from quoting forward US/Hongkong dollar exchange rates as premiums of 100 points replaced discounts of up to 50 points

South China Morning Post

policy ['pɒlɪsi] *noun* **(a)** decisions on the general way of doing something; *government policy on wages or government wages policy*; *the government's prices policy or incomes policy*; *the country's economic policy*; *a company's trading policy*; **the government made a policy statement** *or* **made a statement of policy** = the government declared in public what its plans were; **budgetary policy** = policy of expected income and expenditure; **accounting policies** = the accounting bases used by a company when preparing its financial statements (see FRS 18); **policy cost** = fixed cost, such as advertising cost, which is governed by the management's policy on the amount of advertising to be done **(b) company policy** = the company's agreed plan of action, the company's way of doing things; *what is the company policy on credit?*; *it is against company policy to give more than thirty days' credit*; *our policy is to submit all contracts to the legal department* **(c) insurance policy** = document which shows the conditions of an insurance contract; **an accident policy** = an insurance contract against accidents; **all-risks policy** = insurance which covers risks of any kind, with no exclusions; **a comprehensive** *or* **an all-in policy** = an insurance which covers all risks; **contingent policy** = insurance which pays out only if something happens (as if the person named in the policy dies before the person due to benefit); **endowment policy** = insurance where a sum of money is paid to the insured person on a certain date, or to his estate if he dies earlier; **policy holder** = person who is insured by an insurance company; **to take out a policy** = to sign the contract for an insurance and start paying the premiums; *she took out a life assurance policy* *or* *a house insurance policy*; **the insurance company made out a policy** *or* **drew up a policy** = the company wrote the details of the contract on the policy

poll [pəʊl] *noun* vote using voting papers, used to determine the result of a vote at an AGM where a show of hands is inconclusive

port [pɔːt] *noun* socket or physical connection allowing data transfer between a computer's internal communications channel and another external device; **input port** = circuit or connector that allows a computer to receive data from other external devices; **joystick port** = socket and interfacing circuit into which a joystick can be plugged; **output port** = circuit or connector that allows a computer to output or transmit data to another machine or device; **parallel port** = circuit and connector that allows parallel data to be received or transmitted; **printer port** = output port of a computer with a standard connector to which a printer is connected to receive character data (either serial or parallel); **serial port** = circuit that converts parallel data in a computer to and from a serial form, allowing serial data access

portable ['pɔːtəbl] **1** *adjective* which can be carried; *a portable computer* *or* *a portable typewriter*; **portable pension** = pension rights which a worker can take with him from one company to another as he changes jobs **2** *noun* **a portable** = a computer which can be carried

portfolio [pɔːt'fəʊljəʊ] *noun* **a portfolio of shares** = all the shares owned by a single investor; **portfolio investments** = investments in shares and government stocks (as opposed to investments in property, etc.); **portfolio management** = buying and selling shares to make profits for a single investor; **portfolio theory** = basis for managing a portfolio of investments (a mix of safe stocks and more risky ones)

position [pə'zɪʃən] *noun* **(a)** situation or state of affairs; **what is the cash position?** = what is the state of the company's bank account?; **bargaining position** = statement of position by one group during negotiations **(b)** state of a person's current financial holding in a stock; *(of a marketmaker)*; **to take a position in a share** = to buy shares on one's own account, expecting to sell them later at a profit; **to take a bear position** = to act on the assumption that the market will fall; **bull position** = buying shares in the hope that they will rise; **to close a position** = to arrange one's affairs so that one no longer has any liability to pay (as by selling all one's securities or when a purchaser of a futures contract takes on a sales contract for the same amount to offset the risk); **to cover a position** = to have enough money to pay for a forward purchase; **long position** = situation where an investor sells long (i.e., sells forward shares which he owns); **short position** = situation where an investor sells short (i.e., sells forward shares which he does not own) **(c)** job, paid work in a company; **he is in a key position** = he has an important job

positive ['pɒzətɪv] *adjective* **positive carry** = deal where the cost of the finance is less than the return; **positive cash flow** = situation where more money is coming in than is being spent; *see also* GOODWILL (NOTE: the opposite is **negative**)

possess [pə'zes] *verb* to own; *the company possesses property in the centre of the town*; *he lost all he possessed in the collapse of his company*

possession [pə'zeʃən] *noun* **(a)** action of holding something; **the documents are in his possession** = he is holding the documents; **vacant possession** = being able to occupy a property immediately after buying it because it is empty; *the property is to be sold with vacant possession* **(b)** **possessions** = property, things owned; *they lost all their possessions in the fire*

post [pəʊst] **1** *noun* job; *we have three posts vacant in our accounts department* **2** *verb* **(a)** **to post an entry** = to make an entry in a ledger account based on entries originally written in a book of prime entry; **to post up a**

ledger = to keep a ledger up to date **(b) to post an increase** = to let people know that an increase has taken place

> QUOTE Toronto stocks closed at an all-time high, posting their fifth day of advances in heavy trading
> Financial Times

post-acquisition [ˈpəʊstækwɪˈzɪʃn] *adjective* taking place after a company has been acquired; **post-acquisition profit** = profit of a subsidiary company in the period after it has been acquired, which is treated as revenue and transferred to the consolidated reserves of the holding company; *compare* PRE-ACQUISITION

post-balance sheet event [ˈpəʊstˈbæləns ˈʃiːt ɪˈvent] *noun* something which happens after the date when the balance sheet is drawn up, and before the time when the balance sheet is officially approved by the directors, which affects a company's financial position (see SSAP17)

post-cessation [ˈpəʊstseˈseɪʃn] *adjective* after the ending of a business activity; *royalty income which is received after the business ceased to function, but which comes from contracts entered into while the business was still functioning, should be entered as post-cessation receipts*

postdate [ˈpəʊsˈdeɪt] *verb* to put a later date on a document; *he sent us a postdated cheque*; *his cheque was postdated to June*

postulate [ˈpɒstjuleɪt] *noun* basic assumption on which accounting practice is based

pound [paʊnd] *noun* **(a)** measure of weight (= 0.45 kilos); *to sell oranges by the pound*; *a pound of oranges*; *oranges cost 50p a pound* (NOTE: usually written **lb** after a figure: **25lb**) **(b)** currency used in the UK and many other countries including Cyprus, Egypt, Ireland, Lebanon, Malta, Sudan and Syria **(c)** in particular, the currency of the UK; **pound sterling** = official term for the British currency; *a pound coin*; *a five pound note*; *it costs six pounds*; *the pound/dollar exchange rate* (NOTE: usually written **£** before a figure: **£25**); **pound-cost averaging** = buying securities at different times, but always spending the same amount of money (NOTE: in American English, this is called **dollar-cost averaging**)

poundage [ˈpaʊndɪdʒ] *noun* (i) rate charged per pound in weight; (ii) tax charged per pound in value

power [ˈpaʊə] *noun* **(a)** strength or ability; **purchasing power** = quantity of goods which can be bought by a group of people or with a sum of money; **bargaining power** = strength of one person or group when discussing prices or wages; **earning power** = amount of money someone should be able to earn; *he is such a fine designer that his earning power is very large*; **borrowing power** = amount of money which a company can borrow **(b)** authority, force or legal right; **executive power** = right to act as director or to put decisions into action; **power of appointment** = power of a trustee to dispose of interests in property to another person; **power of attorney** = legal document which gives someone the right to act on someone's behalf in legal matters; **the full power of the law** = the full force of the law when applied; *we will apply the full power of the law to get possession of our property again* **(c)** mathematical term describing the number of times a number is to be multiplied by itself; *5 to the power 2 is equal to 25* (NOTE: written as small figures in superscript: 10^5: say: 'ten to the power five')

PPI *US* = PRODUCERS' PRICE INDEX

practice [ˈpræktɪs] *noun* **(a)** way of doing things; *his practice was to arrive at work at 7.30 and start counting the cash*; **business practices** *or* **industrial practices** *or* **trade practices** = ways of managing or working in business, industry or trade; **private practice** = accounting services offered to clients, as opposed to accounting work carried out as an employee of a company; **restrictive practices** = ways of working which make people less free (such as stopping, by trade unions, of workers from doing certain jobs, or by stores not allowing customers a free choice of product); **sharp practice** = way of doing business which is not honest, but is not illegal; **code of practice** = rules drawn up by an association which the members must follow when doing business **(b)** accountancy firm

> QUOTE the EC demanded international arbitration over the pricing practices of the provincial boards
> Globe and Mail (Toronto)

> QUOTE any professional practice failing to heed the importance of recommendations from clients will not stay in business for very long
> Accountancy

pre-acquisition [ˈpriːækwɪˈzɪʃn] *adjective* before the acquisition of a company; **pre-acquisition profits** = profits of a company in the part of its accounting period before it was acquired by another company (under acquisition accounting methods, the holding company deducts these profits from the combined reserves of the group); *compare* POST-ACQUISITION

pre-acquisition write-down ['priækwɪ'zɪʃn 'raɪtdaʊn] *noun* reduction in the fair value of a new subsidiary in the balance sheet of a holding company against the potential future costs or the possible revaluation of the subsidiary's assets after acquisition

COMMENT: pre-acquisition write-down allows a company to reduce the amount of actual or potential costs in the profit-and-loss account by writing off goodwill on acquisitions from the balance sheet; the lower the holding company's 'fair valuation' of the new subsidiary's assets, the greater the scope for such write-offs

preceding year [prɪ'siːdɪŋ 'jɜː] *noun* the year before the accounting year in question; **taxed on a preceding year basis** = tax on income or capital gains arising in the previous year is payable in the current year

pre-empt [prɪ'empt] *verb* to get an advantage by doing something quickly before anyone else; *they staged a management buyout to pre-empt a takeover bid*

pre-emption right [prɪ'empʃən 'raɪt] *noun* right of an existing shareholder to be first to buy a new stock issue

pre-emptive [prɪ'emptɪv] *adjective* which has an advantage by acting early; **pre-emptive strike against a takeover bid** = rapid action taken to prevent a takeover bid; **a pre-emptive right** = (i) right of a government or of a local authority to buy a property before anyone else; (ii) right of an existing shareholder to be first to buy a new stock issue (so as to be able to maintain his percentage holding)

preference ['prefrəns] *noun* thing which is preferred; thing which has an advantage over something else; **preference dividend** = dividend paid on preference shares; **preference shares** = shares (often with no voting rights) which receive their dividend before all other shares and which are repaid (at face value) before ordinary shares if the company is liquidated; **preference shareholders** = owners of preference shares; **cumulative preference share** = preference share where the dividend will be paid at a later date even if the company cannot pay a dividend in the current year; **non-cumulative**

preference share = preference share where, if the dividend is not paid in the current year, it is lost

COMMENT: preference shares, because they have less risk than ordinary shares, normally carry no voting rights

preferential [prefə'renʃəl] *adjective* showing that something is preferred more than another; **preferential creditor** = creditor who must be paid first if a company is in liquidation; **preferential debt** = debt which is paid before all others; **preferential duty** *or* **preferential tariff** = special low rate of tax; **preferential shares** = shares (part of a new issue) which are set aside for the employees of the company; **preferential terms** *or* **preferential treatment** = terms or way of dealing which is better than usual; *subsidiary companies get preferential treatment when it comes to subcontracting work*

COMMENT: preferential creditors are firstly government departments, such as the Inland Revenue and Customs and Excise (VAT), followed by pension schemes and employee wages

preferred [prɪ'fɜːd] *adjective* **preferred creditor** = creditor who must be paid first if a company is in liquidation; **preferred shares** *US* **preferred stock** = shares which receive their dividend before all other shares, and which are repaid (at face value) if the company is in liquidation; *US* **cumulative preferred stock** = preference share where the dividend will be paid at a later date even if the corporation cannot pay a dividend in the current year

pre-financing ['priːfaɪ'nænsɪŋ] *noun* financing in advance

prelim [prɪ'lɪm] *noun (informal)* = PRELIMINARY ANNOUNCEMENT

preliminary [prɪ'lɪmɪnəri] *adjective* early, happening before anything else; **preliminary discussion** *or* **a preliminary meeting** = discussion or meeting which takes place before the main discussion or meeting starts; **preliminary announcement** = announcement of a company's full-year results, given out to the press before the detailed annual report is released; *US* **preliminary prospectus** = first prospectus for a new share issue, produced to see the market reaction to the proposed issue, but without giving a price for the new shares (also called a 'red herring'; similar to the British 'pathfinder prospectus')

premium ['priːmjəm] *noun* **(a)** payment to encourage someone; **premium offer** = free gift offered to attract more customers **(b) insurance premium** = annual payment made by the insured person or a company to an insurance company; *you pay either an annual premium of £360 or twelve monthly premiums of £32*; **additional premium** = payment made to cover extra items in an existing insurance; **premium income** = income which an insurance company derives from premiums paid by insured persons **(c)** amount to be paid to a landlord or a tenant for the right to take over a lease; *flat to let with a premium of £10,000*; *annual rent: £8,500, premium: £25,000* **(d)** rate above a previous rate; **premium on redemption** = extra amount above the nominal value of a share or debenture paid to the holder by a company buying back (or redeeming) its share or loan stock; **exchange premium** = extra cost above the normal rate for buying foreign currency; *the dollar is at a premium*; **shares sold at a premium** = (i) shares whose price is higher than their asset value or par value; (ii) new shares whose market price is higher than their issue price (NOTE: the opposite is **shares at a discount**) **(e)** *GB* **premium bonds** = government bonds, part of the national savings scheme, which pay no interest, but give the owner the chance to win a monthly prize

prepaid [priːˈpeɪd] *adjective* paid in advance; **carriage prepaid** = note showing that the transport costs have been paid in advance; **prepaid expenses** = expenditure on items such as rent, which is made in one accounting period but covers part of the next period also

prepay [priːˈpeɪ] *verb* to pay in advance (NOTE: **prepaying - prepaid**)

prepayment [priːˈpeɪmənt] *noun* **(a)** payment in advance; **to ask for prepayment of a fee** = to ask for the fee to be paid before the work is done **(b)** *US* repayment of the principal of a loan before it is due; **prepayment penalty** = charge levied on someone who repays a loan (such as a mortgage) before it is due

present 1 ['preznt] *adjective* **(a)** happening now; *the shares are too expensive at their present price*; *what is the present address of the company?* **(b)** being there when something happens; *only six directors were present at the board meeting* **2** [prɪˈzent] *verb* to bring or send and show a document; **to present a bill for acceptance** = to send a bill for payment by the person who has accepted it; **to present a bill for payment** = to send a bill to be paid

presentation [prezənˈteɪʃən] *noun* showing a document; **cheque payable on presentation** = cheque which will be paid when it is presented; **free admission on presentation of the card** = you do not pay to go in if you show this card

present value (PV) ['preznt ˈvæljuː] *noun* **(a)** the value something has now; *in 1974 the pound was worth five times its present value* **(b)** (i) the value now of a specified sum of money to be received in the future, if invested at current interest rates; (ii) price which a share must reach in the future to be the equivalent of today's price, taking inflation into account

COMMENT: the present value of a future sum of money is found by discounting that future sum, and can be used to decide how much money to invest now at current interest rates in order to receive the sum you want to have in a given number of years' time

pressing ['presɪŋ] *adjective* urgent; **pressing bills** = bills which have to be paid

pre-tax *or* **pretax** ['priːtæks] *adjective* before tax has been deducted or paid; **pretax profit** = profit before tax has been calculated; *the dividend paid is equivalent to one quarter of the pretax profit*

previous ['priːvjəs] *adjective* which existed before; **previous balance** = balance in an account at the end of the accounting period before the current one

price [praɪs] **1** *noun* **(a)** money which has to be paid to buy something; **agreed price** = price which has been accepted by both the buyer and seller; **all-in price** = price which covers all items in a purchase (goods, insurance, delivery, etc.); **asking price** = price which the seller is hoping to be paid for the item when it is sold; **bargain price** = very cheap price; **catalogue price** *or* **list price** = price as marked in a catalogue or list; **competitive price** = low price aimed to compete with a rival product; **cost price** = selling price which is the same as the price which the seller paid for the item (either the manufacturing price or the wholesale price); **cut price** = very cheap price; **discount price** = full price less a discount; **factory price** *or* **price ex factory** = price not including transport from the maker's factory; **factory gate prices** = manufacturers' prices in general; **fair price** = good price for both buyer and seller; **firm price** = price which will not change; *they are quoting a firm price of $1.23 a unit*; **going price** *or* **current price** *or* **usual price** = the price which is being charged now; **to sell goods off at half price** = to sell goods at half the price at which they were being sold before; **market price** = price at which a product can be sold; **net price** = price including all discounts and reductions; **retail price** = price at which the retailer sells to the final customer; **Retail Price(s) Index (RPI)** = index which shows how prices of consumer goods have increased or decreased over a period of time; **spot price** = price for immediate delivery of a commodity; *the spot price of oil on the commodity markets*; **wholesale price** = price of a product which is sold by a wholesaler; **Wholesale Price Index** = index showing the rises and falls of wholesale prices of manufactured goods (usually moving about two months before a similar movement takes place on the Retail Price Index) **(b) price ceiling** = highest price which can be reached; **price change** = amount by which the price of a share moves during a day's trading; **price control** = legal measures to stop prices rising too fast; **price cutting** = sudden lowering of prices; **price war** *or* **price-cutting war** = competition between companies to get a larger market share by cutting prices; **price differential** = difference in price between products in a range; **price fixing** = illegal agreement between companies to charge the same price for competing products; **price label** *or* **price tag** = label which shows a price; *the takeover bid put a $2m price tag on the company*; **price list** = sheet giving prices of goods for sale; **price range** = series of prices for similar products from different suppliers; **cars in the £6-7,000 price range** = cars of different makes, selling for between £6,000 and £7,000; **price-sensitive product** = product,

for which demand will change significantly if its price is increased or decreased **(c) to increase in price** = to become more expensive; *petrol has increased in price* *or* *the price of petrol has increased*; **to increase prices** *or* **to raise prices** = to make items more expensive; **we will try to meet your price** = we will try to offer a price which is acceptable to you; **to cut prices** = to reduce prices suddenly; **to lower prices** *or* **to reduce prices** = to make items cheaper **(d)** *(on the Stock Exchange)*; **asking price** = price which sellers are asking for shares; **closing price** = price at the end of a day's trading; **opening price** = price at the start of a day's trading **2** *verb* to give a price to a product; *car priced at £5,000*; **competitively priced** = sold at a low price which competes with that of similar goods from other companies; **the company has priced itself out of the market** = the company has raised its prices so high that its products do not sell

QUOTE that British goods will price themselves back into world markets is doubtful as long as sterling labour costs continue to rise
Sunday Times

QUOTE the average price per kilogram for this season has been 300c
Australian Financial Review

QUOTE European manufacturers rely heavily on imported raw materials which are mostly priced in dollars
Duns Business Month

QUOTE after years of relying on low wages for their competitive edge, Spanish companies are finding that rising costs and the strength of the peseta are pricing them out of the market
Wall Street Journal

price/earnings ratio (P/E ratio *or* **PER)** ['praɪs'ɜːnɪŋz 'reɪʃəʊ] *noun* ratio between the market price of a share and the earnings per share calculated by dividing the market price by the earnings per share; *these shares sell at a P/E ratio of 7* *or* *sell at 7 times earnings*

COMMENT: the P/E ratio is an indication of the way investors think a company will perform in the future, as a high market price suggests that investors expect earnings to grow and this gives a high P/E figure; a low P/E figure implies that investors feel that earnings are not likely to rise

pricing ['praɪsɪŋ] *noun* giving a price to a product; **pricing policy** = a company's policy in giving prices to its products; *our pricing policy aims at producing a 35% gross* *margin*; **common pricing** = illegal fixing of prices by several businesses so that they all charge the same price; **competitive pricing** = putting a low price on a product so that it competes with similar products from other companies; **marginal pricing** = basing the selling price of a product on its variable costs of production plus a margin, but excluding fixed costs

primary ['praɪməri] *adjective* basic; **primary commodities** = raw materials or food; **primary industry** = industry dealing with basic raw materials (such as coal, wood, farm produce); **primary dealer** = marketmaker dealing in government stocks; **primary market** = market where new securities or bonds are issued (if they are resold, it is on the secondary market); **primary products** = products (such as wood, milk, fish) which are basic raw materials

QUOTE farmers are convinced that primary industry no longer has the capacity to meet new capital taxes or charges on farm inputs
Australian Financial Review

prime [praɪm] *adjective* **(a)** most important; **prime sites** = most valuable commercial sites (in main shopping streets, etc.) as opposed to secondary sites; **prime time** = most expensive advertising time for TV commercials; *we are putting out a series of prime-time commercials* **(b)** basic; **prime bills** = bills of exchange which do not involve any risk; **prime cost** = cost involved in producing a product, excluding overheads (it includes direct material costs, direct labour costs and direct expenses) **(c) books of prime entry** = books of account recording a company's financial transactions

COMMENT: the transactions involved in the books of prime entry are: sales (sales day book and sales returns book); purchases (purchases day book and purchases returns book); cash payments and receipts (cash book) and adjustments (journal).

prime rate *or* **prime** [praɪm 'reɪt] *noun* US best rate of interest at which an American bank lends to its customers

QUOTE the base lending rate, or prime rate, is the rate at which banks lend to their top corporate borrowers
Wall Street Journal

COMMENT: not the same as the British bank base rate, which is only a notional rate, as all bank loans in the UK are at a certain percentage point above the base rate

priming ['praɪmɪŋ] *noun see* PUMP PRIMING

principal ['prɪnsəpl] **1** *noun* **(a)** person or company which is represented by an agent; *the agent has come to London to see his principals* **(b)** person acting for himself, such as a marketmaker buying securities on his own account **(c)** money lent or borrowed on which interest is paid; *to repay principal and interest* **2** *adjective* most important; *the principal shareholders asked for a meeting*; *the country's principal products are paper and wood* (NOTE: do not confuse with **principle**)

QUOTE the company was set up with funds totalling NorKr 145m with the principal aim of making capital gains on the secondhand market
Lloyd's List

principle ['prɪnsəpl] *noun* basic point, general rule; **in principle** = in agreement with a general rule; **agreement in principle** = agreement with the basic conditions of a proposal (NOTE: do not confuse with **principal**)

prior ['praɪə] *adjective* earlier; **prior agreement** = agreement which was reached earlier; **without prior knowledge** = without knowing before; **prior charge** = ranking before other capital in terms of distributions of profits and repayment when a company goes into liquidation; **prior-charge capital** = capital in the form of preference shares and debentures; **prior year adjustments** = adjustments made to accounts for previous years, because of changes in accounting policies or because of errors (see FRS 3)

priority [praɪˈɒrəti] *noun* **to have priority** = to have the right to be first; **to have priority over** *or* **to take priority over something** = to be more important than something; *reducing overheads takes priority over increasing turnover*; *debenture holders have priority over ordinary shareholders*; **to give something top priority** = to make something the most important item

private ['praɪvət] *adjective* **(a)** belonging to a single person, not to a company nor to the state; **letter marked 'private and confidential'** = letter which must not be opened by anyone other than the person to whom it is addressed; **private client** *or* **private customer** = (i) client dealt with by a salesman as a person, not as a company; (ii) individual person who is the client of an accountant, stockbroker or tax consultant; **private income** = income from dividends, interest or rents which is not part of a salary; **private investor** = ordinary person with money to invest; **private placing** *US* **private**

placement = placing a new issue of shares with a group of selected financial institutions; **private practice** = accounting services offered to clients, as opposed to accounting work carried out as an employee of a company; **private property** = property which belongs to a private person, not to the public; **private treaty** = agreement between individual persons; **to sell (a house) by private treaty** = to sell (a house) to another person not by auction **(b) private (limited) company** = (i) company with a small number of shareholders whose shares are not traded on the Stock Exchange; (ii) subsidiary company whose shares are not listed on the Stock Exchange, while those of its parent company are; *(of a public company)*; **to go private** = to become a private company again, by concentrating all its shares in the hands of one or a few shareholders and removing its stock exchange listing **(c) private enterprise** = businesses which are owned by private shareholders, not by the state; *the project is funded by private enterprise*; **the private sector** = all companies which are owned by private shareholders, not by the state

QUOTE in the private sector the total number of new house starts was 3 per cent higher than in the corresponding period last year, while public sector starts were 23 per cent lower
Financial Times

QUOTE management had offered to take the company private through a leveraged buyout for $825 million
Fortune

privately held company [ˈpraɪvətli held ˈkʌmpni] *noun US* company controlled by a few shareholders or its directors (also called a 'closed corporation')

pro [prəʊ] *preposition* for; **pro tem** = for the time being, temporarily; **per pro** = with the authority of; *the secretary signed per pro the manager*

probability [prɒbəˈbɪləti] *noun* likelihood that something will happen; *the probability of achieving budgeted sales is about 60%*; *what is the probability of his accepting the offer?*

probable [ˈprɒbəbl] *adjective* likely to happen

probate [ˈprəʊbeɪt] *noun* proving legally that a document, especially a will, is valid; **the executor was granted probate** = the executor was told officially that the will was valid; **probate court** = court which examines wills to see if they are valid

procedure [prəˈsiːdʒə] *noun* way in which something is done; *to follow the proper procedure*; **this procedure is very irregular** = this is not the normal way to do something; **accounting procedures** = a company's methods for maintaining its accounts

proceed [prəˈsiːd] *verb* to go on, to continue; *the negotiations are proceeding slowly*; **to proceed against someone** = to start a legal action against someone; **to proceed with something** = to go on doing something; *shall we proceed with the committee meeting?*

proceedings [prəˈsiːdɪŋz] *plural noun* **(a) conference proceedings** = written report of what has taken place at a conference **(b) legal proceedings** = legal action or lawsuit; *to take proceedings against someone*; *the court proceedings were adjourned*; **to institute proceedings against someone** = to start a legal action against someone

proceeds [ˈprəʊsiːdz] *plural noun* **the proceeds of a sale** = money received from a sale after deducting expenses; *he sold his shop and invested the proceeds in a computer repair business*

process [ˈprəʊses] **1** *noun* **(a) industrial processes** = processes involved in manufacturing products in factories; **decision-making processes** = ways in which decisions are reached; **process costing** = method of costing something which is manufactured from a series of continuous processes, where the total costs of those processes are divided by the number of units produced **(b) the due processes of the law** = the formal work of a legal action **2** *verb* **(a) to process figures** = to sort out information to make it easily understood; *the sales figures are being processed by our accounts department*; *data is being processed by our computer* **(b)** to deal with something in the usual routine way; *to process an insurance claim*; *orders are processed in our warehouse*

processing [ˈprəʊsesɪŋ] *noun* **(a)** sorting of information; *processing of information or of statistics*; **batch processing** = computer system, where information is collected into batches before being loaded into the computer; **data processing** *or* **information processing** = selecting and examining data in a computer to produce information in a special form; **word processing** *or* **text processing** = working with words, using a computer to produce, check and change texts, reports, letters, etc.; **central processing unit (CPU)** = group of circuits that perform the basic functions of a computer, made up of three parts: the control unit, the arithmetic and logic unit (ALU) and the input/output unit **(b) the processing of a claim for insurance** = putting a claim for insurance through the usual office routine in the insurance company; **order processing** = dealing with orders

processor ['prəʊsesə] *noun* **word processor** = small computer which is used for working with words, to produce texts, reports, letters, etc.

producers' price index (PPI) [prə'djuːsəz 'praɪs 'ɪndeks] *noun US* measure of the annual increase in the prices of goods and services charged by producers which is used to indicate the rate of inflation in the US economy

product ['prɒdʌkt] *noun* **(a)** thing which is made or manufactured; **basic product** = main product made from a raw material; **by-product** = secondary product made as a raw material is being processed; **end product** *or* **final product** *or* **finished product** = product made at the end of a production process **(b)** manufactured item for sale; **product advertising** = advertising a particular named product, not the company which makes it; **product analysis** = examining each separate product in a company's range to see why it sells, who buys it, etc.; **product design** = design of consumer products; **product development** = improving an existing product line to meet the needs of the market; **product engineer** = engineer in charge of the equipment for making a product; **product line** *or* **product range** = series of different products made by the same company which form a group (such as cars in different models, pens in different colours, etc.); **product management** = directing the making and selling of a product as an independent item; **product mix** = group of quite different products made by the same company; **banking products** = goods and services produced by banks for customers, such as statements, direct debits, etc.; **treasury products** = financial items produced by the government for sale, such as bonds **(c) gross domestic product (GDP)** = annual value of goods sold and services paid for inside a country; **gross national product (GNP)** = annual value of goods and services in a country, including income from other countries

production [prə'dʌkʃən] *noun* **(a)** showing something; **on production of** = when something is shown; *the case will be released by the customs on production of the relevant documents*; *goods can be exchanged only on production of the sales slip* **(b)** making or manufacturing of goods for sale; *production will probably be held up by industrial action*; *we are hoping to speed up production by installing new machinery*; **batch production** = production in batches; **domestic production** = production of goods in the home market; **mass production** = manufacturing of large quantities of goods; **rate of production** *or* **production rate** = speed at which items are made; **production cost** = cost of making a product; **production department** = section of a company which deals with the making of the company's products; **production line** = system of making a product, where each item (such as a car) moves slowly through the factory with new sections added to it as it goes along; **production manager** = person in charge of the production department; **production overhead** = factory overhead, indirect costs of production which are absorbed into the cost of goods produced; **(total) production overhead cost variance** = difference between the standard cost absorbed and the actual production cost incurred; **production unit** = separate small group of workers producing a certain product; **production unit method** = method of calculating the value of a fixed asset such as a machine, by taking the number of units the asset will produce and dividing this into the depreciated cost of the asset

productive [prə'dʌktɪv] *adjective* which produces; **productive capital** = capital which is invested to give interest; **productive discussions** = useful discussions which lead to an agreement or decision

productivity [prɒdʌk'tɪvəti] *noun* (i) rate of output per worker or per machine in a factory; (ii) rate of return per unit (pound, dollar, etc.) of capital; *bonus payments are linked to productivity*; *the company is aiming to increase productivity*; *productivity has fallen or risen since the company was taken over*; **productivity agreement** = agreement to pay a productivity bonus; **productivity bonus** = extra payments made to workers because of increased production; **productivity drive** = extra effort to increase productivity

QUOTE though there has been productivity growth, the absolute productivity gap between many British firms and their foreign rivals remains

Sunday Times

profession [prə'feʃən] *noun* **(a)** work which needs special skills learnt over a period of time; *the managing director is an accountant by profession* **(b)** group of specialized workers; **the accounting profession** = all qualified accountants; **the banking profession** = all qualified bankers; **the legal profession** = all qualified lawyers

professional [prə'feʃənl] *adjective* referring to one of the professions; *the accountant sent in his bill for professional services*; *we had to ask our lawyer for professional advice on the contract*; **professional fees** = fees paid to lawyers, accountants, architects, etc.; **a professional man** = man who works in one of the professions (such as a lawyer, doctor, accountant); **professional qualifications** = documents showing that someone has successfully finished a course of study which allows him to work in one of the professions

QUOTE one of the key advantages of an accountancy qualification is its worldwide marketability. Other professions are not so lucky: lawyers, for example, are much more limited in where they can work
Accountancy

profit ['prɒfɪt] *noun* **(a)** money gained from a sale which is more than the money spent; **clear profit** = profit after all expenses have been paid; *we made $6,000 clear profit on the deal*; **excess profit** = profit which is higher than what is thought to be normal; **excess profits tax** = tax on excess profits; **gross profit** *or* **gross trading profit** = profit calculated as sales income less the cost of the goods sold (i.e., without deducting any other expenses); **healthy profit** = quite a large profit; **manufacturing profit** = difference between the cost of buying a product from another supplier and the cost to the company of manufacturing it itself; **net profit** *or* **net trading profit** = result where income from sales is larger than all expenditure; **net profit before tax** = profit of a company after expenses have been deducted but before tax has been calculated; **operating profit** = result where sales from normal business activities are higher than the costs; **paper profit** = profit on an asset which has increased in price but has not been sold; *he is showing a paper profit of £25,000 on his investment*; **trading profit** = result where the company's receipts are higher than its expenditure; **profit margin** = percentage difference between sales income and the cost of sales; **pretax profit margin** = the pretax profit shown as a percentage of turnover in a profit and loss

account; **profits tax** *or* **tax on profits** = tax to be paid on profits; **profit before tax** *or* **pretax profit** = profit before any tax has been deducted; **profit before interest and tax (PBIT)** = operating profit shown before deducting interest on borrowings and tax due to the Inland Revenue (NOTE: also called **profit on ordinary activities before tax**); **profit after tax** *or* **net profit** = profit after tax has been deducted **(b) to take one's profit** = to sell shares at a higher price than was paid for them, and so realise the profit, rather than to keep them as an investment; *see also* PROFIT-TAKING; **to show a profit** = to make a profit and state it in the company accounts; *we are showing a small profit for the first quarter*; **to make a profit** = to have more money as a result of a deal; **to move into profit** = to start to make a profit; *the company is breaking even now, and expects to move into profit within the next two months*; **to sell at a profit** = to sell at a price which gives you a profit

QUOTE because capital gains are not taxed and money taken out in profits and dividends is taxed, owners of businesses will be using accountants and tax experts to find loopholes in the law
Toronto Star

profitability [prɒfɪtə'bɪləti] *noun* **(a)** ability to make a profit **(b)** amount of profit made as a percentage of costs or sales revenue; **measurement of profitability** = way of calculating how profitable something is

profitable ['prɒfɪtəbl] *adjective* which makes a profit

profitably ['prɒfɪtəbli] *adverb* making a profit

profit and loss account (P&L account) ['prɒfɪt ənd 'lɒs ə'kaʊnt] *noun* statement of a company's expenditure and income over a period of time, almost always one calendar year, showing whether the company has made a profit or loss; **consolidated profit and loss account** = profit and loss accounts of the holding company and its subsidiary companies, grouped together into a single profit and loss account (NOTE: the American equivalent is the **profit and loss statement** or **income statement**)

QUOTE the bank transferred $5 million to general reserve compared with $10 million in 1983 which made the consolidated profit and loss account look healthier
Hongkong Standard

COMMENT: the balance sheet shows the state of a company's finances at a certain date; the profit and loss account shows the movements which have taken place since the end of the previous accounting period, that is, since the last balance sheet. A profit and loss account can be drawn up either in the horizontal or in the vertical format; most are usually drawn up in the vertical format, as opposed to the more old-fashioned horizontal style, but both styles are allowed by the Companies Act

profit centre ['prɒfɪt 'sentə] *noun* person or department considered separately for the purposes of calculating a profit

profiteer [prɒfɪ'tɪə] *noun* person who makes too much profit, especially when goods are rationed or in short supply

profiteering [prɒfɪ'tɪərɪŋ] *noun* making too much profit

profit-making ['prɒfɪtmeɪkɪŋ] *adjective* which makes a profit; *the whole project was expected to be profit-making by 1990*; **non profit-making** = (organization, such as a club) which is not allowed by law to make a profit; *non profit-making organizations are exempt from tax*

profit-related ['prɒfɪtrɪ'leɪtɪd] *adjective* connected to profit; **profit-related bonus** = bonus paid which is related to the amount of profit a company makes; **profit-related pay** = pay which is related to the amount of profit a company makes (it can be tax free under a scheme agreed with the Inland Revenue)

profit-sharing ['prɒfɪtʃeərɪŋ] *noun* arrangement where workers get a share of the profits of the company they work for; *the company runs a profit-sharing scheme*

profit-taker ['prɒfɪt'teɪkə] *noun* person who sells an investment in order to realise a profit

profit-taking ['prɒfɪt'teɪkɪŋ] *noun* selling investments to realize the profit, rather than keeping them; *share prices fell under continued profit-taking*

QUOTE some profit-taking was seen yesterday as investors continued to lack fresh incentives to renew buying activity

Financial Times

pro forma ['prəʊ 'fɔːmə] **1** *Latin phrase meaning* 'for the sake of form'; **pro forma (invoice)** = invoice sent to a buyer before the goods are sent, so that payment can be made or that goods can be sent to a consignee who is not the buyer; *they sent us a pro forma; we only supply that account on pro forma* **2** *verb*

to issue a pro forma invoice; *can you pro forma this order?*

program ['prəʊɡræm] **1** *noun* **computer program** = instructions to a computer telling it to do a particular piece of work; *to buy a word-processing program*; *the accounts department is running a new payroll program*; **program evaluation and review techniques (PERT)** = definition of tasks or jobs and the time each requires, arranged in order to achieve a goal; **program flowchart** = diagram that graphically describes the various steps in a program; **program library** = collection of useful procedures and programs which can be used for various purposes and included into new software; **program testing** = testing a new program with test data to ensure that it functions correctly **2** *verb* to write a program for a computer; **to program a computer** = to install a program in a computer; *the computer is programmed to print labels*; **programmed trading** = buying and selling shares by computer (the computer is programmed to buy or sell when certain prices are reached or when a certain volume of sales on the market is reached) (NOTE: **programming - programmed)**

programmable [prəʊ'ɡræməbl] *adjective* which can be programmed

programme *US* **program** ['prəʊɡræm] *noun* plan of things which will be done; *development programme*; *research programme*; *training programme*; *to draw up a programme of investment or an investment programme*

programmer ['prəʊɡræmə] *noun* **computer programmer** = person who writes computer programs

programming ['prəʊɡræmɪŋ] *noun* **computer programming** = writing programs for computers; **programming engineer** = engineer in charge of programming a computer system; **programming language** = system of signs, letters and words used to instruct a computer

progress 1 ['prəʊɡres] *noun* movement of work forward; *to report on the progress of the work or of the negotiations*; **to make a progress report** = to report how work is going; **in progress** = which is being done but is not finished; **work in progress** = value of goods being manufactured which are not complete at the end of an accounting period (see SSAP9); **progress payments** = payments made as each stage of a contract is completed; *the fifth progress payment is due in March* **2** [prə'ɡres] *verb* to move forward or to go ahead; *the contract is progressing through various departments*

progressive [prəˈgresɪv] *adjective* which moves forward in stages; **progressive taxation** = taxation system where tax levels increase as the income is higher (also called 'graduated taxation')

prohibitive [prəˈhɪbɪtɪv] *adjective* with a price so high that you cannot afford to pay it; *the cost of redeveloping the product would be prohibitive*

project [ˈprɒdʒekt] *noun* **(a)** plan; *he has drawn up a project for developing new markets in Europe* **(b)** particular job of work which follows a plan; *we are just completing an engineering project in North Africa*; *the company will start work on the project next month*; **project analysis** = examining all costs or problems of a project before work on it is started; **project engineer** = engineer in charge of a project; **project manager** = manager in charge of a project

projected [prəˈdʒektɪd] *adjective* planned or expected; **projected sales** = forecast of sales; *projected sales in Europe next year should be over £1m*

projection [prəˈdʒekʃən] *noun* forecast of something which will happen in the future; *projection of profits for the next three years*; *the sales manager was asked to draw up sales projections for the next three years*

promise [ˈprɒmɪs] **1** *noun* saying that you will do something; **to keep a promise** = to do what you said you would do; *he says he will pay next week, but he never keeps his promises*; **to go back on a promise** = not to do what you said you would do; *the management went back on its promise to increase salaries across the board*; **a promise to pay** = a promissory note **2** *verb* to say that you will do something; *they promised to pay the last instalment next week*

promissory note [prəˈmɪsəri ˈnəʊt] *noun* document stating that someone promises to pay an amount of money on a certain date

promote [prəˈməʊt] *verb* **(a)** to give someone a more important job; *he was promoted from salesman to sales manager* **(b)** to advertise; **to promote a new product** = to increase the sales of a new product by a sales campaign, by TV commercials or free gifts **(c)** **to promote a new company** = to organize the setting up of a new company

promoter [prəˈməʊtə] *noun* **company promoter** = person who organizes the setting up of a new company

promotion [prəˈməʊʃən] *noun* **(a)** moving up to a more important job; *promotion chances or promotion prospects*; *he ruined his chances of promotion when he argued with the managing director*; **to earn promotion** = to work hard and efficiently and so be promoted **(b)** **promotion of a company** = setting up a new company **(c)** **promotion of a product** = selling a new product by publicity, sales campaign, TV commercials or free gifts; *promotion budget*; *promotion team*; *sales promotion*; *special promotion*

promotional [prəˈməʊʃənl] *adjective* used in an advertising campaign; **promotional budget** = forecast cost of promoting a new product

prompt [prɒmpt] *adjective* **(a)** rapid, done immediately; **prompt payer** = company which pays its bills rapidly; **prompt payment** = payment made rapidly; **prompt supplier** = supplier who delivers orders rapidly **(b)** **prompt date** = date for delivery, stated on a futures contract

QUOTE they keep shipping costs low and can take advantage of quantity discounts and other allowances for prompt payment
                    Duns Business Month

proof [pruːf] *noun* thing which shows that something is true; **documentary proof** = proof in the form of a document

-proof [pruːf] *suffix* which prevents something harming; **inflation-proof pension** = pension which will rise to keep pace with inflation

property [ˈprɒpəti] *noun* **(a)** **personal property** = things which belong to a person; *the storm caused considerable damage to personal property*; *the management is not responsible for property left in the hotel rooms* **(b)** land and buildings; *damage to property or property damage*; *the commercial property market is booming*; **property bond** = investment in a fund invested in properties or in property companies; **property company** = company which buys buildings to lease them; **property developer** = person who buys old buildings or empty land and builds new buildings for sale or rent; **the property market** = (i) the market in letting commercial properties; (ii) the market in developing commercial properties as investments; (iii) buying or selling residential properties by individual homeowners;

property shares = shares in property companies; **property tax** = tax paid on buildings or land (such as the uniform business rate in the UK); **commercial property** = building used as offices or shops; **industrial property** = factories or other buildings used for industrial purposes; **investment property** = property which is held for letting (see SSAP19); **private property** = property which belongs to a private person and not to the public; **residential property** = houses or flats owned or occupied by individual residents **(c)** a building; *we have several properties for sale in the centre of the town*

proportion [prə'pɔːʃən] *noun* part (of a total); *a proportion of the pre-tax profit is set aside for contingencies*; *only a small proportion of our sales comes from retail shops*; **in proportion to** = showing how something is related to something else; *profits went up in proportion to the fall in overhead costs*; *sales in Europe are small in proportion to those in the USA*

proportional [prə'pɔːʃənl] *adjective* directly related; *the increase in profit is proportional to the reduction in overheads*

proportionately [prə'pɔːʃənətli] *adverb* in proportion

proprietary [prə'praɪətəri] *adjective* **(a)** product (such as a medicine) which is made and owned by a company; **proprietary drug** = drug which is made by a particular company and marketed under a brand name **(b)** *(in South Africa and Australia)*; **proprietary company** = private limited company

proprietor [prə'praɪətə] *noun* person who owns something, especially property or a business; **proprietors' interest** = amount which the owners of a business have invested in the business

pro rata ['prəʊ 'rɑːtə] *adjective & adverb* at a rate which varies according to the size or importance of something; *a pro rata payment*; *to pay someone pro rata*; **dividends are paid pro rata** = dividends are paid according to the number of shares held

prospect ['prɒspekt] *noun* **prospects** = possibilities for the future; **his job prospects are good** = he is very likely to find a job; **prospects for the market** *or* **market prospects are worse than those of last year** = sales in the market are likely to be lower than they were last year; **growth prospects** = potential for growth in a share or business

prospective [prə'spektɪv] *adjective* which may happen in the future; **prospective dividend** = dividend which a company expects to pay at the end of the current year (NOTE: also called **forecast dividend**); **prospective P/E ratio** = P/E ratio expected in the future on the basis of forecast earnings

prospectus [prə'spektəs] *noun* (i) document which gives information to attract buyers or customers; (ii) document which gives information about a company whose shares are being sold to the public for the first time; **pathfinder prospectus** *US* **preliminary prospectus** = preliminary prospectus about a company which is going to be launched on the Stock Exchange, sent to potential major investors before the issue date, giving details of the company's background, but not giving the price at which shares will be sold (NOTE: plural is **prospectuses**)

QUOTE when the prospectus emerges, existing shareholders and any prospective new investors can find out more by calling the free share information line; they will be sent a leaflet. Non-shareholders who register in this way will receive a prospectus when it is published; existing shareholders will be sent one automatically

Financial Times

prosperity [prɒ'sperəti] *noun* being wealthy; **in times of prosperity** = when people are wealthy

prosperous ['prɒspərəs] *adjective* wealthy; *a prosperous shopkeeper*; *a prosperous town*

protect [prə'tekt] *verb* to defend something against harm; **to protect an industry by imposing tariff barriers** = to stop a local industry from being hit by foreign competition by taxing foreign products when they are imported

protection [prə'tekʃən] *noun* thing which protects; *the legislation offers no protection to part-time workers*; **consumer protection** = protecting consumers against unfair or illegal traders

protectionism [prə'tekʃənɪzm] *noun* restriction of imports into a country to protect the country's own native industry

protective [prə'tektɪv] *adjective* which protects; **protective tariff** = tariff which tries to reduce imports to stop them competing with local products

pro tem ['prəʊ 'tem] *adverb* temporarily, for a time

protest 1 ['prəʊtest] *noun* official document which states that a bill of exchange has not been paid **2** [prə'test] *verb* **to protest a bill** = to draw up a document to prove that a bill of exchange has not been paid

provide [prə'vaɪd] *verb* **(a) to provide for** = to allow for something which may happen in the future; *the contract provides for an annual increase in charges*; *£10,000 of expenses have been provided for in the budget* **(b)** to put money aside in accounts to cover expenditure or loss in the future; *£25,000 is provided against bad debts*

provident ['prɒvɪdənt] *adjective* which provides benefits in case of illness, old age, etc.; *a provident fund*; *a provident society*

provider [prə'vaɪdə] *noun* **provider of capital** = person or company which provides capital to a business (usually by being a shareholder)

provision [prə'vɪʒən] *noun* **(a) to make provision for** = to see that something is allowed for in the future; **there is no provision for** *or* **no provision has been made for car parking in the plans for the office block** = the plans do not include space for cars to park **(b) provisions** = money put aside in accounts for anticipated expenditure where the timing or amount of expenditure but not its actual occurrence is uncertain (if the expenditure is not certain to occur, then the money set aside is called a 'contingent liability'); *the bank has made a £2m provision for bad debts* *or* *a $5bn provision against Third World loans* **(c)** legal condition; **we have made provision to this effect** = we have put terms into the contract which will make this work

provisional [prə'vɪʒənl] *adjective* temporary, not final or permanent; *provisional forecast of sales*; *provisional budget*; *they faxed their provisional acceptance of the contract*; **provisional liquidator** = official appointed by a court to protect the assets of a company which is the subject of a winding up order

provisionally [prə'vɪʒnəli] *adverb* not finally; *the contract has been accepted provisionally*

proxy ['prɒksi] *noun* **(a)** document which gives someone the power to act on behalf of

someone else; *to sign by proxy*; **proxy vote** = votes made by proxy; *the proxy votes were all in favour of the board's recommendation* **(b)** person who acts on behalf of someone else; *to act as proxy for someone*; *shareholders who are unable to attend the AGM are asked to appoint proxies*; **proxy form** *or* **proxy card** *US* **proxy statement** = form which a shareholder receives with his invitation to attend an AGM, which he fills in if he wants to appoint a proxy to vote for him on a resolution

prudence ['pruːdəns] *noun* being careful; **prudence in accounting** = concept that accounts should be prepared on the basis that all anticipated liabilities should be included and that profits should only be included when they are realised

QUOTE FRED 21 warns that prudence may lead to bias if this means that gains and assets are understated and losses and liabilities are overstated

Accountancy

prudent ['pruːdənt] *adjective* careful, not taking any risks; **prudent man rule** = rule that trustees who make financial decisions on behalf of other people should act carefully (as a normal prudent person would)

prudential [pruː'denʃl] *adjective* which is careful or prudent; **prudential ratio** = ratio of capital to assets which it is prudent for a bank to have, according to EC regulations

PSBR = PUBLIC SECTOR BORROWING REQUIREMENT

pseudo-code ['sjuːdəʊ'kəʊd] *noun* English sentence structures, used to describe program instructions which are then coded in the actual programming language

Pte *(Singapore)* = PRIVATE LIMITED COMPANY

Pty = PROPRIETARY COMPANY *(Australia)*; **Pty Ltd** = private limited company

public ['pʌblɪk] *adjective* **(a)** referring to all the people in general; **public holiday** = day when all workers rest and enjoy themselves instead of working; **Public Trustee** = official who is appointed as a trustee of an individual's property; **public utilities** = companies (such as electricity, gas, transport, etc.) which provide a service used by the whole community **(b)** referring to the government or the state; **Public Accounts Committee** = committee of the House of Commons which examines the spending of each department and ministry; **public expenditure** = spending of money by local or central government; **public finance** = the raising of money by governments (by taxes or borrowing) and the spending of it; **public funds** = government money available for expenditure; **public ownership** = situation where the government owns a business, i.e., where an industry is nationalized, or controls a body which provides public services; **public spending** = spending by the government or by local authorities **(c) the company is going public** = the company is going to place some of its shares for sale on the stock market so that anyone can buy them; *US* **public offering** = offering new shares in a corporation for sale to the public as a way of launching the corporation on the Stock Exchange (NOTE: the British equivalent for this is an **offer for sale**); **public placing** = offering a new issue of shares to the public

Public Limited Company (Plc)

['pʌblɪk 'lɪmɪtəd 'kʌmpni] *noun* company in which the general public can invest and whose shares and loan stock can usually be bought and sold on the Stock Exchange (NOTE: also called a **Public Company)**

publicly held company ['pʌblɪkli 'held

'kʌmpni] *noun US* company controlled by a few shareholders or its directors, but which is quoted on the Stock Exchange and where the public hold a few shares

public sector ['pʌblɪk 'sektə] *noun*

nationalized industries and services; *a report on wage rises in the public sector or on public sector wage settlements*; **Public Sector Borrowing Requirement (PSBR)** = amount of money which a government has to borrow to pay for its own spending (i.e., the difference between the government's expenditure and its income)

publish ['pʌblɪʃ] *verb* to make something

public; **published accounts** = accounts of a company which have been prepared and audited and then must be published by sending to the shareholders and other interested parties

pump [pʌmp] *verb* to put something in by

force; *the banks have been pumping money into the company to keep it afloat*

pump priming ['pʌmp 'praɪmɪŋ] *noun*

government investment in new projects which it hopes will benefit the economy

QUOTE in each of the years 1986 to 1989, Japan pumped a net sum of the order of $100bn into foreign securities, notably into US government bonds
Financial Times Review

pur autre vie *or* **per autre vie** ['puːə əutr 'viː *or* 'pɜː 'əutrə 'viː:] *French phrase meaning* 'for the lifetime of another person'

purchase ['pɜːtʃəs] **1** *noun* thing which has been bought; **to make a purchase** = to buy something; *US* **purchase acquisition** = full consolidation, where the assets of a subsidiary company which have been purchased are included into the parent company's balance sheet, and the premium paid for the goodwill is written off against reserves (the British equivalent is 'acquisition accounting'); **purchase book** = records of purchases; **purchase(s) daybook** = book which records the purchases made each day; **purchase(s) ledger** = book in which expenditure is recorded; **purchase order** = official order made out by a purchasing department for goods which a company wants to buy; *we cannot supply you without a purchase order number*; **purchase price** = price paid for something; **purchase requisition** = order to the purchasing department asking it to purchase something; **purchase tax** = tax paid on things which are bought; **bulk purchase** *or* **quantity purchase** = buying of large quantities of goods at low prices; **cash purchase** = purchase made in cash; **hire purchase** = system of buying something on credit by paying a sum regularly each month which includes part debt repayment and part interest; *he is buying a refrigerator on hire purchase*; **hire purchase agreement** = contract to pay for something by instalments **2** *verb* to buy; **to purchase something for cash** = to pay cash for something

purchaser ['pɜːtʃəsə] *noun* person or company which purchases; **the company is looking for a purchaser** = the company is trying to find someone who will buy it; *the company has found a purchaser for its warehouse*

purchasing ['pɜːtʃəsɪŋ] *noun* buying; **purchasing department** = section of a company which deals with the buying of stock, raw materials, equipment, etc.; **purchasing manager** = manager working in the purchasing department; **purchasing officer** = person in a company or organization who is responsible for buying stock, raw materials, equipment, etc.; **purchasing**

power = quantity of goods which can be bought by a group of people or with an amount of money; *the decline in the purchasing power of the pound*; **purchasing routine** = the various stages involved in organizing the purchase of something (sending a purchase requisition to the purchasing department, sending out the official order, etc.); **central purchasing** = purchasing organized by the main office for all departments or branches

put [pʊt] **1** *noun* **put option** = right to sell shares at a certain price at a certain date **2** *verb* to place or to fix; **the accounts put the stock value at £10,000** = the accounts state that the value of the stock is £10,000; **to put a proposal to the vote** = to ask a meeting to vote for or against the proposal; **to put a proposal to the board** = to ask the board to consider a suggestion (NOTE: **putting - put**)

put down ['pʊt 'daʊn] *verb* **(a)** to make a deposit; *to put down money on a house* **(b)** to write an item in a ledger or an account book; *to put down a figure for expenses*

put in ['pʊt 'ɪn] *verb* to put in a bid for something = to offer (usually in writing) to buy something; **to put in an estimate for something** = to give someone a written calculation of the probable costs of carrying out a job; **to put in a claim for damage** = to ask an insurance company to pay for damage suffered by something that was insured

put into ['pʊt 'ɪntʊ] *verb* **to put money into a business** = to invest money in a business

put up ['pʊt 'ʌp] *verb* **(a) who put up the money for the shop?** = who provided the investment money for the shop to start?; **to put something up for sale** = to advertise that something is for sale; *when he retired he decided to put his town flat up for sale* **(b)** to increase, to make higher; *the shop has put up all its prices by 5%*

PV = PRESENT VALUE

pyramid selling ['pɪrəmɪd 'selɪŋ] *noun* illegal way of selling goods or investments to the public, where each selling agent pays for the franchise to sell the product or service, and sells that right on to other agents, so that in the end the person who makes most money is the original franchisor, and sub-agents or investors lose all their investments

Qq

quadruplicate [kwɒˈdruːplɪkət] *noun* **in quadruplicate** = with the original and three copies; *the invoices are printed in quadruplicate*

qualification [kwɒlɪfɪˈkeɪʃn] *noun* **(a)** proof that you have completed a specialized course of study; *to have the right qualifications for the job*; **professional qualifications** = documents which show that someone has successfully finished a course of study which allows him to work in one of the professions **(b) period of qualification** = time which has to pass before someone qualifies for something **(c) auditors' qualification** = a form of words in a report from the auditors of a company's accounts, stating that in their opinion the accounts are not a true reflection of the company's financial position and profit or loss for the year; *see also* QUALIFIED AUDIT REPORT

qualified [ˈkwɒlɪfaɪd] *adjective* **(a)** having passed special examinations in a subject; *she is a qualified accountant*; *we have appointed a qualified designer to supervise the new factory project*; **highly qualified** = with very good results in examinations or possessing particularly relevant experience after qualifying **(b)** with some reservations or conditions; *qualified acceptance of a contract*; *the plan received qualified approval from the board*; **qualified acceptance of a bill** = acceptance of a bill which takes place only if certain conditions are met **(c) qualified accounts** = accounts which have been commented on by the auditors because they contain something with which the auditors do not agree; **qualified auditors' report** *or* **qualified audit report** *US* **qualified opinion** = report from a company's auditors which points out areas in the accounts with which the auditors do not agree or about which they are not prepared to express an opinion, or where the auditors believe the accounts as a whole have not been prepared correctly, or where they are unable to decide whether the accounts are correct or not (see SAS 600); **qualified valuer** = person conducting a valuation who holds a recognised and relevant professional

qualification and has recent post-qualification experience, and sufficient knowledge of the state of the market, with reference to the location and category of the tangible fixed asset being valued (see FRS 15)

qualify [ˈkwɒlɪfaɪ] *verb* **(a) to qualify for** = to be in the right position for, to be entitled to; *the company does not qualify for a government grant*; *she qualifies for unemployment pay* **(b) to qualify as** = to follow a specialized course and pass examinations so that you can do a certain job; *she has qualified as an accountant*; *he will qualify as a solicitor next year* **(c) the auditors have qualified the accounts** = the auditors have found something in the accounts of the company which has made them unable to agree that they show a 'true and fair' view

qualifying [ˈkwɒlɪfaɪɪŋ] *adjective* **qualifying distribution** = money paid as a dividend or bonus which entails a tax liability; **qualifying period** = time which has to pass before something qualifies for a grant, subsidy, etc.; *there is a six-month qualifying period before you can get a grant from the local authority*; **qualifying shares** = number of shares which you need to earn to get a bonus issue or to be a director of the company, etc.; *the opposite is* NON-QUALIFYING

quantifiable [ˈkwɒntɪfaɪəbl] *adjective* which can be quantified; *the effect of the change in the discount structure is not quantifiable*

quantify [ˈkwɒntɪfaɪ] *verb* **to quantify the effect of something** = to show the effect of something in figures; *it is impossible to* *quantify the effect of the new legislation on our turnover*

quantitative [ˈkwɒnɪtətɪv] *adjective* referring to quantities

QUOTE the EC demands that Japan abolish quantitative restrictions and cut import tariffs in three sectors: food, fish products and leather
Times

quantity [ˈkwɒntəti] *noun* large amount; *the company offers a discount for quantity purchase*; **quantity discount** = discount given to a customer who buys large quantities of goods

quantum meruit [ˈkwɒntəm ˈmeruːɪt] *Latin phrase* 'as much as he has deserved': rule that, when claiming for breach of contract, a party is entitled to payment for work done (used in cases where no fixed payment for services has been agreed)

quarter [ˈkwɔːtə] *noun* **(a)** one of four equal parts of a whole; **a quarter of a litre** *or* **a quarter litre** = 250 millilitres; **a quarter of an hour** = 15 minutes; **three quarters** = 75%; *three quarters of the staff are less than thirty years old*; *he paid only a quarter of the list price* **(b)** period of three months; **first quarter, second quarter, third quarter, fourth quarter** *or* **last quarter** = periods of three months from January to the end of March, from April to the end of June, from July to the end of September, from October to the end of the year; *the instalments are payable at the end of each quarter*; *the first quarter's rent is payable in advance*

QUOTE corporate profits for the first quarter showed a 4 per cent drop from last year's final three months
Financial Times

QUOTE economists believe the economy is picking up this quarter and will do better still in the second half of the year
Sunday Times

quarter day [ˈkwɔːtə ˈdeɪ] *noun* day at the end of a quarter, when rents or fees, etc. should be paid

COMMENT: in England, the quarter days are 25th March (Lady Day), 24th June (Midsummer Day), 29th September (Michaelmas Day) and 25th December (Christmas Day)

quarterly [ˈkwɔːtəli] **1** *adjective & adverb* happening every three months, happening four times a year; *there is a quarterly charge for electricity*; *the bank sends us a quarterly*

statement; *we agreed to pay the rent quarterly* or *on a quarterly basis*; **quartery report** = the results of a corporation, produced each quarter **2** *noun US* = QUARTERLY REPORT

quartile [ˈkwɔːtaɪl] *noun* **(a)** one of three figures below which 25%, 50% or 75% of a total falls **(b)** each of the four groups separated by these figures

COMMENT: quartile is used in relation to a frequency distribution, such as the amount of turnover attributable to each customer. It is more common to refer to the upper and lower quartiles (below 25% and above 75%) than to other quartiles

quasi- [ˈkweɪzaɪ] *prefix* almost, which seems like; *a quasi-official body*

quasi-loan [ˈkweɪzaɪˈləʊn] *noun* agreement between two parties where one agrees to pay the other's debts, provided that the second party agrees to reimburse the first at some later date

quasi-public corporation [ˈkweɪzaɪ ˈpʌblɪk kɔːpəˈreɪʃnləʊn] *noun US* American institution which is privately owned, but which serves a public function (such as the Federal National Mortgage Association)

queue [kjuː] **1** *noun* **(a)** line of people waiting one behind the other; *to form a queue* or *to join a queue*; *queues formed at the doors of the bank when the news spread about its possible collapse*; **dole queue** = line of people waiting to collect their unemployment benefit **(b)** series of documents (such as orders, application forms) which are dealt with in order; **his order went to the end of the queue** = his order was dealt with last; **mortgage queue** = list of people waiting for mortgages **2** *verb* to form a line one after the other for something; *when food was rationed, people had to queue for bread*; *we queued for hours to get tickets*; *a list of companies queuing to be launched on the Stock Exchange*; **queuing time** = period of time messages have to wait before they can be processed or transmitted

quick [kwɪk] *adjective* fast, not taking any time; *the company made a quick recovery*; *he is looking for a quick return on his investments*; *we are hoping for a quick sale*; **quick assets** = asset which can easily be changed into cash (including cash in hand, cash in bank accounts, debtors, securities which can be sold on the Stock Exchange); **quick ratio** = ratio of liquid assets (that is, current assets less stocks, but including debtors) to current liabilities, giving an indication of a company's solvency (NOTE: also called **acid test ratio** or **liquidity ratio**)

quid [kwɪd] *noun (slang)* one pound sterling; **to be quids in** = to make a profit, to be in luck; *he was quids in after the sale*

quid pro quo ['kwɪd 'prəʊ 'kwəʊ] *noun* thing given or action carried out in return for something; *he agreed to mention the product in a magazine article and, as a quid pro quo, the company invited him to its golf day*

COMMENT: a quid pro quo is usually an informal agreement, not enforceable in law, that does not involve money

quorum ['kwɔːrəm] *noun* number of people who have to be present at a meeting to make it valid; **to have a quorum** = to have enough people present for a meeting to go ahead; *do we have a quorum?*

COMMENT: if there is a quorum at a meeting, the meeting is said to be 'quorate'; if there aren't enough people present to make a quorum, the meeting is 'inquorate'

quota ['kwəʊtə] *noun* fixed amount of something which is allowed; **import quota** = fixed quantity of a particular type of goods which the government allows to be imported; *the government has imposed a quota on the importation of cars*; *the quota on imported cars has been lifted*; **quota system** = system where imports or supplies are regulated by fixing maximum amounts; **to arrange distribution through a quota system** = to arrange distribution by allowing each distributor only a certain number of items

QUOTE Canada agreed to a new duty-free quota of 600,000 tonnes a year
Globe and Mail (Toronto)

quotation [kwəʊ'teɪʃn] *noun* **(a)** estimate of how much something will cost; *they sent in their quotation for the job*; *to ask for quotations for refitting the shop*; *his quotation was much lower than all the others*; *we accepted the lowest quotation* **(b)** quotation on the Stock Exchange or Stock Exchange quotation = listing of the price of a share on the Stock Exchange; **the company is going for a quotation on the Stock**

Exchange = the company has applied to the Stock Exchange to have its shares listed; *we are seeking a stock market quotation*

quote [kwəʊt] **1** *verb* **(a)** to repeat words used by someone else; to repeat a reference number; *he quoted figures from the annual report*; *in reply please quote this number*; *when making a complaint please quote the batch number printed on the box*; *he replied, quoting the number of the account* **(b)** to estimate, to say what costs may be; *to quote a price for supplying stationery*; *their prices are always quoted in dollars*; *he quoted me a price of £1,026*; *can you quote for supplying 20,000 envelopes?* **2** *noun informal* estimate of how much something will cost; *to give someone a quote for supplying computers*; *we have asked for quotes for refitting the shop*; *his quote was the lowest of three*; *we accepted the lowest quote*; **quote-driven system** = system of working a stock market, where marketmakers quote a price for a stock (as opposed to an order-driven system)

quoted ['kwəʊtɪd] *adjective* **quoted company** = company whose shares can be bought or sold on the Stock Exchange; **quoted investments** = investments in securities which are listed on a Stock Exchange (the opposite is 'unquoted investments'); **quoted shares** = shares which can be bought or sold on the Stock Exchange

QUOTE a Bermudan-registered company quoted on the Luxembourg stock exchange
Lloyd's List

QUOTE banks operating on the foreign exchange market refrained from quoting forward US/Hongkong dollar exchange rates
South China Morning Post

quotient ['kwəʊʃnt] *noun* result of one number divided by another

COMMENT: when two numbers are divided, the answer is made up of a quotient and a remainder (the fractional part), 16 divided by 4 is equal to a quotient of 4 and zero remainder, 16 divided by 5 is equal to a quotient of 3 and a remainder of 1

Rr

R&D [ˈɑːrənˈdiː] = RESEARCH AND DEVELOPMENT *the R&D department; the company spends millions on R&D*

rack rent [ˈræk ˈrent] *noun* (i) very high rent; (ii) full yearly rent of a property let on a normal lease

racket [ˈrækɪt] *noun* series of illegal deals which make a lot of money; *he runs a cut-price ticket racket*

racketeer [rækəˈtɪə] *noun* person who runs a racket

ragioniere [rædʒɪɒˈnjeəri] *Italian* accountant

raid [reɪd] *noun* **dawn raid** = sudden planned purchase of a large number of a company's shares at the beginning of a day's trading (up to 15% of a company's shares may be bought in this way, and the purchaser must wait for seven days before purchasing any more shares; it is assumed that a dawn raid is the first step towards a takeover of the target company); **bear raid** = selling large numbers of shares to try to bring down prices

QUOTE bear raiding involves trying to depress a target company's share price by heavy selling of its shares, spreading adverse rumours or a combination of the two. As an added refinement, the raiders may sell short. The aim is to push down the price so that the raiders can buy back the shares they sold at a lower price
Guardian

raider [ˈreɪdə] *noun* person or company which buys a stake in another company before making a hostile takeover bid (also called a 'corporate raider')

raise [reɪz] **1** *noun US* increase in salary; *he asked the boss for a raise; she is pleased - she has had her raise* (NOTE: British English is **rise**) **2** *verb* **(a) to raise an invoice** = to write out an invoice **(b)** to increase, to make higher; *the government has raised the tax levels; air fares will be raised on June 1st; the company raised its dividend by 10%; when the company raised its prices, it lost half of its* *share of the market* **(c)** to obtain (money) or to organize (a loan); *the company is trying to raise the capital to fund its expansion programme; the government raises more money by indirect taxation than by direct; where will he raise the money from to start up his business?*

QUOTE the company said yesterday that its recent share issue has been oversubscribed, raising A$225.5m
Financial Times

QUOTE investment trusts can raise capital, but this has to be done as a company does, by a rights issue of equity
Investors Chronicle

QUOTE over the past few weeks, companies raising new loans from international banks have been forced to pay more
Financial Times

rally [ˈræli] **1** *noun* rise in price when the trend has been downwards; *shares staged a rally on the Stock Exchange; after a brief rally shares fell back to a new low* **2** *verb* to rise in price, when the trend has been downwards; *shares rallied on the news of the latest government figures*

QUOTE when Japan rallied, it had no difficulty in surpassing its previous all-time high, and this really stretched the price-earnings ratios into the stratosphere
Money Observer

QUOTE bad news for the U.S. economy ultimately may have been the cause of a late rally in stock prices yesterday
Wall Street Journal

random [ˈrændəm] *adjective* done without making any special choice; **random check** = check on items taken from a group without any special choice; **random error** = computer error which has no special reason; **random number** = number that cannot be predicted; **random sample** = sample for testing taken without any deliberate selection; **random sampling** = choosing samples for testing without any special selection; **random**

walk = movement which cannot be predicted (used to describe movements in share prices which cannot be forecast)

range [reɪndʒ] *noun* scale of items from a low point to a high one; **range of prices** *or* **trading range** = difference between the highest and lowest price for a share or bond over a period of time

rank [ræŋk] **1** *noun* position in a company or an organization; *all managers are of equal rank*; **in rank order** = in order according to position of importance **2** *verb* **(a)** to classify in order; *candidates are ranked in order of appearance* **(b)** to be in a certain position; *the non-voting shares rank equally with the voting shares*; *deferred ordinary shares do not rank for dividend*

> QUOTE in a separate development, the Geneva-based bank confirmed that it has accelerated the six Swiss bond issues. Acceleration means the bonds become payable immediately and allows bondholders to rank alongside the company's other creditors
> *Times*

rata [ˈrɑːtə] *see* PRO RATA

rate [reɪt] *noun* **(a)** money charged for time worked, work completed; **all-in rate** = price which covers all items in a purchase (such as delivery, tax and insurance, as well as the goods themselves); **fixed rate** = charge which cannot be changed; **flat rate** = charge which always stays the same; *a flat-rate increase of 10%*; *we pay a flat rate for electricity each quarter*; *he is paid a flat rate of £2 per thousand*; **freight rates** = charges for transporting goods; **full rate** = full charge, with no reductions; **the going rate** = the usual, the current rate of payment; **market rate** = normal price in the market; *we pay the going rate or the market rate for typists*; *the going rate for offices is £20 per square foot* **(b)** **depreciation rate** = rate at which an asset is depreciated each year in the company accounts; **discount rate** = (i) interest rate used to calculate the discount on the sale of commercial bills to a central bank, such as the Bank of England; (ii) rate at which the face value of a bill of exchange is reduced when payment is made before the maturing date; (iii) percentage used in a discounting calculation, as when finding the present value of future income; **insurance rates** = amount of premium which has to be paid per £1000 of insurance **(c)** amount of interest paid; **interest rate** *or* **rate of interest** = percentage charge

for borrowing money; **rate of return** = amount of interest or dividend which comes from an investment, shown as a percentage of the money invested; **bank base rates** = basic rate of interest which a bank uses to calculate the actual rate of interest on loans to customers **(d)** value of one currency against another; *what is today's rate or the current rate for the dollar?*; **cross rate** = exchange rate between two currencies expressed in a third currency; **exchange rate** *or* **rate of exchange** = rate at which one currency is exchanged for another; **to calculate costs on a fixed exchange rate** = to calculate costs on an exchange rate which does not change; **forward rate** = rate for purchase of foreign currency at a fixed price for delivery at a later date **(e)** amount, number or speed compared with something else; *the rate of increase in redundancies*; *the rate of absenteeism or the absenteeism rate always increases in fine weather*; **birth rate** = number of children born per 1,000 of the population; **error rate** = number of mistakes per thousand entries or per page; **rate of sales** = speed at which units are sold **(f)** *GB* **rates** = local taxes on all property; **uniform business rate (UBR)** = tax levied on business property which is the same percentage for the whole country

> QUOTE state-owned banks cut their prime rate a percentage point to 11%
> *Wall Street Journal*

> QUOTE the unions had argued that public sector pay rates had slipped behind rates applying in private sector employment
> *Australian Financial Review*

> QUOTE royalties have been levied at a rate of 12.5% of full production
> *Lloyd's List*

rateable [ˈreɪtəbl] *adjective* **rateable value** = formerly, the value of a commercial property as a basis for calculating local taxes

ratepayer [ˈreɪtpeɪə] *noun* **business ratepayer** = business which pays local taxes on a shop, office, factory, etc.

rating [ˈreɪtɪŋ] *noun* **(a)** putting in order of value or of merit; **credit rating** = amount which a credit agency feels a customer will be able to repay; **merit rating** = judging how well a worker does his work, so that he can be paid according to merit; **performance rating** = judging how well a share or a company has performed; **stock market rating** = price of a share on the stock market, which shows how investors and financial advisers generally consider the value of the company; **rating agency** = organization which gives a credit rating to companies or other organizations issuing bonds **(b)** valuing of property; **rating officer** = official in a local authority who decides the rateable value of a commercial property; *see also* RERATING

ratio ['reɪʃɪəʊ] *noun* proportion or quantity of something compared to something else; *the ratio of successes to failures*; *our product outsells theirs by a ratio of two to one*; **asset turnover ratio** = number of times assets are turned over by sales during the year, calculated as turnover divided by total assets less current liabilities; **capital turnover ratio** = relationship between sales and the capital (i.e. assets less liabilities) used to generate sales; **creditors turnover ratio** = average time taken to pay creditors; **current ratio** = ratio of current assets to current liabilities (showing if a company may not be able to meet its immediate debts); **debtors turnover ratio** = average time which debtors take to pay; **price/earnings ratio (P/E ratio)** = comparison between the market price of a share and the current earnings per share; **stock turnover ratio** = average amount of time stock stays in the warehouse (calculated as the value of sales divided by the average value of stock, showing the number of times stock is turned over during the year); **ratio analysis** = method of analyzing the performance of a company by showing the figures in its accounts as ratios and comparing them with those of other companies

rational number ['ræʃənəl 'nʌmbə] *noun* number that can be written as the ratio of two whole numbers; *24 over 7 is a rational number*; *0.333 can be written as the rational number 1/3*

raw [rɔː] *adjective* in the original state, not processed; **raw data** = data as it is put into a computer, without being analyzed; **raw materials** = substances which have not been manufactured (such as wool, wood, sand)

> QUOTE it makes sense for them to produce goods for sale back home in the US from plants in Britain where raw materials are relatively cheap
> *Duns Business Month*

R/D
= REFER TO DRAWER

re- [riː] *prefix* again

readjust [riːə'dʒʌst] *verb* to adjust again; *to readjust prices to take account of the rise in the costs of raw materials*; *share prices readjusted quickly to the news of the devaluation*

readjustment [riːə'dʒʌstmənt] *noun* act of readjusting; *a readjustment in pricing*; *after the devaluation there was a period of readjustment in the exchange rates*

ready ['redi] *adjective* **ready cash** = money which is immediately available for payment; **these items find a ready sale in the Middle East** = these items sell rapidly or easily in the Middle East

real [rɪəl] *adjective* **(a)** (price, etc.) shown in terms of money adjusted for inflation; **real income** *or* **real wages** = income which is available for spending after tax, etc. has been deducted and after inflation has been taken into account; **real interest rate** = interest rate after taking inflation into account; **real rate of return** = actual rate of return, calculated after taking inflation into account; **real value** = value of an investment which is kept the same (by index-linking, for example); **in real terms** = actually, really; *prices have gone up by 3% but with inflation running at 5% that is a fall in real terms* **(b)** **real time** = time when a computer is working on the processing of data while the problem to which the data refers is actually taking place; **real-time system** = computer system where data is inputted directly into the computer which automatically processes it to produce information which can be used immediately **(c)** **real estate** *or* **real property** = property (land or buildings) considered from a legal point of view; *he made his money from real estate deals in the 1970s* US **real estate agent** = person who sells property for customers; *US* **real estate investment trust (REIT)** = public company which invests only in property on behalf of its shareholders

> QUOTE real wages have been held down dramatically: they have risen as an annual rate of only 1% in the last two years
> *Sunday Times*

> QUOTE sterling M3 rose by 13.5% in the year to August - seven percentage points faster than the rate of inflation and the biggest increase in real terms since 1972-3
> *Economist*

> QUOTE on top of the cost of real estate, the investment in inventory and equipment to open a typical warehouse comes to around $5 million
> *Duns Business Month*

realizable [rɪə'laɪzəbl] *adjective* **realizable assets** = assets which can be sold for money

realization [rɪəlaɪˈzeɪʃən] *noun* **(a)** making real; **the realization of a project** = putting a project into action **(b) realization of assets** = selling of assets for money

realize [ˈrɪəlaɪz] *verb* **(a)** to make something become real; **to realize a project** *or* **a plan** = to put a project or a plan into action **(b)** to sell for money; **to realize property** *or* **assets**; **the sale realized £100,000**; **realized gain** *or* **realized loss** = gain or loss made when assets are sold; **realized profit** = actual profit made when something is sold (as opposed to paper profit) **(c)** to sell the assets of an insolvent company

realtor [ˈrɪəltə] *noun US* person who sells real estate for customers

realty [ˈrɪəlti] *noun* property or real estate

reasonable [ˈriːzənəbl] *adjective* **(a)** sensible, not extreme; **no reasonable offer refused** = we will accept any offer which is not extremely low **(b)** moderate, not expensive; **the restaurant offers good food at reasonable prices**

reassess [riːəˈses] *verb* to assess again

reassessment [riːəˈsesmənt] *noun* new assessment

rebate [ˈriːbeɪt] *noun* **(a)** reduction in the amount of money to be paid; **to offer a 10% rebate on selected goods (b)** money returned to someone because he has paid too much; **tax rebate** = money returned by the Inland Revenue because it was overpaid; **he got a tax rebate at the end of the year**

recapitalization [riːkæpɪtəlaɪˈzeɪʃn] *noun* change in the capital structure of a company (as when new shares are issued), especially when undertaken to avoid the company going into liquidation

recd = RECEIVED

receipt [rɪˈsiːt] **1** *noun* **(a)** paper showing that money has been paid or that something has been received; **customs receipt**; **rent receipt**; **receipt for items purchased**; *please produce your receipt if you want to exchange items*; **receipt book** *or* **book of receipts** = book of blank receipts to be filled in when purchases are made **(b)** act of receiving something; **to acknowledge receipt of a letter** = to write to say that you have received a letter; *we acknowledge receipt of your letter of the 15th*; *goods will be supplied within thirty days of receipt of order*; *invoices are payable within thirty days of receipt*; *on receipt of the notification, the company*

lodged an appeal **(c)** **receipts** = money taken in sales; *to itemize receipts and expenditure*; *receipts are down against the same period last year*; **receipts and payments basis** = method of preparing the accounts of a business, where revenues and costs are shown at the time they are received or paid (as opposed to showing them when they are earned or incurred; also called 'cash basis') **2** *verb* to stamp or to sign a document to show that it has been received

receivable [rɪˈsiːvəbl] *adjective* which can be received; **accounts receivable** = money owed to a company by its customers; **bills (of exchange) receivable** = bills which a creditor will receive in due course

receivables [rɪˈsiːvəblz] *plural noun* money which is owed to a company by its customers

COMMENT: a company can sell its receivables to a debt factor for cash (at a discount to the full amount due)

receive [rɪˈsiːv] *verb* to get something which has been delivered; *we received the payment ten days ago*; *the workers have not received any salary for six months*; *the goods were received in good condition*; **'received with thanks'** = words put on an invoice to show that a sum has been paid

receiver [rɪˈsiːvə] *noun* **(a)** person who receives something; *the receiver of the shipment* **(b)** **administrative receiver** = receiver appointed by a debenture holder to liquidate the assets of a company on his behalf; **official receiver** = official who is appointed by the courts to run a company which is in financial difficulties, to pay off its debts as far as possible, and to close it down; *the court appointed a receiver for the company*; *the company is in the hands of the receiver*

receivership [rɪˈsiːvəʃɪp] *noun* **the company went into receivership** = the company was put into the hands of a receiver; **administrative receivership** = appointment of an administrative receiver by a debenture holder

receiving [rɪ'siːvɪŋ] *noun* **(a)** act of getting something which has been delivered; **receiving clerk** = official who works in a receiving office; **receiving department** = section of a company which deals with incoming goods or payments; **receiving office** = office where goods or payments are received **(b) receiving order** = order from a court appointing a receiver to a company

recession [rɪ'seʃən] *noun* fall in trade or in the economy of a country; *the recession has reduced profits in many companies*; *several firms have closed factories because of the recession*

COMMENT: there a various ways of deciding if a recession is taking place: the usual one is when the GNP falls for three consecutive quarters

reciprocal [rɪ'sɪprəkəl] *adjective* applying from one country, person or company to another and vice versa; *reciprocal agreement*; *reciprocal contract*; **reciprocal holdings** = situation where two companies own shares in each other to prevent takeover bids; **reciprocal trade** = trade between two countries

reciprocate [rɪ'sɪprəkeɪt] *verb* to do the same thing to someone as he has just done to you

QUOTE in 1934 Congress authorized President Roosevelt to seek lower tariffs with any country willing to reciprocate
Duns Business Month

reckon ['rekən] *verb* to calculate; *to reckon the costs at £25,000*; *we reckon the loss to be over £1m*; *they reckon the insurance costs to be too high*

recognize ['rekəgnaɪz] *verb* **recognized agent** = agent who is approved by the company for which he acts; **statement of total recognized gains and losses** = financial statement showing changes in shareholders' equity during an accounting period (see FRS 3); **recognized professional body (RPB)** = professional body which is in charge of the regulation of the conduct of its members; **recognized qualification** = qualification which is well-known to employers and professional bodies

reconcile ['rekənsaɪl] *verb* to make two accounts or statements agree; *to reconcile one account with another*; *to reconcile the accounts*

reconciliation [rekənsɪlɪ'eɪʃən] *noun* making two accounts or statements agree;

bank reconciliation = making sure that the bank statements agree with the company's ledgers; **reconciliation statement** = statement which explains how two accounts can be made to agree

reconstruction [riːkən'strʌkʃən] *noun* new way of organizing; **the reconstruction of a company** = restructuring the finances of a company by transferring the assets to a new company

record 1 ['rekɔːd] *noun* **(a)** report of something which has happened; *the chairman signed the minutes as a true record of the last meeting*; **record book** = book in which minutes of meetings are kept; **for the record** *or* **to keep the record straight** = to note something which has been done; *for the record, I would like these sales figures to be noted in the minutes*; **on record** = correctly reported; *the chairman is on record as saying that profits are set to rise*; **off the record** = unofficially, in private; *he made some remarks off the record about the disastrous home sales figures* **(b) records** = documents which give information; *the names of customers are kept in the company's records*; *we find from our records that our invoice number 1234 has not been paid*; **date of record** *or* **record date** = date when a shareholder must be registered to qualify for a dividend; **holder of record** = person who is registered as the owner of shares in a company at a certain date **(c)** description of what has happened in the past; **track record** = success or failure of a company or individual in the past **(d)** which is better or worse than anything before; **record sales** *or* **record losses** *or* **record profits** = sales, losses or profits which are higher than ever before; *2000 was a record year for the company*; *sales for 2000 equalled the record of 1998*; *our top salesman has set a new record for sales per call*; *we broke our record for June* = we sold more than we have ever sold before in June **2** [rɪ'kɔːd] *verb* to note or to report; *the company has recorded another year of increased profits*; *your complaint has been recorded and will be investigated*

recording [rɪ'kɔːdɪŋ] *noun* making of a note; *the recording of an order* *or* *of a complaint*

recoup [rɪ'kuːp] *verb* **to recoup one's losses** = to get back money which you thought you had lost

recourse [rɪ'kɔːs] *noun* right of a lender to compel a borrower to repay money borrowed; **to decide to have recourse to the courts to**

obtain money due = to decide in the end to sue someone to obtain money owed

recover [rɪ'kʌvə] *verb* **(a)** to get back something which has been lost; *he never recovered his money; the initial investment was never recovered; to recover damages from the driver of the car; to start a court action to recover property* **(b)** to get better, to rise; *the market has not recovered from the rise in oil prices; the stock market fell in the morning, but recovered during the afternoon*

recoverable [rɪ'kʌvərəbl] *adjective* which can be got back; **recoverable ACT** = advance corporation tax which can be set against corporation tax payable for the period; **recoverable amount** = value of an asset, either the price it would fetch if sold, or its value to the company when used (whichever is the larger figure)

recovery [rɪ'kʌvri] *noun* **(a)** getting back something which has been lost; *we are aiming for the complete recovery of the money invested; to start an action for recovery of property* **(b)** movement upwards of shares or of the economy; *the economy staged a recovery; the recovery of the economy after a slump;* **recovery shares** = shares which are likely to go up in value because the company's performance is improving

rectification [rektɪfɪ'keɪʃən] *noun* making changes to a document or register to make it correct; **rectification note** = work which authorizes more work to be done to improve a product which did not originally meet the required standard

rectify ['rektɪfaɪ] *verb* to correct something, to make something right; *to rectify an entry*

recurrent [rɪ'kʌrənt] *adjective* which happens again and again; *a recurrent item of expenditure*

recycle ['riː'saɪkl] *verb* to use something again in a different way (as by investing profits from industry in developing environmental resources)

QUOTE oil producers are probably in a better position to recycle the money than they were in the 1970s, but the money will be spent in different ways
Financial Times Review

QUOTE the balance of payments deficit of the United States (and to a lesser degree, the UK) was being offset by the recycled surpluses of Japan and Germany
Financial Times Review

recycling ['riː'saɪklɪŋ] *noun* deposits made by banks into a bank which is in difficulties, in order to keep it afloat

red [red] *noun* **in the red** = showing a deficit or loss; *my bank account is in the red; the company went into the red in 1999; the company is out of the red for the first time since 1999*

Red Book ['red 'bʊk] *noun* document published on Budget Day, with the text of the Chancellor of the Exchequer's financial statement and budget

red clause credit ['red 'klɔːz 'kredɪt] *noun* letter of credit authorizing the holder to receive an advance payment, usually so that he can continue trading

redeem [rɪ'diːm] *verb* **(a)** to pay off a loan or a debt; *to redeem a mortgage; to redeem a debt* **(b) to redeem a bond** = to sell a bond for cash

redeemable [rɪ'diːməbl] *adjective* which can be sold for cash; **redeemable government stock** = stock which can be redeemed for cash at some time in the future (in the UK, only the War Loan is irredeemable); **redeemable preference share** = preference share which must be bought back by the company at a certain date and for a certain price (the company will set aside money into a special fund for the purpose of redeeming these shares at due date); **redeemable security** = security which can be redeemed at its face value at a certain date in the future

redemption [rɪ'dempʃən] *noun* repayment of a loan or of a debt; **redemption date** = date on which a loan, etc., is due to be repaid; **redemption before due date** = paying back a loan before the date when repayment is due; **redemption value** = value of a security when redeemed; **redemption yield** = yield on a security including interest and its redemption value

red herring ['red 'herɪŋ] *noun US* a preliminary prospectus, the first prospectus for a new share issue, produced to see the market reaction to the proposed issue, but without giving a price for the new shares

(similar to the British 'pathfinder prospectus')

rediscount [riːˈdɪskaʊnt] *verb (of a central bank)* to discount a bill which has already been discounted by the seller

redistribute [riːdɪsˈtrɪbjʊt] *verb* to move items, work or money to different areas or people; *the government aims to redistribute wealth by taxing the rich and giving state benefits to the poor*

redistribution [riːdɪstrɪˈbjuːʃən] *noun* **redistribution of risk** = spreading the risk of an investment or of an insurance among various insurers; **redistribution of wealth** = sharing wealth among the whole population

redlining [ˈredlaɪnɪŋ] *noun* illegal practice of discriminating against prospective borrowers because of the area of the town in which they live

reduce [rɪˈdjuːs] *verb* to make smaller or lower; *to reduce expenditure*; *to reduce a price*; *to reduce taxes*; *prices have been reduced by 15%*; *the government's policy is to reduce inflation to 5%*; **to reduce staff** = to sack employees in order to have a smaller number of staff; **reducing balance method** *US* **reducing installment method** = method of depreciating assets, where the asset is depreciated at a higher rate in the early years and at a lower rate later as repair costs are likely to rise (the depreciation rate is a constant percentage but it is applied to the cost of the asset after each of the previous year's depreciation has been deducted)

reduced [rɪˈdjuːst] *adjective* lower; *reduced prices have increased unit sales*

reduction [rɪˈdʌkʃən] *noun* lowering (of prices, etc.); *price reductions*; *tax reductions*; *staff reductions*; *reduction of expenditure*; *reduction in demand*; *the company was forced to make job reductions*

redundancy [rɪˈdʌndənsi] *noun* being no longer employed, because the job is no longer necessary; **redundancy payment** = payment made to a worker to compensate for losing his or her job; **redundancy rebate** = payment made to a company to compensate for redundancy payments made; **voluntary redundancy** = situation where the worker asks to be made redundant, usually in return for a large payment

redundant [rɪˈdʌndənt] *adjective* **(a)** more than is needed, useless; *redundant capital*; *redundant clause in a contract*; *the new legislation has made clause 6 redundant* **(b)** **to make someone redundant** = to decide that

a worker is not needed any more; **redundant staff** = staff who have lost their jobs because they are not needed any more

re-export 1 [ˈriːˈekspɔːt] *noun* exporting of goods which have been imported; *re-export trade*; *we import wool for re-export*; *the value of re-exports has increased* **2** [riːeksˈpɔːt] *verb* to export something which has been imported

re-exportation [ˈriːekspɔːˈteɪʃən] *noun* exporting goods which have been imported

ref [ref] = REFERENCE

refer [rɪˈfɜː] *verb* **the bank referred the cheque to drawer** = the bank returned the cheque to person who wrote it because there was not enough money in his account to pay it; **'refer to drawer' (R/D)** = words written on a cheque which a bank refuses to pay (NOTE: **referring - referred**)

reference [ˈrefərəns] *noun* **(a)** **terms of reference** = areas which a committee or an inspector can deal with; *under the terms of reference of the committee, it cannot investigate complaints from the public*; *the committee's terms of reference do not cover exports* **(b)** mentioning or dealing with; *with reference to your letter of May 25th* **(c)** numbers or letters which make it possible to find a document which has been filed; *our reference: PC/MS 1234*; *thank you for your letter (reference 1234)*; *please quote this reference in all correspondence*; *when replying please quote reference 1234* **(d)** written report on someone's character, ability, etc.; *to write someone a reference or to give someone a reference*; *to ask applicants to supply references*; **to ask a company for trade references** *or* **for bank references** = to ask for reports from traders or a bank on the company's financial status and reputation; **letter of reference** = letter in which an employer or former employer recommends someone for a job

referral [rɪˈfɜːrəl] *noun* action of referring or recommending someone to someone

QUOTE for the overwhelming majority of firms, the most valuable source of potential work is referrals from satisfied existing clients
Accountancy

refinance [riːˈfaɪnæns] *verb* (i) to replace one source of finance with another; (ii) to extend a loan by exchanging it for a new one

(normally done when the terms of the new loan are better)

refinancing [ri:faɪ'nænsɪŋ] *noun* **refinancing of a loan** = taking out a new loan to pay back a previous loan

> QUOTE the refinancing consisted of a two-for-five rights issue, which took place in September this year, to offer 55.8m shares at 2p and raise about œ925,000 net of expenses
>
> *Accountancy*

refund 1 ['ri:fʌnd] *noun* money paid back; *to ask for a refund*; *she got a refund after she had complained to the manager*; **full refund** *or* **refund in full** = refund of all the money paid; *he got a full refund when he complained about the service* **2** [rɪ'fʌnd] *verb* **(a)** to pay back money; *to refund the cost of postage*; *all money will be refunded if the goods are not satisfactory* **(b)** to borrow money to repay a previous debt

refundable [rɪ'fʌndəbl] *adjective* which can be paid back; *refundable deposit*; *the entrance fee is refundable if you purchase £5 worth of goods*

refunding [rɪ'fʌndɪŋ] *noun* funding of a debt again (as by a government, when it issues new stock to replace stock which is about to mature)

register ['redʒɪstə] **1** *noun* **(a)** official list; *to enter something in a register*; *to keep a register up to date*; **companies' register** *or* **register of companies** = list of companies, showing their directors and registered addresses; **register of debentures** *or* **debenture register** = list of debenture holders of a company; **register of directors** = official list of the directors of a company which has to be sent to the registrar of companies; **register of interests in shares** = list kept by a public company of those shareholders who own more than 5% of its shares; **land register** = list of pieces of land, showing who owns each and what buildings are on it; **register of shareholders** *or* **share register** = list of shareholders in a company with their addresses **(b) cash register** = machine which shows and adds the prices of items bought in a shop, with a drawer for keeping the cash received **2** *verb* **(a)** to write something in an official list; *to register a company*; *to register a sale*; *to register a property*; *to register a trademark* **(b)** to send (a letter) by registered post; *I registered the letter, because it contained some money*

registered ['redʒɪstəd] *adjective* **(a)** which has been noted on an official list; *US*

registered check = cheque written on a bank account on behalf of a client who does not have a bank account himself; **registered company** = company which has been officially incorporated and registered with the Registrar of Companies; **the company's registered office** = the head office of the company as noted in the register of companies; **registered security** = security (such as a share in a quoted company) which is registered with Companies House and whose holder is listed in the company's share register **(b) registered letter** *or* **registered parcel** = letter or parcel which is recorded by the post office before it is sent, so that compensation can be claimed if it is lost; *to send documents by registered mail* *or* *registered post*

registrant ['redʒɪstrənt] *noun US* company applying to register with the Securities and Exchange Commission

registrar [redʒɪs'trɑ:] *noun* person who keeps official records; **the company registrar** = person or company that keeps the share register of a company; **the Registrar of Companies** = government official whose duty is to ensure that companies are properly registered, and that, when registered, they file accounts and other information correctly (he is in charge of the Companies Registration Office)

registration [redʒɪs'treɪʃən] *noun* **(a)** act of having something noted on an official list; *registration of a trademark* *or* *of share ownership*; **certificate of registration** *or* **registration certificate** = document showing that an item has been registered; **registration fee** = money paid to have something registered, or money paid to attend a conference; **registration number** = official number (such as the number of a car); *US* **registration statement** = document sent to the Securities and Exchange Commission which gives information about a company when registering and listing on a stock exchange (the British equivalent is the 'listing particulars') **(b) Companies Registration Office (CRO)** = office of the Registrar of Companies, the official organization where the records of companies must be deposited, so that they can be inspected by the public; **land registration** = system of registering land and its owners

regression analysis [rɪ'greʃn ə'næləsɪs] *noun* method of discovering the relationship between one variable and any number of other variables giving a coefficient by which forecasts can be made, the technique used by statisticians to forecast the way in which something will behave

regressive taxation [rɪ'gresɪv tæk'seɪʃn] *noun* taxation in which tax gets progressively less as income rises (the opposite of 'progressive taxation')

regular ['regjʊlə] *adjective* which happens or comes at the same time each day, each week, each month or each year; **regular income** = income which comes in every week or month; *she works freelance so she does not have a regular income*

regulate ['regjʊleɪt] *verb* **(a)** to adjust something so that it works well or is correct **(b)** to change or to maintain something by law; **prices are regulated by supply and demand** = prices are increased or lowered according to supply and demand; **regulated consumer credit agreement** = credit agreement according to the Consumer Credit Act; **government-regulated price** = price which is imposed by the government

regulation [regjʊ'leɪʃən] *noun* **(a)** act of making sure that something will work well; *the regulation of trading practices*; **regulation agency** = organization (such as FIMBRA) which sees that members of an industry follow government regulations; **audit regulation** = the regulating of auditors by government; *see also* DEREGULATION, SELF-REGULATION **(b)** **regulations** = laws, rules set out by government; *the new government regulations on housing standards*; *fire regulations* or *safety regulations*; *regulations concerning imports and exports*; *US* **Regulation S-X** = rule which governs how companies draw up their reports which are filed with the SEC

QUOTE EC regulations which came into effect in July insist that customers can buy cars anywhere in the EC at the local pre-tax price
Financial Times

QUOTE a unit trust is established under the regulations of the Department of Trade, with a trustee, a management company and a stock of units
Investors Chronicle

QUOTE fear of audit regulation, as much as financial pressures, is a major factor behind the increasing number of small accountancy firms deciding to sell their practices or merge with another firm
Accountancy

regulator ['regjʊleɪtə] *noun* person whose job it is to see that regulations are followed

QUOTE the regulators have sought to protect investors and other market participants from the impact of a firm collapsing
Banking Technology

regulatory [regjʊ'leɪtəri] *adjective* which applies regulations; **regulatory powers** = powers to enforce government regulations; *see also* SELF-REGULATORY

reimburse [riːɪm'bɜːs] *verb* **to reimburse someone his expenses** = to pay someone back for money which he has spent; *you will be reimbursed for your expenses* or *your expenses will be reimbursed*

reimbursement [riːɪm'bɜːsmənt] *noun* paying back money; *reimbursement of expenses*

reinvest [riːɪn'vest] *verb* to invest again; *he reinvested the money in government stocks*

reinvestment [riːɪn'vestmənt] *noun* **(a)** investing again in the same securities **(b)** investing a company's earnings in its own business by using them to create new products for sale, new machinery, etc.

QUOTE many large U.S. corporations offer shareholders the option of reinvesting their cash dividend payments in additional company stock at a discount to the market price. But to some big securities firms these discount reinvestment programs are an opportunity to turn a quick profit
Wall Street Journal

REIT *US* = REAL ESTATE INVESTMENT TRUST

reject 1 ['riːdʒekt] *noun* thing which has been thrown out because it is not of the required standard; *sale of rejects* or *of reject items*; *to sell off reject stock* **2** [rɪ'dʒekt] *verb* to refuse to accept, to say that something is not satisfactory; **the company rejected the takeover bid** = the directors recommended that the shareholders should not accept the bid

related [rɪ'leɪtɪd] *adjective* connected or linked; **related company** = company in which another company makes a long-term capital investment in order to gain control or influence; **related party** = any person or company which controls or participates in the policy decisions of an accounting entity; **earnings-related pension** = pension which is linked to the size of the salary; *see also* PROFIT-RELATED

relative ['relətɪv] *adjective* which is compared to something; **relative error** =

difference between an estimate and its correct value (divided by the estimate)

release [rɪ'li:s] **1** *noun* **(a)** setting free; *release from a contract*; *release of goods from customs*; **release note** *or* **bank release** = note from a bank to say that a bill of exchange has been paid **(b) day release** = arrangement where a company allows a worker to go to college to study for one day each week; *the junior sales manager is attending a day release course* **2** *verb* **(a)** to free; *the customs released the goods against payment of a fine*; *to release a share option* **(b)** to make something public; *the company released information about the new mine in Australia*; *the government has refused to release figures for the number of unemployed women*

> QUOTE pressure to ease monetary policy mounted yesterday with the release of a set of pessimistic economic statistics
> Financial Times

> QUOTE the national accounts for the March quarter released by the Australian Bureau of Statistics showed a real increase in GDP
> Australian Financial Review

relevant ['reləvənt] *adjective* which has to do with what is being discussed; *which is the relevant government department?*; *can you give me the relevant papers?*; **relevant benefits** = benefits (pension, endowment insurance, etc.) provided by a pension scheme; *see also* NET RELEVANT EARNINGS

relief [rɪ'li:f] *noun* **(a)** something which reduces the tax a taxpayer is liable to pay; **mortgage (interest) relief** = allowing someone to pay no tax on the interest payments on a mortgage up to a certain level; **mortgage interest relief at source (MIRAS)** = scheme (scrapped in April 2000) by which the borrower repaid interest on a mortgage less the standard rate tax (i.e., he did not pay the full interest and then reclaim the tax); **tax relief** = allowing someone to pay less tax on certain parts of his income; **double taxation relief** = reduction of tax payable in one country by the amount of tax on income, profits or capital gains already paid in another country; **loss relief** = amount of tax not to be paid on one year's profit to offset a loss in the previous year or years **(b) relief shift** = shift which comes to take the place of another shift, usually the shift between the day shift and the night shift

COMMENT: prior to April 2000, Mortgage Interest Relief at Source (MIRAS) was given in the UK to individuals paying interest on a mortgage; the relief was calculated at the basic rate of income tax multiplied by the interest due on the first £30,000 of the loan and was deducted from the individual's monthly payments

relocation [ri:lə'keɪʃn] *noun* moving to a new place; **relocation package** = payments made by an employer to an employee when the employee is asked to move to a new area in order to work (payments up to certain minimum level are exempt from tax)

remainder [rɪ'meɪndə] *noun* number equal to the dividend minus the product of the quotient and divider; *7 divided by 3 is equal to 2 remainder 1*; *compare with* QUOTIENT

reminder [rɪ'maɪndə] *noun* letter to remind a customer that he has not paid an invoice; *to send someone a reminder*

remission [rɪ'mɪʃən] *noun* **remission of taxes** = refund of taxes which have been overpaid

remit [rɪ'mɪt] *verb* to send (money); *to remit by cheque*; **remitting bank** = bank where a person has an account on which he has written a cheque, the sum of which the bank has to remit to the payee's bank (the 'collecting bank') (NOTE: **remitting - remitted**)

remittance [rɪ'mɪtəns] *noun* money which is sent (to pay back a debt, to pay an invoice, etc.); *please send remittances to the treasurer*; *the family lives on a weekly remittance from their father in the USA*; **remittance advice** *or* **remittance slip** = advice note sent with payment, showing why it is being made (i.e., quoting the invoice number or a reference number)

remunerate [rɪ'mju:nəreɪt] *verb* to pay someone for doing something; *to remunerate someone for their services*

remuneration [rɪmju:nə'reɪʃən] *noun* payment for services; *she has a monthly remuneration of £400*

COMMENT: remuneration can take several forms: the regular monthly salary cheque, as cheque or cash payment for hours worked or for work completed, etc.

render ['rendə] *verb* **to render an account** = to send in an account; *payment for account rendered*; *please find enclosed payment per account rendered*

renegotiate [riːnɪˈgəʊʃieɪt] *verb* to negotiate again; *the company was forced to renegotiate the terms of the loan*

renew [rɪˈnjuː] *verb* to continue something for a further period of time; *to renew a bill of exchange* *or* *to renew a lease*; **to renew a subscription** = to pay a subscription for another year; **to renew an insurance policy** = to pay the premium for another year's insurance

renewal [rɪˈnjuːəl] *noun* act of renewing; *renewal of a lease* *or* *of a subscription* *or* *of a bill; the lease is up for renewal next month; when is the renewal date of the bill?*; **renewal notice** = note sent by an insurance company asking the insured person to renew the insurance; **renewal premium** = premium to be paid to renew an insurance

rent [rent] **1** *noun* money paid to use an office, house or factory for a period of time; **high rent** *or* **low rent** = expensive, cheap rent; *rents are high in the centre of the town; we cannot afford to pay High Street rents; to pay three months' rent in advance*; **back rent** = rent owed; **the flat is let at an economic rent** = at a rent which covers all costs to the landlord; **ground rent** = rent paid by the main tenant to the ground landlord; **nominal rent** = very small rent; **rent control** = government regulation of rents; **income from rents** *or* **rent income** = income from letting office, houses, etc.; **rent review** = increase in rents which is carried out during the term of a lease (most leases allow for rents to be reviewed every three or five years) **2** *verb* **(a)** to pay money to hire an office, house, factory or piece of equipment for a period of time; *to rent an office* *or* *a car; he rents an office in the centre of town; they were driving a rented car when they were stopped by the police* **(b) to rent (out)** = to own a car, office, etc. and let it to someone for money; *we rented part of the building to an American company*; **rent a room** = scheme by which a taxpayer can let a room in his or her house and be exempt from tax on the rental income below a certain level

rental [ˈrentl] *noun* money paid to use an office, house, factory, car, piece of equipment, etc., for a period of time; *the telephone rental bill comes to over £500 a quarter*; **rental income** *or* **income from rentals** = income from letting offices, houses, etc.; **rental value** = full value of the rent for a property if it were charged at the current market rate (i.e., calculated between rent reviews)

renunciation [rɪnʌnsɪˈeɪʃən] *noun* act of giving up ownership of shares; **letter of renunciation** = form sent with new shares, which allows the person who has been allotted the shares to refuse to accept them and so sell them to someone else

reorder [riːˈɔːdə] **1** *noun* further order for something which has been ordered before; **reorder interval** = period of time before a new order for a stock item is placed; **reorder level** = minimum amount of stock of an item which must be reordered when stock falls to this amount; **reorder quantity** = quantity of a product which is reordered, especially the economic order quantity (EOQ), the cheapest quantity of stocks which a company should hold based on the ordering cost and the warehousing costs (lower unit costs because of higher quantities purchased will be offset by higher warehousing costs) **2** *verb* to place a new order for something; *we must reorder these items because stock is getting low*

reorganization [riːɔːɡənaɪˈzeɪʃən] *noun* action of organizing a company in a different way (as in the USA, when a bankrupt company applies to be treated under Chapter 11 to be protected from its creditors while it is being reorganized)

repatriation [riːpætriˈeɪʃn] *noun* return of foreign investments, profits, etc., to the home country of their owner

repay [rɪˈpeɪ] *verb* to pay back; *to repay money owed; the company had to cut back on expenditure in order to repay its debts; he repaid me in full* = he paid me back all the money he owed me (NOTE: **repaying - repaid**)

repayable [rɪˈpeɪəbl] *adjective* which can be paid back; *loan which is repayable over ten years*

repayment [rɪˈpeɪmənt] *noun* paying back; money which is paid back; *the loan is due for repayment next year; he fell behind with his mortgage repayments* = he was late in paying back the instalments on his mortgage; **repayment mortgage** = mortgage where the borrower pays back both interest and capital over the period of the mortgage (as opposed to an endowment mortgage, where only the interest is repaid, and an insurance is taken out to repay the capital at the end of the term of the mortgage)

replacement [rɪ'pleɪsmənt] *noun* **replacement cost** *or* **cost of replacement** = cost of an item to replace an existing asset; **replacement cost accounting** = method of accounting, where assets are valued at the amount it would cost to replace them, rather than at the original cost (NOTE: same as current cost accounting, as opposed to historical cost accounting); **replacement cost depreciation** = depreciation based on the actual cost of replacing the asset in the current year; **replacement price** = price at which the replacement for an asset would have to be bought; **replacement value** = value of something for insurance purposes if it were to be replaced; *the computer is insured at its replacement value*

repo *(informal)* = REPURCHASE AGREEMENT

report [rɪ'pɔːt] **1** *noun* **(a)** statement describing what has happened or describing a state of affairs; *to draft a report*; *to make a report* *or* *to present a report* *or* *to send in a report*; *the sales manager reads all the reports from the sales team*; *the chairman has received a report from the insurance company* **(b)** the company's annual report *or* the chairman's report *or* the directors' report = document sent each year by the chairman of a company or the directors to the shareholders, explaining what the company has done during the year and what its future prospects are (the directors' report is normally part of the annual report, but the chairman's report is optional); **confidential report** = secret document which must not be shown to other people; **feasibility report** = document which says if something can be done; **financial report** = document which gives the financial position of a company, of a club, etc.; **the treasurer's report** = document from the honorary treasurer of a society to explain the financial state of the society to its members; **report form** = balance sheet laid out in vertical form (it is the opposite of 'account' or 'horizontal' form) **2** *verb* **(a)** to make a statement describing something; *he reported the damage to the insurance company*; *we asked the bank to report on his financial status* **(b)** *(of a company)* to present its full-year or half-year accounts to shareholders; **reporting entity** = orgnaization such as a limited company which must report its accounts to its shareholders

repossess [riːpə'zes] *verb* to take back an item which someone is buying under a credit agreement or mortgage, because the purchaser cannot continue the payments; *when he fell behind with the mortgage repayments, the bank repossessed his flat*

repossession [riːpə'zeʃn] *noun* act of repossessing; *repossessions are increasing as people find it difficult to meet mortgage repayments*

re-present ['riː'prɪ'zent] *verb* to present something again; *he re-presented the cheque two weeks later to try to get payment from the bank*

reprice [riː'praɪs] *verb* to change the price on an item (usually, to increase its price)

reproduction cost [riːprə'dʌkʃn 'kɒst] *US* cost of an identical item to replace an existing asset

repurchase ['riː'pɜːtʃəs] *verb* to buy something again, especially something which you have recently bought and then sold; **repurchase agreement** *or* **repo** = agreement, where a company agrees to buy something and sell it back later (in effect, giving a cash loan to the seller; this is used especially to raise short-term finance)

require [rɪ'kwaɪə] *verb* to ask for or to demand something; *to require a full explanation of expenditure*; *the law requires you to submit all income to the tax authorities*

requisition [rekwɪ'zɪʃən] **1** *noun* official order for something; *what is the number of your latest requisition?*; **cheque requisition** = official note from a department to the company accounts staff asking for a cheque to be written; **materials requisition** = official note from a production department, asking for materials to be moved from the store to the workshop; **purchase requisition** = order to the purchasing department asking it to purchase something **2** *verb* to put in an official order for something; to ask for supplies to be sent

resale [ri:'seɪl] *noun* selling goods which have been bought; *to purchase something for resale*; *the contract forbids resale of the goods to the USA*

resale price maintenance (RPM)

[ri:'seɪl 'praɪs 'meɪntənəns] *noun* system where the price for an item is fixed by the manufacturer and the retailer is not allowed to sell it for a lower price (NOTE: the American equivalent is **administered price)**

reschedule [ri:'ʃedju:l] *verb* to arrange new credit terms for the repayment of a loan; *Third World countries which are unable to keep up the interest payments on their loans from western banks have asked for their loans to be rescheduled*

rescind [rɪ'sɪnd] *verb* to annul or to cancel; *to rescind a contract or an agreement*

rescission [rɪ'sɪʃn] *noun* act of rescinding a contract or a winding-up order

research [rɪ'sɜ:tʃ] **1** *noun* trying to find out facts or information; **consumer research** = research into why consumers buy goods and what goods they may want to buy; **market research** = examining the possible sales of a product and the possible customers for it before it is put on the market; **research and development (R & D)** = scientific investigation which leads to making new products or services or improving existing products or services (SSAP 13); *the company spends millions on research and development*; **research and development costs** = the costs involved in R & D; **research and development expenditure** = money spent on R & D **2** *verb* to study, to try to find out information about something

COMMENT: SSAP13 divides research costs into (a) applied research, which is the cost of research leading to a specific aim, and (b) basic, or pure, research, which is research carried out without a specific aim in mind: these costs are written off in the year in which they are incurred. Development costs are the costs of making the commercial products based on the research and, according to SSAP13, may be deferred and matched against future revenues

researcher [rɪ'sɜ:tʃə] *noun* person who carries out research

resell [ri:'sel] *verb* to sell something which has just been bought

reseller [ri:'selə] *noun* person who sells something he has just bought

reserve [rɪ'zɜ:v] *noun* **(a) reserves** = money from profits not paid as dividend, but kept back by a company in case it is needed for a special purpose; **accumulated reserves** = reserves which a company has put aside over a period of years; **bank reserves** = cash and securities held by a bank to cover deposits; **capital reserves** = money which forms part of the capital of a company and can be used for distribution to shareholders only when a company is wound up; **capitalization of reserves** = issuing free bonus shares to shareholders; **cash reserves** = a company's reserves in cash deposits or bills kept in case of urgent need; *the company was forced to fall back on its cash reserves*; *to have to draw on reserves to pay the dividend*; **contingency reserve** *or* **emergency reserves** = money set aside in case it is needed urgently; **reserve for bad debts** = money kept by a company to cover debts which may not be paid; **hidden reserves** = reserves which are not easy to identify in the company's balance sheet; **secret reserves** = reserves which a company keeps hidden illegally; **sums chargeable to the reserves** = sums which can be debited to a company's reserves; **reserve fund** = profits in a business which have not been paid out as dividend but have been ploughed back into the business; **reserve liability** = liability of holders of partly-paid shares to pay them fully in the case where the company goes into liquidation **(b) reserve currency** = strong currency used in international finance, held by other countries to support their own weaker currencies; **currency reserves** = foreign money held by a government to support its own currency and to pay its debts; **a country's foreign currency reserves** = a country's reserves in currencies of other countries; *the UK's gold and dollar reserves fell by $200 million during the quarter* **(c)** *US* **Federal Reserve** *see* FEDERAL **(d)** **reserve price** = lowest price which a seller will accept (at an auction or when selling securities through a broker); *the painting was withdrawn when it did not reach its reserve*

COMMENT: the accumulated profits retained by a company usually form its most important reserve (the profit and loss account), but other reserves include: assets revaluation reserve (used when a company's assets are revalued); share premium account (when shares are issued at a price above par, the difference is credited to the account); capital redemption reserve (if companies buy back their shares they must put the same amount as they have paid to the shareholders into this reserve in order to preserve the funds available to pay the company's creditors)

residence ['rezɪdəns] *noun* **(a)** house or flat where someone lives; *he has a country residence where he spends his weekends* **(b)** act of living or operating officially in a country; **residence permit** = official document allowing a foreigner to live in a country; *he has applied for a residence permit; she was granted a residence permit for one year*

resident ['rezɪdənt] *noun* person or company living or operating in a country; *the company is resident in France*; **dual resident** = person who is legally resident in two countries; **non-resident** = person or company which is not officially resident in a country; *he has a non-resident account with a French bank; she was granted a non-resident visa*

COMMENT: a person is resident in the UK if he or she spends on average at least three months each year in the country

residual [rɪ'zɪdjuəl] *adjective* remaining after everything else has gone; **residual value** = net realisable value of an asset at the end of its useful economic life (usually its sale or scrap value; see FRS 15)

residuary [rɪ'zɪdjuəri] *adjective* referring to what is left; **residuary estate** = (i) estate of a dead person which has not been bequeathed in his will; (ii) what remains of an estate after the debts have been paid and bequests have been made; **residuary beneficiary** *or* **residuary legatee** = person who receives the rest of the personal property after specific legacies have been made

residue ['rezɪdju:] *noun* money left over; *after paying various bequests the residue of his estate was split between his children*

resolution [rezə'lu:ʃən] *noun* decision to be reached at a meeting; **to put a resolution to a meeting** = to ask a meeting to vote on a proposal; *the meeting passed or carried or adopted a resolution to go on strike; the meeting rejected the resolution or the resolution was defeated by ten votes to twenty*

COMMENT: there are three types or resolution which can be put to an AGM: the 'ordinary resolution', usually referring to some general procedural matter, and which requires a simple majority of votes; and the 'extraordinary resolution' and 'special resolution', such as a resolution to change a company's articles of association in some way, both of which need 75% of the votes before they can be carried

resolve [rɪ'zɒlv] *verb* to decide to do something; *the meeting resolved that a dividend should not be paid*

resources [rɪ'sɔ:sɪz] *plural noun* **financial resources** = supply of money for something; *the costs of the London office are a drain on the company's financial resources; the company's financial resources are not strong enough to support the cost of the research programme*; **the cost of the new project is easily within our resources** = we have enough money to pay for the new project

restrict [rɪ'strɪkt] *verb* to limit, to impose controls on; *to restrict credit; we are restricted to twenty staff by the size of our offices; to restrict the flow of trade or to restrict imports*; **to sell into a restricted market** = to sell goods into a market where the supplier has agreed to limit sales to avoid competition

restrictive [rɪ'strɪktɪv] *adjective* which limits; **restrictive covenant** = agreement by a borrower not to sell an asset which he has used as collateral for a loan; **restrictive endorsement** = endorsement on a bill of exchange which restricts the use which can be made of it by the person to whom it is endorsed

restructure [ri:'strʌktʃə] *verb* to reorganize the financial basis of a company

restructuring [ri:'strʌktʃərɪŋ] *noun* **(a)** **the restructuring of a company** = reorganizing the financial basis of a company **(b)** replacing one type of borrowing by another with a longer maturity date

result [rɪ'zʌlt] **1** *noun* **(a)** profit or loss account for a company at the end of a trading period; *the company's results for 1990* **(b)** something which happens because of something else; *what was the result of the price investigation?; the company doubled its sales force with the result that the sales rose by 26%*; **the expansion programme has produced results** = has produced increased sales; **payment by results** = being paid for profits or increased sales **2** *verb* **(a)** **to result in** = to produce as a result **(b)** **to result from** = to happen because of something; *the increase in debt resulted from the expansion programme*

retail ['ri:teɪl] **1** *noun* sale of small quantities of goods to the general public; **retail dealer** = person who sells to the general public; **retail deposit** = deposit placed by an individual with a bank; **retail investor** = private investor, as opposed to institutional investors;

retail price = full price paid by a customer in a shop; **retail shop** *or* **retail outlet** = shop which sells goods to the general public; **the retail trade** = all people or businesses selling goods retail; **the goods in stock have a retail value of £1m** = the value of the goods if sold to the public is £1m, before discounts etc. are taken into account **2** *adverb* **he sells retail and buys wholesale** = he buys goods in bulk at a wholesale discount and sells in small quantities to the public **3** *verb* **(a) to retail goods** = to sell goods direct to the public **(b)** to sell for a price; **these items retail at** *or* **for 25p** = the retail price of these items is 25p

QUOTE I do not see retail investors
overnight becoming big investors in
futures and options. There was a lot
of direct retail interest before
October 1987, but they were badly
hurt in the crash
Financial Weekly

QUOTE statistics from the
international stock exchange show
that retail, or customer, interest
in the equity market has averaged
just under £700m daily in recent
trading sessions
Financial Times

retailer ['riːteɪlə] *noun* person who runs a retail business, selling goods direct to the public

retailing ['riːteɪlɪŋ] *noun* selling of full price goods to the public; *from car retailing the company branched out into car leasing*

retail price ['riːteɪl 'praɪs] *noun* price at which the retailer sells to the final customer; **retail price(s) index (RPI)** = index showing how prices of retail goods have risen over a period of time

COMMENT: in the UK, the RPI is calculated on
a group of essential goods and services; it
includes both VAT and mortgage interest; it is
used as the basis for calculating personal
allowances, pension increases, etc. The
American equivalent is the Consumer Price
Index (CPI)

retain [rɪ'teɪn] *verb* **(a)** to keep; *out of the profits, the company has retained £50,000 as provision against bad debts*; **retained earnings** *or* **retained profit** = amount of profit after tax which a company does not pay out as dividend to the shareholders, but keeps within the business; **retained income** = profit not distributed to the shareholders as dividend; *the balance sheet has £50,000 in retained income* **(b)** **to retain a lawyer to act for a company** = to agree with a lawyer that he will act for you (and pay him a fee in advance)

retainer [rɪ'teɪnə] *noun* money paid in advance to someone so that he will work for you, and not for someone else; *we pay him a retainer of £1,000*

retention [rɪ'tenʃn] *noun* retained earnings, profit which is not paid to the shareholders in the form of dividends, but is kept to be used for future development of the business

retiral [rɪ'taɪərəl] *noun US* = RETIREMENT

retire [rɪ'taɪə] *verb* **(a)** to stop work and take a pension; *she retired with a £6,000 pension*; *the founder of the company retired at the age of 85*; *the shop is owned by a retired policeman* **(b)** to make a worker stop work and take a pension; *they decided to retire all staff over 50*

retirement [rɪ'taɪəmənt] *noun* act of retiring from work; **to take early retirement** = to leave work before the usual age; **retirement age** = age at which people retire; **retirement annuity** = annuity paid to a person at a certain age, from funds paid into a retirement annuity contract; **retirement benefits** = benefits which are payable by a pension scheme to a person on retirement; **retirement pension** = pension which someone receives when he retires, the state pension given to a man who is over 65 or a woman who is over 60 (the pensionable age for women is rising by stages to 65)

retroactive [retrəʊ'æktɪv] *adjective* which takes effect from a time in the past; *retroactive pay rise*; *they got a pay rise retroactive to last January*

retroactively [retrəʊ'æktɪvli] *adverb* going back to a time in the past

return [rɪ'tɜːn] **1** *noun* **(a)** profit or income from money invested; *to bring in a quick return*; *what is the gross return on this line?*; **return on assets (ROA)** *or* **return on capital employed (ROCE)** *or* **return on equity (ROE)** = profit shown as a percentage of the capital in a business; **return on investment (ROI)** = relationship between profit and money invested in a project or company, usually expressed as a percentage; **rate of return** = amount of interest or dividend produced by an investment, shown as a percentage of the original amount invested; **accounting rate of return** *see* ACCOUNTING **(b)** report; **annual return** = official report which a registered company has to make each year to the Registrar of Companies; **bank return** = regular report from a bank on its financial position; **official**

return = official report; **return date** = date by which a company's annual return has to be made to the Registrar of Companies; **to make a return to the tax office** *or* **to make an income tax return** = to send a statement of income to the tax office; **to fill in a VAT return** = to complete the form showing VAT payable on receipts and expenditure; **nil return** = report showing no sales, income, tax etc.; **tax return** = completed tax form, with details of income, expenses and allowances which is sent by a taxpayer to the Inland Revenue **2** *verb* to make a statement; *to return income of £15,000 to the tax authorities*

QUOTE Section 363 of the Companies Act 1985 requires companies to deliver an annual return to the Companies Registration Office. Failure to do so before the end of the period of 28 days after the company's return date could lead to directors and other officers in default being fined up to £2000

Accountancy

QUOTE returns can be sent to any tax office, but the Revenue has stressed that it strongly recommends taking the return back to the issuing office

Accountancy

returns [rɪ'tɜ:nz] *plural noun* unsold goods, especially books, newspapers or magazines sent back to the supplier; *see also* SALES RETURNS

revaluation [ri:vælju'eɪʃən] *noun* act of revaluing; *the balance sheet takes into account the revaluation of the company's properties*; *the revaluation of the dollar against the franc*; **revaluation method** = method of calculating the depreciation of assets, by which the asset is depreciated by the difference in its value at the end of the year over its value at the beginning of the year (used only for small items, and under historic cost principles)

revalue [ri:'vælju:] *verb* to value something again (at a higher value than before); *the company's properties have been revalued*; *the dollar has been revalued against all world currencies*

revenue ['revənju:] *noun* **(a)** money received; *revenue from advertising* *or* *advertising revenue*; *oil revenues have risen with the rise in the dollar*; **revenue account** = equivalent of a profit and loss account for a non-trading organization, such a club or society (it shows income and expenditure

during the year and the surplus or deficit at year-end; often referred to as the 'income and expenditure account'); **revenue accounts** = accounts of a business which record money received as sales, commission etc.; **revenue expenditure** = expenditure on purchasing items which are used, directly or indirectly, to produce revenue in the current accounting period; *compare* CAPITAL EXPENDITURE; **revenue reserves** = retained earnings which are shown in the company's balance sheet as part of the shareholders' funds **(b)** money received by a government in tax; **Inland Revenue** *or* **the Revenue** *US* **Internal Revenue Service** = government department which deals with tax; **revenue officer** = person working in the government tax offices

reverse [rɪ'vɜ:s] **1** *adjective* opposite, in the opposite direction; **reverse bid** = bid for a company, where a acquiring company's shareholders give up their shares in exchange for shares in the target company; **reverse takeover** = OK takeover where the company which has been taken over ends up owning the company which has taken it over (see reverse bid above) **2** *verb* to change a decision to the opposite; *the committee reversed its decision on import quotas*; **reversing entry** = entry in a set of accounts which reverses an entry in the preceding accounts

QUOTE the trade balance sank $17 billion, reversing last fall's brief improvement

Fortune

reversion [rɪ'vɜ:ʃən] *noun* return of property to an original owner; **he has the reversion of the estate** = he will receive the estate when the present lease ends

reversionary [rɪ'vɜ:ʃənəri] *adjective* (property) which passes to another owner on the death of the present one; **reversionary annuity** = annuity paid to someone on the death of another person; **reversionary bonus** = annual bonus on a life assurance policy, declared by the insurer

review [rɪ'vju:] **1** *noun* general examination; *to conduct a review of distributors*; **financial review** = examination of an organization's finances; **rent review** = increase in rents which is carried out during the term of a lease (most leases allow for rents to be reviewed every three or five years); **wage review** *or* **salary review** = examination of salaries or wages in a company to see if the workers should earn more; **she had a salary review last April** = her salary was examined (and increased) in April **2** *verb* to examine something generally; **to review salaries** = to look at all salaries in a company so as to decide on increases; *his salary will be reviewed at the end of the year*; *the company has decided to review freelance payments in the light of the rising cost of living*; *according to the lease, the rent is reviewed every five years*; **to review discounts** = to look at discounts offered to decide whether to change them

revise [rɪ'vaɪz] *verb* to change something which has been calculated or planned; *sales forecasts are revised annually*; *the chairman is revising his speech to the AGM*

revolving credit [rɪ'vɒlvɪŋ 'kredɪt] *noun* system where someone can borrow money at any time up to an agreed amount, and continue to borrow up to that amount as previous borrowings are repaid

rider ['raɪdə] *noun* additional clause; *to add a rider to a contract*

right [raɪt] **1** *adjective* not left; *the credits are on the right side of the page* **2** *noun* **(a)** legal title to something; *right of renewal of a contract*; *she has a right to the property*; *he has no right to the patent*; *the staff have a right to know how the company is doing*; **foreign rights** = legal title to sell something (especially a book) in a foreign country; **right to strike** = legal title for workers to stop working if they have a good reason for it; **right of way** = legal title to go across someone's property **(b)** **rights issue** *US* **rights offering** = giving shareholders the right to buy new shares usually at an advantageous price (the result being that if he takes up the offer, each shareholder still holds proportionately the same percentage of the company's shares as before)

right-hand ['raɪthænd] *adjective* belonging to the right side; *the credit side is the right-hand column in the accounts*; *he keeps the address list in the right-hand drawer of his desk*

rise [raɪz] **1** *noun* **(a)** increase; *rise in the price of raw materials*; *oil price rises brought about a recession in world trade*; *there was a rise in sales of 10%* *or* *sales showed a rise of 10%*; *salaries are increasing to keep up with the rises in the cost of living*; *the recent rise in interest rates has made mortgages dearer* **(b)** increase in salary; *she asked her boss for a rise*; *he had a 6% rise in January* (NOTE: American English for this is **raise**) **2** *verb* to move upwards, to become higher; *prices are rising faster than inflation*; *interest rates have risen to 15%* (NOTE: **rising - rose - has risen**)

risk [rɪsk] *noun* **(a)** possible harm or chance of danger; **to run a risk** = to be likely to suffer harm; **to take a risk** = to do something which may make you lose money or suffer harm; *he is running the risk of overspending his promotion budget*; *the company is taking a considerable risk in manufacturing 25m units without doing any market research* **(b)** **audit risk** = the risk that auditors may give an inappropriate audit opinion on financial statements: audit risk has three components: inherent risk, control risk and detection risk (see SAS 300) **(c)** **financial risk** = possibility of losing money; *there is no financial risk in selling to East European countries on credit*; **risk arbitrage** = buying shares in companies which are likely to be taken over and so rise in price; **(risk) arbitrageur** = person whose business is risk arbitrage; **risk assets** = assets of a bank which are in securities or bonds which may fall in value; **risk-weighted assets** = assets which include off-balance sheet items for insurance purposes; **risk asset ratio** = proportion of a bank's capital which is in risk assets; **risk capital** = capital for investment usually in high-risk projects, but which can also provide high returns (also called 'venture capital'); **risk premium** = extra payment (increased dividend or higher than usual profits) associated with more risky investments **(d)** **at owner's risk** = situation where goods shipped or stored are not insured by the transport company or the storage company, and so must be insured by the owner; *goods left here are at owner's risk*; *the shipment was sent at owner's risk*

risk-free *or* **riskless** ['rɪsk'friː *or* 'rɪskləs] *adjective* with no risk involved; *a risk-free investment*

QUOTE there is no risk-free way of taking regular income from your money higher than the rate of inflation and still preserving its value
Guardian

QUOTE many small investors have also preferred to put their spare cash with risk-free investments such as building societies rather than take chances on the stock market. The returns on a host of risk-free investments have been well into double figures
Money Observer

risky ['rɪski] *adjective* dangerous, which may cause harm; *he lost all his money is some risky ventures in South America*

ROA = RETURN ON ASSETS

ROCE = RETURN ON CAPITAL EMPLOYED

ROE = RETURN ON EQUITY

ROI = RETURN ON INVESTMENT

roll [rəʊl] *verb* to make something go forward by turning it over; **rolling budget** = budget which moves forward on a regular basis (such as a budget covering a twelve-month period, which moves forward each month or quarter); **rolling plan** = plan which runs for a period of time and is updated regularly for the same period

roll over ['rəʊl 'əʊvə] *verb* **to roll over credit** *or* **a debt** = to make credit available over a continuing period, to allow a debt to stand after the repayment date

QUOTE at the IMF in Washington, officials are worried that Japanese and US banks might decline to roll over the principal of loans made in the 1980s to Southeast Asian and other developing countries
Far Eastern Economic Review

rollover ['rəʊləʊvə] *noun* extension of credit or of the period of a loan; **rollover credit** = credit in the form of a medium-term loan, covered by a series of short-term loans; **rollover relief** = tax relief, where profit on the sale of an asset is not taxed if the money realized is used to acquire another asset (the profit on the eventual sale of this second asset will be taxed unless the proceeds of the second sale are also invested in new assets)

roll up ['rəʊl 'ʌp] *verb* to extend a loan, by adding the interest due to be paid to the capital; **rolled-up coupons** = interest coupons on securities, which are not paid out, but added to the capital value of the security

Romalpa clause [rə'mælpæ 'klɔːz] *noun* clause in a contract, whereby the seller provides that title to the goods does not pass to the buyer until the buyer has paid for them

COMMENT: called after the case of *Aluminium Industrie Vaassen BV v. Romalpa Ltd*

root [ruːt] *noun* fractional power of a number; **square root** = number raised to the power one half; *the square root of 25 is 5*

rough [rʌf] *adjective* approximate, not very accurate; **rough calculation** *or* **rough estimate** = approximate answer; *I made some rough calculations on the back of an envelope*

rough out ['rʌf 'aʊt] *verb* to make a draft or a general plan; *the finance director roughed out a plan of investment*

round [raʊnd] *adjective* **in round figures** = not totally accurate, but correct to the nearest 10 or 100

round down ['raʊnd 'daʊn] *verb* to decrease to the nearest full figure

round off ['raʊnd 'ɒf] *verb* to reduce the digits in a decimal number by removing the final zeros above a certain number of digits

round up ['raʊnd 'ʌp] *verb* to increase to the nearest full figure; *to round up the figures to the nearest pound*

QUOTE each cheque can be made out for the local equivalent of £100 rounded up to a convenient figure
Sunday Times

royalty ['rɔɪəlti] *noun* money paid to an inventor, writer or the owner of land for the right to use his property (usually a certain percentage of sales, or a certain amount per sale); *oil royalties*; *he is receiving royalties from his invention*

RPB = RECOGNIZED PROFESSIONAL BODY

RPI [ɑːpiː'aɪ] = RETAIL PRICE(S) INDEX

RPM = RESALE PRICE MAINTENANCE

rubber check ['rʌbə 'tʃek] *noun US* cheque which cannot be cashed because the person writing it does not have enough money in the account to pay it (NOTE: the British equivalent is a **bouncing cheque**)

rule [ruːl] **1** *noun* **(a)** general way of conduct; **as a rule** = usually; *as a rule, we do not give discounts over 20%*; **company rules** =

general way of working in a company; *it is a company rule that smoking is not allowed in the offices* **(b)** **rule of 72** = calculation that an investment will double in value at compound interest after a period shown as 72 divided by the interest percentage (so interest at 10% compound will double the capital invested in 7.2 years) **2** *verb* **(a)** to give an official decision; *the commission of inquiry ruled that the company was in breach of contract*; *the judge ruled that the documents had to be deposited with the court* **(b)** to be in force, to be current; *prices which are ruling at the moment*

rulebook ['ru:lbʊk] *noun* document which lists the rules by which the members of a self-regulatory organization must operate

run [rʌn] **1** *noun* **(a)** making a machine work; **a cheque run** = series of cheques processed through a computer **(b)** rush to buy something; **a run on a bank** = rush by customers to take deposits out of a bank which they think may close down; **a run on the pound** = rush to sell pounds and buy other currencies **2** *verb* **(a)** to be in force; *the lease runs for twenty years*; *the lease has only six months to run*; **run to settlement** = futures

sale which runs until the actual commodity is delivered **(b)** to amount to; *the costs ran into thousands of pounds* **(c)** to work on a machine; *do not run the photocopier for more than four hours at a time*; *the computer was running invoices all night* (NOTE: **running - ran - has run**)

QUOTE applications for mortgages are running at a high level

Times

run into ['rʌn 'ɪntʊ] *verb* **(a)** to run into debt = to start to have debts **(b)** to amount to; *costs have run into thousands of pounds*; **he has an income running into six figures** = he earns more than £100,000

running ['rʌnɪŋ] *noun* **(a)** **running total** = total carried from one column of figures to the next; **running yield** = yield on fixed interest securities, where the interest is shown as a percentage of the price paid **(b)** **running costs** *or* **running expenses** *or* **costs of running a business** = money spent on the day-to-day cost of keeping a business going

run up ['rʌn 'ʌp] *verb* *(informal)* to incur costs at a fast rate; *he quickly ran up a bill for £250*

Ss

SA = SOCIETE ANONYME, SOCIEDAD ANONIMA

S&L = SAVINGS AND LOAN ASSOCIATION

safe [seɪf] **1** *noun* heavy metal box which cannot be opened easily, in which valuable documents, money, etc. can be kept; *put the documents in the safe*; *we keep the petty cash in the safe*; **fire-proof safe** = safe which cannot be harmed by fire; **night safe** = safe in the outside wall of a bank, where money and documents can be deposited at night, using a special door; **wall safe** = safe installed in a wall **2** *adjective* **(a)** out of danger; **keep the documents in a safe place** = in a place where they cannot be stolen or destroyed; **safe keeping** = being looked after carefully; *we put the documents into the bank for safe keeping* **(b) safe investments** = shares, etc., which are not likely to fall in value

safe deposit [ˈseɪf dɪˈpɒzɪt] *noun* bank safe where you can leave jewellery or documents

safe deposit box [ˈseɪf dɪˈpɒzɪt ˈbɒks] *noun* small box which you can rent to keep jewellery or documents in a bank's safe

safety [ˈseɪfti] *noun* **(a)** being free from danger or risk; **safety margin** = time or space allowed for something to be safe; **margin of safety** = units produced (or sales of such units) which are above the breakeven point; **to take safety precautions** *or* **safety measures** = to act to make sure something is safe; **safety regulations** = rules to make a place of work safe for the workers **(b) for safety** = to make something safe, to be safe; *put the documents in the cupboard for safety*; *take a copy of the disk for safety*

salaried [ˈsælərɪd] *adjective* earning a salary; *the company has 250 salaried staff*; **salaried partner** = member of a partnership who is paid a salary

salary [ˈsæləri] *noun* payment for work, made to an employee with a contract of employment, usually in the form of a monthly cheque; *she got a salary increase in June*; *the*

company froze all salaries for a six-month period; **basic salary** = normal salary without extra payments; **gross salary** = salary before tax is deducted; **net salary** = salary which is left after deducting tax and national insurance contributions; **starting salary** = amount of payment for an employee when starting work; **salary cut** = sudden reduction in salary; **salary cheque** = monthly cheque by which an employee is paid; **salary deductions** = money which a company removes from salaries to pay to the government as tax, national insurance contributions, etc.; **salary review** = examination of salaries in a company to see if workers should earn more; **scale of salaries** *or* **salary scale** = list of salaries showing different levels of pay in different jobs in the same company; **the company's salary structure** = organization of salaries in a company, with different rates for different types of job

sale [seɪl] *noun* **(a)** act of selling, act of giving an item or doing a service in exchange for money, or for the promise that money will be paid; **cash sale** = selling something for cash; **credit card sale** = selling something for credit, using a credit card; **firm sale** = sale which does not allow the purchaser to return the goods; **forced sale** = selling something because a court orders it or because it is the only thing to do to avoid a financial crisis; **sale and lease-back** = situation where a company sells a property to raise cash and then leases it back from the purchaser; **sale or return** = system where the retailer sends goods back if they are not sold, and pays the supplier only for goods sold; *we have taken 4,000 items on sale or return*; **bill of sale** = document which the seller gives to the buyer to show that a sale has taken place; **conditions of sale** = agreed ways in which a sale takes place (such as discounts and credit terms) **(b) for sale** = ready to be sold; **to offer something for sale** *or* **to put something up for sale** = to announce that something is ready to be sold; *they put the factory up for sale*; *his shop is for sale*; *these items are not for sale to the general public* **(c) on sale** = ready to be sold in a shop; *these items are on sale in most chemists* **(d)** selling of goods at specially low prices; **bargain sale** = sale of all goods in a store at cheap prices; **clearance sale** = sale of items at low prices to get rid of the stock; **fire sale** = (i) sale of fire-damaged goods; (ii) sale of anything at a very low price; **half-price sale** = sale of items at half the usual price

sales ['seɪlz] *noun* (i) money received for selling something; (ii) number of items sold; *sales have risen over the first quarter*; **sales analysis** = examining the reports of sales to see why items have or have not sold well; **sales book** = record of sales; **book sales** = sales as recorded in the sales book; **sales budget** = plan of probable sales; **cost of sales** = all the costs of a product sold, including manufacturing costs and the staff costs of the production department; **sales day book (SDB)** *or* **sales journal** = book in which non-cash sales are recorded with details of customer, invoice, amount and date; these details are later posted to each customer's account in the sales ledger; **sales department** = section of a company which deals in selling the company's products or services; **domestic sales** *or* **home sales** = sales in the home market; **sales figures** = total sales, or sales broken down by category; **sales forecast** = estimate of future sales; **forward sales** = sales (of shares, commodities, foreign exchange) for delivery at a later date; **sales invoice** = invoice relating to a sale; **sales journal** = SALES DAY BOOK; **sales ledger** = book in which sales to each customer are posted; **sales ledger clerk** = office worker who deals with the sales ledger; **sales manager** = person in charge of a sales department; **sales mix** = the quantity of different products sold by a single company; **sales mix profit variance** = difference in profit from budget caused by selling a non- standard mix of products; **sales price variance** = difference between expected revenue from actual sales and actual revenue; **monthly sales report** = report made showing the number of items sold or the amount of money received from sales; *in the sales reports all the European countries are bracketed together*; **sales return** = report showing sales; **sales returns** = items sold which are returned by the purchaser; **sales returns book (SRB)** = book giving details of goods returned by purchasers, including invoice number, credit notes, quantities, etc.; *US* **sales revenue** = income from sales of goods or services (NOTE: British English is **turnover**); **sales tax** = tax which is paid on each item sold (and is collected when the purchase is made); **sales value** = the amount of money which would be received if something is sold; **sales volume** *or* **volume of sales** = number of units sold; **sales volume**

profit variance = difference in profit from budget caused by selling more or less than the forecast number of units where it is assumed that sales price and production costs are as planned

salvage ['sælvɪdʒ] **1** *noun* **(a)** saving a ship or a cargo from being destroyed; **salvage money** = payment made by the owner of a ship or a cargo to the person who has saved it; **salvage value** *or* **scrap value** = the value of an asset if sold for scrap; **salvage vessel** = ship which specializes in saving other ships and their cargoes **(b)** goods saved from a wrecked ship, from a fire, etc.; *a sale of flood salvage items* **2** *verb* **(a)** to save goods or a ship from being wrecked; *we are selling off a warehouse full of salvaged goods* **(b)** to save something from loss; *the company is trying to salvage its reputation after the managing director was sent to prison for fraud*; *the receiver managed to salvage something from the collapse of the company*

sample ['sɑːmpl] **1** *noun* **(a)** specimen, a small part of an item which is used to show what the whole item is like; *a sample of the cloth or a cloth sample*; **check sample** = sample to be used to see if a whole consignment is acceptable; **free sample** = sample given free to advertise a product **(b)** small group taken to show what a larger group is like; *we interviewed a sample of potential customers*; **a random sample** = a sample taken without any selection **2** *verb* **(a)** to test, to try something by taking a small amount; *to sample a product before buying it* **(b)** to ask a representative group of people questions to find out what the reactions of a much larger group would be; *they sampled 2,000 people at random to test the new drink*

sampling ['sɑːmplɪŋ] *noun* **(a)** testing the attributes of a group (such as people, products, figures) by taking a sample from it; **acceptance sampling** = method of sampling designed to minimize the risk of error from relying on the sample taken **(b)** testing the reactions of a small group of people to find out the reactions of a larger group of consumers

SARL = SOCIETE ANONYME A RESPONSABILITE LIMITEE

SAS = STATEMENT OF AUDITING STANDARDS

save [seɪv] *verb* to keep (money), not to spend (money); *he is trying to save money by walking to work*; *she is saving to buy a house*

save-as-you-earn scheme (SAYE) ['seɪvæzjuːˈɜːn] *noun* scheme where workers can save money regularly by having it deducted automatically from their wages and invested in a savings-related share option scheme

saver ['seɪvə] *noun* person who saves money

savings ['seɪvɪŋz] *plural noun* money saved (i.e. money which is not spent); *GB* **National Savings** = government scheme run by the Post Office, where small investors can invest in government savings certificates, premium bonds, etc.; **savings account** = bank account or building society account where you can put money in regularly and which pays interest, often at a higher rate than a deposit account; **savings certificate** *US* **savings bond** = document showing that you have invested money in a government savings scheme (British savings certificates give an interest which is not taxable; in some cases, interest on US savings bonds is also tax exempt); **savings income** = income in the form of interest on deposits with banks and building societies, government bonds, etc., but not income from dividends or rental income from property; **savings-related share option scheme** = scheme which allows employees of a company to buy shares with money which they have contributed to a regular savings scheme

savings and loan (association) *or* **S&L** ['seɪvɪŋz ən 'laʊn əsəʊsɪ'eɪʃən] *noun US* financial association which accepts and pays interest on deposits from investors and lends money to people who are buying property; the loans are in the form of mortgages on the security of the property being bought (NOTE: the S&Ls are also called **thrifts**)

COMMENT: because of deregulation of interest rates in 1980, many S&Ls found that they were forced to raise interest on deposits to current market rates in order to secure funds, while at the same time they still were charging low fixed-interest rates on the mortgages granted to borrowers. This created considerable problems and many S&Ls had to be rescued by the Federal government

savings bank ['seɪvɪŋz 'bæŋk] *noun* bank where investors can deposit small sums of money and receive interest on it

SAYE ['eseɪwaɪ'i:] = SAVE-AS-YOU-EARN

scale [skeɪl] **1** *noun* **(a)** system which is graded into various levels; **scale of charges** *or* **scale of prices** = list showing various prices; **fixed scale of charges** = rate of charging which does not change; **scale benefit charge**

= levels of tax payable on private use of a company car, or of a mobile telephone; **scale of salaries** *or* **salary scale** = list of salaries showing different levels of pay in different jobs in the same company; *he was appointed at the top end of the salary scale*; **incremental scale** = salary scale with regular annual salary increases **(b) large scale** *or* **small scale** = working with large or small amounts of investment, staff, etc.; **to start in business on a small scale** = to start in business with a small staff, few products or little investment capital; **economies of scale** = making a product more cheaply by manufacturing it in larger quantities; **diseconomies of scale** = situation where increased production actually increases unit cost; *see note at* DISECONOMIES **2** *verb* **to scale down** *or* **to scale up** = to lower or to increase in proportion

COMMENT: if a share issue is oversubscribed, applications may be scaled down; by doing this, the small investor is protected. So, all applications for 1000 shares may receive 300; all applications for 2000 shares may receive 500; applications for 5,000 shares receive 1,000, and applications for more than 5,000 shares will go into a ballot

scatter diagram ['skætə 'daɪəgræm] *noun* chart where points are plotted according to two sets of variables to see if a pattern exists

Sch = SCHEDULE

schedular ['ʃedjuːlə] *adjective* according to a schedule; **schedular tax system** = system of tax where income is classified according to various schedules

schedule ['ʃedjuːl] *noun* **(a)** timetable, a plan of time to be spent of various activities, drawn up in advance; **to be ahead of schedule** = to be early; **to be on schedule** = to be on time; **to be behind schedule** = to be late; *the project is on schedule; the building was completed ahead of schedule; I am sorry to say that we are three months behind schedule; the managing director has a busy schedule of appointments; his secretary tried to fit me into his schedule* **(b)** list (especially additional documents attached to a contract, such as a list attached to an Act of Parliament); *please find enclosed our schedule of charges; schedule of territories to which a contract applies; see the attached schedule or as per the attached schedule* (NOTE: when referring to a schedule to a Finance Act, it is usual to use the abbreviation **Sch: see Sch 5 to FA 1985) (c)** any working paper created by an accountant or auditor, such as a schedule of prepayments **(d)** list of interest rates; *GB* **tax schedules** = the five types of income as classified for tax

COMMENT: the British tax schedules are: **Schedule A:** rental income from land and buildings **Schedule C:** income from public sources such as government stock **Schedule D:** profits of trades and professions, divided into six categories (or Cases) **Schedule E:** salaries, wages, etc., from employment (including directors' fees) and pensions **Schedule F:** dividends from UK companies

scheme [skiːm] *noun* plan, arrangement or way of working; *bonus scheme*; *pension scheme*; *profit-sharing scheme*; **scheme of arrangement** = scheme drawn up by an individual to offer ways of paying his debts, and so avoid bankruptcy proceedings

scorched earth policy [ˈskɔːtʃt ˈɜːθ ˈpɒlɪsi] *noun* way of combating a takeover bid, where the target company sells valuable assets or purchases unattractive assets; *see also* POISON PILL

scrap [skræp] *noun* material left over after an industrial process, and which still has some value (as opposed to waste, which has no value); **scrap value** = the value of an asset if sold for scrap

scrip [skrɪp] *noun* security (a share, bond, or the certificate issued to show that someone has been allotted a share or bond); **scrip dividend** = dividend which takes the form of new shares in the company, as opposed to cash; **scrip issue** = issue of shares, where a company transfers money from reserves to share capital and issues free extra shares to the shareholders (the value of the company remains the same, and the total market value of shareholders' shares remains the same, the market price being adjusted to account for the new shares) (NOTE: also called a **bonus issue** *or* **free issue** *or* **capitalization issue**)

QUOTE under the rule, brokers who fail to deliver stock within four days of a transaction are to be fined 1% of the transaction value for each day of missing scrip
Far Eastern Economic Review

SDB = SALES DAY BOOK

SDRs = SPECIAL DRAWING RIGHTS

seal [siːl] **1** *noun* **(a) common seal** *or* **company's seal** = metal stamp for stamping documents with the name of the company to show they have been approved officially; *to attach the company's seal to a document*; **contract under seal** = contract which has been legally approved with the seal of the company **(b)** piece of paper, metal or wax attached to close something, so that it can be opened only if the paper, metal or wax is removed or broken; **customs seal** = seal attached by customs office to a box, to show that the contents have not passed through customs **2** *verb* **(a)** to close something tightly; **sealed envelope** = envelope where the back has been stuck down to close it; *the information was sent in a sealed envelope*; **sealed tenders** = tenders sent in sealed envelopes, which will all be opened at a certain time **(b)** to attach a seal, to stamp something with a seal; *the customs sealed the shipment*

SEC = SECURITIES & EXCHANGE COMMISSION the official body which regulates the securities markets in the USA (it receives annual reports from companies, and these are regulated by Regulation S-X)

second 1 [ˈsekənd] *adjective* (thing) which comes after the first; **second half-year** = six month period from July to the end of December; **second mortgage** = further mortgage on a property which is already mortgaged; **second quarter** = three month period from April to the end of June **2** *verb* **(a)** [ˈsekənd] **to second a motion** = to be the first person to support a proposal put forward by someone else **(b)** [sɪˈkɒnd] to lend a member of staff to another company, to a government department, etc., for a fixed period of time; *he was seconded to the Department of Trade for two years*

secondary [ˈsekəndri] *adjective* second in importance; **secondary auditor** = auditor for a subsidiary company who has no connection with the primary auditor who audits the accounts of the main company; **secondary banks** = finance companies which provide money for hire-purchase deals; **secondary industry** = industry which uses basic raw materials to make manufactured goods

seconder [ˈsekəndə] *noun* person who seconds a proposal; *there was no seconder for the motion so it was not put to the vote*

second half [ˈsekənd ˈhɑːf] *noun* period of six months from 1st July to the end of December; *the figures for the second half are up on those for the first part of the year*

secondment [sɪˈkɒndmənt] *noun* being seconded to another job for a period; *he is on three years' secondment to an Australian college*

secret [ˈsiːkrət] *noun & adjective* (something) hidden or not known by many people; *the MD kept the contract secret from* *the rest of the board*; *they signed a secret deal with their main rivals*; **secret reserves** = reserves which a company keeps hidden illegally, as opposed to hidden reserves, which are legal reserves which are not easy to identify in the company's balance sheet

secretary ['sekrətri] *noun* **(a)** official of a company or society; **company secretary** = person who is responsible for a company's legal and administrative affairs; **honorary secretary** = person who keeps the minutes and official documents of a committee or club, but is not paid a salary **(b)** *GB* member of the government in charge of a department; *US* **Secretary of the Treasury** *or* **Treasury Secretary** = senior member of the government in charge of financial affairs; *see also* TREASURY

Secretary of State ['sekrətri əv 'steɪt] *noun* **(a)** *GB* one of several members of the government in charge of departments **(b)** *US* senior member of the government in charge of foreign affairs (NOTE: the British equivalent is the **Foreign Secretary**)

section ['sekʃən] *noun* **(a)** part of something; **legal section** = department in a company dealing with legal matters **(b)** one of the parts of an Act of Parliament

sector ['sektə] *noun* **(a)** part of the economy or the business organization of a country; *all sectors of the economy suffered from the rise in the exchange rate*; *technology is a booming sector of the economy*; **public sector** = nationalized industries and public services; **public sector borrowing requirement** = amount of money which a government has to borrow to pay for its own spending; **private sector** = all companies which are owned by private shareholders, not by the state; *the expansion is funded completely by the private sector*; *salaries in the private sector have increased faster than in the public* **(b)** section of a stock market, listing shares in one type of industry (such as the banking sector)

> QUOTE government services form a large part of the tertiary or service sector
> *Sydney Morning Herald*

> QUOTE in the dry cargo sector, a total of 956 dry cargo vessels are laid up - 3% of world dry cargo tonnage
> *Lloyd's List*

secure [sɪ'kjuə] **1** *adjective* safe, which cannot change; **secure job** = job from which you are not likely to be made redundant;

secure investment = investment where you are not likely to lose money **2** *verb* **(a)** **to secure a loan** = to pledge an asset as a security for a loan **(b)** to get (something) safely under your control; *to secure funds*; *he secured the backing of an Australian group*

secured [sɪ'kjuəd] *adjective* **secured creditor** = person who is owed money by someone, and can legally claim the same value of the borrower's property if the money owed is not paid back (a mortgage holder is a secured creditor); **secured debts** = debts which are guaranteed by assets; **secured loan** = loan which is guaranteed by the borrower giving assets as security

securities [sɪ'kjuərətiz] *plural noun* investments in stocks, shares and money market instruments; **gilt-edged securities** *or* **government securities** = investments in British government stock; **listed securities** = shares which can be bought or sold on the Stock Exchange, shares which appear on the official Stock Exchange list; *US* **Securities and Exchange Commission (SEC)** = the official body which regulates the securities markets in the USA (it receives annual reports from companies, and these are regulated by Regulation S-X); *GB* **Securities and Futures Authority (SFA)** = self-regulatory organization which regulates the trading in shares and futures, now part of the FSA; *GB* **Securities and Investments Board (SIB)** = formerly the name of the regulatory body which regulates the securities markets in the UK, now the FSA

securitization [sɪkjuərətaɪ'zeɪʃn] *noun* making a loan or mortgage into a tradeable security by issuing a bill of exchange or other negotiable paper in place of the loan

security [sɪ'kjuərəti] *noun* **(a)** stock, share or money market instrument; *see* SECURITIES **(b)** guarantee that someone will repay money borrowed; **to stand security for someone** = to guarantee that if the person does not repay a loan, you will repay it for him; *to give something as security for a debt*; *to use a house as security for a loan*; *the bank lent him £20,000 without security* **(c)** **job security** = a worker's feeling that he has a right to keep his job, or that he will never be made redundant; **security of employment** = feeling by a worker that he has the right to keep his job until he retires; **security of tenure** = right to keep a job or rented accommodation, provided that certain conditions are met **(d)** **social security** = money or help provided by the government to people who need it; *he lives on social security payments*

seed money ['si:d 'mʌni] *noun* venture capital invested when a new project is starting up (and therefore more risky than secondary finance)

segmental reporting [seg'mentl rɪ'pɔːtɪŋ] *noun* showing in company reports the results of a company or sections of it, separated according to the type of business or geographical area (see SSAP25)

self [self] *pronoun* your own person; *(on cheques)*; '**pay self**' = pay the person who has signed the cheque

self- [self] *prefix* referring to oneself

self-assessment ['selfə'sesmənt] *noun* system where each taxpayer is required to fill in his or her tax return and calculate how much tax is owed for the period

COMMENT: taxpayers in the UK are given a period of five months (to 30th September) during which they can submit details of their income and allowances for the previous year and get the local tax office to prepare their assessment for them. After that period, taxpayers must do the calculations themselves. Taxpayers may receive penalties in the form of fines, for late filing of tax returns

self-employed ['selfɪm'plɔɪd] **1** *adjective* working for yourself, not on the payroll of a company; *a self-employed engineer; he worked for a bank for ten years but now is self-employed;* **self-employed contributions** = Nation Insurance contributions made by self-employed people **2** *noun* **the self-employed** = people who work for themselves

self-financed ['selffaɪ'nænst] *adjective* **the project is completely self-financed** = the project pays its development costs out of its own revenue, with no subsidies

self-financing ['selffaɪ'nænsɪŋ] **1** *noun* the financing of development costs, purchase of capital assets etc., of a company from its own resources **2** *adjective* **the company is completely self-financing** = the company finances its development costs, capital assets, etc. from its own resources

self-regulating organization ['selfregjʊ'leɪtɪŋ ɔːgənaɪ'zeɪʃn] = SELF-REGULATORY ORGANIZATION

self-regulation ['selfregjʊ'leɪʃən] *noun* regulation of an industry by itself, through a committee which issues a rulebook and makes sure that members of the industry follow the rules (as in the case of the regulation of the Stock Exchange by the Stock Exchange Council and the SIB)

self-regulatory ['selfregjʊ'leɪtəri] *adjective* (organization) which regulates itself; **Self-Regulatory Organization (SRO)** = organization which regulates the way in which its own members carry on their business

sell [sel] **1** *noun* act of selling; **to give a product the hard sell** = to make great efforts to persuade customers to buy it; **he tried to give me the hard sell** = he put a lot of effort into trying to persuade me to buy his product; **soft sell** = persuading people to buy, by encouraging and not forcing them to do so **2** *verb* **(a)** to give goods or services in exchange for money; *to sell insurance or to sell refrigerators; they tried to sell their house for £100,000;* **to sell forward** = to sell foreign currency, commodities, etc., for delivery at a later date **(b)** to be bought; *those packs sell for £25 a dozen* (NOTE: **selling - sold**)

sell-by date ['selbaɪ 'deɪt] *noun* date on a food packet which is the last date on which the food is guaranteed to be good

seller ['selə] *noun* vendor, a person who sells; *there were few sellers in the market, so prices remained high;* **seller's market** = market where the seller can ask high prices because there is a large demand for the product

selling ['selɪŋ] *noun* **direct selling** = selling a product direct to the customer without going through a shop; **mail-order selling** = selling by taking orders and supplying a product by post; **selling overhead** = amount of money to be paid for advertising, reps' salaries, travelling expenses and commissions, and other costs involved in selling something; **selling price** = price at which someone is willing to sell; **selling price variance** = SALES PRICE VARIANCE

selling costs ['selɪŋ 'kɒsts] *noun* **(a)** amount of money to be paid for advertising, reps' salaries, travelling expenses and commissions, and other costs involved in selling something **(b)** costs involved in selling an asset, such as a property or shares (these can include fees paid to solicitors, estate agents, brokers, etc.)

semi- [semi] *prefix* half

semiannual ['semi'ænjuəl] *adjective* (interest) paid every six months

semi-fixed cost *or* **semi-variable cost** ['semi'fikst *or* 'semi'veəriəbl 'kɒst] *noun* cost which has both fixed and variable parts (e.g. the rental of a car may consist of a fixed payment plus a sum which is calculated on the number of miles travelled)

senior ['siːnjə] *adjective* (a) (sum) which is repayable before others; **senior capital** = capital in the form of secured loans to a company (it is repaid before junior capital, such as shareholders' equity, in the event of liquidation); **senior debts** = debts which must be repaid in preference to other debts (such as a first mortgage over a second mortgage) (b) older; more important; (worker) who has been employed longer than another; **senior manager** *or* **senior executive** = manager or director who has a higher rank than others; **senior partner** = most important partner in a firm of solicitors or accountants

seniority [siːni'ɒrəti] *noun* being older; being an employee of the company longer; **the managers were listed in order of seniority** = the manager who had been an employee the longest was put at the top of the list

sensitive ['sensətɪv] *adjective* able to feel something sharply; **the market is very sensitive to the result of the elections**; **interest-sensitive purchases** = purchases (such as houses or items bought on hire-purchase) which are influenced by interest rates; **price-sensitive product** = product, for which demand will change significantly if its price is increased or decreased (all products show an increased demand if the price falls and reduced demand if the price rises)

sensitivity analysis [sensə'tɪvəti ə'næləsɪs] *noun* analysis of the effect of changes in the estimated values used in a forecast on the final result of the forecast

separable ['seprəbl] *adjective* which can be separated; **separable net assets** = assets which can be separated from the rest of the assets of a business and sold off (see FRS 10)

separate ['seprət] *adjective* not together; **separate estate** = property of one of the partners in a partnership, as opposed to the property belonging to the partnership itself

separated ['sepəreɪtɪd] *adjective* married, but no longer living together

separation point [sepə'reɪʃən 'pɔɪnt] *noun* point in a manufacturing process when a product becomes separated from other joint products and begins to be processed on its own

sequester *or* **sequestrate** [sɪ'kwestə *or* 'sekwəstreɪt] *verb* to take and keep (property) because a court has ordered it

sequestration [sekwes'treɪʃən] *noun* taking and keeping of property on the order of a court

sequestrator ['sekwəstreɪtə] *noun* person who takes and keeps property on the order of a court

series ['sɪəriːz] *noun* group of bonds or savings certificates, issued over a period of time but all bearing the same interest

Serious Fraud Office (SFO) ['sɪəriəs 'frɔːd 'ɒfɪs] *noun* government department in charge of investigating major fraud in companies

SERPS [sɜːps] = STATE EARNINGS-RELATED PENSION SCHEME

service ['sɜːvɪs] **1** *noun* (a) working for a company, in a shop, etc.; **length of service** = number of years someone has worked; **service agreement** *or* **service contract** = contract between a company and a director showing all conditions of work (b) the work of dealing with customers; payment for help for the customer; **the bill includes service** = includes a charge added for the work involved (c) **services** = business of providing help in some form when it is needed (insurance, banking, etc., as opposed to making or selling goods); **answering service** = office which answers the telephone and takes messages for a company; **24-hour service** = help which is available for the whole day; **service bureau** = office which specializes in helping other offices; **service cost centre** *or* **service centre** = section of a company considered as a cost centre, which provides a service (such as accounting, purchasing, etc.) to other parts of the company; **service costing** = method of costing a service or of allocating the costs of a service department to a production department; **service department** = department of a company which does not deal with production or sales (accounts, personnel, etc.); **service industry** = industry which does not make products, but offers a service (such as banking, insurance, transport) **2** *verb* **to service a debt** = to pay interest on a debt (and also repay the capital at due date); **the company is having problems in servicing its debts**

service charge ['sɜːvɪs 'tʃɑːdʒ] *noun* (a) charge added to the bill in a restaurant to pay for service; amount paid by tenants in a block of flats or offices for general maintenance, insurance, cleaning, etc. **(b)** *US* charges which a bank makes for carrying out work for a customer (the British equivalent is 'bank charges')

set [set] **1** *adjective* fixed, which cannot be changed; *set price* **2** *verb* to fix, to arrange; *we have to set a price for the new computer*; *the price of the calculator has been set low, so as to achieve maximum unit sales*; **the auction set a record for high prices** = the prices at the auction were the highest ever reached (NOTE: **setting - set**)

set against ['set ə'genst] *verb* to balance one group of figures against another group to try to make them cancel each other out; *to set the costs against the invoice*; *can you set the expenses against tax?*

set off ['set 'ɒf] *verb* to use a debt owed by one party to reduce a debt owed to them

settle ['setl] *verb* **(a) to settle an account** = to pay what is owed; **settled account** = arrangement between two parties who agree the accounts between them **(b) to settle a claim** = to agree to pay what is asked for; *the insurance company refused to settle his claim for storm damage*; **the two parties settled out of court** = the two parties reached an agreement privately without continuing the court case **(c)** to place a property in trust; **settled property** = property which is held in trust

settlement ['setlmənt] *noun* **(a)** (i) payment of an account; (ii) payment for shares bought, delivery of share certificates, etc.; **our basic discount is 20% but we offer an extra 5% for rapid settlement** = we take a further 5% off the price if the customer pays quickly; **settlement in cash** *or* **cash settlement** = payment of an invoice in cash, not by cheque; **settlement date** = date when a payment has to be made, such as payment for shares bought; **settlement day** = account day, the day on which shares which have been bought must be paid for (on the London Stock Exchange the account period is three business days from the day of trade); **final settlement** = last payment which settles a debt; *US* **rolling settlement** = payment for shares bought which is carried out a certain number of days after the transaction **(b)** agreement after an argument; **to effect a settlement between two parties** = to bring two parties together to make them agree **(c)** giving of property or cash as a gift

settle on ['setl 'ɒn] *verb* to leave property to someone when you die; *he settled his property on his children*

settlor ['setlə] *noun* person who settles property on someone

set up ['set 'ʌp] *verb* **(a)** to begin (something), to organize (something) new; *to set up an inquiry* *or* *a working party*; **to set up a company** = to start a company **(b) to set up in business** = to start a new business; **set-up time** = period of time between a signal to start an operation and the start

seven-day money ['sevən'deɪ 'mʌni] *noun* investment in financial instruments which mature in seven days' time

several ['sevrəl] *adjective* separate; **joint and several liability** = situation where someone who has a claim against a group of people may sue them separately or as a group

severally ['sevrəli] *adverb* separately, not jointly; **they are jointly and severally liable** = they are liable both as a group and as individuals for the total amount

severance pay ['sevərəns 'peɪ] *noun* money paid as compensation to someone who is losing his job

SFO ['es 'ef 'əʊ] = SERIOUS FRAUD OFFICE

shadow director [ʃædəʊ daɪ'rektə] *noun* person who is not a director of a company, but who tells the directors of a company how to act

share [ʃeə] *noun* one of many equal parts into which a company's capital is divided (the owners of shares are shareholders or, more formally, 'members'); *he bought a block of shares in Marks and Spencer*; *shares fell on the London market*; *the company offered 1.8m shares on the market*; **'A' shares** = ordinary shares with limited or no voting rights; **'B' shares** = ordinary shares with special voting rights (often owned by the founder of the company and his family); **bonus share** = extra share given to an existing shareholder; **deferred shares** = shares which receive a dividend only after all other dividends have been paid; **founder's shares** = special shares issued to the person who starts a company; **ordinary shares** = normal shares in a company, which have no special benefits or restrictions but which carry the right to vote at shareholders' meetings; **preference shares** = shares (often with no voting rights) which receive their dividend before all other shares and are repaid (at face value) before ordinary shares if the company goes into liquidation; **share allocation** *or* **share allotment** = sharing of a number of shares among people who have applied to buy them; **to allot shares** = to give a certain number of shares to people who have applied to buy them; **share capital** = value of the assets of a company held as shares; **share certificate** = document proving that someone owns shares; **share disposals** = selling of shares; **share incentive scheme** = incentive scheme which offers employees shares in the company as a reward for work; **share index** = index figure based on the current market price of certain shares on a stock exchange; **share issue** = selling new shares in a company to the public; **share option** = right to buy or sell shares at a certain price at a time in the future; **share option scheme** = scheme by which employees are given share options which may have tax advantages if approved by the Inland Revenue; **share premium** = amount to be paid above the nominal value of a share in order to buy it; **share premium account** = part of shareholders' funds in a company, formed of the premium paid for new shares sold above par (the par value of the shares is the nominal capital of the company); **share register** = list of shareholders in a company with their addresses; **share warrant** = document which entitles the holder to some shares in a company (NOTE: American English often used the word **stock** where British English uses **share**. See the note at STOCK)

QUOTE falling profitability means falling share prices
Investors Chronicle

QUOTE the share of blue-collar occupations declined from 48 per cent to 43 per cent
Sydney Morning Herald

shareholder ['ʃeəhəʊldə] *noun* person who owns shares in a company (more formally called a 'member'); *to call a shareholders' meeting*; **shareholders' equity** = a company's capital which is owned by its ordinary shareholders (note that preference shareholders are not equity capital; if the company is wound up none of the equity capital would be distributed to the preference shareholders); **shareholders' funds** = the capital and reserves of a company; **majority** *or* **minority shareholder** = person who owns more or less than half the shares in a company; *the solicitor acting on behalf of the minority shareholders* (NOTE: American English is **stockholder**)

QUOTE as of last night the bank's shareholders no longer hold any rights to the bank's shares
South China Morning Post

QUOTE the company said that its recent issue of 10.5% convertible preference shares at A\$8.50 has been oversubscribed, boosting shareholders' funds to A\$700 million plus
Financial Times

shareholding ['ʃeəhəʊldɪŋ] *noun* group of shares in a company owned by one person; **a majority shareholding** *or* **a minority shareholding** = group of shares which are more or less than half the total; *he acquired a minority shareholding in the company; she has sold all her shareholdings*; **dilution of shareholding** = situation where the ordinary share capital of a company has been increased, but without an increase in the assets so that each share is worth less than before (NOTE: American English is **stockholding**)

sharing ['ʃeərɪŋ] *noun* dividing up; **profit-sharing** = dividing profits among workers

sheet [ʃiːt] *noun* **balance sheet** = statement of the financial position of a company at the end of a financial year or at the end of a period; *the company's balance sheet for 2000; the accountants prepared a balance sheet for the first half-year*

shelf [ʃelf] *noun* **off-the-shelf company** = company which has already been registered by an accountant or lawyer, and which is ready for sale to someone who wants to begin trading quickly; *US* **shelf registration** = registration of a corporation with the SEC some time (up to two years is allowed) before it is offered for sale to the public

shelter ['ʃeltə] *noun* protected place; **tax shelter** = financial arrangement (such as a pension scheme) where investments can be made without tax

short [ʃɔːt] **1** *adjective & adverb* **(a)** for a small period of time; **short bill** = bill of exchange payable at short notice; **short credit** = terms which allow the customer only a little time to pay; **in the short term** = in the near future, quite soon; **to borrow short** = to borrow for a short period **(b)** not as much as should be; *the shipment was three items short; when we cashed up we were £10 short* = we had £10 less than we should have had; **to give short weight** = to sell something which is lighter than it should be **2** *noun* **shorts** = government stocks which mature in less than five years' time

shortchange ['ʃɔːt'tʃeɪndʒ] *verb* to give a customer less change than is right, either by mistake or in the hope that he will not notice

short-dated ['ʃɔːt'deɪtɪd] *adjective* **short-dated bills** = bills which are payable within a few days; **short-dated gilts** *or* **gilt-edged securities** = government stocks which mature in less than five years' time

shorten ['ʃɔːtn] *verb* to make shorter; **to shorten a credit period** = to make a credit period shorter, so as to improve the company's cash position

shortfall ['ʃɔːtfɔːl] *noun* amount which is missing which would make the total expected sum; *we had to borrow money to cover the shortfall between expenditure and revenue*

short-range ['ʃɔːt'reɪndʒ] *adjective* **short-range forecast** = forecast which covers a period of a few months

short-term ['ʃɔːt'tɜːm] *adjective* for a short period; *to place money on short-term deposit*; *short-term contract*; **on a short-term basis** = for a short period; **short-term debts** = debts which have to be repaid within a few weeks; **short-term forecast** = forecast which covers a period of a few months; **short-term gains** = gains made over a short period (less than 12 months); **short-term loan** = loan which has to be repaid within a few weeks; **short-term security** = security which matures in less than 5 years

show of hands ['ʃəʊ əv 'hændz] *noun* method of voting (as at an AGM) where members vote on a resolution by raising their hands in the air

COMMENT: if it is difficult to decide which side has won in a show of hands, a ballot may be taken

shrink [ʃrɪŋk] *verb* to get smaller; *the market has shrunk by 20%*; *the company is having difficulty selling into a shrinking market* (NOTE: **shrinking - shrank - has shrunk**)

shrinkage ['ʃrɪŋkɪdʒ] *noun* (a) amount by which something gets smaller; *to allow for shrinkage* (b) *informal* losses of stock through theft (especially by members of the staff of a shop)

shroff [ʃrɒf] *noun (in the Far East)* (i) accountant; (ii) accounts clerk

SI = STATUTORY INSTRUMENT

SIB = SECURITIES AND INVESTMENT BOARD

sick pay ['sɪk 'peɪ] *noun* payment to an employee while he is away from work because of sickness; *see also* STATUTORY

side [saɪd] *noun* part of something; **credit side** = right-hand side of an account; **debit side** = left-hand side of an account

sight [saɪt] *noun* seeing; **bill payable at sight** = bill which must be paid when it is presented; **sight bill** *or* **sight draft** = bill of exchange which is payable at sight; **sight deposit** = bank deposit which can be withdrawn on demand; **sight note** *or* **demand note** = promissory note which must be paid when it is presented; **to buy something sight unseen** = to buy something without having inspected it

sign [saɪn] *verb* to put your signature on a document to show that you have written it or approved it; *to sign a letter or a contract or a document or a cheque*; *the letter is signed by the managing director*; *the cheque is not valid if it has not been signed by the finance director*

signatory ['sɪgnətri] *noun* person who signs a contract, etc.; *you have to get the permission of all the signatories to the agreement if you want to change the terms*

signature ['sɪgnətʃə] *noun* name written in a special way by someone; *a pile of letters waiting for the managing director's signature*; *he found a pile of cheques on his desk waiting for signature*; *all the company's cheques need two signatures*

significant [sɪg'nɪfɪkənt] *adjective* large or important; which has a special meaning; **significant digit** = digit (in a number) that has some meaning (i.e., is not a zero at the beginning or end)

simple ['sɪmpl] *adjective* not complicated, not difficult to understand; **simple average price** = average price calculated by adding different prices and dividing by the number of prices added; **simple contract** = contract which is not under seal, but is made orally or in writing; **simple interest** = interest calculated on the capital only, and not added to it; **simpler basis** = method of calculating business motoring expenses when using your own car, by calculating the number of miles travelled and using tables provided by the Inland Revenue, where cars are classified according to engine size

single ['sɪŋgl] *adjective* one alone; **single-entry bookkeeping** = method of bookkeeping where transactions are recorded by only one entry; **in single figures** = less than ten; *sales are down to single figures*; *inflation is now in single figures*; **single-figure inflation** = inflation rising at less than

10% per annum; **single-parent allowance** = former name for the tax allowance which can be claimed by a single person who has a child of school age living with them (now called the 'additional personal allowance'); **single premium policy** = insurance policy where only one premium is paid rather than regular annual premiums

sink [sɪŋk] *verb* (a) to go down suddenly; *prices sank at the news of the closure of the factory* (b) to invest money (into something); *he sank all his savings into a car-hire business* (NOTE: sinking - sank - sunk)

sinking fund ['sɪŋkɪŋ 'fʌnd] *noun* fund built up out of amounts of money put aside regularly to meet a future need, such as the repayment of a loan; **sinking fund method** = method of providing for depreciation which increases every year by multiplying each previous year's charge by a compound rate of interest

sister ['sɪstə] *adjective* **sister company** = one of several companies which are part of the same group

sleeping partner ['sliːpɪŋ 'pɑːtnə] *noun* partner who has a share in the business but does not work in it

slide [slaɪd] *verb* to move down steadily; *prices slid after the company reported a loss* (NOTE: sliding - slid)

sliding ['slaɪdɪŋ] *adjective* which rises in steps; **a sliding scale of charges** = list of charges which increase gradually according to value, quantity, time, etc.

slip [slɪp] *noun* small piece of paper; **deposit slip** = piece of paper stamped by the cashier to prove that you have paid money into your account; **pay slip** = piece of paper showing the full amount of a worker's pay, and the money deducted as tax, pension and insurance contributions; **paying-in slip** = printed form which is filled in when money is being deposited in a bank; **sales slip** = paper showing that an article was bought at a certain shop

slow payer ['sləʊ 'peɪjə] *noun* company which pays its bills slowly

slump [slʌmp] **1** *noun* (a) rapid fall; *slump in sales*; *slump in profits*; *slump in the value of the pound*; *the pound's slump on the foreign exchange markets* (b) period of economic collapse with high unemployment and loss of trade; *we are experiencing slump conditions*; **the Slump** = the world economic crisis of 1929 - 1933 **2** *verb* to fall fast; *profits*

have slumped; *the pound slumped on the foreign exchange markets*

slush fund ['slʌʃ 'fʌnd] *noun* money kept to one side to give to people as bribes, to persuade them to do what you want

small [smɔːl] *adjective* not large; **small ads** = short private advertisements in a newspaper (selling small items, asking for jobs, etc.); **small businesses** = little companies with low turnover and few employees; **small businessman** = man who runs a small business; *US* **Small Business Administration (SBA)** = federal agency which provides finance and advice to small businesses; **small change** = loose coins; *GB* **small claims court** = court which deals with disputes over small amounts of money; **small and medium-sized enterprises (SMEs)** = the smallest enterprises, with a turnover of less than œ11.2m and fewer than 250 employees; **the small investor** = person who has a small amount of money to invest; **small shopkeepers** = owners of small shops

small company ['smɔːl 'kʌmpni] *noun* company with at least two of the following characteristics: turnover of less than œ2.0m; fewer than 50 staff; net assets of less than œ0.975m (it is allowed to file modified accounts with Companies House); **small companies rate** = rate of corporation tax charged on profits of small companies

SME = SMALL AND MEDIUM-SIZED ENTERPRISES

social ['səʊʃəl] *adjective* referring to society in general; **social costs** = ways in which something will affect people; *the report examines the social costs of building the factory in the middle of the town*; **social security** = money from contributions paid to the National Insurance provided by the government to people who need it; *he gets weekly social security payments*; **social security contributions** = regular payments by workers and employers to the National Insurance scheme; **the social system** = the way society is organized

sociedad anonima (SA) [sɒθieɪˈdæd æˈnɒnɪmæ] *Spanish* Public Limited Company (PLC)

societa per azioni (SpA) [sʊtʃieɪˈtæ peər ætsiˈɔːni] *Italian* Public Limited Company (PLC)

société ['sɒsieɪˈteɪ] *French* company; **société anonyme (SA)** = Public Limited Company (PLC); **société anonyme à**

responsabilité limitée (SARL) = private limited company (Ltd)

society [sə'saɪəti] *noun* club, group of people with the same interests; **building society** = financial institution which accepts and pays interest on deposits, and lends money to people who are buying property; **cooperative society** = organization where customers and workers are partners and share the profits; **friendly society** = group of people who pay regular subscriptions to a fund which is used to help members who are ill or in financial trouble

soft [sɒft] *adjective* not hard; **soft currency** = currency of a country with a weak economy, which is cheap to buy and difficult to exchange for other currencies; **soft loan** = loan (from a company to an employee or from a government to a new business or to another government) at very low or nil interest; **to take the soft option** = to decide to do something which involves least risk, effort or problems

QUOTE the so-called 'soft' commissions whereby fund managers can pay commission out of a fund to stockbrokers, and themselves receive back services as a form of rebate of these commissions
Financial Times Review

software ['sɒftweə] *noun* any program or group of programs which instructs the hardware on how it should perform, including operating systems, word processors, spreadsheets and other applications programs; **accounting software** = programs used to enter and process accounts information on an office computer; **applications software** = programs which are used to perform a certain task

sole [səʊl] *adjective* only; **sole agency** = agreement to be the only person to represent a company, to sell a product in a certain area; *he has the sole agency for Ford cars*; **sole agent** = person who has the sole agency for a product in an area; **sole distributor** = retailer who is the only one in an area who is allowed to sell a certain product; **sole owner** *or* **sole proprietor** = person who owns a business on his own, with no partners and without forming a company; **sole trader** *US* **sole proprietor** = person who runs a business by himself but has not registered it as a company

solvency ['sɒlvənsi] *noun* being able to pay all debts on due date (NOTE: the opposite is **insolvency**)

solvent ['sɒlvənt] *adjective* situation when assets are more than liabilities; *when he bought the company it was barely solvent* (NOTE: the opposite is **insolvent**)

SORP = STATEMENT OF RECOMMENDED PRACTICE

source [sɔːs] *noun* place where something comes from; *source of income*; *you must declare income from all sources to the tax office*; **income which is taxed at source** = where the tax is removed and paid to the government by the employer before the income is paid to the employee; **source and application of funds statement** = statement in a company's annual accounts, showing where new funds came from during the year, and how they were used (see FRS1, formerly SSAP10)

SP = STATEMENT OF PRACTICE

SpA = SOCIETA PER AZIONI

space [speɪs] *noun* gap (printed or displayed in text); **space character** = character code that prints a space; **space bar** = long bar at the bottom of a keyboard, which inserts a space into the text when pressed

spare [speə] *adjective* extra, not being used; *he has invested his spare capital in a computer shop*; **to use up spare capacity** = to make use of time, space or resources which have not been fully used

special ['speʃəl] *adjective* different; not normal; referring to one particular thing; *he offered us special terms*; *the car is being offered at a special price*; **special character** = character which is not a normal one in a certain typestyle (such as a certain accent or a symbol); **Special Commissioner** = official appointed by the Treasury to hear cases where there is a dispute between a taxpayer and the Inland Revenue, as when a taxpayer is appealing against an income tax assessment; **special deposits** = large sums of money which commercial banks have to deposit with the Bank of England; **special notice** = notice of a proposal to be put before a meeting of the shareholders of a company which must be made at least 28 days before the meeting

special drawing rights (SDRs)

['speʃəl 'drɔːɪŋ 'raɪts] *noun* unit of account used by the International Monetary Fund, allocated to each member country for use in loans and other international operations; their value is calculated daily on the weighted values of a group of currencies shown in dollars

special resolution [ˈspeʃəl rezəˈluːʃn] *noun* resolution of the members of a company which is only valid if it is approved by 75% of the votes cast at a meeting (a resolution concerning an important matter, such as a change to the company's articles of association)

COMMENT: 21 days' notice must be given for a special resolution to be put to a meeting, as opposed to an 'extraordinary resolution' for which notice must be given, but no minimum period is specified by law, An extraordinary resolution could be a proposal to wind up a company voluntarily, but changes to the articles of association, such as a change of name, or of the objects of the company, or a reduction in share capital, need a special resolution

specie [ˈspiːʃiː] *plural noun* **(a)** coins, as opposed to paper money **(b)** kind; *the property was divided between the shareholders as a distribution in specie*

specific [spəˈsɪfɪk] *adjective* relating to a particular thing; **specific legacy** = legacy of a particular thing, such as a property, left to a particular individual in a will; **specific order costing** = calculating the cost of a single job or batch of work (also called 'job costing') as opposed to a continuous process; **specific performance** = court order to a party to carry out his obligations in a contract

specifically [spəˈsɪfɪkli] *adverb* in a specific way; *costs are allocated specifically to the various cost centres*

specification [spesɪfɪˈkeɪʃən] *noun* detailed information about what is needed or about a product to be supplied; *to detail the specifications of a computer system*; **job specification** = very detailed description of what is involved in a job; **to work to standard specifications** = to work to specifications which are acceptable anywhere in the industry; **the work is not up to specification** *or* **does not meet our specifications** = the product is not made in the way which was detailed

specify [ˈspesɪfaɪ] *verb* to state clearly what is needed; *to specify full details of the goods ordered*; *do not include VAT on the invoice unless specified*

specimen [ˈspesɪmən] *noun* thing which is given as a sample; **to give specimen signatures on a bank mandate** = to write the signatures of all people who can sign cheques for an account so that the bank can recognise them

spend [spend] *verb* to pay money; *they spent all their savings on buying the shop*; *the company spends thousands of pounds on research*

spending [ˈspendɪŋ] *noun* paying money; *cash spending* *or* *credit card spending*; **consumer spending** = spending by consumers; **spending money** = money for ordinary personal expenses; **spending power** = (i) having money to spend on goods; (ii) amount of goods which can be bought for a certain sum of money; *the spending power of the pound has fallen over the last ten years*; *the spending power of the student market*

split [splɪt] **1** *noun* **(a)** dividing up; **share split** = dividing of shares into smaller denominations; **the company is proposing a five for one split** = the company is proposing that each existing share should be divided into five smaller shares **(b)** lack of agreement; *a split in the family shareholders* **2** *verb* **(a)** to divide shares into smaller denominations; **the shares were split five for one** = five new shares were given for each existing share held **(b) to split the difference** = to come to an agreement over a price by dividing the difference between the amount the seller is asking and amount the buyer wants to pay and agreeing on a price between the two (NOTE: **splitting - split**) **3** *adjective* which is divided into parts; **split commission** = commission which is divided between brokers or agents; **split payment** = payment which is divided into small units

COMMENT: a company may decide to split its shares if the share price becomes too 'heavy' (i.e., each share is priced at such a high level that small investors may be put off, and trading in the share is restricted); in the UK, a share price of £10.00 is considered 'heavy', though such prices are common on other stock markets

split-level investment trust [ˈsplɪtlevl ɪnˈvestmənt ˈtrʌst] *noun* investment trust with two categories of shares: 'income shares' which receive income from the investments, but do not benefit from the rise in their capital value; and 'capital shares', which increase in value as the value of the investments rises, but do not receive any income

spoilage [ˈspɔɪlɪdʒ] *noun* (*of stocks*) items which are not of the correct quality and cannot be sold, except possibly as scrap

spot [spɒt] *noun* price when buying something for immediate delivery; **spot cash** = cash paid for something bought immediately; **the spot market in oil** = the market for buying oil for immediate delivery; **spot price** *or* **spot rate** = current price or rate for something which is delivered immediately (also called 'cash price')

> QUOTE with most of the world's oil now traded on spot markets, Opec's official prices are much less significant than they once were
> *Economist*

> QUOTE the average spot price of Nigerian light crude oil for the month of July was 27.21 dollars per barrel
> *Business Times (Lagos)*

spread [spred] **1** *noun* **(a)** *(in general)* range; **he has a wide spread of investments** *or* **of interests** = he has shares in many different types of companies **(b)** *(banking)* difference between the interest rate a bank pays on deposits and the rate it charges borrowers; *(on the Stock Exchange)* difference between buying and selling prices (i.e. between the bid and offer prices) **2** *verb* to space out over a period of time; *to spread payments over several months*; **to spread a risk** = to make the risk of insurance less great by asking other companies to help cover it (NOTE: **spreading - spread**)

> QUOTE dealers said markets were thin, with gaps between trades and wide spreads between bid and ask prices on the currencies
> *Wall Street Journal*

> QUOTE to ensure an average return you should hold a spread of different shares covering a wide cross-section of the market
> *Investors Chronicle*

spreading ['spredɪŋ] *noun* action of spacing income from artistic work (royalties, etc.) over a period of time, and not concentrating it in the year in which the money is received; **backwards spreading** = spacing income over a period of a certain number of previous years; **forwards spreading** = spreading lump sum income over several years in the future

spreadsheet ['spredʃiːt] *noun* (i) large sheet of paper, laid out in columns, for entering financial data; (ii) computer program in the form of a 'sheet' divided into a grid of memory cells; each cell can store numbers or mathematical formulae which makes the program ideal for processing financial data

Square Mile ['skweə 'maɪl] *noun* the City (of London), the British financial centre

squeeze [skwiːz] **1** *noun* government control carried out by reducing amounts of money available; **credit squeeze** = period when lending by the banks is restricted by the government; **profit squeeze** = situation when a company finds it difficult to make a profit **2** *verb* to crush or to press; to make smaller; *to squeeze margins or profits or credit*; **our margins have been squeezed by the competition** = profits have been reduced because our margins have to be smaller for us to stay competitive

> QUOTE the real estate boom of the past three years has been based on the availability of easy credit. Today, money is tighter, so property should bear the brunt of the credit squeeze
> *Money Observer*

SRO = SELF-REGULATORY ORGANIZATION

SSAPs = STATEMENTS OF STANDARD ACCOUNTING PRACTICE

SSP = STATUTORY SICK PAY

stag [stæg] **1** *noun* person who subscribes for a large quantity of a new issue of shares hoping to sell them immediately to make a profit **2** *verb* **to stag an issue** = to buy a new issue of shares not as an investment, but to sell immediately at a profit (NOTE: **stagging - stagged)**

stage [steɪdʒ] *noun* period, one of several points of development; *the different stages of the production process*; **the contract is still in the drafting stage** = the contract is still being drafted; **in stages** = in different steps; *the company has agreed to repay the loan in stages*

staged payments *noun* ['steɪdʒd 'peɪmənts] payments made in stages

stagger ['stægə] *verb* to arrange (holidays, working hours) so that they do not all begin and end at the same time; *staggered holidays help the tourist industry; we have to stagger the lunch hour so that there is always someone on the switchboard*

stagnant ['stægnənt] *adjective* not active, not increasing; *turnover was stagnant for the first half of the year; a stagnant economy*

stagnate [stæg'neɪt] *verb* not to increase, not to make progress; *the economy is stagnating; after six hours the talks were stagnating*

stagnation [stæg'neɪʃən] *noun* not increasing, not making any progress; *the* *country entered a period of stagnation*; **economic stagnation** = lack of expansion in the economy

stake [steɪk] **1** *noun* money invested; **to have a stake in a business** = to have money invested in a business; **to acquire a stake in a business** = to buy shares in a business; *he acquired a 25% stake in the business* **2** *verb* **to stake money on something** = to risk money on something

QUOTE other investments include a large stake in a Chicago-based insurance company, as well as interests in tobacco products and hotels

Lloyd's List

stale [steɪl] *adjective* (cheque) which is so old, that the bank will not clear it unless it has been confirmed as correct by the payer

stamp [stæmp] **1** *noun* **(a)** device for making marks on documents; mark made in this way; *the invoice has the stamp 'Received with thanks' on it*; *the customs officer looked at the stamps in the passport*; **date stamp** = stamp with rubber figures which can be moved, used for marking the date on documents; **rubber stamp** = stamp made of hard rubber cut to form words; **stamp pad** = soft pad of cloth with ink on which a stamp is pressed, before marking the paper **(b)** **postage stamp** = small piece of gummed paper which you buy from a post office and stick on a letter or parcel to pay for the postage **(c)** **stamp duty** = tax on legal documents (such as the sale or purchase of shares, the conveyance of a property to a new owner) **2** *verb* **(a)** to mark a document with a stamp; *to stamp an invoice 'Paid'*; *the documents were stamped by the customs officials* **(b)** to put a postage stamp on (an envelope, etc.); **stamped addressed envelope** = envelope with your own address written on it and a stamp stuck on it to pay for the return postage; *send a stamped addressed envelope for a catalogue and price list*

standard ['stændəd] **1** *noun* normal quality, or normal conditions which other things are judged against; **current standard** = standard which is only used during the current accounting period (i.e., it is only used in the short term); **ideal standard** = standard which a company wishes to reach (but rarely does so); **standard of living** *or* **living standards** = quality of personal home life (such as amount of food or clothes bought, size of family car, etc.) **2** *adjective* normal or usual; **standard agreement** *or* **standard contract** = normal printed contract form;

standard form contract = contract which states the conditions of carrying out a common commercial arrangement (such as chartering a ship); **standard cost** = estimate of how much something should cost under specified conditions against which actual costs can be measured; **standard costing** = using standard costs to determine the variance between actual and expected results; **standard direct labour** *or* **material** *or* **overhead cost** = expected cost of labour, materials and overheads from the production of a specified quantity of output assuming normal performance by labour and machines, normal quantity of materials used per unit of output and an agreed overhead absorption rate; **standard letter** = letter which is sent to various correspondents without any change to the main text; **standard price** = fixed price per unit, based on the standard cost of production, as opposed to the actual price paid; **standard rate** = basic rate of income tax which is paid by most taxpayers

standby ['stændbaɪ] *noun* **standby credit** = credit which is available if a company needs it, especially credit guaranteed by a euronote

standing ['stændɪŋ] **1** *adjective* **standing order** = order written by a customer asking a bank to pay money regularly to another account; *I pay my subscription by standing order* **2** *noun* good reputation; *the financial standing of a company*; **company of good standing** = very reputable company

start [stɑːt] **1** *noun* beginning; **cold start** = beginning a new business, or opening a new shop, with no previous turnover to base it on **2** *verb* **to start a business from cold** = to begin a new business, with no previous turnover to base it on

starting ['stɑːtɪŋ] *noun* beginning; **starting date** = date on which something starts; **starting rate of tax** = tax rate (currently 10%) paid on the first segment of taxable income, before the basic rate applies; **starting salary** = salary for an employee when he starts work with a company

start-up ['stɑːtʌp] *noun* beginning of a new company, launching a new product (which did not exist before); *start-up costs are high in manufacturing companies*; **start-up financing** = the first stage in financing a new project, which is followed by several rounds of investment capital as the project gets under way (NOTE: plural is **start-ups**)

state [steɪt] **1** *noun* independent country and its government; **state pension** = pension paid to someone by the state (as opposed to a pension paid by an insurance company or by a company); **state retirement pension** = pension paid by the state to people when they reach retirement age **2** *verb* to say clearly; *the document states that all revenue has to be declared to the tax office*; **as per account stated** = the same amount as shown on the account or invoice

statement ['steɪtmənt] *noun* **(a)** saying something clearly; **to make a false statement** = to give wrong details **(b)** **statement of affairs** = financial statement drawn up when a person is insolvent; **statement of expenses** = detailed list of money spent; **statement (of account)** = list of invoices and debits, less any credits, sent by a supplier to a customer at the end of each month; **bank statement** = written document from a bank showing the balance of an account; **monthly** *or* **quarterly statement** = statement which is sent every month or every quarter by a bank or supplier to a customer with an account; **Autumn Statement** = statement on the financial position of the country, with proposals for expenditure, made by the Chancellor of the Exchequer in the autumn **(c)** **financial statements** = documents which show the financial situation of a company at the end of an accounting period as well as the effect of transactions during that period (the primary financial statements are: the balance sheet, the profit and loss account, the statement of total recognized gains and losses and the cash flow statement (see FRS3)); *the accounts department have prepared a financial statement for the shareholders*; **the Financial Statement** = document which sets out the details of the budget presented by the Chancellor of the Exchequer (it is published on Budget Day)

Statements of Auditing Standards (SASs) publications from the Auditing Practices Board (APB) which sets our the basic principles on which external auditors work in the UK and Ireland

Statement of Practice (SP) ['steɪtmənt əv 'præktɪs] recommendation issued by the CCAB regarding accounting practice

Statement of Recommended Practice (SORP) ['steɪtmənt əv rekə'mendɪd 'præktɪs] statement issued with the approval of the ASB which advises companies on how to apply accounting standards to a particular industry

Statements of Standard Accounting Practice (SSAPs) ['steɪtmənts əv 'stændəd ə'kaʊntɪŋ 'præktɪs]

rules laid down by the Accounting Standards Committee (now the Accounting Standards Board) for the preparation of financial statements; *see SUPPLEMENT for a list of SSAPs*

Statement of Value Added (SVA) ['steɪtmənt əv 'vælju: 'ædɪd] statement which shows how a company distributes the difference between sales revenue and the cost of materials and services it buys to generate that revenue

statistical [stə'tɪstɪkəl] *adjective* based on figures; *statistical analysis*; *statistical information*; **statistical discrepancy** = amount by which sets of figures differ

statistician [stætɪ'stɪʃən] *noun* person who analyses statistics

statistics [stə'tɪstɪks] *plural noun* study of facts in the form of figures; *to examine the sales statistics for the previous six months*; *government trade statistics show an increase in imports*

status ['steɪtəs] *noun* **(a)** importance, position in society; **the chairman's car is a status symbol** = the size of the car shows how important the company is; **loss of status** = becoming less important in a group; **status inquiry** = checking on a customer's credit rating **(b)** **legal status** = legal position

status quo ['steɪtəs 'kwəʊ] *noun* state of things as they are now; *the contract does not alter the status quo*

statute ['stætju:t] *noun* law made by parliament; **statute book** = list of laws passed by parliament; **statute of limitations** = law which allows only a certain amount of time (a few years) for someone to claim damages or property

statute-barred ['stætju:t'bɑːd] *adjective* (legal action) which cannot be pursued because the time limit for it has expired

statutory ['stætjʊtəri] *adjective* fixed by law; *there is a statutory period of probation of thirteen weeks*; **statutory holiday** = holiday which is fixed by law; **statutory instrument (SI)** = order (which has the force of law) made under authority granted to a minister by an Act of Parliament; **statutory maternity pay** = payment made each week by an employer to an employee who is pregnant or who has just had a baby; **statutory regulations** = regulations covering financial dealings which are based on Acts of Parliament, such as the Financial Services Act (as opposed to the rules of self-regulatory organizations which are non-statutory); **statutory sick pay (SSP)** = payment made each week by an employer to an employee who is away from work because of sickness

stay of execution ['steɪ əv eksɪ'kju:ʃn] *noun* temporary stopping of a legal order; *the court granted the company a two-week stay of execution*

step [step] *noun* movement; **in step with** = moving at the same rate as; *the pound rose in step with the dollar*; **out of step with** = not moving at the same rate as; *the company's growth was out of step with its competitors*; *wages are out of step with the cost of living*

stepped [stept] *adjective* rising in steps; **stepped costs** = costs which remain fixed up to a certain level of activity but then rise to a new, higher level once that level of activity is exceeded

COMMENT: as an example of stepped costs, the cost of rent remains the same while work is done in a single factory, but when a new factory is needed to achieve greater production capacity a new rental charge is incurred which is added to the rent of the original factory

sterling ['stɜ:lɪŋ] *noun* **(a)** standard currency used in the United Kingdom; *to quote prices in sterling or to quote sterling prices*; **pound sterling** = official term for the British currency; **sterling area** = formerly, area of the world where the pound sterling was the main trading currency; **sterling balances** = a country's trade balances expressed in pounds sterling; **sterling crisis** = sharp fall in the exchange rate of the pound sterling caused by lack of confidence in the UK economy; **sterling index** = index which shows the current value of sterling against a basket of currencies **(b) sterling silver** = official quality of silver articles made and sold (it is 92.5% pure silver)

QUOTE it is doubtful that British goods will price themselves back into world markets as long as sterling labour costs continue to rise faster than in competitor countries
Sunday Times

stewardship ['stjʊədʃɪp] *noun* duty of a person who manages something on behalf of another person, such as his business or finances, etc.; **accounts which are prepared for stewardship purposes** = accounts which are prepared to show to the people for whom the accountant is acting

stock [stɒk] *noun* **(a) stock** *or* **stocks** = quantity of goods for sale or materials for production in hand (see SSAP9); **opening stock** = details of stock at the beginning of an accounting period; **closing stock** = value of stock held at the end of an accounting period; **stock control** = making sure that the correct level of stock is maintained; **stock control program** = software designed to help manage stock in a business; **stock controller** = person who is responsible for maintaining the correct level of stock; **stock depreciation** = reduction in value of stock which is held in a warehouse for some time; **stock figures** = details of how many goods are in the warehouse, store etc.; **stock level** = quantity of goods kept in stock; *we try to keep stock levels low during the summer*; **stock order** = order placed to keep stocks in the warehouse up to the required stock level; **stock record** = card or computer file which shows the quantity of stock held, the date purchased, sales made, etc.; **stock turn** *or* **stock turnround** *or* **stock turnover (ratio)** = total value of goods sold in a year divided by the average value of goods in stock; **stock valuation** = estimating the value of stock at the end of an accounting period; **to buy a shop with stock at valuation** = to pay for the stock the same amount as its value as estimated by the valuer; **stock in hand** = stock held in a shop or warehouse; **to purchase stock at valuation** = to pay for stock the price it is valued at (NOTE: American English for this meaning is usually **inventory) (b)** investments in a company, represented by shares or fixed interest securities; **stocks and shares** = shares and debentures; **stock certificate** = document proving that someone owns stock in a company; *US* **stock option** = option given to an employee to buy stock of the company at a lower price than the current market price, at some time in the future; **debenture stock** = capital borrowed by a company, usually using its fixed assets as security; **dollar stocks** = shares in American companies; **government stock** = government securities; **convertible loan stock** = money lent to a company which can be converted into shares at a later date; *US* **common stock** = ordinary shares in a company giving the shareholders the right to vote at meetings and receive a dividend (NOTE: in Britain, the term **stocks** is generally applied to government stocks and debentures, and **shares** to shares of commercial companies. In the USA, shares in corporations are usually called **stocks** while government stocks are called **bonds**. In practice, **shares** and **stocks** are interchangeable terms, and this can lead to some confusion)

QUOTE US crude oil stocks fell last
week by nearly 2.5m barrels
Financial Times

QUOTE the stock rose to over $20 a
share, higher than the $18 bid
Fortune

stockbroker ['stɒkbrəʊkə] *noun* person
who buys or sells shares for clients;
stockbroker's commission = payment to a
broker for a deal carried out on behalf of a
client

stockbroking ['stɒkbrəʊkɪŋ] *noun* trade
of dealing in shares for clients; *a
stockbroking firm*

stock exchange ['stɒk ɪks'tʃeɪndʒ] *noun*
place where stocks and shares are bought and
sold; one of many stock markets throughout
the world; *he works on the London Stock
Exchange*; *shares in the company are traded
on the Tokyo Stock Exchange*; **stock
exchange listing** = official list of shares
which can be bought or sold on a stock
exchange (NOTE: capital letters are used when
referring to a particular stock exchange: **the
London Stock Exchange;** but **the Stock
Exchange** is generally used to refer to the local
stock exchange of whichever country the
speaker happens to be in)

stockholder ['stɒkhəʊldə] *noun* person
who holds shares in a company

stockholding ['stɒkhəʊldɪŋ] *noun* **(a)**
shares or debentures in a company held by
someone **(b)** keeping stocks of goods;
stockholding cost = holding cost, the cost of
keeping items of stock (including
warehousing and handling costs, insurance,
losses through deterioration, wastage, thefts,
etc., and the cost of capital used to acquire the
stock measured in terms of the interest lost on
the money which was spent on purchasing the
stock in the first place, or the interest paid on
the loans which were needed to finance the
purchase of the stock)

stock-in-trade ['stɒkɪn'treɪd] *noun*
goods held by a business for sale

stock market ['stɒk 'mɑːkɪt] *noun* place
where shares are bought and sold (i.e., a stock
exchange); *stock market price or price on the
stock market*; **stock market valuation** =
value of shares based on the current market
price

stockout ['stɒkaʊt] *noun* situation where
an item is out of stock

stocktaking ['stɒkteɪkɪŋ] *noun* counting
of goods in stock at the end of an accounting
period; *the warehouse is closed for the
annual stocktaking*; **stocktaking sale** = sale
of goods cheaply to clear a warehouse before
stocktaking

stop [stɒp] **1** *noun* not supplying; **account
on stop** = customer which is not supplied
because it has not paid its latest invoices; *to
put an account on stop*; **to put a stop on a
cheque** = to tell the bank not to pay a cheque
which you have written **2** *verb* **(a)** to stop an
account = not to supply an account any more
on credit because bills have not been paid; **to
stop a cheque** = to ask a bank not to pay a
cheque you have written; **to stop payments** =
not to make any further payments **(b) to stop
someone's wages** = to take money out of
someone's wages; *we stopped £25 from his
pay because he was late*

stop-loss order ['stɒp'lɒs 'ɔːdə] *noun*
instruction to a stockbroker to sell a share if
the price falls to a certain level

stoppage ['stɒpɪdʒ] *noun* money take from
a worker's wage packet for insurance, tax,
etc.

store [stɔː] **1** *noun* large shop; **store card** =
credit card issued by a large department store,
which can only be used for purchases in that
store **2** *verb* to keep items of stock

straddle ['strædl] **1** *noun* **(a)** spread, the
difference between bid and offer price **(b)**
buying a put option and a call option at the
same time **2** *verb* to be connected with two or
more accounting periods; *the contract
straddled two financial years*

straight line depreciation ['streɪt 'laɪn
dɪpriː'ʃɪ'eɪʃn] *noun* depreciation calculated by
dividing the cost of an asset, less its residual
value, by the number of years it is likely to be
used

COMMENT: various methods of depreciating
assets are used; under the 'straight line
method', the asset is depreciated at a constant
percentage of its cost each year while with the
'reducing balance method' the asset is
depreciated at a higher rate in the early years
and at a lower rate later

strike [straɪk] *verb* **to strike a bargain with
someone** = to come to an agreement; **a deal
was struck at £25 a unit** = we agreed the
price of £25 a unit; **striking price or strike
price** = (i) price at which a new issue of shares
is offered for sale; (ii) the lowest selling price
when selling a new issue of shares by tender
(applicants who tendered at a higher price will

get shares; those who tendered at a lower price will not) (NOTE: **striking - struck**)

strike out ['straɪk 'aʊt] *verb* to delete or remove an entry from a list

strong [strɒŋ] *adjective* with a lot of force or strength; *a strong demand for the new shares*; *the company needs a strong chairman*; **strong currency** = currency which is high against other currencies (the opposite is a 'weak currency'); **strong market** = market where prices are moving up; **strong pound** = pound which is high against other currencies

QUOTE everybody blames the strong dollar for US trade problems
Duns Business Month

QUOTE in a world of floating exchange rates the dollar is strong because of capital inflows rather than weak because of the nation's trade deficit
Duns Business Month

strongbox ['strɒŋbɒks] *noun* safe, a heavy metal box which cannot be opened easily, in which valuable documents, money, etc., can be kept

strongroom ['strɒŋrʊm] *noun* special room (in a bank) where valuable documents, money, gold, etc., can be kept

structure ['strʌktʃə] *noun* way in which something is organized; *the paper gives a diagram of the company's organizational structure*; *the price structure in the small car market*; *the career structure within a corporation*; *the company is reorganizing its discount structure*; **capital structure of a company** = way in which a company's capital is made up of the various sources of capital; **the company's salary structure** = organization of salaries in a company with different rates of pay for different types of job

stub [stʌb] *noun* **cheque stub** = piece of paper left in a cheque book after a cheque has been written and taken out

sub [sʌb] *noun* **(a)** wages paid in advance **(b)** = SUBSCRIPTION

sub- [sʌb] *prefix* under, less important

subcontract 1 [sʌb'kɒntrækt] *noun* contract between the main contractor for a whole project and another firm who will do part of the work **2** [sʌbkən'trækt] *verb* to agree with a company that they will do part of

the work for a project; *the electrical work has been subcontracted to Smith Ltd*

subcontractor [sʌbkən'træktə] *noun* company which has a contract to do work for a main contractor

subject to ['sʌbdʒɪkt tʊ] *adjective* **(a)** depending on; **the contract is subject to government approval** = the contract will be valid only if it is approved by the government; **agreement** *or* **sale subject to contract** = agreement or sale which is not legal until a proper contract has been signed; **offer subject to availability** = the offer is valid only if the goods are available **(b)** **these articles are subject to import tax** = import tax has to be paid on these articles

subjective [sʌb'dʒektɪv] *adjective* (measure, calculation, etc.) which shows an opinion (NOTE: the opposite is **objective**)

subjectivity [sʌbdʒek'tɪvəti] *noun* showing your opinion (NOTE: the opposite is **objectivity**)

sublease 1 ['sʌbliːs] *noun* lease from a tenant to another tenant **2** [sʌb'liːs] *verb* to lease a leased property from another tenant; *they subleased a small office in the centre of town*

sublessee [sʌble'siː] *noun* person or company which takes a property on a sublease

sublessor [sʌble'sɔː] *noun* tenant who lets a leased property to another tenant

sublet [sʌb'let] *verb* to let a leased property to another tenant; *we have sublet part of our office to a financial consultancy* (NOTE: **subletting - sublet**)

subordinated loan [sə'bɔːdɪneɪtɪd 'ləʊn] *noun* loan which ranks after all other borrowings as regards payment of interest or repayment of capital

subrogation [sʌbrəʊ'geɪʃn] *noun* legal principle whereby someone stands in the place of another person and acquires that person's rights and is responsible for that person's liabilities

subroutine ['sʌbruːtiːn] *noun* section of a computer program which performs a required function and can be called upon at any time from inside the main program

subscribe [səb'skraɪb] *verb* **to subscribe to a share issue** *or* **to subscribe for shares in a company** = to apply for shares in a new company

subscriber [səb'skraɪbə] *noun* **subscriber to a share issue** = person who has applied for shares in a new company

subscription [səb'skrɪpʃən] *noun* **(a)** money paid regularly to belong to a club or association (some subscriptions can be claimed against tax by self-employed people) **(b)** application for new shares in an existing company, or shares in a new company; **subscription to a new share issue** = application for new shares in a company; **subscription list** = list of subscribers to a new share issue; **the subscription lists close at 10.00 a.m. on September 24th** = no new applicants will be allowed to subscribe for the share issue after that time; **subscription price** = price at which new shares are offered for sale

subsidiary [səb'sɪdjəri] **1** *adjective* (thing) which is less important; *they agreed to most of the conditions in the contract but queried one or two subsidiary items*; **subsidiary company** = company which is more than 50% owned by a holding company, and where the holding company controls the board of directors (see FRS2) **2** *noun* company which is owned by a parent company; *most of the group profit was contributed by the subsidiaries in the Far East*

subsidize ['sʌbsɪdaɪz] *verb* to help by giving money; *the government has refused to subsidize the car industry*; **subsidized accommodation** = cheap accommodation which is partly paid for by an employer or a local authority, etc.

subsidy ['sʌbsɪdi] *noun* **(a)** money given to help something which is not profitable; *the industry exists on government subsidies*; *the government has increased its subsidy to the car industry* **(b)** money given by a government to make something cheaper; *the subsidy on butter or the butter subsidy*

substantial [səb'stænʃəl] *adjective* large or important; **to acquire a substantial interest in a company** = to buy a large number of shares in a company

subsystem ['sʌbsɪstəm] *noun* one smaller part of a large system

subtenancy [sʌb'tenənsi] *noun* agreement to sublet a property

subtenant [sʌb'tenənt] *noun* person or company to which a property has been sublet

subtotal ['sʌbtəʊtl] *noun* total of one section of a complete set of figures

subtract [səb'trækt] *verb* to take away (something) from a total; *if the profits from the Far Eastern operations are subtracted, you will see that the group has not been profitable in the European market*

subtraction [səb'trækʃn] *noun* taking one number away from another

subtrahend ['sʌbtrəhend] *noun* in a subtraction operation, the number to be subtracted from the minuend

subvention [səb'venʃn] *noun* subsidy

succeed [sək'siːd] *verb* **(a)** to do well, to be profitable; *the company has succeeded best in the overseas markets*; *his business has succeeded more than he had expected* **(b)** to do what was planned; *she succeeded in passing her shorthand test*; *they succeeded in putting their rivals out of business* **(c)** to follow, especially to take the place of someone who has retired or died; **to succeed to a property** = to become the owner of a property by inheriting it from someone who has died

success [sək'ses] *noun* **(a)** doing something well; *the launch of the new model was a great success*; *the company has had great success in the Japanese market* **(b)** doing what was intended; *we had no success in trying to sell the lease*; *he has been looking for a job for six months, but with no success*

succession [sək'seʃn] *noun* acquiring property or title from someone who has died; **law of succession** = laws relating to how property shall pass to others when the owner dies; **intestate succession** = rules which apply when someone dies without having made a will

sum [sʌm] *noun* **(a)** quantity of money; *a sum of money was stolen from the personnel office*; *he lost large sums on the Stock Exchange*; *she received the sum of £500 in compensation*; **the sum insured** = the largest amount which an insurer will pay under the terms of an insurance; **lump sum** = money paid in one payment, not in several small payments **(b)** total of a series of figures added together; **sum of digits method** *or* **sum of the year's digits** = method of depreciating a fixed asset where the cost of the asset (less its residual value) is multiplied by a fraction based on the number of years of its expected useful life (the fraction changes each year and charges the highest costs to the earliest years)

COMMENT: an example of the sum of digits method of depreciation: if an asset has an expected life of four years, the sum of the digits is ten $(1 + 2 + 3 + 4)$. In the first year, 4/10 of the cost of the asset is charged to depreciation, in the second year 3/10 of the original cost, in the third year 2/10 and in the final year 1/10

summary ['sʌmri] *adjective* **summary administration** = court order making a person bankrupt with debts of less than œ20,000, or where the person has himself petitioned for bankruptcy (the person may be discharged after two years)

sundry ['sʌndri] *adjective & noun* various; **sundry items** *or* **sundries** = small items which are not listed in detail

superannuation [su:pərænjuˈeɪʃn] *noun* pension paid to someone who is too old or too ill to work any more; **superannuation plan** *or* **scheme** = pension plan or scheme

supervisor ['su:pəvaɪzə] *noun* person appointed to supervise the affairs of a person or company in voluntary liquidation

supplementary benefit [sʌplɪˈmentəri 'benɪfɪt] *noun* payments from the government to people with very low incomes

supplier [səˈplaɪə] *noun* person or company which supplies or sells goods or services

supply [səˈplaɪ] **1** *noun* **(a)** providing something which is needed; **supply price** = price at which something is provided; **supply and demand** = amount of a product which is available and the amount which is wanted by customers; **the law of supply and demand** = general rule that the amount of a product which is available and the amount needed by the possible customer are made equal by market prices **(b)** **money supply** = amount of money which exists in a country; *see note at* MONEY SUPPLY; **Supply Bill** = Bill for providing money for government requirements; **supply estimates** = UK government expenditure which is voted by Parliament

supply side economics [səˈplaɪ 'saɪd i:kəˈnɒmɪks] *noun* economic theory, that governments should encourage producers and suppliers of goods by cutting taxes and increasing subsidies, etc., rather than encourage demand by making more money available in the economy

support [səˈpɔːt] *noun* **(a)** giving money to help; *the government has provided support to the electronics industry; we have no financial support from the banks* **(b)** agreement or encouragement; *the chairman has the support of the committee*; **support level** *or* **support point** = level below which a share, a commodity or the stock market will not fall, because of general support from investors; **support price** = price (in the EC) at which a government will buy agricultural produce to stop the price falling

surcharge ['sɜːtʃɑːdʒ] *noun* extra charge; **import surcharge** = extra duty charged on imported goods, to try to stop them from being imported and to encourage local manufacture

surety ['ʃʊərəti] *noun* **(a)** person who guarantees that someone will do something; *to stand surety for someone* **(b)** deeds or share certificates, etc., deposited as security for a loan

surplus ['sɜːpləs] *noun* extra stock, something which is more than is needed; **a budget surplus** = more revenue than was planned for in the budget; **to absorb a surplus** = to take back surplus stock so that it does not affect a business

surrender [səˈrendə] **1** *noun* giving up of an insurance policy before the contracted date for maturity; **surrender value** = money which an insurer will pay if an insurance policy is given up **2** *verb* **to surrender a policy** = to give up an insurance

surtax ['sɜːtæks] *noun* extra tax on high income

suspend [səsˈpend] *verb* to stop (something) for a time; *we have suspended payments while we are waiting for news from our agent; the management decided to suspend negotiations*

suspense account [səsˈpens əˈkaʊnt] *noun* account into which payments are put temporarily when the accountant cannot be sure where they should be posted

suspension [səsˈpenʃən] *noun* stopping something for a time; *suspension of payments*; *suspension of deliveries*

swap [swɒp] *noun* exchanging one thing for another; **currency swap** = (i) agreement to use a certain currency for payments under a contract in exchange for another currency (the two companies involved each can buy one of the currencies at a more favourable rate than the other); (ii) buying (or selling) a fixed amount of foreign currency on the spot market and selling (or buying) the same amount of the same currency on the forward market; **interest rate swap** = agreement between two companies to exchange borrowings (a company with fixed-interest borrowings might swap them for variable interest borrowings of another company; this is also called 'plain vanilla swap')

QUOTE the simplest and most common type of interest rate swap involves the exchange of a fixed for a variable rate obligation, both denominated in the same currency
Accountancy

QUOTE the International Finance Corporation, the World Bank's private sector development arm, became the first borrower to swap funds raised in the Portuguese escudo market
Financial Times

COMMENT: currency swaps are often used when the sale or purchase of foreign currency cannot go ahead as planned, as when dollars which a company had contracted to sell to a bank fail to arrive in time from the customer

sweetener ['swiːtnə] *noun (informal)* bribe, or anything which makes a deal particularly attractive; **equity sweetener** = incentive to encourage people to lend a company money, in the form of a warrant giving the right to buy shares at a later date and at a certain price (NOTE: the American equivalent is **equity kicker)**

switch [swɪtʃ] *verb* to change, especially to change investment money from one type of investment to another; *when war seemed likely, investors switched out of equities into gold*

syndicate 1 ['sɪndɪkət] *noun* group of people or companies working together to make money; *a German finance syndicate*; **arbitrage syndicate** = group of people who together raise the capital to invest in arbitrage deals; **bank syndicate** = group of major international banks which group together to underwrite a massive loan; **underwriting syndicate** = group of underwriters who insure a large risk **2** ['sɪndɪkeɪt] *verb* to arrange for a large loan to be underwritten by several international banks

QUOTE over the past few weeks, companies raising new loans from international banks have been forced to pay more, and an unusually high number of attempts to syndicate loans among banks has failed
Financial Times

synergy ['sɪnədʒi] *noun (of two groups)* producing a greater effect by joining forces than by acting separately

system ['sɪstəm] *noun* **(a)** arrangement, organization of things which work together; *our accounting system has worked well in spite of the large increase in orders*; **decimal system** = system of mathematics based on the number 10; **filing system** = way of putting documents in order for easy reference; **to operate a quota system** = to regulate supplies by fixing quantities which are allowed; *we arrange our distribution using a quota system - each agent is allowed only a certain number of units* **(b)** **computer system** = set of programs, commands, etc., which run a computer; **systems analysis** = (i) analysing a process or system to see if it could be more efficiently carried out by a computer; (ii) examining an existing system with the aim of improving or replacing it; **systems analyst** = person who specializes in systems analysis; **system flowchart** = diagram that shows each step of the computer procedures needed in a system

Tt

tab [tæb] *noun* = TABULATOR

table ['teɪbl] **1** *noun* **(a)** list of figures or facts set out in columns; **table of contents** = list of contents in a book; **actuarial tables** = lists showing how long people of certain ages are likely to live **(b) Table A, B, C, D, E** = specimen articles of association set out in the Companies Act; *see* **A, B, C, D, E 2** *verb* to put items of information on the table before a meeting; *the report of the finance committee was tabled*; **to table a motion** = (i) to put forward a proposal for discussion by putting details of it on the table at a meeting; (ii) *US* to remove a proposal from discussion indefinitely

tabular ['tæbjʊlə] *adjective* **in tabular form** = arranged in a table

tabulate ['tæbjʊleɪt] *verb* to set out in a table

tabulation [tæbjʊ'leɪʃən] *noun* arrangement of figures in a table

tabulator ['tæbjʊleɪtə] *noun* part of a typewriter or computer which sets words or figures automatically in columns

T account ['tiː ə'kaʊnt] *noun* way of drawing up an account, with a line across the top of the paper and a vertical line down the middle, with the debit and credit entries on either side

take [teɪk] **1** *noun* (i) profit from any sale; (ii) cash received in a shop **2** *verb* **(a)** to receive, to get; **the shop takes £2,000 a week** = the shop receives £2,000 a week in cash sales; **he takes home £250 a week** = his salary, after deductions for tax, etc., is £250 a week **(b)** to do a certain action; **to take action** = to do something; *you must take immediate action if you want to stop thefts*; **to take stock** = to count the items in a warehouse, storeroom, etc.; **to take stock of a situation** = to examine the state of things before deciding what to do **(c)** to need (a time or a quantity); *it took the factory six weeks or the factory took six weeks to clear the backlog of orders*; *it will take her all morning to do my letters*; *it took six men and a crane to get the computer*

into the office (NOTE: **taking - took - has taken**)

take away ['teɪk ə'weɪ] *verb* to remove one figure from a total; *if you take away the home sales, the total turnover is down*

take-home pay ['teɪkhəʊm 'peɪ] *noun* amount of money received in wages, after tax, etc., has been deducted

take off ['teɪk 'ɒf] *verb* to remove, to deduct; *he took £25 off the price*

take out ['teɪk 'aʊt] *verb* to remove; **to take out a patent for an invention** = to apply for and receive a patent; **to take out insurance against theft** = to pay a premium to an insurance company, so that if a theft takes place the company will pay compensation

> QUOTE capital gains are not taxed, but money taken out in profits and dividends is taxed
> *Toronto Star*

take-out ['teɪkaʊt] *noun* removing capital which one has originally invested in a new company by selling one's shares

take over ['teɪk 'əʊvə] *verb* **(a)** to start to do something in place of someone else; *the new chairman takes over on July 1st*; *the buyer takes over the company's liabilities* **(b) to take over a company** = to buy (a business) by acquiring most of its shares; *the company was taken over by a large multinational*

takeover ['teɪkəʊvə] *noun* buying a controlling interest in a business by buying more than 50% of its shares; **takeover bid** = offer to buy all or most of the shares in a company so as to control it; **to make a takeover bid for a company** = to offer to buy most of the shares in a company; **to withdraw a takeover bid** = to say that you no longer offer to buy the shares in a company; **the company rejected the takeover bid** = the directors recommended that the shareholders should not accept the offer; *the disclosure of the takeover bid raised share prices*; **contested takeover** = takeover where the board of the company being bought do not recommend it, and try to fight it; **Takeover**

Code = the City Code on Takeovers and Mergers, the code of practice which regulates how takeovers should take place; it is enforced by the Takeover Panel; **Takeover Panel** = the Panel on Takeovers and Mergers, the non-statutory body which examines takeovers and applies the Takeover Code

QUOTE many takeovers result in the new managers/owners rationalizing the capital of the company through better asset management
Duns Business Month

take up ['teɪk 'ʌp] *verb* **to take up an option** = to accept an option which has been offered and put into action; *half the rights issue was not taken up by the shareholders*; **take up rate** = percentage of acceptances for a rights issue

takings ['teɪkɪŋz] *plural noun* money received in a shop or a business; *the week's takings were stolen from the cash desk*

tally ['tælɪ] **1** *noun* note of things counted or recorded; *to keep a tally of stock movements or of expenses*; **tally clerk** = person whose job is to record quantities of cargo; **tally sheet** = sheet on which quantities are recorded **2** *verb* to agree, to be the same; *the invoices do not tally*; *the accounts department tried to make the figures tally*

tangible ['tændʒəbl] *adjective* **tangible assets** *or* **property** = assets which are visible (such as machinery, buildings, furniture, jewellery, etc.); **tangible fixed assets** = assets such as land, buildings, plant and equipment, etc., that have physical substance and are held for use in the production or supply of goods or services, for rental to others, or for administrative purposes on a continuing basis in a reporting entity's activities (see FRS 15); **tangible asset value** *US* **tangible net worth** = value of all the assets of a company less its intangible assets (goodwill, patents, etc.); it is shown as a value per ordinary share

taper relief ['teɪpə rɪ'liːf] *noun* relief for capital gains on assets sold after being held for a certain period of time (the longer the assets has been held, the more relief is given gainst capital gains)

target ['tɑːgɪt] *noun* thing to aim for; **monetary targets** = figures such as the money supply, PSBR, etc., which are given as targets by the government when setting out its budget for the forthcoming year; **production targets** = amount of units a factory is expected to produce; **sales targets** = amount of sales a company, department, or representative is expected to achieve;

takeover target *or* **target company** = company which is the object of a takeover bid; **target market** = market in which a company is planning to sell its goods; **to set targets** = to fix amounts or quantities which workers have to produce or reach; **to meet a target** = to produce the quantity of goods or sales which are expected; **to miss a target** = not to produce the amount of goods or sales which are expected; *they missed the target figure of £2m turnover*

QUOTE in a normal leveraged buyout the acquirer raises money by borrowing against the assets of the target company
Fortune

tax [tæks] **1** *noun* **(a)** money taken by the government or by an official body to pay for government services; **capital gains tax (CGT)** = tax on capital gains; **capital transfer tax** = former name for inheritance tax, i.e. the tax on gifts or bequests of money or property; **corporation tax** = tax on profits made by companies; **advance corporation tax (ACT)** = tax paid by a company in advance of its main corporation tax payments; it is paid when dividends are paid to shareholders and is deducted from the main tax payment when that falls due; it appears on the tax voucher attached to a dividend warrant; **mainstream corporation tax (MCT)** = total tax paid by a company on its profits (less any ACT which the company will already have paid); **excess profits tax** = tax on profits which are higher than what is thought to be normal; **income tax** = tax on salaries and wages; **inheritance tax** = tax on gifts or bequests of money or property; **land tax** = tax on the amount of land owned; **sales tax** = tax on the price of goods sold; **turnover tax** = tax on company turnover; **windfall tax** = tax on companies that have made large profits because of circumstances outside their normal trading activities (a windfall tax was imposed on the privatized utility companies in 1997); **value added tax (VAT)** = tax on goods and services, added as a percentage of the net invoiced sales price **(b)** **ad valorem tax** = tax calculated according to the value of the goods taxed; **back tax** = tax which is owed from previous years; **basic tax** = tax paid at the normal rate; **direct tax** = tax which is deducted from income directly; **indirect tax** = tax paid on purchases, not from income directly (such as VAT); **to levy a tax** *or* **to impose a tax** = to make a tax payable; *the government has imposed a 15% tax on petrol*; **to lift a tax** = to remove a tax; *the tax on company profits has been lifted*; **exclusive of tax** = not including tax; **tax abatement** =

reduction of tax; **tax accountant** = qualified accountant who prepares tax returns for clients and advises them on tax matters; **tax adjustments** = changes made to tax; **tax advantage** = possible reduction in tax payable or relief from tax allowed by tax law, such as qualifying for capital allowances by purchasing certain fixed assets; **tax adviser** or **tax consultant** = person who gives advice on tax problems; **tax allowance** or **allowances against tax** = part of income which a person is allowed to earn and not pay tax on; **tax avoidance** = trying (legally) to minimize the amount of tax to be paid; **in the top tax bracket** = paying the highest level of tax; **tax code** = number given to indicate the amount of tax allowances a person has; **tax concession** = allowing less tax to be paid; **tax credit** = part of a dividend on which the company has already paid advance corporation tax which is deducted from the shareholder's income tax charge; **tax deductions** = (i) money removed from a salary to pay tax; (ii) US business expenses which can be claimed against tax; **tax deducted at source** = tax which is removed from a salary or interest before the money is paid out; **tax deposit certificate** = certificate showing that a taxpayer has deposited money in advance of a tax payment (the money earns interest while on deposit); **tax evasion** = trying illegally not to pay tax; **tax exemption** = (i) being free from payment of tax; (ii) US part of income which a person is allowed to earn and not pay tax on; **tax form** = blank form to be filled in with details of income, expenses and allowances and sent to the tax office each year; **tax haven** = country where taxes are low, encouraging companies to set up their main offices there (countries such as the Bahamas are tax havens); **tax holiday** = period when a new company pays no tax; **tax inspector** or **inspector of taxes** = official of the Inland Revenue who examines tax returns and decides how much tax someone should pay; **tax loophole** = legal means of not paying tax; **tax loss** = loss made by a company during an accounting period, for which relief from tax is given; **tax office** = local office of the Inland Revenue (it does not necessarily deal with the tax affairs of people who live locally); **tax planning** = trying (legally) to minimize the amount of tax to be paid; **tax rates** = percentage rates of tax on different bands of taxable income; *see also* BASIC RATE, HIGHER RATE, STARTING RATE; **tax rebate** = money returned by the Inland Revenue because it was overpaid; **tax relief** = allowing someone not to pay tax on certain parts of his income; **tax return** or **tax declaration** = completed tax form, with

details of income, expenses and allowances which is sent by a taxpayer to the Inland Revenue; **Tax Return Guide** = booklet sent by the Inland Revenue to each taxpayer, giving instructions on how to complete the tax return; **tax shelter** = financial arrangement (such as a pension scheme) where investments can be made without tax; **tax year** = twelve month period on which taxes are calculated (in the UK, from 6th April to 5th April of the following year) **2** *verb* to make someone pay a tax, to impose a tax on something; *the government is proposing to tax businesses at 50%*; *income is taxed at 25%*; *luxury items are heavily taxed*

taxable ['tæksəbl] *adjective* which can be taxed; **taxable benefit** = benefit which is included in a person's taxable income and is subject to tax; **taxable items** = items on which a tax has to be paid; **taxable income** = income on which a person has to pay tax; **taxable person** = person who is registered for VAT, and who charges VAT on goods or services supplied; **taxable supply** = supply of goods which are subject to VAT

taxation [tæk'seɪʃən] *noun* act of taxing; **direct taxation** = taxes (such as income tax) which are deducted directly from income; **indirect taxation** = taxes (such as sales tax) which are paid on purchases and not deducted directly from income; **double taxation** = taxing the same income twice; **double taxation agreement** = agreement between two countries that a person living in one country will not be taxed in both countries on the income earned in the other country; **graduated taxation** or **progressive taxation** = taxation system where tax levels increase as income rises; **regressive taxation** = system of taxation in which tax gets progressively less as income rises

tax-deductible ['tæksdɪ'dʌktəbl] *adjective* which can be deducted from total income before tax is calculated; **these expenses are not tax-deductible** = tax has to be paid on these expenses

tax-exempt ['tæksɪg'zempt] *adjective* not required to pay tax; (income or goods) which are not subject to tax; **Tax-Exempt Special Savings Account (TESSA)** = prior to April 1999, account into which money could be placed to earn interest free of tax, provided it was left untouched for a certain period of time (usually five years); US **tax-exempt bond** = bond issued by a town or local area where the interest is not subject to state tax (also called a 'municipal bond': the British equivalent is a 'local authority bond')

tax-free ['tæks'friː] *adjective* on which tax does not have to be paid

taxpayer ['tækspeɪə] *noun* person or company which has to pay tax; *basic taxpayer or taxpayer at the basic rate*; *corporate taxpayers*

tax point ['tæks 'pɔɪnt] *noun* (i) time when goods are supplied and VAT is charged; (ii) time at which a tax begins to be applied

T-bill ['tiː'bɪl] *US (informal)* = TREASURY BILL

T-bond ['tiː'bɒnd] = TREASURY BOND

technical ['teknɪkəl] *adjective* **(a)** referring to a particular machine or process; *the document gives all the technical details on the new computer* **(b)** referring to influences inside a market (volumes traded, forecasts based on market analysis, etc.), as opposed to external factors, such as oil-price rises, wars, etc.; **technical analysis** = study of the price movements and volumes traded on a stock exchange; **technical correction** = situation where a share price or a currency moves up or down because it was previously too low or too high; **technical decline** = fall in share prices because of technical analysis

QUOTE market analysts described the falls in the second half of last week as a technical correction
Australian Financial Review

QUOTE at the end of the day, it was clear the Fed had not loosened the monetary reins, and Fed Funds forged ahead on the back of technical demand
Financial Times

technical department ['teknɪkəl dɪ'pɑːtmənt] *noun* department in a practising firm of accountants that does research and development, and interprets new professional developments

COMMENT: the technical department writes the audit and assurance manual, decides on the standard accounts, maintains documentation and provides news and in-depth coverage of technical developments, such as a new FRS. Query answering and a formal dispute resolution service are also usually provided by this department. Marketing may be done through writing books and articles and providing speakers for conferences. The department also provides input to various professional bodies and committees to maintain the firm's commitment to the development of the accountancy profession

technician [tek'nɪʃən] *noun* **accounting technician** = person who assists in the

preparation of accounts but who is not a fully qualified accountant

telegraphic transfer ['telɪgræfɪk 'trɑːnsfə] *noun* transfer of money from one account to another by telex (used often for sending money abroad, it is quicker but more expensive than sending a draft through the post)

teller ['telə] *noun* person who takes cash from or who pays cash to customers at a bank

tem *see* PRO TEM

tenancy ['tenənsi] *noun* (i) agreement by which a tenant can occupy a property; (ii) period during which a tenant has an agreement to occupy a property; **joint tenancy** = situation where two or more persons acquire interests in a property together where, if one of the joint tenants dies, his share goes to the others who survive him

tenant ['tenənt] *noun* person or company which rents a house, flat or office to live or work in; *the tenant is liable for repairs*; **sitting tenant** = tenant who is living in a house when the freehold or lease is sold

tender ['tendə] **1** *noun* **(a)** offer to do something for a certain price; **to put a project out to tender** *or* **to ask for** *or* **to invite tenders for a project** = to ask contractors to give written estimates for a job; **to put in a tender** *or* **to submit a tender** = to make an estimate for a job; **sealed tenders** = tenders sent in sealed envelopes which will all be opened together at a certain time **(b)** to sell shares by **tender** = to ask people to offer in writing a price for shares; **tender offer** = method of selling new securities or bonds by asking investors to make offers for them, and accepting the highest offers **(c) legal tender** = coins or notes which can be legally used to pay a debt (small denominations cannot be used to pay large debts) **2** *verb* **to tender for a contract** = to put forward an estimate of cost for work to be carried out under contract; *to tender for the construction of a hospital*

tenderer ['tendərə] *noun* person or company which tenders for work; *the company was the successful tenderer for the project*

tendering ['tendrɪŋ] *noun* act of putting forward an estimate of cost; *to be successful, you must follow the tendering procedure as laid out in the documents*

tenor ['tenə] *noun* time before a financial instrument matures or before a bill is payable

term [tɜ:m] *noun* **(a)** period of time when something is legally valid; *the term of a lease*; *the term of the loan is fifteen years*; *to have a loan for a term of fifteen years*; *during his term of office as chairman*; **term deposit** = money invested for a fixed period at a higher rate of interest; **term assurance** *or* **term insurance** = life assurance which covers a person's life for a period of time (at the end of the period, if the person is still alive he receives nothing from the insurance); *he took out a ten-year term insurance*; **term loan** = loan for a fixed period of time; **term of years** = fixed period of several years (of a lease); **term shares** = type of building society deposit for a fixed period of time at a higher rate of interest; **short-term** = for a short period of time; **long-term** = for a long period of time; **medium-term** = for a period between short-term and long-term **(b) terms** = conditions, duties which have to be carried out as part of a contract; arrangements which have to be agreed before a contract is valid; *he refused to agree to some of the terms of the contract*; *by* **or** *under the terms of the contract, the company is responsible for all damage to the property*; *to negotiate for better terms*; **terms of payment** *or* **payment terms** = conditions for paying something; **terms of sale** = conditions attached to a sale; **terms of trade** = difference between a country's exports and imports; **cash terms** = lower terms which apply if the customer pays cash; **'terms: cash with order'** = terms of sale showing that payment has to be made in cash when the order is placed; **easy terms** = terms which are not difficult to accept, price which is easy to pay; *the shop is let on very easy terms*; *to pay for something on easy terms*; **on favourable terms** = on especially good terms; *the shop is let on very favourable terms*; **trade terms** = special discount for people in the same trade

terminal bonus ['tɜ:mɪnl 'bəʊnəs] *noun* bonus received when an insurance comes to an end

termination clause ['tɜ:mɪ'neɪʃn 'klɔ:z] *noun* clause which explains how and when a contract can be terminated

TESSA ['tesə] = TAX-EXEMPT SPECIAL SAVINGS ACCOUNT

testament ['testəmənt] *noun* **last will and testament** = will, document by which a person says what he wants to happen to his property when he dies

testamentary [testə'mentəri] *adjective* *adjective* referring to a will; **testamentary disposition** = passing of property to someone in a will

testate ['testeɪt] *adjective* having made a will; *did he die testate?*; *see also* INTESTATE

testator [te'steɪtə] *noun* man who has made a will

testatrix [te'steɪtrɪks] *noun* woman who has made a will

thing in action, thing in possession *see* CHOSE

third party ['θɜ:d 'pɑ:ti] *noun* any person other than the two main parties involved in a contract (i.e., in an insurance contract, not the insurance company nor the person who is insured); **third-party insurance** = insurance to cover damage to any person who is not one of the people named in the insurance contract; **the case is in the hands of a third party** = the case is being dealt with by someone who is not one of the main interested parties

third quarter ['θɜ:d 'kwɔ:tə] *noun* three months' period from 1st July to 30th September

threshold ['θreʃəʊld] *noun* limit, the point at which something changes; **threshold agreement** = contract which says that if the cost of living goes up by more than a certain amount, pay will go up to match it; **pay threshold** = point at which pay increases because of a threshold agreement; **tax threshold** = point at which another percentage of tax is payable; *the government has raised the minimum tax threshold from £6,000 to £6,500*

thrift [θrɪft] *noun* **(a)** saving money by spending carefully **(b)** *US* private local bank, savings and loan association or credit union, which accepts and pays interest on deposits from small investors

thrifty ['θrɪfti] *adjective* careful not to spend too much money

tied [taɪd] *adjective* **tied financial adviser** = qualified person, authorized to act by the

Personal Investment Authority, who advises private clients on the financial products offered by a single company (as opposed to an independent financial adviser, who only advises on a wide range of products)

tight [taɪt] *adjective* which is controlled, which does not allow any movement; *the manager has a very tight schedule today - he cannot fit in any more appointments*; *expenses are kept under tight control*; **tight money** = money which is borrowed at high interest rates because credit is being squeezed; **tight money policy** = government policy to restrict money supply

QUOTE mortgage money is becoming tighter
Times

QUOTE a tight monetary policy by the central bank has pushed up interest rates and drawn discretionary funds into bank deposits
Far Eastern Economic Review

QUOTE the UK economy is at the uncomfortable stage in the cycle where the two years of tight money are having the desired effect on demand
Sunday Times

tighten ['taɪtn] *verb* to make (something) tight, to control (something); *the accounts department is tightening its control over departmental budgets*

QUOTE the decision by the government to tighten monetary policy will push the annual inflation rate above the previous high
Financial Times

tighten up on ['taɪtn 'ʌp ɒn] *verb* to control (something) more; *the government is tightening up on tax evasion*; *we must tighten up on the reps' expenses*

till [tɪl] *noun* drawer for keeping cash in a shop; **cash till** = cash register, a machine which shows and adds prices of items bought, with a drawer for keeping the cash received; *there was not much money in the till at the end of the day*; **till float** *or* **cash float** = cash put into the cash box at the beginning of the day to allow change to be given to customers; **till money** = cash held by banks

time [taɪm] *noun* **(a)** period when something takes place (such as one hour, two days, fifty minutes, etc.); **time and motion study** = study in an office or factory of how long it takes to do certain jobs and the movements workers have to make to do them; **time and motion expert** = person who analyses time

and motion studies and suggests changes in the way work is done **(b)** hours worked; **he is paid time and a half on Sundays** = he is paid the normal rate plus 50% extra when he works on Sundays; **full-time** = working for the whole normal working day; **overtime** = hours worked more than the normal working time; **part-time** = not working for a whole working day **(c)** period before something happens; **time bill** = bill of exchange which is payable at a specific time after acceptance; **time deposit** = deposit of money for a fixed period, during which it cannot be withdrawn; **lead time** = time between placing an order and receiving the goods; **time limit** = period during which something should be done; **to keep within the time limits** *or* **within the time schedule** = to complete work by the time stated

time-keeping ['taɪmkiːpɪŋ] *noun* being on time for work; *he was warned for bad time-keeping*

time rate ['taɪm 'reɪt] *noun* rate for work which is calculated as money per hour or per week, and not money for work completed

times [taɪmz] *preposition* number of times something is multiplied by another; **shares selling at 10 times earnings** = shares selling at a P/E ratio of 10

timescale ['taɪmskeɪl] *noun* time which will be taken to complete work; *our timescale is that all work should be completed by the end of August*; *he is working to a strict timescale*

time sheet ['taɪm 'ʃiːt] *noun* paper showing when a worker starts work in the morning and leaves work in the evening, or one which shows how much time a worker spends on various jobs in different locations

time work ['taɪm 'wɜːk] *noun* work which is paid for at a rate per hour or per day, not per piece of work completed

tip [tɪp] *noun* a gratuity, money given to someone who has helped you (the person receiving tips must declare them on his or her tax return); *the staff are instructed not to accept tips*

title ['taɪtl] *noun* right to own a property; *she has no title to the property*; *he has a good title to the property*; **title deeds** = document showing who is the owner of a property

token ['təʊkən] *noun* **(a)** thing which acts as a sign or symbol; **token charge** = small charge which does not cover the real costs; *a token charge is made for heating*; **token**

payment = small payment to show that a payment is being made; **token rent** = very low rent payment to show that a rent is being asked, even though it does not cover real costs **(b) book token** or **flower token** = card bought in a shop which is given as a present and which must be exchanged for books or flowers; **gift token** = card bought in a shop which is given as a present and which must be exchanged in that shop for goods

toll [təʊl] *noun* payment for using a service (usually a bridge or a road); *we had to cross a toll bridge to get to the island; you have to pay a toll to cross the bridge*

toll call ['təʊl 'kɔːl] *noun US* long-distance telephone call

toll free ['təʊl 'friː] *adverb US* without having to pay a charge for a long-distance telephone call; *to call someone toll free; a toll-free number*

COMMENT: toll-free numbers usually start with the digits 800

tools [tuːlz] *noun* small portable pieces of equipment used to make something (they are valued as tangible fixed assets)

top-hat pension ['tɒphæt 'penʃən] *noun* special extra pension for senior managers

top up ['tɒp 'ʌp] *verb* to add to something to make it more complete; *he topped up his pension contributions to make sure he received the maximum allowable pension when he retired*

tort [tɔːt] *noun* harm done to someone or property which can be the basis of a lawsuit; **action in tort** = action brought by a plaintiff who has suffered damage or harm caused by the defendant; **proceedings in tort** = court action for damages for a tort

tortious ['tɔːʃəs] *adjective* referring to a tort; **tortious act** = a tort; **tortious liability** = liability for harm caused by a breach of duty

total ['təʊtl] **1** *adjective* complete, with everything added together; **total charge for credit** = total cost of borrowing money when buying something on credit; **total income** = all income from all sources; **the cargo was written off as a total loss** = the cargo was so badly damaged that the insurers said it had no value **2** *noun* amount which is complete, with everything added up; *the total of the charges comes to more than £1,000*; **grand total** = final total made by adding several subtotals **3** *verb* to add up to; *costs totalling more than £25,000* (NOTE: **totalling - totalled** but American English **totaling - totaled**)

tracker fund ['trækə 'fʌnd] *noun* investment fund which tracks (i.e. follows closely) one of the stock market indices, such as the Footsie

track record ['træk 'rekɔːd] *noun* success or failure of a company or salesman in the past; *he has a good track record as an insurance salesman; the company has no track record in the computer market*

trade [treɪd] **1** *noun* **(a)** business of buying and selling; **export trade** or **import trade** = the business of selling to other countries or buying from other countries; **foreign trade** or **overseas trade** or **external trade** = trade with other countries; **home trade** = trade in the country where a company is based; **trade cycle** = period during which trade expands, then slows down, then expands again; **balance of trade** or **trade balance** = international trading position of a country in merchandise, excluding invisible trade; **adverse balance of trade** = situation when a country imports more than it exports; **favourable balance of trade** = situation where a country's exports are larger than its imports; **trade deficit** = difference in value between a country's low exports and higher imports; **trade surplus** = difference in value between a country's high exports and lower imports **(b) to do a good trade in a range of products** = to sell a large number of the range of products; **fair trade** = international business system where countries agree not to charge import duties on certain items imported from their trading partners; **free trade** = system where goods can go from one country to another without any restrictions; **free trade area** = group of countries practising free trade; *see also* EFTA **(c) trade agreement** = international agreement between countries over general terms of trade; **trade barriers** = controls placed by a government to prevent imports coming into the country; **trade bill** = bill of exchange between two companies who are trading partners (it is issued by one company and accepted by the other); **trade credit** = credit offered by one company when trading with another; **trade creditors** = companies which are owed money by a company in the normal course of trading (the amount owed to trade creditors is shown in the annual accounts); **trade debtors** = debtors who owe money to a company in the normal course of that company's trading; **trade deficit** or **trade gap** = difference in value between a country's high imports and low exports; **trade description** = description of a product to attract customers; *GB* **Trade Descriptions**

Act = act which limits the way in which products can be described so as to protect customers from wrong descriptions made by manufacturers; **trade directory** = book which lists all the businesses and business people in a town; **trade mission** = visit to a country by a group of foreign businessmen to discuss trade **(d)** people or companies dealing in the same type of product; **trade association** = group which links together companies in the same trade; **trade counter** = shop in a factory or warehouse where goods are sold to retailers; **trade discount** *or* **trade terms** = reduction in price given to a customer in the same trade; **trade fair** = large exhibition and meeting for advertising and selling a certain type of product; **trade price** = special wholesale price paid by a retailer to a manufacturer or wholesaler; **to ask a company to supply trade references** = to ask a company to give names of traders who can report on the company's financial situation and reputation **2** *verb* to buy and sell, to carry on a business; **traded options** = options to buy or sell shares at a certain price at a certain date in the future, which themselves are bought or sold (in London, this is done through the Traded Options Market or TOM)

> QUOTE a sharp setback in foreign trade accounted for most of the winter slowdown. The trade balance sank $17 billion
>
> *Fortune*

> QUOTE at its last traded price, the bank was capitalized around $1.05 billion
>
> *South China Morning Post*

> QUOTE with most of the world's oil now traded on spot markets, Opec's official prices are much less significant than they once were
>
> *Economist*

trademark *or* **trade name** ['treɪdmɑːk *or* 'treɪd 'neɪm] *noun* particular name, design, etc., which has been registered by the manufacturer and which cannot be used by other manufacturers (it is an 'intangible asset')

trade-off ['treɪdɒf] *noun* exchanging one thing for another as part of a business deal

trader ['treɪdə] *noun* person who does business by buying and selling; person who buys or sells stocks, shares, options, etc.; **commodity trader** = person whose business is buying and selling commodities; *US* **floor trader** = independent trader on a stock exchange, who buys and sells on his own

account; **sole trader** = person who runs a business, usually by himself, but has not registered it as a company

trade-weighted index ['treɪd'weɪtɪd 'ɪndeks] *noun* index of the value of a currency calculated against a basket of currencies

> QUOTE the trade-weighted dollar chart shows there has been a massive devaluation of the dollar since the mid-'80s and the currency is at its all-time low. In terms of purchasing power, it is considerably undervalued
>
> *Financial Weekly*

trading ['treɪdɪŋ] *noun* **(a)** business of buying and selling; **trading account** = account of a company's trading (showing sales, costs of sales and gross profit or loss) as opposed to a manufacturing account which refers to costs of production only; **trading area** = group of countries which trade with each other; **trading company** = company which specializes in buying and selling goods; **adverse trading conditions** = bad conditions for trade; **trading estate** = area of land near a town specially for factories and warehouses; **trading limit** = maximum amount of something which can be traded by a single trader; **trading loss** = situation where a company's receipts are less than its expenditure; **trading partner** = company or country which trades with another; **trading pattern** = general way in which trade is carried on; *the company's trading pattern shows high export sales in the first quarter and high home sales in the third quarter*; **trading profit** = situation where a company's turnover exceeds its cost of sales; **trading stamp** = special stamp given away by a shop, which the customer can collect and exchange later for free goods; **fair trading** = way of doing business which is reasonable and does not harm the customer; *GB* **Office of Fair Trading** = government department which protects consumers against unfair or illegal business **(b)** buying and selling on a stock exchange or commodities exchange; **fair trading** = legal trade in shares, the legal buying and selling of shares; **forward trading** = buying or selling commodities forward; **insider trading** = illegal buying or selling of shares in a company by people who have secret information about the company's plans; **option trading** = buying and selling share options; **trading floor** = (i) area of a broking house where dealing in securities is carried out by phone, using monitors to display current prices and stock exchange transactions; (ii) part of a stock exchange where dealers trade in securities (NOTE: American English for this is also **pit**)

train [treɪn] *verb* to show someone how to do a particular task; **staff training** = teaching staff better and more profitable ways of working; **training levy** = tax paid by companies to fund the government's training schemes

trainee [treɪ'niː] *noun* person who is learning how to do something; *we employ a trainee accountant to help in the office at peak periods*; *graduate trainees come to work in the accounts department when they have finished their courses at university*; **management trainee** = young member of staff being trained to be a manager

traineeship [treɪ'niːʃɪp] *noun* post of trainee

tranche [trɑːnʃ] *noun* one of series of instalments (used when referring to loans to companies, government securities which are issued over a period of time, or money withdrawn by a country from the IMF); *the second tranche of interest on the loan is now due for payment*

transact [træn'zækt] *verb* **to transact business** = to carry out a piece of business

transaction [træn'zækʃən] *noun* **business transaction** = piece of business, buying or selling; **cash transaction** = transaction paid for in cash; **a transaction on the stock exchange** = purchase or sale of shares on the stock exchange; *the paper publishes a daily list of stock exchange transactions*; **exchange transaction** = purchase or sale of foreign currency; **fraudulent transaction** = transaction which aims to cheat someone

transfer 1 ['trænsfə] *noun* moving someone or something to a new place; *he applied for a transfer to our branch in Scotland*; **transfer of property** *or* **transfer of shares** = moving the ownership of property or shares from one person to another; **airmail transfer** = sending money from one bank to another by airmail; **bank transfer** = moving money from a bank account to another account; **credit transfer** *or* **transfer of funds** = moving money from one account to another; **stock transfer form** = form to be signed by the person transferring shares; **telegraphic transfer** *or* **wire transfer** = transfer of money from one account to another by telex (used often for sending money abroad, it is quicker but more expensive than sending a draft through the post) **2** [træns'fɜː] *verb* to move someone or

something to a new place; *the accountant was transferred to our Scottish branch*; *the sum was transferred to your Madrid account*; *he transferred his shares to a family trust*; *she transferred her money to a deposit account*; **transferred charge call** = phone call where the person receiving the call agrees to pay for it
(NOTE: **transferring - transferred**)

transferable [træns'fɜːrəbl] *adjective* (document, such as a bearer bond) which can be passed to someone else

transferee [trænsfə'riː] *noun* person to whom property or goods are transferred

transferor [trænsfə'rɔː] *noun* person who transfers goods or property to another

translate [træns'leɪt] *verb* to change into another form (such as into another currency; see SSAP20)

> QUOTE the normal accounting policy of translating assets and liabilities of overseas subsidiaries into sterling at the exchange rate prevailing at balance sheet date
>
> *Accountancy*

translation [træns'leɪʃən] *noun* changing into another form

> QUOTE translation of an overseas subsidiary's financial statements into sterling using the net investment method gives rise to an exchange difference
>
> *Accountancy*

traveller's cheques *US* **traveler's checks** ['trævləz 'tʃeks] *noun* cheques taken by a traveller which can be cashed in a foreign country

treasurer ['treʒərə] *noun* **(a)** person who looks after the money or finances of a club or society, etc.; **honorary treasurer** = treasurer who does not receive any fee **(b)** *GB* company official responsible for providing new finance for the company and using its existing financial resources in the best possible way **(c)** *US* main financial officer of a company **(d)** *(Australia)* finance minister

treasury ['treʒəri] *noun* **(a) the Treasury** = government department which deals with the country's finance (the term is used in both the UK and the USA; in most other countries this department is called the 'Ministry of Finance'); **treasury bill** = short-term financial instrument which does not give any interest and is sold by the government at a discount through the central bank (in the UK, their term varies from three to six months; in the USA, they are for 91 or 182 days, or for 52 weeks. In American English they are also called 'Treasuries' or 'T-bills'); **treasury bonds** = long-term bonds issued by the British or American governments; **treasury notes** = medium-term bonds issued by the US government; **treasury products** = financial items produced by the government for sale, such as bonds; **treasury stocks** = bonds issued by the British government (NOTE: also called **exchequer stocks**) *US* **Treasury Secretary** = member of the US government in charge of finance (NOTE: the equivalent of the **Finance Minister** in most countries, or of the **Chancellor of the Exchequer** in the UK) *GB* **Chief Secretary to the Treasury** = government minister responsible to the Chancellor of the Exchequer for the control of public expenditure (NOTE: in the USA, this is the responsibility of the Director of the Budget) **(b)** *(in a company)*; **treasury function** = tasks involved in dealing with the finances of the organization

trend [trend] *noun* general way things are going; *a downward trend in investment*; *we notice a general trend to sell to the student market*; *the report points to inflationary trends in the economy*; *an upward trend in sales*; **economic trends** = way in which a country's economy is moving; **market trends** = gradual changes taking place in a market; **trend line** = line on a graph or chart which shows which way a trend is going

> QUOTE the quality of building design and ease of accessibility will become increasingly important, adding to the trend towards out-of-town office development
> Lloyd's List

trial ['traɪəl] *noun* **(a)** court case to judge a person accused of a crime; *he is on trial* or *is standing trial for embezzlement* **(b)** test to see if something is correct; **trial balance** = draft calculation of debits and credits to see if they balance

tribunal [traɪ'bjuːnl] *noun* official court which examines special problems and makes judgements; **adjudication tribunal** = group which adjudicates in industrial disputes; **industrial tribunal** = court which can decide in disputes about employment; **rent tribunal** = court which can decide if a rent is too high or low

trillion ['trɪljən] *number* one million millions (NOTE: British English now uses the same meaning as American English; formerly in British English it meant one million million

millions, and it is still sometimes used with this meaning; see also the note at BILLION)

> QUOTE if land is assessed at roughly half its current market value, the new tax could yield up to ¥10 trillion annually
> Far Eastern Economic Review

triplicate ['trɪplɪkət] *noun* **in triplicate** = with an original and two copies; *to print an invoice in triplicate*; **invoicing in triplicate** = preparing three copies of invoices

true [truː] *adjective* correct or accurate; **true copy** = exact copy; *I certify that this is a true copy*; *certified as a true copy*; **true and fair view** = appropriate statement of a company's financial position as shown in its accounts and confirmed by the auditors

> COMMENT: accounts drawn up in accordance with the Companies Act 1985 are required to give a true and fair view of the state of affairs of a company at the end of the financial year in question and of the profit or loss of the company for that financial year. The true and fair requirement is overriding. Where in special circumstances compliance with the requirements of the Companies Act 1985 as to the matters to be included in the accounts would be inconsistent with the true and fair requirement there must be a departure from the requirements of the law

truncate [trʌŋ'keɪt] *verb* to operate a simplified banking system by not returning physical cheques to the paying bank

truncation [trʌŋ'keɪʃn] *noun* simplified banking system, where actual cheques are not sent to the paying bank, but held in the receiving bank which notifies the paying bank by computer of the details of cheques received

trust [trʌst] **1** *noun* **(a)** being confident that something is correct, will work, etc.; **we took his statement on trust** = we accepted his statement without examining it to see if it was correct **(b)** legal arrangement to pass goods, money or valuables to someone who will look after them well; *he left his property in trust for his grandchildren*; **he was guilty of a breach of trust** = he did not act correctly or honestly when people expected him to; **he has a position of trust** = his job shows that people believe he will act correctly and honestly **(c)** management of money or property for someone; *they set up a family trust for their grandchildren US* **trust company** = organization which supervises the financial affairs of private trusts, executes wills, and acts as a bank to a limited number of customers; **trust deed** = document which sets out the details of a private trust; **trust fund** =

assets (money, securities, property) held in trust for someone; **investment trust** = company whose shares can be bought on the Stock Exchange and whose business is to make money by buying and selling stocks and shares; **unit trust** = organization which takes money from investors and invests it in stocks and shares for them under a trust deed **(d)** *US* monopoly, a small group of companies which control the supply of a product **2** *verb* **to trust someone with something** = to give something to someone to look after; *can he be trusted with all that cash?*

trustee [trʌs'tiː] *noun* person who has charge of money in trust, person who is responsible for a family trust; *the trustees of the pension fund*; **trustee in bankruptcy** = person who is appointed by a court to run the affairs of a bankrupt and pay his creditors

Truth in Lending Act ['truːθ ɪn 'lendɪŋ 'ækt] US Act of 1969, which forces lenders to state the full terms of their interest rates to borrowers

TSA = THE SECURITIES ASSOCIATION

turn [tɜːn] *noun* **(a)** movement in a circle, change of direction **(b)** profit or commission **(c) stock turn** = total value of stocks sold in a year divided by the average value of goods in stock; *the company has a stock turn of 6.7*

turn down ['tɜːn 'daʊn] *verb* to refuse; *the board turned down their takeover bid*; *the bank turned down their request for a loan*; *the application for a licence was turned down*

turn over ['tɜːn 'əʊvə] *verb* **(a)** to have a certain amount of sales; *we turn over £2,000 a week* **(b)** *US* to pass something to someone; *she turned over the documents to the lawyer* (NOTE: in this meaning, British English is usually **hand over**)

> QUOTE a 100,000 square foot warehouse can turn its inventory over 18 times a year, more than triple a discounter's turnover
> *Duns Business Month*

> QUOTE he is turning over his CEO title to one of his teammates, but will remain chairman for a year
> *Duns Business Month*

turnover ['tɜːnəʊvə] *noun* **(a)** *GB* (i) amount of sales of goods or services produced by a company; (ii) amount of sales or income of the business of a self-employed person; *the company's turnover has increased by 235%*; *we based our calculations on the forecast turnover* (NOTE: the American equivalent is sales volume); **gross turnover** = turnover including VAT and discounts; **net turnover** = turnover before VAT and after trade discounts have been deducted; **asset turnover ratio** = number of times assets are turned over by sales during the year; **capital turnover ratio** = turnover divided by average capital during the year; **creditors turnover** *or* **creditor days ratio** = average time taken to pay for credit purchases calculated as average creditors divided by average daily purchases during the year; **debtors turnover** *or* **debtor days ratio** = average time which debtors take to pay for credit sales calculated as average debtors divided by average daily sales during the year **(b)** number of times something is used or sold in a period (usually one year), expressed as a percentage of a total; **stock turnover (ratio)** = total value of goods sold in a year divided by the average value of goods held in stock; **turnover of shares** = total value of shares bought and sold on the Stock Exchange during the year (it covers both sales and purchases, so each transaction is counted twice)

turn round ['tɜːn 'raʊnd] *verb* to make (a company) change from making a loss to become profitable; **he turned the company round in less than a year** = he made the company profitable in less than a year

turnround *US* **turnaround** ['tɜːnraʊnd *or* 'tɜːnəraʊnd] *noun* **(a)** value of goods sold during a year divided by the average value of goods held in stock **(b)** action of emptying a ship, plane, etc., and getting it ready for another commercial journey **(c)** making a company profitable again

> QUOTE the US now accounts for more than half our world-wide sales; it has made a huge contribution to our earnings turnaround
> *Duns Business Month*

two-bin system ['tuːbɪn 'sɪstəm] *noun* warehousing system, where the first bin contains the current working stock, and the second bin has the backup stock (when the first bin is empty, it is time to reorder proe stock)

Uu

UBR = UNIFORM BUSINESS RATE

UITF = URGENT ISSUES TASK FORCE

ultra vires [ˈʌltrə ˈvaɪriːz] *Latin phrase meaning* 'beyond powers'; **their action was ultra vires** = they acted in a way which exceeded their legal powers; *see* INTRA VIRES

umbrella organization [ʌmˈbrelə ˈɔːgənaɪzeɪʃn] *noun* large organization which includes several smaller ones

unaccounted for [ʌnəˈkaʊntɪd fɔː] *adjective* lost, without any explanation; *several thousand units are unaccounted for in the stocktaking*

unadjusted [ʌnəˈdʒʌstɪd] *adjective* (balance) which has not been adjusted

unamortized [ʌnˈæmɔːtaɪzd] *adjective* (cost) which has not been amortized

unaudited [ʌnˈɔːdɪtɪd] *adjective* which has not been audited; *unaudited accounts*

unauthorized [ʌnˈɔːθəraɪzd] *adjective* not permitted; *unauthorized access to the company's records*; *unauthorized expenditure*; *no unauthorized persons are allowed into the laboratory*; **unauthorized unit trust** = private unit trust operated by a stockbroking firm for its clients

unbalanced [ʌnˈbælənst] *adjective* (budget) which does not balance or which is in deficit

unbanked [ʌnˈbæŋkt] *adjective* (cheque) which has not been deposited in a bank account

uncalled [ʌnˈkɔːld] *adjective* (capital) which a company is authorized to raise and has been issued but for which payment has not yet been requested

uncashed [ʌnˈkæʃt] *adjective* which has not been cashed; *uncashed cheques*

uncertainty [ʌnˈsɜːtənti] *noun* **fundamental uncertainty** = a type of inherent uncertainty that gives rise to a particular form of modified auditors' report; *an inherent uncertainty is fundamental when the magnitude of its potential impact is so great that, without clear disclosure of the nature and implications of the uncertainty, the view given by the financial statements would be seriously misleading*

unchanged [ʌnˈtʃeɪndʒd] *adjective* which has not changed

QUOTE the dividend is unchanged at L90 per ordinary share
Financial Times

unchecked [ʌnˈtʃekt] *adjective* which has not been checked; *unchecked figures*

uncontrollable [ʌnkənˈtrəʊləbl] *adjective* which cannot be controlled; *uncontrollable costs*

uncrossed cheque [ˈʌnkrɒst ˈtʃek] *noun* cheque which does not have two lines across it, and can be cashed anywhere (NOTE: also called an **open cheque:** they are no longer used in the UK, but are still found in other countries)

undated [ʌnˈdeɪtɪd] *adjective* with no date indicated or written; *he tried to cash an undated cheque*; **undated bond** = bond with no maturity date

| COMMENT: the only British government stock which is undated are the War Loan

under- [ˈʌndə] *prefix* less important than, lower than or less than expected

underabsorbed overhead [ˈʌndəəbˈzɔːbd ˈəʊvəhed] *noun* absorbed overhead which ends up by being lower than the actual overhead incurred (NOTE: the opposite is **overabsorbed)**

underabsorption [ʌndəəbˈzɔːpʃn] *noun* situation where the actual overhead incurred is higher than the absorbed overhead (NOTE: the opposite is **overabsorption)**

underbid [ʌndəˈbɪd] *verb* to bid less than someone (NOTE: **underbidding - underbid)**

underbidder [ʌndəˈbɪdə] *noun* person who bids less than the person who buys at an auction

undercapitalized [ʌndəˈkæpɪtəlaɪzd] *adjective* without enough capital; *the company is severely undercapitalized*

undercharge [ʌndəˈtʃɑːdʒ] *verb* to ask for too little money; *he undercharged us by £25*

underemployed [ʌndərɪmˈplɔɪd] *adjective* with not enough work; **underemployed capital** = capital which is not producing enough income

underestimate 1 [ʌndərˈestɪmɪt] *noun* estimate which is less than the actual figure; *the figure of £50,000 in turnover was a considerable underestimate* **2** [ʌndərˈestɪmeɪt] *verb* to think that something is smaller or not as bad as it really is; *they underestimated the effects of the strike on their sales*; *he underestimated the amount of time needed to finish the work*

underlease [ˈʌndəliːs] *noun* lease from a tenant to another tenant

underspend [ʌndəˈspend] *verb* to spend less; **he has underspent his budget** = he has spent less than was allowed in the budget (NOTE: **underspending - underspent**)

understate [ʌndəˈsteɪt] *verb* to make something seem less than it really is; *the company accounts understate the real profit*

understatement [ʌndəˈsteɪtmənt] *noun* showing something as being less than it really is

undersubscribed [ʌdəsʌbˈskraɪbd] *adjective* (share issue) where applications are not made for all the shares on offer, and part of the issue remains with the underwriters

undertake [ʌndəˈteɪk] *verb* to agree to do something; *to undertake to investigate market irregularities*; *they have undertaken not to sell into our territory* (NOTE: **undertaking - undertook - has undertaken**)

undertaking [ʌndəˈteɪkɪŋ] *noun* **(a)** a business (usually not a limited company) **(b)** (legally binding) promise; *they have given us a written undertaking not to sell their products in competition with ours*; **general undertaking** = undertaking signed by the directors of a company applying for a stock

exchange listing, promising to work within the regulations of the Stock Exchange

undervaluation [ʌndəvæljuˈeɪʃən] *noun* being valued at a lower amount than is justified

undervalued [ʌndəˈvæljuːd] *adjective* not valued highly enough; *the properties are undervalued on the balance sheet*; *the dollar is undervalued on the foreign exchanges* (NOTE: the opposite is **overvalued**)

QUOTE in terms of purchasing power, the dollar is considerably undervalued, while the US trade deficit is declining month by month
Financial Weekly

underwrite [ʌndəˈraɪt] *verb* **(a)** to accept financial responsibility for the purchase of something; **to underwrite a share issue** = to guarantee that a share issue will be sold by agreeing to buy all shares which are not subscribed; *the issue was underwritten by three underwriting companies* **(b)** to insure, to cover (a risk); **to underwrite an insurance policy (c)** to agree to pay for costs; *the government has underwritten the development costs of the project* (NOTE: **underwriting - underwrote - has underwritten**)

underwriter [ˈʌndəraɪtə] *noun* person or company which underwrites a share issue or an insurance; **Lloyd's underwriter** = member of an insurance group at Lloyd's who accepts to underwrite insurances; **marine underwriter** = person who insures ships and their cargoes

underwriting [ˈʌndəraɪtɪŋ] *noun* action of guaranteeing to purchase shares in a new issue if no one purchases them; **underwriting fee** = fee paid by a company to the underwriters for guaranteeing the purchase of new shares in that company

COMMENT: when a major company flotation or share issue or loan is prepared, a group of companies (such as merchant banks) will form a syndicate to underwrite the action: the syndicate will be organized by the 'lead underwriter', together with a group of main underwriters; these in turn will ask others ('sub-underwriters') to share in the underwriting

undischarged bankrupt [ˈʌndɪstʃɑːdʒd ˈbæŋkrʌpt] *noun* person who has been declared bankrupt and has not been released from that state

undisclosed [ʌndɪsˈkləʊzd] *adjective* not identified; **undisclosed principal** = principal who has not been identified by his agent

COMMENT: the doctrine of the undisclosed principal means that the agent may be sued as well as the principal (if his identity is discovered)

undistributable reserves [ˌʌndɪsˈtrɪbjuːtəbl rɪˈzɜːvz] *noun* reserves of a company which cannot be distributed to the shareholders, except if the company is wound up (also known as 'capital reserves')

undistributed profit [ˌʌndɪsˈtrɪbjuːtɪd ˈprɒfɪt] *noun* profit which has not been distributed as dividends to shareholders but is retained in the business

unearned income [ˈʌnɜːnd ˈɪnkʌm] *noun* income (such as interest and dividends) from investments, not from salary, wages or profits of one's business (also called 'investment income'); *compare* EARNED INCOME

unemployed [ˌʌnɪmˈplɔɪd] *adjective* not employed, without any work; **unemployed office workers** = office workers with no jobs; **the unemployed** = the people without any jobs

unemployment [ˌʌnɪmˈplɔɪmənt] *noun* lack of work; **mass unemployment** = unemployment of large numbers of workers; **unemployment benefit** *US* **unemployment compensation** = payment made to someone who is unemployed

QUOTE tax advantages directed toward small businesses will help create jobs and reduce the unemployment rate
Toronto Star

unencumbered [ˌʌnɪnˈkʌmbəd] *adjective* (property) which is not mortgaged

unfair competition [ʌnˈfeə kɒmpəˈtɪʃn] *noun* trying to do better than another company by using techniques which are not fair, such as importing foreign goods at very low prices or by wrongly criticizing a competitor's products

unfavourable *US* **unfavorable** [ʌnˈfeɪvərəbl] *adjective* not favourable; **unfavourable balance of trade** = situation where a country imports more than it exports; **unfavourable exchange rate** = exchange rate which gives an amount of foreign currency for the home currency which is not good for trade; *the unfavourable exchange rate hit the country's exports*; **unfavourable variance** = adverse variance, one which produces an unexpected loss

ungeared [ʌnˈgɪəd] *adjective* with no borrowings

unified credit *noun US* estate and gift tax credit which permits the transfer of assets free of federal estate and gift tax

COMMENT: in accordance with the Taxpayer Relief Act of 1997, the asset credit amount gradually increases so that by the year 2006 the first $1 million of an estate will be excluded from taxation

uniform business rate (UBR) *noun* tax levied on business property which is the same percentage for the whole country

unincorporated [ʌnɪnˈkɔːpəreɪtɪd] *adjective* business which has not been made into a company (i.e., a partnership or a sole trader)

unissued capital [ʌnˈɪʃuːd ˈkæpɪtl] *noun* capital which a company is authorized to issue by its articles of association but has not issued as shares

unissued stock [ʌnˈɪʃuːd ˈstɒk] *noun* capital stock which a company is authorised to issue but has not issued

unit [ˈjuːnɪt] *noun* (a) single product for sale; **unit cost** = the cost of one item (i.e total product costs divided by the number of units produced); **unit price** = the price of one item (b) **accounting unit** = accounting entity, any unit which takes part in financial transactions which are recorded in a set of accounts (it can be a department, a sole trader, a plc, etc.); **units of service method** *or* **production unit method** = method of depreciating a machine, by dividing its cost less residual value by the number of units it is expected to produce during its useful life (c) **monetary unit** *or* **unit of currency** = main item of currency of a country (a dollar, pound, yen, etc.); **unit of account** = standard unit used in financial transactions among members of a group, such as SDRs in the IMF (d) single share in a unit trust; **accumulation units** = units in a unit trust, where the dividend is left to accumulate as new units; **income units** = units in a unit trust, where the investor receives dividends in the form of income; **unit-linked insurance** = insurance policy which is linked to the security of units in a unit trust or fund

unitholder [ˈjuːnɪthəʊldə] *noun* person who holds units in a unit trust

unit trust [ˈjuːnɪt ˈtrʌst] *noun* organization which takes money from small investors and invests it in stocks and shares for them under a trust deed, the investment being in the form of shares (or units) in the trust

COMMENT: unit trusts have to be authorized by the Department of Trade and Industry before they can offer units for sale to the public, although unauthorized private unit trusts exist. The US equivalent is the 'mutual fund'

unlawful [ʌnˈlɔːfʊl] *adjective* against the law, not legal

unlimited [ʌnˈlɪmɪtɪd] *adjective* with no limits; *the bank offered him unlimited credit*; **unlimited company** = company where the shareholders have no limit as regards liability; **unlimited liability** = situation where a sole trader or each partner is responsible for all the firm's debts with no limit to the amount each may have to pay

unliquidated claim [ʌnˈlɪkwɪdeɪtɪd ˈkleɪm] *noun* claim for unliquidated damages

unliquidated damages [ʌnˈlɪkwɪdeɪtɪd ˈdæmɪdʒɪz] *plural noun* damages which are not for a fixed amount of money but are awarded by a court as a matter of discretion

COMMENT: torts give rise to claims for unliquidated damages

unlisted [ʌnˈlɪstɪd] *adjective* **unlisted company** = company whose shares are not listed on a stock exchange; **unlisted securities** = shares which are not listed on a stock exchange; *see also* DELISTING

unpaid [ʌnˈpeɪd] *adjective* not paid; **unpaid balance** = balance of a loan or invoice which still has to be paid after a part payment or instalment payment has been made; **unpaid invoices** = invoices which have not been paid; **unpaid tax** = tax which should have been paid and has not been paid

unprofitable [ʌnˈprɒfɪtəbl] *adjective* which is not profitable

QUOTE the airline has already eliminated a number of unprofitable flights

Duns Business Month

unquoted [ˈʌnkwəʊtɪd] *adjective* **unquoted company** = company whose shares are not listed on the stock exchange; **unquoted investments** = investments which are difficult to value, such as shares which have no stock exchange listing or land of which the asset value is difficult to estimate; **unquoted shares** = shares which have no stock exchange quotation

unrealized [ʌnˈrɪəlaɪzd] *adjective* which has not been realized; **unrealized gain** = gain which exists on paper but which has not been realized

unredeemed pledge [ʌnrɪˈdiːmd ˈpledʒ] *noun* pledge which the borrower has not taken back by paying back his loan

unregistered [ʌnˈredʒɪstəd] *adjective* (company) which has not been registered

unsecured [ʌnsɪˈkjʊəd] *adjective* **unsecured creditor** = creditor who is owed money, but has no security (such as a mortgage) from the debtor for the debt; **unsecured debt** = debt which is not guaranteed by a charge on assets or by any collateral; **unsecured loan** = loan made with no security

unsubsidized [ʌnˈsʌbsɪdaɪzd] *adjective* with no subsidy

unused allowances [ʌnˈjuːzd əˈlaʊwənsɪz] *noun* part of the married couple's allowance or the blind person's allowance which is not used because the recipient does not have enough income, and which can then be passed to their spouse

up *adverb & preposition* in a higher potition, to a higher position; *the inflation rate is going up steadily*; *security prices were up slightly at the end of the day*

up front [ˈʌp ˈfrʌnt] *adverb* in advance; **money up front** = payment in advance; *they are asking for £100,000 up front before they will consider the deal*; *he had to put money up front before he could clinch the deal*

upside [ˈʌpsaɪd] *noun* **upside potential** = possibility for a share to increase in value (NOTE: the opposite is **downside)**

uptick [ˈʌptɪk] *noun US* price of a share sold, which is higher than the previous price

upturn [ˈʌptɜːn] *noun* movement towards higher sales or profits; *an upturn in the economy*; *an upturn in the market*

Urgent Issues Task Force (UITF) [ˈɜːdʒənt ˈɪʃuːz ˈtɑːsk ˈfɔːs] *noun* a committee of the UK Accounting Standards Board that considers major urgent and emerging accounting issues; its pronouncements are known as UITF Abstracts

usage [ˈjuːzɪdʒ] *noun* way in which something is used (such as stock or equipment); **usage method** = method of depreciating a machine, by dividing its cost less residual value by the number of units it is expected to produce or the length of time it is expected to be used

use 1 [juːs] *noun* way in which something can be used; **directions for use** = instructions on how to run a machine; **to make use of something** = to use something; **in use** = being worked; **items for personal use** = items which a person will use for himself, not on behalf of the company; **he has the use of a company car** = he has a company car which he uses privately; **land zoned for industrial use** = land where planning permission has been given to build factories **2** [ju:z] *verb* to take a machine, a company, a process, etc., and work with it; *we use airmail for all our overseas correspondence*; *the photocopier is being used all the time*; *they use freelancers for most of their work*

useful economic life [ˈjuːsfʊl iːkəˈnɒmɪk ˈlaɪf] *noun* the period during which an entity expects to derive economic benefit from using an asset such as a machine and over which it can be depreciated

user [ˈjuːzə] *noun* person who uses something; **end user** = person who actually uses a product; **user's guide** *or* **handbook** = book showing someone how to use something

usury [ˈjuːʒəri] *noun* lending money at very high interest

utilization [juːtɪlaɪˈzeɪʃən] *noun* making use of something; **capacity utilization** = the extent to which something is being used

QUOTE control permits the manufacturer to react to changing conditions on the plant floor and to keep people and machines at a high level of utilization
Duns Business Month

utilize [ˈjuːtɪlaɪz] *verb* to use

Vv

valorem [və'lɔ:rəm] *see* AD VALOREM

valuation [vælju'eɪʃən] *noun* estimate of how much something is worth; *to ask for a valuation of a property before making an offer for it*; **stock valuation** = estimating the value of stock at the end of an accounting period; *to buy a shop with stock at valuation* = to pay for the stock the same amount as its value as estimated by a valuer; **valuation of a business** = estimating the value of a business (this can be done on various bases, such as an assets basis, its break-up value, its value as a going concern, etc.)

value ['vælju:] **1** *noun* amount of money which something is worth; *he imported goods to the value of £250*; *the fall in the value of sterling*; *the valuer put the value of the stock at £25,000*; **value for money (VFM)** = degree to which spending money on something achieves economy (spending the minimum to get the required result); **good value (for money)** = a bargain, something which is worth the price paid for it; *that restaurant gives value for money*; *buy that computer now - it is very good value*; *holidays in Italy are good value because of the exchange rate*; **to rise in value** *or* **to fall in value** = to be worth more or less; **added value** *or* **value added** = amount added to the value of a product or service, being the difference between its cost and the amount received when it is sold (wages, taxes, etc., are deducted from the added value to give the retained profit); *see also* VALUE ADDED TAX; **asset value** = value of a company calculated by adding together all its assets; **book value** = value as recorded in the company's accounts; **'sample only - of no commercial value'** = not worth anything if sold; **declared value** = value of goods entered on a customs declaration form; **discounted value** = difference between the face value of a share and its lower market price; **face value** = value written on a coin, banknote or share; **future value (FV)** = the value to which a sum of money will increase if invested for a certain period of time at a certain rate of interest; **market value** = value of an asset, of a product or of a company, if sold today; **par value** = value written on a share certificate; **present value (PV)** = the value something has now, the value now of a specified sum of money to be received in the future, if invested at current interest rates; **scarcity value** = value of something which is worth a lot because it is rare and there is a large demand for it; **surrender value** = money which an insurer will pay if an insurance policy is given up before maturity date **2** *verb* to estimate how much money something is worth; *he valued the stock at £25,000*; *we are having the jewellery valued for insurance*

Value Added Tax (VAT) ['vælju: 'ædɪd 'tæks] *noun* tax imposed as a percentage of the net invoice value of goods and services (see SSAP5)

> QUOTE the directive means that the services of stockbrokers and managers of authorized unit trusts are now exempt from VAT; previously they were liable to VAT at the standard rate. Zero-rating for stockbrokers' services is still available as before, but only where the recipient of the service belongs outside the EC
>
> *Accountancy*

COMMENT: In the UK, VAT is organized by the Customs and Excise Department, and not by the Treasury. It is applied at each stage in the process of making or selling a product or service. Company 'A' charges VAT for their work, which is bought by Company 'B', and pays the VAT collected from 'B' to the Customs and Excise; Company 'B' can reclaim the VAT element in Company 'A''s invoice from the Customs and Excise, but will charge VAT on their work in their invoice to Company 'C'. Each company along the line charges VAT and pays it to the Customs and Excise, but claims back any VAT charged to them. The final consumer pays a price which includes VAT, and which is the final VAT revenue paid to the Customs and Excise

valuer ['væljʊə] *noun* person who estimates how much money something is worth; *see also* QUALIFIED VALUER

vanilla [və'nɪlə] *see* SWAP

variable ['veəriəbl] **1** *adjective* which changes; **variable costs** = money paid to produce a product which increases with the quantity made (such as direct labour costs and direct materials costs); **variable rate** *or* **floating rate** = rate of interest on a loan which is not fixed, but can change with the current bank interest rates **2** *noun (computers)* (computer program identifier for a) register or storage location which can contain any number or characters and which may vary during the program run; **global variable** = number that can be accessed by any routine or structure in a program; **local variable** = number which can only be accessed by certain routines in a certain section of a computer program

variance ['veəriəns] *noun* difference; **adverse variance** = variance which shows that the actual result is worse than expected; **budget variance** = difference between the cost as estimated for the budget, and the actual cost; **calendar variance** = variance which occurs if a company uses calendar months for the financial accounts but uses the number of actual working days to calculate overhead expenses in the cost accounts; **capacity variance** = variance caused by the difference between planned and actual hours worked; **favourable variance** = variance which shows that the actual result is better than expected; **at variance with** = which does not agree with; *the actual sales are at variance with the sales reported by the reps*; **overhead capacity variance** = difference between the overhead absorbed based on budgeted hours and actual hours worked; **(total) overhead cost variance** = difference between the overhead cost absorbed and the actual overhead costs (both fixed and variable); **overhead efficiency variance** = difference between the overhead absorbed by actual production at the standard rate of absorption and the overhead that should have been incurred given actual hours worked; **overhead expenditure variance** = difference between the budgeted overhead costs and the actual expenditure; **overhead volume variance** = difference in fixed overheads allocated to the production of more or less units than the standard quantity on which the overhead absorption rate has been calculated; **sales price variance** = difference between expected revenue from actual sales and actual revenue; **sales mix profit variance** = difference in profit from budget caused by selling a non-standard mix of products; **sales volume profit variance** = difference in profit from budget, caused by selling more or less than the forecast number of units where it is

assumed that sales price and production costs are as planned

VAT ['viːeɪˈtiː: *or* væt] = VALUE ADDED TAX *the invoice includes VAT at 17.5%*; *the government is proposing to increase VAT to 17.5%*; *some items (such as books) are zero-rated for VAT*; *he does not charge VAT because he asks for payment in cash*; **VAT declaration** = statement declaring VAT income to the VAT office; **VAT invoicing** = sending of an invoice including VAT; **VAT invoice** = invoice which shows VAT separately; **VAT inspector** = government official who examines VAT returns and checks that VAT is being paid; **VAT office** = government office dealing with the collection of VAT in an area

VATman *or* **vatman** ['vætmæn] *noun* VAT inspector

VCT = VENTURE CAPITAL TRUST

vending ['vendɪŋ] *noun* selling; **(automatic) vending machine** = machine which provides drinks, cigarettes, etc., when a coin is put in

vendor ['vendə] *noun* **(a)** person who sells (a property); *the solicitor acting on behalf of the vendor* **(b)** company selling its shares on a stock market for the first time

venture ['ventʃə] **1** *noun* business, commercial deal which involves a risk; *he lost money on several import ventures*; *she has started a new venture - a computer shop*; **joint venture** = a business project jointly controlled by two or more companies (see FRS 9); **venture capital** = capital for investment which may easily be lost in risky projects, but can also provide high returns; **Venture Capital Trust (VCT)** = quoted company that invests in smaller firms which need capital to grow (money invested by purchasing shares in a VCT must remain there for five years, and in return no capital gains are paid on £100,000 worth of VCT shares sold) **2** *verb* to risk (money)

QUOTE along with the stock market boom of the 1980s, the venture capitalists piled more and more funds into the buyout business, backing bigger and bigger deals with ever more extravagant financing structures

Guardian

vertical ['vɜːtɪkəl] *adjective* upright, straight up or down; **vertical communication** = communication between senior managers via the middle management to the workers;

vertical integration = joining two businesses together which deal with different stages in the production or sale of a product (as a shoe manufacturer buying a shoe retail chain)

vertical form ['vɜːtɪkəl 'fɔːm] *noun* one of the two styles of presenting a balance sheet allowed by the Companies Act (NOTE: also called 'report form') *see comment at* BALANCE SHEET

vested interest ['vestɪd 'ɪntrest] *noun* special interest in keeping an existing state of affairs; **she has a vested interest in keeping the business working** = she wants to keep the business working because she will make more money if it does

VFM = VALUE FOR MONEY

virement ['vaɪəmənt] *noun* (administration) transfer of money from one account to another or from one section of a budget to another

visible ['vɪzəbl] *adjective* which can be seen; **visible imports** *or* **exports** *or* **visible trade** = real products which are imported or exported; *compare* INVISIBLE

visual display terminal (VDT) *or* **visual display unit (VDU)** ['vɪzjuəl dɪs'pleɪ 'tɜːmɪnəl *or* 'vɪzjuəl dɪs'pleɪ 'juːnɪt] *noun* screen, similar to a television screen, connected to a computer to enable the user to see the instructions given to and results received form the computer

vivos ['vaɪvəʊs] *Latin word meaning* 'living people'; **gift inter vivos** = present given by one living person to another

void [vɔɪd] **1** *adjective* not legally valid; **the contract was declared null and void** = the contract was said to be no longer valid **2** *verb* **to void a contract** = to make a contract invalid

COMMENT: a contract is void where it never had legal effect, but is voidable if it is apparently of legal effect and remains of legal effect until one or both parties take steps to rescind it

voidable ['vɔɪdəbl] *adjective* (contract) which can be rescinded

volenti non fit injuria [və'lenti nɒn fɪt ɪn'dʒʊəriə] *Latin phrase meaning* 'there can be no injury to a person who is willing': rule that if someone has agreed to take the risk of an injury he cannot sue for it (as in the case of someone injured in a boxing match)

volume ['vɒljuːm] *noun* quantity of items sold; quantity of shares traded on a stock market; **volume discount** = discount given to a customer who buys a large quantity of goods; **volume of output** = number of items produced; **volume of trade** *or* **volume of business** = number of items sold; *the company has maintained the same volume of business in spite of the recession*

volume of sales *or* **sales volume** ['vɒljuːm əv 'seɪlz *or* 'seɪlz 'vɒljuːm] *noun* **(a)** *GB* number of items sold; **low** *or* **high volume of sales** = small or large number of items sold **(b)** *US* amount of money produced by sales (the British equivalent is 'turnover')

QUOTE daily trading volumes on the major markets suggest there was no great avalanche of selling; but there was little or no buying either and, hence, no support on the downside

Financial Times Review

voluntary ['vɒləntəri] *adjective* **(a)** done without being forced; **voluntary liquidation** *or* **voluntary winding up** = situation where a company itself decides it must close and sell its assets; **voluntary redundancy** = situation where a worker asks to be made redundant **(b)** done without being paid; **voluntary organization** = organization which has no paid staff

vote [vəʊt] **1** *noun* marking a paper, holding up your hand, etc., to show your opinion or to show who you want to be elected; **to take a vote on a proposal** *or* **to put a proposal to the vote** = to ask people present at a meeting to say if they do or do not agree with the proposal; **casting vote** = vote used by the chairman in the case where the votes for and against a proposal are equal; *the chairman has the casting vote*; *he used his casting vote to block the motion*; **postal vote** = election where the voters send in their voting papers by post **2** *verb* to show an opinion by marking a paper or by holding up your hand at a meeting; *the meeting voted to close the factory*; *52% of the members voted for Mr Smith as chairman*; **to vote for a proposal** *or* **to vote against a proposal** = to say that you agree or do not agree with a proposal; **two directors were voted off the board at the AGM** = the AGM voted to dismiss two directors; **she was voted on to the committee** = she was elected a member of the committee

voter ['vəʊtə] *noun* person who votes

voting ['vəʊtɪŋ] *noun* act of making a vote; **voting paper** = paper on which the voter puts a cross to show for whom he wants to vote; **voting rights** = rights of shareholders to vote at company meetings; **voting shares** = shares which give the holder the right to vote at company meetings; **non-voting shares** = shares which do not allow the shareholder to vote at company meetings

voucher ['vautʃə] *noun* **(a)** paper which is given instead of money; **cash voucher** = paper which can be exchanged for cash; *with every £20 of purchases, the customer gets a cash voucher to the value of £2*; **gift voucher** = card, bought in a shop, which is given as a present and which must be exchanged in that shop for goods; **luncheon voucher** = ticket, given by an employer to a worker, which can be exchanged in a restaurant for food **(b)** written document to show that money has really been paid (such as a petty cash voucher)

COMMENT: vouchers given by a company to its employees are counted as taxable income

Ww

wage [weɪdʒ] *noun* money paid (usually in cash each week) to a worker for work done; *she is earning a good wage or good wages in the supermarket*; **basic wage** = normal pay without any extra payments; *the basic wage is £110 a week, but you can expect to earn more than that with overtime*; **hourly wage** *or* **wage per hour** = amount of money paid for an hour's work; **minimum wage** = lowest hourly wage which a company can legally pay its workers; **wage adjustments** = changes made to wages; **wage claim** = asking for an increase in wages; **wages clerk** = office worker who deals with the pay of other workers; **wage differentials** = differences in salary between workers in similar types of jobs; **wage drift** = difference between wages and money actually earned (the difference being made up by bonus payments, overtime payments, etc.); **wage freeze** *or* **freeze on wages** = period when wages are not allowed to increase; **wage indexation** = linking of increases to the percentage rise in the cost of living; **wage levels** = rates of pay for different types of work; **wage negotiations** = discussions between management and workers about pay; **wage packet** = envelope containing money and pay slip; **wages payable account** = account showing gross wages and employer's National Insurance contributions paid during a certain period; **wages policy** = government policy on what percentage increases should be paid to workers; **wage scale** = list of wages, showing different rates of pay for different jobs in the same company

QUOTE European economies are being held back by rigid labor markets and wage structures
Duns Business Month

QUOTE real wages have been held down dramatically: they have risen at an annual rate of only 1% in the last two years
Sunday Times

COMMENT: the term 'wages' refers to weekly or hourly pay for workers, usually paid in cash. For workers paid by a monthly cheque, the term used is 'salary'

wage-earner ['weɪdʒˌɜːnə] *noun* person who earns money in a job

wage-earning ['weɪdʒˌɜːnɪŋ] *adjective* **the wage-earning population** = people who have jobs and earn money

war [wɔː] *noun* battle or fight or argument between countries or companies; *they launched a tariff war against the neighbouring countries*; *a bitter circulation war between newspapers*

warehouse ['weəhaʊs] *noun* large building where goods are stored; **bonded warehouse** = warehouse where goods are stored until excise duty has been paid; **warehouse capacity** = space available in a warehouse; **price ex warehouse** = price for a product which is to be collected from the manufacturer's or agent's warehouse and so does not include delivery

warrant ['wɒrənt] **1** *noun* official document which allows someone to do something; **dividend warrant** = cheque which makes payment of a dividend; **share warrant** = document which says that someone has the right to a number of shares in a company **2** *verb* to guarantee; *all the spare parts are warranted*; *the car is warranted in perfect condition*

QUOTE the rights issue will grant shareholders free warrants to subscribe for further new shares
Financial Times

warrantee [wɒrən'tiː] *noun* person who is given a warranty

warrantor ['wɒrəntɔː] *noun* person who gives a warranty

warranty ['wɒrənti] *noun* **(a)** guarantee, a legal document which promises that a machine will work properly or that an item is of good quality; *the car is sold with a twelve-month warranty*; *the warranty covers spare parts but not labour costs* **(b)** promise in a contract; **breach of warranty** = failing to do something which is a part of a contract **(c)** statement made by an insured person which declares that the facts stated by him are true

wash sale ['wɒʃ 'seɪl] *noun US* sale and then repurchase of a block of shares

waste [weɪst] **1** *noun* material left over from an industrial process which has no value (as opposed to scrap which has some value) **2** *verb* to use more than is needed; *to waste money or paper or electricity or time*; *the MD does not like people wasting his time with minor details*; *we turned off all the heating so as not to waste energy*

wasting asset ['weɪstɪŋ 'æsɪt] *noun* asset which becomes gradually less valuable as time goes by (for example a short lease on a property)

wealth tax ['welθ 'tæks] *noun* tax on money, property or investments owned by a person

the Web or World Wide Web (www) [web] *noun* the millions of dites and pages that make up the internet; **web page** = page of information on the World Wide Web; **web site** = internet site containing various web pages linked together; **WebTrust** = a product evidenced by a special active graphic through which a website that sells on-line can show that independent accountants have concluded that it provides transaction integrity and protects information collected from its customers

weight [weɪt] **1** *noun* **(a)** measurement of how heavy something is; **to sell fruit by weight** = the price is per pound or per kilo of the fruit; **false weight** = weight on a shop scales which is wrong and so cheats customers; **gross weight** = weight of both the container and its contents; **net weight** = weight of goods after deducting the packing material and container; **to give short weight** = to give less than one should; **inspector of weights and measures** = government official who inspects goods sold in shops to see if the quantities and weights are correct; *see also* UNDERWEIGHT **(b)** **weight of money** = amount of money which is in the system as cash, and is available for investment **2** *verb* to give an extra value to a certain factor; **weighted average** = average which is calculated taking several factors into account, giving some more value than others; **weighted average cost or price** = average price per unit of stock delivered in a period calculated either at the end of the period ('periodic weighted average') or each time a new delivery is received ('cumulative weighted average'); **weighted index** = index where some important items are given more value than less important ones

weighting ['weɪtɪŋ] *noun* additional salary or wages paid to compensate for living in an expensive part of the country; *salary plus a London weighting*

white knight ['waɪt 'naɪt] *noun* person or company which rescues a firm in financial difficulties, especially saving a firm from being taken over by an unacceptable purchaser

White Paper ['waɪt 'peɪpə] *noun GB* report from the government on a particular problem

whole-life insurance or policy ['həʊllaɪf ɪn'ʃʊərəns] *noun* insurance policy where the insured person pays a fixed premium each year and the insurance company pays a sum when he dies

wholesale ['həʊlseɪl] *noun & adverb* buying goods from manufacturers and selling in large quantities to traders who then sell in smaller quantities to the general public; **wholesale banking** = banking services between merchant banks and other financial institutions (as opposed to 'retail banking'); **wholesale dealer** = person who buys in bulk from manufacturers and sells to retailers; **wholesale price** = price of a product which is wholesale; **Wholesale Price Index** = index showing the rises and falls of wholesale prices of manufactured goods (usually moving about two months before a similar movement takes place on the Retail Price Index); **he buys wholesale and sells retail** = he buys goods in bulk at a wholesale discount and then sells in small quantities to the public

wholesaler ['həʊlseɪlə] *noun* person who buys goods in bulk from manufacturers and sells them to retailers

wholly-owned subsidiary ['həʊlliəʊnd səb'sɪdjəri] *noun* company which is owned completely by another company

widow ['wɪdəʊ] *noun* woman whose husband has died; **widow's pension** = pension paid to a widow

will [wɪl] *noun* legal document where someone says what should happen to his property when he dies; *he wrote his will in 1999*; *according to her will, all her property is left to her children*

windfall profit ['wɪnfɔːl 'prɒfɪt] *noun* sudden profit which is not expected; **windfall (profits) tax** = tax on sudden profits

windmill ['wɪndmɪl] *(informal)* = ACCOMMODATION BILL

winding up ['waɪndɪŋ 'ʌp] *noun* liquidation, the closing of a company and selling of its assets; **a compulsory winding up order** = order from a court saying that a company must be wound up; *see also* VOLUNTARY

window ['wɪndəʊ] *noun* **(a) shop window** = large window in a shop front, where customers can see goods displayed; **window envelope** = envelope with a hole in it covered with plastic like a window, so that the address on the letter inside can be seen; **window shopping** = looking at goods in shop windows, without buying anything **(b)** short period when something is available; **window of opportunity** = short period which allows an action to take place

window dressing ['wɪndəʊ 'dresɪŋ] *noun* **(a)** putting goods on display in a shop window, so that they attract customers **(b)** showing transactions in financial statements whose purpose is only to make a business seem better *or* more profitable or more efficient than it really is

wind up ['waɪnd 'ʌp] *verb* **(a)** to end (a meeting); *he wound up the meeting with a vote of thanks to the committee* **(b)** to wind up a company = to put a company into liquidation; *the court ordered the company to be wound up* (NOTE: **winding - wound**)

WIP = WORK IN PROGRESS

wire transfer ['waɪə 'trɑːsfə] *noun* = TELEGRAPHIC TRANSFER

Wirtschaftsprüfer ['viətʃɑːftspruːfə] *German* accountant

withdraw [wɪθ'drɔː] *verb* **(a)** to take (money) out of an account; *to withdraw money from the bank or from your account*; *you can withdraw up to £50 from any bank on presentation of a bank card* **(b)** to take back (an offer); *one of the company's backers has withdrawn* = he stopped supporting the company financially; *to withdraw a takeover bid*; *the chairman asked him to withdraw the remarks he has made about the finance director* (NOTE: **withdrawing - withdrew - has withdrawn**)

withdrawal [wɪθ'drɔːəl] *noun* removing money from an account; **withdrawal without**

penalty at seven days' notice = money can be taken out of a deposit account, without losing any interest, provided that seven days' notice has been given; *to give seven days' notice of withdrawal*; **early withdrawal** = removing money from a term deposit account before due date (usually incurring a penalty)

withholding tax [wɪθ'həʊldɪŋ 'tæks] *noun* (i) tax which takes money away from interest or dividends before they are paid to the investor (usually applied to non-resident investors); (ii) any amount deducted from a person's income which is an advance payment of tax owed (such as PAYE); (iii); *US* income tax deducted from the paycheck of a worker before he is paid

with profits ['wɪθ 'prɒfɪts] *adverb* (insurance policy) which guarantees the policyholder a share in the profits of the fund in which the premiums are invested

work [wɜːk] *noun* **(a)** things done using the hands or brain; **casual work** = work where the workers are hired for a short period; **clerical work** = work done in an office; **work in progress (WIP)** = value of service on a contract which has not been completed, or value of goods being manufactured which are not complete at the end of an accounting period (see SSAP9) **(b)** job, something done to earn money; **work permit** = official document which allows someone who is not a citizen to work in a country

QUOTE the control of materials from purchased parts through work in progress to finished goods provides manufacturers with an opportunity to reduce the amount of money tied up in materials
Duns Business Month

QUOTE the quality of the work environment demanded by employers and employees alike
Lloyd's List

worker ['wɜːkə] *noun* person who is employed; **casual worker** = worker who can be hired for a short period; **clerical worker** = person who works in an office; **factory worker** = person who works in a factory; **worker director** = director of a company who is a representative of the workforce; **worker representation on the board** = having a representative of the workers as a director of the company

workforce ['wɜːkfɔːs] *noun* all the workers (in an office or factory)

working ['wɜːkɪŋ] *adjective* **(a)** which works; **working control of a company** =

having enough shares in a company to able to control all its actions (usually, this means 51% of shares); **working partner** = partner who works in a partnership; **working underwriter** = member of a Lloyd's syndicate who actively generates business (as opposed to the 'names' who put up the security) **(b)** referring to work; **working capital** = capital in the form of cash, stocks and debtors (less creditors) used by a company in its day-to-day operations (normally defined as the excess of current assets over current liabilities); **working conditions** = general state of the place where people work (if it is hot, noisy, dark, dangerous, etc.); **working papers** = papers on which calculations have been made before a final result is reached (these are useful at a later stage if you need to check how calculations were carried out, the accounting policy used, etc.); **the normal working week** = the usual number of hours worked per week; *even though he is a freelance, he works a normal working week*

work out ['wɜːk 'aut] *verb* to calculate; *he worked out the costs on the back of an envelope*; *he worked out the discount at 15%*; *she worked out the discount on her calculator*

works [wɜːks] *noun* factory; *an industrial works*; *an engineering works*; **works committee** *or* **works council** = committee of workers and management which discusses the organization of work in a factory; **price ex works** = price not including transport from the manufacturer's factory; **the works manager** = person in charge of a works

workstation ['wɜːksteɪʃn] *noun* desk with a computer terminal, printer, telephone, etc., where a computer operator works

World Bank ['wɜːld 'bæŋk] *noun* central bank, controlled by the United Nations, whose funds come from the member states of the UN and which lends money to member states

World Trade Organization (WTO)
['wɜːld 'treɪd ɑːɡənaɪ'zeɪʃn] international organization set up with the aim of reducing restrictions in trade between countries

worldwide [wɜːld'waɪd] *adjective & adverb* everywhere in the world; *the company has a worldwide network of distributors*; *worldwide sales or sales worldwide have topped two million units*; *this make of computer is available worldwide*

World Wide Web ['wɜːld 'waɪd 'web] *see* WEB

worth [wɜːθ] **1** *adjective* having a value or a price; *do not get it repaired - it is only worth £25*; *the car is worth £6,000 on the secondhand market*; *he is worth £10m* = his property or investments, etc. would sell for £10m; **what are ten pounds worth in dollars?** = what is the equivalent of £10 in dollars? (NOTE: always follows the verb **to be**) **2** *noun* value; *give me thirty pounds' worth of petrol* = give me as much petrol as £30 will buy

worthless ['wɜːθləs] *adjective* having no value; *the cheque is worthless if it is not signed*

writ [rɪt] *noun* legal document ordering someone to do something or not to do something; *the court issued a writ to prevent the trade union from going on strike*; **to serve someone with a writ** *or* **to serve a writ on someone** = to give someone a writ officially, so that he has to obey it

write down ['raɪt 'daun] *verb* to note an asset at a lower value than previously; *the car is written down in the company's books*; **written-down value** = value of an asset in a company's accounts after it has been written down; **closing written-down value** *or* **opening written-down value** = the written-down value of an asset at the end or the beginning of an accounting period; **writing-down allowance** = a form of capital allowance giving tax relief to companies acquiring fixed assets which are written down on a year-by-year basis; **written-down allowance (WDA)** = allowance which can be claimed on capital expenditure by a business or self-employed person in the years after the purchase was made (in the first year, the first year allowance (FYA) applies)

write-down ['raɪtdaun] *noun* recording of an asset at a lower value; *see also* PRE-ACQUISITION

> QUOTE the holding company has seen its earnings suffer from big writedowns in conjunction with its $1 billion loan portfolio
> *Duns Business Month*

write off ['raɪt 'ɒf] *verb* (i) to cancel (a debt); (ii) to remove an asset from the accounts as having no value; *to write off bad debts*; *two cars were written off after the accident* = the insurance company considered that both cars were a total loss; **the**

cargo was **written off as a total loss** = the cargo was so badly damaged that the insurers said it had no value

QUOTE $30 million from usual company borrowings will either be amortized or written off in one sum
Australian Financial Review

write-off ['raɪtɒf] *noun* total loss, cancellation of a bad debt, removal of an asset's value in a company's accounts; *the car was a write-off*; *to allow for write-offs in the yearly accounts*; **direct write-off** = method of dealing with possible bad debts, where they are written off totally, and if they are finally paid, this amount is written back into the accounts

write out ['raɪt 'aʊt] *verb* to write in full; *she wrote out the minutes of the meeting from her notes*; **to write out a cheque** = to write the words and figures on a cheque and then sign it

write up ['raɪt 'ʌp] *verb* to post final entries into an accounts ledger

written resolution ['rɪtən rezə'luːʃn] *noun* decision to be reached by postal vote of the members of a UK private company equivalent to a resolution at a meeting

WTO WORLD TRADE ORGANIZATION

WWW WORLD WIDE WEB

Xx Yy Zz

xa (ex-all) ['eks 'ɔːl] *noun* share price where the share is sold without the right to receive a dividend, rights issue, or any other current issue; **xc (ex-capitalization)** = share price where the share is sold without the right to receive a recent scrip issue; **xd (ex dividend)** = share price not including the right to receive the current dividend; **xr (ex-rights)** = share price where the share is sold without the right to benefit from a recent rights issue

year [jɜː] *noun* period of twelve months; **calendar year** = year from January 1st to December 31st; **current year** = the year in which an accounting period falls; *under self-assessment, income is taxed on a current year basis - i.e. it is taxed in the year in which it is received*; **financial year** = the twelve month period for a firm's accounts; **year of assessment** *or* **fiscal year** = twelve-month period on which income tax is calculated (in the UK it is April 6th to April 5th of the following year); **year end** = the end of the financial year, when a company's accounts are prepared

year-end ['jɜːend] *adjective* referring to the end of a financial year; *the accounts department has started work on the year-end accounts*

yearly ['jɜːli] *adjective* happening once a year; *yearly payment*; *yearly premium of £250*

Yellow Book ['jeləʊ 'bʊk] *noun* publication by the London Stock Exchange which gives details of the regulations covering the listing of companies on the exchange

yellow pages ['jeləʊ 'peɪdʒɪz] *plural noun* section of a telephone directory (printed on yellow paper) which lists businesses under various headings (such as computer stores or banks, etc.)

yen [jen] *noun* money used in Japan (NOTE: usually written as ¥ before a figure: **¥2,700** (say 'two thousand seven hundred yen')

yield [jiːld] **1** *noun* money produced as a return on an investment, shown as a percentage of the money invested; **current yield** = income from a security calculated as a percentage of its current market price; *share with a current yield of 5%*; **dividend yield** = dividend per share expressed as a percentage of the price of a share; **earnings yield** = earnings per share expressed as a percentage of the current market price of the share; **effective yield** = actual yield shown as a percentage of the price paid; **fixed yield** = fixed percentage return which does not change; **flat yield** = interest rate as a percentage of the price paid for fixed-interest stock; **gross yield** = profit from investments before tax is deducted; **income yield** = actual percentage yield of government stocks, the fixed interest being shown as a percentage of the market price; **initial yield** = expected yield on a new unit trust; **interest yield** = yield on a fixed-interest investment; **maturity yield** *US* **yield to maturity** = calculation of the yield on a fixed-interest investment, assuming it is bought at a certain price and held to maturity; **negative yield curve** = situation where the yield on a long-term investment is less than on a short-term investment; **positive yield curve** = situation where the yield on a long-term investment is more than on a short-term investment; **running yield** = yield on fixed interest securities, where the interest is shown as a percentage of the price paid; **(dividend) yield basis** = method of valuing shares in a company, calculated as the dividend per share divided by the expected dividend yield **2** *verb* to produce (as interest, dividend, etc.); *government stocks which yield a small interest*; *shares which yield 10%*

COMMENT: to work out the yield on an investment, take the gross dividend per annum, multiply it by 100 and divide by the price you paid for it (in pence): an investment paying a dividend of 20p per share and costing £3.00, is yielding 6.66%

YTD YEAR TO DATE

zero ['zɪərəʊ] *noun* nought, number 0; **zero inflation** = inflation at 0%; **zero compression** *or* **zero suppression** = shortening of a file by the removal of unnecessary zeros

zero-based budgeting (ZBB) ['zɪərəʊbeɪst 'bʌdʒətɪŋ] method of budgeting which makes no assumptions about the possible uses of money (they all begin at zero), and each plan of action has to be justified in terms of the benefits it brings compared to its total cost (other budgeting methods assume that past activities are justified, without assessing their value)

zero-coupon bond *or* **zero-rated bond** ['zɪərəʊkuːpɒn 'bɒnd *or* 'zɪərəʊ'reɪtɪd 'bɒnd] *noun* bond which carries no interest, but which is issued at a discount and so provides a capital gain when it is redeemed at face value

zero fill *or* **zeroize** ['zɪərəʊ 'fɪl *or* 'zɪərəʊaɪz] *verb* to fill a section of memory with zero values

zero-rated ['zɪərəʊ'reɪtɪd] *adjective* (item) which has a VAT rate of 0%

zero-rating ['zɪərəʊ'reɪtɪŋ] *noun* rating of an item at 0% VAT

zone [zəʊn] *noun* area of a town or country (for administrative purposes); **development zone** *or* **enterprise zone** = area which has been given special help from the government to encourage businesses and factories to set up there; **free trade zone** = area where there are no customs duties

ABBREVIATIONS

AAA = AMERICAN ACCOUNTING ASSOCIATION

AAIA = ASSOCIATE OF THE ASSOCIATION OF INTERNATIONAL ACCOUNTANTS

AAPA = ASSOCIATE OF THE ASSOCIATION OF AUTHORIZED PUBLIC ACCOUNTANTS

AAT = ASSOCIATION OF ACCOUNTING TECHNICIANS

a/c *or* **acc** = ACCOUNT

ACA = ASSOCIATE OF THE INSTITUTE OF CHARTERED ACCOUNTANTS IN ENGLAND AND WALES

ACAUS = ASSOCIATION OF CHARTERED ACCOUNTANTS IN THE UNITED STATES

ACCA = ASSOCIATE OF THE ASSOCIATION OF CHARTERED CERTIFIED ACCOUNTANTS, ASSOCIATION OF CHARTERED CERTIFIED ACCOUNTANTS

acct = ACCOUNT

ACH (US) = AUTOMATED CLEARING HOUSE

ACMA = ASSOCIATE OF THE CHARTERED INSTITUTE OF MANAGEMENT ACCOUNTANTS

ACT = ADVANCE CORPORATION TAX

ADP = AUTOMATIC DATA PROCESSING

ADR = AMERICAN DEPOSITARY RECEIPT

AFA = ASSOCIATE OF THE INSTITUTE OF FINANCIAL ACCOUNTANTS

AFBD = ASSOCIATION OF FUTURES BROKERS AND DEALERS

AFOF = AUTHORIZED FUTURES AND OPTIONS FUND

AGM = ANNUAL GENERAL MEETING

AICPA = AMERICAN INSTITUTE OF CERTIFIED PUBLIC ACCOUNTANTS

ALU = ARITHMETIC LOGIC UNIT

AOB = ANY OTHER BUSINESS

APB (GB) = AUDITING PRACTICES BOARD; **(US)** *(formerly)* = ACCOUNTING PRINCIPLES BOARD

APR = ANNUAL PERCENTAGE RATE

ARM = ADJUSTABLE RATE MORTGAGE

ARPS = ADJUSTABLE RATE PREFERRED STOCK

ARR = ACCOUNTING RATE OF RETURN

ASB = ACCOUNTING STANDARDS BOARD

ASC *(formerly)* = ACCOUNTING STANDARDS COMMITTEE

ASCII = AMERICAN STANDARD CODE FOR INFORMATION INTERCHANGE

AST = AUTOMATED SCREEN TRADING

ASX = AUSTRALIAN STOCK EXCHANGE

ATM = AUTOMATED TELLER MACHINE

AVC = ADDITIONAL VOLUNTARY CONTRIBUTION

BASIC = BEGINNER'S ALL-PURPOSE SYMBOLIC INSTRUCTION CODE

BCD = BINARY CODED DECIMAL

b/d = BROUGHT DOWN

BES = BUSINESS EXPANSION SCHEME

b/f = BROUGHT FORWARD

BIN = BANK IDENTIFICATION NUMBER

BIS = BANK FOR INTERNATIONAL SETTLEMENTS

bn = BILLION

BOP = BALANCE OF PAYMENTS

B/P = BILL PAYABLE

B/R = BILL RECEIVABLE

BV = BESLOTEN VENOOTSCHAP

CA = CHARTERED ACCOUNTANT

CACA = CHARTERED ASSOCIATION OF CERTIFIED ACCOUNTANTS

CAPM = CAPITAL ASSET PRICING MODEL

CAT = CERTIFIED ACCOUNTING TECHNICIAN

CB = CASH BOOK

CCA = CURRENT COST ACCOUNTING

CCAB = CONSULTATIVE COMMITTEE OF ACCOUNTANCY BODIES

CD = CERTIFICATE OF DEPOSIT

c/d = CARRIED DOWN

CE = CHIEF EXECUTIVE

CEO = CHIEF EXECUTIVE OFFICER

c/f = CARRIED FORWARD

CFA = CASH FLOW ACCOUNTING

CFO = CHIEF FINANCIAL OFFICER

CGT = CAPITAL GAINS TAX

CHAPS = CLEARING HOUSE AUTOMATED PAYMENTS SYSTEM

CHIPS = CLEARING HOUSE INTERBANK PAYMENTS SYSTEM

c.i.f. or **CIF** = COST, INSURANCE AND FREIGHT

CIMA = CHARTERED INSTITUTE OF MANAGEMENT ACCOUNTANTS

CIPFA = CHARTERED INSTITUTE OF PUBLIC FINANCE AND ACCOUNTANCY

C/N = CREDIT NOTE

c/o = CARE OF

Co. = COMPANY

COBOL = COMMON ORDINARY BUSINESS ORIENTED LANGUAGE

COD or **c.o.d.** = CASH ON DELIVERY

COLA (US) = COST OF LIVING ADJUSTMENT

COM = COMPUTER OUTPUT ON MICROFILM

COP = CURRENT OPERATING PROFIT

COSA = COST OF SALES ADJUSTMENT

CP = COMMERCIAL PAPER

CPA (US) = CERTIFIED PUBLIC ACCOUNTANT

CPI = CONSUMER PRICE INDEX

CPM = CRITICAL PATH METHOD

CPP = CURRENT PURCHASING POWER

CPU = CENTRAL PROCESSING UNIT

Cr or **CR** = CREDIT

CRO = COMPANIES REGISTRATION OFFICE

CT = CORPORATION TAX

CVP = COST-VOLUME-PROFIT

CWO = CASH WITH ORDER

DBA = DATABASE ADMINISTRATOR

DBMS = DATABASE MANAGEMENT SYSTEM

DCF = DISCOUNTED CASH FLOW

dept = DEPARTMENT

DP = DATA PROCESSING

Dr or **DR** = DEBTOR

DTI = DEPARTMENT OF TRADE AND INDUSTRY

e.& o.e. = ERRORS AND OMISSIONS EXCEPTED

EBCDIC = EXTENDED BINARY CODED DECIMAL INTERCHANGE CODE

EC = EUROPEAN COMMUNITY

ECB = EUROPEAN CENTRAL BANK

ECGD = EXPORT CREDITS GUARANTEE DEPARTMENT

ECP = EUROCOMMERCIAL PAPER

ecu *or* **ECU** = EUROPEAN CURRENCY UNIT

ED = EXPOSURE DRAFT

EDI = ELECTRONIC DATA INTERCHANGE

EDP = ELECTRONIC DATA PROCESSING

EEA = EUROPEAN ECONOMIC AREA

EEC = EUROPEAN ECONOMIC COMMUNITY

EEIG = EUROPEAN ECONOMIC INTEREST GROUPING

EFT = ELECTRONIC FUNDS TRANSFER

EFTA = EUROPEAN FREE TRADE ASSOCIATION

EFTPOS = ELECTRONIC FUNDS TRANSFER AT POINT OF SALE

EGM = EXTRAORDINARY GENERAL MEETING

EIB = EUROPEAN INVESTMENT BANK

EIS = ENTERPRISE INVESTMENT SCHEME

ELS = ELECTRONIC LODGEMENT SERVICE

EMH = EFFICIENT MARKET HYPOTHESIS

EMU = EUROPEAN MONETARY UNION

EOQ = ECONOMIC ORDER QUANTITY

epos *or* **EPOS** = ELECTRONIC POINT OF SALE

eps *or* **EPS** = EARNINGS PER SHARE

ERDF = EUROPEAN REGIONAL DEVELOPMENT FUND

ERM = EXCHANGE RATE MECHANISM

ESOP = EMPLOYEE SHARE OWNERSHIP PLAN

EV = EXPECTED VALUE

EVR = ELECTRONIC VERSION OF THE TAX RETURN

exor = EXECUTOR

FA = FINANCE ACT

FAE = FINAL ADMITTING EXAM

FAS = FINANCIAL ACCOUNTING STANDARDS

FASB = FINANCIAL ACCOUNTING STANDARDS BOARD

FCA = FELLOW OF THE INSTITUTE OF CHARTERED ACCOUNTANTS IN ENGLAND AND WALES

FCCA = FELLOW OF THE ASSOCIATION OF CHARTERED CERTIFIED ACCOUNTANTS

FCMA = FELLOW OF THE CHARTERED INSTITUTE OF MANAGEMENT ACCOUNTANTS

FEE = FEDERATION DES EXPERTS COMPTABLES EUROPEENS

FIFO = FIRST IN FIRST OUT

FIMBRA = FINANCIAL INTERMEDIARIES, MANAGERS AND BROKERS REGULATORY ASSOCIATION

FOB *or* **f.o.b.** = FREE ON BOARD

FOR = FREE ON RAIL

FRED = FINANCIAL REPORTING EXPOSURE DRAFT

FRN = FLOATING RATE NOTE

FRRP = FINANCIAL REPORTING REVIEW PANEL

FRS = FINANCIAL REPORTING STANDARD

FSAVCs = FREESTANDING ADDITIONAL VOLUNTARY CONTRIBUTIONS

FT = FINANCIAL TIMES

FV = FUTURE VALUE

FYA = FIRST YEAR ALLOWANCE

GAAP = GENERALLY ACCEPTED ACCOUNTING PRINCIPLES

GAO (US) = GENERAL ACCOUNTING OFFICE

GDP = GROSS DOMESTIC PRODUCT

GmbH = GESELLSCHAFT MIT BESCHRANKTER HAFTUNG

GNP = GROSS NATIONAL PRODUCT

GST = GOODS AND SERVICES TAX

HLL = HIGH-LEVEL LANGUAGE

HP = HIRE PURCHASE

IAPC = INTERNATIONAL AUDITING PRACTICES COMMITTEE

IAS = INTERNATIONAL ACCOUNTING STANDARD

IASC = INTERNATIONAL ACCOUNTING STANDARDS COMMITTEE

ICAEW = INSTITUTE OF CHARTERED ACCOUNTANTS IN ENGLAND AND WALES

ICAI = INSTITUTE OF CHARTERED ACCOUNTANTS IN IRELAND

ICAS = INSTITUTE OF CHARTERED ACCOUNTANTS OF SCOTLAND

IFA = INDEPENDENT FINANCIAL ADVISER, INSTITUTE OF FINANCIAL ACCOUNTANTS

IMF = INTERNATIONAL MONETARY FUND

IMRO = INVESTMENT MANAGEMENT REGULATORY ORGANIZATION

Inc = INCORPORATED

I/O = INPUT/OUTPUT

IOU = I OWE YOU

IP = INFORMATION PROVIDER

IPO = INITIAL PUBLIC OFFERING

IR = INFORMATION RETRIEVAL

IRA (US) = INDIVIDUAL RETIREMENT ACCOUNT

IRC = INLAND REVENUE COMMISSIONER * COMMISSIONER OF INLAND REVENUE

IRR = INTERNAL RATE OF RETURN

IRS (US) = INTERNAL REVENUE SERVICE

IT = INFORMATION TECHNOLOGY

IVA = INDIVIDUAL VOLUNTARY ARRANGEMENT

JIT = JUST-IN-TIME

LAN = LOCAL AREA NETWORK

LAUTRO = LIFE ASSURANCE AND UNIT TRUST REGULATORY ORGANIZATION

LBO = LEVERAGED BUYOUT

L/C = LETTER OF CREDIT

LDT = LICENSED DEPOSIT-TAKER

LIBID = LONDON INTERBANK BID RATE

LIBOR = LONDON INTERBANK OFFERED RATE

LIFO = LAST IN FIRST OUT

LLL = LOW-LEVEL LANGUAGE

LSE = LONDON STOCK EXCHANGE

Ltd = LIMITED

m = METRE, MILE, MILLION

MB = MEGABYTE

MBI = MANAGEMENT BUYIN

MBO = MANAGEMENT BUYOUT

MCR = MAGNETIC CHARACTER RECOGNITION

MCT = MAINSTREAM CORPORATION TAX

MICR = MAGNETIC INK CHARACTER RECOGNITION

min = MINUTE, MINIMUM

MIRAS = MORTGAGE INTEREST RELIEF AT SOURCE

MIS = MANAGEMENT INFORMATION SYSTEMS

MMC = MONOPOLIES AND MERGERS COMMISSION

MRD = MUTUAL RECOGNITION DIRECTIVE

MWCA = MONETARY WORKING

CAPITAL ADJUSTMENT

NAO = NATIONAL AUDIT OFFICE

NASDAQ = NATIONAL ASSOCIATION OF SECURITIES DEALERS AUTOMATED QUOTATIONS

NAV = NET ASSET VALUE

NBV = NET BOOK VALUE

NIC = NATIONAL INSURANCE CONTRIBUTIONS

NIF = NOTE ISSUANCE FACILITY

NIFO = NEXT IN FIRST OUT

No. = NUMBER

NPV = NET PRESENT VALUE

NRV = NET REALIZABLE VALUE

NYSE = NEW YORK STOCK EXCHANGE

O & M = ORGANIZATION AND METHODS

o.b.o. = OR BEST OFFER

Oeics = OPEN-ENDED INVESTMENT COMPANIES

OFT = OFFICE OF FAIR TRADING

OMB = OFFICE OF MANAGEMENT AND BUDGET

o.n.o. = OR NEAR OFFER

OPM = OTHER PEOPLE'S MONEY

OTC = OVER-THE-COUNTER MARKET

P&L = PROFIT AND LOSS

p.a. = PER ANNUM

PAYE = PAY AS YOU EARN

PBIT = PROFIT BEFORE INTEREST AND TAX

PCB = PETTY CASH BOOK

P/E = PRICE/EARNINGS

PEP = PERSONAL EQUITY PLAN

PER = PRICE/EARNINGS RATIO

PERT = PROGRAM EVALUATION AND REVIEW TECHNIQUES

PIN = PERSONAL IDENTIFICATION NUMBER

PLC *or* **plc** = PUBLIC LIMITED COMPANY

pm = PREMIUM

PPI (US) = PRODUCERS' PRICE INDEX

PSBR = PUBLIC SECTOR BORROWING REQUIREMENT

Pte = PRIVATE LIMITED COMPANY

Pty = PROPRIETARY COMPANY

PV = PRESENT VALUE

qty = QUANTITY

R&D = RESEARCH AND DEVELOPMENT

RAM = RANDOM ACCESS MEMORY

R/D = REFER TO DRAWER

recd = RECEIVED

ref = REFERENCE

REIT (US) = REAL ESTATE INVESTMENT TRUST

repo = REPURCHASE AGREEMENT

ROA = RETURN ON ASSETS

ROCE = RETURN ON CAPITAL EMPLOYED

ROE = RETURN ON EQUITY

ROI = RETURN ON INVESTMENT

ROM = READ ONLY MEMORY

RPB = RECOGNIZED PROFESSIONAL BODY

RPI = RETAIL PRICE(S) INDEX

RPM = RESALE PRICE MAINTENANCE

SA = SOCIETE ANONYME, SOCIEDAD ANONIMA

S&L = SAVINGS AND LOAN ASSOCIATION

SARL = SOCIETE ANONYME A RESPONSABILITE LIMITEE

SAS = STATEMENT OF AUDITING STANDARDS

SAYE = SAVE-AS-YOU-EARN

Sch = SCHEDULE

SDB = SALES DAY BOOK

SDRs = SPECIAL DRAWING

RIGHTS

SEC = SECURITIES & EXCHANGE COMMISSION

SERPS = STATE EARNINGS-RELATED PENSION SCHEME

SFO = SERIOUS FRAUD OFFICE

SI = STATUTORY INSTRUMENT

SIB = SECURITIES AND INVESTMENT BOARD

SME = SMALL AND MEDIUM-SIZED ENTERPRISES

SORP = STATEMENT OF RECOMMENDED PRACTICE

SP = STATEMENT OF PRACTICE

SpA = SOCIETA PER AZIONI

SRO = SELF-REGULATORY ORGANIZATION

SSAPs = STATEMENTS OF STANDARD ACCOUNTING PRACTICE

SSP = STATUTORY SICK PAY

SVA = STATEMENT OF VALUE ADDED

TESSA = TAX-EXEMPT SPECIAL SAVINGS ACCOUNT

TOM = TRADED OPTIONS MARKET

TSA = THE SECURITIES ASSOCIATION

UBR = UNIFORM BUSINESS RATE

UITF = URGENT ISSUES TASK FORCE

VAT = VALUE ADDED TAX

VCT = VENTURE CAPITAL TRUST

VDU = VISUAL DISPLAY UNIT

VFM = VALUE FOR MONEY

WIP = WORK IN PROGRESS

ZBB = ZERO-BASED BUDGETING

Supplement

UK ACCOUNTING STANDARDS

STATEMENTS OF STANDARD ACCOUNTING PRACTICE (SSAPs)

SSAP 4 Accounting for government grants

SSAP 5 Accounting for VAT

SSAP 8 Treatment of taxation issued under the imputation system in the accounts of companies

SSAP 9 Stocks and long-term contracts

SSAP 13 Accounting for research and development

SSAP 17 Accounting for post balance sheet events

SSAP 19 Accounting for investment properties

SSAP 20 Foreign currency translation

SSAP 21 Accounting for leases and hire purchase contracts

SSAP 25 Segmental reporting

FINANCIAL REPORTING STANDARDS (FRSs)

FRS 1 Cash flow statements

FRS 2 Accounting for subsidiary undertakings

FRS 3 Reporting financial performance

FRS 4 Capital instruments

FRS 5 Reporting the substance of transactions

FRS 6 Acquisitions and mergers

FRS 7 Fair values in acquisition accounting

FRS 8 Related party disclosures

FRS 9 Associates and joint ventures

FRS 10 Goodwill and intangible assets

FRS 11 Impairment of fixed assets and goodwill

FRS 12 Provisions, contingent liabilities and contingent assets

FRS 13 Derivatives and other financial instruments: disclosures

FRS 14 Earnings per share

FRS 15 Tangible fixed assets

FRS 16 Current tax

FRS 17 Retirement benefits

FRS 18 Accounting policies

FRS 19 Deferred tax

FRSSE Financial reporting standard for smaller entities

The SSAPs were issued by the Accounting Standards Committee (ASC) which was replaced in August 1990 by the Accounting Standards Board (ASB). The ASB adopted all existing SSAPs but declared that it would review and amend them if necessary as well as issue new standards of its own. Accounting standards issued by the ASB are known as Financial Reporting Standards (FRSs). Exposure drafts of FRSs are Financial Reporting Exposure Drafts and are referred to as FREDs (pronounced 'freds').

A sub-committee of the ASB, the Urgent Issues Task Force (UITF) issues authoritative pronouncements known as UIFT Abstracts.

UITF ABSTRACTS

UITF Abstract 3 Treatment of goodwill on disposal of a business

UITF Abstract 4 Presentation of long-term debtors in current assets

UITF Abstract 5 Transfers from current assets to fixed assets

UITF Abstract 6 Accounting for post-retirement benefits other than pensions

UITF Abstract 7 True and fair view override disclosures

UITF Abstract 9 Accounting for operations in hyper-inflationary economies

UITF Abstract 10 Disclosure of directors' share options

UITF Abstract 11 Capital instruments: issuer call options

UITF Abstract 12 Lessee accounting for reverse premiums and similar incentives

UITF Abstract 13 Accounting for ESOP Trusts

UITF Abstract 14 Disclosure of changes in accounting policy

UITF Abstract 15 Disclosure of substantial acquisitions

UITF Abstract 16 Income and expenses subject to non-standard rates of tax

UITF Abstract 17 Employee share schemes

UITF Abstract 18 Pension costs following the 1997 tax changes in respect of dividend income

UITF Abstract 19 Tax on gains and losses on foreign currency borrowings that hedge an investment in a foreign enterprise

UITF Abstract 20 Year 2000 issues: accounting and disclosures

UITF Abstract 21 Accounting issues arising from the proposed introduction of the euro

UITF Abstract 22 The acquisition of a Lloyd's business

The Auditing Practices Board issues a series of Statements of Auditing Standards for the guidance of external auditors.

STATEMENTS OF AUDITING STANDARDS (SASs)

100 Objective and General Principles Governing an Audit of Financial Statements

110 Fraud and Error

120 Consideration of Law and Regulations

130 The Going Concern Basis in Financial Statements

140 Engagement Letters

150 Subsequent Events

160 Other Information in Documents Containing Audited Financial Statements

200 Planning

210 Knowledge of the Business

220 Materiality and the Audit

230 Working Papers

240 Quality Control for Audit Work

300 Accounting and Internal Control Systems and Audit Risk Assessments

400 Audit Evidence

410 Analytical Procedures

420 Audit of Accounting Estimates

430 Audit Sampling

440 Management Representations

450 Opening Balances and Comparatives

460 Related Parties

470 Overall View of Financial Statements

480 Service Organizations

500 Considering the Work of Internal Audit

510 The Relationship between Principal Auditors and other Auditors

520 Using the Work of An Expert

600 Auditors' Reports on Financial Statements

601 Imposed Limitation of Audit Scope

610 Reports to Directors or Management

620 The Auditors' Right and Duty to Report to Regulators in the Financial sector

ACCOUNTING STANDARDS IN THE USA

FASB STATEMENT OF FINANCIAL ACCOUNTING STANDARDS (SFAS)

SFAS 1 Disclosure of Foreign Currency Translation Information

SFAS 2 Accounting for Research and Development Costs

SFAS 3 Reporting Accounting Changes in Interim Financial Statements--an amendment of APB Opinion No. 28

SFAS 4 Reporting Gains and Losses from Extinguishment of Debt--an amendment of APB Opinion No. 30

SFAS 5 Accounting for Contingencies

SFAS 6 Classification of Short-Term Obligations Expected to Be Refinanced--an amendment of ARB No. 43, Chapter 3A

SFAS 7 Accounting and Reporting by Development Stage Enterprises

SFAS 8 Accounting for the Translation of Foreign Currency Transactions and Foreign Currency Financial Statements

SFAS 9 Accounting for Income Taxes: Oil and Gas Producing Companies--an amendment of APB Opinions No. 11 and 23

SFAS 10 Extension of "Grandfather" Provisions for Business Combinations--an amendment of APB Opinion No. 16

SFAS 11 Accounting for Contingencies: Transition Method--an amendment of FASB Statement No. 5

SFAS 12 Accounting for Certain Marketable Securities

SFAS 13 Accounting for Leases

SFAS 14 Financial Reporting for Segments of a Business Enterprise

SFAS 15 Accounting by Debtors and Creditors for Troubled Debt Restructurings

SFAS 16 Prior Period Adjustments

SFAS 17 Accounting for Leases: Initial Direct Costs--an amendment of FASB Statement No. 13

SFAS 18 Financial Reporting for Segments of a Business Enterprise: Interim Financial Statements--an amendment of FASB Statement No. 14

SFAS 19 Financial Accounting and Reporting by Oil and Gas Producing Companies

SFAS 20 Accounting for Forward Exchange Contracts--an amendment of FASB Statement No. 8

SFAS 21 Suspension of the Reporting of Earnings per Share and Segment Information by Nonpublic Enterprises--an amendment of APB Opinion No. 15 and FASB Statement No. 14

SFAS 22 Changes in the Provisions of Lease Agreements Resulting from Refundings of Tax-Exempt Debt--an amendment of FASB Statement No. 13

SFAS 23 Inception of the Lease--an amendment of FASB Statement

amendment of APB Opinion No. 17, an interpretation of APB Opinions 16 and 17, and an amendment of FASB Interpretation No. 9

SFAS 73 Reporting a Change in Accounting for Railroad Track Structures--an amendment of APB Opinion No. 20

SFAS 74 Accounting for Special Termination Benefits Paid to Employees

SFAS 75 Deferral of the Effective Date of Certain Accounting Requirements for Pension Plans of State and Local Governmental Units--an amendment of FASB Statement No. 35

SFAS 76 Extinguishment of Debt--an amendment of APB Opinion No. 26

SFAS 77 Reporting by Transferors for Transfers of Receivables with Recourse

SFAS 78 Classification of Obligations That Are Callable by the Creditor--an amendment of ARB No. 43, Chapter 3A

SFAS 79 Elimination of Certain Disclosures for Business Combinations by Nonpublic Enterprises--an amendment of APB Opinion

SFAS 80 Accounting for Futures Contracts

SFAS 81 Disclosure of Postretirement Health Care and Life Insurance Benefits

SFAS 82 Financial Reporting and Changing Prices: Elimination of Certain Disclosures--an amendment of FASB Statement No. 33

SFAS 83 Designation of AICPA Guides and Statement of Position on Accounting by Brokers and Dealers in Securities, by Employee Benefit Plans, and by Banks as Preferable for Purposes of Applying APB Opinion 20--an amendment FASB Statement No. 32 and APB Opinion No. 30 and a rescission of FASB Interpretation No. 10

SFAS 84 Induced Conversions of Convertible Debt--an amendment of APB Opinion No. 26

SFAS 85 Yield Test for Determining whether a Convertible Security is a Common Stock Equivalent--an amendment of APB Opinion

SFAS 86 Accounting for the Costs of Computer Software to Be Sold, Leased, or Otherwise Marketed

SFAS 87 Employers' Accounting for Pensions

SFAS 88 Employers' Accounting for Settlements and Curtailments of Defined Benefit Pension Plans and for Termination Benefits

SFAS 89 Financial Reporting and Changing Prices

SFAS 90 Regulated Enterprises-Accounting for Abandonments and Disallowances of Plant Costs--an amendment of FASB Statement No. 71

SFAS 91 Accounting for Nonrefundable Fees and Costs Associated with Originating or Acquiring Loans and Initial Direct Costs of Leases--an amendment of FASB Statements No. 13, 60, and 65 and a rescission of FASB Statement No. 17

SFAS 92 Regulated Enterprises-Accounting for Phase-in Plans--an amendment of FASB Statement No. 71

SFAS 93 Recognition of Depreciation by Not-for-Profit Organizations

SFAS 94 Consolidation of All Majority-owned Subsidiaries--an amendment of

ARB No. 51, with related amendments of APB Opinion No. 18 and ARB No. 43, Chapter 12

SFAS 95 Statement of Cash Flows

SFAS 96 Accounting for Income Taxes

SFAS 97 Accounting and Reporting by Insurance Enterprises for Certain Long-Duration Contracts and for Realized Gains and Losses from the Sale of Investments

SFAS 98 Accounting for Leases: Sale-Leaseback Transactions Involving Real Estate, Sales-Type Leases of Real Estate, Definition of the Lease Term, and Initial Direct Costs of Direct Financing Leases--an amendment of FASB Statements No. 13, 66, and 91 and a rescission of FASB Statement No. 26 and Technical Bulletin No. 79-11

SFAS 99 Deferral of the Effective Date of Recognition of Depreciation by Not-for-Profit Organizations--an amendment of FASB Statement No. 93

SFAS 100 Accounting for Income Taxes-Deferral of the Effective Date of FASB Statement No. 96--an amendment of FASB Statement

SFAS 101 Regulated Enterprises-Accounting for the Discontinuation of Application of FASB Statement No. 71

SFAS 102 Statement of Cash Flows-Exemption of Certain Enterprises and Classification of Cash Flows from Certain Securities Acquired for Resale--an amendment of FASB Statement No. 95

SFAS 103 Accounting for Income Taxes-Deferral of the Effective Date of FASB Statement No. 96--an amendment of FASB Statement

SFAS 104 Statement of Cash Flows-Net Reporting of Certain Cash Receipts and Cash Payments and Classification of Cash Flows from Hedging Transactions--an amendment of FASB Statement

SFAS 105 Disclosure of Information about Financial Instruments with Off-Balance-Sheet Risk and Financial Instruments with Concentrations of Credit Risk

SFAS 106 Employers' Accounting for Postretirement Benefits Other Than Pensions

SFAS 107 Disclosures about Fair Value of Financial Instruments

SFAS 108 Accounting for Income Taxes-Deferral of the Effective Date of FASB Statement No. 96--an amendment of FASB Statement

SFAS 109 Accounting for Income Taxes

SFAS 110 Reporting by Defined Benefit Pension Plans of Investment Contracts--an amendment of FASB Statement No. 35

SFAS 111 Rescission of FASB Statement No. 32 and Technical Corrections

SFAS 112 Employers' Accounting for Postemployment Benefits--an amendment of FASB Statements No. 5 and 43

SFAS 113 Accounting and Reporting for Reinsurance of Short-Duration and Long-Duration Contracts

SFAS 114 Accounting by Creditors for Impairment of a Loan--an amendment of FASB Statements No. 5 and 15

SFAS 115 Accounting for Certain Investments in Debt and Equity Securities

SFAS 116 Accounting for Contributions Received and Contributions Made

SFAS 117 Financial Statements of Not-for-Profit Organizations

SFAS 118 Accounting by Creditors for Impairment of a Loan-Income Recognition and Disclosures--an amendment of FASB Statement No. 114

SFAS 119 Disclosure about Derivative Financial Instruments and Fair Value of Financial Instruments

SFAS 120 Accounting and Reporting by Mutual Life Insurance Enterprises and by Insurance Enterprises for Certain Long-Duration Participating Contracts--an amendment of FASB Statements 60, 97, and 113 and Interpretation No. 40

SFAS 121 Accounting for the Impairment of Long-Lived Assets and for Long-Lived Assets to Be Disposed Of

SFAS 122 Accounting for Mortgage Servicing Rights--an amendment of FASB Statement No. 65

SFAS 123 Accounting for Stock-Based Compensation

SFAS 124 Accounting for Certain Investments Held by Not-for-Profit Organizations

SFAS 125 Accounting for Transfers and Servicing of Financial Assets and Extinguishments of Liabilities

SFAS 126 Exemption from Certain Required Disclosures about Financial Instruments for Certain Nonpublic Entities--an amendment to FASB Statement No. 107

SFAS 127 Deferral of the Effective Date of Certain Provisions of FASB Statement No. 125--an amendment to FASB Statement No. 125

SFAS 128 Earnings per Share

SFAS 129 Disclosure of Information about Capital Structure

SFAS 130 Reporting Comprehensive Income

SFAS 131 Disclosures about Segments of an Enterprise and Related Information

SFAS 132 Employers' Disclosures about Pensions and Other Postretirement Benefits--an amendment of FASB Statements No. 87, 88, and 106

SFAS 133 Accounting for Derivative Instruments and Hedging Activities

SFAS 134 Accounting for Mortgage-Backed Securities Retained after the Securitization of Mortgage Loans Held for Sale by a Mortgage Banking Enterprise--an amendment of FASB Statement No. 65

SFAS 135 Rescission of FASB Statement No. 75 and Technical Corrections

SFAS 136 Transfers of Assets to a Not-for-Profit Organization or Charitable Trust That Raises or Holds Contributions for Others

SFAS 137 Accounting for Derivative Instruments and Hedging Activities-Deferral of the Effective Date of FASB Statement No. 133--an amendment of FASB Statement No. 133

SFAS 138 Accounting for Certain Derivative Instruments and Certain Hedging Activities--an amendment of FASB Statement No. 133

SFAS 139 Rescission of FASB Statement No. 53 and amendments to FASB Statements No. 63, 89 and 121

SFAS 140 Accounting for Transfers and Servicing of Financial Assets and Extinguishments of Liabilities--a replacement of FASB Statement No. 125

The Accounting Equation

Assets = Capital + Liabilities

which can be restated as: Capital = Assets - Liabilities

or: Liabilities = Assets - Capital

Assets are: the resources owned by the company (cash, debtors, machinery, stocks, etc.)

Liabilities and capital are: the amounts of money owed to people who have provided those resources (banks, trade creditors, shareholders, debenture holders, etc.)

'T' Accounts

Name of Account

DR	CR
Entries on the debit side of an account account represent any of the following:	Entries on the credit side of an represent any of the following:
a) Increase in assets b) Decrease in liabilities c) Decrease in capital	a) Increase in liabilities b) Increase in capital c) Decrease in assets

Example: Cash/Bank Account

		£			£
1 April	Bal b/d	1,500			
20 April	Debtors A/c	2,000	25 April Creditors A/c		2,200
(received from customers)			(paid to suppliers)		
			30 April Bal c/d		3,500
		3,500			3,500

About the Profit and Loss Account

The Fourth Directive of the EC adopted in 1978 allows member countries to prepare profit and loss accounts in four possible ways: two vertical formats and two horizontal. In the UK the 1981 Companies Act incorporated the EC directive into law. However, whilst all four profit and loss formats are permissabte most UK companies use the vertical format illustrated. The horizontal profit and loss account format may be summarised as follows:

	£		£
Cost of sales	X	Sales	X
Gross profit	X		
	———		———
	X		X
Expenses	X	Gross profit	X
	———		———
	X		X
	═══		═══

In Germany and Italy only the vertical format is allowed.

According to the UK Companies Act a company must show all the items marked with * on the face of the profit and loss account. It must also disclose the value of certain items in the notes to the profit and loss account, such as:

a) interest owed on bank and other loans
b) rental income
c) costs of hire of plant and machinery
d) amounts paid to auditors
e) turnover for each class of business and country in which sales are made
f) number of employees and costs of employment

Specimen Co Ltd

Profit and Loss Account for the Year to 31 December 2000

	£000	£000
* Turnover		9,758
* Cost of sales		6,840
* Gross profit		2,918
* Distribution costs	585	
* Administrative expenses	407	
		992
		1,926
* Other operating income		322
		2,248
* Income from shares in group companies	200	
* Income from other fixed asset investments	75	
* Other interest receivable and similar income	36	
		311
		2,559
* Amounts written off investments	27	
* Interest payable and similar charges	26	
		53
Profit on ordinary activities before taxation		2,506
* Tax on profit on ordinary activities		916
* Profit on ordinary activities after taxation		1,590
* Extraordinary income	153	
* Extraordinary charges	44	
* Extraordinary profit	109	
* Tax on extraordinary profit	45	
		64
* Profit for the financial year		1,654
Transfers to Reserves	400	
Dividends Paid and Proposed	750	
		1,150
Retained profit for the financial year		504

About the Balance Sheet

Both UK law (1989 Companies Act) and the EC Fourth Directive allow companies to produce vertical or horizontal balance sheets although most UK companies prefer the vertical format as illustrated above. The conventional form of horizontal balance sheet can be summarised as follows:

	£		£
Capital brought forward	X	Fixed Assets	X
Profit for the year	X		
Capital at year end	X		
	X		
Long term liabilities	X		
Current liabilities	X	Current Assets	X
	X		X

Of the EC states, Italy and Germany allow companies to use the horizontal format only

The Companies Act requires UK companies to show all the items marked with * in the example on the face of the balance sheet: the other items can be shown either on the balance sheet or in the notes to the accounts. In addition, the law requires companies to show the value of certain items in separate notes to the balance sheet such as details of fixed assets purchased and sold during the year.

The notes to the published accounts almost always begin with a description of the accounting policies used by the company in the accounts e.g. the depreciation policy. In the UK most accounts are prepared on a historical cost basis but this is not compulsory and other bases, such as current cost or historical cost modified by revaluation of certain assets, are also allowed.

Modified Accounts

Criteria used	Small sized	Medium sized
Total assets	< £0.975m	< £3.9m
Turnover	< £2m	< £8m
Average number of employees	< 50	< 250

If two of any three criteria apply to any company it will be regarded as a small or medium sized company and will therefore be able to prepare modified accounts as follows:

Size of company   **Exemptions allowed**

Small   Only the balance sheet items marked with * in the example need be shown
No profit and loss account required
No Directors report required

Medium   Profit and loss account can begin from gross profit
No analysis of turnover required in the notes

Specimen Co Ltd

Balance Sheet for the Year to 31 December 2000

	£000	£000	£000
* FIXED ASSETS			
* Intangible assets			
Development costs	1,255		
Goodwill	850		
		2,105	
* Tangible assets			
Land and buildings	4,758		
Plant and machinery	2,833		
Fixtures and fittings	1,575		9,166
* Investments		730	
			12,001
* CURRENT ASSETS			
* Stocks	975		
* Debtors	2,888		
* Cash at bank	994		
		4,857	
* CREDITORS: AMOUNTS FALLING DUE WITHIN ONE YEAR			
Bank loans	76		
Trade creditors	3,297		
Accruals	20		
		3,393	
* NET CURRENT ASSETS			1,464
* TOTAL ASSETS LESS CURRENT LIABILITIES			13,465
* CREDITORS: AMOUNTS FALLING DUE AFTER MORE THAN ONE YEAR			
Debenture loans		1,875	
Finance leases		866	
Bank and other loans		124	
			2,865
* PROVISIONS FOR LIABILITIES AND CHARGES			
Taxation including deferred taxation	33		
Other provisions	557		
			590
			10,010
* CAPITAL AND RESERVES			
* Called-up share capital		5,000	
" Share premium account		500	
" Revaluation reserve		1,158	
• Other reserves		262	
			6,920
• PROFIT AND LOSS ACCOUNT			3,090
			10.010

Specimen Co Ltd

Statement of Source and Application of Funds

For the year to 31 December 2000

	£000	£000
Source of Funds		
Profit before tax		2,615
Adjustment for items not involving the movement of funds:		
Depreciation	772	
Profit on the sale of fixed assets	(12)	
Provision for bad debts	3	
Development expenditure	45	
		808
Total generated from operations		3,423
Funds from other sources		
Issue of shares	250	
Sale of fixed assets	75	
Dividends received	240	
		565
		3,988
Application of funds		
Dividends paid	550	
Taxation paid	777	
Purchase of fixed assets	1,437	
		2,764
Increase in working capital		1,224
Increase in stock	82	
Decrease in debtors	82	
Decrease in creditors	545	
		383
Decrease in bank overdraft	297	
Increase in cash balances	544	
		841
		1,224

NB For accounting periods ending after September 1991 companies are required to prepare cash flow statements according to FRS1—see next page.

Specimen Co Ltd

Cash Flow Statement for the year to 31 December 2000

	£000	£000
Operating activities		
Cash received from customers		8,804
Interest and dividends received		276
Cash paid to suppliers		(3,642)
Cash paid to and on behalf of employees		(1,789)
Interest paid		(26)
Net cashflow from operations		3,423
Corporation tax paid		(777)
Investing activities		
Purchase of investments	(866)	
New fixed assets acquired	(1,437)	
Sale of fixed assets	75	
Net cashflow from investing activities		(2,228)
Financing activities		
New share capital	250	
Repayment on finance leases	(65)	
Dividends paid	(550)	
Net cashflow from financing activities		(365)
Net cash inflow		53

Specimen Co Ltd

Statement of Value Added for the Year to 31 December 2000

	£000	£000
Turnover		9,758
Bought-in materials and services		5.233
Value Added		4.525
Applied the following way:		
To pay employees' wages, pensions and other benefits		1,827
To pay providers of capital		
Interest on loans	26	
Dividends to shareholders	750	
		776
To pay government		
Corporation tax payable		961
To provide for maintenance and expansion of assets		
Depreciation	772	
Retained Profits	189	
		961
		4,525

About the Value Added Statement

Value added statements are not required by UK law or the SSAPs and are rarely found in company annual reports. However, many people consider them very useful indicators of a company's operational efficiency and it is possible that they will become more widely reported in future.

'Value added' means the difference between the total value of output and the total cost of materials and services used in production. The value added statement shows how this added value is applied: to pay works and managers, taxes and dividends, to maintain operating capacity (i.e. depreciation) and the amount added to reserves.

BASIC DOUBLE-ENTRY BOOKKEEPING

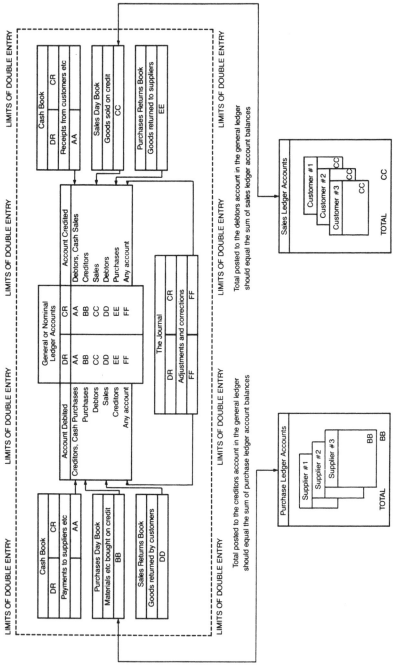

Check Your Vocabulary for Business

We publish a wide range of specialist workbooks that help teach, improve and test English vocabulary. This title includes word games, puzzles and tests to help students study and improve their business English vocabulary. Each book provides full instructions and answers for teachers and students. Each workbook has a corresponding English dictionary. For a full list of titles, visit our website.

Check your vocabulary for:

Banking & Finance	ISBN 0-948549-96-3
Business	ISBN 1-901659-22-4
Computing	ISBN 1-901659-28-3
English for FCE	ISBN 1-901659-11-9
English for IELTS	ISBN 1-901659-60-7
English for TOEFL	ISBN 1-901659-68-2
Hotels, Tourism	ISBN 0-948549-75-0
Law	ISBN 1-901659-21-6
Marketing	ISBN 1-901659-48-8
Medicine	ISBN 1-901659-47-X

Dictionary of Banking & Finance

This dictionary provides comprehensive coverage of the terms used in banking and finance, ranging from personal bank accounts to international money markets. Over 9,000 entries cover both British and American English; includes clear definitions of complex terms together with example sentences, parts of speech, and phonetic pronunciation guides.

Dictionary of Banking & Finance:
ISBN 1-901659-30-5   360pages   paperback
CD-ROM edition:
ISBN 1-901659-35-6   MS-Windows software

Bilingual Business Dictionaries

This range of respected bilingual business dictionaries is based on the English *Dictionary of Business* and provides processionals, teachers, students and translators with accurate translations of current international business terms. Each title includes over 50,000 entries.

Business Spanish Dictionary:
ISBN 0-948549-90-4   680pages   hardback
Business French Dictionary:
ISBN 0-948549-64-5   600pages   hardback
Business German Dictionary:
ISBN 0-948549-50-5   650pages   hardback

For details on your local stockist or a complete catalogue of our range of over 80 dictionaries and workbooks, please contact:

Peter Collin Publishing Ltd
32-34 Great Peter Street, London, SW1P 2DB
tel: (+44) 020 7222 1155   fax: (+44) 020 7222 1551
email: info@petercollin.com   website: www.petercollin.com